Kaplan Publishing are constantly finding new
difference to your studies and our exciting o
offer something different to students lookin

This book comes with free MyKaplan online
study anytime, anywhere. **This free online resourc... separately and is included in the price of the book.**

Having purchased this book, you have access to the following online study materials:

CONTENT	ACCA (including FBT, FMA, FFA)		FIA (excluding FBT, FMA, FFA)	
	Text	Kit	Text	Kit
Electronic version of the book	✓	✓	✓	✓
Knowledge checks with instant answers	✓		✓	
Material updates	✓	✓	✓	✓
Latest official ACCA exam questions*		✓		
Timed questions with an online tutor debrief using video icon***		✓		
Consolidation Test including questions and answers	✓		✓	

* Excludes BT, MA, FA, FBT, FMA, FFA; for all other papers includes a selection of questions, as released by ACCA

*** Excludes BT, MA, FA, LW, FBT, FMA and FFA

How to access your online resources

Kaplan Financial students will already have a MyKaplan account and these extra resources will be available to you online. You do not need to register again, as this process was completed when you enrolled. If you are having problems accessing online materials, please ask your course administrator.

If you are not studying with Kaplan and did not purchase your book via a Kaplan website, to unlock your extra online resources please go to www.mykaplan.co.uk/addabook (even if you have set up an account and registered books previously). You will then need to enter the ISBN number (on the title page and back cover) and the unique pass key number contained in the scratch panel below to gain access. You will also be required to enter additional information during this process to set up or confirm your account details.

If you purchased through the Kaplan Publishing website you will automatically receive an e-mail invitation to MyKaplan. Please register your details using this email to gain access to your content. If you do not receive the e-mail or book content, please contact Kaplan Publishing.

Your Code and Information

This code can only be used once for the registration of one book online. This registration and your online content will expire when the final sittings for the examinations covered by this book have taken place. Please allow one hour from the time you submit your book details for us to process your request.

Please scratch the film to access your unique code.

Please be aware that this code is case-sensitive and you will need to include the dashes within the passcode, but not when entering the ISBN.

ACCA

Strategic Professional

Strategic Business Reporting (INT & UK) (SBR)

EXAM KIT

British Library Cataloguing-in-Publication Data

A catalogue record for this book is available from the British Library.

Published by:
Kaplan Publishing UK
Unit 2 The Business Centre
Molly Millar's Lane
Wokingham
Berkshire
RG41 2QZ

ISBN: 978-1-83996-149-6

Acknowledgements

These materials are reviewed by the ACCA examining team. The objective of the review is to ensure that the material properly covers the syllabus and study guide outcomes, used by the examining team in setting the exams, in the appropriate breadth and depth. The review does not ensure that every eventuality, combination or application of examinable topics is addressed by the ACCA Approved Content. Nor does the review comprise a detailed technical check of the content as the Approved Content Provider has its own quality assurance processes in place in this respect.

CONTENTS

Versions of some questions in this Exam Kit may also be available on the ACCA Practice Platform on the ACCA website. They are a very useful reference, in particular to attempt using ACCA's exam software. However, you should be aware that ACCA will decide when those questions will be amended for syllabus changes or replaced, so they may differ slightly from the versions in this Exam Kit

This document references IFRS® Standards and IAS Standards®, which are authored by the International Accounting Standards Board (the Board), and published in the 2022 IFRS Standards Red Book.

Key features in this edition

In addition to providing a wide ranging bank of real past exam questions, we have also included in this edition:

- Paper specific information and advice on exam technique.
- Our recommended approach to make your revision for this particular subject as effective as possible.

  This includes step by step guidance on how best to use our Kaplan material (Study Text, Pocket Notes and Exam Kit) at this stage in your studies.
- Enhanced tutorial answers packed with specific key answer tips, technical tutorial notes and exam technique tips from our experienced tutors.
- Complementary online resources including full tutor debriefs and question assistance to point you in the right direction when you get stuck.

You will find a wealth of other resources to help you with your studies on the following sites:

www.MyKaplan.co.uk

www.**acca**global.com/students/

UK GAAP focus

The majority of the UK syllabus exam will be the same as the international exam, which is based on International Financial Reporting Standards (IFRS® Standards and IAS® Standards). The UK exam will also test some differences between UK GAAP and International Financial Reporting Standards. There could also be a focus on the requirements of Companies Act. It is anticipated that the differences will account for no more than 20% of the SBR UK paper.

UK syllabus students should refer to the list of examinable documents for the UK examination. This document is available on the ACCA web site at www.accaglobal.com

To assist UK syllabus students, additional questions and answers based on examinable UK content are included in this Exam Kit.

Quality and accuracy are of the utmost importance to us so if you spot an error in any of our products, please send an email to mykaplanreporting@kaplan.com with full details.

Our Quality Co-ordinator will work with our technical team to verify the error and take action to ensure it is corrected in future editions.

INDEX TO QUESTIONS AND ANSWERS

KEY TO THE INDEX

PAPER ENHANCEMENTS

We have added the following enhancements to the answers in this Exam Kit:

Key answer tips

All answers include key answer tips to help your understanding of each question.

Tutorial note

All answers include more tutorial notes to explain some of the technical points in more detail.

Top tutor tips

For selected questions, we 'walk through the answer' giving guidance on how to approach the questions with helpful 'tips from a top tutor', together with technical tutor notes.

These answers are indicated with the 'footsteps' icon in the index.

ONLINE ENHANCEMENTS

Answer debrief

For selected questions, we recommend that they are to be completed in full exam conditions (i.e. properly timed in a closed book environment).

In addition to the examining team's technical answer, enhanced with key answer tips and tutorial notes in this exam kit, online you can find an answer debrief by a top tutor that:

- works through the question in full
- explains key elements of the answer
- ensures that the easy marks are obtained as quickly as possible.

These questions are indicated with the 'video' icon in the index.

Answer debriefs will be available on MyKaplan at:

www.mykaplan.co.uk

SECTION A QUESTIONS

Group financial statements

Reporting and ethical implications

SECTION B QUESTIONS

UK GAAP focus

ANALYSIS OF PAST EXAMS

The table below summarises the key topics that have been tested in recent examinations.

Note that the references are to the number of the question in this edition of the exam kit.

	Sep 2018	Dec 2018	Mar/Jun 2019	Sep/Dec 2019	Mar 2020	Sep/Dec 2020	Mar/Jun 2021	Sep/Dec 2021
Groups question								
Goodwill calculations	Q8		Q6	Q5	Q4	Q3	Q2	Q1
Goodwill impairments				Q5				
Step acquisitions						Q3		Q1
Disposals		Q7	Q6					
Control-to-control								
Overseas subsidiaries			Q6		Q4			
Definition of a business	Q8							
Definition of control							Q2	Q1
Acquisition accounting							Q2	
Associates	Q8							Q1
Joint arrangements								Q33
Statement of cash flows		Q7				Q3		
Ethical issues	Q28	Q27	Q26	Q25	Q24	Q23	Q22	Q21
Conceptual Framework	Q47	Q7 Q45 Q46		Q41				
Accounting standards								
IAS 1								
IAS 2		Q45						
IAS 7	Q48	Q7						
IAS 8								
IAS 10								
IAS 12		Q46	Q26	Q25				Q1
IAS 16							Q36	
IAS 19			Q26	Q41	Q40	Q3 Q38	Q2	
IAS 20								
IAS 21			Q6		Q4			Q21
IAS 23						Q23		
IAS 24				Q25	Q24			
IAS 27							Q35	
IAS 28	Q8		Q43	Q41 Q42				Q33
IAS 32				Q25			Q22	Q34
IAS 33								
IAS 34								
IAS 36	Q28	Q45		Q5	Q39	Q37	Q22 Q36	
IAS 37	Q28	Q45	Q22		Q24 Q40	Q37	Q36	Q34
IAS 38	Q47				Q39	Q37	Q35	Q21 Q34
IAS 40								
IAS 41								
IFRS 1								
IFRS 2				Q5				
IFRS 3	Q8	Q45	Q6	Q5				

	Sep 2018	Dec 2018	Mar/Jun 2019	Sep/Dec 2019	Mar 2020	Sep/Dec 2020	Mar/Jun 2021	Sep/Dec 2021
IFRS 5	Q28	Q7	Q6		Q4	Q37		
IFRS 7								
IFRS 8								
IFRS 9	Q8		Q43	Q41	Q4		Q36	
IFRS 10			Q43	Q42				
IFRS 11		Q45	Q43	Q41				
IFRS 12								
IFRS 13				Q5 Q41	Q4		Q2 Q35	
IFRS 15	Q47	Q27	Q44	Q41		Q23	Q35	Q21
IFRS 16		Q27	Q43		Q39 Q40		Q35	Q33
SMEs Standard						Q38		
Analysis								
APMs	Q48							
Ratios			Q43	Q42				Q33
Disclosures		Q46						Q34
Integrated reporting	Q47					Q38		
Sustainability			Q44 (A)		Q40		Q36	
Current issues	*	Q46	*	*	*		Q36	Q34

* The current issue examined is no longer an examinable topic and so does not feature in this Exam Kit, or the particular current issue examined now falls within another area of the syllabus.

EXAM TECHNIQUE

- **Divide the time** you spend on questions in proportion to the marks on offer:

  Whatever happens, always keep your eye on the clock and **do not over run on any part of any question!**

- If you **get completely stuck** with a question:
  - move on
  - **return to it later.**

- Stick to the question and **tailor your answer** to what you are asked.
  - pay particular attention to the verbs in the question.

- If you do not understand what a question is asking, **state your assumptions**.

  Even if you do not answer in precisely the way the examiner hoped, you should be given some credit, if your assumptions are reasonable.

- You should do everything you can to make things easy for the marker.

  The marker will find it easier to identify the points you have made if you leave plenty of space between the points that you are making.

- **Discursive questions**:

  Your answer should have a clear structure. Use headings and paragraphs to provide focus.

  Be concise and stay on topic. You will score no marks if you do not answer the question.

- **Workings**:

  It is essential to include all your workings in your answers – method marks are available even if your final answer is incorrect.

  If your exam is computer based, make sure you reference any calculations performed in the spreadsheet.

PAPER SPECIFIC INFORMATION

THE EXAM

FORMAT OF THE EXAM

	Number of marks
Section A: Two compulsory questions	50
Section B: Two compulsory questions of 25 marks each	50
	100
Total time allowed: 3 hours 15 minutes.	

Note that:

- The first question in Section A will be worth 30 marks. It will always test group accounting. In addition to the consideration of the numerical aspects of group accounting (max 25 marks), a discussion and explanation of these numbers will be required. This question will also test other areas of the syllabus.
- The second question in Section A will be worth 20 marks. It requires consideration of (i) the reporting implications and (ii) the ethical implications of specific events in a given scenario. Two professional marks will be awarded in this question for the application of ethical principles to the scenario.
- Section B consists of two questions, which may be scenario or case-study or essay based and will contain both discursive and computational elements. Section B could deal with any aspect of the syllabus but will always include either a full question, or part of a question, that tests the analysis section of the syllabus. Two professional marks will be awarded in the Section B question that requires analysis.

PASS MARK

The pass mark for all ACCA Qualification examinations is 50%.

The UK exam

The Examiner has indicated that Section B questions in the UK exam will be adapted to assess UK specific content. These questions may be based on either a single entity or a group and will be worth approximately 15-20 marks. They may have discursive and/or numerical content and requirements, and could cover the following syllabus areas:

- The financial reporting requirements for UK and Republic of Ireland entities (UK GAAP) and their interaction with the Companies Act requirements
- The reasons why an entity might choose to adopt FRS 101 or FRS 102
- The scope and basis of preparation of financial statements under UK GAAP
- The concepts and pervasive principles set out in FRS 102
- The principal differences between UK GAAP and International Financial Reporting Standards.

Note that the UK syllabus exam will be denominated in dollars (identified as $); this Exam Kit adopts the same notation and style for UK syllabus content.

DETAILED SYLLABUS

The detailed syllabus and study guide written by the ACCA can be found at:

www.**acca**global.com/student

KAPLAN'S RECOMMENDED REVISION APPROACH

QUESTION PRACTICE IS THE KEY TO SUCCESS

Success in professional examinations relies upon you acquiring a firm grasp of the required knowledge at the tuition phase. In order to be able to do the questions, knowledge is essential.

However, the difference between success and failure often hinges on your exam technique on the day and making the most of the revision phase of your studies.

The **Kaplan Study Text** is the starting point, designed to provide the underpinning knowledge to tackle all questions. However, in the revision phase, pouring over text books is not the answer.

Kaplan Online progress tests help you consolidate your knowledge and understanding and are a useful tool to check whether you can remember key topic areas.

Kaplan Pocket Notes are designed to help you quickly revise a topic area, however you then need to practice questions. There is a need to progress to full exam standard questions as soon as possible, and to tie your exam technique and technical knowledge together.

The importance of question practice cannot be over-emphasised.

The recommended approach below is designed by expert tutors in the field, in conjunction with their knowledge of the examining team and their recent real exams.

The approach taken for the Applied Skills exams is to revise by topic area. However, with the Strategic Professional exams, a multi topic approach is required to answer the scenario based questions.

You need to practice as many questions as possible in the time you have left.

OUR AIM

Our aim is to get you to the stage where you can attempt exam standard questions confidently, to time, in a closed book environment, with no supplementary help (i.e. to simulate the real examination experience).

Practising your exam technique on examination-style questions, in timed conditions, is also vitally important for you to assess your progress and identify areas of weakness that may need more attention in the final run up to the examination.

In order to achieve this we recognise that initially you may feel the need to practice some questions with open book help and exceed the required time.

The approach below shows you which questions you should use to build up to coping with exam standard question practice, and references to the sources of information available should you need to revisit a topic area in more detail.

EXAMINER'S COMMENTS

We have included many of the examiner's comments to the examination questions in this kit for you to see the main pitfalls that students fall into with regard to technical content.

However, too many times in the general section of the report, the examiner comments that students had failed due to:

- 'misallocation of time'
- 'running out of time' and
- showing signs of 'spending too much time on an earlier question and clearly rushing the answer to a subsequent question'.

Good exam technique and time management is vital.

The examiners have also stressed the importance of carrying forward knowledge from FR. This is highlighted as a common weakness in candidate's scripts and is often the difference between a pass and a fail. Do not neglect the financial reporting topics and skills garnered within FR as they are imperative to SBR success.

Another regularly raised point by the examiner's team is the need to apply knowledge to the scenarios. It is not enough to merely state the required rules and knowledge learnt from the study material. Application to the scenario carries a substantially greater number of marks than just knowledge of the relevant rules.

STRATEGIC PROFESSIONAL COMPUTER BASED EXAMINATIONS

We advise consulting the ACCA Global website for additional CBE revision resources. On the ACCA website there is a CBE demonstration. It is **ESSENTIAL** that you attempt this before your real CBE. You will become familiar with how to move around the SBE screens and the way that questions are formatted, increasing your confidence and speed in the actual exam.

Be sure you understand how to use the **software** before you start the exam. If in doubt, ask the assessment centre staff to explain it to you.

Questions are **displayed on the screen** and answers are entered using keyboard and mouse.

For additional support with your studies please also refer to the ACCA Global website.

THE KAPLAN SBR REVISION PLAN

Stage 1: Assess areas of strengths and weaknesses

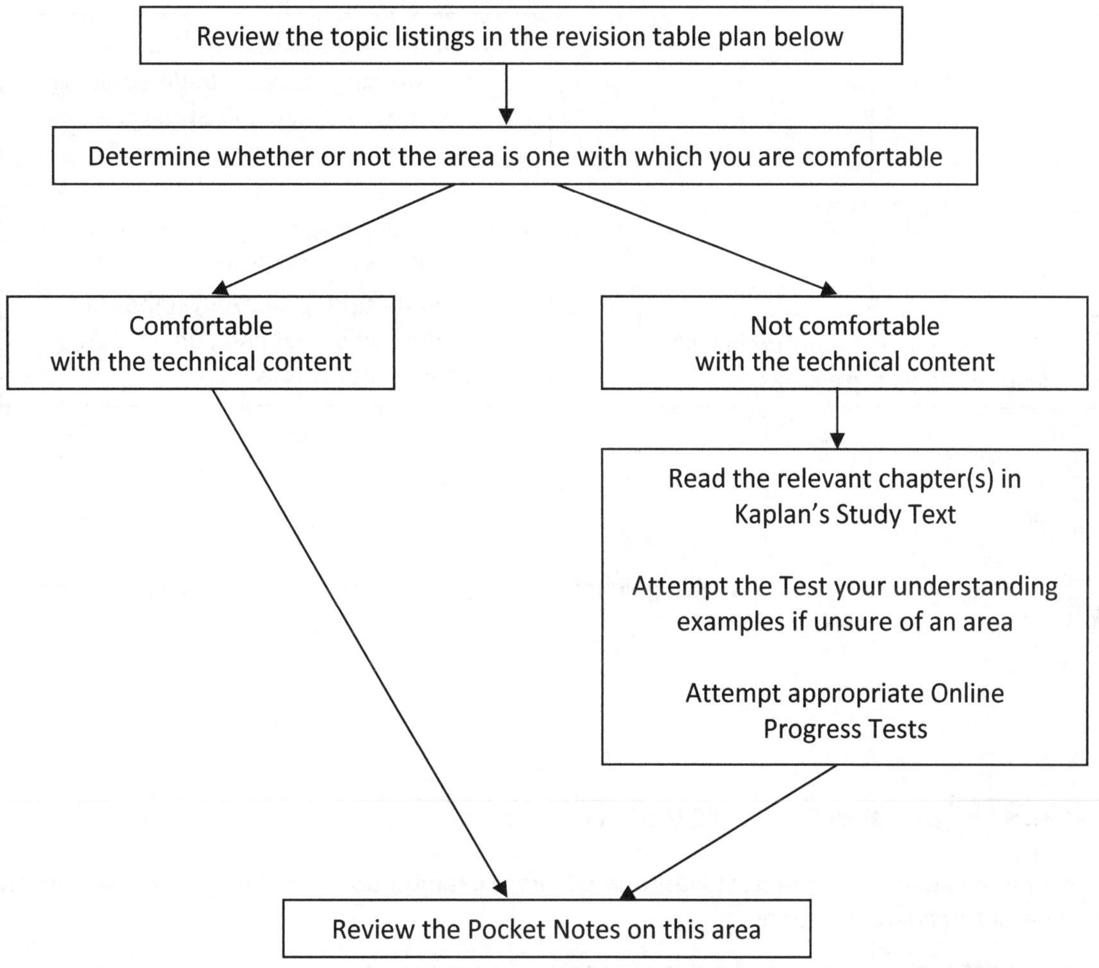

Stage 2: Practice questions

Follow the order of revision of topics as recommended in the revision table plan below and attempt the questions in the order suggested.

Try to avoid referring to text books and notes and the model answer until you have completed your attempt.

Try to answer the question in the allotted time.

Review your attempt with the model answer and assess how much of the answer you achieved in the allocated exam time.

Fill in the self-assessment box below and decide on your best course of action.

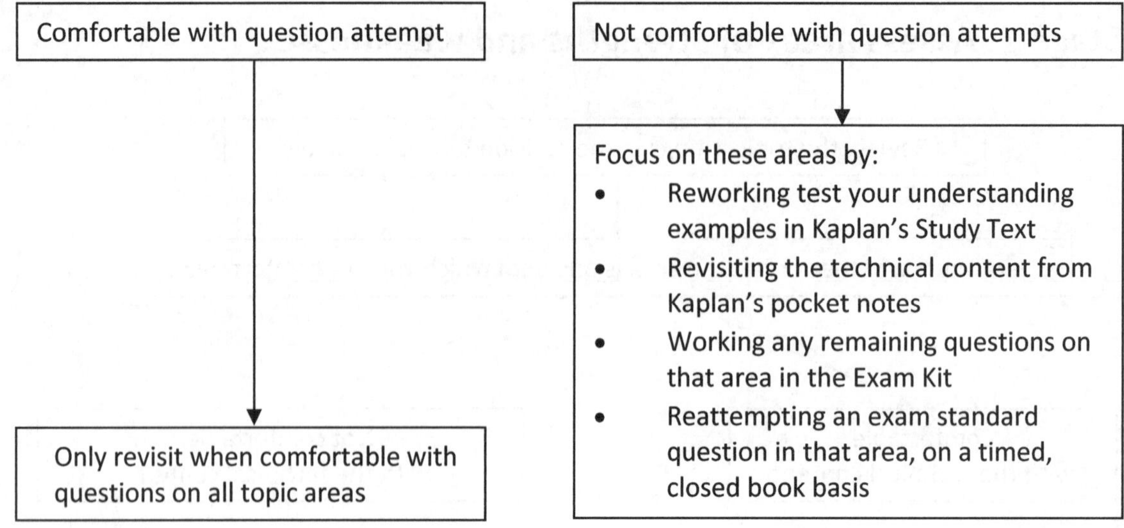

Note that:

The 'footsteps questions' give guidance on exam techniques and how you should have approached the question.

Stage 3: Final pre-exam revision

We recommend that you **attempt at least one full mock examination** containing a set of previously unseen exam standard questions.

It is important that you get a feel for the breadth of coverage of a real exam without advanced knowledge of the topic areas covered – just as you will expect to see on the real exam day.

Ideally this mock should be sat in timed, closed book, real exam conditions and could be:

- a mock examination offered by your tuition provider, and/or
- one of the specimen exams.

KAPLAN'S DETAILED REVISION PLAN

Topic	*Study Text Chapter*	*Pocket Note Chapter*	*Questions to attempt*	*Tutor guidance*	*Date attempted*	*Self-assessment*
The financial reporting framework	1	1	Q45 Q46(a) Q47(a)	Ensure that you know the contents of the *Conceptual Framework* and that you are able to apply it to transactions.		
Ethical and professional principles	2	2	Q21 Q22 Q23 Q24	Ensure that you can apply the ACCA *Code of Ethics and Conduct* to practical scenarios.		
Reporting financial performance						
Fair value measurement	1	1	Q50(a)	You must know the definition of fair value and be able to apply it. Make sure that you know the markets used to measure fair value and the levels of inputs to fair value measurement.		
Performance reporting and revenue	3, 4	3, 4	11(b) Q23(a) Q27(b) Q41(a)	This could include revenue recognition or the presentation of discontinued activities.		
Non-current assets, agriculture and inventories.	5, 6	5, 6	Q37 Q39 Q61(b)	There are several reporting standards within this heading. In particular, issues around property, plant and equipment, intangible assets, and impairment are regularly examined. Don't forget smaller areas, like government grants.		

Topic	*Study Text Chapter*	*Pocket Note Chapter*	*Questions to attempt*	*Tutor guidance*	*Date attempted*	*Self-assessment*
Foreign currency transactions	7	7	Q9(b) Q63(c)	Ensure that you know how to account for exchange differences arising on overseas transactions within an individual company's financial statements.		
Leases	8	8	Q33 Q39(a) Q43(b)	Ensure that you know how to determine when a contract contains a lease. You must be able to account for leases from the perspective of the lessee and the lessor, as well as sale and leaseback transactions.		
Employee benefits	9	9	Q2(b) Q26(a) Q34(d) Q40(b) Q41(c)	Ensure that you understand how to account for defined benefit and defined contribution schemes.		
Share-based payment	10	10	Q5(c) Q55(a)	Ensure that you understand how to account for both cash-settled transactions and equity-settled transactions.		
Provisions and events after the reporting period	11	11	Q36(c) Q40(b) Q50(b)	Ensure that you know when a legal or constructive obligation arises, and that you can apply the definition of an adjusting and non-adjusting event per IAS 10.		
Financial instruments	12	12	Q43(a) Q58 Q63	Ensure that you understand and can apply recognition, measurement and classification rules relating to financial instruments per IAS 32 and IFRS 9.		

Topic	*Study Text Chapter*	*Pocket Note Chapter*	*Questions to attempt*	*Tutor guidance*	*Date attempted*	*Self-assessment*
Income taxes	13	13	Q1 (b) Q25(a) Q46(b)	The main focus is likely to be the recognition and measurement of deferred tax assets and liabilities.		
Segment reporting	14	14	Q59(a)	Ensure that you can define a reportable segment and apply the definition to information provided. It is also important to know whether two segments can be aggregated.		
Related parties	15	15	Q24(a)	Ensure you can identify related parties per IAS 24, and the implications for any transactions which they may enter into.		
Small entities	17	17	Q38(a) Q53(a)	Ensure that you know the key differences between full IFRS Standards and the IFRS for SMEs Standard.		
Changes in accounting regulation	16, 23	16, 23	Q44(b) Q53(b) Q62(b)	You must be able to discuss the implications of adopting new accounting regulation. You should also ensure you are up-to-date with current issues in the profession.		

Topic	*Study Text Chapter*	*Pocket Note Chapter*	*Questions to attempt*	*Tutor guidance*	*Date attempted*	*Self-assessment*
Group financial statements						
Basic groups, including associates and joint arrangements	18	18	Q1 Q5 Q8	Ensure that you understand the standard workings required for subsidiaries in group financial statements, as well as key definitions – such as 'control', 'joint control' and 'significant influence'.		
Changes in group structure	19	19	Q1 Q11 Q12	Ensure that you know how to account for share transactions where control is either gained, lost or retained.		
Foreign currency subsidiaries	20	20	Q4 Q6	Ensure that you can consolidate a foreign subsidiary and can calculate the exchange differences that arise on its net assets, profit and goodwill.		
Statements of cash flows	21	21	Q3 Q7	Ensure that you know the format of a statement of cash flows and can deal with changes in group structure within the statement.		
Interpretation for stakeholders	22	22	Q38(a) Q40(a) Q42(b) Q46(b) Q48	Ensure that you are happy with the interpretation of financial and non-financial information, including additional performance measures. You must also be able to discuss the framework for integrated reporting and sustainability.		

Note that not all of the questions are referred to in the programme above. The remaining questions in the Exam Kit are for extra practice for those who require more questions on some areas.

Section 1

PRACTICE QUESTIONS

SECTION A QUESTIONS – GROUP FINANCIAL STATEMENTS

1 CHUCKLE (SEP/DEC 2021)  *Walk in the footsteps of a top tutor*

Background

Chuckle Co has an equity interest in a number of entities including Grin Co. Chuckle Co has recently acquired additional equity in Grin Co and the directors of Chuckle Co are unsure as to how this may impact upon their consolidated financial statements. The year end is 31 March each year.

Initial acquisition of Grin Co

On 1 April 20X2, Chuckle Co acquired 30% of the equity shares of Grin Co. The consideration consisted of $100 million cash. The carrying amount of the net assets of Grin Co on 1 April 20X2 were $286 million which was the same as their fair value. Since then, Grin Co has been correctly treated as an associate in the consolidated financial statements of Chuckle Co.

The remaining 70% of the equity of Grin Co at 1 April 20X2 is owned by a few other investors, none of which own more than 10% of the equity of Grin Co. Analysis shows that all shareholders have voted independently in the past. Chuckle Co and Grin Co share some key management personnel.

Subsequent acquisition of Grin Co

Chuckle Co acquired a further 18% of Grin Co's equity on 1 April 20X6. The consideration for the further 18% of the equity shares of Grin Co on 1 April 20X6 was $66 million in cash. The fair value of the original 30% equity interest was $127 million at 1 April 20X6. The carrying amount of the net assets of Grin Co on 1 April 20X6 was $348 million which included some land which had been revalued upwards by $15 million and correctly accounted for on 1 April 20X5.

Deferred tax at 20% had also been correctly accounted for on this gain in the individual statement of financial position of Grin Co as at 31 March 20X6. The rest of the increase in the net assets of Grin Co since acquisition was solely due to profits. Grin Co paid no dividends during this period.

The remaining 52% of the equity of Grin Co at 1 April 20X6 is owned by a few other investors, none of which own more than 10% of the equity of Grin Co.

On 1 April 20X6, Chuckle Co also acquired some share options in Grin Co exercisable any time until 31 March 20X7. The exercise price of the options at 1 April 20X6 was just above the market price of Grin Co's shares. Grin Co has been profitable for a number of years and the share price has been on an upwards trend which is expected to continue. Chuckle Co would increase its ownership to 60% should it exercise its rights. It is believed that there would be additional cost savings should the additional shares be acquired as decisions at board level could be made more efficiently.

Fair value of net assets of Grin Co

The carrying amounts of the net assets of Grin Co on 1 April 20X6 were as follows:

	$m
Non-current assets	355
Current assets	214
Deferred tax	(16)
Other liabilities	(205)
Total	348

Included within the non-current assets was the land which had been previously revalued upwards by $15 million on 1 April 20X5. The carrying amount of this land at 1 April 20X5 and 20X6 was $50 million but its fair value was assessed to be $60 million at 1 April 20X6.

Current assets include finished goods with a cost of $84 million. The fair value of these goods is $131 million.

On 1 April 20X6, the directors of Chuckle Co also identified that Grin Co had an internally generated database of customers who were likely to be interested in purchasing their products. Although there were no contractual or legal rights associated with this database, a professional expert has estimated that competitors of Grin Co would be prepared to pay $5 million for this database. Grin Co has not recognised the database as an asset within their individual financial statements.

The current rate of tax is 20%. This rate should be applied to any fair value adjustments deemed necessary.

Chuckle Co has a policy of measuring the non-controlling interest as the proportionate share of the net assets.

Required:

Draft an explanatory note to the directors of Chuckle Co to address the following issues:

(a) (i) why it was correct to initially classify Grin Co as an associate, as opposed to a subsidiary, on 1 April 20X2 **(4 marks)**

(ii) how Grin Co should be accounted for as an associate using the equity method in the consolidated statement of financial position of Chuckle Co at 31 March 20X6. Your answer should also explain how the revaluation of the land at 1 April 20X5 was accounted for and include all relevant calculations **(5 marks)**

(iii) whether the classification of Chuckle Co's investment in Grin Co should change on April 20X6. **(5 marks)**

On the assumption that Chuckle Co obtains control on 1 April 20X6, explain:

(b) (i) how the fair value of the non-current and current assets at acquisition (including any deferred tax adjustments) should be calculated, and **(8 marks)**

(ii) how goodwill/gain on bargain purchase should be calculated at 1 April 20X6. Your discussion should include a brief description of the accounting treatment arising from the additional purchase of the 18% equity in Grin Co. **(8 marks)**

(Total: 30 marks)

2 COLUMBIA (MAR/JUN 2021)  *Walk in the footsteps of a top tutor*

Background

Columbia Co is the parent of a listed group which operates within the telecommunications industry. During the year ended 31 December 20X5, Columbia Co acquired a new subsidiary and made adjustments to its pension scheme. The group's current year end is 31 December 20X5.

Acquisition of Peru Co

Brazil Co is a competitor of Columbia Co. On 1 July 20X5, both Brazil Co and Columbia Co acquired 50% of the 5 million ordinary $1 shares of Peru Co. The consideration paid by Columbia Co consisted of cash of $8 per share and also a 1 for 20 share exchange when the market price of Columbia Co's shares was $10 each. Brazil Co also paid $8 per share for their interest but did not issue any shares to the original shareholders of Peru Co. The ordinary shares of Peru Co have one voting right each.

Following the acquisition, Columbia Co had the contractual right to appoint 60% of the board of Peru Co with the remaining 40% appointed by Brazil Co. Brazil Co has veto rights over any amendments to the articles of incorporation and also over the appointment of auditors. Brazil Co and Columbia Co each appointed one member to Peru Co's senior management team. It is the senior manager appointed by Columbia Co who makes the key decisions regarding the development of Peru Co's new technologies, its principle revenue stream, the markets that it will operate in and how it is financed. The senior manager appointed by Columbia Co also provides a supervisory role and has the right to request that significant activities get board approval, such as imposing restrictions on Peru Co from undertaking activities that would significantly increase credit risk.

Peru Co: net assets at 1 July 20X5

The net assets of Peru Co reported in the individual financial statements had a carrying amount of $32 million on 1 July 20X5. However, on the acquisition of Peru Co, the directors of Columbia Co discovered the following:

On 1 January 20X5, Peru Co acquired 6 million 6% coupon bonds for $6 million in an unquoted company at par ($1). Bond interest is paid annually on 31 December. Due to a premium on redemption the effective rate of interest was 8%. Peru Co has a business model to collect the contractual cash-flows from the bonds and therefore measures them at amortised cost. Columbia Co holds similar unquoted assets but has a business model whereby they may either collect the contractual cash-flows or sell the asset. Bonds with a similar risk profile for a similar quoted company were trading at $2 per bond on 1 July 20X5. A discount of 30% is considered reasonable to reflect the difference in liquidity of the two types of bonds.

One of the identifiable intangible assets of Peru Co at acquisition was a brand. The brand had a carrying amount of $4 million on 1 July 20X5. Columbia Co has a similar branded product and is, therefore, planning to discontinue the trade of Peru Co's branded product with immediate effect. The future cash-flows from the Peru Co's product post-acquisition are therefore considered to be $nil. If the trade of the branded product were to be sold to a competitor in order to continue the trade, it is estimated that it could be sold for around $5 million.

Peru Co has several technical support service contracts for which there are outstanding performance obligations at 1 July 20X5. Included in contract liability (deferred income) at this date is a balance of $2.8 million in respect of these contracts. It is estimated that these contracts will cost $1.7 million for Peru co (and any other market participants) to complete. A mark-up of 30% is considered reasonable for this type of contract.

Columbia Co has a policy of measuring the non-controlling interest at fair value.

Columbia Co: Pension scheme

Columbia Co has, for many years, operated a defined benefit pension scheme. At 1 January 20X5, the fair value of the pension scheme assets were estimated to be $260 million and the present value of the pension scheme liabilities were $200 million. The total of the present value of future refunds and reductions in future contributions (asset ceiling) was $20 million at 1 January 20X5. This table provides details of the scheme for the year ended 31 December 20X5 when there was a curtailment to the scheme.

Discount rate on good quality corporate bonds	5%
	$m
Current service costs	30
Cash contributions	21
Benefits paid during the year	25
Scheme curtailment (31 December 20X5)	28
Payment to employees as settlement for curtailment (paid 31 December 20X5)	16

At 31 December 20X5, the fair value of the pension scheme assets were estimated to be $242 million and the present value of the pension scheme liabilities were $195 million. The total of the present value of future refunds and reductions in future contributions (asset ceiling) was $25 million at 31 December 20X5.

Columbia Co intends all new employees to be offered a defined contribution rather than a defined benefit pension scheme. Contributions of $0.5 million were paid into a defined contribution scheme for new employees over the last 3 months of the year.

Required:

Draft an explanatory note to the directors of Columbia Co to address the following issues:

(a) (i) whether Columbia Co should be considered the acquirer in a business combination with Peru Co (9 marks)

(ii) a calculation of goodwill at 1 July 20X5, explaining how fair values of both the consideration and the net assets have been determined, and (11 marks)

(b) how the defined benefit and the defined contribution pension schemes should be accounted for in the year ended 31 December 20X5. (10 marks)

(Total: 30 marks)

3 SUGAR (SEP/DEC 2020) 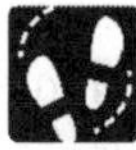 *Walk in the footsteps of a top tutor*

Background

At 30 June 20X7, Sugar Co has investments in several associate companies, including Flour Co. On 1 July 20X7 Sugar Co acquired additional shares in Flour Co and obtained control. On 1 October 20X7 Sugar Co also acquired an associate, Butter Co. The group is preparing the consolidated statement of cash flows for the year ended 30 June 20X8.

Acquisition of Flour Co

Flour Co has 10 million shares in issue. A 40% shareholding in Flour Co was purchased several years ago at a cost of $10 million. This investment gave Sugar Co significant influence in Flour Co. The consideration to acquire an additional three million shares (30% shareholding) in Flour Co on 1 July 20X7 was in two parts: (i) cash and; (ii) a one for two share exchange when the market price of Sugar Co shares was $6 each. In Flour Co's individual financial statements, the net assets had increased by $12 million between the two acquisition dates. The carrying amount of Flour Co's net assets on 1 July 20X7 was as follows: licenses

	$000
Intangible assets (licenses and patents)	6,781
Property, plant and equipment	18,076
Cash and cash equivalents	1,234
Other net current assets	9,650
Total net assets carrying amount	35,741

The carrying amounts of the net assets at 1 July 20X7 were equal to the fair values except for land which had a fair value $600,000 above the carrying amount. The Sugar group values non -controlling interests (NCI) at fair value and the share price of Flour Co at 1 July 20X7 was $3.80. This share price should be used to value NCI at that date and to value the initial 40% equity interest in Flour Co.

Goodwill at 1 July 20X7 was correctly calculated as $2,259,000 and has been correctly accounted for in the consolidated statement of financial position.

Asset acquisitions and disposals

Including its purchase of the additional investment in Flour Co which it correctly consolidated from 1 July 20X7, the Sugar group also purchased various assets during the year.

There were no disposals or impairments of intangible assets during the year but amortisation of $3.5 million had been deducted from profit from operations.

The only additions to property, plant and equipment during the year were as a result of the acquisition of Flour Co. The group disposed of some plant and machinery at a loss on disposal of $2 million. Depreciation deducted from the profit from operations was $10 million.

Sugar Co purchased a 25% equity interest in Butter Co on 1 October 20X7 for $5 million cash which gave significant influence. Butter Co paid a dividend in the post-acquisition period and Sugar Co also received dividends from other associates during the year ended 30 June 20X8. Sugar Co did not pay any dividends during the year.

There were no acquisitions of investments measured at fair value through profit or loss (FVTPL) during the year but there were disposals which had a carrying amount of $4 million. These were sold at a profit of $500,000 which was included, alongside fair value gains, in investment income in the consolidated statement of profit or loss. The investment income figure also includes dividends received from these investments and any fair value gains or losses recognised on the initial investment in Flour Co.

In addition to the shares issued to purchase Flour Co, Sugar Co issued some ordinary $1 shares for cash during the year ended 30 June 20X8.

Group financial statement extracts

The group's consolidated financial statements have been calculated correctly. Extracts, together with relevant comparative figures at 30 June, are provided below:

Consolidated statement of financial position as at 30 June (extracts):

	20X8	20X7
	$000	$000
Non-current assets		
Intangible assets	33,456	15,865
Property, plant and equipment	55,124	52,818
Investment in associates	26,328	23,194
Financial assets (measured at FVTPL)	3,000	6,000
Equity		
Ordinary share capital ($1 shares)	23,000	20,000
Other components of equity (all share premium)	33,600	18,000
Non-controlling interest	30,152	12,914

Consolidated statement of profit or loss for the year ended 30 June 20X8 (extract):

	$000
Investment income	3,891
Share of profit from associate companies	15,187
Profit attributable to the non-controlling interest	9,162

Pension scheme

Sugar Co is the only entity of the group which operates a defined benefit pension scheme. The pension scheme obligation increased during the year from $1.175m to $6.368m. The movement on the pension liability represents the service cost component, the net interest component and also the remeasurement component for the year. Sugar Co usually makes cash contributions into the scheme on an annual basis towards the year end. The significant increase in the pension scheme obligation for the year ended 30 June 20X8 was because the contributions to the scheme did not follow normal practice and were instead made in July 20X8. Benefits paid during the year were $2 million in cash.

Required:

(a) **Draft an explanatory note to the directors of Sugar Co, addressing how the initial 40% investment in Flour Co and the additional purchase of the equity shares on 1 July 20X7 should be accounted for in the consolidated financial statements (including the statement of cash flows). Using the goodwill figure of $2,259,000, calculate the cash paid to acquire control of Flour Co and include a brief explanation as to how that cash should be accounted for in the consolidated statement of cash flows.**

(10 marks)

(b) Prepare extracts of the cash flows generated from (i) investing activities and (ii) financing activities in the consolidated statement of cash flows for the Sugar group for the year ended 30 June 20X8. No explanations are required in part (b).

(16 marks)

(c) Describe the impact, if any, that the defined benefit pension scheme will have on the consolidated statement of cash flows for the Sugar group for the year ended 30 June 20X8 assuming that cash flows from operating activities are calculated by the indirect method. **(4 marks)**

(Total: 30 marks)

4 HUMMINGS (MAR 2020)  *Walk in the footsteps of a top tutor*

Background

Hummings Co is the parent company of a multinational listed group of companies. Hummings Co uses the dollar ($) as its functional currency. Hummings Co acquired 80% of the equity shares of Crotchet Co on 1 January 20X4 and 100% of Quaver Co on the same date. The group's current financial year end is 31 December 20X4.

Crotchet Co: functional currency

The head office of Crotchet Co is located in a country which uses the dinar as its main currency. However, its staff are located in a variety of other locations. Consequently, half of their employees are paid in dinars and the other half are paid in the currency of grommits. Crotchet Co has a high degree of autonomy and is not reliant on finance from Hummings Co, nor do sales to Hummings Co make up a significant proportion of their income. All of its sales and purchases are invoiced in grommits and therefore Crotchet Co raises most of its finance in grommits. Cash receipts are retained in both grommits and dinars. Crotchet Co does not own a dollar ($) bank account. Crotchet Co is required by law to pay tax on its profits in dinars.

The acquisition of Crotchet Co

Hummings Co paid cash of $24 million for the 80% holding in Crotchet Co on 1 January 20X4. Hummings Co has a policy of measuring non-controlling interests at fair value. The fair value of the non-controlling interests in Crotchet Co on 1 January 20X4 was $6 million. Since Crotchet Co has a range of net assets held domestically and overseas, the fair values of the net assets at acquisition were determined in their local currency. Hence, the fair value of some assets have been determined in dinars and others in grommits. The total fair value of the net assets denominated in grommits at 1 January 20X4 was 43 million grommits. The total fair value of the net assets denominated in dinars at 1 January 20X4 was 50 million dinars.

Excluded from these fair values are several contracts with the customers of Crotchet Co. These contractual relationships prohibit the customers of Crotchet Co from obtaining services from any of the main competitors of Crotchet Co. They have an estimated fair value at 1 January 20X4 of 15 million grommits.

At 31 December 20X4, it was decided to impair goodwill by 30%.

The following is a summary of the exchange rates between the dollar, grommits and dinars at 1 January 20X4 and 31 December 20X4:

1 January 20X4	**31 December 20X4**
\$1:8 grommits	\$1:7 grommits
\$1: 4 dinar	\$1: 3.5 dinar
1 dinar:2 grommits	1 dinar:2 grommits

The acquisition of Quaver Co

On 1 January 20X4, Hummings Co purchased a 100% equity interest in Quaver Co. Hummings Co made the acquisition with the intention to sell and therefore did not wish to have an active involvement in the business of Quaver Co. Hummings Co immediately began to seek a buyer for Quaver Co and felt that the sale would be completed by 31 October 20X4 at the latest. A buyer for Quaver Co was located in August 20X4 but, due to an unforeseen legal dispute over a contingent liability disclosed in Quaver Co's financial statements, the sale had not yet been finalised as at 31 December 20X4. The sale is expected to be completed in early 20X5.

Impairment of bonds

On 31 December 20X3, Hummings Co purchased \$10 million 5% bonds in Stave Co at par value. The bonds are repayable on 31 December 20X6 and the effective rate of interest is 8%. Hummings Co's business model is to collect the contractual cash flows over the life of the asset. At 31 December 20X3, the bonds were considered to be low risk and as a result the 12-month expected credit losses are expected to be \$10,000.

On 31 December 20X4, Stave Co paid the coupon interest. However, at that date, the risks associated with the bonds were deemed to have increased significantly. The present value of the cash shortfalls arising on default in the year ended 31 December 20X5 is \$462,963 and the probability of default is 3%. The present value of cash shortfalls arising on default in the year ended 31 December 20X6 is \$6,858,710 and the probability of default is 5%.

Required:

Draft an explanatory note to the directors of Hummings Co, addressing the following:

(a) how the functional currency of Crotchet Co should be determined. (5 marks)

(b) (i) how Crotchet Co's customer contracts should be accounted for in the consolidated financial statements of Hummings Co, which are presented in dollars (\$), for the year ended 31 December 20X4. (4 marks)

(ii) a calculation of the goodwill on acquisition of Crotchet Co (in grommits) and how it would be accounted for in the consolidated statement of financial position of Hummings Co at 31 December 20X4 after translation. Include a brief explanation and calculation of how the impairment and exchange difference on goodwill will impact on the consolidated financial statements. (6 marks)

(c) how Quaver Co should be accounted for in the consolidated financial statements at 31 December 20X4. (4 marks)

(d) a calculation and discussion of how the bonds should be accounted for in the financial statements of Hummings Co as at 31 December 20X3 and for the year ended 31 December 20X4, including any impairment losses. (11 marks)

(Total: 30 marks)

5 LUPLOID (SEP/DEC 2019)  *Walk in the footsteps of a top tutor*

Background

Luploid Co is the parent company of a group undergoing rapid expansion through acquisition. Luploid Co has acquired two subsidiaries in recent years, Colyson Co and Hammond Co. The current financial year end is 30 June 20X8.

Acquisition of Colyson Co

Luploid Co acquired 80% of the five million equity shares ($1 each) of Colyson Co on 1 July 20X4 for cash of $90 million. The fair value of the non-controlling interest (NCI) at acquisition was $22 million. The fair value of the identifiable net assets at acquisition was $65 million, excluding the following asset. Colyson Co purchased a factory site several years prior to the date of acquisition. Land and property prices in the area had increased significantly in the years immediately prior to 1 July 20X4. Nearby sites had been acquired and converted into residential use. It is felt that, should the Colyson Co site also be converted into residential use, the factory site would have a market value of $24 million. $1 million of costs are estimated to be required to demolish the factory and to obtain planning permission for the conversion. Colyson Co was not intending to convert the site at the acquisition date and had not sought planning permission at that date. The depreciated replacement cost of the factory at 1 July 20X4 has been correctly calculated as $17.4 million.

Impairment of Colyson Co

Colyson Co incurred losses during the year ended 30 June 20X8 and an impairment review was performed. The carrying amount of the net assets of Colyson Co at 30 June 20X8 (including fair value adjustments on acquisition but excluding goodwill) are as follows:

	$m
Land and buildings	60
Plant and machinery	15
Intangibles other than goodwill	9
Current assets (at recoverable amount)	22
Total	106

The recoverable amount of Colyson Co's assets was estimated to be $100 million. Included in this assessment was a building owned by Colyson Co which had been damaged in a storm and needs to be impaired by $4 million. Other land and buildings are held at recoverable amount. None of the assets of Colyson Co including goodwill have been impaired previously. Colyson Co does not have a policy of revaluing its assets.

Acquisition of Hammond Co and share-based payments

Luploid Co acquired 60% of the 10 million equity shares of Hammond Co on 1 July 20X7. Two Luploid Co shares are to be issued for every five shares acquired in Hammond Co. These shares will be issued on 1 July 20X8. The fair value of a Luploid Co share was $30 at 1 July 20X7.

Hammond Co had previously granted a share-based payment to its employees with a three-year vesting period. At 1 July 20X7, the employees had completed their service period but had not yet exercised their options. The fair value of the options granted at 1 July 20X7 was $15 million. As part of the acquisition, Luploid Co is obliged to replace the share-based payment scheme of Hammond Co with a scheme that has a fair value of $18 million at 1 July 20X7. There are no vesting conditions attached to this replacement scheme.

Unrelated to the acquisition of Hammond, Luploid Co issued 100 options to 10,000 employees on 1 July 20X7. The shares are conditional on the employees completing a further two years of service. Additionally, the scheme required that the market price of Luploid Co's shares had to increase by 10% from its value of $30 per share at the acquisition date over the vesting period. It was anticipated at 1 July 20X7 that 10% of staff would leave over the vesting period but this was revised to 4% by 30 June 20X8. The fair value of each option at the grant date was $20. The share price of Luploid Co at 30 June 20X8 was $32 and is anticipated to grow at a similar rate in the year ended 30 June 20X9.

Required:

Draft an explanatory note to the directors of Luploid Co, addressing the following:

(a) (i) How the fair value of the factory site should be determined at 1 July 20X4 and why the depreciated replacement cost of $17.4 million is unlikely to be a reasonable estimate of fair value. **(7 marks)**

(ii) A calculation of goodwill arising on the acquisition of Colyson Co measuring the non-controlling interest at:

- **fair value**
- **proportionate share of the net assets.** **(3 marks)**

(b) The calculation and allocation of Colyson Co's impairment loss at 30 June 20X8 and a discussion of why the impairment loss of Colyson Co would differ depending on how non-controlling interests are measured. Your answer should include a calculation and an explanation of how the impairments would impact upon the consolidated financial statements of Luploid Co. **(11 marks)**

(c) (i) How the consideration for the acquisition of Hammond Co should be measured on 1 July 20X7. Your answer should include a discussion of why only some of the cost of the replacement share-based payment scheme should be included within the consideration. **(4 marks)**

(ii) How much of an expense for share-based payment schemes should be recognised in the consolidated statement of profit or loss of Luploid Co for the year ended 30 June 20X8. Your answer should include a brief discussion of the relevant principles and how the vesting conditions impact upon the calculations. **(5 marks)**

Note: Any workings can either be shown in the main body of the explanatory note or in an appendix to the explanatory note.

(Total: 30 marks)

6 CARBISE (MAR/JUN 2019)  *Walk in the footsteps of a top tutor*

Background

Carbise is the parent company of an international group which has a presentation and functional currency of the dollar. The group operates within the manufacturing sector. On 1 January 20X2, Carbise acquired 80% of the equity share capital of Bikelite, an overseas subsidiary. The acquisition enabled Carbise to access new international markets. Carbise transfers surplus work-in-progress to Bikelite which is then completed and sold in various locations. The acquisition was not as successful as anticipated and on 30 September 20X6 Carbise disposed of all of its holding in Bikelite. The current year end is 31 December 20X6.

Bikelite trading information

Bikelite is based overseas where the domestic currency is the dinar. Staff costs and overhead expenses are all paid in dinars. However, Bikelite also has a range of transactions in a number of other currencies. Approximately 40% of its raw material purchases are in dinars and 50% in the yen. The remaining 10% are in dollars of which approximately half were purchases of material from Carbise. This ratio continued even after Carbise disposed of its shares in Bikelite.

Revenue is invoiced in equal proportion between dinars, yen and dollars. To protect itself from exchange rate risk, Bikelite retains cash in all three currencies. No dividends have been paid by Bikelite for several years. At the start of 20X6 Bikelite sought additional debt finance. As Carbise was already looking to divest, funds were raised from an issue of bonds in dinars, none of which were acquired by Carbise.

Acquisition of Bikelite

Carbise paid dinar 100 million for 80% of the ordinary share capital of Bikelite on 1 January 20X2. The net assets of Bikelite at this date had a carrying amount of dinar 60 million. The only fair value adjustment deemed necessary was in relation to a building which had a fair value of dinar 20 million above its carrying amount and a remaining useful life of 20 years at the acquisition date. Carbise measures non-controlling interests (NCI) at fair value for all acquisitions, and the fair value of the 20% interest was estimated to be dinar 22 million at acquisition. Due to the relatively poor performance of Bikelite, it was decided to impair goodwill by dinar 6 million during the year ending 31 December 20X5.

Rates of exchange between the $ and dinar are given as follows:

1 January 20X2:	$1:0.5 dinar
Average rate for year ended 31 December 20X5	$1:0.4 dinar
31 December 20X5:	$1:0.38 dinar
30 September 20X6:	$1:0.35 dinar
Average rate for the nine-month period ended 30 September 20X6	$1:0.37 dinar

Disposal of Bikelite

Carbise sold its entire equity shareholding in Bikelite on 30 September 20X6 for $150 million. Further details relating to the disposal are as follows:

Carrying amount of Bikelite's net assets at 1 January 20X6 in its separate financial statements	dinar 48 million
Bikelite loss for the year ended 31 December 20X6 in its separate financial statements	dinar 8 million
Cumulative exchange gains on Bikelite at 1 January 20X6	$74.1 million
Non-controlling interest in Bikelite at 1 January 20X6	$47.8 million

Required:

(a) Prepare an explanatory note for the directors of Carbise which addresses the following issues:

(i) The meaning of an entity's presentation and functional currency Explain your answer with reference to how the presentation and functional currency of Bikelite should be determined. (7 marks)

(ii) A calculation of the goodwill on the acquisition of Bikelite and what the balance would be at 30 September 20X6 immediately before the disposal of the shares. Your answer should include a calculation of the exchange difference on goodwill for the period from 1 January 20X6 to 30 September 20X6. (5 marks)

(iii) An explanation of your calculation of goodwill and the treatment of exchange differences on goodwill in the consolidated financial statements. You do not need to discuss how the disposal will affect the exchange differences. (4 marks)

Note: Any workings can either be shown in the main body of the explanatory note or in an appendix to the explanatory note.

(b) Explain why exchange differences will arise on the net assets and profit or loss of Bikelite each year and how they would be presented within the consolidated financial statements. Your answer should include a calculation of the exchange differences which would arise on the translation of Bikelite (excluding goodwill) in the year ended 31 December 20X6. (7 marks)

(c) (i) Calculate the group profit or loss on the disposal of Bikelite. (3 marks)

(ii) Briefly explain how Bikelite should be treated and presented in the consolidated financial statements of Carbise for the year ended 31 December 20X6. (4 marks)

(Total: 30 marks)

7 MOYES (DEC 2018)  *Walk in the footsteps of a top tutor*

Background

The following are extracts from the consolidated financial statements of the Moyes group.

Group statement of profit or loss for the year ended 30 September 20X8:

	$m
Revenue	612
Cost of sales	(347)
Gross profit	265
Operating expenses	(123)
Share of profit of associate	67
Profit before tax	209

Extracts from the group statement of financial position:

	30 September 20X8	**30 September 20X7**
	$m	$m
Inventories	126	165
Trade receivables	156	149
Trade payables	215	197

The following information is also relevant to the year ended 30 September 20X8:

Pension scheme

Moyes operates a defined benefit scheme. A service cost component of $24 million has been included within operating expenses. The remeasurement component for the year was a gain of $3 million. Benefits paid out of the scheme were $31 million. Contributions into the scheme by Moyes were $15 million.

Goodwill

Goodwill was reviewed for impairments at the reporting date. Impairments arose of $10 million in the current year.

Property, plant and equipment

Property, plant and equipment (PPE) at 30 September 20X8 included cash additions of $134 million. Depreciation charged during the year was $99 million and an impairment loss of $43 million was recognised. Prior to the impairment, the group had a balance on the revaluation surplus of $50 million of which $20 million related to PPE impaired in the current year.

Inventory

Goods were purchased for Dinar 80 million cash when the exchange rate was $1:Dinar 5. Moyes had not managed to sell the goods at 30 September 20X8 and the net realisable value was estimated to be Dinar 60 million at 30 September 20X8. The exchange rate at this date was $1:Dinar 6. The inventory has been correctly valued at 30 September 20X8 with any expense correctly included within cost of sales.

Changes to group structure

During the year ended 30 September 20X8, Moyes acquired a 60% subsidiary, Davenport, and also sold all of its equity interests in Barham for cash. The consideration for Davenport consisted of a share for share exchange together with some cash payable in two years. 80% of the equity shares of Barham had been acquired several years ago but Moyes had decided to sell as the performance of Barham had been poor for a number of years. Consequently, Barham had a substantial overdraft at the disposal date. Barham was unable to pay any dividends during the financial year but Davenport did pay an interim dividend on 30 September 20X8.

Discontinued operations

The directors of Moyes wish advice as to whether the disposal of Barham should be treated as a discontinued operation and separately disclosed within the consolidated statement of profit or loss. There are several other subsidiaries which all produce similar products to Barham and operate in a similar geographical area. Additionally, Moyes holds a 52% equity interest in Watson. Watson has previously issued share options to other entities which are exercisable in the year ending 30 September 20X9. It is highly likely that these options would be exercised which would reduce Moyes' interest to 35%. The directors of Moyes require advice as to whether this loss of control would require Watson to be classified as held for sale and reclassified as discontinued.

Required:

(a) Draft an explanatory note to the directors of Moyes which should include:

(i) a calculation of cash generated from operations using the indirect method; and

(ii) an explanation of the specific adjustments required to the group profit before tax to calculate the cash generated from operations.

Note: Any workings can either be shown in the main body of the explanatory note or in an appendix to the explanatory note. (12 marks)

(b) Explain how the changes to the group structure and dividend would impact upon the consolidated statement of cash flows at 30 September 20X8 for the Moyes group. You should not attempt to alter your answer to part (a). (6 marks)

(c) Advise the directors as to whether Watson should be classified as held for sale and whether both it and Barham should be classified as discontinued operations. (6 marks)

(d) The recognition criteria in the 2010 *Conceptual Framework* stated that a flow of economic benefits must be probable before an element can be recognised in the financial statements. However, IFRS and IAS Standards were criticised for applying this probability criterion inconsistently. The 2018 *Conceptual Framework* addressed these concerns.

Required:

Explain how the probability criterion has been inconsistently applied across accounting standards. Illustrate your answer with reference to the measurement of assets held for sale, provisions, and contingent consideration transferred in a business combination. Your answer should discuss the Board's recognition criteria in the 2018 *Conceptual Framework*. (6 marks)

(Total: 30 marks)

8 BANANA (SEP 2018)  *Walk in the footsteps of a top tutor*

 ***Answer debrief***

Background

Banana is the parent of a listed group of companies which have a year end of 30 June 20X7. Banana has made a number of acquisitions and disposals of investments during the current financial year and the directors require advice as to the correct accounting treatment of these acquisitions and disposals.

The acquisition of Grape

On 1 January 20X7, Banana acquired an 80% equity interest in Grape. The following is a summary of Grape's equity at the acquisition date.

	$m
Equity share capital ($1 each)	20
Retained earnings	42
Other components of equity	8
	——
Total	70
	——

The purchase consideration comprised 10 million of Banana's shares which had a nominal value of $1 each and a market price of $6.80 each. Additionally, cash of $18 million was due to be paid on 1 January 20X9 if the net profit after tax of Grape grew by 5% in each of the two years following acquisition. The present value of the total contingent consideration at 1 January 20X7 was $16 million. It was felt that there was a 25% chance of the profit target being met. At acquisition, the only adjustment required to the identifiable net assets of Grape was for land which had a fair value $5 million higher than its carrying amount. This is not included within the $70 million equity of Grape at 1 January 20X7.

Goodwill for the consolidated financial statements has been incorrectly calculated as follows:

	$m
Share consideration	68
Add NCI at acquisition (20% × $70 million)	14
Less net assets at acquisition	(70)
	——
Goodwill at acquisition	12
	——

The financial director did not take into account the contingent cash since it was not probable that it would be paid. Additionally, he measured the non-controlling interest using the proportional method of net assets despite the group having a published policy to measure non-controlling interest at fair value. The share price of Grape at acquisition was $4.25 and should be used to value the non-controlling interest.

The acquisition and subsequent disposal of Strawberry

Banana had purchased a 40% equity interest in Strawberry for $18 million a number of years ago when the fair value of the identifiable net assets was $44 million. Since acquisition, Banana had the right to appoint one of the five directors on the board of Strawberry. The investment has always been equity accounted for in the consolidated financial statements of Banana.

Banana disposed of 75% of its 40% investment on 1 October 20X6 for $19 million when the fair values of the identifiable net assets of Strawberry were $50 million. At that date, Banana lost its right to appoint one director to the board. The fair value of the remaining 10% equity interest was $4.5 million at disposal but only $4 million at 30 June 20X7. Banana has recorded a loss in reserves of $14 million calculated as the difference between the price paid of $18 million and the fair value of $4 million at the reporting date. Banana has stated that they have no intention to sell their remaining shares in Strawberry and wish to classify the remaining 10% interest as fair value through other comprehensive income in accordance with IFRS 9 *Financial Instruments*.

The acquisition of Melon

On 30 June 20X7, Banana acquired all of the shares of Melon, an entity which operates in the biotechnology industry. Melon was only recently formed and its only recognised asset consists of a licence to carry out research activities. Melon has no employees because research activities were outsourced to other companies, although these contracts expired on 30 June 20X7. The research activities are still at a very early stage and it is not clear whether any definitive product would result from the activities. A management company provides personnel for Melon to supply supervisory activities and administrative functions. Banana believes that Melon does not constitute a business in accordance with IFRS 3 *Business Combinations*. The directors of Banana believe that Melon should be treated as an asset acquisition.

The acquisition of bonds

On 1 July 20X5, Banana acquired $10 million 5% bonds at par with interest being due at 30 June each year. The bonds are repayable at a substantial premium so that the effective rate of interest was 7%. Banana intended to hold the bonds to collect the contractual cash flows arising from the bonds and measured them at amortised cost.

On 1 July 20X6, Banana sold the bonds to a third party for $8 million. The fair value of the bonds was $10.5 million at that date. Banana has the right to repurchase the bonds on 1 July 20X8 for $8.8 million and it is likely that this option will be exercised. The third party is obliged to return the coupon interest to Banana and to pay additional cash to Banana should bond values rise. Banana will also compensate the third party for any devaluation of the bonds.

Required:

(a) Draft an explanatory note to the directors of Banana, discussing the following:

(i) how goodwill should have been calculated on the acquisition of Grape and show the accounting entry which is required to amend the financial director's error (8 marks)

(ii) why equity accounting was the appropriate treatment for Strawberry in the consolidated financial statements up to the date of its disposal showing the carrying amount of the investment in Strawberry just prior to disposal (4 marks)

(iii) how the gain or loss on disposal of Strawberry should have been recorded in the consolidated financial statements and how the investment in Strawberry should be accounted for after the part disposal. (4 marks)

Note: Any workings can either be shown in the main body of the explanatory note or in an appendix to the explanatory note.

(b) Discuss whether the directors are correct to treat Melon as an asset acquisition. (7 marks)

(c) Discuss how the derecognition requirements of IFRS 9 *Financial Instruments* should be applied to the sale of the bond including calculations to show the impact on the consolidated financial statements for the year ended 30 June 20X7. (7 marks)

(Total: 30 marks)

Calculate your allowed time, allocate the time to the separate parts..............

9 BUBBLE *Walk in the footsteps of a top tutor*

Background

The following extracts from draft financial statements relate to Bubble, a public limited company, and Tyslar, a company in which it has an investment.

Extracts from draft statements of financial position as at 31 October 20X5

	Bubble	**Tyslar**
	$m	Dinars m
Assets		
Non-current assets		
Property, plant and equipment	280	390
Investment in Tyslar	46	–
Financial assets	122	98
Total non-current assets	448	488
Equity		
Equity shares ($1 each)	80	210
Retained earnings	230	292
Other components of equity	40	–
Total equity	350	502

The following information is relevant to the preparation of the consolidated statement of financial position as at 31 October 20X5.

Tyslar

Bubble owns 60% of the equity shares of Tyslar, a company located overseas which has presented its financial statements in dinars. The shares in Tyslar were acquired on 1 November 20X4.

At the date of acquisition, retained earnings were 258 million dinars and Tyslar had no other components of equity. On this date, non-depreciable land was carried in the financial statements of Tyslar at 50 million dinars but it had a fair value of 70 million dinars.

The non-controlling interest at acquisition is to be calculated at fair value by reference to the quoted share price of Tyslar. At the acquisition date, the quoted share price was 2.62 dinars per share.

An impairment review of goodwill was undertaken as at 31 October 20X5. The goodwill of Tyslar is to be impaired by 20%. Tyslar has not issued any equity shares since acquisition.

The following exchange rates have been provided:

	Dinars to $
1 November 20X4	8
1 May 20X5	9
31 October 20X5	9.5
Average for the year to 31 October 20X5	8.5

Overseas property

Bubble wished to expand its overseas operations and on 1 May 20X5 acquired an overseas property with a fair value of 58.5 million dinars. In exchange for the building, Bubble paid the supplier with land which Bubble had held but for which it had yet to determine its use. The carrying amount of the land was $5 million but it had an open market value of $7 million. Bubble was unsure as to how to deal with this transaction and so has transferred $5 million from investment properties to property, plant and equipment. The transaction has commercial substance.

In addition, Bubble spent $0.5 million to help relocate staff to the new property and added this amount to the cost of the building. Bubble has made no other entries in its financial statements in relation to the property. Bubble has a policy of depreciating properties over 35 years and follows the revaluation model under IAS 16 *Property, Plant & Equipment*. As a result of a surge in the market, it is estimated that the fair value of the property is 75 million dinars as at 31 October 20X5.

Required:

(a) (i) **Calculate, with supporting explanations, the value of goodwill arising on the acquisition of Tyslar that should be reported in the consolidated statement of financial position as at 31 October 20X5. (7 marks)**

(ii) **Explain why foreign exchange differences arise on the retranslation of Tyslar and how they are accounted for in the consolidated financial statements. As part of your answer you should calculate the balance on the group translation reserve as at 31 October 20X5. (10 marks)**

(iii) **Advise the directors of Bubble on how to correct the accounting treatment of the overseas property, showing the adjustments needed, and calculate the 'property, plant and equipment' balance as it would appear in the consolidated statement of financial position as at 31 October 20X5. (7 marks)**

(b) **Functional currency**

Tyslar operates a mine. Its income is denominated and settled in dinars. The output of the mine is routinely traded in dinars and its price is determined initially by local supply and demand. Tyslar pays 40% of its costs and expenses in dollars with the remainder being incurred locally and settled in dinars. Tyslar's management has a considerable degree of authority and autonomy in carrying out the operations of Tyslar and is not dependent upon group companies for finance.

Required:

Discuss and apply the principles set out in IAS 21 *The Effects of Changes in Foreign Exchange Rates* in order to determine the functional currency of Tyslar. (6 marks)

(Total: 30 marks)

10 JOCATT *Walk in the footsteps of a top tutor*

Background

The following draft group financial statements relate to Jocatt, a public limited company, with a reporting date of 30 November 20X2.

Jocatt Group: Extracts from statement of financial position as at 30 November

	20X2	**20X1**
	$m	$m
Non-current assets		
Property, plant and equipment	502	412
Investment property	8	6
Goodwill	40	68
Financial assets	4	–
Current assets		
Inventories	105	128
Trade receivables	62	113
Non-current liabilities:		
Long-term borrowings	67	71
Deferred tax	32	41
Defined benefit pension deficit	25	22
Current liabilities:		
Trade payables	144	55
Current tax payable	33	30

Jocatt Group: Extract from statement of profit or loss and other comprehensive income for the year ended 30 November 20X2

	$m
Profit from operations	52
Finance costs	(8)
Profit before tax	44
Income tax expense	(11)
Profit for the year	34
Other comprehensive income after tax – items that will not be reclassified to profit or loss in future accounting periods:	
Changes in revaluation surplus (PPE)	(4)
Net remeasurement gain on defined benefit plan	8
Tax on the above	(1)
Other comprehensive income for the year	3

Jocatt Group: Statement of changes in equity for the year ended 30 November 20X2

	Share capital	Retained earnings	Revaluation surplus (PPE)	Total	Non-controlling interest	Total equity
	$m	$m	$m	$m	$m	$m
Balance at 1 Dec 20X1	275	328	16	619	36	655
Share capital issued	15			15		15
Dividends		(5)		(5)	(11)	(16)
Acquisitions					20	20
Total comp inc for year		30	(3)	27	10	37
Balance at 30 Nov 20X2	290	353	13	656	55	711

Additional information

The following information relates to the financial statements of Jocatt:

1 On 1 December 20X1, Jocatt acquired 8% of the ordinary shares of Tigret for $4 million and recorded it as a financial asset at the cost of purchase. This investment was measured at fair value through profit or loss.

On 30 June 20X2, Jocatt acquired a further 52% of the ordinary shares of Tigret and gained control of the company. The purchase consideration transferred on 30 June 20X2 comprised cash of $15 million and shares of $15 million. The fair value of the non-controlling interest in Tigret on 30 June 20X2 was correctly determined to be $20 million. The fair value of Tigret's identifiable net assets at the acquisition date, excluding deferred tax, was $45 million and included:

	$m
Trade receivables	5
Trade payables	6

Jocatt has calculated and accounted for goodwill arising on the acquisition of Tigret of $5 million ($30m + $20m – $45 million). However, the following has not been taken into account:

- At 30 June 20X2, the fair value of the 8% holding in Tigret had risen to $5 million. In the consolidated statement of financial position as at 30 November 20X2, this investment is still classified as a financial asset and is measured at $4 million.
- The tax base of the identifiable net assets of Tigret was $35 million at 30 June 20X2. The tax rate of Tigret is 30%.

2 Goodwill relating to all subsidiaries had been impairment tested in the year to 30 November 20X2 and any impairment correctly calculated and accounted for.

3 Jocatt operates a defined benefit scheme. The service cost component for the year ended 30 November 20X2 is $16 million. The net interest component of $2 million is included within finance costs.

4 Jocatt uses the fair value model for measuring investment property. No investment properties have been purchased or sold in the current period.

5 Jocatt sold property, plant and equipment with a carrying amount of $10 million for cash of $19 million. Depreciation for the period was $27 million.

Required:

(a) (i) Discuss, with calculations, how goodwill arising on the acquisition of Tigret should have been calculated. Show the adjustments which need to be made to the consolidated financial statements. (7 marks)

(ii) In accordance with IAS 7 *Statement of Cash Flows*, prepare:

- **Cash flows from operating activities (using the indirect method)**
- **Cash flows from financing activities.**

Note: Ignore deferred taxation other than where it is mentioned in the question. (17 marks)

(b) Direct and indirect methods

The directors of Jocatt have commented that the indirect method of reporting cash flows from operating activities is more useful and informative to users of financial statements than the direct method.

Required:

Discuss the extent to which the directors' comment is valid. (6 marks)

(Total: 30 marks)

11 ZIPPY  *Walk in the footsteps of a top tutor*

Background

Zippy is a manufacturing company with a reporting date of 30 June 20X6. It has a wide portfolio of investment properties, as well as investments in many other entities. The draft statement of profit or loss and other comprehensive income for one of those entities, Ginny, is provided below

Draft statement of profit or loss and other comprehensive income for the year ended 30 June 20X6

	$m
Revenue	132
Cost of sales	(76)
Gross profit	56
Investment income	19
Administrative costs	(12)
Other expenses	(18)
Operating profit	45
Net finance costs	(6)
Profit before tax	39
Income tax expense	(7)
Profit for the year	32

	$m
Other comprehensive income	
Items that will not be reclassified to profit or loss	
Gains on property revaluation	16
Total comprehensive income for year	48

The following information is relevant to the preparation of the group statement of profit or loss and other comprehensive income:

Ginny

On 1 July 20X4, Zippy acquired 60% of the equity interests of Ginny, a public limited company. The purchase consideration comprised cash of $90 million and the fair value of the identifiable net assets acquired was $114 million at that date. Zippy uses the 'full goodwill' method for all acquisitions and the fair value of the non-controlling interest in Ginny was $50 million on 1 July 20X4. Goodwill had been reviewed annually for impairment and no impairment was deemed necessary.

Zippy disposed of a 20% equity interest in Ginny on 31 March 20X6 for cash consideration of $44 million. On the disposal date the remaining 40% holding had a fair value of $62 million and Zippy was left with significant influence over Ginny. Zippy accounts for investments in subsidiaries at cost and has included a gain in investment income of $14 million within its individual financial statements to reflect the disposal. The net assets of Ginny had a fair value of $118 million at 1 July 20X5 and this was reflected in the carrying amounts of the net assets. All gains and losses of Ginny have accrued evenly throughout the year. The disposal is not classified as a separate major line of business or geographical operation.

Office blocks

Zippy holds properties for investment purposes. At 1 July 20X5, Zippy held a 10-floor office block at a fair value of $90 million with a remaining useful life of 15 years. The first floor was occupied by Zippy's staff and the second floor was let to Boo, a subsidiary of Zippy, free of charge. The other eight floors were all let to unconnected third parties at a normal commercial rent. When Boo vacates the property next year, it will be let out to third parties. It was estimated that the fair value of the office block was $96 million at 30 June 20X6. Zippy has a policy of restating all land and buildings to fair value at each reporting date. The only accounting entries for the year ended 30 June 20X6 in relation to this office block have been to correctly include the rental income in profit or loss. It can be assumed that each floor is of equal size and value. Depreciation is charged to administrative costs.

During April 20X6, an explosion at a different office block caused substantial damage and it was estimated that the fair value fell from $20 million at 30 June 20X5 to $14 million at 30 June 20X6. Zippy has estimated that costs of $3 million would be required to repair the block but is unsure whether to carry out the repairs or whether to sell the block for a reduced price. The property has been left in the financial statements at a value of $20 million. A provision of $3 million for the repair costs was charged to other expenses.

Required:

(a) (i) **Explain, with suitable calculations, how the investment in Ginny should be accounted for in the consolidated statement of profit or loss and other comprehensive income of the Zippy group for the year ended 30 June 20X6.** **(11 marks)**

(ii) **Explain, with suitable calculations, how the two office blocks should be accounted for in the consolidated financial statements of the Zippy group for the year ended 30 June 20X6.** **(8 marks)**

(iii) **Explain why the accounting treatment of the 10 floor office block in Zippy's individual (non-consolidated) financial statements will differ from the treatment in the consolidated financial statements of the Zippy group. Calculations are not required.** **(4 marks)**

(b) **Other comprehensive income**

The directors of Zippy are unsure as to the differences between other comprehensive income and profit or loss and the rationale as to why some gains can be and others cannot be reclassified to profit or loss. Zippy has a defined benefit pension scheme and the directors have heard that local GAAP in some countries allows actuarial gains and losses (the remeasurement component) to be deferred using an applicable systematic method rather than being recognised immediately.

Required:

Discuss the differences between other comprehensive income and profit or loss and the rationale as to why some gains and losses can be and others cannot be reclassified to profit or loss. Include in your answer a brief discussion of the benefits of immediate recognition of the remeasurement component under IAS 19 *Employee Benefits*. **(7 marks)**

(Total: 30 marks)

12 ASHANTI

Background

The following financial statement extracts relate to Ashanti, a public limited company, and its investments.

Extracts from the statements of profit or loss for the year ended 30 April 20X9.

	Ashanti	**Bochem**	**Ceram**
	$m	$m	$m
Revenue	810	235	142
Cost of sales	(686)	(137)	(84)
Gross profit	124	98	58

The following information is relevant to the preparation of the group statement of profit or loss.

Sale of shares in Bochem

On 1 May 20X7, Ashanti acquired 70% of the equity interests of Bochem, a public limited company. The fair value of the identifiable net assets at that date was $160 million. The share capital and retained earnings of Bochem were $55 million and $85 million respectively and other components of equity were $10 million at the date of acquisition. The excess of the fair value of the identifiable net assets at acquisition is due to an increase in the value of plant, which is depreciated on the straight-line method and has a five year remaining life at the date of acquisition. Depreciation is charged to cost of sales.

Ashanti disposed of a 10% equity interest to the non-controlling interests (NCI) of Bochem on 30 April 20X9 for a cash consideration of $34 million. The carrying amount of the net assets of Bochem at 30 April 20X9 was $210 million before any adjustments on consolidation. Goodwill arising on the acquisition of Bochem was $44 million but had reduced in value by 20% before the sale of the equity interest to the NCI.

Sale of shares in Ceram

Ashanti acquired 80% of the equity interests of Ceram, a public limited company, on 1 May 20X7. The purchase consideration was cash of $95.2 million. Ceram's identifiable net assets were fair valued at $115 million and the NCI of Ceram had a fair value of $26 million at that date. On 1 November 20X8, Ashanti disposed of 50% of the equity of Ceram for a consideration of $90 million. Ceram's identifiable net assets were $160 million and the NCI was $35 million at the date of disposal. The remaining equity interest of Ceram held by Ashanti was fair valued at $45 million. After the disposal, Ashanti can still exert significant influence. Goodwill had been impairment tested and no impairment had occurred. Ceram's total profit for the year ended 30 April 20X9 was $14 million and can be assumed to have accrued evenly.

Additional transactions

Ashanti sold inventory to both Bochem and Ceram in October 20X8. The sale price of the inventory was $10 million and $5 million respectively. Ashanti sells goods at a gross profit margin of 20% to group companies. At the year-end, half of the inventory sold to Bochem remained unsold but the entire inventory sold to Ceram had been sold to third parties.

At the year end, Ashanti sold goods on credit to Spice, an unrelated company, and recognised revenue of $5 million. Before the date of the sale, the customer had made an announcement that it would be restructuring its debts. At the date of the sale, it was deemed improbable that Ashanti would recover the amounts outstanding.

Required:

(a) (i) **Explain, with suitable calculations, how Ashanti should deal with the sale of the equity interests in Bochem in the consolidated financial statements.** **(6 marks)**

(ii) **Explain, with suitable calculations, how Ashanti should deal with the sale of the equity interests in Ceram and its remaining investment in Ceram in the consolidated statement of profit or loss.** **(8 marks)**

(iii) **Taking into account all of the information presented, calculate the 'revenue' and 'cost of sales' figures that would appear in the consolidated statement of profit or loss. Your answer should include an explanation of the correct treatment of Ashanti's sale to Spice.** **(9 marks)**

(b) Night

The directors of Ashanti are considering acquiring 49.9% of the equity shares of Night. The next biggest shareholders will be Night's two original founders, who will hold 21% and 8% of the equity shares respectively. The original founders are not related. The remaining 21.1% of the shares will be held by 11 shareholders, who are acquaintances of the original founders but whom have a remote relationship to one another. There has not been complete owner representation at the last three annual general meetings of Night. Ashanti will have the ability to appoint four of the six members of Night's Board of Directors ('the Board'). The Board of Night have overall responsibility for decisions that affect the entity's operations.

Required:

Discuss whether the proposed share purchase will lead to Ashanti obtaining control over Night. (7 marks)

(Total: 30 marks)

13 TRAILER  *Walk in the footsteps of a top tutor*

Background and financial statement extracts

Trailer, a public limited company, operates in the manufacturing sector. Trailer purchased an investment in part during the reporting period. Extracts from the draft statements of financial position at 31 May 20X3 are as follows:

	Trailer	Park
	$m	$m
Equity:		
Share capital	1,750	1,210
Retained earnings	1,240	930
Other components of equity	125	80
Total equity	3,115	2,220

The following information is relevant to the preparation of the group financial statements:

Loan to charity

Trailer has made a loan of $50 million to a charitable organisation for the building of new sporting facilities. The loan was made on 1 June 20X2 and is repayable on maturity in three years' time. The interest rate on the loan is 3%, but Trailer assesses that an unsubsidised rate for such a loan would have been 6%. The first interest payment was made on 31 May 20X3. Trailer initially recorded a financial asset at $50 million and reduced this by the interest received during the period. The loss allowance has been correctly dealt with.

Restructuring plans

Trailer has announced two major restructuring plans. The first plan is to reduce its capacity by the closure of some of its smaller factories, which have already been identified. This will lead to the redundancy of 500 employees, who have all individually been selected and communicated with. The costs of this plan are $14 million in redundancy costs and $4 million in retraining costs. The second plan is to re-organise the finance and information technology department over a one-year period but it does not commence for two years. The plan results in 20% of finance staff losing their jobs during the restructuring. The costs of this plan are $10 million in redundancy costs and $6 million in retraining costs. No entries have been made in the financial statements for the above plans.

Acquisition of Park

On 1 June 20X2, Trailer acquired 60% of the equity interests of Park, a public limited company. The purchase consideration comprised cash of $1,250 million.

On 1 June 20X2, the fair value of the identifiable net assets acquired was $1,950 million and retained earnings of Park were $650 million and other components of equity were $55 million. The excess in fair value is due to plant and machinery with a remaining useful life of 7 years as at the acquisition date. It is the group's policy to measure the non-controlling interest (NCI) at acquisition at its proportionate share of the fair value of the subsidiary's net assets.

The goodwill of Park was impairment tested at 31 May 20X3. The recoverable amount of the net assets of Park was $2,083 million. There was no impairment of the net assets of Park before this date.

Required:

(a) (i) Discuss, with suitable workings, how the loan to the charitable organisation should be dealt with in the consolidated financial statements for the year ended 31 May 20X3. (6 marks)

(ii) Discuss how the restructuring plans should be dealt with in the consolidated financial statements for the year ended 31 May 20X3. (5 marks)

(iii) Prepare the equity section of the consolidated statement of financial position as at 31 May 20X3. (12 marks)

(b) NCI at fair value

It is the Trailer group's policy to measure the NCI at acquisition at its proportionate share of the fair value of the subsidiary's net assets. The directors of Trailer have used this policy for several years and do not know the implications, if any, of accounting for the NCI at fair value. The fair value of the NCI of Park at 1 June 20X2 was $800 million.

Required:

Explain to the directors, with suitable calculations, the impact on the financial statements if goodwill arising on the acquisition of Park had been calculated using the fair value of the NCI. (7 marks)

(Total: 30 marks)

14 WESTON  *Walk in the footsteps of a top tutor*

Background

Weston has appointed a new financial controller. Weston calculates 'cash generated from operations' using the indirect method. The following information relates to the financial statements of the Weston Group:

Extracts from Weston Group: Statement of financial position as at 31 January

	20X6	20X5
	$m	$m
Non-current assets		
Property, plant and equipment	389	413
Goodwill	4	19
Investment in associate	102	–
Current assets		
Inventories	108	165
Trade and other receivables	106	104
Cash and cash equivalents	39	43
Non-current liabilities		
Retirement benefit liability	60	72
Net deferred tax liability	14	15
Current liabilities		
Trade and other payables	36	41
Current tax payable	47	92

Extracts from statement of profit or loss and other comprehensive income for the year ended 31 January 20X6

Continuing operations	$m
Profit from operations	167
Share of profit of associate	16
Profit before tax	183
Income tax expense	(40)
Profit for the year from continuing operations	143
Discontinued operations	
Loss for the year from discontinued operations (see note 2)	(25)
Total profit for the year	118

Other comprehensive income for the year (after tax) which will not be reclassified to profit or loss in future years	
Remeasurement gains on defined benefit plan	3
	–––
Total comprehensive income for the year	121
	–––

Additional information for preparation of statement of cash flows

1 On 31 July 20X5, Weston disposed of its entire 80% equity holding in Northern for cash. The shares had been acquired on 31 July 20X1 for a consideration of $132 million when the fair value of the net assets was $124 million. This included a fair value uplift of $16 million in relation to plant with a remaining useful life of eight years. Deferred tax at 25% on the fair value adjustment was also correctly provided for in the group accounts and is included within the fair value of net assets. The fair value of the non-controlling interest at acquisition was $28 million. Goodwill, calculated under the full fair value method, was tested annually for impairment.

At 31 January 20X5, goodwill relating to Northern had been impaired by 75%. A goodwill impairment charge has been included within administration expenses for the current year but does not relate to Northern.

The carrying amounts in the individual accounts of Northern at disposal are listed below. The fair value adjustment and subsequent deferred tax were not incorporated into the individual accounts of Northern.

	$m
Property, plant and equipment	80
Inventories	38
Trade receivables	23
Trade and other payables	(10)
Deferred tax liability	(6)
Bank overdraft	(2)

2 The loss for the period from discontinued operations in the consolidated statement of profit or loss and other comprehensive income relates to Northern and can be analysed as follows:

	$m
Profit before tax	6
Income tax expense	(2)
Loss on disposal	(29)
	–––
	(25)
	–––

3 Weston purchased a 40% interest in an associate for cash on 1 February 20X5. The associate paid a dividend of $10 million in the year ended 31 January 20X6.

4 The retirement benefit liability relates to Weston as other companies in the group operate defined contribution schemes. The latest actuarial valuation is as follows:

	$m
Net obligation at 1 February 20X5	72
Service cost component	11
Contributions to scheme	(19)
Remeasurement gains	(4)
	——
Net obligation at 31 January 20X6	60
	——

The benefits paid in the period by the trustees of the scheme were $7 million. Weston operates in a country which only allows tax relief when contributions are paid into the scheme. The tax base was therefore zero at 31 January 20X5 and 31 January 20X6. The tax rate paid by Weston is 25%. The service cost component is included within administrative expenses.

5 There were no disposals of property, plant and equipment during the year except on the sale of Northern. Depreciation for the year was $20 million and is included within cost of sales.

Required:

(a) **(i)** **In accordance with IAS 7 *Statement of Cash Flows*, prepare:**

- **Cash flows from operating activities (using the indirect method)**
- **Cash flows from investing activities.** **(18 marks)**

(ii) **Using your answer to part (a) (i), explain how to calculate cash generated from operations using the indirect method.** **(6 marks)**

The Finance Director is considering the acquisition of a 30% investment in Abuelo Co. The acquisition is proposed to occur on 31 July 20X6. Abuelo Co has a functional currency of Dinars. The Financial Controller is uncertain of the accounting treatment of the proposed investment within the Weston Group accounts. The proposed consideration consists of 6m dinars in cash and 1million shares in Weston. The current share price of Weston is $1.50 per share. It is anticipated that, by the acquisition date, the shares will have grown in value to $2.00. Weston will exert significant influence on Abuelo Co under the terms of the deal. Abuelo's forecasted information for the year ended 31 January 20X7 shows a profit after tax of 40m dinars.

Exchange rates	dinars: $1
1 Feb 20X6	5.0
31 July 20X6	6.0
31 January 20X7	7.0
Average exchange rate for year ended 31 January 20X7	5.8

(b) **Explain to the Financial Controller, using illustrative calculations when needed, the accounting treatment of the proposed investment in Abuelo Co within the Weston Group statement of financial position and statement of profit or loss and other comprehensive income for the year ended 31 January 20X7. For any calculations, assume that the forecasted figures are accurate representations.** **(6 marks)**

(Total: 30 marks)

15 JOEY  *Walk in the footsteps of a top tutor*

Joey, a public limited company, operates in the media sector. Joey has investments in a number of companies. The draft consolidated statement of financial position at 30 November 20X4 is as follows:

	$m
Assets:	
Non-current assets	
Property, plant and equipment	6,709
Goodwill	40
Investment in associate (Margy)	700
	7,449
Current assets	2,011
Total assets	9,460
Equity and liabilities:	
Equity attributable to owners of parent	
Share capital	850
Retained earnings	4,086
Other components of equity	258
	5,194
Non-controlling interest	908
Non-current liabilities	2,770
Current liabilities	588
Total liabilities	3,358
Total equity and liabilities	9,460

The following information is required to correct the draft consolidated financial statements:

Acquisition of Hulty

On 1 December 20X3, Joey acquired 80% of Hulty's 600 million $1 equity shares in exchange for cash of $750 million. The carrying amount of Hulty's net assets at the acquisition date was $960 million. Joey determined that the fair value of the 20% non-controlling interest in Hulty at that date was $250 million. It is group policy to measure the non-controlling interest at fair value. Joey recorded a goodwill asset arising on the acquisition of Hulty of $40 million ($750m + $250m – $960m).

However, shortly after the acquisition date, the accountant of Joey realised the following:

- Deferred cash consideration of $50 million arising on the acquisition of Hulty had not been recorded by Joey. This payment is due on 30 November 20X5. An appropriate discount rate is 10%.
- The fair value of Hulty's identifiable net assets had been calculated to be $980 million as at 1 December 20X3. The excess in the fair value of the net assets over their carrying amounts was due to an unrecognised franchise right with a remaining useful life of four years at 1 December 20X3. No entries have been recorded in respect of this franchise right.

Acquisition of Margy

On 1 December 20X1, Joey acquired 30% of the ordinary shares of Margy for a cash consideration of $600 million. Joey treated Margy as an associate and has equity accounted for Margy up to 1 December 20X3. Joey's investment in Margy as at 1 December 20X3 is still included in the draft consolidated statement of financial position. At 1 December 20X3, the fair value of the 30% equity interest in Margy held by Joey was $705 million.

On 1 December 20X3, Joey acquired a further 40% of the ordinary shares of Margy for a cash consideration of $975 million and gained control of the company. At 1 December 20X3, the fair value of Margy's identifiable net assets was $2,250 million. The fair value of the non-controlling interest was assessed as $620 million. A gain on bargain purchase of $655 million ($975m + $620m – $2,250m) has been recorded in profit or loss.

Additionally, buildings with a carrying amount of $200 million had been included in the fair valuation of Margy at 1 December 20X3. The buildings have a remaining useful life of 20 years at 1 December 20X3. However, Joey had commissioned an independent valuation of the buildings of Margy which was not complete at 1 December 20X3 and therefore not considered in the fair value of the identifiable net assets at the acquisition date. The valuations were received on 1 April 20X4 and resulted in a decrease of $40 million in the fair value of property, plant and equipment at the date of acquisition. This fair value decrease, which does not affect the fair value of the non-controlling interest at acquisition, has not been entered into the financial statements of Margy or the draft consolidated statements. Buildings are depreciated on the straight-line basis.

Agreement with CP

Joey is looking to expand into publishing and entered into an arrangement with Content Publishing (CP), a public limited company, on 1 December 20X3. CP will provide content for a range of books and online publications.

CP is entitled to a royalty calculated as 10% of sales and 30% of gross profit of the publications. Joey has sole responsibility for all printing, binding, and platform maintenance of the online website. The agreement states that key strategic sales and marketing decisions must be agreed jointly. Joey selects the content to be covered in the publications but CP has the right of veto over this content. However on 1 June 20X4, Joey and CP decided to set up a legal entity, JCP, with equal shares and voting rights. CP continues to contribute content into JCP but does not receive royalties. Joey continues the printing, binding and platform maintenance. The sales and cost of sales in the period were $5 million and $2 million respectively. The whole of the sale proceeds and the costs of sales were recorded in Joey's financial statements with no accounting entries being made for JCP or amounts due to CP. Joey currently funds the operations. Assume that the sales and costs accrue evenly throughout the year and that all of the transactions relating to JCP have been in cash.

Shares

Joey's share capital is comprised of 'A' class shares. These shares have been correctly classified as equity. Joey is considering issuing the following instruments:

- 'B' class shares that are not mandatorily redeemable but contain a call option allowing Joey to repurchase them. Dividends would be payable on the B shares if, and only if, dividends are paid on the A ordinary shares.
- Share options which will give the counterparty rights to buy a fixed number of ordinary shares for a fixed amount of $10 million.

The directors of Joey require advice as to whether these financial instruments should be classified as debt or equity in accordance with IAS 32 *Financial Instruments: Presentation*.

Required:

(a) **Explain, with suitable workings, how to correct the errors that have arisen when accounting for the acquisition of Hulty. Show the adjusting entries required to correct the consolidated statement of financial position. (9 marks)**

(b) **Explain, with suitable workings, how to correct the errors that have arisen when accounting for the acquisition of Margy. Show the adjusting entries required to correct the consolidated statement of financial position. (9 marks)**

(c) **Discuss, with suitable workings, how the agreement with CP should have been accounted for in the consolidated financial statements. (8 marks)**

(d) **In accordance with IAS 32 *Financial Instruments: Presentation,* discuss whether the 'B' class shares and the share options should be classified as financial liabilities or equity. (4 marks)**

(Total: 30 marks)

16 PARSLEY  *Walk in the footsteps of a top tutor*

 *Answer debrief*

Background and draft financial statements

Parsley, a public limited company, has investments in Sage and Saffron. All three companies prepare their financial statements in accordance with International Financial Reporting Standards. The presentation currency of the group is the dollar ($). Saffron's functional currency is the Franc (FR). The draft statements of profit or loss for the year ended 30 April 20X4 are presented below:

	Parsley	Sage	Saffron
	$m	$m	FRm
Revenue	143	68	210
Cost of sales	(61)	(42)	(126)
Gross profit	82	26	84
Distribution costs	(10)	(6)	(14)
Administrative expenses	(23)	(10)	(29)
Operating profit	49	10	41
Investment income	1	2	–
Finance costs	(2)	(4)	(3)
Profit before taxation	48	8	38
Taxation	(11)	(2)	(8)
Profit for the period	37	6	30

The following information is relevant to the preparation of the consolidated financial statements:

Sale of shares in Sage

Parsley acquired 70% of Sage's one million $1 ordinary shares for $6 million many years ago. At the acquisition date, the carrying value of Sage's net assets was $5 million, and this was deemed to be the same as their fair value. The non-controlling interest was measured using the proportion of net assets method. Goodwill arising on the acquisition of Sage has never been impaired. On 31 October 20X3, Parsley sold 300,000 of its shares in Sage for $6.5 million. The fair value of the interest retained was $9.5 million. The retained earnings of Sage were $9 million as at 30 April 20X3. The only entry posted in Parsley's individual financial statements is to record the cash received and to credit these proceeds to a suspense account.

Acquisition of Saffron

On 1 May 20X3, Parsley purchased 60% of Saffron's one million FR1 ordinary shares for FR71 million. The non-controlling interest at acquisition was valued at FR29 million using the fair value method. At 1 May 20X3, the carrying value of Saffron's net assets was FR60 million but the fair value was FR70 million. The excess in fair value was due to an unrecognised brand with a remaining useful economic life of five years at the acquisition date.

At 30 April 20X4, it was determined that goodwill arising on the acquisition of Saffron was impaired by FR4 million.

The following exchange rates are relevant:

	FR: $1
1 May 20X3	5.0
30 April 20X4	4.0
Average for year ended 30 April 20X4	4.6

Lease

On 1 May 20X2, Parsley signed a lease to use an item of machinery. The useful economic life of the machine and the lease term were both five years. Lease payments are due annually in advance. The lease payment for the first year was $1.2 million. Parsley's rate of borrowing is 10%. The present value of the lease payments, excluding the payment made on 1 May 20X2, was $3.8 million.

Lease payments increase annually by the rate of inflation over the previous 12 months. On 1 May 20X3, inflation for the prior 12 months was 8%.

The lease was correctly accounted for in accordance with IFRS 16 *Leases* in the year ended 30 April 20X3. The only entry made in the current year is to record the cash payment made to the lessor within cost of sales.

Required:

(a) (i) Discuss, with calculations, how Parsley should account for Sage in the consolidated statement of profit or loss and other comprehensive income for the year ended 30 April 20X4. (8 marks)

(ii) Discuss, with calculations, how Parsley should account for Saffron in the consolidated statement of profit or loss and other comprehensive income for the year ended 30 April 20X4. (8 marks)

(iii) Explain how the lease agreement should be accounted for in the consolidated financial statements for the year ended 30 April 20X4. Show the adjusting entries required. (8 marks)

Related parties

Related party relationships are a particularly key concern when preparing financial statements for group entities. The objective of IAS 24 *Related Party Disclosures* is to ensure that financial statements contain the necessary disclosures to make users aware of the possibility that financial statements may have been affected by the existence of related parties.

Required:

(b) Describe the main circumstances that give rise to related parties and explain why the disclosure of related party relationships and transactions is important.

(6 marks)

(Total: 30 marks)

Calculate your allowed time, allocate the time to the separate parts..............

17 MARCHANT  *Walk in the footsteps of a top tutor*

Tutorial note

This question requires the preparation of a consolidated statement of profit or loss and other comprehensive income. The examining team have said that the preparation of full consolidated financial statements is unlikely to appear in the Strategic Business Reporting exam. However this question still provides important revision of a range of consolidation issues.

The following draft financial statements relate to Marchant, a public limited company, and companies it has investments in.

Marchant Group: Draft statements of profit or loss and other comprehensive income for the year ended 30 April 20X4.

	Marchant	**Nathan**	**Option**
	$m	$m	$m
Revenue	400	115	70
Cost of sales	(312)	(65)	(36)
Gross profit	88	50	34
Other income	21	7	2
Administrative costs	(15)	(9)	(12)
Other expenses	(35)	(19)	(8)
Operating profit	59	29	16
Finance costs	(5)	(6)	(4)
Finance income	6	5	8
Profit before tax	60	28	20
Income tax expense	(19)	(9)	(5)
Profit for the year	41	19	15
Other comprehensive income – revaluation gains	10	2	–
Total comprehensive income for year	51	21	15

The following information is relevant to the preparation of the group statement of profit or loss and othercomprehensive income:

1 On 1 May 20X2, Marchant acquired 60% of the equity interests of Nathan, a public limited company. The purchase consideration comprised cash of $80 million and the fair value of the identifiable net assets acquired was $110 million at that date. The fair value of the non-controlling interest (NCI) in Nathan was $45 million on 1 May 20X2. Marchant wishes to use the 'full goodwill' method for all acquisitions. The share capital and retained earnings of Nathan were $25 million and $65 million respectively and other components of equity were $6 million at the date of acquisition. The excess of the fair value of the identifiable net assets at acquisition is due to non-depreciable land.

Goodwill has been impairment tested annually and as at 30 April 20X3 had reduced in value by 20%. However at 30 April 20X4, the impairment of goodwill had reversed and goodwill was valued at $2 million above its original value. This upward change in value has already been included in above draft financial statements of Marchant prior to the preparation of the group accounts.

2 Marchant disposed of an 8% equity interest in Nathan on 30 April 20X4 for a cash consideration of $18 million and had accounted for the gain or loss in other income. The carrying amount of the net assets of Nathan at 30 April 20X4 was $120 million before any adjustments on consolidation. Marchant accounts for investments in subsidiaries using IFRS 9 *Financial Instruments* and has made an election to show gains and losses in other comprehensive income. The carrying amount of the investment in Nathan was $90 million at 30 April 20X3 and $95 million at 30 April 20X4 before the disposal of the equity interest.

3 Marchant acquired 60% of the equity interests of Option, a public limited company, on 30 April 20X2. The purchase consideration was cash of $70 million. Option's identifiable net assets were fair valued at $86 million and the NCI had a fair value of $28 million at that date. On 1 November 20X3, Marchant disposed of a 40% equity interest in Option for a consideration of $50 million. Option's identifiable net assets were $90 million and the value of the NCI was $34 million at the date of disposal. The remaining equity interest was fair valued at $40 million. After the disposal, Marchant exerts significant influence. Any increase in net assets since acquisition has been reported in profit or loss and the carrying amount of the investment in Option had not changed since acquisition. Goodwill had been impairment tested and no impairment was required. No entries had been made in the financial statements of Marchant for this transaction other than for cash received.

4 Marchant sold inventory to Nathan for its fair value of $12 million. Marchant made a loss on the transaction of $2 million. Nathan still holds $8 million of this inventory at the year end.

5 Ignore the taxation effects of the above adjustments. Any expense adjustments should be amended in other expenses.

Required:

(a) (i) Prepare a consolidated statement of profit or loss and other comprehensive income for the year ended 30 April 20X4 for the Marchant Group.

Note: Do not adjust your answer for the information presented in part (b)

(18 marks)

(ii) Explain, with suitable calculations, how the sale of the 8% interest in Nathan should be dealt with in the group statement of financial position at 30 April 20X4. (5 marks)

(b) Marchant held a portfolio of trade receivables with a carrying amount of $4 million at 30 April 20X4. At that date, the entity entered into a factoring agreement with a bank, whereby it transferred the receivables in exchange for $3.6 million in cash. Marchant has agreed to reimburse the factor for any shortfall between the amount collected and $3.6 million. Once the receivables have been collected, any amounts above $3.6 million, less interest on this amount, will be repaid to Marchant. Marchant has derecognised the receivables and charged $0.4 million as a loss to profit or loss.

Required:

Outline the rules in IFRS 9 *Financial Instruments* relating to the derecognition of a financial asset and discuss how these rules affect the treatment of the portfolio of trade receivables in Marchant's financial statements. (7 marks)

(Total: 30 marks)

18 ANGEL  *Walk in the footsteps of a top tutor*

Tutorial note

This question requires the preparation of a consolidated statement of cash flows. The examining team have said that the preparation of full consolidated financial statements is unlikely to appear in the Strategic Business Reporting exam. However this question still provides important revision of a range of consolidation issues.

The following draft group financial statements relate to Angel, a public limited company:

Angel Group: Statement of financial position as at 30 November 20X3

	30 November 20X3	**30 November 20X2**
	$m	$m
Assets		
Non-current assets		
Property, plant and equipment	475	465
Goodwill	105	120
Other intangible assets	150	240
Investment in associate	80	
Financial assets	215	180
	1,025	1,005
Current assets		
Inventories	155	190
Trade receivables	125	180
Cash and cash equivalents	465	355
	745	725
Total assets	1,770	1,730

Equity and liabilities		
Share capital	850	625
Retained earnings	456	359
Other components of equity	29	20
	1,335	1,004
Non-controlling interest	90	65
Total equity	1,425	1,069
Non-current liabilities		
Long-term borrowings	26	57
Deferred tax	35	31
Retirement benefit liability	80	74
Total non-current liabilities	141	162
Current liabilities		
Trade payables	155	361
Current tax payable	49	138
Total current liabilities	204	499
Total liabilities	345	661
Total equity and liabilities	1,770	1,730

Angel Group: Statement of profit or loss and other comprehensive income for the year ended 30 November 20X3

	$m
Revenue	1,238
Cost of sales	(986)
Gross profit	252
Other income	30
Administrative expenses	(45)
Other expenses	(50)
Operating profit	187
Finance costs	(11)
Share of profit of associate	12
Profit before tax	188
Income tax expense	(46)
Profit for the year	142
Profit attributable to:	
Owners of parent	111
Non-controlling interest	31
	142

	$m
Other comprehensive income:	
Items that will not be reclassified to profit or loss	
Revaluation of property, plant and equipment	8
Actuarial losses on defined benefit plan	(4)
Tax relating to items not reclassified	(2)
Total items that will not be reclassified to profit or loss	2
Items that may be reclassified to profit or loss	
Financial assets	4
Tax relating to items that may be reclassified	(1)
Total items that may be reclassified to profit or loss	3
Other comprehensive income (net of tax) for the year	5
Total comprehensive income for year	147
Total comprehensive income attributable to:	
Owners of the parent	116
Non-controlling interest	31
	147

Angel Group: Extracts from statement of changes in equity for the year ended 30 November 20X3

	Share capital	Retained earnings	Other components of equity – financial assets reserve	Other components of equity – revaluation reserve	Non-controlling interest
	$m	$m	$m	$m	$m
Balance 1 December 20X2	625	359	15	5	65
Share capital issued	225				
Dividends for year		(10)			(6)
Total comprehensive income for the year		107	3	6	31
Balance 30 November 20X3	850	456	18	11	90

The following information relates to the financial statements of the Angel Group:

(i) On 1 December 20X2, Angel acquired all of the share capital of Sweety for $30 million. The carrying amounts of the identifiable net assets in Sweety's individual financial statements and the fair values are set out below, together with their tax base. Goodwill arising on acquisition is not deductible for tax purposes. There were no other acquisitions in the period. The tax rate is 30%.

The fair values in the table below have been reflected in the year-end balances of the Angel Group.

	Carrying amounts $ million	Tax base $ million	Fair values $million (excluding deferred taxation)
Property, plant and equipment	12	10	14
Inventories	5	4	6
Trade receivables	3	3	3
Cash and cash equivalents	2	2	2
Total assets	22	19	25
Trade payables	(4)	(4)	(4)
Retirement benefit obligations	(1)		(1)
Deferred tax liability	(0.6)		
Net assets at acquisition	16.4	15	20

(ii) The retirement benefit is classified as a non-current liability in the statement of financial position and comprises the following:

	$m
Net obligation at 1 December 20X2	74
Net interest cost	3
Current service cost	8
Contributions to scheme	(9)
Remeasurements – actuarial losses	4
Net obligation at 30 November 20X3	80

The benefits paid in the period by the trustees of the scheme were $6 million. Angel had included the obligation assumed on the purchase of Sweety in current service cost above, although the charge to administrative expenses was correct in the statement of profit and loss and other comprehensive income. There were no tax implications regarding the retirement benefit obligation. Defined benefit costs are included in administrative expenses.

(iii) Property, plant and equipment (PPE) with a carrying amount of $49 million was disposed of for cash proceeds of $63 million. The gain on disposal is included in administrative expenses. Depreciation charged to profit or loss in the year was $29 million.

(iv) Angel purchased a 30% interest in an associate for cash on 1 December 20X2. The net assets of the associate at the date of acquisition were $280 million. The associate made a profit after tax of $40 million and paid a dividend of $10 million out of these profits in the year ended 30 November 20X3. Angel does not hold investments in any other associate entities.

(v) An impairment test carried out at 30 November 20X3 showed that goodwill and other intangible assets were impaired. The impairment of goodwill relates to 100% owned subsidiaries.

(vi) The following schedule relates to the financial assets owned by Angel:

	$m
Balance 1 December 20X2	180
Less carrying amount of financial assets disposed	(26)
Add purchases of financial assets	57
Add gain on revaluation of financial assets	4
Balance at 30 November 20X3	215

The sale proceeds of the financial assets were $40 million. Profit on the sale of the financial assets is included in 'other income' in the financial statements.

(vii) The finance costs were all paid in cash in the period.

Required:

(a) **Prepare a consolidated statement of cash flows using the indirect method for the Angel Group plc for the year ended 30 November 20X3 in accordance with the requirements of IAS 7 *Statement of Cash Flows*.**

Note: The notes to the statement of cash flows are not required. **(25 marks)**

(b) The directors of Angel have deposited funds with a bank in two accounts as follows:

(i) $3 million into a 12-month term account, earning 3.5% interest. The cash can be withdrawn by giving 14 days' notice but Angel will incur a penalty, being the loss of all interest earned.

(ii) $7 million into a 12-month term account earning 3% interest. The cash can be withdrawn by giving 21 days' notice. Interest will be paid for the period of the deposit but if money is withdrawn, the interest will be at the rate of 2%, which is equivalent to the bank's stated rate for short-term deposits.

Angel is confident that it will not need to withdraw the cash from the higher-rate deposit within the term, but wants to keep easy access to the remaining $7 million to cover any working capital shortfalls which might arise.

Required:

Advise Angel on whether each of the funds meets the definition of a 'cash equivalent'. **(5 marks)**

(Total: 30 marks)

19 TRAVELER  *Walk in the footsteps of a top tutor*

Tutorial note

This question requires the preparation of a consolidated statement of financial position. The examining team have said that the preparation of full consolidated financial statements is unlikely to appear in the Strategic Business Reporting exam. However this question still provides important revision of a range of consolidation issues.

Traveler, a public limited company, operates in the manufacturing sector. The draft statements of financial position are as follows at 30 November 20X1:

	Traveler	**Data**	**Captive**
	$m	$m	$m
Assets:			
Non-current assets			
Property, plant and equipment	439	810	620
Investments in subsidiaries			
Data	820		
Captive	541		
Financial assets	108	10	20
	1,908	820	640
Current assets	1,067	781	350
Total assets	2,975	1,601	990
Equity and liabilities:			
Share capital	1,120	600	390
Retained earnings	1,066	442	169
Other components of equity	60	37	45
Total equity	2,246	1,079	604
Non-current liabilities	455	323	73
Current liabilities	274	199	313
Total equity and liabilities	2,975	1,601	990

The following information is relevant to the preparation of the group financial statements:

1 On 1 December 20X0, Traveler acquired 60% of the equity interests of Data, a public limited company. The purchase consideration comprised cash of $600 million. At acquisition, the fair value of the non-controlling interest in Data was $395 million. Traveler wishes to use the 'full goodwill' method. On 1 December 20X0, the fair value of the identifiable net assets acquired was $935 million and retained earnings of Data were $299 million and other components of equity were $26 million. The excess in fair value is due to non-depreciable land.

On 30 November 20X1, Traveler acquired a further 20% interest in Data for a cash consideration of $220 million.

2 On 1 December 20X0, Traveler acquired 80% of the equity interests of Captive for a consideration of $541 million. The consideration comprised cash of $477 million and the transfer of non-depreciable land with a fair value of $64 million. The carrying amount of the land at the acquisition date was $56 million. At the year end, this asset was still included in the non-current assets of Traveler and the sale proceeds had been credited to profit or loss.

At the date of acquisition, the identifiable net assets of Captive had a fair value of $526 million, retained earnings were $90 million and other components of equity were $24 million. The excess in fair value is due to non-depreciable land. This acquisition was accounted for using the partial goodwill method in accordance with IFRS 3 *Business Combinations*.

3 Goodwill was impairment tested after the additional acquisition in Data on 30 November 20X1. The recoverable amount of the net assets and goodwill of Data was $1,099 million and that of Captive was $700 million.

Required:

(a) Prepare a consolidated statement of financial position for the Traveler Group for the year ended 30 November 20X1. (23 marks)

(b) At the start of the year to 30 November 20X2, Traveler acquired a major subsidiary. The inventory acquired in this business combination was valued at its fair value at the acquisition date in accordance with IFRS 3 *Business Combinations*. The inventory increased in value as a result of the fair value exercise. A significant part of the acquired inventory was sold shortly after the acquisition.

In the consolidated statement of profit or loss and other comprehensive income, the directors of Traveler intend to split the cost of inventories acquired in the business combination and sold by the acquirer after the business combination over two different lines: cost of sales, and a 'non-recurring item' within operating income. The part presented under cost of sales will correspond to the inventory's carrying amount in the subsidiary's financial statements. The part to be presented as a 'non-recurring item' corresponds to the fair value increase recognised on the business combination. The 'non-recurring item' amounted to 25% of Traveler's earnings before interest and tax (EBIT).

Traveler intends to disclose this accounting policy in the notes to the financial statements and to explain that showing the full fair value of the inventory within cost of sales would result in a fall in the gross margin. Traveler argues that isolating this part of the margin in the 'non-recurring items', whose nature is transparently presented in the notes, will enable users to evaluate changes in gross margin.

Required:

Discuss whether Traveler's proposal is in accordance with IFRS© Standards.

(7 marks)

(Total: 30 marks)

20 ROSE  *Walk in the footsteps of a top tutor*

Tutorial note

This question requires the preparation of a consolidated statement of financial position where one of the subsidiaries presents its financial statements in a different currency to the group. The examining team have said that the preparation of full consolidated financial statements is unlikely to appear in the Strategic Business Reporting exam. However this question still provides important revision of a range of consolidation issues.

Rose, a public limited company, operates in the mining sector. The draft statements of financial position are as follows, at 30 April 20X1:

	Rose	**Petal**	**Stem**
	$m	$m	Dinars m
Assets			
Non-current assets			
Property, plant and equipment	385	117	430
Investments in subsidiaries			
Petal	113		
Stem	46		
	544	117	430
Current assets	118	100	330
Total assets	662	217	760
Equity and liabilities			
Share capital	158	38	200
Retained earnings	256	56	300
Other components of equity	7	4	–
Total equity	421	98	500
Non-current liabilities	56	42	160
Current liabilities	185	77	100
Total liabilities	241	119	260
Total equity and liabilities	662	217	760

The following information is relevant to the preparation of the group financial statements:

1 On 1 May 20X0, Rose acquired 70% of the equity interests of Petal, a public limited company. The purchase consideration comprised cash of $94 million. The fair value of the identifiable net assets recognised by Petal was $120 million excluding the patent below. The identifiable net assets of Petal at 1 May 20X0 included a patent which had a fair value of $4 million. This had not been recognised in the financial statements of Petal. The patent had a remaining term of four years to run at that date and is not renewable. The retained earnings of Petal were $49 million and other components of equity were $3 million at the date of acquisition. The remaining excess of the fair value of the net assets is due to an increase in the value of land.

   Rose wishes to use the 'full goodwill' method. The fair value of the non-controlling interest in Petal was $46 million on 1 May 20X0. There have been no issues of ordinary shares since acquisition and goodwill on acquisition is not impaired.

   Rose acquired a further 10% interest from the non-controlling interest in Petal on 30 April 20X1 for a cash consideration of $19 million.

2 Rose acquired 52% of the ordinary shares of Stem on 1 May 20X0 when Stem's retained earnings were 220 million dinars. The fair value of the identifiable net assets of Stem on 1 May 20X0 was 495 million dinars. The excess of the fair value over the net assets of Stem is due to an increase in the value of land. Rose wishes to use the 'full goodwill' method. The fair value of the non-controlling interest in Stem at 1 May 20X0 was 250 million dinars. There have been no issues of ordinary shares and no impairment of goodwill since acquisition.

   The following exchange rates are relevant to the preparation of the group financial statements:

	Dinars to $
1 May 20X0	6
30 April 20X1	5
Average for year to 30 April 20X1	5.8

Required:

(a) **Prepare a consolidated statement of financial position of the Rose Group at 30 April 20X1, in accordance with International Financial Reporting Standards, showing the exchange difference arising on the translation of Stem's net assets. Ignore deferred taxation.** **(22 marks)**

(b) The directors of Rose are not fully aware of the requirements of IAS 21 *The Effects of Changes in Foreign Exchange Rates* in relation to exchange rate differences. They would like advice on how exchange differences should be recorded on both monetary and non-monetary assets in the financial statements and how these differ from the requirements for the translation of an overseas entity. The directors also wish advice on what would happen to the exchange differences if Rose sold all of its equity shares in Stem.

Required:

Provide a brief memo for the directors of Rose which identifies the correct accounting treatment for the various issues raised. **(8 marks)**

(Total: 30 marks)

SECTION A QUESTIONS – REPORTING AND ETHICAL IMPLICATIONS

21 AGENCY GROUP (SEP/DEC 2021)  *Walk in the footsteps of a top tutor*

Background

The Agency Group manufactures products for the medical industry. They have been suffering increased competition and, therefore, have sold a licence to distribute an existing product. They have also developed a new product which they hope will improve their market reputation. They have recently employed an ACCA student accountant. The year end is 31 December 20X7.

Ethical issues and foreign exchange

On 1 October 20X7, the finance director, Ms Malgun, a financial accountant, recruited Mr Raavi as an ACCA student accountant on a temporary employment contract which can be terminated by either party without reason. Mr Raavi has found it difficult to find employment and accepted the risk attached to the employment contract. However, the jurisdiction has laws which protect employees from termination due to discrimination. Mr Raavi has been told by Ms Malgun that there has been a global slowdown in business and that the biggest uncertainty is customer demand. She has therefore impressed upon Mr Raavi that the company profitability targets are based upon achieving 30% higher net profit than their nearest competitors. Ms Malgun is partly remunerated through profit related pay.

Ms Malgun has been under significant pressure from the board of directors to meet performance targets and would normally prepare the year-end financial statements. However, for the current year end, she has delegated this task to Mr Raavi.

Mr Raavi has included in profit or loss the foreign exchange gains arising on the re-translation of a foreign subsidiary which is held for sale. Mr Raavi has emailed Ms Malgun informing her of the accounting treatment. Although Ms Malgun is an expert in IFRS standards, she did not comment on this incorrect accounting treatment of the foreign exchange gains.

After the financial statements had been published, Ms Malgun disciplined Mr Raavi for the incorrect accounting treatment of the foreign exchange gains. However, despite this, she is prepared to make his employment contract permanent.

Sale of licence

On 1 January 20X7, Agency Co granted (sold) Kokila Co a licence with no end date to sell a headache product (Headon) in South America. Agency Co has retained the rights to sell Headon in the rest of the world. The South American market's relative value compared to the rest of the world is 20%. The manufacturing process used to produce Headon is not specialised and several other entities could also manufacture it for Kokila Co. Kokila Co will purchase Headon directly from Agency Co at cost plus 50%. The product has been sold for many years.

On 1 January 20X7, Kokila Co made an up-front payment of $15 million and will make an additional payment of $3 million when South American sales exceed $35 million. Agency Co had correctly capitalised development costs for Headon as an intangible asset at a carrying amount of $30 million.

Drug development

Agency Co is developing a biosimilar product for the treatment of a particular medical condition. A biosimilar product is one which is highly similar to another which has already been given regulatory approval. The existing approved product's (Xudix) patent is expiring and AgencyCo has applied to the government for regulatory approval of its new product. The submission includes an analysis which compares Xudix to Agency Co's proposed product in order to demonstrate biosimilarity. The government has reviewed the analysis and allowed Agency Co to undertake initial medical trials. Agency Co feels that the trials are going well. The product is used in the treatment of a very specific condition which affects only a small group of people, and Agency Co has decided to develop this product for reputational reasons. A person using the product will only pay a notional amount for the product if it is proven to be effective.

Required:

(a) (i) **Discuss the appropriateness of Mr Raavi's accounting treatment of the foreign exchange gains on the re-translation of the foreign subsidiary which is held for sale. (3 marks)**

(ii) **Discuss any ethical issues raised by Ms Malgun's actions regarding her management of Mr Raavi. (6 marks)**

(b) **Discuss how the granting (sale) of the licence to Kokila Co should be accounted for by Agency Co on 1 January 20X7. (5 marks)**

(c) **Discuss the accounting treatment of the costs incurred to date in developing the biosimilar drug. (4 marks)**

Professional marks will be awarded in part (a)(ii) for the quality of the discussion. **(2 marks)**

(Total: 20 marks)

22 BISMUTH (MAR/JUN 2021)  *Walk in the footsteps of a top tutor*

Background

Bismuth Co is a mining company. Investors in Bismuth Co receive earnings from mining projects as a return on their investment. The year end is 31 December 20X7.

Impairment testing of mines

At 31 December 20X7, Bismuth Co owns mines which have a carrying amount of $200 million. The company has committed itself to decommissioning its mines at the end of their useful life (five years or less) and has created a decommissioning provision of $53 million. However, the directors are unsure how the decommissioning provision will impact on the impairment testing of the mines. At the end of the useful life of a mine, its reusable components will be dismantled and sold.

The following information relates to the decommissioning of the mines at 31 December 20X7:

	$million
Carrying amount of decommissioning provision	53
Present value of future cash inflows from:	
– sale of reusable components at decommission date (inflows)	20
– sale of mining output from 31 December 20X7 to decommission date (inflows)	203
– operating costs from 31 December 20X7 to decommission date (outflows)	48

Class A and Class B shares

Bismuth Co has issued two classes of shares, class A and class B, in exchange for a cryptocurrency, Bitcoin. Both types of shares permit the holder to vote and give an entitlement to 'rewards'. Bismuth Co has discretion over whether 'rewards' are payable on class A and class B shares. Bitcoin can be readily converted into cash in Bismuth Co's jurisdiction.

Class A shares are redeemable at par in the event of Bismuth Co obtaining a listing on a formal stock exchange which is highly probable. On listing, Bismuth Co has a choice as to the method of redemption either:

(i) cash to the value of 1 Bitcoin per 1000 class A shares, or

(ii) shares to the value of 2 Bitcoins per 1000 class A shares.

Note: 1 Bitcoin equates to approximately $12,000

The share settlement option, option (ii) above, would involve exchanging class A shares for the equivalent number of class B shares. Class B shares have never fluctuated in value.

Bismuth Co is not compelled to redeem the class B shares but these shares do contain an option allowing Bismuth Co to repurchase them. However, if within two years, Bismuth Co fails to exercise its call option on the class B shares, it must pay an additional reward to the holders of class B shares.

Blockchain technology

Bismuth Co plans to implement Blockchain technology to store all of its data relating to its mines, trading and to certify the ethical sourcing of all its raw materials. The chief accountant, Ms Pleasant, is currently developing a blockchain technology that will be filed for patent. Ms Pleasant has only recently taken up the post and has discovered that work done at her previous employer, Gypsam Co, is relevant to the project. If Ms Pleasant discloses this information, it will compromise a patent process at Gypsam Co but will consolidate her position as chief accountant in Bismuth Co. When she left the employment of Gypsam Co, she signed a confidentiality agreement but the clauses were not clear or specific about what information could be shared and with whom.

Ms Pleasant has significant knowledge of Blockchain technology but the finance director, Mr Fricklin has limited knowledge of it or the new business model that Bismuth Co is trying to develop. Mr Fricklin has told her that there is no need to spend a significant amount of time creating a technology to ethically source materials. Ms Pleasant is worried about Mr Fricklin's lack of technical and legal knowledge as she feels that it will affect the development of the technology. In addition, some of the data concerning ethically sourced materials has gone missing and she thinks that Mr Fricklin has erased the data to try and sabotage the project. Mr Fricklin has told the Board of Directors that he has an 'in depth knowledge' of the technology.

Required:

(a) **Discuss, with suitable calculations, whether Bismuth Co should recognise an impairment loss for the mines. (5 marks)**

(b) **Discuss whether the class A and B shares should be classified as either equity or liability in accordance with IAS 32 *Financial Instruments: Presentation.* (5 marks)**

(c) **Discuss the ethical issues raised by the implementation of the blockchain technology for both the chief accountant and the finance director, including any appropriate actions which should be considered to resolve these issues. (8 marks)**

Professional marks will be awarded in part (c) for the quality of the discussion. **(2 marks)**

(Total: 20 marks)

23 CALIBRA (SEP/DEC 2020)  *Walk in the footsteps of a top tutor*

Calibra Co operates in the property sector and has invested in new technology, distributed ledgers/blockchain, to trade and to support property transactions. The financial year end of Calibra Co is 31 December 20X8.

Apartment blocks

Calibra Co builds apartment blocks which normally take two years to complete from the date of signing the contract. The performance obligation is satisfied at a point in time. The title and possession, and therefore control, of the apartment blocks pass to the customer upon completion of construction. The price which is payable on completion of each apartment block is $9.55 million. Alternatively, customers can pay $8.5 million cash on the day that the contract is signed. The chief accountant has calculated that this represents an appropriate borrowing rate of 6% for Calibra Co.

Calibra Co immediately recognises $8.5 million as revenue if customers pay when they sign the contract.

Chief accountant and Bodoni Co

The chief accountant does not hold a permanent employment contract with Calibra Co. He has applied for the position on a permanent basis and is to be interviewed in the near future. Bodoni Co, a customer of Calibra Co, wanted to take advantage of the $8.5 million reduced price for an apartment block but was having problems with cash flow. The chief accountant therefore allowed Bodoni Co to pay $8.5 million and to delay payment until one month after the contract was signed. In return, Bodoni Co has agreed to provide a good employment reference. The chief accountant of Calibra Co was afraid that he might lose Bodini Co as a customer and referee if he did not agree to the delay in payment.

Distributed ledger technology

Calibra Co has recently used distributed ledger technology/blockchain to sell shares in a property to investors. These digitised transactions are only visible to the authorised parties. The chief accountant publicly supports this technology and is to manage the new system. However, he has private concerns over the reliability of the due diligence carried out on the sale of property shares and the potential violation of local regulations. The directors of Calibra Co want to increase the number of transactions on the distributed ledger by offering digital shares in the whole of the entity's property portfolio. Although the chief accountant has very basic knowledge of distributed ledgers, he has assured the directors that he can facilitate this move. The project has been approved by the board despite the chief accountant's private reservations. The chief accountant has only recently qualified as an accountant and wishes to be employed with Calibra Co on a permanent basis.

Required:

(a) **Discuss how Calibra Co should have accounted for the sale of the apartment blocks in accordance with IFRS 15 *Revenue from Contracts with Customers* and IAS 23 *Borrowing Costs*. (5 marks)**

(b) **Provide the accounting entries that would be required to record the contractual sale of an apartment block on 1 January 20X8 at the discounted amount over the two-year construction period. (3 marks)**

(c) **Discuss the way in which the chief accountant should have acted to ensure that he maintained ethical standards in dealing with the issues described. (10 marks)**

Professional marks will be awarded in part (c) for the quality of the ethical discussion. (2 marks)

(Total: 20 marks)

24 BAGSHOT (MAR 2020)  *Walk in the footsteps of a top tutor*

Background

Bagshot Co has a controlling interest in a number of entities. Group results have been disappointing in recent years and the directors of Bagshot Co have been discussing various strategies to improve group performance. The current financial year end is 31 December 20X5.

The following personnel are relevant to the scenario:

Mr Shaw: Head accountant of Bagshot Co

Mrs Dawes: Chief executive of Bagshot Co

Mike Starr: Nephew of Mr Shaw

Mrs Shaw: Wife of Mr Shaw

Group restructure

Mr Shaw, an ACCA member, is the head accountant of Bagshot Co. He is not a member of the board of directors. Mrs Dawes, the chief executive of Bagshot Co, is also an ACCA member. During December 20X5, Mrs Dawes revealed plans to Mr Shaw of a potential restructure of the Bagshot group which had been discussed at board meetings. The restructuring plans included a general analysis of expected costs which would be incurred should the restructure take place. These include legal fees, relocation costs for staff and also redundancy costs for a number of employees. One such employee to be made redundant, Mike Starr, is the nephew of Mr Shaw.

Mrs Dawes is insistent that Mr Shaw should include a restructuring provision for all of the expenditure in the financial statements of Bagshot Co for the year ended 31 December 20X5. Mrs Dawes argues that, even if the restructure did not take place exactly as detailed, similar levels of expenditure are likely to be incurred on alternative strategies. It would therefore be prudent to include a restructuring provision for all expenditure. None of the staff other than Mr Shaw have been notified of the plans although Mrs Dawes has informed Mr Shaw that she expects a final decision and public announcement to be made prior to the authorisation of the financial statements.

Mrs Shaw

Mrs Shaw is the wife of Mr Shaw, the head accountant of Bagshot Co. She is not an employee of Bagshot Co and does not know about the proposed restructure. However, Mrs Shaw recently acquired 5% of the equity shares in Bagshot Co. Mr Shaw is considering informing his wife of the proposed restructure so that she can make an informed decision as to whether to divest her shareholding or not. Mr Shaw is concerned that, in the short term at least, the inclusion of any restructuring costs would be harmful to the profitability of Bagshot Co. It is also uncertain as to how the market may react should the restructure take place. It is, however, anticipated that in the long term, shareholder value would be enhanced.

Required:

(a) (i) Discuss the appropriate accounting treatment of the restructuring costs in the financial statements of Bagshot Co for the year ended 31 December 20X5. (6 marks)

(ii) Discuss what is meant by good stewardship of a company and whether the restructure and the recognition of a restructuring provision in the financial statements are examples of good stewardship. (4 marks)

(iii) Discuss briefly whether Mrs Shaw's acquisition of the equity shares in Bagshot Co should be disclosed as a related party transaction. (3 marks)

(b) Identify and discuss the ethical issues arising from the scenario which Mr Shaw needs to consider and what actions he should take as a consequence. (5 marks)

Professional marks will be awarded in part (b) for the clarity of discussion. (2 marks)

(Total: 20 marks)

25 STENT (SEP/DEC 2019)  *Walk in the footsteps of a top tutor*

 ***Answer debrief***

Stent Co is a consumer electronics company which has faced a challenging year due to increased competition. Stent Co has a year end of 30 September 20X9 and the unaudited draft financial statements report an operating loss. In addition to this, debt covenant limits based on gearing are close to being breached and the company is approaching its overdraft limit.

Cash advance from Budster Co

On 27 September 20X9, Stent Co's finance director asked the accountant to record a cash advance of $3 million received from a customer, Budster Co, as a reduction in trade receivables. Budster Co is solely owned by Stent Co's finance director. The accountant has seen an agreement signed by both companies stating that the $3 million will be repaid to Budster Co in four months' time. The finance director argues that the proposed accounting treatment is acceptable because the payment has been made in advance in case Budster Co wishes to order goods in the next four months. However, the accountant has seen no evidence of any intent from Budster Co to place orders with Stent Co. **(4 marks)**

Preference shares

On 1 October 20X8, the CEO and finance director each paid $2 million cash in exchange for preference shares from Stent Co which provide cumulative dividends of 7% per annum. These preference shares can either be converted into a fixed number of ordinary shares in two years' time, or redeemed at par on the same date, at the choice of the holder. The finance director suggests to the accountant that the preference shares should be classified as equity because the conversion is into a fixed number of ordinary shares on a fixed date ('fixed for fixed') and conversion is certain (given the current market value of the ordinary shares).

(4 marks)

Deferred tax asset

Stent Co includes a deferred tax asset in its statement of financial position, based on losses incurred in the current and the previous two years. The finance director has asked the accountant to include the deferred tax asset in full. He has suggested this on the basis that Stent Co will return to profitability once its funding issues are resolved. **(3 marks)**

Required:

(a) Discuss appropriate accounting treatments which Stent Co should adopt for all issues identified above and their impact upon gearing.

Note: The mark allocation is shown against each issue above.

The accountant has been in her position for only a few months and the finance director has recently commented that 'all these accounting treatments must be made exactly as I have suggested to ensure the growth of the business and the security of all our jobs'. Both the finance director and the accountant are fully qualified members of ACCA.

Required:

(b) Discuss the ethical issues arising from the scenario, including any actions which the accountant should take to resolve the issues. (7 marks)

Professional marks will be awarded in this question for the application of ethical principles. (2 marks)

(Total: 20 marks)

Calculate your allowed time, allocate the time to the separate parts..............

26 HUDSON (MAR/JUN 2019)  *Walk in the footsteps of a top tutor*

Background

Hudson has a year end of 31 December 20X2 and operates a defined benefit scheme for all employees. In addition, the directors of Hudson are paid an annual bonus depending upon the earnings before interest, tax, depreciation and amortisation (EBITDA) of Hudson.

Hudson has been experiencing losses for a number of years and its draft financial statements reflect a small loss for the current year of $10 million. On 1 May 20X2, Hudson announced that it was restructuring and that it was going to close down division Wye. A number of redundancies were confirmed as part of this closure with some staff being reallocated to other divisions within Hudson. The directors have approved the restructuring in a formal directors' meeting. Hudson is highly geared and much of its debt is secured on covenants which stipulate that a minimum level of net assets should be maintained. The directors are concerned that compliance with IFRS Standards could have significant implications for their bonus and debt covenants.

Redundancy and settlement costs

Hudson still requires a number of staff to operate division Wye until its final expected closure in early 20X3. As a consequence, Hudson offered its staff two packages in relation to the curtailment of the defined benefit scheme. A pension enhancement was offered for all staff who leave before the final closure of division Wye. An additional pension enhancement was offered for staff who remained in employment until the final closure of division Wye. The directors of Hudson have only included an adjustment in the financial statements for those staff who left prior to 31 December 20X2. The directors have included this adjustment within the remeasurement component of the defined benefit scheme. They do not wish to provide for any other enhancements until employment is finally terminated, arguing that an obligation would only arise once the staff were made redundant. On final termination, the directors intend to include the remaining basic enhancement and the additional pension enhancement within the remeasurement component.

The directors and accountant are aware that the proposed treatment does not conform to IFRS Standards. The directors believe that the proposed treatment is justified as it will help Hudson maintain its debt covenant obligations and will therefore be in the best interests of their shareholders who are the primary stakeholder. The directors have indicated that, should the accountant not agree with their accounting treatment, then he will be replaced.

Tax losses

The directors of Hudson wish to recognise a material deferred tax asset in relation to $250 million of unused trading losses which have accumulated as at 31 December 20X2. Hudson has budgeted profits for $80 million for the year ended 31 December 20X3. The directors have forecast that profits will grow by 20% each year for the next four years. The market is currently depressed and sales orders are at a lower level for the first quarter of 20X3 than they were for the same period in any of the previous five years. Hudson operates under a tax jurisdiction which allows for trading losses to be only carried forward for a maximum of two years.

Required:

(a) Explain why the directors of Hudson are wrong to classify the basic and additional pension enhancements as part of the remeasurement component, including an explanation of the correct treatment for each of these items. Also explain how any other restructuring costs should be accounted for. (8 marks)

(b) Explain whether a deferred tax asset can be recognised in the financial statements of Hudson in the year ended 31 December 20X2. (5 marks)

(c) Identify any ethical issues which arise from the directors' proposed accounting treatments and behaviour. Your answer should also consider the implications for the accountant arising from the directors' behaviour. (5 marks)

Professional marks will be awarded in part (c) for quality of discussion. (2 marks)

(Total: 20 marks)

27 FISKERTON (DEC 2018)  *Walk in the footsteps of a top tutor*

Background

The following is an extract from the statement of financial position of Fiskerton, a public limited entity as at 30 September 20X8.

	$000
Non-current assets	160,901
Current assets	110,318
Equity share capital ($1 each)	10,000
Other components of equity	20,151
Retained earnings	70,253
Non-current liabilities (bank loan)	50,000
Current liabilities	120,815

The bank loan has a covenant attached whereby it will become immediately repayable should the gearing ratio (long-term debt to equity) of Fiskerton exceed 50%. Fiskerton has a negative cash balance as at 30 September 20X8.

Halam property

Included within the non-current assets of Fiskerton is a property in Halam which has been leased to Edingley under a 40-year lease. The property was acquired for $20 million on 1 October 20X7 and was immediately leased to Edingley.

The asset was expected to have a useful life of 40 years at the date of acquisition and have a minimal residual value. Fiskerton has classified the building as an investment property and has adopted the fair value model.

The property was initially revalued to $22 million on 31 March 20X8. Interim financial statements had indicated that gearing was 51% prior to this revaluation. The managing director was made aware of this breach of covenant and so instructed that the property should be revalued. The property is now carried at a value of $28 million which was determined by the sale of a similar sized property on 30 September 20X8. This property was located in a much more prosperous area and built with a higher grade of material. An independent professional valuer has estimated the value to be no more than $22 million. The managing director has argued that fair values should be referenced to an active market and is refusing to adjust the financial statements, even though he knows it is contrary to international accounting standards.

Sales contract

Fiskerton has entered into a sales contract for the construction of an asset with a customer whereby the customer pays an initial deposit. The deposit is refundable only if Fiskerton fails to complete the construction of the asset. The remainder is payable on delivery of the asset. If the customer defaults on the contract prior to completion, Fiskerton has the right to retain the deposit. The managing director believes that, as completion of the asset is performed over time, revenue should be recognised accordingly. He has persuaded the accountant to include the deposit and a percentage of the remaining balance for construction work in revenue to date.

Required:

(a) **Discuss how the Halam property should have been accounted for and explain the implications for the financial statements and the debt covenant of Fiskerton.** **(7 marks)**

(b) **In accordance with IFRS 15 *Revenue from Contracts with Customers*, discuss whether revenue arising from the sales contract should be recognised on a stage of completion basis.** **(4 marks)**

(c) **Explain any ethical issues which may arise for the managing director and the accountant from each of the scenarios.** **(7 marks)**

Professional marks will be awarded in part (c) for the quality of the discussion. **(2 marks)**

(Total: 20 marks)

28 FARHAM (SEP 2018)  *Walk in the footsteps of a top tutor*

Background

Farham manufactures white goods such as washing machines, tumble dryers and dishwashers. The industry is highly competitive with a large number of products on the market. Brand loyalty is consequently an important feature in the industry. Farham operates a profit related bonus scheme for its managers based upon the consolidated financial statements but recent results have been poor and bonus targets have rarely been achieved. As a consequence, the company is looking to restructure and sell its 80% owned subsidiary Newall which has been making substantial losses. The current year end is 30 June 20X8.

Factory subsidence

Farham has a production facility which started to show signs of subsidence since January 20X8. It is probable that Farham will have to undertake a major repair sometime during 20X9 to correct the problem. Farham does have an insurance policy but it is unlikely to cover subsidence. The chief operating officer (COO) refuses to disclose the issue at 30 June 20X8 since no repair costs have yet been undertaken although she is aware that this is contrary to international accounting standards. The COO does not think that the subsidence is an indicator of impairment. She argues that no provision for the repair to the factory should be made because there is no legal or constructive obligation to repair the factory.

Farham has a revaluation policy for property, plant and equipment and there is a balance on the revaluation surplus of $10 million in the financial statements for the year ended 30 June 20X8. None of this balance relates to the production facility but the COO is of the opinion that this surplus can be used for any future loss arising from the subsidence of the production facility. **(5 marks)**

Sale of Newall

At 30 June 20X8 Farham had a plan to sell its 80% subsidiary Newall. This plan has been approved by the board and reported in the media. It is expected that Oldcastle, an entity which currently owns the other 20% of Newall, will acquire the 80% equity interest. The sale is expected to be complete by December 20X8. Newall is expected to have substantial trading losses in the period up to the sale. The accountant of Farham wishes to show Newall as held for sale in the consolidated financial statements and to create a restructuring provision to include the expected costs of disposal and future trading losses. The COO does not wish Newall to be disclosed as held for sale nor to provide for the expected losses. The COO is concerned as to how this may affect the sales price and would almost certainly mean bonus targets would not be met. The COO has argued that they have a duty to secure a high sales price to maximise the return for shareholders of Farham. She has also implied that the accountant may lose his job if he were to put such a provision in the financial statements. The expected costs from the sale are as follows:

	$m
Future trading losses	30
Various legal costs of sale	2
Redundancy costs for Newall employees	5
Impairment losses on owned assets	8

Included within the future trading losses is an early termination penalty of $6 million for a leased asset which is deemed surplus to requirements. **(6 marks)**

Required:

(a) **Discuss the accounting treatment which Farham should adopt to address each of the issues above for the consolidated financial statements.**

Note: The mark allocation is shown against each of the two issues above.

(b) **Discuss the ethical issues arising from the scenario, including any actions which Farham and the accountant should undertake.** **(7 marks)**

Professional marks will be awarded in part (b) for the quality of the discussion. **(2 marks)**

(Total: 20 marks)

29 CLOUD  *Walk in the footsteps of a top tutor*

 ***Answer debrief***

Background

Cloud, a public limited company, is preparing financial statements for the year ended 31 December 20X1. The profit figure reported in the interim financial statements was lower than shareholders expected, and net operating cash flows for the year are below budget. The directors of Cloud receive a bonus if Cloud's operating cash flow and profit before tax exceed a predetermined target for the year. The finance director is perceived to be a dominant personality, and members of the accounts department, many of whom are ACCA members, follow his instructions without question.

Presentation of loan in statement of cash flows

Cloud has entered into a long-term contract with a major customer and negotiated a new bank loan on the strength of this contract. The proceeds of the loan were received in the current period and are to be repaid over four years to 31 December 20X5. Cloud has reported the loan proceeds as an operating cash flow because it relates to a long-term trading contract.

Share sale

During the period Cloud sold 5% of the equity shares of Fog for $2 million. Prior to the sale, Cloud owned 100% of the shares of Fog. This transaction has improved Cloud's cash position while enabling it to retain control over Fog. At the date of the share sale, the goodwill and net assets of Fog were carried in the consolidated statement of financial position at $5 million and $25 million respectively. The non-controlling interest at acquisition was measured at fair value. Cloud has recorded a profit on the disposal of the shares in the consolidated statement of profit or loss.

Revaluation of property, plant and equipment

Cloud purchased an item of property, plant and equipment for $10 million on 1 January 20X0. The useful economic life was estimated to be five years. At 31 December 20X0, the asset was revalued to $12 million. At 31 December 20X1, the asset's value had fallen to $4 million. The downwards revaluation was recorded in other comprehensive income.

Required:

Explain, with suitable calculations, how the above transactions should be dealt with in the financial statements for the year ended 31 December 20X1 and discuss the ethical and professional issues raised. (18 marks)

Professional marks will be awarded in this question for the application of ethical principles. (2 marks)

(Total: 20 marks)

 ***Calculate your allowed time, allocate the time to the separate parts..............***

30 GARDEN  *Walk in the footsteps of a top tutor*

Background

Garden is a public listed company with a reporting date of 30 November 20X6. It owns and operates various online businesses. Its customers order goods through Garden's websites, and these goods are delivered by third party couriers. At 30 November 20X6, the finance director owns 15% of Garden's ordinary shares and the operations director owns 10%. The rest of the shares are owned by numerous other shareholders. All ordinary shares carry equal voting rights. At the most recent annual general meeting, some of the shareholders expressed dis-satisfaction with the financial performance of Garden. They also complained that the directors were overpaid and were not demonstrating effective stewardship of the company's assets The accountant of Garden started her employment during the year ended 30 November 20X6 and has encountered a number of issues.

Share-based payment

On 1 December 20X5, a share-based payment scheme was introduced for Garden's six directors. The directors are entitled to 600,000 share options each if they remain employed by the company until 30 November 20X8. The fair value of each share option was $4 at 1 December 20X5 and $5 at 30 November 20X6. At 1 December 20X5 it was estimated that none of the directors would leave before the end of three years but, as at 30 November 20X6, the estimated number of leavers was revised to one. The finance director has told the accountant that no entries or disclosures are required for this scheme in the current year's financial statements because it has not yet vested. **(4 marks)**

The directors' son

The wife of the finance director is the sales director of Garden. Their son is undertaking an internship with Garden and receives a salary of $30,000 per annum, which is in line with market rates. The finance director has ordered the accountant to omit any reference to his son's salary from the financial statements. **(3 marks)**

Operating segments

At the start of the current year, Garden purchased the trade and assets of a fashion retail chain that operates a number of shops in large towns and cities. The chain did not sell its products online. The press were critical of Garden's decision, accusing them of over-paying for the chain and of expanding into a sector in which they lack experience and expertise. The performance of the shops, which is monitored internally by Garden's chief operating decision makers, has been poor. When reviewing the operating segment disclosure note prepared by the finance director the accountant noticed that the new retail business has been aggregated with the rest of Garden's trading operations and disclosed as a single reportable segment. The gross profit margins made from the retail outlets are much lower than those made from Garden's online operations. From overhearing conversations, the accountant is aware that Garden's finance director is a good friend of the former owner of the retail chain. **(4 marks)**

Required:

(a) Discuss the correct accounting treatment of the above three issues in Garden's financial statements for the year ended 30 November 20X6.

Note: The mark allocation is shown against each of the three issues above.

(b) Discuss the accounting and ethical implications of the above from the perspective of the accountant. (7 marks)

Professional marks will be awarded in part (b) for the application of ethical principles. (2 marks)

(Total: 20 marks)

31 CHERRY  *Walk in the footsteps of a top tutor*

Background

Cherry is a large public limited company. It prepares its financial statements using IFRS Standards and has a reporting date of 30 November 20X6. A bonus is paid to the directors each year which is based upon the operating profit margin of Cherry.

Change in accounting policy for pension scheme

On 1 December 20X5, there was an amendment to Cherry's defined benefit scheme whereby the promised pension entitlement was increased from 10% of final salary to 15%. The directors believe that the pension scheme, which is in deficit, is not an integral part of the operating activities of Cherry. As such they have changed their accounting policy so that, from the current year, all gains and losses on the pension scheme are recognised in other comprehensive income. They believe that this will make the financial statements more consistent, more understandable and can be justified on the grounds of fair presentation.

(3 marks)

Trademark

On 1 December 20X2, Cherry acquired a trademark, Golfo, for a line of golf clothing for $3 million. Initially, because of the difficulty in determining its useful life, Cherry decided to amortise the trademark over a 10-year life, using the straight-line method. On 1 December 20X5, a competitor unexpectedly revealed a technological breakthrough which is expected to result in a product which, when launched in May 20X8, will significantly reduce the demand for the Golfo product-line. Cherry now intends to continue manufacturing Golfo products until 31 May 20X8. Amortisation of $300,000 in relation to the Golfo trademark has been charged in the financial statements for the year ended 30 November 20X6.

(4 marks)

Sale and leaseback

Cherry sold a building for its fair value of $5 million to a finance company on 30 November 20X6 when its carrying amount was $3.5 million. The building was leased back from the finance company for a period of 5 years. The remaining useful life of the building was deemed to be 25 years so it can be concluded that control of the building has transferred to the finance company. Lease rentals are $440,000 payable annually in arrears. The interest rate implicit in the lease is 7%. The present value of the annual lease payments is $1.8 million. Cherry has recorded the cash proceeds, derecognised the building, and recorded a profit on disposal of $1.5 million in the statement of profit or loss. No other accounting entries have been posted.

The directors have told the financial controller that the accounting treatments outlined above are correct. Any further time that the financial controller spends reviewing these transactions will be looked on unfavourably when deciding her bonus for the year.

(5 marks)

Required:

(a) **Discuss the correct accounting treatment of the above transactions in the financial statements of Cherry for the year ended 30 November 20X6.**

Note: The mark allocation is shown against each of the three issues above.

(b) **Discuss the ethical implications of the above scenario.** **(6 marks)**

Professional marks will be awarded in part (b) for the application of ethical principles.

(2 marks)

(Total: 20 marks)

32 ANOUK

Background

Anouk is a public limited entity with a reporting date of 31 December 20X1. It has covenants attached to some of the bank loan balances included within liabilities on its statement of financial position. The covenants create a legal obligation to repay the loans in full if Anouk's liabilities exceed a specified level. A new financial controller was appointed in January 20X2 and has discovered some financial reporting issues in relation to the year ended 31 December 20X1.

Receivables factoring

On 31 December 20X1 Anouk sold some of its trade receivables to a debt factor. The factor advanced 20% of the $40 million receivables sold. Further amounts become payable to Anouk but are subject to an imputed interest charge so that Anouk receives progressively less of the remaining balance the longer it takes the factor to recover the funds. The factor has full recourse to Anouk for a six-month period after which Anouk has no further obligations and has no rights to receive any further payments from the factor.

The directors are concerned about the negative impact that any potential debt factoring arrangements may have on its loan covenants. As such, they have ordered the financial controller to treat the factoring arrangement in accordance with its legal form.

B-shares

One of Anouk's subsidiaries, Vianne, has two classes of shares: A and B. A-shares carry voting powers and B-shares are issued to meet regulatory requirements. Vianne's shareholder agreement stipulates that the minority B shareholders can exercise a put option every three years which requires Anouk to buy their shares. The exercise price is the original cost paid by the shareholders. In Anouk's consolidated statement of financial position, the B-shares owned by minority shareholders are reported in equity as a non-controlling interest.

Crane

On the 31 December 20X1, Anouk signed a contract to use a crane for the next five years. The supplier of the crane is permitted to substitute the crane for an alternative model during the period of use, and is required to do so if the crane develops a fault. Due to the size of the crane, the supplier would have to incur significant costs to substitute it. The contract states that Anouk can use the crane for any construction activities it wishes. However, the contract also states that the crane cannot be used if wind speed exceeds 14 metres per second. Anouk must pay a fixed monthly rental fee for use of the crane. Anouk has posted no accounting entries in respect of this contract. The financial controller found this contract by accident and suspects that the directors had attempted to conceal it.

Required:

Discuss the accounting and ethical implications of the above. (18 marks)

Professional marks will be awarded in this question for the application of ethical principles. (2 marks)

(Total: 20 marks)

SECTION B QUESTIONS

33 STEM (SEP/DEC 2021)  *Walk in the footsteps of a top tutor*

Stem Co is a manufacturing company and is considering providing cars for its senior management. It has also entered into an agreement with two other companies to develop a new technology through a separate legal entity, Emphasis Co. The financial year end of Stem Co is 31 December 20X7.

Company cars

On 1 January 20X7, Stem Co is considering providing company cars for its senior management and is comparing three options.

Option 1

The cars can be leased for a period of four years starting on 1 January 20X7. The cars have a total market value of $75,274 on this date. The lease requires payments of $1,403 on a monthly basis for the duration of the lease term of which $235 is a servicing charge. Stem Co wishes to show the servicing charge as a separate line item in profit or loss.

At the end of the four-year period, there is no option to renew the lease or purchase the cars, and there is no residual value guarantee. The interest to be charged for the year ended 31 December 20X7 is correctly calculated at $2,274 based upon the implicit interest rate in the lease. The net present value of the lease payments over four years is $50,803 excluding the service charge.

Option 2

The cars can be purchased for $75,274 with a 100% bank loan. The cars would be purchased on 1 January 20X7 and held for four years. The estimated residual value is $29,753. Monthly service costs would still be $235 per month. The loan would be repayable in four annual instalments commencing 1 January 20X8. Assume that an average annual percentage rate on a loan is 5%.

Option 3

A final alternative is to lease the cars with a 12-month agreement on 1 January 20X7 with no purchase option. The cost would be $1,900 per month in advance including servicing charge. Stem Co would take advantage of the short-term lease exemption under IFRS 16 Leases.

Other relevant information

The profit before tax and before accounting for any of the three options for cars is likely to be $100,000 for the year ended 31 December 20X7. Stem Co depreciates cars over a four-year period using straight line depreciation.

Emphasis Co

On 1 January 20X7, Stem Co has contributed cash to a new legal entity, Emphasis Co, and holds an interest of 40%. The other two companies contributing have retained equity interests of 40% and 20%, respectively. The purpose of the entity is to share risks and rewards in developing a new technology. The holders of a 40% interest can appoint three members each to a seven-member board of directors. All significant decisions require the unanimous consent of the board. The holder of the 20% interest can appoint only one board member and can only participate in the significant decisions of the entity through the board. There are no related parties.

Stem Co contributed cash of $150,000 to Emphasis Co. The entity will use the cash invested by Stem Co to gain access to new markets and to develop new products. At 1 January 20X7, the carrying amount of the net assets contributed by the three companies was $310,000 but the fair value of the net assets contributed was $470,000.

Required:

(a) Explain, with suitable calculations, the impact of the three alternative company car options on:

- **earnings before interest, tax, depreciation and amortisation (EBITDA)**
- **profit before tax, and**
- **the statement of financial position for the year ended 31 December 20X7.**

Note: Candidates should refer to IFRS 16 *Leases* where appropriate. **(13 marks)**

(b) (i) Discuss briefly principles of the equity method of accounting and whether it is a more relevant measurement basis than cost or fair value of an investment in an associate company.

Note: There is no need to refer to any exhibit when answering part (b)(i). **(4 marks)**

(ii) Discuss why Stem Co's investment in Emphasis Co should be classified as a joint venture and how Stem Co should account for its interest at 1 January 20X7 in accordance with IAS 28 *Investments in Associates and Joint Ventures*.

Note: Candidates should show any relevant entries required in the accounting records of Stem Co. **(8 marks)**

(Total: 25 marks)

34 SYMBAL (SEP/DEC 2021)  *Walk in the footsteps of a top tutor*

Symbal Co develops cryptocurrency funds and is a leading authority on crypto investing. Symbal Co specialises in Initial Coin Offerings ('ICO') that raises funds from investors in the form of cash or a crypto asset such as Bitcoin.

The year-end of Symbal Co is 31 March 20X7.

Development costs

The diagram below illustrates how the ICO is used by Symbal Co.

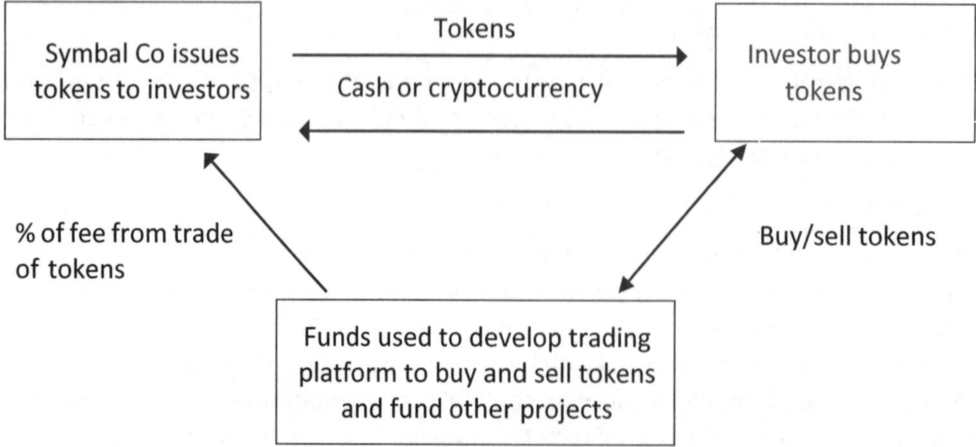

Note: The terms token and coin mean the same and investors are often referred to as supporters.

An ICO issues tokens to investors for cryptocurrency or cash. For each ICO, Symbal Co establishes a separate payment platform on which the investors can trade the tokens. These tokens do not represent an ownership interest in the entity. Symbal Co promises to produce gains for investors from trading the tokens on the platform and in return, the company takes a percentage of the profit as a fee.

As at 31 March 20X7, Symbal Co has incurred significant cost in promoting the issue of the ICO tokens, and developing the trading platform for dealing with the purchase and sale of the ICO tokens. These costs have been met from its own capital and expensed to profit or loss. Symbal Co will earn revenue from supporting the purchase and sale of tokens.

ICO arrangements

Occasionally, Symbal Co enters into pre-sale agreements to raise funding from selected investors prior to a public sale of tokens. Symbal Co has entered into a pre-sale agreement with an investor which entitles the investor to a 10% discount on the price for tokens compared to other investors at the time of the ICO. On 1 March 20X7, the investor paid Symbal Co $1 million in cash. The issue date of the ICO is 30 April 20X7. The cash is only refundable if the ICO is abandoned before 30 April 20X7 because the minimum funding level of $9 million has not been achieved.

Once the tokens are issued, ICO investors can readily convert them into cash or cryptocurrencies on Symbal Co's platform but they do not entitle the holder to future goods and services from Symbal Co other than supporting the purchase and sale of tokens. The inflows received for tokens are used by Symbal Co to fund the future development of the payment platform and other projects.

In order to induce investment in the ICO, Symbal Co has made a commitment to the holders of tokens to pay a single payment of 10% of any annual profit for the year ended 31 March 20X8. The holders do not have any other rights such as redemption of their tokens or any residual interest in the assets of Symbal Co.

The ICO raised $10 million on 30 April 20X7.

Tokens granted to directors

Symbal Co sometimes does not issue all the tokens from an ICO to investors but retains some to use to reward their employees. On 1 March 20X7, Symbal Co granted tokens to its five directors from the issue on 30 April 20X7. The award vests on 31 March 20X7 to directors who were in Symbal Co's employment at 31 March 20X7. The tokens give the directors the right to receive a car of their choice up to a value of $50,000 at any time in the next 12 months to 31 March 20X8 if they remain as directors of Symbal Co. All five directors were still with Symbal Co on 31 March 20X7.

Required:

(a) Explain the principles of good disclosure which should be used to inform investors regarding the company's holding of crypto assets.

Note: There is no need to refer to any exhibit when answering part (a). **(6 marks)**

Professional marks will be awarded in part (a) for clarity and quality of discussion. **(2 marks)**

(b) Advise whether the various development and promotional costs related to the ICO can be accounted for as an intangible asset at 31 March 20X7. (5 marks)

(c) **Discuss how the receipt of $1 million cash in the pre-sale agreement should be accounted for in the financial statements for the year ended 31 March 20X7 and how the $10 million raised in the ICO should be accounted for in the financial statements for the year ended 31 March 20X8.** **(6 marks)**

(d) **Discuss why the granting of the tokens to the five directors should be accounted for in accordance with IAS 19 *Employee Benefits* rather than IFRS 2 *Share-based Payment* in the financial statements for the year ended 31 March 20X7.** **(6 marks)**

(Total: 25 marks)

35 SITKA (MAR/JUN 2021)  *Walk in the footsteps of a top tutor*

Sitka Co is a software development company which operates in an industry where technologies change rapidly. Its customers use the cloud to access the software and Sitka Co generates revenue by charging customers for the software license and software updates. It has recently disposed of an interest in a subsidiary, Marlett Co, and purchased a controlling interest in Billing Co. The year end of the company is 31 December 20X7.

Software contract and updates

On 1 January 20X7, Sitka Co agreed a four-year contract with Cent Co to provide access to licence Sitka Co's software including customer support in the form of monthly updates to the software. The total contract price is $3 million for both licensing the software and the monthly updates. Sitka Co licenses the software on a stand-alone basis for between $1 million and $2 million over a four-year period and regularly sells the monthly updates separately for $2·5 million over the same period. The software can function on its own without the updates. Although, the monthly updates improve its effectiveness, they are not essential to its functionality. However, because of the rapidly changing technology in the industry, if Cent Co does not update the software regularly, the benefits of using the software would be significantly reduced. In the year to 31 December 20X7, Cent Co has only updated the software on two occasions. Cent Co must access the software via the cloud and does not own the rights to the software.

Part-disposal of Marlett Co

Sitka Co prepares separate financial statements in accordance with IAS 27 *Separate Financial Statements*. At 31 December 20X6, it held a 60% controlling equity interest in Marlett Co and accounted for Marlett Co as a subsidiary. In its separate financial statements, Sitka Co had elected to measure its investment in Marlett Co using the equity method. On 1 July 20X7, Sitka Co disposed of 45% of its equity interest in Marlett Co for $10 million and lost control. At the date of disposal, the carrying amount of Marlett Co in its separate financial statements was $12 million. After the partial disposal, Sitka Co does not have joint control of, or significant influence over Marlett Co and its retained interest of 15% is to be treated as an investment in an equity instrument. At 1 July 20X7, the fair value of the retained interest of 15% in Marlett Co was $3.5 million. Sitka Co wishes to recognise any profit or loss on the disposal of the 45% interest in other comprehensive income.

Acquisition of Billing Co

Sitka Co has acquired two assets in a business combination with Billing Co. The first asset is 'Qbooks' which is an accounting system developed by Billing Co for use with the second asset which is 'Best Cloud' software. The directors of Sitka Co believe that the fair value of the assets is higher if valued together rather than individually. If the assets were to be sold, there are two types of buyers that would be interested in purchasing the assets. One buyer group would be those who operate in the same industry and have similar assets. This group of buyers would eventually replace Qbooks with their own accounting system which would enhance the value of their assets. The fair values of the individual assets in the industry buyer group would be $30 million for Qbooks and $200 million for 'Best Cloud', therefore being $230 million in total. Another type of buyer is the financial investor who would not have a substitute asset for Qbooks. They would licence Qbooks for its remaining life and commercialise the product. The indicated fair values for Qbooks and Best Cloud within the financial investor group are $50million and $150 million, being $200 million in total.

Required:

(a) (i) **Discuss whether the four-year software contract with Cent Co is a single performance obligation in accordance with IFRS 15 *Revenue from Contracts with Customers* including how the revenue from the contract would be accounted for in Sitka Co's financial statements for the year ended 31 December 20X7. Your answer should include whether the revenue should be recognised at a point in time or over time. (8 marks)**

(ii) **Discuss briefly why the right to receive access to Sitka Co's software is unlikely to be accounted for as an intangible asset or a lease in Cent Co's financial statements. (4 marks)**

(b) **Discuss and demonstrate how the disposal of 45% interest and the retained interest of 15% in Marlett Co should be accounted for in the separate financial statements of Sitka Co at the date of disposal. (9 marks)**

(c) **Discuss how the two assets acquired on the acquisition of Billing Co should be valued in accordance IFRS 13 *Fair Value Measurement.* (4 marks)**

(Total: 25 marks)

36 COLAT (MAR/JUNE 2021)  *Walk in the footsteps of a top tutor*

Colat Co manufactures aluminium products and operates in a region that has suffered a natural disaster on 1 November 20X7. There has been an increase in operating costs as the company had to replace a regional supplier with a more costly international supplier. The year-end of Colat Co is 31 December 20X7.

Non-current assets

As a result of the natural disaster, the share price of Colat Co has declined as a significant amount of non-current assets were destroyed, including the manufacturing facility. In addition, Colat Co has suffered reputational damage resulting in a decline in customer demand. The non-current assets of Colat Co that were destroyed had a carrying amount of $250 million on 31 October 20X7 and the fair value of these non-current assets was $280 million based on an independent appraisal shortly before that date. In addition, Colat Co determined that a power plant will have to be closed and decommissioned earlier than previously expected. The remaining useful life of the power plant has reduced from 25 years to 8 years. Non-current assets are valued using the cost model.

Other natural disaster consequences

Environmental damage and government compensation

Colat Co has, in the past, repaired minor environmental damage that it has caused but it has never suffered a natural disaster on this scale. There is no legal obligation for Colat Co to repair and restore damage caused by the disaster as this will be the responsibility of the government.

The government announced on 1 December 20X7 that there would be compensation of $50 million available to repair the environmental damage only and that companies should apply for the compensation by 31 December 20X7. By 1 March 20X8, when the financial statements were approved, Colat Co had only received an acknowledgement of their application but no approval.

Hedge of commodity price risk in aluminium

Colat Co hedges commodity price risk in aluminium and such transactions were classified as 'highly probable' in accordance with IFRS 9 *Financial Instruments*. However, the purchases which were considered highly probable prior to the natural disaster, are no longer expected to occur.

Potential insurance policy proceeds

Colat Co's insurance policy provides compensation for losses based on the fair value of non-current assets, any temporary relocation costs estimated at $2million and any revenue lost during the two-month period from 1 November 20X7. At 31 December 20X7, it is unclear which events and costs are covered by insurance policies and significant uncertainty exists as to whether any compensation will be paid. Before the financial statements were approved, it was probable that the insurance claim for the loss of the non-current assets would be paid but no further information was available about other insured losses.

The insurance policy does not cover environmental damage which is the responsibility of the government.

Required (25 marks):

Investors need to understand a variety of factors when making an investment decision. The nature of the companies in which they are looking to invest is an important consideration, as is the need to incorporate sustainability factors into investment decisions.

(a) **Discuss why sustainability has become an important aspect of the investors' analysis of companies.**

Note: there is no requirement to refer to any exhibit when answering part (a). **(4 marks)**

Professional marks will be awarded in part (a) for clarity and quality of discussion. **(2 marks)**

(b) **Discuss any events affecting Colat Co which might indicate that an impairment test ought to be conducted in accordance with IAS 36 *Impairment of Non-Current Assets*.** **(3 marks)**

(c) **Discuss how the following should be accounted for in the financial statements for the year ended 31 December 20X7:**

(i) **the destruction of the non-current assets and decommissioning of the power plant** **(4 marks)**

(ii) **the cost of repairing the environmental damage and the potential receipt of government compensation** **(4 marks)**

(iii) **the hedge of the commodity price risk in aluminium, and** **(4 marks)**

(iv) **the potential insurance policy proceeds.** **(4 marks)**

(Total: 25 marks)

37 CORBEL (SEP/DEC 2020)  *Walk in the footsteps of a top tutor*

Corbel Co trades in the perfume sector. It has recently acquired a company for its brand 'Jengi', purchased two additional brand names, and has announced plans to close its Italian stores. Corbel Co also opened a new store on a prime site in Paris. The current financial year end is 31 December 20X7.

Acquisition of Jengi Co

On 1 January 20X7, Corbel Co acquired 100% of Jengi Co. Both companies operate in the perfume sector. Corbel Co intends to merge the manufacture of Jengi Co's products into its own facilities and close Jengi Co's manufacturing unit. Jengi Co's brand name is well known in the sector, retailing at premium prices, and therefore, Corbel Co will continue to sell products under the Jengi brand name after its registration has been transferred and its manufacturing units have been integrated. The directors of Corbel Co believe that most of the value of Jengi Co was derived from the brand and there is no indication of the impairment of the brand at 31 December 20X7.

Acquisition of perfume brands

In addition to now owning the Jengi Co brand, Corbel Co has acquired two other perfume brand names to prevent rival companies acquiring them. The first perfume (Locust) has been sold successfully for many years and has an established market. The second is a new perfume which has been named after a famous actor (Clara) who intends to promote the product. The directors of Corbel Co believe that the two perfume brand names have an indefinite life.

Plan to close and sell stores

Corbel Co approved and announced a plan to close and sell all six Italian stores on 31 December 20X7. The six stores will close after a liquidation sale which will last for three months. Management has committed to a formal plan for the closure of the six stores and has also started an active search for a single buyer for their assets. The stores are being closed because of the increased demand generated by Corbel Co's internet sales.

A local newspaper has written an article suggesting that up to 30 stores may be closed with a loss of 500 jobs across the world, over the next five years. The directors of Corbel have denied that this is the case.

Corbel Co's primary store

Corbel Co's primary store is located in central Paris. It has only recently been opened at a significant cost with the result that management believes it will make a loss in the current financial year to 31 December 20X7. This loss-making is not of concern as the performance is consistent with expectations for such a new and expensive store and management believes that the new store will have a positive effect on Corbel Co's brand image.

If impairment testing of the primary store were to be required, then Corbel Co would include the cash flows from all internet sales in this assessment. The goods sold via the internet are sourced from either Corbel Co's central distribution centre or individual stores. Internet sales are either delivered to the customer's home or collected by the customer from the store supplying the goods.

Required:

(a) **Describe the main challenges in recognising and measuring intangible assets, such as brands, in the statement of financial position.** **(5 marks)**

(b) **Discuss the following accounting issues relating to Corbel Co's financial statements for the year ended 31 December 20X7 in accordance with IFRS standards:**

(i) **whether the Jengi Co brand name will be accounted for separately from goodwill on acquisition and whether it should be accounted for as a separate cash generating unit after the integration of the manufacturing units** **(4 marks)**

(ii) **how to account for intangible assets with an indefinite life and whether the Locust and Clara perfume brand names can be regarded as having an indefinite life** **(6 marks)**

(iii) **how to account for the proposed closure of the six stores and the suggested closure of the remaining stores; and** **(6 marks)**

(iv) **whether the primary store should be tested for impairment at 31 December 20X7 and whether the internet sales can be attributed to this store.** **(4 marks)**

(Total: 25 marks)

38 HANDFOOD (SEP/DEC 2020)  *Walk in the footsteps of a top tutor*

Handfood Co is a small and medium-sized enterprise (SME) which has introduced a benefit to encourage employees to remain with the entity. The company's financial year end is 31 December and it prepares its financial statements using IFRS Standards but is interested in the differences with the SMEs Standard.

SMEs

It can be argued that small and medium-sized enterprises (SMEs) face financing difficulties because there is serious information asymmetry between SMEs and investors. Information asymmetry, in the context of SMEs, means that the SME has access to relevant information, while the investor suffers from a lack of relevant information. It can be argued that the SMEs Standard decreases information asymmetry between the entity and investors.

Where SMEs lead in product and service innovation, they can also lead in innovation for integrated reporting. There is a clear, concise and persuasive case for why SMEs and their stakeholders stand to benefit greatly by using integrated reporting.

Employee benefit

On 1 January 20X2, Handfood Co introduced a benefit to encourage employees to remain in its employment for at least five years. Handfood Co has promised its employees a lump-sum benefit, payable on 1 January 20X7, which is equal to 1% of their salary at 31 December 20X6, provided they remain employed until that date.

The current salaries of employees on 1 January 20X2 are $1.1 million per annum. The directors of Handfood Co have used the following assumptions:

- Salaries for year ended 31 December 20X2 will remain at $1.1 million.
- Salaries should increase by 3% each year from 1 January 20X3.
- There is a 75% probability that all employees will still be employed by Handfood Co at 31 December 20X6.

The discount rate is 5% per year.

Handfood Co recognises actuarial gains and losses in other comprehensive income. Interest is recognised by Handfood Co on an annual basis. Handfood Co uses the projected unit credit method to measure its benefit obligations which means that the current service cost is the increase in the present value of the future benefit liabilities. The benefit will be payable from the balance on Handfood Co's business bank account at 1 January 20X7.

Present value factors	5%
Periods (years)	
4	0.823
5	0.784

Required:

(a) (i) Discuss the nature of the SMEs Standard and the principal differences between the SMEs Standard and full IFRS Standards. (4 marks)

(ii) Discuss the effect that information asymmetry can have on the decision to invest in SMEs. (4 marks)

(iii) Discuss how integrated reporting could help SMEs better understand and better communicate how they create value to investors. (5 marks)

Professional marks will be awarded in part (a) for clarity and quality of discussion. **(2 marks)**

(b) (i) Discuss, with suitable calculations, the principles of how Handfood Co should account for the current service cost of its employee benefit for the year ended 31 December 20X2. (6 marks)

(ii) Discuss the impact on the additional employee benefit for the year ended 31 December 20X3 if Handfood Co were to take into account the following changes in assumptions:

- **an increase in employees' salaries above 3% per annum; and**
- **a decrease in the probability of employees leaving the company.**

Note: there is no need to provide any calculations in your answer to (b) (ii). (4 marks)

(Total: 25 marks)

39 LERIA CO (MAR 2020)  *Walk in the footsteps of a top tutor*

Background

Leria Co is an internationally successful football club. Leria Co is preparing the financial statements for the year ending 31 October 20X5 but is currently facing liquidity problems.

Stadium sale/leaseback and improvements

Leria Co has entered into a contract regarding its stadium whereby it will sell the stadium on 30 November 20X6 and immediately lease it back. The directors of Leria Co wish to classify the stadium as a non-current asset 'held for sale' in its financial statements for the year ended 31 October 20X5 as they believe the sale to be highly probable at that date. The sale contract requires the disposal of the stadium for its fair value (market value) of $30 million and for Leria Co to lease it back over 10 years. The present value of the lease payments at market rates on 30 November 20X6 will be $26 million. The market value for a stadium of this type has not changed in several years and is unlikely to change in the near future. The stadium is being depreciated by 5% per annum using the reducing balance method.

In the year to 31 October 20X6, it is anticipated that $2 million will be spent to improve the crowd barriers in the stadium. There is no legal requirement to improve the crowd barriers. Leria Co has incorrectly treated this amount as a reduction of the asset's carrying amount at 31 October 20X5 and the corresponding debit has been made to profit or loss. At 31 October 20X5, the carrying amount of the stadium, after depreciation and deduction of the crowd barrier improvements, is $18 million.

Television programme content rights

Leria Co has its own subscription-based television station. As a result, it has material intangible assets which relate to the content rights associated with the television programmes. The budgeted costs of production are based on the estimated future revenues for the television programme. These costs of production are then capitalised as an intangible asset and called 'contents rights'. The directors of Leria Co believe that the intellectual property in the content rights is consumed as customers view the television programmes. Consequently, Leria Co currently amortises the content rights based upon estimated future revenues from the television programme. For example, if a television programme is expected to generate $8 million of revenue in total and $4 million of that revenue is generated in year 1, then the intangible asset will be amortised by 50% in year 1. However, the industry practice is to amortise the capitalised cost of the programme, less its recoverable amount, over its remaining useful life.

Players' contract costs

Players' registration contract costs are shown as intangible assets and are initially recognised at the fair value of the consideration paid for their acquisition. However, subsequently, players' contracts are often re-negotiated at a cost. Also, players' contracts may contain contingent performance conditions where individual players may be paid a bonus based on their success in terms of goals scored or the success of the football team as a whole. These bonuses represent additional contract costs.

For impairment purposes, Leria Co does not consider that it is possible to determine the value-in-use of an individual player unless the player were to suffer a career threatening injury and cannot play in the team. Players only generate direct cash flows when they are sold to another football club.

Required:

(a) Discuss with reference to IFRS Standards:

(i) whether the directors can classify the stadium as held for sale at 31 October 20X5

(ii) Leria Co's accounting treatment of the crowd barrier improvements at 31 October 20X5; and

(iii) the principles of the accounting treatment for the sale and leaseback of the stadium at 30 November 20X6. (13 marks)

(b) Discuss:

(i) whether the amortisation of the intangible assets relating to television programme content rights by Leria Co and by the industry are acceptable policies in accordance with IFRS standards; and

(ii) how to account for the players' contract costs (including the contingent performance conditions), any impairment which might be required to these non-current assets and whether a player can be considered a single cash generating unit. (12 marks)

(Total: 25 marks)

40 ECOMA CO (MAR 2020)  *Walk in the footsteps of a top tutor*

(a) Sustainability

There is a global trend towards more extensive and more meaningful narrative reporting. Improvements in the quality and scope of this reporting are driven by regulatory demands as well as market demands for transparency. Many investors now adhere to 'sustainable investing', an approach to investment where environmental, social or governance (ESG) factors, in combination with financial considerations, guide the selection and management of investments.

Required:

Discuss why the disclosure of sustainable information has become an important and influential consideration for investors. (8 marks)

(b) Background

The directors of Ecoma Co consider environmental, social and governance issues to be extremely important in a wide range of areas, including new product development, reputation building and overall corporate strategy. The company is taking a proactive approach to managing sustainability and is actively seeking opportunities to invest in sustainable projects and embed them in their business practices. The company's financial year end is 30 September 20X5.

Head office

Ecoma Co is committed to a plan to move its head office to a building which has an energy efficient green roof that acts as a natural temperature controller. The move from the current head office, which is leased, will take place at the company's year end of 30 September 20X5. The new green roof building requires less maintenance than a conventional building and produces oxygen which offsets Ecoma Co's CO_2 emissions.

The directors of Ecoma Co believe that the green roof building will save the company $2 million per annum over the useful life of the building. However, over the next two years, it anticipates that the disruption of the move will cause the company to make a loss of $10 million per annum. The company wishes to make a provision of $16 million which comprises the loss to be incurred over the next two years net of the saving created by the green roof.

Meanwhile, the company will have to vacate its currently leased head office building. At 30 September 20X5, the lease has two years to run with rentals payable in advance on 1 October each year.

The pre-tax discount rate is 5%.

Defined benefit pension scheme

Ecoma Co is worried that the poor remuneration package offered to employees is putting the company at risk of reputational damage. Consequently, Ecoma Co changed its pension scheme on 30 September 20X5 to include all of its staff. The benefits accrue from the date of their employment but only vest after two years additional service from 30 September 20X5. The net pension obligation at 30 September 20X5 of $78 million has been updated to include this change. During the year, benefits of $6 million were paid under the scheme and Ecoma Co contributed $10 million to the scheme. These payments had been recorded in the financial statements but no other entries for the year have been made. The following information relates to the pension scheme:

Net pension obligation at 30 September 20X5	$78m
Net pension obligation at 30 September 20X4	$59m
Current service cost for year	$18m
Past service cost relating to scheme amendment at 30 September 20X5	$9m
Discount rate at 30 September 20X4	5.5%
Discount rate at 30 September 20X5	5.9%

Required:

(i) **In accordance with relevant IFRS Standards, discuss how the $16 million provision associated with Ecoma Co's move to a new head office and the vacation of its old head office should be accounted for. (6 marks)**

(ii) **Advise Ecoma Co on the principles of accounting for the pension scheme, including calculations, for the year to 30 September 20X5. (7 marks)**

(iii) **Calculate the impact which the above adjustments in (b) (ii) will have on profit before tax of $25 million for the year ended 30 September 20X5. Ignore potential tax implications. (2 marks)**

Professional marks will be awarded in part (a) for clarity and quality of discussion. (2 marks)

(Total: 25 marks)

41 DIGIWIRE (SEP/DEC 2019)  *Walk in the footsteps of a top tutor*

Digiwire Co has developed a new business model whereby it sells music licences to other companies which then deliver digital music to consumers.

Revenue: sale of three-year licence

Digiwire Co has agreed to sell Clamusic Co, an unlisted technology start-up company, a three-year licence to sell Digiwire Co's catalogue of classical music to the public. This catalogue contains a large selection of classical music which Digiwire Co will regularly update over the three-year period.

As payment for the three-year licence, Clamusic Co has issued shares to Digiwire Co equivalent to a 7% shareholding. Voting rights are attached to these shares. Digiwire Co received the shares in Clamusic Co on 1 January 20X6, which is the first day of the licence term.

Digiwire Co will also receive a royalty of 5% of future sales of Clamusic Co as additional revenue for the licence.

Clamusic Co valuation and revenue

On 1 January 20X6, Clamusic Co was valued at between $4–$5 million by a professional valuer who used a market-based approach. The valuation was based on the share price of a controlling interest in a comparable listed company.

For the financial year end of 31 December 20X6, sales of the classical music were $1 million. At 31 December 20X6, a further share valuation report had been produced by the same professional valuer which indicated that Clamusic Co was valued in the region of $6–$7 million.

Investment in FourDee Co

Digiwire Co has agreed to work with TechGame Co to develop a new music platform. On 31 December 20X6, the companies created a new entity, FourDee Co, with equal shareholdings and shares in profit. Digiwire Co has contributed its own intellectual property in the form of employee expertise, cryptocurrency with a carrying amount of $3 million (fair value of $4 million) and an office building with a carrying amount of $6 million (fair value of $10 million). The cryptocurrency has been recorded at cost in Digiwire Co's financial statements. TechGame Co has contributed the technology and marketing expertise. The board of FourDee Co will comprise directors appointed equally by Digiwire Co and TechGame Co. Decisions are made by a unanimous vote.

Pension plan

Digiwire Co provides a defined benefit pension plan for its employees. From 1 September 20X6, Digiwire Co decided to curtail the plan and to limit the number of participants. The monthly service cost calculated using assumptions at the start of the year is $9 million. The monthly service cost calculated using assumptions at 1 September 20X6 is $6 million. The relevant financial information relating to the plan is as follows:

Date	**Net deficit**	**Discount rate**
	$m	%
1 January 20X6	30	3
1 September 20X6	36	3.5
31 December 20X6	39	3.7

Required:

(a) Advise the directors of Digiwire Co on the recognition and measurement of the:

(i) Clamusic Co shares received as revenue for the sale of the three-year licence and how they should be accounted for in the financial statements for the year ended 31 December 20X6; and

(ii) royalties which Clamusic Co has agreed to pay in respect of the three-year licence in the financial statements for the year ended 31 December 20X6. Your answer to (a) (ii) should demonstrate how recognition and measurement of the royalties is supported by the *Conceptual Framework for Financial Reporting*. (10 marks)

(b) Based on International Financial Reporting Standards, advise the directors on the following:

(i) the classification of the investment which Digiwire Co has in FourDee Co

(ii) the derecognition of the assets exchanged for the investment in FourDee Co and any resulting gain/loss on disposal in the financial statements of Digiwire Co at 31 December 20X6; and

(iii) whether the cryptocurrency should be classified as a financial asset or an intangible asset. Your answer should also briefly consider whether fair value movements on the cryptocurrency should be recorded in profit or loss. (10 marks)

(c) Discuss the accounting repercussions of the pension plan curtailment, including a calculation of the net interest component and current service cost for the year ended 31 December 20X6. (5 marks)

(Total: 25 marks)

42 GUIDANCE (SEP/DEC 2019)  *Walk in the footsteps of a top tutor*

Guidance Co is considering the financial results for the year ended 31 December 20X6. The industry places great reliance on the return on equity (ROE) as an indicator of how well a company uses shareholders' funds to generate a profit.

Return on equity (ROE)

Guidance Co analyses ROE in order to understand the fundamental drivers of value creation in the company. ROE is calculated as:

$$\text{Return on equity} = \frac{\text{Net profit before tax}}{\text{Sales}} \times \frac{\text{Sales}}{\text{Assets}} \times \frac{\text{Assets}}{\text{Equity}}$$

Guidance Co uses year-end equity and assets to calculate ROE.

The following information relates to Guidance Co for the last two years:

	20X5	20X6
	$m	$m
Net profit before tax	30	38
Sales	200	220
Assets at 31 December	250	210
Equity at 31 December	175	100

Special purpose entity (SPE)

During the year ended 31 December 20X6, Guidance Co stated that it had reorganised its assets and set up a SPE. Guidance Co transferred property to the SPE at its carrying amount of $50 million, but had incorrectly charged revaluation reserves with this amount rather than showing the transfer as an investment in the SPE. The property was the SPE's only asset. However, Guidance Co still managed the property, and any profit or loss relating to the assets of the entity was remitted directly to Guidance Co. Guidance Co had no intention of consolidating the SPE.

Miscellaneous transactions

Guidance Co has bought back 25 million shares of $1 for $1.20 per share during the year ended 31 December 20X6 for cash and cancelled the shares. This transaction was deemed to be legal.

Guidance Co purchased a 25% interest in an associate company on 1 July 20X6 for cash. The investment had cost $15 million and the associate had made profits of $32 million in the year to 31 December 20X6. Guidance Co accounted for the purchase of the associate correctly.

These miscellaneous transactions have been accounted for in the financial information provided for the year ended 31 December 20X6.

(a) Management's intent and motivation will often influence accounting information. However, corporate financial statements necessarily depend on estimates and judgement. Financial statements are intended to be comparable but their analysis may not be the most accurate way to judge the performance of any particular company. This lack of comparability may be due to different accounting policy choices or deliberate manipulation.

Required:

Discuss the reasons why an entity may choose a particular accounting policy where an IFRS Standard allows an accounting policy choice and whether faithful representation and comparability are affected by such choices. (6 marks)

(b) (i) Discuss the usefulness to investors of the ROE ratio and its component parts provided above and calculate these ratios for the years ended 31 December 20X5 and 20X6. These calculations should be based upon the information provided in table 1. (5 marks)

(ii) Discuss the impact that the setting up of the SPE and miscellaneous transactions have had on ROE and its component parts. Given these considerations, adjust table 1 and recalculate the ROE for 20X6 thereby making it more comparable to the ROE of 20X5. (12 marks)

Professional marks will be awarded in part (b) for clarity and quality of discussion. (2 marks)

(Total: 25 marks)

43 CRYPTO (MAR/JUN 2019)  *Walk in the footsteps of a top tutor*

(a) **(i)** Crypto operates in the power industry, and owns 45% of the voting shares in Kurran. Kurran has four other investors which own the remaining 55% of its voting shares and are all technology companies. The largest of these holdings is 18%. Kurran is a property developer and purchases property for its renovation potential and subsequent disposal. Crypto has no expertise in this area and is not involved in the renovation or disposal of the property.

The board of directors of Kurran makes all of the major decisions but Crypto can nominate up to four of the eight board members. Each of the remaining four board members are nominated by each of the other investors. Any major decisions require all board members to vote and for there to be a clear majority. Thus, Crypto has effectively the power of veto on any major decision. There is no shareholder agreement as to how Kurran should be operated or who will make the operating decisions for Kurran. The directors of Crypto believe that Crypto has joint control over Kurran because it is the major shareholder and holds the power of veto over major decisions.

The directors of Crypto would like advice as to whether or not they should account for Kurran under IFRS 11 *Joint Arrangements.* **(6 marks)**

(ii) On 1 April 20X7, Crypto entered into a contract to purchase a fixed quantity of electricity at 31 December 20X8 for 20 million euros. Both Crypto and the supplier have a functional currency of dollars. The electricity will be used in Crypto's production processes.

Crypto has separated out the foreign currency embedded derivative from the electricity contract and measured it at fair value through other comprehensive income (FVTOCI). However, on 31 December 20X7, there was a contractual modification, such that the contract is now an executory contract denominated in dollars. At this date, Crypto calculated that the embedded derivative had a negative fair value of 2 million euros.

The directors of Crypto would like advice as to whether they should have separated out the foreign currency derivative and measured it at FVTOCI, and how to treat the modification in the contract. **(5 marks)**

Required:

Advise the directors of Crypto as to how the above issues should be accounted for with reference to relevant IFRS Standards.

Note: The split of the mark allocation is shown against each of the two issues above.

(b) Previous leasing standards were heavily criticised by financial statement users. One reason for this was that lessees were often not required to recognise lease liabilities on the statement of financial position. This approach would lead to significant off-balance sheet finance. IFRS 16 *Leases* was issued in response to such criticisms and rectified the problem.

Required:

(i) Discuss some of the key effects to the financial statements as observed by investors caused by the improved accounting treatment adopted by IFRS 16, as described above.

(6 marks)

(ii) If a company were to apply the improved accounting treatment for leases under IFRS 16 for the first time, discuss the likely impact that IFRS 16 will have generally on accounting ratios and particularly on:

- **Earnings before interest and tax to interest expense (interest cover)**
- **Earnings before interest and tax to capital employed (return on capital employed)**
- **Debt to earnings before interest, tax, depreciation and amortisation (EBITDA). (6 marks)**

Professional marks will be awarded in this question for clarity and quality of discussion. (2 marks)

(Total: 25 marks)

44 ZEDTECH (MAR/JUN 2019)

(a) Zedtech is a software development company, listed on a local stock exchange, which provides data hosting and other professional services. As part of these services, Zedtech also securely hosts a range of inventory management software online which allows businesses to manage inventory from anywhere in the world. It also sells hardware in certain circumstances.

Zedtech sells two distinct software packages. The first package, named 0inventory, gives the customer the option to buy the hardware, professional services and hosting services as separate and distinct contracts. Each element of the package can be purchased without affecting the performance of any other element. Zedtech regularly sells each service separately and generally does not integrate the goods and services into a single contract.

With the second package, InventoryX, the hardware is always sold along with the professional and hosting services and the customer cannot use the hardware on its own. The hardware is integral to the delivery of the hosted software. Zedtech delivers the hardware first, followed by professional services and finally, the hosting services. However, the professional services can be sold on a stand-alone basis as this is a distinct service which Zedtech can offer any customer.

Zedtech has decided to sell its services in a new region of the world which is suffering an economic downturn. The entity expects the economy to recover and feels that there is scope for significant growth in future years. Zedtech has entered into an arrangement with a customer in this region for promised consideration of $3 million. At contract inception, Zedtech feels that it may not be able to collect the full amount from the customer and estimates that it may collect 80% of the consideration.

Required:

(i) Discuss the principles in IFRS 15 *Revenue from Contracts with Customers* which should be used by Zedtech to determine the recognition of the above contracts. (5 marks)

(ii) Discuss how the above contracts should be recognised in the financial statements of Zedtech under IFRS 15. (7 marks)

The directors of Zedtech have heard through industry forums and think-tanks that sustainability reporting is becoming a primary focus for the executives within Zedtech's industry. Zedtech's management are keen to promote the ways that Zedtech positions sustainability at the core of its operations.

(b) Discuss the specific factors that Zedtech must consider to ensure they operate in a sustainable fashion and how sustainability reporting could be important to Zedtech's management and stakeholders. (8 marks)

Zedtech has a reporting date of 31 December 20X1. On the reporting date, it enters into a 5-year lease agreement to hire a new server to improve software performance and deal with increased data storage requirements. The present value of the lease payments to be made is $15 million. Lease rentals are paid in advance and the first $4m has already been paid. In Zedtech's tax jurisdiction, tax relief on leases is given in respect of the lease liability as payments are made. The tax rate is 20%.

(c) Explain the deferred tax implications caused by the lease arrangement entered into by Zedtech. (5 marks)

(Total: 25 marks)

45 FILL (DEC 2018)

(a) Fill is a coal mining company and sells its coal on the spot and futures markets. On the spot market, the commodity is traded for immediate delivery and, on the forward market, the commodity is traded for future delivery. The inventory is divided into different grades of coal. One of the categories included in inventories at 30 November 20X6 is coal with a low carbon content which is of a low quality. Fill will not process this low quality coal until all of the other coal has been extracted from the mine, which is likely to be in three years' time. Based on market information, Fill has calculated that the three-year forecast price of coal will be 20% lower than the current spot price.

The directors of Fill would like advice on two matters:

(i) whether the *Conceptual Framework* affects the valuation of inventories

(ii) how to calculate the net realisable value of the coal inventory, including the low quality coal. **(7 marks)**

(b) At 30 November 20X6, the directors of Fill estimate that a piece of mining equipment needs to be reconditioned every two years. They estimate that these costs will amount to $2 million for parts and $1 million for the labour cost of their own employees. The directors are proposing to create a provision for the next reconditioning which is due in two years' time in 20X8, along with essential maintenance costs. There is no legal obligation to maintain the mining equipment.

As explained above, it is expected that there will be future reductions in the selling prices of coal which will affect the forward contracts being signed over the next two years by Fill.

The directors of Fill require advice on how to treat the reconditioning costs and whether the decline in the price of coal is an impairment indicator. **(8 marks)**

(c) Fill jointly controls coal mines with other entities. The Theta mine was purchased by three participants during the year. Fill owns 40%, and the other two participants own 35% and 25% of the mine. The operating agreement requires any major decisions to be approved by parties representing 72% of the interest in the mine.

The directors of Fill wish advice on whether the *Conceptual Framework* will affect the decision as to whether Fill controls the mine.

The directors are also wondering whether the acquisition of the 40% interest would be considered a business combination under IFRS Standards. **(10 marks)**

Required:

Advise the directors of Fill on how the above transactions should be dealt with in its financial statements with reference to relevant IFRS Standards and the *Conceptual Framework*.

Note: The split of the mark allocation is shown against each of the three issues above.

(Total: 25 marks)

46 HOLLS (DEC 2018)  *Walk in the footsteps of a top tutor*

 ***Answer debrief***

(a) The IFRS *Practice Statement Management Commentary* provides a broad, non-binding framework for the presentation of management commentary which relates to financial statements which have been prepared in accordance with IFRS Standards. The management commentary is within the scope of the *Conceptual Framework* and, therefore, the qualitative characteristics will be applied to both the financial statements and the management commentary.

Required:

(i) **Discuss briefly the arguments for and against issuing the IFRS *Practice Statement Management Commentary* as a non-binding framework or as an IFRS Standard.** **(4 marks)**

(ii) **Discuss how the qualitative characteristics of understandability, relevance and comparability should be applied to the preparation of the management commentary.** **(5 marks)**

(b) Holls Group is preparing its financial statements for the year ended 30 November 20X7. The directors of Holls have been asked by an investor to explain the accounting for taxation in the financial statements.

The Group operates in several tax jurisdictions and is subject to annual tax audits which can result in amendments to the amount of tax to be paid.

The profit from continuing operations was $300 million in the year to 30 November 20X7 and the reported tax charge was $87 million. The investor was confused as to why the tax charge was not the tax rate multiplied by the profit from continuing operations. The directors have prepared a reconciliation of the notional tax charge on profits as compared with the actual tax charge for the period.

	$ million
Profit from continuing operations before taxation	300
Notional charge at local corporation tax rate of 22%	66
Differences in overseas tax rates	10
Tax relating to non-taxable gains on disposals of businesses	(12)
Tax relating to the impairment of brands	9
Other tax adjustments	14
Tax charge for the year	87

The amount of income taxes paid as shown in the statement of cash flows is $95 million but there is no current explanation of the tax effects of the above items in the financial statements.

The tax rate applicable to Holls for the year ended 30 November 20X7 is 22%. There is a proposal in the local tax legislation that a new tax rate of 25% will apply from 1 January 20X8. In the country where Holls is domiciled, tax laws and rate changes are enacted when the government approves the legislation. The government approved the legislation on 12 November 20X7. The current weighted average tax rate for the Group is 27%. Holls does not currently disclose its opinion of how the tax rate may alter in the future but the government is likely to change with the result that a new government will almost certainly increase the corporate tax rate.

At 30 November 20X7, Holls has deductible temporary differences of $4.5 million which are expected to reverse in the next year. In addition, Holls also has taxable temporary differences of $5 million which relate to the same taxable company and the tax authority. Holls expects $3 million of those taxable temporary differences to reverse in 20X8 and the remaining $2 million to reverse in 20X9. Prior to the current year, Holls had made significant losses.

Required:

With reference to the above information, explain to the investor, the nature of accounting for taxation in financial statements.

Note: Your answer should explain the tax reconciliation, discuss the implications of current and future tax rates, and provide an explanation of accounting for deferred taxation in accordance with relevant IFRS Standards. (14 marks)

Professional marks will be awarded in part (b) for clarity and quality of discussion. (2 marks)

(Total: 25 marks)

Calculate your allowed time, allocate the time to the separate parts..............

47 SKIZER (SEP 2018)  *Walk in the footsteps of a top tutor*

(a) Skizer is a pharmaceutical company which develops new products with other pharmaceutical companies that have the appropriate production facilities.

Stakes in development projects

When Skizer acquires a stake in a development project, it makes an initial payment to the other pharmaceutical company. It then makes a series of further stage payments until the product development is complete and it has been approved by the authorities. In the financial statements for the year ended 31 August 20X7, Skizer has treated the different stakes in the development projects as separate intangible assets because of the anticipated future economic benefits related to Skizer's ownership of the product rights. However, in the year to 31 August 20X8, the directors of Skizer decided that all such intangible assets were to be expensed as research and development costs as they were unsure as to whether the payments should have been initially recognised as intangible assets. This write off was to be treated as a change in an accounting estimate.

Sale of development project

On 1 September 20X6, Skizer acquired a development project as part of a business combination and correctly recognised the project as an intangible asset. However, in the financial statements to 31 August 20X7, Skizer recognised an impairment loss for the full amount of the intangible asset because of the uncertainties surrounding the completion of the project. During the year ended 31 August 20X8, the directors of Skizer judged that it could not complete the project on its own and could not find a suitable entity to jointly develop it. Thus, Skizer decided to sell the project, including all rights to future development. Skizer succeeded in selling the project and, as the project had a nil carrying value, it treated the sale proceeds as revenue in the financial statements. The directors of Skizer argued that IFRS 15 *Revenue from Contracts with Customers* states that revenue should be recognised when control is passed at a point in time. The directors of Skizer argued that the sale of the rights was part of their business model and that control of the project had passed to the purchaser.

Required:

(i) Outline the criteria in IAS 38 *Intangible Assets* for the recognition of an intangible asset and discuss whether these are consistent with the *Conceptual Framework*. (5 marks)

(ii) Discuss the implications for Skizer's financial statements for both the years ended 31 August 20X7 and 20X8 if the recognition criteria in IAS 38 for an intangible asset were met as regards the stakes in the development projects above. Your answer should also briefly consider the implications if the recognition criteria were not met. (5 marks)

(iii) Discuss whether the proceeds of the sale of the development project above should be treated as revenue in the financial statements for the year ended 31 August 20X8. (4 marks)

(b) External disclosure of information on intangibles is useful only insofar as it is understood and is relevant to investors. It appears that investors are increasingly interested in and understand disclosures relating to intangibles. A concern is that, due to the nature of IFRS disclosure requirements, investors may feel that the information disclosed has limited usefulness, thereby making comparisons between companies difficult. Many companies spend a huge amount of capital on intangible investment, which is mainly developed within the company and thus may not be reported. Often, it is not obvious that intangibles can be valued or even separately identified for accounting purposes. The Integrated Reporting Framework may be one way to solve this problem.

Required:

(i) Discuss the potential issues which investors may have with:

- **accounting for the different types of intangible asset acquired in a business combination**
- **the choice of accounting policy of cost or revaluation models, allowed under IAS 38 *Intangible Assets* for intangible assets**
- **the capitalisation of development expenditure.** **(7 marks)**

(ii) Discuss whether integrated reporting can enhance the current reporting requirements for intangible assets. **(4 Marks)**

(Total: 25 marks)

48 TOOBASCO (SEP 2018)  *Walk in the footsteps of a top tutor*

(a) Toobasco is in the retail industry. In the reporting of financial information, the directors have disclosed several alternative performance measures (APMs), other than those defined or specified under International Financial Reporting Standards. The directors have disclosed the following APMs:

(i) 'Operating profit before extraordinary items' is often used as the headline measure of the Group's performance, and is based on operating profit before the impact of extraordinary items. Extraordinary items relate to certain costs or incomes which are excluded by virtue of their size and are deemed to be non-recurring. Toobasco has included restructuring costs and impairment losses in extraordinary items. Both items had appeared at similar amounts in the financial statements of the two previous years and were likely to occur in future years.

(ii) 'Operating free cash flow' is calculated as cash generated from operations less purchase of property, plant and equipment, purchase of own shares, and the purchase of intangible assets. The directors have described this figure as representing the residual cash flow in the business but have given no detail of its calculation. They have emphasised its importance to the success of the business. They have also shown free cash flow per share in bold next to earnings per share in order to emphasise the entity's ability to turn its earnings into cash.

(iii) 'EBITDAR' is defined as earnings before interest, tax, depreciation, amortisation and rent. EBITDAR uses operating profit as the underlying earnings. In an earnings release, just prior to the financial year end, the directors disclosed that EBITDAR had improved by $180 million because of cost savings associated with the acquisition of an entity six months earlier. The directors discussed EBITDAR at length describing it as 'record performance' but did not disclose any comparable IFRS information and there was no reconciliation to any IFRS measure. In previous years, rent had been deducted from the earnings figure to arrive at this APM.

(iv) The directors have not taken any tax effects into account when calculating the remaining APMs.

Required:

Advise the directors whether the above APMs would achieve fair presentation in the financial statements. (10 marks)

(b) Daveed is a car retailer who leases vehicles to customers under operating leases and often sells the cars to third parties when the lease ends. Net cash generated from operating activities for the year ended 31 August 20X8 for the Daveed Group is as follows:

Year ended 31 August 20X8	$m
Cash generated from operating activities	345
Income taxes paid	(21)
Pension deficit payments	(33)
Interest paid	(25)
Associate share of profits	12
Net cash generated from operating activities	278

Cash generated from operating activities was calculated using the indirect method.

Net cash flows generated from investing activities included interest received of $10 million and net capital expenditure of $46 million excluding the business acquisition at (iii) below.

There were also some errors in the presentation of the statement of cash flows which could have an impact on the calculation of net cash generated from operating activities.

The directors have provided the following information as regards any potential errors:

(i) Cars are treated as property, plant and equipment when held under operating leases and when they become available for sale, they are transferred to inventory at their carrying amount. In its statement of cash flows for the year ended 31 August 20X8, cash flows from investing activities included cash inflows relating to the disposal of cars ($30 million).

(ii) On 1 September 20X7, Daveed purchased a 25% interest in an associate for cash. The associate reported a profit after tax of $16 million and paid a dividend of $4 million out of these profits in the year ended 31 August 20X8. As can be seen in the calculation above, the directors included a figure of $12 million when calculating net cash generated from operating activities. The associate was correctly recorded at $23 million in the statement of financial position at 31 August 20X8 and profit for the year of $4 million was included in the statement of profit or loss. No adjustment was made for Daveed's share of the associate's profit when calculating cash generated from operating activities.

(iii) Daveed also acquired a digital mapping business during the year ended 31 August 20X8. The statement of cash flows showed a loss of $28 million in net cash inflow generated from operating activities as the effect of changes in foreign exchange rates arising on the retranslation of this overseas subsidiary. The assets and liabilities of the acquired subsidiary had been correctly included in the calculation of the cash movement during the year.

(iv) During the year to 31 August 20X8, Daveed made exceptional contributions to the pension plan assets of $33 million but the statement of cash flows had not recorded the cash tax benefit of $6 million.

(v) Additionally, Daveed had capitalised the interest paid of $25 million into property, plant and equipment ($18 million) and inventory ($7 million).

(vi) Daveed has defined operating free cash flow as net cash generated by operating activities as adjusted for net capital expenditure, purchase of associate and dividends received, interest received and paid. Any exceptional items should also be excluded from the calculation of free cash flow.

Required:

Prepare:

(i) a schedule that calculates net cash generated from operating activities to correct any errors above (4 marks)

(ii) a reconciliation from net cash generated by operating activities to operating free cash flow (as described in note (vi) above) (4 marks)

(iii) an explanation of the adjustments made in parts (i) and (ii) above. (5 marks)

Professional marks will be awarded in part (b) for clarity and quality of discussion. (2 marks)

(Total: 25 marks)

49 PLAYER TWO

(a) Player Two, a public limited company, operates a number of retail stores that sell computer and video games. It prepares financial statements in accordance with IFRS Standards. In its financial statement disclosure notes for the year ended 31 December 20X1 it has reported an additional performance measure: adjusted basic EPS (earnings per share). This performance measure does not feature on the face of its statement of profit or loss and other comprehensive income. The following is an extract from its financial statement disclosures:

	20X1
Profit after tax ($m)	2.5
Adjusting items ($m)	10.3
Adjusted profit after tax ($m)	12.8
Shares outstanding (m)	122.2
Adjusted basic EPS	10.5c

Player Two also discloses similar information for the prior period.

The disclosure note states that 'adjusting items' comprise:

- $6.8 million amortisation charge in relation to acquired brands and intangible assets (20X0: $6.9 million).
- $1.4 million restructuring costs (20X0: $0.9 million)
- $2.1 million impairment charge relating to retail stores.

The directors of Player Two are aware that the Board has published ED/2019/7 *General Presentation and Disclosures.* This exposure draft outlines the Board's proposals regarding the disclosure of management performance measures – such as 'adjusted profit after tax'.

Required:

With reference to Player Two's disclosure of adjusted EPS, discuss the benefits and limitations of disclosing additional performance measures in the financial statements. (15 marks)

(b) Wrap is a public limited company that operates in the media industry. This industry is currently experiencing little economic growth. Wrap's market capitalisation (the market price per share multiplied by the number of shares outstanding) is less than its net asset value per the financial statements.

In accordance with IAS 36 *Impairment of Assets,* Wrap has carried out various impairment reviews. Cash generating unit D, a magazine publishing business to which goodwill has been allocated, was tested for impairment and was deemed not to be impaired. Wrap has produced the following disclosure note for inclusion in the financial statements:

'The recoverable amount of cash generating unit D has been determined as its value in use. The calculation of value in use was based on cash flow projections that were approved by management. The average discount rate used by Wrap during the year was 10%. The future cash flows of unit D beyond the budgeted period were extrapolated using an 8 per cent growth rate. Management believes that any reasonably possible change in the key assumptions on which D's recoverable amount is based would not cause D's carrying amount to exceed its recoverable amount.'

Required:

Discuss why the information contained in this disclosure may be of limited use to the users of Wrap's financial statements. (8 marks)

Professional marks will be awarded in this question for clarity and quality of presentation. (2 marks)

(Total: 25 marks)

50 MEHRAN  *Walk in the footsteps of a top tutor*

(a) Mehran is a public limited company. It operates in a number of business sectors, including farming, mining and retail. The directors require advice about how to apply IFRS 13 *Fair Value Measurement.*

(i) Mehran has just acquired a company, which comprises a farming and mining business. Mehran wishes advice on how to fair value some of the assets acquired.

One such asset is a piece of land, which is currently used for farming. The fair value of the land if used for farming is $5 million. If the land is used for farming purposes, a tax credit of $0.1 million arises.

Mehran has determined that market participants would consider that the land could have an alternative use for residential purposes. The fair value of the land for residential purposes before associated costs is thought to be $7.4 million. In order to transform the land from farming to residential use, there would be legal costs of $200,000, a viability analysis cost of $300,000 and costs of demolition of the farm buildings of $100,000. Additionally, permission for residential use has not been formally given by the legal authority and because of this, market participants have indicated that the fair value of the land, after the above costs, would be discounted by 20% because of the risk of not obtaining planning permission.

In addition, Mehran has acquired the brand name associated with the produce from the farm. Mehran has decided to discontinue the brand on the assumption that it is similar to its existing brands. Mehran has determined that if it ceases to use the brand, then the indirect benefits will be $20 million. If it continues to use the brand, then the direct benefit will be $17 million. Other companies in this market do not have brands that are as strong as Mehran's and so would not see any significant benefit from the discontinuation. **(9 marks)**

(ii) Mehran owns a non-controlling equity interest in Erham, a private company, and wishes to fair value it as at its financial year end of 31 March 20X6. Mehran acquired the ordinary share interest in Erham on 1 April 20X4. During the current financial year, Erham has issued further equity capital through the issue of preferred shares to a venture capital fund. As a result of the preferred share issue, the venture capital fund now holds a controlling interest in Erham. The terms of the preferred shares, including the voting rights, are similar to those of the ordinary shares, except that the preferred shares have a cumulative fixed dividend entitlement for a period of four years and the preferred shares rank ahead of the ordinary shares upon the liquidation of Erham. The transaction price for the preferred shares was $15 per share. Mehran wishes to know the factors which should be taken into account in measuring the fair value of their holding in the ordinary shares of Erham at 31 March 20X6 using a market-based approach. **(6 marks)**

Required:

Discuss the way in which Mehran should fair value the above assets with reference to the principles of *IFRS 13 Fair Value Measurement.*

Note: The mark allocation is shown against each of the two issues above.

(b) Mehran has recognised provisions in its financial statements for the year ended 31 March 20X6. It has produced the following provisions disclosure note:

	Customer refunds	**Reorganisations**	**Total**
	$m	$m	$m
1 April 20X5	10.2	8.0	18.2
Charged to profit or loss	13.1	10.2	23.3
Utilised	(9.1)	(9.6)	(18.7)
31 March 20X6	14.2	8.6	22.8
Of which:			
Current	14.2	8.0	22.2
Non-current	–	0.6	0.6

Provisions for customer refunds reflect the company's expected liability for returns of goods sold in retail stores based on experience of rates of return. Provisions for reorganisations reflect restructuring and redundancy costs, principally in relation to our retail operations as well as restructurings in Finance and IT.

The directors of Mehran have been asked by an investor to explain the accounting for provisions in the financial statements and to explain why the information provided in the provisions disclosure note is useful.

Required:

Explain to the investor the nature of accounting for provisions in financial statements. Your answer should explain the benefits and limitations of the information provided in Mehran's disclosure note. (8 marks)

Professional marks will be awarded in part (b) for clarity and quality of presentation. (2 marks)

(Total: 25 marks)

51 CARSOON

Carsoon Co is a public limited. It constructs premises for third parties. It has a year end of 28 February 20X7.

(a) **(i)** On 1 March 20X6, Carsoon invested in a debt instrument with a fair value of $6 million and has assessed that the financial asset is aligned with the fair value through other comprehensive income business model. The instrument has an interest rate of 4% over a period of six years. The effective interest rate is also 4%. On 1 March 20X6, the debt instrument is not impaired in any way. During the year to 28 February 20X7, there was a change in interest rates and the fair value of the instrument seemed to be affected. The instrument was quoted in an active market at $5.3 million but the price based upon an in-house model showed that the fair value of the instrument was $5.5 million. This valuation was based upon the average change in value of a range of instruments across a number of jurisdictions.

The directors of Carsoon felt that the instrument should be valued at \$5.5 million and that this should be shown as a Level 1 measurement under IFRS 13 *Fair Value Measurement*. There has not been a significant increase in credit risk since 1 March 20X6, and expected credit losses should be measured at an amount equal to 12-month expected credit losses of \$400,000. Carsoon sold the debt instrument on 1 March 20X7 for \$5.3 million.

The directors of Carsoon wish to know how to account for the debt instrument until its sale on 1 March 20X7. **(8 marks)**

(ii) Carsoon constructs retail vehicle outlets and enters into contracts with customers to construct buildings on their land. The contracts have standard terms, which include penalties payable by Carsoon if the contract is delayed.

In the year ended 28 February 20X7, Carsoon incurred general and administrative costs of \$10 million, and costs relating to wasted materials of \$5 million. These have been recognised as contract assets.

Due to poor weather, one of the projects was delayed. As a result, Carsoon faced contractual penalties. Carsoon felt that the penalties should be shown as a contingent liability. Additionally, during the year, Carsoon agreed to construct a storage facility on the same customer's land for \$7 million at a cost of \$5 million. This was completed during the current financial year.

The directors of Carsoon wish to know how to account for the \$15 million costs, the penalties, and the storage facility in accordance with IFRS 15 *Revenue from Contracts with Customers*. **(7 marks)**

Required:

Advise Carsoon on how the above transactions should be dealt with in its financial statements with reference to relevant International Financial Reporting Standards.

Note: The mark allocation is shown against each of the two issues above.

(b) Carsoon owns the entire share capital of Sinkton, a company that operates in the manufacturing industry and also has a reporting date of 28 February 20X7. Heavy rain in the month prior to the reporting date caused several rivers surrounding Sinkton to burst their banks. As a result, Sinkton's only owned building, in which its factory and head office functions are housed, was flooded. At the start of the reporting period the building was believed to have a remaining useful life of twenty years.

The flooding damaged key plant and machinery as well as some finished goods. Production did not cease, but production volumes declined by two-thirds. The inventory was not insured for flood damage but the machinery was. The directors believe it is probable that the insurers will compensate Sinkton for the machinery damage, but there is doubt about the amount of insurance proceeds that will be received. Confirmation will not be received from the insurers until after the authorisation of the financial statements.

As a result of the flood, Sinkton expects to make an operating loss in the next financial year. The flood has caused a strain on cash flow and the board of directors believe that they will need to make some staff redundancies. However, no firm redundancy plans have been drafted. The directors of Sinkton are worried about the increasing incidence of flooding and expect to move to new premises in five years' time.

Required:

Discuss the financial reporting repercussions of the above in Sinkton's financial statements for the year ended 28 February 20X7. (10 marks)

(Total: 25 marks)

52 SKYE

(a) Skye is a public limited company which has a functional currency of dollars ($). It has entered into a number of transactions in the year ended 31 May 20X7. The directors require advice about how they should be accounted for.

(i) Skye has B shares in issue which allow the holders to request redemption at specified dates and amounts. The legal charter of Skye states that the entity has a choice whether or not to accept the request for repayment of the B shares. There are no other conditions attached to the shares and Skye has never refused to redeem any of the shares up to the current year end of 31 May 20X7. In all other respects the instruments have the characteristics of equity.

Skye also has preference shares in issue which are puttable by the holders at any time after 31 May 20X7. Under the terms of the shares, Skye is only permitted to satisfy the obligation for the preference shares when it has sufficient distributable reserves. Local legislation is quite restrictive in defining the profits available for distribution.

The directors of Skye wish to know if the above financial instruments should be classified as equity items or financial liabilities as at 31 May 20X7. **(6 marks)**

(ii) Skye has a foreign branch which has a functional currency of dollars ($). The branch's taxable profits are determined in dinars. On 1 June 20X6, the branch acquired a property for 6 million dinars. The property had an expected useful life of 12 years with a zero residual value. The asset is written off for tax purposes over eight years. The tax rate in Skye's jurisdiction is 30% and in the branch's jurisdiction is 20%. The foreign branch uses the cost model for valuing its property and measures the tax base at the exchange rate at the reporting date.

Exchange rates	$1 = dinars
1 June 20X6	5
31 May 20X7	6

The directors require advice as to the deferred tax implications of the above. **(7 marks)**

Required:

Advise the directors of Skye on how the above transactions should be dealt with in its financial statements with reference to relevant International Financial Reporting Standards.

(b) The 2010 *Conceptual Framework* was criticised for its many notable omissions. One such omission that the 2018 *Conceptual Framework* addressed was the role of prudence. The revised *Conceptual Framework* also details factors to consider when selecting a measurement basis. This information should assist the preparers of financial statements when applying an accounting standard that offers a measurement choice (such as IAS 40 *Investment Property)*.

Required:

(i) Discuss what is meant by prudence and the extent to which prudence is consistent with the fundamental qualitative characteristic of faithful representation. (6 marks)

(ii) With reference to the *Conceptual Framework* discuss the factors that preparers of the financial statements should consider when an accounting standard offers a choice of measurement basis. (6 marks)

(Total: 25 marks)

53 WHITEBIRK

(a) Whitebirk meets the definition of a small entity in its jurisdiction and complies with the *IFRS for SMEs Standard* (the SMEs Standard). Whitebirk has entered into the following transactions during the year ended 31 May 20X6.

(i) Whitebirk requires a new machine, which will be included as part of its property, plant and equipment. Whitebirk therefore commenced construction of the machine on 1 February 20X6, and this continued until its completion which was after the year end of 31 May 20X6. The direct costs were $2 million in February 2016 and then $1 million in each subsequent month until the year end. Whitebirk has incurred finance costs on its general borrowings during the period, which could have been avoided if the machine had not been constructed. Whitebirk has calculated that the weighted average cost of borrowings for the period 1 February – 31 May 20X6 on an annualised basis amounted to 9% per annum.

(ii) Whitebirk has incurred $1 million of research expenditure to develop a new product in the year to 31 May 20X6. Additionally, it incurred $0.5 million of development expenditure to bring another product to a stage where it is ready to be marketed and sold.

Required:

(i) In accordance with IAS 23 *Borrowing Cost* and IAS 38 *Intangible Assets,* advise the directors of Whitebirk on how the borrowing costs (note i) and the research and development expenditure (note ii) would be accounted for in the year ended 31 May 20X6. (8 marks)

(ii) Discuss how the two transactions would be dealt with under the SMEs Standard in the year ended 31 May 20X6. (4 marks)

(b) One of the reasons why Whitebirk prepares its financial statements using the SMEs Standard is because of the difficulties involved every time a new IFRS Standard is issued. The directors believe that the practicalities and financial statement implications of regularly implementing new IFRS Standards are overly onerous to an entity the size of Whitebirk. However, Whitebirk may have to transition to full IFRS Standards if it continues to grow in size.

Required:

(i) Discuss the key practical considerations and financial statement implications that an entity must consider when implementing a new IFRS Standard.

(10 marks)

(ii) Briefly explain the principles outlined in IFRS 1 *First Time Adoption of IFRS* that must be applied when an entity adopts full IFRS Standards for the first time. **(3 marks)**

(Total: 25 marks)

54 BUSINESS COMBINATIONS  *Walk in the footsteps of a top tutor*

(a) You work for an accountancy firm. You have asked to provide advice to clients about the following transactions:

(i) On 1 October 20X4, Saag, a listed company, purchased 90% of the ordinary shares of Aloo. Aloo, which ceased trading one week prior to the share purchase, owns a manufacturing facility comprising of land and buildings as well as related equipment. The fair value of the land and buildings is similar to the fair value of the equipment. The acquisition of Aloo only gained legal approval on the basis that all employees who worked at the facility are retained. There are no other assets, including any inventories, or processes transferred as part of the sale.

Saag proposes to account for the purchase of Aloo as a business combination. **(7 marks)**

(ii) On 1 September 20X4, Bimbi, a listed bank, entered into a business combination with another listed bank, Lental. The business combination has taken place in two stages, which were contingent upon each other. On 1 September 20X4, Bimbi acquired 45% of the share capital and voting rights of Lental for cash. On 1 November 20X4, Lental merged with Bimbi and Bimbi issued new A-shares to Lental's shareholders for their 55% interest.

On 31 August 20X4, Bimbi had a market value of $70 million and Lental a market value of $90 million. Bimbi's business represents 45% and Lental's business 55% of the total value of the combined businesses.

After the transaction, the former shareholders of Bimbi excluding those of Lental owned 51% and the former shareholders of Lental owned 49% of the votes of the combined entity. The Chief Operating Officer (COO) of Lental is the biggest individual owner of the combined entity with a 25% interest. The purchase agreement provides for a board of six directors for the combined entity, five of whom will be former board members of Bimbi with one seat reserved for a former board member of Lental. The board of directors nominates the members of the management team. The management comprised the COO and four other members, two from Bimbi and two from Lental. Under the terms of the purchase agreement, the COO of Lental is the COO of the combined entity.

Bimbi proposes to identify Lental as the acquirer in the business combination but requires advice as to whether this is correct. **(8 marks)**

Required:

Advise whether the proposed treatments of the above two transactions are in accordance with IFRS Standards.

Note: The mark allocation is shown against each of the two transactions above.

(b) On 1 January 20X4, Bolo purchased 45% of the ordinary shares of Kata. Consideration paid was $3 million. The carrying amounts of the net assets of Kata at that date were $2.4 million and approximated their fair values. The statement of financial position for Kata as at 31 December 20X4 was as follows:

	$m
Property, plant & equipment	14
Inventories	1
Total assets	15
Share capital	1
Retained earnings	2
Loans	12
Equity and liabilities	15

The directors of Bolo are unsure whether to treat Kata as an associate or a subsidiary in the consolidated financial statements. When relevant, Bolo measures non-controlling interests using the proportion of net assets method.

Required:

Discuss and compare the impact on the consolidated financial statements of Bolo for the year ended 31 December 20X4 if the investment in Kata is accounted for as:

- **a subsidiary, or**
- **an associate.** **(8 marks)**

Professional marks will be awarded in part (b) for clarity and quality of presentation. **(2 marks)**

(Total: 25 marks)

55 MARGIE  *Walk in the footsteps of a top tutor*

(a) Margie, a public limited company, has entered into several share related transactions during the period and wishes to obtain advice on how to account for them.

(i) On 1 May 20X2, Margie granted 500 share appreciation rights (SARs) to its 300 managers. All of the rights vested on 30 April 20X4 but they can be exercised from 1 May 20X4 up to 30 April 20X6. At the grant date, the value of each SAR was $10 and it was estimated that 5% of the managers would leave during the vesting period. The fair value of each SAR is as follows:

Date	**Fair value ($)**
30 April 20X3	9
30 April 20X4	11
30 April 20X5	12

All of the managers who were expected to leave employment did leave the company as expected before 30 April 20X4. On 30 April 20X5, 60 managers exercised their options when the intrinsic value of the right was $10.50 and were paid in cash.

Margie is confused as to whether to account for the SARs under IFRS 2 *Share-based Payment* or IFRS 13 *Fair Value Measurement*, and would like advice as to how the SARs should have been accounted for between the grant date and 30 April 20X5. **(6 marks)**

(ii) Margie issued shares during the financial year. Some of those shares were subscribed for by employees who were existing shareholders, and some were issued to an entity, Grief, which owned 5% of Margie's share capital. Before the shares were issued, Margie offered to buy a building from Grief and agreed that the purchase price would be settled by the issue of shares.

Margie requires advice about how to account for these two transactions. **(5 marks)**

(iii) Margie has entered into a contract with a producer to purchase 350 tonnes of wheat. The purchase price will be settled in cash at an amount equal to the value of 2,500 of Margie's shares. Margie may settle the contract at any time by paying the producer an amount equal to the current market value of 2,500 of Margie shares, less the market value of 350 tonnes of wheat. Margie has no intention of taking physical delivery of the wheat.

The directors of Margie are unsure as to whether this transaction is a share-based payment and require advice as to how it should be accounted for in the financial statements. **(7 marks)**

Required:

Advise the directors of Margie on their various requests above.

Note: The mark allocation is shown against each of the three issues.

(b) The directors of Margie believe that some International Financial Reporting Standards are inconsistent with the *Conceptual Framework*. They have made the following comments:

- The recognition of an expense in respect of an equity-settled share-based payment scheme with employees is not in line with the *Conceptual Framework's* definition of an expense.
- The recognition of a liability, rather than income, in respect of non-refundable deposits received from customers is not in line with the *Conceptual Framework's* definition of a liability.
- Internally generated brands meet the definition of an asset, and so the fact that IAS 38 *Intangible Assets* prohibits their recognition in the financial statements contradicts the *Conceptual Framework*.

Required:

Discuss the extent to which each of the directors' comments is valid. (7 marks)

(Total: 25 marks)

56 KAYTE

Kayte, a public limited company, operates in a number of industries. It has a reporting date of 30 November 20X3.

(a) One of the industries that Kayte operates in is shipping. Kayte's owns shipping vessels – classified as property, plant and equipment and measured using the cost model-which constitute a material part of its total assets. The economic life of the vessels is estimated to be 30 years, but the useful life of some of the vessels is only 10 years because Kayte's policy is to sell these vessels when they are 10 years old. Kayte estimated the residual value of these vessels at sale to be half of acquisition cost and this value was assumed to be constant during their useful life. Kayte argued that the estimates of residual value used were conservative in view of an immature market with a high degree of uncertainty and presented documentation which indicated some vessels were being sold for a price considerably above carrying value. Broker valuations of the residual value were considerably higher than those used by Kayte. Kayte argued against broker valuations on the grounds that it would result in greater volatility in reporting.

Kayte keeps some of the vessels for the whole 30 years and these vessels are required to undergo an engine overhaul in dry dock every 10 years to restore their service potential, hence the reason why some of the vessels are sold. The residual value of the vessels kept for 30 years is based upon the steel value of the vessel at the end of its economic life. In the current period, one of the vessels had to have its engine totally replaced after only eight years. Normally, engines last for the 30-year economic life if overhauled every 10 years. Additionally, one type of vessel was having its funnels replaced after 15 years but the funnels had not been depreciated separately.

Required:

Advise the directors of Kayte on the accounting issues above. **(11 marks)**

(b) Throughout its other business operations, Kayte is reliant on skilled workers to design and manufacture high-tech products. Because of the importance of Kayte's workforce to its business operations, the directors wish to disclose the following key performance indicators (KPIs) in the annual integrated report <IR>.

	20X3	**20X2**
Average employee salary ($)	30,325	29,956
Revenue per employee ($)	116,432	102,124
Sick days per employee	4.9	2.1
Employee turnover (%)	18.7	13.9

The national rate of inflation is currently 2%.

Employee turnover has been calculated as the number of employees who left Kayte during the year as a % of the average number of employees throughout the year. The average rate of employee turnover in the industry is 14.1%.

Required:

(i) Briefly discuss some of the factors that management should consider when disclosing KPIs in the reporting entity's <IR>. (4 marks)

(ii) Discuss how the KPIs might be interpreted by users of the <IR>. (8 marks)

Professional marks will be awarded in part (b) for clarity and quality of presentation. (2 marks)

(Total: 25 marks)

57 VERGE  *Walk in the footsteps of a top tutor*

(a) (i) In its annual financial statements for the year ended 31 March 20X3, Verge, a public limited company, had identified the following operating segments:

(i) Segment 1 local train operations

(ii) Segment 2 inter-city train operations

(iii) Segment 3 railway constructions

The company disclosed two reportable segments. Segments 1 and 2 were aggregated into a single reportable operating segment. Operating segments 1 and 2 have been aggregated on the basis of their similar business characteristics, and the nature of their products and services. In the local train market, it is the local transport authority which awards the contract and pays Verge for its services. In the local train market, contracts are awarded following a competitive tender process, and the ticket prices paid by passengers are set by and paid to the transport authority. In the inter-city train market, ticket prices are set by Verge and the passengers pay Verge for the service provided.

(7 marks)

(ii) Verge entered into a contract with a government body on 1 April 20X1 to undertake maintenance services on a new railway line. The total revenue from the contract is $5 million over a three-year period. The contract states that $1 million will be paid at the commencement of the contract but although invoices will be subsequently sent at the end of each year, the government authority will only settle the subsequent amounts owing when the contract is completed. The invoices sent by Verge to date (including $1 million above) were as follows:

Year ended 31 March 20X2 $2.8 million

Year ended 31 March 20X3 $1.2 million

The balance will be invoiced on 31 March 20X4. Verge has only accounted for the initial payment in the financial statements to 31 March 20X2 as no subsequent amounts are to be paid until 31 March 20X4. The amounts of the invoices reflect the work undertaken in the period. Verge wishes to know how to account for the revenue on the contract in the financial statements to date.

Market interest rates are currently at 6%. **(7 marks)**

Required:

Advise Verge on how the above accounting issues should be dealt with in its financial statements for the years ending 31 March 20X2 (where applicable) and 31 March 20X3.

Note: The mark allocation is shown against each of the two issues above.

(b) The directors of Verge have prepared forecasts for the next five years and they are concerned that the company does not have sufficient liquid assets to fulfil its expansion plans. The directors propose to raise the required funds on 1 April 20X3 in one of the following ways:

(i) The issue of 5 million ordinary shares.

(ii) The issue of 10 million convertible bonds in exchange for cash proceeds. Interest is payable annually in arrears. The bond holders will be able to redeem the bonds on 31 March 20X6 in the form of cash or a fixed number of Verge's ordinary shares.

The directors are unsure of the impact of the proposals on the financial statements.

Required:

Discuss the impact of the above proposals on the financial statements of Verge. Your answer should consider the potential impact on basic and diluted earnings per share and on the primary users' perception of Verge's financial performance and position.
(9 marks)

Professional marks will be awarded in part (b) for clarity and quality of presentation.
(2 marks)

(Total: 25 marks)

58 ARON

The directors of Aron would like advice about the financial reporting treatment of some financial instrument transactions that took place during the year ended 31 May 20X7.

Convertible bonds

Aron issued one million convertible bonds on 1 June 20X6. The bonds had a term of three years and were issued for their fair value of $100 million, which is also the par value. Interest is paid annually in arrears at a rate of 6% per annum. Bonds without the conversion option attracted an interest rate of 9% per annum on 1 June 20X6. The company incurred issue costs of $1 million. The impact of the issue costs is to increase the effective interest rate to 9.38%. At 31 May 20X9 the bondholders can opt to be repaid the par value in cash, or they can opt to receive a fixed number of ordinary shares in Aron.

Share exchange

Aron held 3% holding of the shares in Smart, a public limited company. The investment was designated upon recognition as fair value through other comprehensive income and as at 31 May 20X7 was measured at its fair value of $5 million. The cumulative gain reported in other comprehensive income and held in equity relating to this investment was $400,000. On 31 May 20X7, the whole of the share capital of Smart was acquired by Given, a public limited company. Aron received shares in Given with a fair value of $5.5 million in exchange for its holding in Smart.

Winston bonds

On 1 June 20X6, Aron purchased $10 million of listed bonds at par and paid in cash. These bonds had been issued by Winston, an entity operating in the video games industry. The bonds are due to be redeemed at a premium on 31 May 20X9, with Aron also receiving 5% interest annually in arrears. The effective rate of interest on the bonds is 15%. Aron often holds bonds until the redemption date, but will sell prior to maturity if investments with higher returns become available. Winston's bonds were deemed to have a low credit risk at inception.

On 31 May 20X7, Aron received the interest due on the bonds. However, there were wider concerns about the economic performance and financial stability of the video games industry. As a result, the quoted price of Aron's investment at 31 May 20X7 was $9 million, although a pricing model developed by the financial controller that relies on management estimates valued the holding at $9.5 million. Based on Winston's strong working capital management and market optimism about the entity's forthcoming products, the bonds were still deemed to have a low credit risk.

The financial controller of Aron calculated the following expected credit losses for the Winston bonds as at 31 May 20X7:

12 month expected credit losses	$0.2m
Lifetime expected credit losses	$0.4m

Required:

(a) **Discuss the accounting treatment of the convertible bonds in the financial statements for the year ended 31 May 20X7.** **(9 marks)**

(b) **Discuss the accounting treatment of the share exchange in the financial statements for the year ended 31 May 20X7.** **(6 marks)**

(c) **Discuss the accounting treatment of the Winston bonds in the financial statements for the year ended 31 May 20X7. Your answer should explain the impact of the bonds in Aron's statement of cash flows.** **(10 marks)**

(Total: 25 marks)

59 KLANCET  *Walk in the footsteps of a top tutor*

Klancet, a public limited company, is a pharmaceutical company and is seeking advice on several financial reporting issues.

(a) **(i)** Klancet produces and sells its range of drugs through three separate divisions. In addition, there are two laboratories which carry out research and development activities.

In the first of these laboratories, the research and development activity is funded internally and centrally for each of the three sales divisions. It does not carry out research and development activities for other entities. Each of the three divisions is given a budget allocation which it uses to purchase research and development activities from the laboratory. The laboratory is directly accountable to the division heads for this expenditure.

The second laboratory performs contract investigation activities for other laboratories and pharmaceutical companies. This laboratory earns 75% of its revenues from external customers and these external revenues represent 18% of the organisation's total revenues.

The performance of the second laboratory's activities and of the three separate divisions is regularly reviewed by the chief operating decision maker (CODM). In addition to the heads of divisions, there is a head of the second laboratory. The head of the second laboratory is directly accountable to the CODM and they discuss the operating activities, allocation of resources and financial results of the laboratory.

Klancet is uncertain as to whether the research and development laboratories should be reported as two separate segments under IFRS 8 *Operating Segments*, and would like advice on this issue. **(8 marks)**

(ii) Klancet has agreed to sell a patent right to another pharmaceutical group, Jancy. Jancy would like to use the patent to develop a more complex drug. Klancet will receive publicly listed shares of the Jancy group in exchange for the right. The value of the listed shares represents the fair value of the patent. If Jancy is successful in developing a drug and bringing it to the market, Klancet will also receive a 5% royalty on all sales.

Additionally, Klancet won a competitive bidding arrangement to acquire a patent. The purchase price was settled by Klancet issuing new publicly listed shares of its own.

Klancet's management would like advice on how to account for the above transactions. **(6 marks)**

Required:

Advise Klancet on how the above transactions should be dealt with in its financial statements with reference to relevant International Financial Reporting Standards.

Note: The mark allocation is shown against each of the two issues above.

(b) On 1 July 20X6, Klancet purchased a debt instrument for its nominal value of $5 million. The transaction was at fair value. Klancet's business model is to hold financial assets to collect the contractual cash flows but also sell financial assets if investments with higher returns become available. Interest is received at a rate of 4% annually in arrears. The effective rate of interest is 10%.

On 30 June 20X7, the fair value of the debt instrument was $4.5 million. There has not been a significant increase in credit risk since inception. Expected credit losses are immaterial.

The directors are unsure how to account for this financial instrument. They also wish to know if the correct accounting treatment is consistent with the *Conceptual Framework*.

Required:

(i) Discuss, with reference to IFRS 9 *Financial Instruments*, how the above transactions should be dealt with in Klancet's financial statements for the year ended 30 June 20X7. (4 marks)

(ii) Discuss whether the accounting treatment of this transaction is consistent with the *Conceptual Framework*. (7 marks)

(Total: 25 marks)

60 EMCEE  *Walk in the footsteps of a top tutor*

(a) **(i)** Emcee, a public limited company, is a sports organisation which owns several football and basketball teams. It has a financial year end of 31 May 20X6.

Emcee purchases and sells players' registrations on a regular basis. Emcee must purchase registrations for that player to play for the club. Player registrations are contractual obligations between the player and Emcee. The costs of acquiring player registrations include transfer fees, league levy fees, and player agents' fees incurred by the club. Also, players' contracts can be extended and this incurs additional costs for Emcee.

At the end of every season, which also is the financial year end of Emcee, the club reviews its playing staff and makes decisions as to whether they wish to sell any players' registrations. These registrations are actively marketed by circulating other clubs with a list of players' registrations and their estimated selling price. Players' registrations are also sold during the season, often with performance conditions attached. Occasionally, it becomes clear that a player will not play for the club again because of, for example, a player sustaining a career threatening injury or being permanently removed from the playing squad for another reason. The playing registrations of certain players were sold after the year end, for total proceeds, net of associated costs, of \$25 million. These registrations had a carrying amount of \$7 million.

Emcee would like to know the financial reporting treatment of the acquisition, extension, review and sale of players' registrations in the circumstances outlined above. **(9 marks)**

(ii) In the consolidated financial statements for 20X6, Emcee recognised a net deferred tax asset of \$16 million. This asset was made up of \$3 million relating to taxable temporary differences and \$19 million relating to the carry-forward of unused tax losses. The local tax regulation allows unused tax losses to be carried forward indefinitely. Emcee expects that within five years, future taxable profits before tax would be available against which the unused tax losses could be offset. This view was based on the budgets for the years 20X6-20Y1. The budgets were primarily based on general assumptions about economic improvement indicators. Additionally, the entity expected a substantial reduction in the future impairments which the entity had recently suffered and this would result in a substantial increase in future taxable profit.

Emcee had recognised material losses during the previous five years, with an average annual loss of \$19 million. A comparison of Emcee's budgeted results for the previous two years to its actual results indicated material differences relating principally to impairment losses. In the interim financial statements for the first half of the year to 31 May 20X6, Emcee recognised impairment losses equal to budgeted impairment losses for the whole year. In its financial statements for the year ended 31 May 20X6, Emcee disclosed a material uncertainty about its ability to continue as a going concern. The current tax rate in the jurisdiction is 30%. **(8 marks)**

Required:

Discuss how the above matters should be dealt with in Emcee's financial statements.

Note: The mark allocation is shown against each of the two issues above.

(b) Developing a framework for disclosure is at the forefront of current debate and there are many bodies around the world attempting to establish an overarching framework to make financial statement disclosures more effective, coordinated and less redundant. Some argue that disclosure notes are too lengthy and numerous. Others argue that there is no such thing as too much 'useful' information for users.

Required:

Discuss why it is important to ensure the optimal level of disclosure in annual reports, and the role of materiality when preparing financial statement disclosure notes. (8 marks)

(Total: 25 marks)

61 GASNATURE  *Walk in the footsteps of a top tutor*

Answer debrief

(a) Gasnature is a public limited company involved in the production and trading of natural gas and oil. It prepares its financial statements using International Financial Reporting Standards. The directors require advice about the accounting treatment of some of the transactions that Gasnature has entered into during the year.

(i) Gasnature jointly owns an underground storage facility with another entity, Gogas. Both parties extract gas from offshore gas fields, which they own and operate independently from each other. Gasnature owns 55% of the underground facility and Gogas owns 45%. They have agreed to share services and costs accordingly, with decisions regarding the storage facility requiring unanimous agreement of the parties. Local legislation requires the decommissioning of the storage facility at the end of its useful life.

Gasnature wishes to know how to treat the agreement with Gogas including any obligation or possible obligation arising on the underground storage facility.

(7 marks)

(ii) Gasnature has entered into a 10-year contract with Agas for the purchase of natural gas. Gasnature has made an advance payment to Agas for an amount equal to the total quantity of gas contracted for 10 years which has been calculated using the forecasted price of gas. The advance carries interest of 6% per annum, which is settled by way of the supply of extra gas. Fixed quantities of gas have to be supplied each month and there is a price adjustment mechanism in the contract whereby the difference between the forecasted price of gas and the prevailing market price is settled in cash monthly. If Agas does not deliver gas as agreed, Gasnature has the right to claim compensation at the current market price of gas.

Gasnature wishes to know whether the contract with Agas should be accounted for under IFRS 9 *Financial Instruments*. **(6 marks)**

Required:

Discuss, with reference to IFRS Standards, how Gasnature should account for the above agreement and contract

(b) Gasnature's institutional shareholders invest in a wide-range of entities. Gasnature's directors are concerned that certain IFRS and IAS Standards permit entities to choose between different measurement bases and presentation methods. They believe that these choices hinder its shareholders from comparing Gasnature to other entities on a like-for-like basis.

Required:

Outline the main accounting choices permitted by IAS 16 *Property, Plant and Equipment* and IAS 20 *Accounting for Government Grants and Disclosure of Government Assistance* and discuss the potential impact of these on investors' analysis of financial statements. **(10 marks)**

Professional marks will be awarded in part (b) for clarity and quality of presentation. **(2 marks)**

(Total: 25 marks)

 ***Calculate your allowed time, allocate the time to the separate parts..............***

62 EVOLVE  *Walk in the footsteps of a top tutor*

 ***Answer debrief***

(a) Evolve is a real estate company, which is listed on the stock exchange and has a year end of 31 August.

(i) At 31 August 20X6, Evolve controlled a wholly owned subsidiary, Resource, whose only assets were land and buildings, which were all measured in accordance with International Financial Reporting Standards. On 1 August 20X6, Evolve published a statement stating that a binding offer for the sale of Resource had been made and accepted and, at that date, the sale was expected to be completed by 31 August 20X6. The non-current assets of Resource were measured at the lower of their carrying amount or fair value less costs to sell at 31 August 20X6, based on the selling price in the binding offer. This measurement was in accordance with IFRS 5 *Non-current Assets Held for Sale and Discontinued Operations*. However, Evolve did not classify the non-current assets of Resource as held for sale in the financial statements at 31 August 20X6 because there were uncertainties regarding the negotiations with the buyer and a risk that the agreement would not be finalised. There was no disclosure of these uncertainties and the original agreement was finalised on 20 September 20X6. **(7 marks)**

(ii) Evolve operates in a jurisdiction with a specific tax regime for listed real estate companies. Upon adoption of this tax regime, the entity has to pay a single tax payment based on the unrealised gains of its investment properties. Evolve purchased Monk whose only asset was an investment property for $10 million. The purchase price of Monk was below the market value of the investment property, which was $14 million, and Evolve chose to account for the investment property under the cost model. However, Evolve considered that the transaction constituted a 'bargain purchase' under IFRS 3 *Business Combinations*. As a result, Evolve accounted for the potential gain of $4 million in profit or loss and increased the 'cost' of the investment property to $14 million. At the same time, Evolve opted for the specific tax regime for the newly acquired investment property and agreed to pay the corresponding tax of $1 million. Evolve considered that the tax payment qualifies as an expenditure necessary to bring the property to the condition necessary for its operations, and therefore was directly attributable to the acquisition of the property. Hence, the tax payment was capitalised and the value of the investment property was stated at $15 million. **(6 marks)**

Required:

Advise Evolve on how the above transactions should be correctly dealt with in its financial statements with reference to relevant International Financial Reporting Standards.

Note: The mark allocation is shown against each of the two issues above.

(b) The International Accounting Standards Board (the Board) is undertaking a broad-based initiative to explore how disclosures in financial reporting can be improved. The Disclosure Initiative is made up of a number of implementation and research projects, one of which is concerned with materiality. The Board have now issued a Practice Statement in which it provides further guidance on the application of materiality to financial statements.

Required:

Discuss why the concept of materiality is so important to preparers and users of financial statements.

Your answer should include reference to the Board's materiality Practice Statement.

(10 marks)

Professional marks will be awarded in part (b) for clarity and quality of presentation.

(2 marks)

(Total: 25 marks)

Calculate your allowed time, allocate the time to the separate parts..............

63 ARTWRIGHT

(a) Artwright trades in the chemical industry. The entity has development and production operations in various countries. It has entered into an agreement with Jomaster under which Artwright will licence Jomaster's know-how and technology to manufacture a chemical compound, Volut. The know-how and technology has a fair value of $4 million. Artwright cannot use the know-how and technology for manufacturing any other compound than Volut. Artwright has not concluded that economic benefits are likely to flow from this compound but will use Jomaster's technology for a period of three years. Artwright will have to keep updating the technology in accordance with Jomaster's requirements. The agreement stipulates that Artwright will make a non-refundable payment of $4 million to Jomaster for access to the technology. Additionally, Jomaster will also receive a 10% royalty from sales of the chemical compound.

Additionally, Artwright is interested in another compound, Yacton, which is being developed by Jomaster. The compound is in the second phase of development. The intellectual property of compound Yacton has been put into a newly formed shell company, Conew, which has no employees. The compound is the only asset of Conew. Artwright is intending to acquire a 65% interest in Conew, which will give it control over the entity and the compound. Artwright will provide the necessary resources to develop the compound.

The directors of Artwright require advice about how the above events are accounted for in accordance with International Financial Reporting Standards. **(8 marks)**

(b) Artwright has entered into three derivative contracts during the year ended 30 April 20X4, details of which are as follows:

	Initial recognition at fair value	**Fair value 30 April 20X4**	**Details**
A	Nil	$20m (liability)	Artwright believes that oil prices are due to rise in the future so during the year has entered into futures contracts to buy oil at a fixed price. Artwright has no exposure to oil prices in the course of its business. In fact, oil prices have fallen resulting in the loss at the year-end.
B	$1m	$9m (liability)	Artwright has an investment in equity designated to be measured at fair value through other comprehensive income. Artwright is concerned the investment will fall in value and it wishes to cover this risk. Thus during the year it entered into derivative B to cover any fall in value and designated this as a hedging instrument as part of a fair value hedge. In fact, by the reporting date, the asset increased in value by $8.5 million.
C	Nil	$25m (asset)	Artwright is concerned about the potential for raw material prices to rise. It managed this risk by entering into derivative C – a futures contract. This arrangement has been designated as a cash flow hedge. At the year-end the raw material prices have risen, potentially giving the company an increased future cost of $24 million.

Assume that all designated hedges meet the effectiveness criteria outlined in IFRS 9 *Financial Instruments.*

The directors of Artwright would like an outline of the hedge effectiveness criteria and also require advice on how the three derivatives should be accounted for in the financial statements for the year ended 30 April 20X4. **(9 marks)**

(c) Artwright's functional currency is the dollar. Artwright took out a foreign currency loan of 5 million dinars at a fixed interest rate of 8% on 1 May 20X3. The effective rate of interest on the loan is also 8%. Annual interest payments commenced on 30 April 20X4. The loan will be repaid on 30 April 20X5. Currency rates during the year are as follows:

Exchange rates	dinars: $1
1 May 20X3	5.0
30 April 20X4	6.0
Average exchange rate for year ended 30 April 20X4	5.6

The average currency exchange rate for the year is not materially different from the actual rate.

The directors of Artwright require advice on how to account for the loan and interest in the financial statements for the year ended 30 April 20X4. **(8 marks)**

Required:

With reference to relevant IFRS Standards, respond to the directors requests.

Note: The mark allocation is shown against each of the three issues above.

(Total: 25 marks)

64 LUCKY DAIRY

(a) (i) The Lucky Dairy, a public limited company, produces milk for supply to various customers. It is responsible for producing twenty five per cent of the country's milk consumption. The company owns cows and heifers (young female cows).

The herd as at 31 May 20X2 is comprised as follows:

70,000 – 3 year old cows (all purchased before 1 June 20X1)

25,000 – 2 year old heifers purchased for $46 each on 1 December 20X1

There were no animals born or sold in the year. The per unit values less estimated costs to sell were as follows:

	$
2 year old animal at 31 May 20X1	50
2 year old animal at 31 May 20X2	55
3 year old animal at 31 May 20X2	60

The directors would like advice on how the herd should be accounted for in its primary financial statements for the year ended 31 May 20X2. Advice about disclosure notes is not required. **(6 marks)**

(ii) On 1 December 20X1 Lucky Dairy purchased interest-bearing bonds in Jags, another listed company, for $10 million and classified these assets to be measured at amortised cost. Just prior to the date of the bond purchase, Jags had released an interim financial report that demonstrated encouraging year-on-year growth and a strong financial position. As such, external agencies had graded the bonds as having a low credit risk. In May 20X2, Jags released its annual financial statements and these showed a weak trading performance in the final six months of its reporting period as well as a large decline in the cash generated from its operations compared to the prior year. These financial statements show that, at the period end, Jags was relatively close to breaching its loan covenants. The listed bond price of Jags has fallen by 20% since December 20X1 despite an overall increase in bond prices for other listed entities in the same sector. It has been reported that external agencies are reviewing and re-assessing the credit rating of Jags. Despite encountering financial difficulties, Jags has met all of its obligations to its lenders and bond holders.

The directors of Lucky Dairy would like advice on how the above information will impact the carrying amount of its financial assets. **(8 marks)**

Required:

Advise Lucky Dairy on how the above transactions should be correctly dealt with in its financial statements with reference to relevant International Financial Reporting Standards.

Note: The mark allocation is shown against each of the two issues above.

(b) Lucky Dairy's directors have been reviewing the International Integrated Reporting Council's *Framework for Integrated Reporting*. The directors believe that International Financial Reporting Standards are already extensive and provide stakeholders with a comprehensive understanding of an entity's financial position and performance for the year. In particular, statements of cash flow enable stakeholders to assess the liquidity, solvency and financial adaptability of a business. They are concerned that any additional disclosures could be excessive and obscure the most useful information within a set of financial statements. They are therefore unsure as to the rationale for the implementation of a separate, or combined, integrated report.

Required:

Discuss the extent to which statements of cash flow provide stakeholders with useful information about an entity and whether this information would be improved by the entity introducing an Integrated Report. (9 marks)

Professional marks will be awarded in part (b) for clarity and quality of presentation. (2 marks)

(Total: 25 marks)

UK GAAP FOCUS

65 STEM (SEP/DEC 2021)

Stem Co is a parent of a manufacturing company. It has entered into an agreement with two other companies to develop a new technology through a separate legal entity, Emphasis Co. The financial year end of Stem Co is 31 December 20X7.

Emphasis Co

On 1 January 20X7, Stem Co has contributed cash to a new legal entity, Emphasis Co, and holds an interest of 40%. The other two companies contributing have retained equity interests of 40% and 20% respectively. The purpose of the entity is to share risks and rewards in developing a new technology. The holders of a 40% interest can appoint three members each to a seven-member board of directors. All significant decisions require the unanimous consent of the board. The holder of the 20% interest can appoint only one board member and can only participate in the significant decisions of the entity through the board. There are no related parties.

Stem Co contributed cash of $150,000 to Emphasis Co. The entity will use the cash invested by Stem Co to gain access to new markets and to develop new products. At 1 January 20X7, the carrying amount of the net assets contributed by the three companies was $310,000 but the fair value of the net assets contributed was $470,000.

Emphasis Co is not held by Stem Co as part of an investment portfolio.

Required:

(a) **Explain the key differences between IFRS 3 *Business Combinations* and FRS 102 *The Financial Reporting Standard applicable in the UK and Republic of Ireland*.**

Note: there is no need to refer to any exhibit when answering part (a). **(7 marks)**

(b) **In accordance with FRS 102, discuss why Stem Co's investment in Emphasis Co should be classified as a jointly controlled entity and how Stem Co should account for its interest at 1 January 20X7 in the consolidated financial statements.**

Note: candidates should show any relevant entries required in the accounting records of Stem Group. **(8 marks)**

(Total: 15 marks)

66 SITKA (MAR/JUN 2021)

Sitka Co is a software development company which operates in an industry where technologies change rapidly. Its customers use the cloud to access the software and Sitka Co generates revenue by charging customers for the software license and software updates. It has recently disposed of an interest in a subsidiary, Marlett Co, and purchased a controlling interest in Billing Co. Sitka Co uses FRS 102 *The Financial Reporting Standard applicable in the UK and Republic of Ireland* in its individual financial statements and IFRS in the group financial statements. The year end of the company is 31 December 20X7.

Software contract and updates

On 1 January 20X7, Sitka Co agreed a four-year contract with Cent Co to provide access to licence Sitka Co's software including customer support in the form of monthly updates to the software. Cent Co is a UK company.

The total contract price is $3 million for both licensing the software and the monthly updates. Sitka Co licenses the software on a stand-alone basis for between $1 million and $2 million over a four-year period and regularly sells the monthly updates for $2.5 million over the same period. The software can function on its own without the updates. Although, the monthly updates improve its effectiveness, they are not essential to its functionality. However, because of the rapidly changing technology in the industry, if Cent Co does not update the software regularly, the benefits of using the software would be significantly reduced. In the year to 31 December 20X7, Cent Co has only updated the software on two occasions. Cent Co must access the software via the cloud and does not own the rights to the software.

Part disposal of Martlett

Sitka Co prepares separate financial statements in accordance with FRS 102. At 31 December 20X6, it held a 60% controlling equity interest in Marlett Co and accounted for Marlett Co as a subsidiary. In its separate financial statements, Sitka Co had elected to measure its investment in Marlett Co at cost less any impairment. On 1 July 20X7, Sitka Co disposed of 45% of its equity interest in Marlett Co for $10 million and lost control. At the date of disposal, the carrying amountof Marlett Co in its separate financial statements was $12 million. After the partial disposal, Sitka Co does not have joint control of, or significant influence over Marlett Co and its retained interest of 15% is to be treated as an investment in an equity instrument.

At 1 July 20X7, the fair value of the retained interest of 15% in Marlett Co was $3.5 million. Sitka Co wishes to recognise any profit or loss on the disposal of the 45% interest in other comprehensive income.

Acquisition of Billing Co

Sitka Co has acquired two assets in a business combination with Billing Co. The first asset is 'Qbooks' which is an accounting system developed by Billing Co for use with the second asset which is 'Best Cloud' software. The directors of Sitka Co believe that the fair value of the assets is higher if valued together rather than individually. If the assets were to be sold, there are two types of buyers that would be interested in purchasing the assets. One buyer group would be those who operate in the same industry and have similar assets. This group of buyers would eventually replace Qbooks with their own accounting system which would enhance the value of their assets. The fair values of the individual assets in the industry buyer group would be $30 million for Qbooks and $200 million for 'Best Cloud', therefore being $230 million in total.

Another type of buyer is the financial investor who would not have a substitute asset for Qbooks. They would licence Qbooks for its remaining life and commercialise the product. The indicated fair values for Qbooks and Best Cloud within the financial investor group are $50 million and $150 million, being $200 million in total.

Required:

(a) Discuss briefly why the right to receive access to Sitka Co's software is unlikely to be accounted for as an intangible asset or a lease in Cent Co's financial statements in accordance with FRS 102. (4 marks)

(b) Discuss and demonstrate how the disposal of a 45% interest and the retained interest of 15% in Martlett Co should be accounted for in the separate financial statements of Sitka Co at the date of disposal in accordance with FRS 102. (8 marks)

(c) Discuss briefly whether the fair value of the two assets acquired on the acquisition of Billing Co would be different if accounted for in accordance with FRS 102 and IFRS 13 *Fair Value Measurement.* (5 marks)

(Total: 17 marks)

67 CORBEL (SEP/DEC 2020)

Corbel Co is a UK small and medium enterprise (SME) trading in the perfume sector. It has recently acquired a company for its brand 'Jengi', purchased two additional brand names, and has announced plans to close its Italian stores. Corbel Co also opened a new store on a prime site in London. The current financial year end is 31 December 20X7.

Acquisition of Jengi Co

On 1 January 20X7, Corbel Co acquired 100% of Jengi Co. Both companies operate in the perfume sector. Corbel Co intends to merge the manufacture of Jengi Co's products into its own facilities and close Jengi Co's manufacturing unit. Jengi Co's brand name is well known in the sector, retailing at premium prices, and therefore, Corbel Co will continue to sell products under the Jengi brand name after its registration has been transferred and its manufacturing units have been integrated. The directors of Corbel Co believe that most of the value of Jengi Co was derived from the brand and there is no indication of the impairment of the brand at 31 December 20X7.

Acquisition of perfume brands

In addition to owning the Jengi Co brand, Corbel Co has acquired two other perfume brand names to prevent rival companies acquiring them. The first perfume (Locust) has been sold successfully for many years and has an established market. The second is a new perfume which has been named after a famous actor (Clara) who intends to promote the product. The directors of Corbel Co believe that the two perfume brand names have an indefinite life.

Plan to close and sell stores

Corbel Co approved and announced a plan to close and sell all six Italian stores on 31 December 20X7. The six stores will close after a liquidation sale which will last for three months. Management has committed to a formal plan for the closure of the six stores and has also started an active search for a single buyer for their assets. The stores are being closed because of the increased demand generated by Corbel Co's internet sales. A local newspaper has written an article suggesting that up to 30 stores may be closed with a loss of 500 jobs across the world, over the next five years. The directors of Corbel have denied that this is the case.

Corbel Co's primary store

Corbel Co's primary store is located in central London. It has only recently been opened at a significant cost with the result that management believes it will make a loss in the current financial year to 31 December 20X7. This loss making is not of concern as the performance is consistent with expectations for such a new and expensive store and management believes that the new store will have a positive effect on Corbel Co's brand image. If impairment testing of the primary store were to be required, then Corbel Co would include the cash flows from all internet sales in this assessment. The goods sold via the internet are sourced from either Corbel Co's central distribution centre or individual stores. Internet sales are either delivered to the customer's home or collected by the customer from the store supplying the goods.

Required:

Discuss the following accounting issues relating to Corbel Co's financial statements for the year ended 31 December 20X7 in accordance with FRS 102, *The Financial Reporting Standard applicable in the UK and Republic of Ireland*:

(a) whether the Jengi Co brand name should be tested for impairment, and whether it can be accounted for as a separate cash generating unit after the integration of the manufacturing units (4 marks)

(b) whether the two perfume brand names (Locust and Clara) can be accounted for as if they have an indefinite life and how to determine their useful life (6 marks)

(c) how to account for the proposed closure of the six stores and the suggested closure of the remaining stores, and how this contrasts with IFRS 5 *Non-current Assets Held for Sale and Discontinued Operations*; and (6 marks)

(d) whether the primary store should be tested for impairment at 31 December 20X7 and whether the internet sales can be attributed to this store. (4 marks)

(Total: 20 marks)

68 LERIA (MAR 2020)

Leria Co owns a football club, Real Verde, in the UK. The football club reports under FRS 102 *The Financial Reporting Standard applicable in the UK and Republic of Ireland*. As a result, it has material intangible assets which relate to the contract costs of its players.

Players' registration contract costs are shown as intangible assets and are initially recognised at the fair value of the consideration paid for their acquisition. However, subsequently, players' contracts are often re-negotiated at a cost. Also, players' contracts may contain contingent performance conditions where individual players may be paid a bonus based on their success in terms of goals scored or the success of the football team as a whole. These bonuses represent additional contract costs.

For impairment purposes, Leria Co does not consider that it is possible to determine the value-in-use of an individual player unless the player were to suffer a career threatening injury and cannot play in the team. Players only generate direct cash flows when they are sold to another football club.

Required:

(a) Discuss the key differences between accounting for intangible assets in accordance with FRS 102 and IFRS Standards. (5 marks)

(b) Discuss how to account, in accordance with FRS 102, for the players' contract costs (including the contingent performance conditions), any impairment which might be required to these non-current assets and whether a player can be considered a single cash generating unit. (7 marks)

(Total: 12 marks)

69 DIGIWIRE (SEP/DEC 2019)

Pension plan

Digiwire Co has a UK subsidiary which provides a pension plan for its employees. From 1 September 20X6, Digiwire Co decided to curtail the plan and to limit the number of participants. The employees were paid compensation from the plan assets and some received termination benefits due to redundancy. Due to the curtailment, the current monthly service cost changed from $9 million to $6 million. The relevant financial information relating to the plan is as follows:

Date	**Net defined liability**	**Discount rate**
	$m	%
1 January 20X6	30	3
1 September 20X6	36	3.5
31 December 20X6	39	3.7

True and fair override

Concerns have been raised about the operation of the true and fair override in UK law. The importance of the true and fair requirement in corporate financial statements is fundamental and is necessarily dependent on estimates and judgement.

Required:

(a) **Describe the differences in the guidance on accounting for termination benefits under FRS 102 *The Financial Reporting Standard applicable in the UK and Republic of Ireland* and IAS 19 *Employee Benefits*.** **(3 marks)**

(b) **If amendments to IAS 19 in respect of plan amendments, curtailments and settlements were adopted by FRS 102, calculate and discuss the impact on the FRS 102 calculation of net interest and current service cost of the subsidiary for the year ended 31 December 20X6.** **(8 marks)**

(c) **Discuss the issues which may arise in the application of the true and fair override in financial statements in the UK and whether faithful representation and comparability may be affected by such a regulation.** **(6 marks)**

(Total: 17 marks)

70 CRYPTO (MAR/JUN 2019)

Crypto operates in the power industry, and owns 45% of the voting shares in Kurran. Kurran has four other investors which own the remaining 55% of its voting shares and are all technology companies. The largest of these holdings is 18%. Kurran is a property developer and purchases property for its renovation potential and subsequent disposal. Crypto has no expertise in this area and is not involved in the renovation or disposal of the property.

The board of directors of Kurran makes all of the major decisions but Crypto can nominate up to four of the eight board members. Each of the remaining four board members are nominated by each of the other investors. Any major decisions require all board members to vote and for there to be a clear majority. Thus, Crypto has effectively the power of veto on any major decision. There is no shareholder agreement as to how Kurran should be operated or who will make the operating decisions for Kurran.

The directors of Crypto believe that Crypto has joint control over Kurran because it is the major shareholder and holds the power of veto over major decisions.

Crypto has also entered into a contract to purchase 80% of the shares of an overseas subsidiary. The directors are concerned about the procedures required to translate the results of a foreign subsidiary into Crypto's presentational currency to prepare the consolidated financial statements. Specifically, the directors are concerned about the translation process and the treatment of cumulative foreign exchange gains and losses, particularly as regards the non-controlling interest (NCI).

Required:

(a) **As far as the definition of control is concerned, discuss the key differences between FRS 102 *The Financial Reporting Standard applicable in the UK and Republic of Ireland* and IFRS 10 *Consolidated Financial Statements*. Your answer should also briefly explain the classification of joint arrangements in IFRS 11 *Joint Arrangements*.** **(6 marks)**

(b) **Discuss the advice which should be given to Crypto regarding how Kurran should be accounted for under FRS 102.** **(6 marks)**

(c) **Advise Crypto on the FRS 102 procedures to be followed when translating the results of a foreign subsidiary into the presentation currency of the group. Your answer should also set out any differences between FRS 102 and IAS 21 *The Effects of Changes in Foreign Exchange Rates* as regards the treatment of cumulative foreign exchange gains and losses including those relating to the NCI.** **(5 marks)**

(Total: 17 marks)

71 FILL (DEC 2018)

(a) On 1 December 20X6, Fill purchased an open cast coal mine in the UK. The negotiation and purchase of a coal mining licence took a substantial amount of time to complete, and resulted in Fill incurring significant borrowing costs. Fill also acquired equipment which will be used for the construction of various mines throughout the UK. Fill wishes to capitalise the borrowing costs on the acquisition of the licence and the equipment.

However, during the last six months of the year ended 30 November 20X8, there has been a significant decline in the spot price of coal and it is expected that future reductions in selling prices may occur. Currently, the forward contracts being signed over the next two years by Fill indicate a reduction in the price of coal. At 30 November 20X8, the mine has a useful remaining life of four years. As a result of the decline in the price of coal, Fill has decided to sell the mine and has approached several potential buyers.

Required:

Advise the directors of Fill on how to treat the above events under FRS 102 *The Financial Reporting Standard applicable in the UK and Republic of Ireland*. **(8 marks)**

(b) Several years ago, Fill had purchased an interest of 10% in another mining company. However, over the last two years, Fill has made several other purchases of shares with the result that, at 30 November 20X8, it owned 51% of the equity of the mining company. Fill had incurred significant legal and advisory costs in acquiring control. The mining company has reserves which contain different grades of coal. As the entity cannot process some high quality coal for several years, contingent consideration for the purchase of the entity has been agreed. On the date that Fill gained control of the mining company, the fair value of the contingent consideration was estimated at $10 million.

Required:

Advise the directors of Fill on the differences in treatment of the above purchase of the mining company between IFRS 3 *Business Combinations* and FRS 102 *The Financial Reporting Standard applicable in the UK and Republic of Ireland*. (7 marks)

(Total: 15 marks)

72 SKIZER (SEP 2018)

Skizer is a pharmaceutical company which develops new products with other pharmaceutical companies that have the appropriate production facilities. Stakes in development projects When Skizer acquires a stake in a development project, it makes an initial payment to the other pharmaceutical company. It then makes a series of further stage payments until the product development is complete and it has been approved by the authorities. In the financial statements for the year ended 31 August 20X7, Skizer has treated the different stakes in the development projects as separate intangible assets because of the anticipated future economic benefits related to Skizer's ownership of the product rights. However, in the year to 31 August 20X8, the directors of Skizer decided that all such intangible assets were to be expensed as research and development costs as they were unsure as to whether the payments should have been initially recognised as intangible assets. This write off was to be treated as a change in an accounting estimate.

Required:

(a) Outline the criteria in FRS 102 *The Financial Reporting Standard applicable in the UK and Republic of Ireland* for the recognition of an intangible asset and discuss whether these are consistent with the *Conceptual Framework*. (6 marks)

(b) Discuss the required treatment under FRS 102 for the stakes in the development projects for both the years ended 31 August 20X7 and 20X8 assuming that the recognition criteria for an intangible asset were met. Your answer should also briefly consider the implications if the recognition criteria were not met. (5 marks)

(c) Discuss the key differences between International Financial Reporting Standards and FRS 102 with regards to the recognition of intangible assets. (4 marks)

(Total: 15 marks)

73 BOBARRA

(a) Shortly before the financial year-end, Bobarra signed a letter of intent to buy a group of companies in the United Kingdom (UK). The UK group was diverse in nature and included subsidiaries, which the entity was prepared to sell. One subsidiary was operating in a country that was engaged in civil war and so the group had lost managerial control over the entity. Another subsidiary was being held by the group specifically to make a profit on its resale. Bobarra has little experience of UK company legislation and UK Generally Accepted Accounting Practice (UK GAAP).

The directors require advice on the requirements to prepare group financial statements in the UK and any relevant exemptions and exclusions from consolidation available in the UK. **(9 marks)**

(b) At 30 November 20X6, three people own the shares of Bobarra. The finance director owns 60%, and the operations director owns 30%. The third owner is a passive investor who does not help manage the entity. All ordinary shares carry equal voting rights. The wife of the finance director is the sales director of Bobarra. Their son is currently undertaking an apprenticeship with Bobarra and receives a salary of $30,000 per annum, which is normal compensation. The finance director and sales director have set up a trust for the sole benefit of their son. The trust owns 60% of the ordinary shares of Santarem which carry voting rights. The finance director and sales director are trustees of the trust.

Finally, Bobarra owns 100% of the shares in Alucant, which in turn owns 100% of the shares in Cantor. Alucant also has a 80% holding of the shares of Drumby. There have been transactions in the year between Bobarra and Drumby.

The directors of Bobarra require advice on the identification of related parties and the preparation of related party disclosure in respect of its separate financial statements for the year ending 30 November 20X6 in accordance with IAS 24 *Related Party Disclosures* and FRS 102 *The Financial Reporting Standard applicable in the UK and Republic of Ireland* **(7 marks)**

Required:

Advise Bobarra on the matters set out above. (Total: 16 marks)

74 HARRIS

The directors of Harris are looking at the requirements of IFRS 3 *Business Combinations* and FRS 102 *The Financial Reporting Standard applicable in the UK and Republic of Ireland*. The directors would like advice on the accounting treatment of goodwill because the entity is preparing to purchase a UK subsidiary at a competitive price.

The directors are also concerned about the differences between IAS 12 *Income Taxes* and FRS 102 with regards to the recognition of deferred tax assets and liabilities.

Required:

(a) Discuss the key differences with regards to accounting for goodwill under IFRS 3 and FRS 102. (9 marks)

(b) Discuss the differences in the general recognition principles between IAS 12 and FRS 102 in accounting for deferred tax. (6 marks)

(Total: 15 marks)

75 ROWLING

Rowling, a public limited company, purchases and develops numerous intangible assets. Two of the directors of Rowling are qualified accountants who were trained in International Financial Reporting Standards. The directors of Rowling are aware that the UK Financial Reporting Council in the UK has published a range of Financial Reporting Standards (FRSs) – FRS 100, 101, 102 and 105 – but do not understand the scope of these or what entities they apply to. Moreover they require an explanation of how International Financial Reporting Standards and FRS 102 differ with regards to the recognition of intangible assets.

Required:

Prepare a draft memorandum to the directors setting out:

- **the scope of FRS 100, FRS 101, FRS 102 and FRS 105** **(9 marks)**
- **the differences between IFRS Standards and FRS 102 with regards to the recognition of intangible assets.** **(6 marks)**

(Total: 15 marks)

76 TOTO

On 1 January 20X1, Toto enters into a lease. The lease term is three years and the asset, which is not specialised, has a useful economic life of ten years. Ownership of the asset does not transfer to Toto at the end of the lease term. Toto must make lease payments annually in arrears. No other fees or costs are required. The lease payments are material to Toto's financial statements.

Required:

Compare the impact of the above on the financial statements of Toto for the year ended 31 December 20X1 if the lease is accounted for in accordance with:

- **IFRS 16 *Leases*, or**
- **FRS 102 *The Financial Reporting Standard applicable in the UK and Republic of Ireland.***

Your answer should make reference to key financial statement ratios. **(15 marks)**

77 HOWEY

Howey, a public limited company, intends to dispose of part of its business. This meets the criteria in IFRS 5 *Non-current Assets Held for Sale and Discontinued Operations* to be classified as a discontinued operation. They are also considering acquiring a subsidiary exclusively with a view to resale.

Required:

(a) **Discuss the differences between the treatment of non-current assets held for sale and discontinued operations under FRS 102 *The Financial Reporting Standard applicable in the UK and Republic of Ireland* and International Financial Reporting Standards.** **(9 marks)**

(b) **Discuss why a UK entity might choose to adopt FRS 102 instead of applying IFRS Standards.** **(6 marks)**

(Total: 15 marks)

78 LOKI

On 1 January 20X1, Loki purchased 70% of the ordinary shares of Odin for cash consideration of $300 million. The identifiable net assets of Odin at this date had a carrying amount of $200 million and a fair value of $280 million. If accounting standards permit, Loki measures non-controlling interests (NCI) at acquisition at fair value. The fair value of the NCI at acquisition was $120 million.

On 31 December 20X2, Loki performed an impairment review. Odin was deemed to be a cash generating unit. The net assets of Odin (excluding goodwill) were carried in the consolidated financial statements of the Loki group at $260 million. The recoverable amount of Odin was calculated as $350 million.

If required, you should assume that the goodwill arising on the acquisition of Odin was attributed a useful economic life of ten years as at the acquisition date.

Required:

(a) Discuss, with calculations, how the impairment review should be accounted for in accordance with IFRS Standards. (6 marks)

(b) Discuss, with calculations, how the impairment review should be accounted for if Loki prepared its financial statements in accordance with FRS 102. (9 marks)

(Total: 15 marks)

Section 2

ANSWERS TO PRACTICE QUESTIONS

SECTION A QUESTIONS – GROUP FINANCIAL STATEMENTS

1 CHUCKLE (SEP/DEC 2021)  *Walk in the footsteps of a top tutor*

Key answer tips

This is a very groups heavy Q1, with less emphasis on non-group IFRS knowledge compared to previous sittings. This shows how important it is not to question spot as variances between mark allocations can arise between exam sittings. However, what is always guaranteed is that groups will be set within Q1.

This question considered a group with complicated classification issues, caused by changing levels of investment over a period of time and has a statement of financial position emphasis. The question required the understanding and discussion of the basic concepts underpinning the classification of investments within the group (e.g. associates requiring significant influence, subsidiaries requiring control) and how they could be affected by chages in the group structure (in this case, a step acquisition). It also included more complicated calculations of group accounting treatments (equity accounting and goodwill calculations).

The required calculation elements do still specify that explanations are needed. Narrative marks will be given for addressing these areas.

Keep an eye on the dates in the requirements. Part (a)(i) is interested in the classifications on **1 April 20X2**, part (a)(ii) is concerned with **31 March 20X6** (both dates being prior to the step-acquisition of 18% and so shareholdings are 30%), whilst (a)(iii) and (b) are concerned with issues at **1 April 20X6** (which is after the step acquisition, when shareholdings of 48% were held).

It may help to attempt part (b)(i) and (b)(ii) simulatenously. Set up a template for the goodwill calculation (needed for (b)(ii). Then fill in the template with any relevant figures you spot as you attempt to explain the affects on the net assets at acquisition of the fair value adjustments in (b)(i).

(a) **(i)** Significant influence is the ability to participate in the financial and operating policy decisions of the investee, but is not control or joint control over these policies.

IFRS 10 *Consolidated Financial Statements* states that an investor controls an investee only if the investor has all of the following:

- power over the investee,
- exposure to or rights to variable returns from its involvement with the investee, and
- the ability to use its power over the investee to affect the amount of the investor's returns.

Control is presumed to exist where the investor has a majority of the voting rights of the investee. This would usually give the investor the ability to direct the relevant activities, i.e. the activities which significantly affect the investee's returns. An ownership of 50% or less of the voting rights does not necessarily preclude an investor from obtaining control.

Tutorial note

*As well as discussing the factors contributing to the correct accounting treatment (in this case, the elements suggesting significant influence over Grin), you should also address why alternative treatments are **not appropriate**, particularly if factors in the scenario can be used to support these conclusions. This is alluded to in the requirement with the 'as oppose to a subsidiary' comment, but can be applied more generally.*

Marks will be allocated for highlighting why Grin is not a subsidary of Chuckle (due to the lack of control), as well as why Grin is an associate (due to the significant influence).

The strategy applied to this particular model answer is to prove that control does not exist first and foremost, and then to address the issue of significant influence (see below). Do not fret if your approach was the opposite (to focus on why significant influence is exerted, and then to discuss why control is not appropriate). You'll still get the credit!

Prior to 1 April 20X6, Chuckle Co only owned 30% of the equity and no share options. Where an investor has a significant minority, close consideration should be given as to whether the voting rights alone or whether a combination of factors is deemed sufficient to obtain power. Chuckle Co and Grin Co do share some key management personnel which can sometimes be evidence of control. However, there has been no clear past voting pattern suggesting that Chuckle Co is unable to directly influence the economic decisions of the other investors. With only 30% of the equity and no additional potential rights, it would appear that Chuckle Co was only able to exercise significant influence rather than control. It can be concluded that it was correct to classify Grin Co as an associate.

(ii) Grin Co is an associate and would have been accounted for using the equity method in the consolidated financial statements of Chuckle Co. The initial investment is measured at cost and the carrying amount is increased to recognise the investors' share of the profits and other comprehensive income after the date of acquisition. One line would be included within non-current assets under the heading 'Investment in associate' which at 31 March 20X6 would be valued at $118.6 million ($100m + (30% × ($348m – $286m))).

Tutorial note

The points above should represent the achievable marks within this requirement. Make sure you understand the accounting of an associate.

The subsequent points below are more complicated. They address the additional explanations as specified in the requirement. Note that they are not adjustments to the equity accounting described above (as the revaluation is already correctly accounted for within the $348m net assets of Grin).

Candidates need to appreciate that an upwards revaluation of land would create entries to the revaluation surplus (and OCI) of the associate. In the group accounts, equity accounting leads to a share (30%) of the post-acquisition revaluation surplus being incorporated in the group equity within the CSOFP.

Commonly in exam questions, movements in an associate's net assets are created by impacts to profits, the parent's share of which will affect the CSOFP within retained earnings. In this question, there is enough information to identify that the post-acquisition movements in the associate's net assets are accounted for within different reserves.

Well done if you have noted the deferred tax impacts caused by the revaluation in the associate. It is fair to suggest that this is a higher skill mark compared to the other issues addressed in the answer.

The revaluation gain of $15 million would be recorded within other components of equity and deferred tax at 20% of $3 million would be netted off within equity in the individual financial statements of Grin Co. In the consolidated financial statements Chuckle Co should include $3.6 million (30% of the net gain of $12 million ($15m × 80%)) within other components of equity. As the remaining increase in net assets is due to profits (i.e. $50 million ($348m – $286m – $12m)), Chuckle Co should include $15 million (30% × $50m) within consolidated retained earnings.

(iii) The acquisition of the extra 18% of the equity on 1 April 20X6 would now unquestionably make Chuckle Co a significant minority investor. No other investor owns more than 10% of the equity, so Chuckle Co owns a much higher proportional share (48%). Where the other shareholdings are owned by a large number of unconnected, dispersed holders, it would be clear that power has been obtained. However, the other shares are owned by just a few other investors which is unlikely to be considered a large, dispersed group of unconnected shareholders.

Potential voting rights should be considered in the assessment of control. For these to be included in the assessment, the rights should be substantive. That would usually mean that they are currently exercisable and have an exercise price which is below the market price of the shares so that they are 'in the money'. In that sense, it is worthwhile for the investor to acquire the extra shares. In the case of Chuckle Co, they own share options that are currently exercisable but not in the money. This is because the exercise price is above the share price of Grin Co. However, it can be seen that they are only just out of the money. In addition, the share price of Grin Co is expected to increase and cost savings are expected from a further acquisition of shares. It seems, therefore, that the share options would be deemed to be substantive. Since exercising these options would enable Chuckle Co to obtain a 60% shareholding, it can be concluded that Chuckle Co is able to exercise power over Grin Co from 1 April 20X6. Grin Co should be reclassified from an associate to a subsidiary at this date.

Tutorial note

For (b)(i) and (b)(ii) candidates must apply the assumption that Chuckle has control of Grin after the step acquisition. This creates a step acquisition where control is achieved. Grin is now a subsidiary. This assumption is provided within the requirement.

Do not perservere with any conclusions that you may have made from (a)(iii) that contradict the assumption.

Also, the assumption does provide a good hint as to what the conclusion of a(iii) should have been!

(b) **(i)** It is necessary for the calculation of goodwill that Chuckle Co measures the identifiable assets acquired and the liabilities assumed at their acquisition date fair values. IFRS 13 *Fair Value Measurement* should be considered in the assessment of the fair values. It has been identified that, at the point control is achieved, the fair value of the land is $10 million above carrying amount. The valuation should be representative of the amount which market participants would be willing to sell the asset or transfer the liability in an orderly transaction under current market conditions.

Tutorial note

Fair value adjustments are very common issues within the SBR exam. Candidates must be well-versed in the need for fair value adjustments upon consolidation. The basic effects of the fair value adjustments to land, inventory and intangibles should be easy marks for well-prepared students. (Note: not quite so easy if this is your first attempt at an exam standard question, but trust me, you'll see fair value adjustments again and again as you continue to practice exam-standard questions.)

The effect of fair value adjustments upon deferred tax is less commonly tested. In the group accounts, fair value adjustments cause changes in the carrying amount which are not reflected in the tax base. Therefore, temporary differences arise, causing deferred tax. Remember, the accounting treatment of the deferred tax should match the accounting treatment of the transaction causing the deferred tax. Therefore, any entry to record deferred tax on fair value adjustments is allocated to goodwill (see part (b)(ii)).

The increase in value of $10 million will create an additional taxable temporary difference. In effect, the carrying amount of the land is increased by $10 million with no alteration to the tax base. An additional deferred tax liability arises at the acquisition date of $2 million. Since the deferred tax is an identifiable liability at the acquisition date, it should be recognised on acquisition as part of Grin's net assets. An overall increase in net assets of $8 million ($10m – $2m) arises.

Finished goods should be valued at their estimated sales price less the sum of the costs of disposal and a reasonable profit allowance for the selling effort of the acquiring entity. The fair value of the finished goods is $131 million and so a fair value adjustment of $47 million ($131m – $84m) is required. This creates a further taxable temporary difference in the consolidated financial statements of Chuckle Co with a corresponding deferred tax liability at 20% of $9.4 million.

It is correct that the database as an internally generated intangible asset is not recognised in the individual financial statements of Grin Co. On acquisition, Chuckle Co should recognise the database as a separate intangible asset from goodwill in the consolidated financial statements, providing that the database satisfies the criteria for recognition as an intangible asset and a reliable estimate of the fair value can be determined. Although there are no contractual or legal rights associated with the database, the database still appears to be identifiable as it could be sold separately to Grin Co's competitors. The professional expert's valuation of $5 million would appear to provide a reliable estimate of fair value. The database should therefore be recognised in the consolidated financial statements at $5 million with a further increase to the deferred tax liability at 20% equal to $1 million.

(ii) The additional purchase of the 18% equity would constitute a piecemeal or step acquisition. Goodwill will be calculated as the amount by which the fair value of the consideration exceeds the fair value of the identifiable net assets on acquisition.

Tutorial note

In the group accounts, treat a step acquisition that achieves control as if the group has:

- *sold the initial investment (the 30%)*
- *bought back the entire investment (the 48%) in one go at the point control is achieved.*

This means the 30% is revalued to fair value (in this case, with gains or losses taken to profit or loss) and the goodwill is calculated as if the entire 48% was purchased in one go. Consideration will include the amount paid for the 18% and the newly revalued fair value of the 30%.

Chuckle Co must therefore remeasure its previously held equity interest in Grin Co at its acquisition fair value and recognise the resulting gain or loss in profit or loss. The previously held equity interest would have a carrying amount of \$118.6 million (part (a)(ii)). The fair value is \$127 million, so a gain of \$8.4 million is recognised in the consolidated statement of profit or loss. Goodwill will be calculated including both the fair value of the original consideration and the fair value of the additional consideration.

The previous revaluation gain (net of deferred tax) which was included within other comprehensive income should be recognised on the same basis as would be required if Chuckle Co had disposed directly of the previously held equity interest. Since gains on revaluation are not reclassified to profit or loss on disposal, \$3.6 million (see part (a) (ii)) should be transferred from the revaluation surplus of the group to retained earnings on 1 April 20X6.

Goodwill will be calculated as follows:

	\$m	**\$m**
Consideration of 18% holding		66
Fair value of original 30% holding		127
Non-controlling interest at acquisition (397.6 × 52%)		206.8
Less net assets at acquisition:		
Net assets per question	348	
Fair value adjustment land	10	
Subsequent deferred tax	(2)	
Fair value adjustment inventory	47	
Subsequent deferred tax	(9.4)	
Database	5	
Subsequent deferred tax	(1)	(397.6)
Goodwill on acquisition of Grin Co		**2.2**

Marking scheme			
			Marks
(a)	(i)	Discussion of control (IFRS 10 and other factors) v significant influence and application to the scenario	4
	(ii)	Discussion of equity accounting and application to the scenario	2
		– Calculation of investment in associate	2
		– Calculation of reserves	1
			5
	(iii)	Application of the following discussion to the scenario:	
		– Acquisition of 18% equity	2
		– Share options	3
			5
(b)	(i)	Discussion and calculation of the following FV adjustments	
		– Land and DT	2
		– Inventory and DT	3
		– Customer list	3
			8
	(ii)	Application of the following discussion to the scenario:	
		– Piecemeal acquisition	3
		– Gain on step acquisition calculation	1
		– Impact on revaluation gain	1
		– Goodwill calculation	3
			8
Total			**30**

Examiner's comments

Chuckle Co was a 30-mark question which translates (using 1.8 minutes per mark) into 54 minutes of the SBR exam. Candidates invariably spend too long on Q1 as it has more marks than any other question. However, there may be easier marks in other parts of the exam paper which are not achieved because of the excess time spent on Q1. The SBR exam states that all questions are compulsory and the consequences from not answering all questions are that it makes it much more difficult to pass the exam

a)i) Candidates generally could define significant influence as the ability to participate in the financial and operating policy decisions of the investee but not have control or joint control over these policies. In addition, many candidates expanded their answer to discuss control with the result that half marks (2 marks) were readily gained by many candidates. The difficulty came when candidates attempted to apply these principles to the scenario. Candidates needed to consider whether voting rights alone or whether a combination of factors was sufficient to obtain power. As Chuckle Co only held 30% of the equity and no additional voting rights, many candidates concluded that the correct classification was that of an associate. However, those candidates that concentrated on simply discussing why significant influence was demonstrated whilst ignoring why control was not indicated, did not perform as well on the question. Ensuring you have addressed all aspects of a requirement before moving on is important – candidates were directed to discuss 'as opposed to a subsidiary'.

a)ii) Many candidates explained that the initial investment is measured using equity accounting. However, candidates often could not apply the principle to the scenario. The application of the equity method of accounting is a basic requirement of the SBR exam and candidates could have scored at least half marks for its correct application in this question. It was surprising how many candidates did not provide a basic explanation of the equity method of accounting or make a reasonable attempt at the calculation.

The revaluation element was answered well by some and those that considered the treatment in the individual financial statements scored high marks. Several candidates incorrectly dealt with the revaluation via profit or loss. The treatment of revaluation gains and losses is again fundamental to this examination and is assumed knowledge. Candidates are losing relatively easy marks if they do not understand nor apply basic assumed knowledge of financial reporting principles. Candidates must be able to take advantage of the application of these basic principles as there are much more difficult areas of the SBR syllabus which candidates have to deal with.

a)iii) The acquisition of the extra 18% of the equity on 1 April 20X6 made Chuckle Co a significant minority investor as they now held 48% of the equity shares. Many candidates concentrated on the ownership of 48% and concluded that this was not enough to control and therefore, incorrectly concluded that the status should not change.

To gain a good mark, candidates not only needed to consider the purchase of the additional holding but also the potential voting rights. In this case, candidates should have observed that the share options were substantive and that exercising these options would enable Chuckle Co to obtain a 60% shareholding. Therefore, Chuckle Co is able to exercise power over the associate from 1 April 20X6. Thus, candidates should have concluded that the associate needs to be reclassified as a subsidiary at this date.

b)i) This requirement carried 8 marks and therefore a substantial answer was expected. As soon as fair value is mentioned in a requirement, the principles of IFRS 13 *Fair Value Measurement* should be used. This does not mean that definitions of level 1, 2 and 3 are required every time but it does mean that the relevant sections of the IFRS standard should be quoted in the answer.

Some candidates confused the fair value of finished goods with the net realisable value principle. Net realisable value refers to the net amount that an entity expects to realise from the sale of inventory in the ordinary course of business. Fair value reflects the price at which an orderly transaction to sell the same inventory in the principal or most advantageous market for that inventory would take place between market participants at the measurement date. The former is an entity-specific value, the latter is not. Net realisable value for inventories may not equal fair value less costs to sell. The fair valuation of finished goods created a further taxable temporary difference in the consolidated financial statements of Chuckle Co with a corresponding deferred tax liability at 20%.

As regards the database, many candidates realised that it would not be recognised in the individual financial statements of the subsidiary but would be recognised as a separate intangible asset from goodwill in the consolidated financial statements as the database appeared to be identifiable. Again, this valuation would result in a further increase in the deferred tax liability.

Candidates' knowledge of IFRS 13 was surprisingly limited. However, most candidates could apply the information given in the question and made a good attempt at calculating the fair values of the net assets acquired. A significant number of candidates did not consider the deferred tax implications, despite being specifically asked to, and as a result, could not gain full marks for the question.

b) ii) The discussion needed to include a brief description of the accounting treatment arising from the additional purchase of the 18% equity in the associate. The additional purchase of the 18% equity constituted a piecemeal or step acquisition which means that the previously held equity interest should be remeasured at its acquisition fair value with any resulting gain or loss going to profit or loss. Where the step acquisition was recognised by candidates, the accounting treatment was generally well documented. However, many candidates did not realise that the purchase of shares was a step acquisition.

The revaluation gain on land (net of deferred tax) would also be transferred from the revaluation surplus of the group to retained earnings on 1 April 20X6. Very few candidates mentioned this point.

The calculation of non-controlling interest (NCI) was dependent upon the correct calculation of the fair value of the net assets at acquisition and therefore the own figure rule was used to award marks on this part of the question. However, some candidates used incorrect NCI percentages. The NCI held 52% of the equity and this confused many candidates as they assumed that the NCI could not hold more than 50%. Many also failed to consider the deferred tax implications.

Overall, the calculation of goodwill was generally well answered. Answers on how to treat the additional purchase of 18% could have been improved as it was often too brief. Only the strongest candidates discussed the step acquisition and the fair value of the original consideration. Not many stated the gain would be recognised in profit or loss.

2 COLUMBIA (MAR/JUN 2021)  *Walk in the footsteps of a top tutor*

Key answer tips

This question is a typical 'Q1' style question. It tests the groups syllabus area, but also includes requirements covering other syllabus areas – this time the topic areas tested is IAS 19 *Employee Benefits.*

The group content (seen in requirements (a) (i) & (ii)) consisted of **discussion** and **explanation** of group issues, not just group calculations. More marks are typically afforded to narrative elements of the answer than the calculation elements. Candidates should remember this when attempting answers – the focus should be on the explaination of the thought processes and rationales used when performing calculations, rather than just presenting an answer consisting solely of inexplicable calculations.

If you justify your point by applying reasonable assumptions but have calculated the figures incorrectly, credit will still be given for your rationale. If presented with only an incorrect calculation to mark, bereft of any justification as to how the numbers were derived, markers cannot awards any marks at all.

(a) **(i)** An acquirer is the entity which has assumed control over another entity. In accordance with IFRS® 10 *Consolidated Financial Statements,* an investor controls an investee where it has:

- power over the investee,
- exposure or rights to variable returns from its involvement with the investee,
- the ability to use its power over the investee to affect the amount of the investor's returns.

Tutorial note

To detemine whether Columbia is the acquirer requires contemplation of who has control of Peru Co. This is a great illustration of the type of requirement where candidates should:

(i) outline the rules from the standard (e.g. as above re control definition)

(ii) apply the rules to the specific details in the questions (e.g. how does the particular arrangement illustrate control, which factors do not indicate control)

(iii) provide a conclusion that addresses the requirement (e.g. based on the factors identifed do you think that Columbia is the acquirer or not?).

Throughout the proceeding paragraphs, you'll see reference to how the factors in the scenario illustrate 'power', the 'rights to variable returns' and 'the ability to affect the amount of variable returns'. The examiner is applying the rules from the standard to the specific scenario to allow a conclusion to be made.

There are a significant number of factors to consider when determining which entity should be treated as the acquirer. The first factor to consider is the consideration transferred for the relative share of ownership. It may look at first that Columbia Co and Brazil Co have undertaken a joint venture where the two parties share control over the investee. This is because both Columbia Co and Brazil Co have paid an equal amount of $8 per share. Additionally, Columbia Co and Brazil Co have each obtained 50% of the equity interests and have equal voting rights of one vote per share. Both entities satisfy the criteria for rights to a variable return. However, a joint venture relies upon there being joint control over all the key operating and financing decisions of the entity. The scenario does not indicate that unanimous consent is required because decision-making responsibilities appear to be split between Columbia Co and Brazil Co.

Tutorial note

When discussing accounting issues, it is important to consider any possible alternative outcomes. In this requirement, you are asked to determine whether Columbia is the acquirer. Do not let any initial assumptions you make restrict your answer. As in, do not assume the examiner only wants to hear that Columbia is the acquirer. Confirmation bias can be displayed in many candidates answers, which can limit the marks awarded e.g. only mentioning the factors that suggest Columbia is the acquirer and ignoring any suggestions that Columbia may not be the acquirer.

Scenarios will regularly provide information that point towards different conclusions from what you may originally expect but which may (or may not) be able to be refuted when applying the rules of the standard. Here the answer addresses the potential for the acquisition of Peru Co to be a joint venture, rather than an acquired subsidiary which is fully controlled by Columbia (where Columbia would be the acquirer.

Some factors may confirm your hypothesis, others may indicate that alternative approaches may be relevant. Easy marks can be awarded by outlining why an accounting treatment is not relevant too (e.g.'Peru Co is not a joint venture because...'.) A really good answer will be able to consider conflicting information and address whether it impacts on the candidate's overall conclusions.

A second factor to consider is who has the rights to appoint the majority of the governing body. Columbia Co can appoint 60% of the board suggesting they may be the acquirer. It is true that Brazil Co does have additional rights in terms of the power to veto amendments to the articles of incorporation and the appointment of auditors. In the assessment of control, it is important to consider whether these rights give Brazil Co power over the investee and whether it can use this power to affect their return. In this assessment, it is important to distinguish between substantive rights and protective rights. Only rights which are substantive are said to give the investor control. These rights are more likely to be considered protective since they appear to prohibit changes in the activities of the investee which Brazil Co does not agree with rather than give Brazil Co power. Additionally, these are not rights which would allow Brazil Co to affect the profitability of Peru Co and subsequently their return. Protective rights do not prevent Columbia Co from obtaining control.

A similar argument can be applied to the appointment of the senior managers. The entity which has the right to appoint the majority of the senior management team is more likely to be the acquirer. Whilst each entity can appoint one senior manager each, the rights of the senior management appointed by Brazil Co appear to be protective while all key decisions are made by the senior manager appointed by Columbia Co. The rights of the senior manager appointed by Columbia Co therefore appear substantive including requesting board approval for significant activities. They have the rights over decisions affecting the key revenue earning capabilities of Peru Co including technological development, markets to operate it and ways of raising finance. Thus Columbia Co has power over the investee and these rights enable them to affect their return.

Further evidence that Columbia Co is the acquirer is reflected by the share issue which Columbia paid as additional consideration. To obtain control, it is often the case that the acquirer has to pay a premium on acquisition for their equity interests. Columbia Co has in effect had to pay additional consideration equal to $1.25 million (50% × $5 million × 1/20 × $10) despite each investor acquiring 50% of the equity shares. It can be concluded that Columbia is the acquirer in a business combination and that Brazil Co, in effect, is the non-controlling interest.

Tutorial note

Make sure you give a conclusion. Tell the examiner, based on the factors you identified in your explanation, whether you think Columbia is, or is not, the acquirer. Do not be afraid to have an opinion!

(ii) Goodwill at acquisition should be calculated as follows:

	$m	$m
Consideration		
– Cash (5m × 50% × $8)		20
– Shares ((5m × 50%)/20 × $10)		1.25
		21.25
FV of NCI at acquisition (5m × 50% × $8)		20
Less		
Fair value of net assets at acquisition		
Per question	32	
FV adjustment – bonds	2.16	
FV adjustment – brand	1	
FV adjustment – deferred income	0.59	
		(35.75)
Goodwill at acquisition		5.5

Tutorial note

The requirement asks for a calculation of goodwill. This should be a familiar calculation at this point. Therefore, set up a goodwill working template within the CBE software before reading the detail in the question. You can then fill in sections as you go through the detail rather than attempting the goodwill calculation all in one go (which can be inefficent from a timing perspective).

However, the question also asks for explanations of the fair values. The narrative is likely to carry a greater number of marks than the calculation.

IFRS 13 *Fair Value Measurement* states that the fair value is the price which would be received to sell an asset or paid to transfer a liability in an orderly transaction between market participants at the measurement date. This means that fair value is not entity specific but rather should take into account a market participant's ability to generate economic benefits by using the asset in its highest and best use or by selling it to another market participant who would use the asset in its highest and best use. Goodwill should be measured by deducting the fair value of the identifiable net assets at acquisition from the fair value (including any non-controlling interest) of the consideration paid.

Tutorial note

The question requires explanations of the fair values used in a goodwill calculation. However, as well as discussing the relevant standards to help calculate goodwill (IFRS 3), other standards may be relevant too. To determine fair values, IFRS 13 Fair Value Measurement needs to be applied. It is easy to get pigeon-holed into only discussing one particular standard which can limit your discussion marks.

In terms of the consideration paid by Columbia Co for the acquisition of Peru Co, the fair value of the cash paid will be equal to face value. Columbia Co has paid $8 per share for their 50% equity interest resulting in a cash consideration of $20 million (50% × 5 million × $8). The most reliable evidence of fair value is where an observable price for an identical asset or liability is traded on an active market. The fair value of Columbia Co's equity should therefore be measured using the market price of their own shares at the acquisition date of $10 per share. This results in a fair value measurement of $1.25 million (50% × 5 million × 1/20 × $10) for the share for share exchange.

Tutorial note

Discuss and explain the fair value of ***both*** *the consideration paid (as above) and the various fair value adjustments required to determine the fair value of the net assets on acquisition (as below). The more issues you discuss, the more marks you can be awarded even if you make mistakes.*

There are two main issues to identify in the consideration paid – the cash paid and the share exchange.

Since the non-controlling interest is also to be measured at fair value and Brazil Co paid $8 per share for their 50% equity interest, this will have a fair value of $20 million.

Tutorial note

*Some students get very confused about what measuring the non-controlling interest at fair value actually means. Keep it simple – we are trying to value the shares that the parent entity **did not** purchase.*

In assessing the fair value of the identifiable net assets at acquisition, it is important that the net assets of Peru Co are measured using the same accounting policies of the group. Since Columbia Co has similar bonds where their business model is to either collect the cash flows or to sell, the bonds should be measured at their acquisition date fair values and treated as a fair value through other comprehensive income investment rather than amortised cost. The carrying amount of the bonds in the individual financial statements of Peru Co on 1 July 20X5 would be \$6.24 million (\$6 million + (6/12 × \$6 million × 8%)). Since the bonds are in an unquoted company and an active market for an identical asset is not observable, it appears reasonable to use the market value for a similar asset as adjusted for differences in their liquidity. The bonds would have a fair value of \$8.4 million (6 million × \$2 × 70%). A fair value uplift to the net assets of Peru Co of \$2.16 million (\$8.4 million – \$6.24 million) is required.

Tutorial note

Remember, Goodwill is calculated at acquisition. As identified in the requirement, this is 1 July 20X5. Subsequent treatment of the financial asset at the year-end is irrelevant in this particular requirement so there is no need to discuss it.

The fair value of the brand has to be determined in accordance with its highest and best use for market participants. Since it is not entity specific, the intention by Columbia Co to discontinue the brand is not relevant unless it is what other market participants would also do with the brand. Since it is estimated that a competitor would be prepared to pay \$5 million to continue the trade of the brand, this is not the case. The highest and best use of the brand from a market perspective would appear to be continue the trade at a value of \$5 million. A \$1 million increase is required to the fair value of the brand.

The deferred income must be measured from the market's perspective. Since the market would expect to incur direct and incremental costs of \$1.7 million in the performance of their obligations, the fair value should be determined by adding the 30% mark-up to this estimate. The fair value of the deferred income should be \$2.21 million (\$1.7 million × 130/100). This will result in a decrease in the liabilities at acquisition and therefore an increase in the net assets of Peru Co equal to \$590,000 (\$2.8 million – \$2.21 million).

Tutorial note

There are three separate fair value adjustments to consider. The bond, the brand and the contract liability. Make sure you attempt to discuss them all as each one will have its own mark allocation. Marks can still be obtained even if you make a mistake but leaving an issue out entirely will definitely cost you credit. So, if you're not sure, have a guess and move on.

(b) Defined benefit plan

Where a defined benefit pension scheme is in surplus, IAS® 19 *Employee Benefits* requires the surplus to be measured as the lower of:

- The surplus in the plan, and
- The present value of the economic benefits in the form of refunds from the plan or reductions in the future contributions to the plan (known as the asset ceiling).

At 1 January 20X5, the surplus of the scheme is $60 million ($260 million – $200 million) but the asset ceiling is only $20 million, so the defined benefit pension asset would have been restricted to $20 million. Interest on the opening asset would therefore be adjusted and only $1 million (5% × $20 million) interest income will be recorded in profit or loss for the year. The cash contributions of $21 million should be added to the scheme assets, benefits paid of $25 million are deducted from both the scheme's assets and the scheme's liabilities and the current service cost of $30 million is charged to profit or loss.

IAS 19 states that an entity must first determine any past service cost arising from a gain or loss on settlement without considering the effect on the asset ceiling. A gain therefore should be recognised in the profit or loss of Columbia Co on the settlement equal to $12 million ($28 million – $16 million). The pension scheme surplus at 31 December 20X5 is summarised as follows:

	Asset	Liabilities	Net plan assets before ceiling adjustment	Ceiling adjustment	Net plan assets after ceiling adjustment
	$m	$m	$m	$m	$m
Before 1 January 20X5	260	200	60	(40)	20
Net interest at 5%	13	10	3	(2)	1
Cash contributions	21		21	–	21
Benefits paid	(25)	(25)	–	–	
Current service costs		30	(30)	–	(30)
Curtailment and settlement	(16)	(28)	12	–	12
Total at 31 December 20X5	253	187	66	(42)	24

Tutorial note

Candidates are not required to produce this table in its entirety and the detail provided here is for tutorial purposes only.

*An abbreviated version would directly use the **'Net plan assets after ceiling adjustment'** column and still provide the conclusions shown below.*

The actuary has valued the scheme as a surplus of $47 million ($242 million – $195 million) immediately after the curtailment which would result in a remeasurement loss of $19 million ($66 million – $47 million) on 31 December 20X5. However, the effect of the asset ceiling is that the pension scheme would only be recognised at a value of $24 million following the curtailment (see table above). Since the scheme is valued at the lower of the surplus of the scheme and the present value of the economic benefits in the form of refunds from the plan or reductions in the future combinations, the scheme will be restated to $25 million. A net gain of $1 million ($25 million – $24 million) will be recognised in other comprehensive income.

The pension scheme asset should be included in the financial statements of Columbia Co at $25 million (the lower of $25 million and $47 million).

Defined contribution plan

With a defined contribution scheme, it is the employee who undertakes all of the risk should the pension plan not perform to expectations. Columbia Co would have no obligations further to their contributions into the scheme.

This means that, provided the correct contributions have been paid into the scheme, no asset or liability would be recognised within their statement of financial position. The cash contributions of $0.5 million are instead recognised as an expense in profit or loss.

Tutorial note

Do not neglect the much simpler defined contribution scheme. It is easy to take too long on the defined benefit scheme and miss out the defined contribution entirely. The defined contribution will definitely carry its own mark allocation. Maybe do it first!

Marking scheme

			Marks
(a)	(i)	Definition of control	1
		Application of the following to the scenario:	
		– voting rights	2
		– governance structure	2
		– key management	2
		– premium on consideration	2
			9
	(ii)	IFRS 13 discussion	2
		Application of IFRS 13 to the following:	
		– bonds	2
		– brand	2
		– deferred income	2
		Goodwill calculation	3
			11
(b)		Discussion of defined benefit scheme and asset ceiling	4
		Defined benefit calculations	5
		Discussion of the defined contribution scheme	1
			10
Total			**30**

Examiner's comments

Overall this question was very well answered with some candidates scoring full marks.

Columbia Co was a 30-mark question. It is important to allow yourself time for reading, thinking and checking your answer within the allocated timeframe to ensure you have the opportunity to gain the maximum marks across the question. You should avoid the temptation to expand your answer to one requirement beyond the allotted time. For example, some candidates spent too long on Q1(a), meaning that they reached the maximum mark allocation well before the end of their answer. This meant they used time that should have been spent answering the remaining requirements, especially part (b). Markers cannot allocate more marks to a requirement than is available, even if the comments may otherwise be worthy of marks. So, in short, stick to your allotted time.

a) (i) Many candidates cut and pasted information from the question. Marks were awarded as long as sensible comments were made by the candidates as to why the information was important in the determination of the acquirer – the candidate **must add** their own comments to the cut and pasted information. There were many points that could be raised by candidates and the marking scheme flexibly allocated marks based upon the application of the control principle. As a result, many candidates scored full marks on this part of the question, demonstrating a good knowledge of the principles and their application.

a) (ii) This part of the question attracted a significant number of marks (11 marks) and therefore there was an expectation of an in depth discussion of the principles of fair values and their application. The calculation of goodwill was well answered but it seldom attracts more than 2/3 marks as generally the calculation is relatively straightforward.

Candidates answered this part of the question satisfactorily. Consideration was usually calculated correctly as was the non-controlling interest. However, various errors were made when trying to correctly account for the fair values of identifiable net assets. Many candidates struggled with the fair valuation of the bond, although the concept of fair values was generally well understood.

Dealing with the accounting for the brand was the best answered part of the question, although a common mistake was to use the full fair value rather than the fair value adjustment when calculating goodwill.

b) Candidates showed a good knowledge an understanding of both defined benefit and defined contribution schemes and were able to make a good attempt at the calculations, although the discussion was lacking at times. The defined contribution element was well answered.

3 SUGAR (SEP/DEC 2020)  *Walk in the footsteps of a top tutor*

Key answer tips

This question tests consolidated statements of cash flow. This is a topic that students find difficult. However, in part (b), there are lots of easy marks for simply picking up figures from the scenario. Read the question carefully so that you are able to identify these easy marks.

Pay careful attention to verbs. Part (a) asks for you to 'address' the accounting treatment. Part (b) requires you to 'prepare extracts'. This means that explanations will score you marks in part (a), but will not in part (b).

Parts (a) and (b) involve calculations. Set out workings clearly – this will help the markers give you credit even if you have made mistakes.

(a) Cash paid to acquire Flour Co

The acquisition of Flour Co is a step acquisition. This means the original 40% equity interest is treated as if it is disposed and then reacquired at fair value. The difference between the carrying amount of the original 40% equity interest in the consolidated financial statements and its fair value would be included as a gain within profit or loss.

Tutorial note

Gains and losses arising on step acquisitions are recorded in profit or loss unless the previous shareholding was an investment in shares that had been designated to be measured at fair value through other comprehensive income.

As an associate, the investment would have been accounted for using the equity method and would be carried at $14.8 million as at 1 July 20X7:

	$000
Cost	10,000
Share of post-acquisition net asset increase ($12m × 40%)	4,800
Investment in associate as at 1 July 20X7	14,800

Tutorial note

Any associate impairments would have been deducted from the carrying amount of the investment.

The fair value of the original 40% interest would be $15.2 million (10m × 40% × $3.80) and so gain of $400,000 ($15.2m – $14.8m) would be included in profit or loss.

Tutorial note

Goodwill is always calculated on the date control is achieved. It is not recalculated, even if the parent increases its shareholding.

Goodwill will be calculated at 1 July 20X7, the date that control is gained, as the difference between the fair value of the consideration and non-controlling interest and the fair value of the identifiable net assets at acquisition. The consideration must include the fair value of the original 40% equity interest as well as the fair value of the additional consideration.

Tutorial note

*Some students get very confused about what measuring the non-controlling interest at fair value actually means. Keep it simple – we are trying to value the shares that the parent entity **did not** purchase.*

The fair value of the non-controlling interest at 1 July 20X7 will be $11.4 million (10m × 30% × $3.80). The fair value of the share exchange will be $9 million. (3 million shares acquired × ½ × $6).

Tutorial note

Put all the relevant figures into the goodwill calculation. Remember that the subsidiary's identifiable net assets at acquisition are measured at fair value. The 'cash consideration' is the balancing figure.

Goodwill has been determined to be $2,259,000 which means the cash paid to acquire Flour Co on 1 July 20X7 must be $3 million as follows:

	$000
Cash consideration (bal. fig.)	3,000
Fair value of original 40% equity interest	15,200
Fair value of share exchange	9,000
Fair value of non-controlling interest at acquisition	11,400
Fair value of identifiable net assets at acquisition including FV uplift ($35,741 + $600)	(36,341)
Goodwill on acquisition per question	2,259

Tutorial note

The share exchange is not a cash flow and so will not be reported in the statement of cash flows.

The debit entry for the share exchange is recorded in goodwill. The credit entry is recorded in equity (share capital and premium).

Cash paid to acquire Flour Co will be included within the investing activities of the consolidated statement of cash flows. However, the cash held by Flour Co comes under group control, so the net outflow presented in the consolidated statement of cash flows is $1,766,000 ($3m – $1.234m).

(b) Extracts from the consolidated statement of cash flows for the Sugar Group year ended 30 June 20X8

Tutorial note

Remember to put brackets around the cash outflows. Try and reference figures to your workings – this will help the marker award credit if you have made a mistake.

Cash flows from investing activities

	$000
Net cash paid on acquisition of Flour Co (part a)	(1,766)
Cash paid to acquire intangible assets (W1)	(12,051)
Proceeds from disposal of property plant and equipment (W2)	4,370
Cash paid on acquisition of Butter Co	(5,000)
Dividends received from associates (W3)	2,253
Proceeds from disposal of FVTPL investment ($4m + $0.5m)	4,500
Investment income received (W5)	1,991

Cash flows from financing activities

	$000
Issue of ordinary shares during the year (W6)	9,600
Dividends paid to the non-controlling interest (W7)	(3,324)

Workings

Tutorial note

Set out your workings clearly. This will help you to score marks even if you make mistakes.

(W1) Intangibles

Tutorial note

Remember to include the intangible assets owned by Sugar Co. These are now under group control.

	$000
Intangibles b/f	15,865
Goodwill on acquisition of Sugar Co	2,259
Licences and patents on acquisition of Sugar Co	6,781
Amortisation	(3,500)
Cash purchase (bal. fig.)	12,051
Intangibles c/f	33,456

(W2) Property, plant and equipment

	$000
Property, plant and equipment b/f	52,818
Acquisition of Flour Co (at fair value)	18,676
Depreciation	(10,000)
Carrying amount of disposal (bal. fig.)	(6,370)
Property, plant and equipment c/f	55,124

The asset was sold at a loss of $2 million, so disposal proceeds must have been $4.37 million ($6.37m – $2m).

(W3) Dividends received from associates

Tutorial note

As a result of the step acquisition, Sugar Co is a subsidiary rather than an associate. As such, the investment in the associate must be derecognised.

When accounting using the equity method, dividends received are deducted from the carrying amount of the investment.

	$000
Investment in associates b/f	23,194
Associate profit for the year	15,187
Acquisition of Butter Co	5,000
Step acquisition Sugar Co (part a)	(14,800)
Dividends received (bal. fig.)	(2,253)
Investment in associate c/f	26,328

(W4) FVTPL financial asset

Tutorial note

This working will enable you to work out the gain arising on remeasurement of these assets to fair value. This gain has been reported in investment income, but it is not a cash flow. When working out cash from investments (W5), you will need to remove this gain from investment income.

	$000
FVTPL asset b/f	6,000
Carrying amount of disposal	(4,000)
Fair value gains (bal. fig.)	1,000
FVTPL asset c/f	3,000

(W5) Investment income

Tutorial note

This is probably the trickiest working. The investment income line in the statement of profit or loss includes lots of non-cash income. These need to be removed in order to calculate the cash received from investments.

	$000
Investment income per PL	3,891
FV gains on FVTPL investments (W4)	(1,000)
Fair value gains on step acquisition (part (a))	(400)
Profit on disposal of FVTPL	(500)
Investment income received	1,991

Proceeds from the disposal of the FVTPL asset are $4.5 million ($4m + $0.5m)

(W6) Issue of ordinary shares during the year

Tutorial note

Remember to reconcile the total of share capital and premium year-on-year. Lots of students will forget about the impact of the share exchange in part (a).

	$000
Share capital and premium b/f ($20m + $18m)	38,000
Share for share exchange (part a)	9,000
Cash proceeds (bal. fig.)	9,600
Share capital and premium c/f ($23m + $33.6m)	56,600

(W7) Dividends paid to non-controlling interest

Tutorial note

Many students struggle with this working. If you find it tricky then try and memorise the items that are included.

	$000
Non-controlling interest b/f	12,914
Acquisition of Flour Co (part a)	11,400
Non-controlling interest profit for the year	9,162
Dividends paid to non-controlling interest (bal. fig.)	(3,324)
Non-controlling interest c/f	30,152

(c) Defined benefit scheme

Tutorial note

To answer this question, you need to nail down the accounting treatment of a defined benefit pension scheme. Once you have done that, you should be able to identify the cash flow and the non-cash expenses.

The only cash flow that should be recorded in the consolidated statement of cash flows in relation to defined benefit pension schemes is the contributions paid into the scheme. This is typically included within the operating activities of the group statement of cash flows.

Since Sugar Co did not make any contributions until after the year-end there will be no cash flows to include in the consolidated statement of cash flows for the year ended 30 June 20X8. The $2 million benefits paid out of the scheme are an outflow of cash from the pension scheme itself, a separate entity, rather than a cash outflow of Sugar Co.

This does not mean that the pension scheme will not have any impact upon the consolidated statement of cash flows of the Sugar group. Since operating activities are being calculated using the indirect method it is necessary to adjust for any items that effect operating profit but are not cash flows. The service cost component would need to be added back to group profits. Finance costs in profit and loss would include the net interest component – this is not a cash flow and so would require adjusting.

The remeasurement component does not impact the group statement of cash flows since it is not a cash flow, nor does it impact operating profit.

Tutorial note

The remeasurement component is reported in other comprehensive income. It is presented as an item that will never be reclassified to profit or loss.

In SBR exam questions, the remeasurement component is normally accumulated in other components of equity. However, the question states that other components of equity wholly relate to share premium. This must mean that the remeasurement component has been accumulated in retained earnings. Per IAS 1 Presentation of Financial Statements, this treatment is allowed and is, in fact, the treatment adopted by many real-life companies.

ACCA marking guide		
		Marks
(a)	Application of the following discussion to the scenario:	
	– Treatment as an associate including FV 40% and share exchange at 1 July 20X7	5
	– FV NCI and identifiable net assets at 1 July 20X7	3
	– Goodwill calculation and treatment of cash consideration	2
		10
(b)	Marks for calculations as follows:	
	Acquisition of Intangibles	3
	Proceeds on disposal of PPE	3
	Cash paid for Butter Co	1
	Dividends received from associates	2
	Investment income received	3
	Issue of ordinary shares	2
	Non-controlling interest dividend	2
		16
(c)	Application of the following discussion to the scenario:	
	- Cash flows to include/exclude	2
	- Other elements of defined benefit scheme	2
		4
Total		**30**

Examiner's comments

Overall, part (a) was well-answered. Most candidates provided clear explanations, and a significant number of answers calculated the correct cash consideration. Many answers explained where the cash outflow would appear in the statement of cash flows, although very few worked out the net outflow.

Part (b) required collating information from various sources, and there was evidence from some candidates' answers that they found this challenging. A well-presented answer would include a list of additions or deductions leading from opening to closing balances, with a balancing item for the cash item. Some spreadsheet answers did not use the functionality available which meant basic arithmetic errors occurred. Similarly, some candidates did not show the workings behind a figure – this could have been presented as a typed out working or as formula within a cell. Not showing any supporting workings means it is not possible to award partial marks.

For part (c), weaker answers tended to focus too much on the benefits paid in the next year, which was not relevant for answering the question on cash flow impact. Some candidates incorrectly suggested this represented an adjusting event and missed the cash flow focus of the requirement.

4 HUMMINGS (MAR 2020)  *Walk in the footsteps of a top tutor*

Key answer tips

Only 14 of the 30 available marks in this question test group accounting. In fact, the requirement worth the most marks tests financial instruments. There is no point attempting to guess which topics will be examined in your SBR exam – instead, you must cover, and feel comfortable with, the whole syllabus. Although this question tests many different accounting standards, well-prepared students should not find it too tough.

The easiest marks are on the topic of foreign exchange – 5 marks in part (a) for a discussion of functional currency and 6 marks in part (b) on accounting for goodwill. Concentrate on these if you are struggling.

(a) Functional currency

Tutorial note

Start by stating the definition of functional currency and the principles used to determine it.

Remember that a subsidiary would have the same functional currency as its parent if it acted with little autonomy.

The functional currency is the currency of the primary economic environment in which the entity operates. With a foreign acquisition, consideration should be given as to whether Crotchet Co should adopt the same functional currency as its parent, Hummings Co. However, Crotchet Co appears to be largely independent and is not reliant on Hummings Co for either sales or finance. It is not required therefore for Crotchet Co to adopt the same functional currency as Hummings Co. Crotchet Co does not appear to have transactions in dollars or have a dollar bank account and it can be concluded that the dollar should not be their functional currency.

Tutorial note

Make sure that you reach an explicit conclusion – what is the functional currency of Crotchet Co?

In determining its functional currency, Crotchet Co should consider the currency which mainly influences its sales price of goods and the currency which mainly influences its labour and other costs. This is likely to be the currency which goods are invoiced in and the currency in which costs are settled. The location of the entity's head office is irrelevant except to the extent that it is likely that the costs of running the head office are likely to be settled in the domestic currency. For Crotchet Co, whilst there are a number of transactions in dinars and tax has to be paid in dinars, it appears that the vast majority of their transactions are in grommits. All sales and purchases are invoiced in grommits as well as approximately half of their staff being paid in grommits. Funds for finance are raised in grommits which further suggests that grommits should be chosen as the functional currency of Crotchet Co.

(b) (i) Customer contracts

Tutorial note

This question is only worth 4 marks so your answer should be less detailed than the one below, otherwise you would be wasting time.

You score easy marks for stating the key principles – the subsidiary's identifiable net assets at acquisition are recognised at fair value.

IFRS 3 *Business Combinations* requires the investor to recognise the investee's identifiable net assets at acquisition at fair value.

To be identifiable, a customer contract must either be capable of being used or sold separately, or it must arise from legal or contractual rights. A reliable estimate of its fair value is also necessary to be recognised as a separate asset rather than subsumed within the goodwill figure. This is the case regardless of whether the contracts had been recognised within the individual financial statements of Crotchet Co or not.

The contracts provide Crotchet Co with a legal right to prevent their customers from obtaining goods and services from their competitors and a reliable estimate of fair value appears to be obtainable. The contracts should therefore be recognised as a separate intangible asset.

Identifiable net assets should be recognised at fair value as at the acquisition date. For the contracts, this amounts to 15 million grommits. This would be translated at the spot rate of exchange of $1 to 8 grommits and would be recognised initially in the consolidated financial statements at $1.875 million.

Tutorial note

The question asks for the accounting treatment in the year ended 31 December 20X4. As such, you should discuss the accounting treatment subsequent to initial recognition – i.e. amortisation. Many students concentrate on initial recognition issues only.

The contracts need to be examined to determine their average unexpired useful life and amortised over this period. This amortisation expense should be translated at the average rate of exchange and recorded in consolidated profit or loss. The carrying amount of the contracts would need to be retranslated at the closing rate of exchange of $1 to 7 grommits, with a corresponding exchange gain recognised in other comprehensive income.

(ii) Calculation of goodwill

Tutorial note

Set out your workings neatly.

You will only be penalised for errors once, so do not worry if you make a mistake early in the calculation (such as with the net assets figure).

In SBR, goodwill impairments are normally translated at the average rate of exchange. However, this rate was not provided and so the closing rate was used instead.

Goodwill at 31 December 20X4 would be $8·2 million calculated as follows:

	Grommits millions	**Rate**	**$ millions**
Consideration ($24m × 8)	192		
NCI at acquisition ($6m × 8)	48		
Net assets at acquisition (W1)	(158)		
Goodwill at 1 January 20X4	82	8	10.25
Impairment (30%)	(24.6)	7	(3.51)
Exchange gain (bal. fig.)			**1.46**
Goodwill at 31 December 20X4	57.4	7	8.2

(W1) Net assets at acquisition

Net assets at acquisition are 43 million grommits plus 15 million grommits for the contractual relationships plus 100 million grommits for the dinar assets translated at 1 dinar to 2 grommits (50m × 2).

Explanation of accounting treatment

Tutorial note

*Be explicit about **where** income and expenses are recognised – the statement of profit or loss, or in other comprehensive income.*

Many students forget to discuss whether income or expenses should be attributed to non-controlling interests.

Goodwill is initially recognised at the spot rate of exchange of $1:8 grommits and so would initially be $10.25 million.

The impairment loss of $3.51 million will be expensed to the consolidated statement of profit or loss.

Goodwill will be retranslated using the closing rate of exchange of $1:7 grommits with the exchange gain of $1.46 million included in other comprehensive income.

Since non-controlling interests at acquisition are measured at fair value, both the impairment and the exchange gain will be apportioned 80/20 between the shareholders of Hummings Co and the non-controlling interest respectively.

(c) Quaver Co

Tutorial note

IFRS 5 Non-current Assets Held for Sale and Discontinued Operations is regularly tested in the SBR exam. Make sure that you know the definition of an asset held for sale, as well as the qualifying criteria. Applying these criteria to the scenario is relatively straightforward.

An asset or disposal group should be classified as held for sale if the carrying amount will be primarily recovered through a sales transaction. For this to be the case, IFRS 5 *Non-current Assets Held for Sale and Discontinued Operations* states that:

- The asset must be available for immediate sale in its present condition and the sale must be highly probable
- The sale must be expected to be complete within 12 months
- The asset must be actively marketed at a reasonable price
- Management must be committed to a plan of sale and it is unlikely that any significant changes to the plan will be made.

The sale has not taken place within 12 months of acquisition; however, an exception is permitted where the sale is still deemed to be highly probable and the delay was caused by events which were unforeseen and beyond the control of management. The sale is still expected early in 20X5 and the legal dispute was unforeseen, so this exception seems applicable. As such, Quaver should be classified as a disposal group held for sale. Quaver Co should initially be measured at fair value less costs to sell with any subsequent decreases in fair value less costs to sell taken to consolidated profit or loss.

It appears clear that management was immediately committed to the sale as Hummings Co did not wish to have active involvement in the activities of Quaver Co. Quaver Co is therefore a subsidiary acquired exclusively with a view to resale. In accordance with IFRS 5, Quaver should be presented as a discontinued operation and so its earnings for the year must be disclosed separately in the consolidated statement of profit or loss.

Tutorial note

Students are generally good at spotting issues about assets held for sale, but tend to omit discussion of discontinued operations. Remember that disposing of (or holding for sale) a separate major line of business, or the operations within a specific geographical area, would also qualify as a discontinued operation.

(d) Year ended 31 December 20X3

Tutorial note

The question asks you to consider the accounting treatment as at 31 December 20X3 and for the year ended 31 December 20X4.

Make sure that you discuss the accounting treatment of the bond itself, as well as the impairment rules.

The business model of Hummings Co is to collect the contractual cash flows of the bonds over the life of the asset, so the bonds should be measured at amortised cost.

The financial asset should be recognised at fair value (plus fees if applicable), which is equal to the $10,000,000 paid to purchase the bonds.

Tutorial note

State the relevant principles in IFRS 9 Financial Instruments with respect to financial asset impairments before applying them to the scenario.

IFRS 9 *Financial Instruments* requires entities to calculate expected credit losses for investments in debt instruments that are measured at amortised cost or fair value through other comprehensive income.

On acquisition, the bonds are low risk and are not credit impaired. This means that Hummings Co should calculate 12-month expected credit losses. The 12-month expected credit loss is defined as a portion of the lifetime expected credit losses which represent the expected credit losses resulting from a default within the next 12 months.

Hummings Co should therefore recognise an allowance of $10,000 as at 31 December 20X3. This will be expensed to profit or loss and a separate allowance created. The allowance is netted off the $10,000,000 bond in the statement of financial position of Hummings Co as at 31 December 20X3. The carrying amount of the bonds in the statement of financial position at 31 December 20X3 will be $9.99 million ($10 million – $10,000).

Year ended 31 December 20X4

Interest income at the effective rate of 8% should be recognised in profit or loss and added to the carrying amount of the financial asset. This is calculated on the gross carrying amount of the financial asset ($10m) and amounts to $800,000 ($10m × 8%).

The coupon interest of $500,000 ($10m × 5%) is deducted from the carrying amount of the bonds. This means that the bonds would have a carrying amount of $10,300,000 ($10m + $0.8m – $0.5m) at 31 December 20X4 before considering any impairment issues.

Tutorial note

Discuss the principles regarding the measurement of the loss allowance before you calculate it.

At 31 December 20X4, there has been a significant increase in credit risk. This means that Hummings Co should make an allowance to recognise the lifetime expected credit losses. This is defined as the expected credit losses (cash shortfalls) which result from all possible default events over the expected life of the bonds. An allowance is required equal to the present value of the expected loss in contractual cash flows as weighted by the probability of default. The expected default losses are discounted using the original effective rate of interest of 8%.

Date	Cash flow working	PV of default ($)
31/12/X5	3% × $462,963	13,889
31/12/X6	5% × $6,858,710	342,936
		356,825

Tutorial note

Don't stop with the calculation of the loss allowance; discuss how it is accounted for.

The expected loss allowance should be increased to $356,825 with an expense recorded in profit or loss of $346,825 ($356,825 – $10,000). The net carrying amount of the bonds reported in the statement of financial position as at 31 December 20X4 would be $9,943,175 ($10,300,000 – $356,825).

Marking scheme

			Marks
(a)		Autonomy from parent	2
		Determination of functional currency	3
			5
(b)	(i)	Identifiable criteria and recognition	3
		Need to amortise	1
			4
	(ii)	Goodwill calculation	4
		Discussion of impairment and exchange	1
		Recognition of split between shareholders	1
			6
(c)		Discussion of asset held for sale criteria	2
		Application of above to Quaver Co	2
			4
(d)		Amortised cost identification	1
		12 month credit loss discussion	2
		12 month credit loss calculation	1
		Amortised cost calculation	1
		Explanation of lifetime credit losses	3
		Calculation of lifetime credit losses	3
			11
Total			**30**

Examiner's comments

Answers to part (a) were generally good, with most candidates displaying a good application of primary economic environment principles by which the functional currency is determined, leading to a valid conclusion.

In part (b) (i), weaker answers expanded beyond the requirement, to include general consolidation techniques, or erroneously focused on IFRS 15 *Revenue from Contracts with Customers* rather than IFRS 3 *Business Combinations*. In part (b) (ii), the calculation at the acquisition date was generally well-answered, provided candidates followed the guidance: calculating goodwill first at local currency, including a fair value adjustment highlighted in part (b) (i), and then translating. Fewer candidates achieved full marks as they neglected to explain the impact of both impairment and exchange difference on the consolidated financial statements.

Answers to part (c) in general showed a good appreciation of the rules and applied these to the scenario. Most candidates were able to score well from applying their knowledge.

Part (d) had the most marks allocated to it but was often the shortest answer compared to the other parts. Few candidates demonstrated a clear understanding of the expected value approach to impairment losses under IFRS 9 *Financial Instruments*, and a general lack of confidence in this area is evident. The second year treatment was less-well explained, with very few candidates calculating the appropriate probability-weighted allowance. The net increase in this allowance was rarely presented. Explanations tended to be too brief or, if provided, were not applicable to the scenario. The focus tended to be on calculations despite the requirement explicitly asking for "calculation and discussion". Weaker answers presented a table of discounted cashflows, or recommended treatment at fair value through profit or loss, which illustrated a lack of preparation in this area.

5 LUPLOID (SEP/DEC 2019)  *Walk in the footsteps of a top tutor*

Key answer tips

Question 1 always examines group accounting, but other issues will be tested as well. This question requires a good knowledge of IFRS 13 *Fair Value Measurement,* IAS 36 *Impairment of Assets* and IFRS 2 *Share-based Payment.*

Part (b) is worth 11 marks. To score well your answer must contain more than just a series of calculations. Explain how the impairment review is performed, which assets are written down, and where the impairment loss is recorded.

(a) (i) Fair value measurement

Tutorial note

Fair value measurement is a popular exam topic. Make sure that you know the definition of fair value.

IFRS 13 *Fair Value Measurement* defines fair value as the price which would be received to sell an asset or paid to transfer a liability in an orderly transaction between market participants at the measurement date. Fair value is therefore not supposed to be entity specific but rather market focused. Essentially the estimate is the amount that the market would be prepared to pay for the asset.

Tutorial note

The fair value of a non-financial asset should be determined based on its highest and best use. Non-financial assets include property, plant and equipment, inventories, intangible assets, and investment properties.

The market would consider all alternative uses for the assessment of the price which they would be willing to pay. For non-financial assets, fair value should therefore be measured by consideration of the highest and best use of the asset. There is a presumption that the current use would be the highest and best use unless evidence exists to the contrary.

The highest and best use of the asset appears to be as residential property and not the current industrial use. The intentions of Colyson Co are not relevant as fair value is not entity specific. The alternative use would need to be based upon fair and reasonable assumptions. In particular, it would be necessary to ensure that planning permission to demolish the factory and convert into residential properties would be likely. Since several nearby sites have been given such permission, this would appear to be the case.

The fair value of the factory site should be valued as if converted into residential use. Since this cannot be determined on a stand-alone basis, the combined value of the land and buildings is calculated. The $1 million demolition and planning costs should be deducted from the market value of $24 million. The fair value of the land and buildings should be $23 million. The fair value of the identifiable net assets at acquisition are $88 million ($65m + $23m).

Depreciated replacement cost

Depreciated replacement cost should only be considered as a possible method for estimating the fair value of the asset when other more suitable methods are not available. This may be the case when the asset is highly specialised. This is not the case with the factory site. Depreciation is unlikely to be an accurate reflection of all forms of obsolescence including physical deterioration. Moreover, the rise in value of land and properties particularly for residential use would mean that to use depreciated replacement cost would most likely undervalue the asset.

(ii) Goodwill calculations

Tutorial note

This part of the question only asked for 'calculations'. No marks are awarded for discussion of the goodwill calculations.

Goodwill should be calculated as follows:

	Fair value method	Proportional method
	$m	$m
Consideration	90	90
Non-controlling interest (NCI) at acquisition	22	17.6
Net assets at acquisition	(88)	(88)
Goodwill	24	19.6

NCI at acquisition under proportional method is $17.6m (20% × $88m).

The fair value of the net assets at acquisition is $88m as per part (a) (i) ($65m + $23m).

(b) Impairment

An impairment arises where the carrying amount of the net assets exceeds the recoverable amount.

Where the cash flows cannot be independently determined for individual assets, they should be assessed as a cash generating unit. That is the smallest group of assets which independently generate cash flows. Impairments of cash generating units are allocated first to goodwill and then to the other assets in proportion to their carrying amounts. No asset should be reduced below its recoverable amount.

Fair value method

The overall impairment of Colyson Co is $30 million ($106m + goodwill $24m – $100m).

The damaged building should be impaired by $4 million with a corresponding charge to profit or loss. Since $4 million has already been allocated to the land and buildings, $26 million of impairment loss remains to be allocated.

The full $24 million of goodwill should be written off and expensed in the consolidated statement of profit or loss.

Of the remaining $2 million impairment ($30m – $4m – $24m), $1.25 million will be allocated to the plant and machinery ((15/(15 + 9)) × 2m) and $0.75 million will be allocated to the remaining intangibles ((9/(9 + 15)) × 2m). As no assets have been previously revalued, all the impairments are charged to profit or loss.

Tutorial note

If the NCI has been measured at fair value at acquisition then 'full goodwill' has been calculated (i.e. the goodwill attributable to the owners of the parent company and the goodwill attributable to the NCI). As such, the NCI must be attributed its share of the goodwill impairment charge.

Of the impairment loss, $24 million (80% × $30m) will be attributable to the owners of Luploid Co and $6 million (20% × $30m) to the NCI in the consolidated statement of profit or loss.

The allocation of the impairment is summarised in this table:

	Original CA	**Impairment**	**Revised CA**
	$m	$m	$m
Land and buildings	60	(4.00)	56
Plant and machinery	15	(1.25)	13.75
Intangibles other than goodwill	9	(0.75)	8.25
Goodwill	24	(24.00)	0
Current assets (at recoverable amount)	22	–	22
Total	130	(30)	100

Proportionate method

The basic principles and rule for impairment is the same as the fair value method and so $4 million will again first be written off against the land and buildings.

When NCI is measured using the proportional share of net assets, no goodwill attributable to the NCI is recognised. This means that the goodwill needs to be grossed up when an impairment review is performed so that it is comparable with the recoverable amount.

The goodwill of $19.6 million is grossed up by 100/80 to a value of $24.5 million. This extra $4.9 million is known as notional goodwill. The overall impairment is now $30.5 million ($106m + $24.5m – $100m) of which $4 million has already been allocated to land and buildings.

Since the remaining impairment of $26.5 million ($30.5m – $4m) exceeds the total notional goodwill, this is written down to zero. However, as only $19.6 million goodwill is recognised within the consolidated accounts, the impairment attributable to the notional goodwill is not recognised. The impairment charged in the consolidated statement of profit or loss is therefore $19.6 million and this is fully attributable to the owners of Luploid Co.

Of the remaining $2 million ($30.5m – $4m – $24.5m), $1.25 million will be allocated to the plant and machinery (15/(15 + 9) × 2m) and $0.75 million will be allocated to the remaining intangibles (9/(9 + 15) × 2m). As no assets have been previously revalued, all the impairments are charged to profit or loss.

Tutorial note

If goodwill is calculated using the proportionate method, then the goodwill impairment recognised in the consolidated financial statements is all attributable to the owners of the parent company. However, any impairment loss related to other assets must be allocated between the owners of the parent company and the non-controlling interest.

The impairment expense attributable to the owners of Luploid Co is $24.4 million ($19.6m goodwill impairment + (80% × ($4m building + $2m plant and machinery and other intangibles))). The impairment expense attributable to the NCI is $1.2 million (20% × $6m). This is summarised below:

	Original CA	**Impairment**	**Revised CA**
	$m	$m	$m
Land and buildings	60	(4.00)	56
Plant and machinery	15	(1.25)	13.75
Intangibles other than goodwill	9	(0.75)	8.25
Goodwill	19.6	(19.60)	0
(Notional goodwill)	4.9	(4.90)	0
Current assets (at recoverable amount)	22	–	22
Total	130.5	(30.5)	100

(c) (i) Consideration

IFRS 3 *Business Combinations* requires all consideration to be measured at fair value on acquisition of a subsidiary.

Deferred shares should be measured at the fair value at the acquisition date with subsequent changes in fair value ignored. Luploid Co will issue 2.4 million (60% × 10m × 2/5) shares as consideration. The market price at the date of acquisition was $30, so the total fair value is $72 million (2.4m × $30).

Since Luploid Co is obliged to replace the share-based scheme of Hammond Co on acquisition, the replacement scheme should also be included as consideration (but only up to the fair value of the original scheme as at 1 July 20X7). The fair value of the replacement scheme at the grant date was $18 million. However the fair value of the original Hammond Co scheme at the acquisition date was only $15 million. As such, only $15 million should be added to the consideration.

The total consideration should be valued as $87 million ($72m + $15m).

(ii) Expense related to replacement scheme

The $3 million ($18m – $15m) not included within the consideration (see above) should be treated as part of the post-acquisition remuneration package for the employees and measured in accordance with IFRS 2 *Share-based Payment*. As there are no further vesting conditions it should be recognised as a post-acquisition expense immediately.

Expense related to additional scheme

Tutorial note

When dealing share-based payment questions, students tend to provide answers that are wholly numerical. Make sure that you discuss and apply the principles from IFRS 2 Share-based Payments or you will miss out on some very easy marks.

The condition relating to the share price of Luploid Co is a market based vesting condition. These are adjusted for in the calculation of the fair value at the grant date of the option. An expense is therefore recorded in the consolidated profit or loss of Luploid Co (and a corresponding credit to equity) irrespective of whether the market based vesting condition is met or not.

The additional two years' service is a non-market based vesting condition. The expense and credit to equity should be adjusted over the vesting period as expectations change regarding the non-market based vesting condition.

The correct charge to the profit or loss and credit to equity in the year ended 30 June 20X8 is $9.6 million ((10,000 × 96%) × 100 × $20 × ½).

ACCA marking guide

			Marks
(a)	(i)	– application of the following discussion to the scenario:	
		how FV should be determined	5
		why depreciation replacement cost is unsuitable	2
			7
	(ii)	– calculation marks for:	
		correct FV of net assets	1
		correct NCI figures	2
			3
(b)		– discussion of what constitutes an impairment and CGUs	2
		– correct calculation of impairment losses for both methods	2
		– notional goodwill	1
		– impairment allocation	3
		– discussion of how and why methods differ	3
			11
(c)	(i)	– calculation FV of deferred shares	1
		– calculation of FV of options	1
		– discussion of the above calculations and application to the scenario	2
			4
	(ii)	– calculation share expense	1
		– application of the following discussion to the scenario:	
		Calculations	2
		vesting conditions	2
			5
Total			**30**

Examiner's comments

Answers to part (a) (i) were generally good, with most candidates outlining the methods by which fair value is determined under IFRS 13. 11 marks were available for part (b) and most answers allocated an appropriate amount of their answer to this part. Whilst almost all answers described the basic impairment process, a surprising number of candidates excluded goodwill from their impairment calculation. This may have limited their opportunities for marks, particularly where their explanations did not explain the process by which an impairment loss is allocated to assets of a cash generating unit. Very few candidates explained the need for grossing-up goodwill under the net assets NCI valuation method, and how this is then allocated between group and NCI. Explanations of how the impairment loss is apportioned between group and NCI were generally quite basic. Indeed, most candidates identified that there is no goodwill attributable to NCI under the proportion of net assets valuation, but then suggested none of the impairment need be apportioned to NCI).

Part (c) (i) required an explanation of how consideration in the form of shares in a second acquisition should be valued. Most answers correctly calculated the fair value of the share exchange. Part (c) (ii) asked for the resulting share-based expense and a discussion of the vesting conditions; unfortunately this was less-well answered.

6 CARBISE (MAR/JUN 2019)  *Walk in the footsteps of a top tutor*

Key answer tips

This question examines the topic of overseas subsidiaries. As should be expected, the question requires the calculation of key figures in the consolidated financial statements (such as goodwill and foreign exchange differences), but also explanations of the accounting principles behind those calculations.

(a) Subject: Foreign subsidiary Bikelite

(i) Presentation currency

Tutorial note

Start off with the definition of presentation currency.

The presentation currency is the currency in which the financial statements are presented. IAS 21 *The Effects of Changes in Foreign Exchange Rates* permits an entity to present its individual financial statements in any currency. It would therefore be up to the directors of Bikelite to choose a presentation currency for its individual financial statements. Factors which might be considered include the currency used by major shareholders and the currency in which debt finance is primarily raised.

Functional currency

Tutorial note

Start off with the definition of functional currency.

The functional currency is the currency of the primary economic environment in which the entity operates. Since transactions are initially recorded in an entity's functional currency, the results and financial position would need to be retranslated where this differed to the presentation currency.

Tutorial note

Remember that a subsidiary is likely to have the same functional currency as its parent if certain factors apply – such as if the subsidiary operates with little autonomy from its parent.

When determining the functional currency of Bikelite, consideration should first be given to whether the functional currency of Bikelite should be the same as Carbise, at least whilst under the control of Carbise.

It appears that Bikelite has considerable autonomy over its activities. Despite being acquired to make more efficient use of the surplus inventory of Carbise, purchases from Carbise were only 5% of Bikelite's total purchases. Revenue is invoiced in a range of currencies suggesting a geographically diverse range of customers which, although this allows Carbise access to new international markets, is unlikely to be classified as an extension of the parent's operations. The volume of the transactions involved between Carbise and Bikelite would seem to be far too low to come to this conclusion. Bikelite also appears free to retain cash in a range of currencies and is not obliged to remit the cash to Carbise in the form of dividends. Nor does Bikelite appear to be dependent on financing from Carbise with other investors taking up the bond issue at the start of 20X6. The functional currency of Bikelite is not necessarily the same as Carbise.

Tutorial note

State the primary factors used to determine functional currency and then apply them to the scenario.

In determining its functional currency, Bikelite should consider the following primary factors: the currency which mainly influences the sales price for their goods, the currency of the country whose competitive forces and regulations determine the sales price and also the currency which influences labour, material and overhead costs. The key determinant here is the currency which the majority of the transactions are settled in. Bikelite invoices and is invoiced in a large range of currencies and so it would not be immediately clear as to the appropriate functional currency. Nor is there detail about whether there is a currency in which competitive forces and regulations could be important. We do not know, for example, what currency Bikelite's major competitors invoice in.

Tutorial note

If the primary factors used to determine functional currency are inconclusive then an entity must apply secondary factors.

Secondary factors include the currency in which financing activities are obtained and the currency in which receipts from operating activities are retained. Funds were raised in dinars from the bond issue and so it would appear that the dinar should probably be the functional currency for Bikelite.

(ii) Goodwill

Tutorial note

Be careful – the acquisition of the subsidiary was not in the current year. The question asks you for the current year foreign exchange gain on goodwill, not the cumulative gain.

Goodwill in dinars on the acquisition of Bikelite would be dinar 42 million. This is calculated as follows:

	Dinars millions
Consideration	100
FV of NCI	22
Less net assets at acquisition (60 + 20)	(80)
Goodwill at acquisition	42

On acquisition, the goodwill in dollars would have been $84 million (dinar 42m/0.5).

An impairment of dinars 6 million arose in the year ended 31 December 20X5.

Tutorial note

This would have been translated at the average rate in the prior reporting period. The impairment charge of $15 million (dinar 6m/0.4) would have been recorded in the statement of profit or loss in the prior period.

The remaining goodwill of dinars 36 million (dinars 42m – dinars 6m) would have been translated as at 31 December 20X5 using the closing rate of $1:0.38. Goodwill in the consolidated statement of financial position as at 31 December 20X5 would have been $94.7 million (dinars 36m/0.38).

Goodwill of dinar 36 million at 30 September 20X6 will be translated at the rate on that date of $1:0.35. This amounts to $102.9 million (dinars 36m/0.35).

This is summarised below:

	Dinar millions	**rate**	**$ millions**
Goodwill at 31 December 20X5 (dinar 42m – dinar 6m)	36	0.38	94.7
Exchange gain (bal. fig.)			**8.2**
Goodwill at 30 September 20X6	36	0.35	102.9

The exchange gain arising in the current year is therefore $8.2 million ($102.9m – $94.7m).

(iii) Explanation of goodwill calculation and exchange gain

Tutorial note

You need to briefly explain how to calculate goodwill ***and*** *the treatment of the foreign exchange differences arising on its retranslation. Make sure you identify all the requirements or you will lose easy marks.*

On a business combination, goodwill is calculated by comparing the fair value of the consideration plus non-controlling interests (NCI) at acquisition with the fair value of the identifiable net assets at acquisition.

An adjustment of dinar 20 million is required to the property of Bikelite to ensure the net assets at acquisition are properly measured at fair value.

Carbise measures NCI using the fair value method. This means that goodwill attributable to the NCI is included within the overall calculation of goodwill.

At each year end, all assets (including goodwill) and liabilities are retranslated using the closing rate of exchange. Exchange differences arising on the retranslation are recorded within other comprehensive income. Since the non-controlling interest is measured under the fair value method, the exchange difference would be apportioned 80%/20% between the owners of Carbise and the non-controlling interest.

Tutorial note

If the non-controlling interest had been valued at its proportionate share of the fair value of the subsidiary's identifiable net assets, then the foreign exchange gain on goodwill would have been wholly attributable to the owners of Cabrise.

Only the current year exchange difference would be recorded within other comprehensive income for the year ended 31 December 20X6. The cumulative exchange differences on goodwill at 30 September 20X6 (i.e. the exchange gain in the prior and current period) would be held in equity prior to the disposal of Bikelite.

(b) Exchange differences on net assets and profit

Tutorial note

Easy marks are available for explaining ***why*** *foreign exchange differences arise.*

The net assets of Bikelite would have been retranslated each year at the closing rate of exchange. There is therefore an exchange difference arising each year by comparing the opening net assets at the opening rate of exchange with the opening net assets at the closing rate of exchange.

An additional exchange difference arises through the profit or loss of Bikelite each year being translated at the average rate of exchange in the consolidated statement of comprehensive income. The profit or loss will increase or decrease the net assets of Bikelite respectively which, as is indicated above, will be translated at the closing rate of exchange for inclusion in the consolidated statement of financial position.

As with goodwill, the current year exchange differences are presented in other comprehensive income with 80% attributable to the shareholders of Carbise and 20% to the NCI. Cumulative exchange differences will be included in equity on the consolidated statement of financial position.

Tutorial note

The figures from the separate financial statements of Bikelite will not include any consolidation adjustments.

The carrying amount of the net assets of Bikelite in the separate financial statements on 1 January 20X6 was dinar 48 million. This would not include the dinar 20 million fair value adjustment, or subsequent depreciation arising on this. The carrying amount of Bikelite's opening net assets in the consolidated financial statements would therefore be dinar 64 million (dinar 48 + (dinar 20 million × 16/20)).

Bikelite would only be consolidated for the first nine months of the year because Carbise loses control on 30 September 20X6. Losses per the separate financial statements for the year ended 31 December 20X6 were dinar 8 million, so only dinar 6 million would be consolidated. Additional depreciation of dinar 0.75 million (dinar 20m/20 × 9/12) would be charged for the first nine months of the year in the consolidated financial statements. Therefore, the total loss of Bikelite in the consolidated financial statements is dinar 6.75 million.

Net assets at disposal in dinars would therefore be dinar 57.25 million (dinar 64 – dinar 6.75).

Tutorial note

It is important to learn the pro-formas for calculating foreign exchange differences. Remember that a profit in the period will increase the opening net assets, but a loss will reduce the opening net assets. Profits and losses are translated at the average rate.

The exchange gain for the year ended 31 December 20X6 would be $13.4 million calculated as follows:

	$ millions
Opening net assets at opening rate (dinar 64/0.38)	168.4
Loss for 9 months at average rate (dinar 6.75/0.37)	(18.2)
Current year exchange gain (bal. fig.)	13.4
Net assets at 30 September 20X6 (dinar 57.25/0.35)	163.6

This exchange gain is presented in other comprehensive income. Of the total, $10.7 million is attributable to the shareholders of Carbise (80% × $13.4m) and $2.7 million to the NCI.

Tutorial note

Don't be too disheartened if you make mistakes in your calculations. Lots of students would forget to adjust the opening net assets and loss of Bakelite for the impact of the fair value adjustment. Those students would still score marks for demonstrating knowledge of the key principles involved when translating an overseas subsidiary.

(c) (i) Group profit or loss on disposal on Bikelite

Tutorial note

This is an important pro-forma to learn. You will not be penalised if your figures from previous parts of the question are incorrect. Lots of students would forget to reclassify the group's share of the previously recognised foreign exchange gains to profit or loss.

	$ millions
Proceeds	150
Net assets at disposal (see (b))	(163.6)
Goodwill at disposal (see (a)(ii))	(102.9)
NCI at disposal (see calc. below)	48.5
Exchange gains recycled to profit and loss	76.6
Group profit on disposal	8.6

Workings

Exchange gains at 1 January 20X6 per the question are $74.1 million. Current year exchange differences on goodwill are $8.2 million (see (a)(ii)) and on the net assets are $13.4 million (see (b)). Cumulative exchange gains at 30 September 20X6 are therefore $95.7 million ($74.1m + $8.2m + $13.4m). On disposal, the parent's share should be recycled to profit or loss. This amounts to $76.6 million (80% × $95.7m).

NCI at disposal is calculated as follows:

	$ millions
NCI at 1 January 20X6 per question	47.8
NCI share of loss to 30 September 20X6 (20% × $18.2m (part (b)))	(3.6)
NCI share exchange gains for 9 months to 30 September 20X6 (20% × ($13.4m + $8.2m))	4.3
NCI at 30 September 20X6	48.5

(ii) Treatment and presentation of Bikelite

For the year ended 31 December 20X6, Carbise will consolidate Bikelite for the first nine months of the year up to the date of disposal of the shares and subsequent loss of control.

Exchange differences on the translation of the net assets, profits and goodwill in relation to the nine months to 30 September 20X6 will initially be recognised in other comprehensive income.

On 30 September 20X6, a consolidated profit or loss on disposal will be calculated in the consolidated financial statements of Carbise. In effect, the proceeds are compared to the net assets and unimpaired goodwill not attributable to the non-controlling interest at the disposal date. The cumulative exchange differences on the translation of Bikelite would be reclassified to profit or loss.

Tutorial note

The presentation of a subsidiary that has been sold during the period, or which is held for sale, depends on whether it qualifies as a discontinued operation. State the relevant principles used to determine whether a component of a business is a 'discontinued operation', and then apply these to the scenario.

Consideration should be given as to whether the disposal of Bikelite would be presented as a discontinued operation. According to IFRS 5 *Non-current Assets Held for Sale and Discontinued Operations,* for Bikelite to be classified as a discontinued operation, it would need to represent a separate major line of business or geographical area of operations. Since Bikelite was initially acquired by Carbise to gain easier access to international markets, it is likely that the criterion would be met.

ACCA marking guide			
			Marks
(a)	(i)	– discussion of presentation and functional currency	2
		– application of the above discussion to the scenario	5
		Maximum	7
	(ii)	– calculation of goodwill	2
		– calculation of the exchange difference on goodwill	3
			5
	(iii)	– explanation of the goodwill calculation and application to the scenario	2
		– explanation of the exchange gain and application to the scenario	2
		Maximum	4
(b)	– explanation of Bikelite exchange differences		3
	– calculation of Bikelite exchange differences for y/e 20X6:		
	translation		3
	split between parent and NCI		1
		Maximum	7
(c)	– calculation of group profit or loss on disposal		3
	– explanation of the accounting treatment of Bikelite		4
Total			**30**

Examiner's comments

In the first part, weak answers tended to list the factors determining the functional currency with little application to the scenario.

The technical parts of a consolidation, in this case part (ii), are generally well-answered although some candidates are often less prepared to perform a translation from a foreign currency. Likewise, explanations of calculations within the consolidation process, part (iii), are often well-answered provided that the calculations have been performed well. Although the question is broken into several sections, some candidates insist on answering as if it is one question. Candidates are advised against this because it makes it difficult for markers to mark.

7 MOYES (DEC 2018)  *Walk in the footsteps of a top tutor*

Key answer tips

This question examines consolidated statements of cash flow. However, note that the calculation of cash generated from operations was only worth six marks. In contrast, discussion of the adjustments made to profit before tax (part (a) (ii)) and discussion of the impact of a change in group structure (part (b)) were worth twelve marks. To succeed in SBR, you must feel confident with the discursive requirements.

When preparing a statement of cash flows (or extracts from the statement), pay careful attention to whether the figures need brackets.

(a) Explanatory note to: The directors of Moyes

Subject: Cash flows generated from operations

(i) Cash generated from operations

Tutorial note

Make sure that your reconciliation is clearly labelled. This will help the markers to award you credit if you have made mistakes.

	$m
Profit before tax	209
Share of profit of associate	(67)
Service cost component	24
Contributions into the pension scheme	(15)
Impairment of goodwill	10
Depreciation	99
Impairment of property, plant and equipment ($43m – $20m)	23
Reduction in inventories ($126m – $165m + $6m)	33
Loss on inventory	6
Increase in receivables	(7)
Increase in payables	18
Cash generated from operations	333

Tutorial note

Note that the same answer would have been obtained if no separate adjustment was made for the $6 million loss on inventories and if the reduction in inventories was presented as $39 million ($126m – $165m).

(ii) Explanation of adjustments

Tutorial note

Work through your calculation of cash generated from operations and discuss the rationale behind each adjustment you have made to profit before tax.

Indirect method

Cash flows from operating activities are principally derived from the key trading activities of the entity. This would include cash receipts from the sale of goods, cash payments to suppliers and cash payments on behalf of employees. The indirect method adjusts profit or loss for the effects of transactions of a non-cash nature, any deferrals or accruals from past or future operating cash receipts or payments and any items of income or expense associated with investing or financing cash flows.

Associate

The share of profit of associate is an item of income associated with investing activities and so has been deducted.

Non-cash flows

Non-cash flows which have reduced profit and must subsequently be added back include the service cost component, depreciation, exchange losses and impairments. With the impairment of property, plant and equipment, the first $20 million of impairment will be allocated to the revaluation surplus so only $23 million would have reduced operating profits and should be added back.

Pension

In relation to the pension scheme, the remeasurement component can be ignored as it is neither a cash flow nor an expense to operating profits. Cash contributions should be deducted, though, as these represent an operating cash payment ultimately to be received by Moyes' employees. Benefits paid to retired employees are a cash outflow for the pension scheme rather than for Moyes and so should be ignored.

Working capital

The movements on receivables, payables and inventory are adjusted so that the timing differences between when cash is paid or received and when the items are accrued in the financial statements are accounted for.

Inventory is measured at the lower of cost and net realisable value. The inventory has suffered an overall loss of $6 million (Dinar 80 million/5 – Dinar 60 million/6). This is not a cash flow and would be added back to profits in the reconciliation. However, the loss of $6 million should also be adjusted in the year-on-year inventory movements. The net effect of this on the statement of cash flows will be nil.

(b) Change in structure

Tutorial note

Students are generally good at dealing with changes in group structures in numerical questions. Make sure that you understand the principles behind the numerical treatment so that you are able to address discursive questions as well.

When the parent company acquires or sells a subsidiary during the financial year, cash flows arising from the acquisition or disposal are presented as investing activities.

In relation to Davenport, no cash consideration has been paid during the current year because the consideration consisted of a share for share exchange and deferred cash. The deferred cash would be presented as a negative cash flow within investing activities when paid in two years' time.

This does not mean that there would be no impact on the current year's statement of cash flows. On gaining control, Moyes would consolidate 100% of the assets and liabilities of Davenport which would presumably include some cash or cash equivalents at the date of acquisition. These would be presented as a cash inflow at the date of acquisition net of any overdrafts held at acquisition.

Adjustments would also need to be made to the opening balances of assets and liabilities by adding the fair values of the identifiable net assets at acquisition to the respective balances. This would be necessary to ensure that only the cash flow effects are reported in the consolidated statement of cash flows.

On the disposal of Barham, the net assets at disposal, including goodwill, are removed from the consolidated financial statements. Since Barham is overdrawn, this will have a positive cash flow effect for the group. The overdraft will be added to the proceeds (less any cash and cash equivalents at disposal) to give an overall inflow presented in investing activities. Care would once again be necessary to ensure that all balances at the disposal date are removed from the corresponding assets and liabilities so that only cash flows are recorded within the consolidated statement of cash flows.

Dividends

Tutorial note

The question asked about changes in group structure and dividends. Make sure that you address both aspects. The examining team regularly comment that students fail to address all parts of the exam questions.

Dividends received by Moyes from Davenport are not included in the consolidated statement of cash flows since cash has in effect been transferred from one group member to another.

The non-controlling interest's share of the dividend would be presented as a cash outflow in financing activities.

(c) Assets held for sale

Tutorial note

Start with the definition of an asset held for sale and then apply it to the scenario.

IFRS 5 *Non-current Assets Held for Sale and Discontinued Operations* defines an asset held for sale as one where the carrying amount will be recovered principally through a sales transaction. To be classified as held for sale, a sale has to be highly probable and the asset should be available for sale in its present condition.

At face value, Watson would not appear to meet this definition as no sales transaction is to take place.

IFRS 5 does not explicitly extend the requirements for held for sale to situations where control is lost. However, the Board have confirmed that in instances where control is lost, the subsidiary's assets and liabilities should be derecognised. Loss of control is a significant economic event and fundamentally changes the investor–investee relationship. Therefore situations where the parent is committed to lose control should trigger a reclassification as held for sale. Whether this should be extended to situations where control is lost to other causes would be judgemental. It is possible therefore that Watson should be classified as held for sale.

Discontinued operations

Tutorial note

Start with the definition of an asset held for sale and then apply it to the scenario. Remember you were asked to discuss both Barham and Watson.

IFRS 5 defines a discontinued operation as a component of an entity which either has been disposed of or is classified as held for sale, and

(i) represents a separate major line of business or geographical area of operations, or

(ii) is a single co-ordinated plan to dispose of a separate major line or area of operations, or

(iii) is a subsidiary acquired exclusively for resale.

Barham has been sold during the year but there appears to be other subsidiaries which operate in similar geographical regions and produce similar products. Little guidance is given as to what would constitute a separate major line of business or geographical area of operations. The definition is subjective and the directors should consider factors such as materiality and relevance before determining whether Barham should be presented as discontinued or not.

The same is true for Watson. Assuming it can be classified as held for sale, it would need to be a separate major line of business or geographical area of operation to be presented as a discontinued operation.

(d) Probability

Tutorial note

This question requires knowledge of the recognition criteria in a range of IFRS and IAS Standards, as well as in the Conceptual Framework. This content is core. If your knowledge here is lacking then you should revisit the Study Text.

Different accounting standards use different levels of probabilities to discuss when assets and liabilities should be recognised in the financial statements. For example, economic benefits from property, plant and equipment and intangible assets need to be probable to be recognised; to be classified as held for sale, the sale has to be highly probable.

Under IAS 37 *Provisions, Contingent Liabilities and Contingent Assets,* a provision should only be recognised if an outflow of economic resources is probable. Contingent assets, on the other hand, can only be recognised if the inflow is economic benefits is virtually certain. This could lead to a situation where two sides of the same court case have two different accounting treatments despite the likelihood of pay-out being identical for both parties.

Contingent consideration transferred on a business combination is recognised in the financial statements regardless of the level of probability. Instead the fair value is adjusted to reflect the level of uncertainty of the contingent consideration.

Tutorial note

The Conceptual Framework has been recently revised. Ensure your knowledge is up-to-date.

In the 2018 *Conceptual Framework*, the Board confirmed a new approach to recognition which requires decisions to be made with reference to the qualitative characteristics of financial information. The *Conceptual Framework* says than an item is recognised if it meets the definition of an element and if recognition provides users of financial statements with:

- relevant information
- a faithful representation of the asset or liability.

The key change in the 2018 *Conceptual Framework* was therefore to remove the probability criterion. The *Conceptual Framework* will inform the revision of current IFRS and IAS Standards as well as the development of new standards, and this may mean that more assets and liabilities with a low probability of inflow or outflow of economic resources will be recognised in the future. The Board accepts that prudence could still mean there will be inconsistencies in the recognition of assets and liabilities within financial reporting standards but may be a necessary consequence of providing investors and lenders with the most useful information.

Marking guide

			Marks
(a)	–	calculation of cash flow generated from operations	6
	–	explanation of the adjustments and use of the scenario	6
			12
(b)	–	application of the following discussion to the scenario:	
		purchase consideration (shares and deferred cash)	1
		impact on consolidated statement of cash flows of:	
		subsidiary acquisition (including dividend)	3
		subsidiary disposal	2
			6
(c)	–	IFRS 5 definition of discontinued operation and application to the scenario	3
	–	consideration of held for sale and application to the scenario	1
	–	consideration of loss of control and application to the scenario	2
			6
(d)	–	inconsistent application of the probability criterion (including examples)	3
	–	Conceptual Framework	3
			6
Total			**30**

Examiner's comments

Statements of cash flow will be examined regularly in the SBR exam as they form part of the group accounting aspect of the syllabus. Many candidates ignored the fact that they had to draft an explanatory note and simply showed the calculation of cash generated from operations. Some candidates showed the accounting entries for the various elements set out in the question even though this was not required. The maximum marks available for simply showing the calculation was 6 marks which represented only half of the marks for this part of the question. To gain these marks, candidates had to ensure that the cash flow adjustments were in the right direction. For example, depreciation had to be added back to profit before tax and not deducted in order to gain credit. Candidates performed well on this part of the question, gaining full marks in many cases.

The second part of the question required an explanation of how the changes to the group structure and dividend would impact upon the consolidated statement of cash flows. This aspect of the syllabus has historically been examined as a calculation but in this exam, candidates were required to explain the principles behind the adjustments to the statement of cash flows. Where attempts were made at explanations in this question then candidates performed quite well.

The third part of the question required candidates to advise the directors as to the held for sale and discontinued operation classifications. It is important for candidates to realise that there is only a small number of marks available for simply setting out the rules in IFRS 5 and that the majority of the marks are awarded for the application of the principles in the standard. Also, the question asked for a discussion of both held for sale and discontinued operation criteria and thus it is important for candidates to deal with both issues. However, several candidates focussed on held for sale with little discussion of discontinued operations.

8 BANANA (SEP 2018)  *Walk in the footsteps of a top tutor*

Key answer tips

This question examines core issues in group accounting, such as the calculation of goodwill and the accounting treatment of associates.

In SBR you will be asked to 'discuss' the correct accounting treatment of transactions. Calculations are not enough to pass the exam.

Part (c) tests financial instrument derecognition issues. This is a common exam topic. Make sure that you know the key principles that govern the classification, recognition, measurement, derecognition and impairment of financial instruments.

(a) (i) Goodwill

Tutorial note

This answer involves some calculations but the majority of it is discursive. If you neglect the discussion element then you will not pass.

According to IFRS 3 *Business Combinations*, goodwill should be calculated by comparing the fair value of the consideration with the fair value of the identifiable net assets at acquisition.

The shares have been correctly valued using the market price of Banana at acquisition.

Contingent consideration should be included at its fair value which should be assessed taking into account the probability of the targets being achieved as well as being discounted to present value. It would appear reasonable to measure the consideration at a value of $4 million ($16 million × 25%). A corresponding liability should be included within the consolidated financial statements with subsequent remeasurement. This would be adjusted prospectively to profit or loss rather than adjusting the consideration and goodwill.

The finance director has measured the non-controlling interest using the proportional method rather than at fair value. Although either method is permitted on an acquisition by acquisition basis, the accounting policy of the Banana group is to measure non-controlling interest at fair value. The fair value of the non-controlling interest at acquisition is $17 million (20% × 20 million × $4.25).

Net assets at acquisition were incorrectly included at their carrying amount of $70 million. This should be adjusted to fair value of $75 million with a corresponding $5 million increase to land in the consolidated statement of financial position.

Tutorial note

Goodwill calculations are a common exam topic. Learn the pro-forma.

Goodwill should have been calculated as follows:

	$m
Fair value of share exchange	68
Contingent consideration	4
Add NCI at acquisition	17
Less net assets at acquisition	(75)
Goodwill at acquisition	14

The correcting entry required to the consolidated financial statements is:

Dr Goodwill	\$2 million
Dr Land	\$5 million
Cr Non-controlling interest	\$3 million
Cr Liabilities	\$4 million

Tutorial note

Make sure that your debits and credits balance.

If you don't feel comfortable with debits and credits then you could refer to increases or decreases instead.

(ii) Equity accounting

Tutorial note

There is only one mark available for the correct calculation of the associate's carrying amount. The discussion element is crucial.

If an entity holds 20% or more of the voting power of the investee, it is presumed that the entity has significant influence unless it can be clearly demonstrated that this is not the case. The existence of significant influence by an entity is usually evidenced by representation on the board of directors or participation in key policy making processes. Banana has 40% of the equity of Strawberry and can appoint one director to the board. It would appear that Banana has significant influence but not control. Strawberry should be classified as an associate and be equity accounted for within the consolidated financial statements.

The equity method is a method of accounting whereby the investment is initially recognised at cost and adjusted thereafter for the post-acquisition change in the investor's share of the investee's net assets. The investor's profit or loss includes its share of the investee's profit or loss and the investor's other comprehensive income includes its share of the investee's other comprehensive income. At 1 October 20X6, Strawberry should have been included in the consolidated financial statements at a carrying amount of \$20.4 million (\$18 million + (40% × (\$50 million – \$44 million))).

(iii) Disposal

Tutorial note

Show all of your workings. Make sure they are clearly labelled.

On disposal of 75% of the shares, Banana no longer exercises significant influence over Strawberry and a profit on disposal of $3.1 million should have been calculated.

Tutorial note

You can still score full marks if you answer to part (ii) was incorrect. Markers apply the 'own figure rule'.

	$m
Proceeds	19.0
Fair value retained	4.5
Carrying amount of associate (part (ii))	(20.4)
Profit on disposal	3.1

Banana is incorrect to have recorded a loss in reserves of $14 million and this should be reversed. Instead, a gain of $3.1 million should have been included within the consolidated statement of profit or loss.

Tutorial note

The definition of a financial asset includes an investment in the equity shares of another entity. Lots of students forget this.

If no designation was made to measure the shares at fair value through other comprehensive income then Banana would measure them at fair value through profit or loss.

The retained 10% investment is a financial asset. Per IFRS 9 *Financial Instruments* it is initially recognised at fair value of $4.5 million. Banana does not intend to sell their remaining interest so, as long as they make an irrecoverable election, they can treat the remaining interest at fair value through other comprehensive income. The investment will be restated to its fair value of $4 million at the reporting date with a corresponding loss of $0.5 million reported in other comprehensive income.

(b) Melon

Tutorial note

If your conclusion differs from the one below then you can still score well. Make sure that you state the relevant rules from the accounting standard and then apply them to the scenario.

Melon should only be treated as an asset acquisition if it does not meet the definition of a business.

Tutorial note

State the definition of a business and then apply it to the scenario.

IFRS 3 *Business Combinations* defines a business as an integrated set of activities and assets that can be managed to provide goods or services, generate investment income (such as dividends or interest), or generate other income from ordinary activities. To meet this definition, the acquisition must comprise inputs and processes that significantly contribute to the **ability** to turn those inputs into outputs. To qualify as a business, outputs are not required.

Tutorial note

Don't forget the optional concentration test.

The Board has introduced an optional concentration test that helps entities to conclude whether an acquisition is **not** a business. The concentration test is met if substantially all of the fair value of the total assets acquired is concentrated in a single identifiable asset or group of similar identifiable assets.

In the case of Melon, two types of assets appear to have been acquired: a licence, and research activities. The research activities appear to be at a very early stage and, whilst in substance are very different in nature to the licence itself, are likely to be of relatively low value. It is therefore plausible that substantially all of the fair value is concentrated in the licence itself. If so, the acquisition would not be treated as a business combination.

Should it be determined that the research activities are of sufficient value then this means that not all the fair value is concentrated in a single asset. This would necessitate a more detailed assessment of the inputs and processes acquired.

The licence and the research activities are inputs. However, to qualify as a business, a process must have been acquired that would significantly contribute to the ability to turn these into output. Per IFRS 3 an acquired process is only substantive if:

- it is critical to convert an input to an output, and
- inputs acquired include a knowledgeable, skilled, organised workforce able to perform that process on other acquired inputs to produce outputs.

A skilled and knowledgeable workforce with the ability to complete the research has not been acquired because there are no employees and the outsourcing contracts have expired. As such, Banana has not acquired a substantive process. The directors' proposal to treat Melon as an asset purchase, rather than a business combination, was therefore correct.

(c) Bonds

Tutorial note

The bonds have been 'sold' so a key issue in this question concerns derecognition. In other words, should the financial asset be removed from the statement of financial position? Begin your answer with the rules governing derecognition from IFRS 9 Financial Instruments. Then apply these rules to the bond sale.

IFRS 9 *Financial Instruments* requires that a financial asset only qualifies for derecognition once the entity has transferred the contractual rights to receive the cash flows from the asset or where the entity has retained the contractual rights but has an unavoidable obligation to pass on the cash flows to a third party. The substance of the disposal of the bonds needs to be assessed by a consideration of the risks and rewards of ownership.

Banana has not transferred the contractual rights to receive the cash flows from the bonds. The third party is obliged to return the coupon interest to Banana and to pay additional amounts should the fair values of the bonds increase. Consequently, Banana still has the rights associated with the interest and will also benefit from any appreciation in the value of the bonds. Banana still retains the risks of ownership as it has to compensate the third party should the fair value of the bonds depreciate in value.

If the sale were a genuine transfer of risks and rewards of ownership, then the sales price would be approximate to the fair value of the bonds. It would only be in unusual circumstances, such as a forced sale of Banana's assets arising from severe financial difficulties, that this would not be the case. The sales price of $8 million is well below the current fair value of the bonds of $10.5 million. Additionally, Banana is likely to exercise their option to repurchase the bonds.

It can be concluded that no transfer of rights has taken place and therefore the asset should not be derecognised.

Tutorial note

Once you have reached a conclusion about derecognition then you need to think in more detail about the specific financial statement impact of the transaction in the year ended 30 June 20X7.

To measure the asset at amortised cost, the entity must have a business model where they intend to collect the contractual cash flows over the life of the asset. Banana maintains these rights and therefore the sale does not contradict its business model. The bonds should continue to be measured at amortised cost in the consolidated financial statements of Banana.

The carrying amount of the bonds at 30 June 20X6 would have been $10.2 million ($10 million + (7% × $10m) – (5% × $10m)). Amortised cost prohibits restatement to fair value. The carrying amount of the bonds at 30 June 20X7 should be $10.4 million ($10.2m + (7% × $10.2m) – (5% × $10m)).

The proceeds received of $8 million should be recognised as a financial liability measured at amortised cost. An interest charge of $0.8 million would accrue between 1 July 20X6 and 1 July 20X8, being the difference between the sale and repurchase price of the bonds.

Marking scheme

			Marks
(a)	(i)	Goodwill and contingent consideration	3
		Why existing goodwill calculation is incorrect	3
		Correct calculation and entry	2
			8
	(ii)	Significant influence	2
		Equity accounting	1
		Carrying amount	1
			4
	(iii)	Calculation of gain	1
		Rationale for gain	1
		Correct treatment after disposal	2
			4
(b)		Discussion of business combinations	**7**
(c)		Consideration of IFRS 9 principles	4
		Transfer of rights/conclusions	1
		Carrying amount of bonds	2
			7
Total			**30**

Examiner's comments

Many candidates gained high marks in the first part, provided they separated the complex calculations from their explanations. Techniques such as producing the calculations on one page whilst simultaneously explaining them on a second page proved an efficient exam technique. Whilst most candidates are naturally drawn to the numbers, most of the marks in this section were allocated to the explanation and the application of IFRS 3 *Business Combinations*. Weak answers to (i) provided insufficient explanation of the accounting treatment relating to each aspect of the goodwill calculation, for which marks were available if explained. Part (ii) was generally well-answered although in some cases the carrying amount of the associate was overlooked or incorrect. In part (iii) explanations were generally good, although the disposal calculation was often incorrect (for example, omitting the fair value of the retained investment).

Part (b) was generally weak. Many answers focused on defining an asset, with minimal reference to the requirements of a business combination under IFRS 3. In part (c), providing that candidates identified the key aspect of substance, marks were awarded accordingly.

9 BUBBLE  *Walk in the footsteps of a top tutor*

Key answer tips

It is important to be able to calculate the exchange differences that arise when an overseas subsidiary is translated into the presentation currency of the group. Memorise the necessary pro-formas before attempting this question.

The consolidation question in the Strategic Business Reporting exam is likely to require both discussion and calculations. Easy marks can be obtained on the former, but students tend to prioritise the latter.

(a) (i) Goodwill

Tutorial note

The question asks you to 'advise'. Calculations alone are not sufficient to score full marks.

IFRS 3 *Business Combinations* says that goodwill is recognised at the acquisition date. It is calculated as the difference between:

- the total of the fair value of the consideration transferred to acquire control and the non-controlling interest, and
- the fair value of the subsidiary's identifiable net assets.

According to IAS 21 *The Effects of Changes in Foreign Exchange Rates*, goodwill arising on acquisition of foreign operations is treated as the foreign operation's asset. At each reporting date, it is translated at the closing rate of exchange. Goodwill should be reviewed for impairment annually.

Goodwill is calculated initially in foreign currency as follows:

	Dm
Fair value of consideration ($46m × 8)	368
NCI at acquisition (210m shares × 40% × 2.62 dinars)	220
Fair value of identifiable net assets (W1)	(488)
Goodwill at acquisition	100
Impairment (20%)	(20)
Goodwill at reporting date	80

The goodwill of Tyslar as at 31 October 20X5 is therefore $8.4 million (D80m/9.5).

(W1) Net assets at acquisition

	Dinars m
Share capital	210
Retained earnings	258
Fair value adjustment (70m – 50m)	20
	488

The subsidiary's net assets should be measured in the consolidated financial statements at fair value at the acquisition date. As such, the land carried at 50m dinars in the separate financial statements should be remeasured to 70m dinars (and then translated into dollars at the appropriate rate).

(ii) Translation reserve

Foreign exchange differences arise when translating Tyslar into the presentation currency of the group. This is because:

- goodwill is retranslated every year at the closing rate
- the opening net assets are retranslated every year at the closing rate
- profit for the year is translated in the statement of profit or loss at the average rate but net assets in the statement of financial position are translated at the closing rate.

Exchange differences arising on the retranslation of an overseas subsidiary are recorded in other comprehensive income. They are presented as an item that may be reclassified to profit or loss in the future.

Exchange differences arising on the translation of the subsidiary's opening net assets and profit are attributable to the owners of the group and the non-controlling interest (NCI). Exchange differences arising on the translation of goodwill are attributable to the owners of the group and the NCI if the NCI at acquisition was valued at its fair value.

The exchange differences attributable to the owners of the group are held in a translation reserve in equity. This is calculated as follows:

	$m
Group share of goodwill forex loss (W2)	(1.0)
Group share of net asset and profit forex loss (W3)	(6.1)
	(7.1)

(W2) Exchange loss on Tyslar's goodwill

Tutorial note

If goodwill is calculated using the fair value method, the exchange gain or loss and any impairment must be apportioned between the group and the NCI.

	Dm	**Exchange rate**	$m
Opening (acquisition) goodwill (part (a) (i))	100	8.0	12.5
Impairment (part (a) (i))	(20)	8.5	(2.4)
Exchange loss (bal. fig)			(1.7)
Closing goodwill	80	9.5	8.4

Goodwill has been calculated using the fair value method. Therefore, the exchange loss must be allocated between the group and the NCI based on their respective shareholdings.

Group: $1.7m × 60% = $1.0m

NCI: $1.7m × 40% = $0.7m

(W3) Exchange loss on Tyslar's opening net assets and profit

Tutorial note

Make sure that you learn this pro-forma.

	Dm	**Exchange rate**	$m
Net assets at 1 Nov 20X4 (part (a) (i))	488	8.0	61.0
Profit for the year (D522m (W4) – D488m)	34	8.5	4.0
Exchange loss (bal. fig)			(10.1)
Net assets at 31 Oct 20X5 (W4)	522	9.5	54.9

The exchange loss on the opening net assets and profit must be allocated between the group and the NCI based on their respective shareholdings:

Group: $10.1m × 60% = $6.1m

NCI: $10.1m × 40% = $4.0m

(W4) Net assets at reporting date

	Dm
Share capital	210
Retained earnings	292
Fair value adjustment	20
	522

(iii) Overseas property

The property should have been recognised at $7 million, which is the fair value of the consideration transferred to acquire it. A profit on the disposal of the land of $2 million ($7m – $5m) should also have been recorded. The correcting entry is:

Dr PPE $2m

Cr P/L $2m

The staff relocation costs should not have been capitalised. The correcting entry is:

Dr P/L $0.5m

Cr PPE $0.5m

The building should be depreciated over its useful life, giving a current year charge of $0.1 million ($7m/35 × 6/12):

Dr P/L $0.1m

Cr PPE $0.1m

At the reporting date, the building should be revalued from its carrying amount of $6.9 million ($7m – $0.1m) to its fair value of $7.9 million (D75m/9.5). The gain is recorded in other comprehensive income. The entry to record it is:

Dr PPE $1.0m

Cr OCI $1.0m

The total property, plant and equipment balance is calculated as follows:

	$m
Bubble	280.0
Tyslar (D390/9.5)	41.1
Tyslar fair value adjustment (D20m/9.5)	2.1
PPE cost adjustment	2.0
Removal of incorrect costs	(0.5)
Depreciation	(0.1)
Revaluation	1.0
	325.6

(b) Functional currency

Tutorial note

Remember to state the rules (how is a functional currency determined) and then apply those rules to the scenario.

IAS 21 *The Effects of Changes in Foreign Exchange Rates* says that the functional currency is the currency of the primary economic environment in which the entity operates. The primary economic environment in which an entity operates is normally the one in which it primarily generates and expends cash.

The following factors should be considered in determining Tyslar's functional currency:

- The currency that mainly influences the determination of the sales prices
- The currency of the country whose competitive forces and regulations mainly influences operating costs.

The currency that dominates the determination of sales prices will normally be the currency in which the sales prices for goods and services are denominated and settled. In Tyslar's case, sale prices are influenced by local demand and supply, and are traded in dinars. Analysis of the revenue stream points to the dinar as being the functional currency. The cost analysis is indeterminate because the expenses are influenced by the dinar and the dollar.

IAS 21 also requires entities to consider secondary factors when determining the functional currency. These factors include the degree of autonomy and the independence of financing. Tyslar operates with a considerable degree of autonomy both financially and in terms of its management. Tyslar does not depend on the group for finance.

In conclusion, Tyslar's functional currency will be the dinar because its revenue is clearly influenced by the dinar.

Marking scheme		
		Marks
(a)	Goodwill calculation and discussion	7
	Group translation reserve	10
	Property, plant and equipment	7
(b)	Functional currency discussion – 1 mark per point	6
Total		**30**

10 JOCATT  *Walk in the footsteps of a top tutor*

Key answer tips

There are always easy marks in cash flow questions – read the question very carefully and you should find lots of figures that can be put straight into your pro-forma. Make sure that you get your brackets the right way around or you will lose marks.

(a) (i) Acquisition of Tigret

Jocatt obtained control over Tigret in stages (also known as a 'step acquisition'). On 30 June 20X2, Jocatt should have revalued the previous 8% investment to its fair value of $5 million and it in the goodwill calculation. This adjustment will increase goodwill by $5 million. A gain of $1 million ($5m – $4m) should have been recorded in the consolidated statement of profit or loss. The adjusting entry is:

Dr Goodwill $5m

Cr Financial assets $4m

Cr Profit or loss $1m

The identifiable net assets of TIgret at acquisition are consolidated at their fair value of $45 million. This creates a taxable temporary difference of $10 million because the carrying amount of the net assets in the consolidated financial statements exceeds the tax base of $35 million. A deferred tax liability arises for $3 million ($10m × 30%) in the consolidated statement of financial position. This is treated as part of the subsidiary's acquisition net assets and therefore goodwill at acquisition will also increase by $3 million:

Dr Goodwill $3m

Cr Deferred tax liabilities $3m

Goodwill at the acquisition date is calculated as follows:

	$m
Fair value of consideration ($15m + $15m)	30
Fair value of previous equity interest	5
Fair value of non-controlling interest	20
Fair value of net assets at acquisition (excl. deferred tax)	(45)
Deferred tax	3
Goodwill on acquisition	13

Tutorial note

An alternative calculation for goodwill would be:

$5m draft + $5m step acquisition adjustment + $3m deferred tax adjustment = $13 million

(ii) Extracts from Jocatt Group: Statement of Cash flows for the year ended 30 November 20X2

	$m	$m
Cash flows from operating activities:		
Profit before tax ($44m + $1m gain on Tigret)	45	
Finance costs	8	
Retirement benefit service cost	16	
Depreciation	27	
Gain on investment property (W2)	(2)	
Profit on sale of land ($19m – $10m)	(9)	
Impairment of goodwill (W1)	33	
Gain on Tigret	(1)	
Cash paid to retirement benefit scheme (W4)	(7)	
Decrease in trade receivables ($62m – $113m – $5m)	56	
Decrease in inventories ($105m – $128m)	23	
Increase in trade payables ($144m – $55m – $6m)	83	
Cash generated from operations		272
Interest paid ($8m – $2m interest on defined benefit plan)		(6)
Income taxes paid (W3)		(18)
		248
Cash flows from financing activities:		
Repayment of long-term borrowings ($71m – $67m)		(4)
Non-controlling interest dividend (per SOCIE)		(11)
Dividends paid by Jocatt (per SOCIE)		(5)
		(20)

Workings

(W1) Goodwill

Tutorial note

Reconcile the movement in the carrying amount of goodwill between the two reporting dates to calculate the impairment. This should be added back in the reconciliation between profit before tax and cash generated from operations.

	$m
Opening balance at 1 December 20X1	68
Acquisition of Tigret (part (i))	13
Impairment (bal. fig.)	(33)
Closing balance at 30 November 20X2 ($40m + $8m (part (i)))	48.0

(W2) Investment property

Tutorial note

Fair value gains and losses on investment properties are recorded in the statement of profit or loss.

	$m
Opening balance at 1 December 20X1	6
Gain (bal. fig.)	2
Closing balance at 30 November 20X2	8

(W3) Taxation

Tutorial note

Reconcile the opening and closing balances for both the income tax liability and the deferred tax liability in a single working. Remember to include any charge for the year included in profit or loss and also in other comprehensive income. You should also ensure that you correctly deal with any tax-related balances on a subsidiary acquired or disposed of during the year.

	$m
Opening tax balances at 1 December 20X1 ($41m + $30m)	71
Deferred tax on acquisition (part (i))	3
Charge for year per profit or loss	11
Charge for year in OCI	1
Tax paid (bal. fig.)	(18)
Closing tax balances at 30 November 20X2 ($32m + $3m (part (i)) + $33m)	68

(W4) Defined benefit scheme

Tutorial note

The movement on the defined benefit plan during the year comprises the service cost component, the net interest component, and the remeasurement component. Remember that the remeasurement component is taken to other comprehensive income for the year – it is therefore not an item that should be adjusted for within operating activities. The cash contributions paid into the plan are presented in operating activities.

	$m
Opening balance at 1 December 20X1	22
Service cost component	16
Net interest component	2
Net remeasurement component gain for year (per OCI)	(8)
Contributions paid (bal. fig.)	(7)
Closing balance at 30 November 20X2	25

(b) Indirect and direct method

The direct method presents separate categories of cash inflows and outflows whereas the indirect method is a reconciliation of profit before tax reported in the statement of profit or loss to the cash flow from operations. The adjustments include non-cash items in the statement of profit or loss plus operating cash flows that were not included in profit or loss.

A problem for users is the fact that entities can choose the method used. This limits comparability.

The majority of companies use the indirect method for the preparation of statements of cash flow. Most companies justify this on the grounds that the direct method is too costly.

Users often prefer the direct method because it reports operating cash flows in understandable categories, such as cash collected from customers, cash paid to suppliers, cash paid to employees and cash paid for other operating expenses. When presented in this way, users can assess the major trends in cash flows and can compare these to the entity's competitors.

The complicated adjustments required by the indirect method are difficult to understand and can be confusing to users. In many cases these adjustments cannot be reconciled to observed changes in the statement of financial position.

Marking scheme

			Marks
(a)	(i)	Acquisition of TIgret – 1 mark per point	**7**
	(ii)	Profit before tax	1
		Finance costs	1
		Retirement benefit expense	1
		Depreciation on PPE	1
		Revaluation gain on investment property	1
		Profit on sale of land	1
		Impairment of goodwill	1
		Gain on Tigret	1
		Decrease in trade receivables	1
		Decrease in inventories	1
		Increase in trade payables	1
		Cash paid to defined benefit scheme	1
		Finance costs paid	1
		Income taxes paid	2
		Repayment of long-term borrowings	1
		Non-controlling interest dividend	1
		Dividends paid	1
			17 max
(b)		1 mark per point	**6**
Total			**30**

11 ZIPPY  *Walk in the footsteps of a top tutor*

Key answer tips

In the Strategic Business Reporting exam, it is unlikely that you will be asked to produce full consolidated statements. The questions are more likely to involve explanation and/or the preparation of extracts. Students tend to find this harder, and often say that they are unsure what they need to write. It is therefore crucial to carefully debrief the answer to this question, and learn from the things that you missed. Remember, practice makes perfect.

(a) (i) Ginny

First nine months

Tutorial note

Don't jump straight to the disposal calculation. After all, Zippy did not dispose of the shares until nine months into the reporting period.

For the first nine months' of the year Zippy had control over Ginny and so Ginny was a subsidiary during this time. Zippy must consolidate Ginny's incomes and expenses and other comprehensive income (OCI) on a line-by-line basis for the first nine months' of the year.

Ginny made a profit of $32 million for the 12 month period so $24 million (9/12 × $32 million) of this must be consolidated. Of this $9.6 million ($24m × 40%) is attributable to the non-controlling interest.

Ginny recorded OCI of $16 million for the 12 month period so $12 million (9/12 × $16m) must be consolidated. Of this $4.8 million ($12m × 40%) is attributable to the non-controlling interest.

Loss of control

Tutorial note

Remember that not all share sales lead to a loss of control. If control is retained then no profit or loss arises and the transaction is instead accounted for in equity.

The share sale results in Zippy's holding in Ginny falling from 60% to 40% of the equity shares. Zippy has therefore lost control of Ginny. The difference between the proceeds from the disposal (including the fair value of the shares retained) and the goodwill, net assets and NCI of Ginny at the disposal date will give rise to profit or loss on disposal.

This is calculated as follows:

Tutorial note

It is important to remember the following pro-forma. It is worth a lot of marks.

	$m	$m
Proceeds		44
Fair value of remaining interest		62
		106
Goodwill at disposal (W1)	26	
Net assets at disposal (W2)	154	
Non-controlling interest at disposal (W3)	(66)	
Carrying amount of sub at disposal		(114)
Loss on disposal		(8)

When preparing the consolidated statement of profit or loss, the gain of $14 million reported in Ginny's individual financial statements must be removed from investment income. The group will instead report an $8 million loss on disposal.

The remaining investment

Tutorial note

After a subsidiary disposal, students commonly forget to account for the remaining investment. Very easy marks can be scored here.

The remaining 40% investment in Ginny gives Zippy significant influence. As such, Ginny is an associate of Zippy and should be accounted for using the equity method. This means that the group recognises its share of the associate's profit after tax, and its share of the associate's OCI.

Tutorial note

Don't forget to account for the group's share of the associate's other comprehensive income.

The consolidated statement of profit or loss and OCI will show the following amounts:

	$m
Share of profits of associate (40% × 3/12 × $32m)	3.2
Share of other comprehensive income of associate (40% × 3/12 × $16m)	1.6

Workings

Tutorial note

Set out your workings clearly.

(W1) Goodwill at disposal

	$m
Fair value of consideration	90
Fair value of non-controlling interest	50
Fair value of identifiable net assets acquired	(114)
Goodwill	26

(W2) Net assets at disposal

Tutorial note

The question tells you the net assets of Ginny at the start of the year. You need to add on nine months' of total comprehensive income in order to work out the net assets at the disposal date.

	$m
Net assets at 1 July 20X5 –- per question	118
Profit to 31 March 20X6 (9/12 × $32m)	24
OCI to 31 March 20X6 (9/12 × $16m)	12
	154

(W3) NCI at disposal

Tutorial note

When working out the group profit or loss on disposal it is normally wise to leave the NCI at disposal until last. This is because the calculation requires the subsidiary's net assets at the disposal date.

	$m
Non-controlling interest at acquisition	50
NCI share of post-acquisition net asset movement (40% × ($154m (W2) – $114m))	16
	66

(ii) Ten floor office block

Tutorial note

In this part of the question, there are more marks available for the discussion than for calculations.

IAS 40 *Investment Property* says that portions of a property can be classified as investment property if they can be sold or leased out separately from the rest of the building.

Property occupied by a subsidiary does not qualify as investment property in the consolidated financial statements, because it is being used by the group. The first two floors of Zippy's office block should therefore be classified as property, plant and equipment in the consolidated financial statements.

Depreciation of $1.2 million (($90m × 0.2)/15 years) should therefore be charged to administrative costs.

The first two floors should be revalued to $19.2 million ($96m × 0.2) in the statement of financial position. A revaluation gain should be recorded within other comprehensive income of $2.4 million ($19.2m – (($90m × 0.2) – $1.2m)).

The remaining eight floors qualify as investment property. Investment property measured at fair value is not depreciated. Fair value gains relating to investment properties are recorded in profit or loss.

These eight floors should be revalued to $76.8 million ($96m × 0.8) in the statement of financial position. A revaluation gain of $4.8 million will be recorded in investment income in the statement of profit or loss ($76.8m – ($90m × 0.8)).

Explosion

IAS 36 *Impairment of Assets* does not apply to investment property that is measured at fair value. Investment properties under the fair value model are simply restated to fair value with the gains and losses recorded in profit or loss.

The building should be revalued to $14 million and a $6 million loss ($20m – $14m) should be charged to investment income.

IAS 37 *Provisions, Contingent Liabilities and Contingent Assets* says that a provision should be recognised if there is an obligation from a past event that will lead to a probable outflow of economic benefits that can be measured reliably. The provision of $3 million should be reversed through other expenses as there is no obligation to carry out the repairs.

(iii) Individual financial statements

According to IFRS 10 *Consolidated Financial Statements,* consolidated financial statements present the parent and its subsidiaries as a single economic entity.

The second floor of the ten floor office block is being used by another group member. This means that it is being used within the single economic entity for administrative purposes. The second floor must therefore be classified as property, plant and equipment in the consolidated financial statements.

In the individual financial statements of Zippy, the second floor qualifies as an investment property because it is part of a building held to earn rental income (even though no rent is currently charged on the second floor).

As a result of this classification difference, the depreciation charge in the individual financial statements will be lower than in the consolidated financial statements. The carrying amount of investment properties will be higher than in the consolidated financial statements. The revaluation gain in OCI will be lower and the gain in profit or loss will be higher than in the consolidated financial statements.

(b) Other comprehensive income

Tutorial note

Other comprehensive income is a popular exam topic. Make sure that you are aware of current debates around its nature and use.

Profit or loss includes all items of income and expense except those which are recognised in other comprehensive income (OCI) as required or permitted by IFRS Standards.

The *Conceptual Framework* states that profit or loss is the primary source of information about the financial performance of an entity and so income and expenses are normally recognised in that statement. According to the *Conceptual Framework*, an income or expense is presented in other comprehensive if it results from remeasuring an item to current value and if it means that:

- profit or loss provides more relevant information, or
- a more faithful representation is provided of an entity's performance.

The Board makes decisions about OCI on a standard-by-standard basis, as these are revised or issued.

Income and expenditure included in other comprehensive income should be reclassified to profit or loss when doing so results in profit or loss providing more relevant information. Again these decisions are made on a standard-by-standard basis. The Board may decide that reclassification is not appropriate if there is no clear basis for identifying the amount or timing of the reclassification.

With regards to defined benefit pension schemes, the service cost is immediately recognised in profit or loss. The remeasurement component is recognised as other comprehensive income and presented as an item not to be reclassified to the profit or loss in the future. The remeasurement component comprises errors within actuarial assumptions about life expectancy, wage inflation, service lives as well as differences between actual and expected returns. It can be argued that there is no correlation between such items and the underlying performance of an entity, thus justifying the decision that this should never be reclassified to profit or loss.

That said, reclassification is criticised for adding unnecessary complexity to financial reporting and potentially enabling earnings management. Reclassification could be easily misunderstood as essentially the same gain gets reported twice, once within OCI and once within profit or loss. Additionally it is likely that there will be a mismatch on reclassification as the gains or losses may be reported in a different period to when the underlying change in value of the asset or liability took place.

Pensions and immediate recognition

Actuarial gains and losses vary significantly from one year to the next. Immediate recognition may create volatility within the statement of financial position and other comprehensive income. It is, however, important that users are fully aware as to the extent of an entity's pension scheme obligations. This may not be evident if there is a deferral of the remeasurement component. It can be argued therefore that the immediate recognition leads to greater transparency of the financial statements.

Marking scheme			
			Marks
(a)	(i)	Discussion – 1 mark per point	5
		Calculations	6
			11
	(ii)	Property discussion and calcs – 1 mark per point	**8**
	(iii)	Individual financial statements – 1 mark per point	**4**
(b)	OCI – 1 mark per point		**7**
Total			**30**

12 ASHANTI

Key answer tips

Parts (a) (i) and (ii) require you to explain the treatment of the share sales. Easy marks are available for your discussion – do not jump straight into calculations or you will miss these.

Present workings clearly. You can still score highly even if you get the wrong answer.

If you don't know how to deal with a specific number or a transaction then leave it out (or guess!). There is no negative marking.

(a) (i) Sale of shares in Bochem

Tutorial note

When dealing with the sale of shares in a subsidiary company, it is vital to establish whether or not the parent has lost control.

Ashanti's sale of shares in Bochem does not lead to a loss of control. Consequently there is no gain or loss to the group arising on this transaction and goodwill is not recalculated. Instead, the transaction is accounted for within equity, as an increase in the non-controlling interest (from 30% to 40%).

The non-controlling interest (NCI) in equity will be increased by $25.1 million (W1). The proceeds received from the sale exceed the increase in the NCI by $8.9 million (W1), and so other components of equity will be increased by this amount.

(W1) Control-to-control calculation

		$m
Proceeds of share disposal		34.0
Carrying amount of Bochem at sale date:		
Net assets (W2)	216.0	
Goodwill (80% × $44m)	35.2	
	251.2	
Change in NCI (10% × 251.2)		25.1
Increase in OCE		8.9

(W2) Net assets

	Acquisition date	**Reporting date**
	$m	$m
Equity shares	55	
Retained earnings	85	210
Other equity components	10	
FVA – plant (bal fig)	10	10
Dep'n ($10m/5 × 2 years)		(4)
	160	216

(ii) Sale of shares in Ceram

Tutorial note

If control over a company is lost then a profit or loss on disposal must be calculated. Take time to memorise the pro-forma for calculating this profit or loss.

Ashanti controlled Ceram for the first 6 months of the year, and so will consolidate 6/12 of its revenues and costs.

Mid-way through the year, Ashanti has lost control over Ceram. At this point Ceram is derecognised from the consolidated statement of financial position and a gain or loss on disposal arises in the consolidated statement of profit or loss.

This is calculated as follows:

	$m	$m
Proceeds		90.0
Fair value of residual holding at disposal date		45.0
		135.0
Carrying amount of Ceram at disposal:		
Net assets at disposal	160.0	
Goodwill at disposal (W3)	6.2	
NCI at disposal	(35.0)	
		(131.2)
Profit on disposal		3.8

Tutorial note

Don't forget to discuss the treatment of the remaining shares.

The remaining 30% interest in Ceram gives Ashanti significant influence. Therefore, from this date, Ceram is an associate and is accounted for using the equity method. The consolidated statement of profit or loss will report profits from associates of $2.1 million (6/12 × $14m × 30%).

(W3) Goodwill calculation

	$m
Consideration	95.2
Fair value of NCI at acquisition	26.0
	121.2
Fair value of net assets at acquisition	(115.0)
Goodwill at acquisition/reporting date	6.2

(iii) Revenue and cost of sales

Tutorial note

Set out your workings clearly.

Revenue and cost of sales are calculated as follows:

Revenue

	$m
Ashanti	810
Bochem	235
Ceram ($142m × 6/12)	71
Intra-group (W5)	(15)
Sale to Spice (W6)	(5)
	1,096

Cost of sales

	$m
Ashanti	686
Bochem	137
Ceram ($84m × 6/12)	42
Depreciation (W4)	2
Intra-group (W5)	(15)
Unrealised profits (W5)	1
	853

(W4) Depreciation

The fair value adjustment relating to Bochem's plant is $10 million (W2).

One year's worth of depreciation must be charged in the consolidated statement of profit or loss. This amounts to $2 million ($10m / 5 years).

Dr Cost of sales $2m

Cr Property, plant and equipment $2m

(W5) Intra-group trading

Tutorial note

Most consolidated profit or loss questions involve intra-group trading. Make sure that you are happy with the required adjustments because they are a source of easy marks.

Ashanti has sold goods to both Bochem and Ceram. Group revenue and cost of sales will need to be reduced by $15 million ($10m + $5m).

Dr Revenue $15m

Cr Cost of sales $15m

An adjustment is required to remove the unrealised profits within group inventory as a result of the sale to Bochem. The unrealised profits amount to $1 million ($10m × 20% × ½).

Dr Cost of sales $1m

Cr Inventory $1m

(W6) Sale to Spice

IFRS 15 *Revenue from Contracts with Customers* says that a contract with a customer should only be accounted for if:

- The parties have approved the contract
- Rights and obligations can be identified from the contract
- Payment terms can be identified
- The contract has commercial substance
- It is probable that the seller will collect the consideration they are entitled to

Based on the information available, it would seem that the final criterion was not met. Therefore, the contract cannot be accounted for and no revenue should have been recognised.

The revenue recognised by Ashanti on this date must be reversed:

Dr Revenue $5m

Cr Receivables $5m

(b) Control

Tutorial note

Start by stating the definition of control, as found in IFRS 10 Consolidated Financial Statements. Apply this definition to the scenario and reach an explicit conclusion about whether Ashanti will assume control over Night.

According to IFRS 10 *Consolidated Financial Statements*, an investor controls an investee if the investor has:

- power over the investee
- exposure, or rights, to variable returns from its involvement with the investee
- the ability to use its power over the investee to affect the amount of the investor's returns

When assessing whether control exists, the following should be considered:

- The size of the entity's holding compared to the size of the holding of other investors
- Whether the entity can direct the relevant activities of the investee (such as decisions about operations, capital expenditure, and the appointment and remuneration of key personnel)
- How dispersed the other shareholdings are
- Any potential voting rights (such as those arising from convertible instruments or options) held by the entity or by other entities
- Whether investors are related parties of one another, or if they have close business relationships.

A 49.9% holding is less than 50%, meaning that Ashanti will not have a controlling holding in the voting shares of Night. However, a 49.9% holding is very close to a majority shareholding.

One of the investors will have a holding of greater than 20%, which suggests significant influence. This might place doubt on the ability of Ashanti to control Night. However, IFRS 10 states that it is possible to control an entity when another investor has significant influence. Whilst the other shareholders could vote together as a block and therefore have the controlling vote, this is unlikely. This is because:

- The shareholdings are relatively dispersed
- The other investors do not have a close relationship with one another
- Based on past practice, it is likely that at least one of the other investors will not attend the Annual General Meeting, thus giving Ashanti the majority of the voting rights.

Ashanti controls the board of directors, thus enabling it to make key operating decisions that will affect the profits and returns of Night.

All things considered, it would seem that Ashanti will control Night. Night should therefore be accounted for as a subsidiary from the acquisition date.

Marking scheme			
			Marks
(a)	(i)	Discussion – 1 mark per point	3
		Calculations	3
			6
	(ii)	Discussion – 1 mark per point	4
		Calculations	4
			8
	(iii)	Pro-rating	1
		Intra-group	2
		PURP	1
		Depreciation	2
		Sale to Spice – narrative	2
		Sale to Spice – adjustment	1
			9
(b)	Control – 1 mark per point		**7**
Total			**30**

13 TRAILER  *Walk in the footsteps of a top tutor*

Key answer tips

Parts (a) (i) and (ii) require you to discuss the treatment of financial reporting issues. Keep an eye on the clock, otherwise you will not have enough time to make a decent attempt at the rest of the question.

Part (a) (iii) asks you to prepare the equity section of the statement of financial position. The easiest way to do this would be to use the standard workings for a consolidated statement of financial position (W1 – W5). Don't forget about the adjustments you have proposed in your answer to the earlier parts of the question. Show all your workings – this will enable you to score highly even if you make a few mistakes.

In part (b), you need to talk about the impact of NCI measurement on the calculation of goodwill arising on the acquisition date as well as the impact on the goodwill impairment review.

(a) (i) Loan to charity

Tutorial note

The loan is a financial instrument because Trailer has a contractual right to receive cash.

IFRS 9 *Financial Instruments* says that financial assets should be recognised initially at fair value. According to IFRS 13 *Fair Value Measurement,* this is the selling price of an asset in an orderly transaction between market participants.

Market rate loans attract interest of 6%, whereas the loan advanced to the charity only attracts interest at 3%. As such, the price paid by Trailer of $50 million is not indicative of the asset's fair value. The fair value of the financial asset must therefore be determined. This can be achieved by calculating the present value of all future cash receipts using the prevailing market interest rate for a similar instrument.

Fair value of the financial asset

	Cash flows	**Discount factor**	**Present value**
	$m		$m
20X3	1.5	1/1.06	1.4
20X4	1.5	$1/1.06^2$	1.3
20X5	51.5	$1/1.06^3$	43.3
			46.0

The financial asset should have been recognised at $46 million rather than $50 million. The $4 million difference between the fair value of the asset and the amount of cash advanced should have been recognised as an expense in profit or loss.

The correcting entry is:

Dr Profit or loss $4.0m

Cr Financial assets $4.0m

The financial asset is then measured at amortised cost because, as per IFRS 9, Trailer intends to hold it the asset to maturity to collect the contractual cash flows. Interest is credited to profit or loss using the effective rate. Cash receipts reduce the carrying amount of the asset.

1 June 20X2	**Interest credit (6%)**	**Cash received**	**31 May 20X3**
$m	$m	$m	$m
46.0	2.8	(1.5)	47.3

The cash receipt has been correctly accounted for. The correcting entry should therefore be:

Dr Financial assets $2.8m

Cr Profit or loss $2.8m

(ii) Provision for restructuring

Tutorial note

Remember the criteria for recognising a provision. All three of the criteria must be met before a provision can be recognised.

According to IAS 37 *Provisions, Contingent Liabilities and Contingent Assets*, a provision is recognised if:

- there is an obligation from a past event
- an outflow of economic benefits is probable
- the outflow can be measured reliably.

The first plan has been communicated to those directly affected, creating a constructive obligation to incur expenditure on the restructuring.

IAS 37 says that costs can only be included in a restructuring provision if they result directly from, and are necessarily entailed by, a restructuring. This includes costs such as employee redundancy costs. Expenses that relate to ongoing activities, such as relocation and retraining, are excluded. With regard to the first plan, a provision should be recognised for the redundancy costs of $14 million.

The adjustment required is:

Dr Profit or loss $14m

Cr Provisions $14m

In contrast, Trailer should not recognise a provision for the finance and IT department's re-organisation. The re-organisation is not due to start for two years. External parties are unlikely to have a valid expectation that management is committed to the re-organisation as the time frame allows significant opportunities for management to change the details of the plan or even to decide not to proceed with it. Additionally, identification of the staff that will lose their jobs is not sufficiently detailed to support the recognising of a redundancy provision.

(iii) Extract from consolidated Statement of Financial Position at 31 May 20X3

	$m
Equity attributable to owners of parent	
Share capital	1,750.0
Retained earnings (W5)	1,209.6
Other components of equity (W5)	140.0
	3,099.6
Non-controlling interest (W4)	833.2
Total equity	3,932.8

Workings

(W1) Group structure

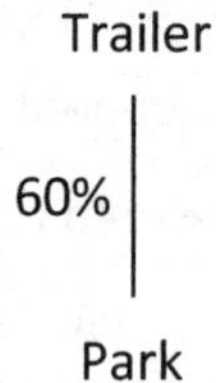

(W2) Net assets

Tutorial note

If you are told the fair value of the net assets of the subsidiary at acquisition then you can calculate the fair value adjustments using a balancing figure approach.

	Acq'n date	**Rep date**
	$m	$m
Share capital	1,210	1,210
Other components	55	80
Retained earnings	650	930
Fair value adjustment – plant (bal. fig)	35	35
Depreciation ($35m/7)		(5)
	1,950	2,250

Of the $300 million ($2,250m – $1,950m) post-acquisition net asset movement, $25 million ($80m – $55m) relates to other components of equity and $275 million ($300m – $25m) relates to retained earnings.

(W3) Goodwill

Tutorial note

Goodwill needs to be calculated so that an impairment review can be performed.

	$m
Fair value of consideration	1,250
NCI at acquisition (40% × $1,950m)	780
Fair value of identifiable net assets acquired (W2)	(1,950)
Goodwill at acquisition	80

(W4) Non-controlling interest

Tutorial note

There are easy marks available here as long as you know your standard workings.

	$m
NCI in Park at acquisition (W3)	780
NCI % of post-acquisition net assets (40% × $300m (W2))	120
Impairment of other assets (40% × $167m (W6))	(66.8)
	833.2

(W5) Reserves

Retained earnings

Tutorial note

Any adjustments to the statement of profit or loss will impact retained earnings.

	$m
Trailer	1,240
Park: 60% × $275m (W2)	165
Impairment of goodwill (W6)	(80)
Impairment of other assets (60% × $167m (W6))	(100.2)
Financial asset write down (part a (i))	(4.0)
Interest credit (part a (i))	2.8
Restructuring provision (part a (ii)	(14)
	1,209.6

Other components of equity

	$m
Trailer	125
Park: 60% × $25m (W2)	15
	140

(W6) Impairment of Park

Tutorial note

In note 2 of the question, we are told the recoverable amount of the net assets of Park. We therefore need to compare this to the carrying amount of Park's net assets.

Remember that goodwill has been calculated using the proportionate basis. This means that, when performing an impairment review, the goodwill must be grossed up to include the NCI's interest.

	$m	$m
Goodwill (W3)	80	
Notional NCI ($80m × 40/60)	53.3	
Total notional goodwill		133.3
Net assets at reporting date (W2)		2,250
Total carrying amount of assets		2,383.3
Recoverable amount		(2,083.0)
Impairment		300.3

The impairment is firstly allocated to the total notional goodwill of $133.3m. However, only 60% of the total notional goodwill has been recognised in the statements and therefore only 60% ($80m) of the impairment is accounted for. This expense is all attributable to the owners of Trailer.

The remaining impairment of $167m ($300.3m – $133.3m) is allocated against the other assets of Park in proportion to their carrying amounts. This impairment loss is attributable to the owners of the Trailer and the NCI based on their respective shareholdings.

(b) Impact of measuring the NCI at air value

Tutorial note

When calculating goodwill in this part of the question, you will not be penalised for any mistakes that you made in part (a).

Remember that goodwill calculated under the fair value method ***does not*** *need grossing up when performing an impairment review.*

Goodwill calculation

	$m
Fair value of consideration	1,250
Fair value of NCI	800
Fair value of identifiable net assets acquired (W2)	(1,950)
Goodwill at acquisition	100

Goodwill impairment review

	$m
Goodwill	100
Net assets at reporting date (W2)	2,250
Total carrying amount	2,350
Recoverable amount	(2,083)
Impairment	267
Allocated to:	
Goodwill	100
Other assets	167
Total	267

Under the previous method used by Trailer, the NCI was recognised at its share of the subsidiary's net assets and so did not include any goodwill. The full goodwill method means that non-controlling interest and goodwill are both increased by the goodwill that relates to the non-controlling interest.

In the case of Park, measuring the NCI at its fair value increases the goodwill arising at acquisition from $80 million to $100 million. The figure used for NCI under the proportionate method of $780m has also increased by $20 million, to $800m at 1 June 20X2.

The full goodwill method increases reported net assets, and so any impairment of goodwill will be greater. Thus in the case of Park, the impairment of goodwill will be \$100m. This will be charged \$60 million to retained earnings and \$40 million to the NCI. Under both methods, the impairment of the other assets is \$167 million, which is split between retained earnings and the NCI.

Although measuring non-controlling interest at fair value may prove difficult, goodwill impairment testing is easier under full goodwill. This is because there is no need to gross up goodwill.

Marking scheme			
			Marks
(a)	(i)	Discussion – 1 mark per point	3
		Calculations	3
			6
	(ii)	Discussion – 1 mark per point	**5**
	(iii)	Share capital	1
		NCI	2
		Retained earnings	4
		Fair value adjustment	1
		Goodwill calculation	1
		Goodwill impairment	2
		Other components of equity	1
			12
(b)	NCI discussion – 1 mark per point		4
	Goodwill calculation		1
	Impairment calculation		2
			7
Total			**30**

14 WESTON  *Walk in the footsteps of a top tutor*

Key answer tips

Read the question carefully and you should be able to find several figures that you can put straight into your cash flow extracts (e.g. the associate's profits, the service cost component, and depreciation). Prioritise these quick, easy marks – they are essential to pass the exam.

(a) (i) Weston Group Statement of cash flows for year ended 31 January 20X6

	$m
Cash flow from operating activities	
Profit before tax (W1)	189
Associate's profits	(16)
Service cost component	11
Depreciation	20
Impairment of goodwill (W5)	6
Cash contributions to pension scheme	(19)
Movements in working capital	
Increase in trade and other payables ($36m – $41m + $10m)	5
Increase in trade and other receivables ($106m – $104m + $23m)	(25)
Decrease in inventories ($108m – $165m + $38m)	19
Cash generated from operations	190
Income taxes paid (W7)	(81)
	109
Cash flows from investing activities	
Purchase of property, plant and equipment (W8)	(84)
Dividends received from associate (W6)	4
Purchase of associate (W6)	(90)
Net proceeds on disposal of Northern (W2)	87.4
	(82.6)

Workings

(W1) Profit

Tutorial note

You need to use the profit before tax from both continuing and discontinued operations.

Total profit before tax is:

	$m
Profit before tax – continuing operations	183
Profit before tax – discontinued operations	6
	189

(W2) Proceeds on disposal of Northern

Tutorial note

The question tells you the loss on the disposal of the subsidiary and gives you enough information to calculate the goodwill, net assets and non-controlling interest at the disposal date. You then need to work backwards, to deduce the cash proceeds received from the subsidiary disposal.

	$m
Cash proceeds from sale (bal. fig.)	85.4
Goodwill at disposal (W3)	(9)
Fair value of net assets at disposal (W4)	(129)
Non-controlling interest at disposal (W4)	23.6
Loss on disposal (per question)	(29)

The net cash impact of the disposal is therefore $87.4 million ($85.4m proceeds + $2m overdraft disposed).

(W3) Goodwill – Northern

Tutorial note

Goodwill calculations are a source of easy marks.

	$m
Consideration	132
Fair value of non-controlling interest	28
	160
Identifiable net assets at acquisition	(124)
Goodwill on acquisition	36
Impairment of goodwill (75%)	(27)
Carrying amount of goodwill at disposal	9

(W4) Net assets and NCI at disposal

Tutorial note

The question gives you the carrying amount of the net assets in Northern's individual financial statements. However, this will not include the fair value uplift that arises on consolidation, or the deferred tax on this uplift.

The carrying amount of the property, plant and equipment at disposal will be \$80m, as per the question, plus \$16 million fair value uplift less 4/8 depreciation. This amounts to \$88 million.

The deferred tax liability recorded on the fair value uplift would have been \$4 million (25% × \$16m). This will have been released in line with the extra depreciation, so the carrying amount at disposal will be only \$2 million (\$4m – (\$4m × 4/8)). The carrying amount of the entire deferred tax liability at disposal is therefore \$8m (\$6m per question + \$2m above).

The revised carrying amounts at disposal are:

	\$m
Property, plant and equipment	88
Inventory	38
Trade receivables	23
Trade and other payables	(10)
Deferred tax	(8)
Bank overdraft	(2)
	129

The non-controlling interest in Northern at disposal will be:

	\$m
Non-controlling interest at acquisition	28
NCI share of post-acquisition net assets (20% × (\$129m – \$124m))	1
NCI share of goodwill impairment (20% × \$27m) (W3)	(5.4)
	23.6

(W5) Goodwill

Tutorial note

Reconcile goodwill year-on-year to identify the impairment charge. This needs to be added back to profit when calculating cash generated from operations.

	$m
Balance at 1 February 20X5	19
Disposal of subsidiary (W3)	(9)
Impairment (bal. fig.)	(6)
Balance at 31 January 20X6	4

(W6) Associate

Tutorial note

Lots of students forget that dividends received from an associate reduce the carrying amount of the group's investment.

	$m
Balance at 1 February 20X5	–
Share of associate profit	16
Dividend received ($10m × 40%)	(4)
Cost of acquisition (bal. fig.)	90
Balance at 31 January 20X6	102

(W7) Taxation

Tutorial note

Deferred tax can be charged to profit or loss, or to other comprehensive income. Don't forget the tax charge relating to the discontinued operation (note (ii) in the question).

	$m
Balance at 1 February 20X5 ($15m + $92m)	107
Charge for year – continuing	40
Charge for year – discontinued	2
Deferred tax at disposal (W4)	(8)
Deferred tax on remeasurement gain (25% × $4m)	1
Cash paid (bal. fig.)	(81)
Balance at 31 January 20X6 ($14m + $47m)	61

Tutorial note

Since the actuarial gain of $4m would be recorded in other comprehensive income, the deferred tax on the actuarial gain of $1m (25% × $4m) will also be in other comprehensive income. Any remaining movement in the deferred tax on the pension will be included within the charge to profit or loss for the year.

(W8) Property, plant and equipment

	$m
Balance at 1 February 20X5	413
Disposal of subsidiary (W4)	(88)
Depreciation charge	(20)
Cash additions (bal. fig.)	84
Balance at 31 January 20X6	389

(ii) The indirect method

IAS 7 *Statement of Cash Flows* states that the indirect method of calculating cash generated from operations involves adjusting the profit (or loss) for the period for the effects of:

- changes in inventories, payables and receivables
- non-cash items
- items which relate to investing or financing.

With regards to Weston:

- Associate's profits – undistributed profits of an associate are not a cash flow and so must be deducted from the group's profit before tax. Moreover, an associate is a type of investment rather than a part of the entity's operating activities and so any cash flows with associate entities are reported within 'cash flows from investing activities'.

- Service cost, depreciation and impairment – these are non-cash expenses and so are eliminated by adding them back to profit.
- Movements in working capital – businesses buy and sell goods on credit, but only cash receipts and cash payments should be reported in the statement of cash flows. Adjusting for the movement in working capital items eliminates the impact of accruals accounting. In the current year. Some of the year-on-year movement in working capital relates to the disposal of Northern, rather than because of cash flows with customers and suppliers, and so the effect of this disposal has been eliminated.

(b) Investment in Abuelo Co

Tutorial note

This part of the question tests a foreign associate. This is a new addition to the 22/23 syllabus. Make sure you understand these concepts as, historically, the examiners have included scenarios based upon the new topics at the earliest possible opportunity.

Weston Group's proposed 30% investment in Abuelo Co will cause Weston to exert significant influence on Abuelo Co. Therefore, Abuelo will be accounted for as an associate, using equity accounting.

Equity accounting recognises an 'Investment in associate' under Non-current assets within the statement of financial position. This consists of the consideration paid, plus the parent's share of any post-acquisition movement in the net assets of the associate. No consolidation of the assets or liabilities of the associate occurs as no control is exerted.

As Abuelo Co is a foreign currency associate, the investment in associate must be translated at the closing rate for inclusion within the group accounts. This may create foreign currency gains or losses on translation that will be recorded within group equity and other comprehensive income. The investment in associate line is calculated as \$3.4m (see W1) for inclusion within the Weston Group non-current assets as at 31 January 20X7.

The statement of profit or loss and other comprehensive income includes, in separate lines, the parent's share of the associate's profit after tax (above group profit before tax) and the associate's other comprehensive income (within group OCI).

The share of Abuelo Co's profits would be translated at the average rate for inclusion in the group accounts. Thus a share of associate's profit figure of \$1m ((30% × (40 × 6/12))/5.8) would be recorded above group profit before tax.

The group OCI would include the annual foreign currency loss of \$0.6m (see W1) arising from the translation of the foreign currency associate. This would also be debited to a translation reserve within the group statement of financial position (located within the equity section). Abuelo Co does not anticipate recording any items of OCI for the year ended 31 January 20X7 so no share of associate's OCI is required.

Working

	Dinars m	**Exchange rate**	**$m**
Cost of associate			
– Cash	6.0	6	1.0
– Shares (1m × $2m) translated at 6 dinars (HR)	12.0	6	2.0
Share of profit (30% × (40m dinars × 6/12))	6.0	5.8	1.0
Exchange gain		bal. fig	(0.6)
Closing investment in associate	24.0	7	3.4

Marking scheme

			Marks
(a)	(i)	Cash flows from operating activities	
		Profit	1
		Associate's profit	1
		Pension scheme service cost	1
		Depreciation	1
		Goodwill impairment	1
		Working capital movements	3
		Tax paid	2
		Pension contributions	1
		Cash flows from investing activities	
		Property, plant and equipment	1
		Associate dividend	1
		Purchase of associate	1
		Disposal of Northern	4
			18
	(ii)	Indirect method	**6**
(b)	Foreign currency associate		
	SOFP		**3**
	P/L		**1**
	OCI		**2**
Total			**30**

15 JOEY  *Walk in the footsteps of a top tutor*

Key answer tips

Remember to allocate your time carefully when attempting question 1 in the SBR exam. It would be very easy to get bogged down in a particular issue or adjustment and to then run out of time. Spend your time on the areas of the question that you are most confident with.

(a) Hulty

Tutorial note

Consideration transferred in a business combination and the identifiable net assets of the subsidiary at the acquisition date should both be measured at fair value. If you struggle to think about the double entries required for these adjustments then think about how you would process them through the standard consolidation workings and what impact this would have on the SFP balances.

Deferred consideration

IFRS 3 *Business Combinations* says that the consideration transferred to achieve control over another business must be measured at fair value. Deferred consideration should be measured at its present value.

The present value of the deferred consideration as at 1 December 20X3 was $41.3 million ($50m × $1/1.10^2$). Goodwill should be increased by this amount and a corresponding liability recognised. The correcting entry is:

Dr Goodwill	$41.3m
Cr Liabilities	$41.3m

Tutorial note

Don't forget to unwind the discount on the liability.

Interest on the liability should be charged to profit or loss in the year. This amounts to $4.1 million ($41.3m × 10%). The entry to record this in the consolidated statement of financial position is:

Dr Retained earnings	$4.1m
Cr Liabilities	$4.1m

Franchise right

IFRS 3 *Business Combinations* says that the identifiable net assets of a subsidiary should be measured at fair value at the acquisition date.

The fair value of the identifiable net assets exceeds their carrying amounts by $20 million ($980m – $960m). This relates to an unrecognised intangible franchise right that must be recognised in the consolidated financial statements as at the acquisition date. This adjustment reduces the amount of goodwill recognised. The correcting adjustment is:

Dr Intangible asset – franchise right	$20m
Cr Goodwill	$20m

The intangible asset should be amortised over its remaining useful life. The current year charge that needs to be recorded in consolidated profit or loss is $5 million ($20m/4 years). The franchise right is an asset held by the subsidiary, so the charge in profit or loss should be allocated between the owners of the parent company and the non-controlling interest based on their respective shareholdings. The entry required to record this in the consolidated statement of financial position is:

Dr Retained earnings ($5m × 80%)	$4m
Dr NCI ($5m × 20%)	$1m
Cr Intangible asset – franchise right	$5m

Total goodwill arising on Hulty

Total goodwill arising on the acquisition of Hulty is therefore $61.3 million ($40m draft + $41.3m – $20m).

(b) Margy

Step acquisition

Joey has achieved control over Margy in stages. On the date that control was achieved the previous shareholding should been included in the goodwill calculation at its fair value. Any gain or loss on revaluing this shareholding to fair value is recorded in the consolidated statement of profit or loss (or in other comprehensive income if the previously held shares were measured at fair value through other comprehensive income).

The equity accounted investment in Margy of $700 million should therefore have been eliminated and included in the goodwill calculation at its fair value of $705 million. A $5 million gain would arise in consolidated profit or loss.

This adjustment means that the gain on bargain purchase of $655 million is eliminated. The adjusting entry required in the statement of financial position is:

Dr Retained earnings (to remove gain on bargain purchase)	$655m
Dr Goodwill ($705m – $655m)	$50m
Cr Investment in associate	$700m
Cr Retained earnings (gain on step acquisition)	$5m

Building adjustment

During the measurement period, the acquirer must retrospectively adjust the amounts recognised at the acquisition date if further facts and information are obtained. The measurement period ends 12 months after the acquisition date.

The revision of the building's fair value at the acquisition date was determined within 12 months of the business combination so it must therefore be adjusted for as at the acquisition date. This will reduce the amount of property, plant and equipment (PPE) in the consolidated statement of financial position and will increase the goodwill arising on the acquisition of Margy. The adjustment required is:

Dr Goodwill	\$40m
Cr PPE	\$40m

If the building is worth less than originally estimated then it increases the risk that Joey overpaid for Margy and therefore that goodwill might be impaired. However, no information is provided about this.

Tutorial note

It is common in exams to have to charge depreciation on a fair value uplift. However, if a building was over-valued as at the acquisition date then it is likely that the depreciation subsequently charged is also too high.

The property, plant and equipment has been included in the consolidated financial statements at \$200 million, rather than \$160 million, and so too much depreciation will have been charged. Depreciation of \$2 million (\$40m/20 years) must be removed from consolidated profit or loss. The PPE is held by a subsidiary and so this adjustment must be allocated to the owners of the parent and the non-controlling interest based on their respective shareholdings. The adjustment required in the consolidated statement of financial position is:

Dr PPE	\$2m
Cr Retained earnings (\$2m × 70%)	\$1.4m
Cr NCI (\$2m × 30%)	\$0.6m

Total goodwill arising on Margy

Total goodwill arising on the acquisition of Margy is therefore \$90 million (\$50m + \$40m).

(c) Joint arrangement

Tutorial note

A joint arrangement is an arrangement over which two or more parties have joint control. Remember that joint arrangements may take the form of joint operations or joint ventures. A joint venture, which normally involves the establishment of a separate entity, is accounted for using the equity method.

For the period to 31 May 20X4, the requirement for unanimous key strategic decisions means this is a joint arrangement. Since there is no legal entity, it would be classified as a joint operation. Joey should therefore account for its direct rights to the underlying results and assets.

Up until 31 May 20X4, the joint operation had the following results:

	$m
Revenue (5m × 6/12)	2.5
Cost of sales (2m × 6/12)	(1.0)
Gross profit	1.5

The amount that belongs to CP is therefore:

	$m
10% × Sales (10% × 2.5m)	0.25
30% of gross profit 30% × $1.5m)	0.45
Amount due to CP	0.7

Joey has recorded all of the sales proceeds and costs for the six month period, hence recording a profit of $1.5 million. Joey's profits must therefore be reduced by $0.7 million, and a payable to CP recorded for the same amount. The adjustment required is:

Dr Profit or loss	$0.7m
Cr Accounts payable CP	$0.7m

Tutorial note

The question requires you to 'discuss'. Easier marks are available for the narrative part of your answer.

From 1 June 20X4, Joey has a share of the net assets of the joint arrangement rather than direct rights. This means that the joint arrangement would be classified as a joint venture and must be accounted for in the consolidated financial statements using the equity method.

Joey has accounted for all proceeds and costs of the joint venture. This should be removed from its statement of profit or loss and a payable recorded to transfer this back to JCP

Dr Profit or loss	$1.5 m
Cr Payable to JCP	$1.5 m

Joey should then equity-for its share of JCP's profit of $0.75 million ($1.5m × 50%). This will be recorded in profit or loss and recognised as an investment in the statement of financial position.

Dr Investment in joint venture	$0.75 m
Cr Profit or loss	$0.75 m

(d) Debt and equity

Tutorial note

This is a very common exam requirement. You must memorise the definition of a financial liability.

IAS 32 *Financial Instruments: Presentation* says that a financial liability is a contractual obligation to deliver either cash or another financial asset to the holder. Equity is any contract which evidences a residual interest in the entity's assets after deducting all of its liabilities.

However, a contract may involve the delivery of the entity's own equity instruments. A contract which will be settled by the entity delivering a fixed number of its own equity instruments in exchange for cash or another financial asset is an equity instrument. If there is any variability in the number of own equity instruments to be delivered then the contract is a financial liability.

B shares

The B shares should be classified as equity because there is no contractual obligation to pay the dividends or to redeem the instrument. Dividends can only be paid on the B shares if dividends have been declared on the A shares. However, there is no contractual obligation to declare A share dividends.

Share options

The classification of the share options is dependent on whether there is variability in the number of equity shares delivered. Joey will settle the contract by issuing a fixed number of its own equity instruments in exchange for cash, so the share options would be classified as an equity instrument.

Marking scheme

		Marks
(a)	Hulty – 1 mark per point	9
(b)	Margy – 1 mark per point	9
(c)	CP – 1 mark per point	8
(d)	IAS 32 classifications	4
Total		**30**

16 PARSLEY  *Walk in the footsteps of a top tutor*

Key answer tips

Part (a) focusses on group accounting issues. Parsley lost control of Sage during the year. Sage is therefore consolidated until the disposal date and a profit or loss on disposal must be calculated. Saffron is an overseas subsidiary, which must be translated into the group's presentation currency. Exchange differences on the retranslation of Saffron's opening net assets, profit and goodwill are recorded in other comprehensive income.

(a) Group structure

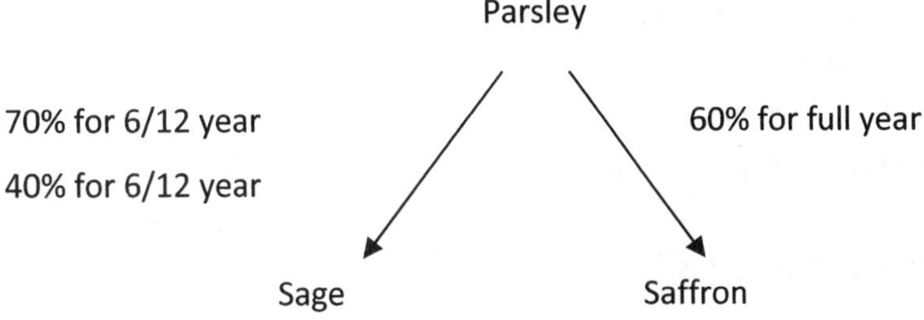

(i) Sage

Tutorial note

Memorise the pro-forma for calculating the profit or loss arising on the disposal of a subsidiary. This can be worth a lot of marks in the exam.

Parsley lost control over Sage halfway through the year. This means that Parsley must consolidate the line-by-line results of Sage for the first 6 months of the year.

Sage made a profit for the year of \$6 million, of which Parsley will consolidate \$3 million (\$6 million × 6/12). Of this, \$2.1 million (\$3 million × 70%) is attributable to the equity owners of the Parsley group and the remaining \$0.9 million is attributable to the non-controlling interest.

A profit or loss on the disposal of Sage must be reported in the consolidated statement of profit or loss.

This is calculated as follows:

	$m	$m
Proceeds from disposal	6.5	
Fair value of interest retained	9.5	
		16.0
Goodwill disposed:		
Consideration	6.0	
NCI at acquisition ($5m × 30%)	1.5	
Net assets at acquisition	(5.0)	
Goodwill at disposal		(2.5)
Net assets at disposal:		
Share capital	1.0	
Retained earnings bfd	9.0	
Profit to disposal date ($6m × 6/12)	3.0	
Net assets at disposal		(13.0)
NCI at disposal:		
NCI at acquisition	1.5	
NCI % of post-acquisition net assets (30% × ($13m – $5m))	2.4	
		3.9
Profit on disposal		4.4

After the share sale, Parsley retains significant influence over Sage. This means that Sage is an associate for the final six months of the year and must be accounted for using the equity method. The group will show its share of the associate's profit as a single line in the consolidated statement of profit or loss. This amounts to $1.2 million ($6m × 6/12 × 40%).

(ii) Saffron

Profit or loss

IFRS 3 *Business Combinations* says that the identifiable net assets of a subsidiary should be consolidated at fair value. It would seem that Saffron has a brand that is unrecognised in its individual financial statements but which must be consolidated at its fair value.

The fair value of this brand is calculated as follows:

	FRm
Fair value of net assets	70
Carrying amount of net assets	(60)
Fair value of brand	10

Amortisation must be charged on the brand. In the current period, this will be FR2 million (FR10m/5 years).

Saffron is an overseas subsidiary. Its results, including the above amortisation adjustment, must be translated for inclusion in the consolidated statement of profit or loss and other comprehensive income at the average rate. The results of Saffron will then be consolidated line-by-line. The net impact on consolidated profit will be $6.1 million ((FR30 per P/L – FR2 amortisation)/4.6)). Of this $3.7 million ($6.1m × 60%) is attributable to the equity owners of the parent. The remaining $2.4 million is attributable to the non-controlling interest.

Goodwill impairment and foreign exchange

Tutorial note

Calculate goodwill in the subsidiary's currency and then translate it at the closing rate. The foreign exchange gain or loss is recorded in other comprehensive income, as an item that may be reclassified to profit or loss in the future.

The goodwill of Saffron is calculated as follows:

	FRm
Cost of acquisition	71
FV of NCI at acquisition	29
	100
Less FV net assets at acquisition	(70)
Goodwill at acquisition	30
Impairment	(4)
Goodwill at reporting date	26

Goodwill is translated at the reporting date at the closing rate. This gives rise to a foreign exchange gain, calculated below:

FX gain on retranslation	FRm	Rate	$m
Acquisition	30	5.0	6.0
Impairment	(4)	4.6	(0.9)
FX gain on retranslation		**Bal fig**	**1.4**
Rep date	26	4.0	6.5

The impairment of $0.9 million is recorded in profit or loss. Of this, $0.5 million ($0.9m × 60%) is attributable to the equity owners of the parent. The remaining $0.4 million is attributable to the non-controlling interest.

The gain of $1.4 million is recorded in other comprehensive income. The forex gain attributable to the equity owners of the parent is $0.8 million ($1.4m × 60%) and the remaining $0.6 million is attributable to the non-controlling interest.

Foreign exchange gain on opening net assets and profit

A foreign exchange gain arises on the translation of Saffron's opening net assets and profit:

	FRm	Rate	$m
Opening net assets	70	5.0	14.0
Profit (FR30m – FR2m (W1))	28	4.6	6.1
FX gain on retranslation		**Bal fig**	**4.4**
Rep date	98	4.0	24.5

The gain of $4.4 million is recorded in other comprehensive income. The forex gain attributable to the equity owners of the parent is $2.6 million ($4.4m × 60%) and the remaining $1.8 million is attributable to the non-controlling interest.

(iii) Lease

Tutorial note

To determine the accounting entries in the second year of the lease you will need to determine the carrying amounts of the lease liability and right-of-use asset at the end of the first year.

The year ended 30 April 20X3

IFRS 16 *Leases* says that lease liabilities are recognised at the present value of payments yet to be made. This includes fixed lease payments, as well as variable payments based on the relevant index or rate at the start of the lease. The liability is reduced by cash payments. Interest on the liability increases its carrying amount and is charged to profit or loss.

A right-of-use asset is recognised at the value of the initial lease liability plus payments made before or at commencement and initial direct costs. Assuming the cost model is chosen, the asset is depreciated over the lower of the lease term and its remaining useful economic life.

In the prior year, the right of use asset would have been recognised at $5 million ($3.8m + $1.2m). The depreciation charge in the prior year would have been $1 million ($5m/5 years), and the carrying amount of the asset at the end of the prior year was, therefore, $4 million.

The lease liability would have been recorded at $3.8 million. Interest of $0.38 million ($3.8m × 10%) would have been charged to profit or loss. As such, the liability at 30 April 20X3 was $4.18 million ($3.8m + $0.38m).

The year ended 30 April 20X4

Tutorial note

Remember that you are asked to provide an 'explanation'. Calculations and double entries are not enough to score a high mark.

If changes to lease payments occur then the liability must be recalculated and adjusted. A corresponding entry is made against the carrying amount of the right-of-use asset.

Based on inflation for the last 12 months, the lease payments now due each year are $1.3 million ($1.2m × 108%).

The revised liability is calculated as follows:

	Cash ($m)	**Disc.**	**PV** ($m)
1/5/20X3	1.3	1	1.30
1/5/20X4	1.3	$1/1.10^1$	1.18
1/5/20X5	1.3	$1/1.10^2$	1.07
1/5/20X6	1.3	$1/1.10^3$	0.98
Revised liability			4.53

The lease liability must be increased from $4.18 million to $4.53 million. The entry required is:

Dr Right-of-use asset	$0.35m
Cr Lease liability	$0.35m

After this adjustment, the right-of use asset is held at $4.35 million ($4m + $0.35m). Depreciation for the year ended 30 April 20X4 is $1.09 million ($4.35m/4 years).

Dr Depreciation expense	$1.09m
Cr Right-of-use asset	$1.09m

The carrying amount of the right-of use asset at the year-end is $3.26 million ($4.35m – $1.09m).

The current year cash repayment has been incorrectly charged to profit or loss.

Dr Lease liability	$1.3m
Cr Cost of sales	$1.3m

Interest on the outstanding lease liability is $0.32 million (($4.53m – $1.3m) × 10%).

Dr Finance costs	$0.32m
Cr Lease liability	$0.32m

The carrying amount of the lease liability at the year-end is $3.55 million ($4.53m – $1.3m + $0.32m).

(b) IAS 24 *Related Party Disclosures* states that a person or a close member of their family is related to the reporting entity if that person:

- has control, joint control or significant influence over the reporting entity
- is a member of key management personnel of the reporting entity or its parent.

The main circumstances that lead to an entity being related to the reporting entity are as follows:

- the entity and the reporting entity are members of the same group
- one entity is an associate or joint venture of the other
- both entities are joint ventures of the same third party
- the entity is controlled or jointly controlled by a person who is a related party of the reporting entity.

In the absence of related party disclosures, users of financial statements would assume that an entity has acted independently and in its own best interests. Most importantly, they would assume that all transactions have been entered into willingly and at arm's length (i.e. on normal commercial terms at fair value). Where related party relationships and transactions exist, this assumption may not be justified.

Related party relationships and transactions may distort financial position and performance, both favourably and unfavourably. The most obvious example of this type of transaction would be the sale of goods from one party to another on non-commercial terms.

It is a common misapprehension that related party transactions need only be disclosed if they are not on market terms. This is not the case. For example, a parent may instruct all members of its group to buy certain products or services (on commercial terms) from one of its subsidiaries. If the parent were to sell the subsidiary, it would be important for the prospective buyer to be aware that the related party transactions would probably not occur in the future.

Even where there have been no related party transactions, it is still important for some related party relationships to be disclosed. A subsidiary may obtain custom, receive favourable credit ratings, and benefit from a superior management team simply by being a part of a well-respected group. As such, an entity must always disclose information about its parent.

Marking scheme			
			Marks
(a)	(i)	Sage – 1 mark per point	8
	(ii)	Saffron – 1 mark per point	8
	(iii)	Lease – 1 mark per point	8
(b)		Related parties – 1 mark per point	6
Total			**30**

17 MARCHANT  *Walk in the footsteps of a top tutor*

Key answer tips

When producing a consolidated statement of profit or loss and other comprehensive income it is important to understand the group structure. Marchant disposed of shares in Nathan but did not lose control. Therefore, Nathan's incomes and expenses must be consolidated for the full year and no profit or loss on disposal is recorded in the group's financial statements. However, Marchant lost control over Option half way through the year. This means that Option's incomes and expenses must be consolidated for the first 6 months and then a profit on disposal calculated. Marchant retained significant influence over Option, so must account for the remaining holding using the equity method for the second half of the year.

(a) (i) Marchant Group: Statement of profit or loss and other comprehensive income for the year ended 30 April 20X4

Tutorial note

If a subsidiary has been disposed of during the year, remember to consolidate its income and expenses up to the disposal.

When producing a statement of profit or loss, you need to split profit and total comprehensive income for the period between the owners of the parent and the non-controlling interest.

	$m
Revenue ($400 + $115 + (6/12 × $70) – $12 (W6))	538.0
Cost of sales ($312 + $65 + (6/12 × $36) – $12 (W6))	(383.0)
Gross profit	155.0
Other income ($21 + $7 + (6/12 × $2) – $5.3 (W3))	23.7
Administrative costs ($15 + $9 + (6/12 × $12)	(30.0)
Other expenses ($35 + $19 + (6/12 × $8) + $5 (W2))	(63.0)
Operating profit	85.7
Share of profits of associates (20% × (6/12 × $15))	1.5
Profit on disposal of subsidiary (W4)	22.0
Finance costs ($5 + $6 + (6/12 × $4))	(13.0)
Finance income ($6 + $5 + (6/12 × $8))	15.0
Profit before tax	111.2
Income tax expense ($19 + $9 + (6/12 × $5)	(30.5)
Profit for the year	80.7
Other comprehensive income:	
Items which will not be reclassified to profit or loss	
Changes in revaluation surplus ($10 + $2 –$5 (W3))	7.0
Total comprehensive income for the year	87.7
Profit attributable to:	
Owners of the parent (bal. fig.)	70.1
Non-controlling interest (W7)	10.6
	80.7
Total comprehensive income attributable to:	
Owners of the parent (bal. fig.)	76.3
Non-controlling interest (W7)	11.4
	87.7

Workings

(W1) Group structure

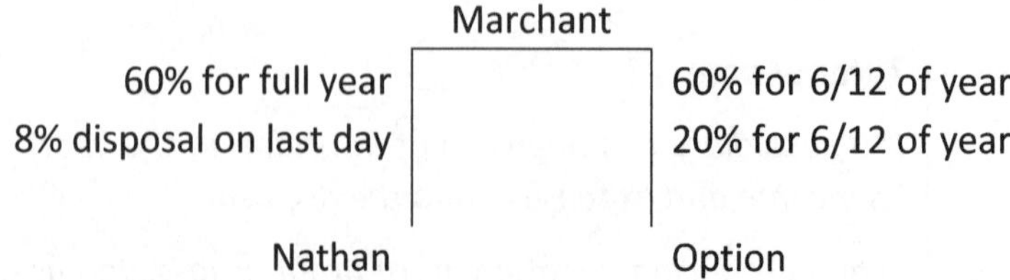

(W2) Nathan's goodwill

Tutorial note

Remember, impairments recorded against goodwill can never be reversed.

	$m
Fair value of consideration	80
Fair value of non-controlling interest	45
	125
Fair value of identifiable net assets acquired	(110)
Goodwill at acquisition	15
Impairment (20%)	(3)
Goodwill	12

Goodwill has been increased to $17 million ($15m + $2m). However, impairments recorded against goodwill are not allowed to be reversed. Therefore, $5 million ($17m – $12m) must be charged to profit or loss to reduce goodwill to the correct amount of $12 million.

(W3) Disposal of shares in Nathan

Tutorial note

Control over Nathan has not been lost. Therefore, no profit or loss on disposal should be recorded in the consolidated financial statements.

A profit on disposal will have been recorded in the individual accounts of Marchant, calculated as follows:

	$m
Proceeds	18.0
Carrying amount of investment disposed (8/60 × $95m)	(12.7)
Profit	5.3

This profit on disposal must be removed from other income. There will be no profit or loss on disposal in the consolidated financial statements because control over the subsidiary has not been lost.

The current year gain on the investment in Nathan of $5 million ($95m – $90m) must also be removed from other comprehensive income.

(W4) Disposal of Option

Tutorial note

If control over an investment has been lost, a profit or loss on disposal must be calculated and included in the consolidated statement of profit or loss. This calculation is normally worth a lot of marks so it is important to learn the pro-forma.

As Marchant has sold a controlling interest in Option, a gain or loss on disposal should be calculated. Additionally, the results of Option should only be consolidated in the statement of profit or loss and other comprehensive income for the six months to 1 November 20X3. Thereafter Option should be accounted for using the equity method.

The gain recognised in profit or loss would be as follows:

	$m	$m
Fair value of consideration		50
Fair value of residual interest		40
		90
Less carrying amount of subsidiary:		
Net assets at disposal	90	
Goodwill at disposal (W5)	12	
Non-controlling interest at disposal	(34)	
		(68)
Gain on disposal to profit or loss		22

(W5) Goodwill of Option

Tutorial note

Goodwill calculations are a source of easy marks. Make sure that you know the pro-forma.

	$m
Fair value of consideration	70
Fair value of non-controlling interest	28
Fair value of identifiable net assets acquired	(86)
Goodwill	12

(W6) Intra-group sale

Tutorial note

Intra-group trading must be eliminated from consolidated revenue and costs of sales. Any unrealised profits should also be eliminated by increasing cost of sales. However, if a loss is made on intra-group trading, it may suggest that the value of the goods have fallen and therefore that the loss is actually realised.

The loss on the sale of the inventory is not eliminated from group profit or loss. Because the sale is at fair value, the inventory value must have been impaired and therefore the loss on sale must remain realised. However, the revenue and cost of sales of $12 million will be eliminated.

(W7) Profit and TCI attributable to the NCI

Tutorial note

When calculating the NCI's share of Nathan's profit and TCI, it is important to think about the date of the share disposal. The 8% holding of Nathan was not sold to the NCI until the very last day of the year. Therefore, when the profits and OCI of Nathan were earned, the NCI share was 40% rather than 48%.

	Nathan	**Option**
	$m	$m
Profit (6/12 Option)	19.0	7.5
× NCI % (40%)	7.6	3.0

The total profit attributable to the NCI is therefore $10.6 million ($7.6m + $3.0m).

	Nathan	**Option**
	$m	$m
TCI (6/12 Option)	21.0	7.5
× NCI % (40%)	8.4	3.0

The TCI attributable to the NCI is therefore $11.4 million ($8.4m + $3.0m).

(ii) Sale of shares in Nathan

Tutorial note

If control over an investment is retained, then a profit or loss on disposal is not included in the consolidated financial statements. Instead, equity is adjusted.

Note that part (ii) asks you to ***explain*** *how the sale of the shares will be treated. Calculations are not enough to score full marks.*

Once control has been achieved, transactions whereby the parent entity acquires further equity interests from non-controlling interests, or disposes of equity interests without losing control, are accounted for as equity transactions. Therefore:

- the carrying amount of the non-controlling interests is adjusted to reflect the changes in its interest in the subsidiary
- any difference between the amount by which the non-controlling interests is adjusted and the fair value of the consideration paid or received is recognised directly in equity attributed to the owners of the parent; and
- there is no consequential adjustment to the carrying amount of goodwill, and no gain or loss is recognised in profit or loss or in other comprehensive income.

Sale of equity interest in Nathan

	$m
Fair value of consideration received	18
Increase in non-controlling interest ($120m net assets + fair value adjustment of $14m (see below) + $12m goodwill) × 8%)	(11.7)
Positive movement in parent equity	6.3

The fair value adjustment at acquisition is calculated as follows:

	$m
Share capital	25
Retained earnings	65
Other components of equity	6
Fair value adjustment (bal. fig.)	14
Fair value of net assets	110

(b) Derecognition

Tutorial note

Start your answer by stating the de-recognition rules from IFRS 9. You would not be expected to know the same level as detail as is provided below.

Derecognition is required if either:

- the contractual rights to the cash flows from the financial asset have expired, or
- the financial asset has been transferred, and the transfer of that asset is eligible for derecognition.

An asset is transferred if the entity has transferred the contractual rights to receive the cash flows.

Once an entity has determined that the asset has been transferred, it then determines whether or not it has transferred substantially all of the risks and rewards of ownership of the asset. If substantially all the risks and rewards have been transferred, the asset is derecognised. If substantially all the risks and rewards have been retained, derecognition of the asset is precluded.

Tutorial note

Now apply the rules that you have stated to the information in the scenario.

Marchant has transferred its rights to receive cash flows. However, it has guaranteed that it will compensate the bank up to $3.6 million. As such, it has retained credit risk associated with the asset.

Additionally, Marchant would seem to have some late payment risk as it will be charged interest on amounts received over $3.6 million.

It would seem that Marchant has not transferred substantially the risks associated with the receivable. Therefore the receivables of $4 million should still be re-instated in the financial statements. Marchant should recognise a liability of $3.6 million for the cash proceeds received and remove the charge of $0.4 million from profit or loss.

Marking scheme		
		Marks
(a)	Consolidation	1
	Pro-rating of Option	1
	Intra-group trade	2
	Goodwill impairment adjustment	3
	Removal of gain on Nathan	2
	Removal of OCI gain	1
	Gain on disposal of Option	3
	Goodwill calculation for Option	1
	Associate	2
	NCI	2
	Sale of equity interest in Nathan	5
		23
(b)	IFRS 9 *Financial Instruments* derecognition – 1 mark per point	**7**
Total		**30**

18 ANGEL  *Walk in the footsteps of a top tutor*

Key answer tips

Students generally dislike statements of cash flows. However, there are lots of easy marks available because many of the cash flows do not require any workings – find these in the question and slot them straight into your pro-forma. Think about whether the figures need brackets – you will lose marks if you get this wrong.

To answer part (b) it is essential to know the definition of a 'cash equivalent'. State this definition and then apply it to each of the two deposits in the question.

(a) Statement of cash flows for the year ended 30 November 20X3

	$m
Profit before tax	188
Adjustments to operating activities	
Finance costs	11
Associate's profit	(12)
Depreciation	29
Financial assets – profit on sale ($40m – $26m)	(14)
Profit on sale of PPE ($63m – $49m)	(14)
Impairment of goodwill and intangible assets (W2)	116.5
Retirement benefit expense (W6)	10
	314.5
Movements in working capital	
Decrease in trade receivables ($125m – $180m – $3m)	58
Decrease in inventories ($155m – $190m – $6m)	41
Decrease in trade payables ($155m – $361m – $4m)	(210)
Cash generated from operations	203.5
Cash paid to retirement benefit scheme (W6)	(9)
Interest paid	(11)
Income taxes paid (W5)	(135.5)
Net cash generated by operating activities	48
Cash flows from investing activities	
Sale of financial assets	40
Purchase of financial assets	(57)
Purchase of property, plant and equipment (W1)	(66)
Purchase of subsidiary ($30m – $2m)	(28)
Proceeds from sale of property, plant and equipment	63
Dividend received from associate (W4)	3
Purchase of associate (W4)	(71)
Net cash flows used by investing activities	(116)
Cash flows from financing activities	
Proceeds from issue of shares (SOCIE)	225
Repayment of long-term borrowings ($26m – $57m)	(31)
Dividends paid (SOCIE)	(10)
Dividend paid to non-controlling interests (SOCIE)	(6)
Net cash generated by financing activities	178
Net increase in cash and cash equivalents	110
Cash and cash equivalents at beginning of period	355
Cash and cash equivalents at end of period	465

Workings

(W1) Property, plant and equipment

	$m
Balance at 1 December 20X2	465
Disposals	(49)
Depreciation	(29)
Revaluation	8
Acquisition of sub	14
Purchase of PPE (bal. fig.)	66
Balance at 30 November 20X3	475

(W2) Impairments

Tutorial note

Reconcile the goodwill balance year-on-year to find the impairment charge. This is a non-cash expense so must be added back in the reconciliation between profit before tax and cash generated from operations.

	$m
Opening balance at 1 December 20X2	120.0
Current year amount on subsidiary (W3)	11.5
Impairment (bal. fig.)	(26.5)
Closing balance at 30 November 20X3	105.0

Impairments of other intangibles amount to $90m ($240m – 150m).

Total impairments are therefore $116.5m ($90m + $26.5m).

(W3) Purchase of subsidiary

Tutorial note

The subsidiary's identifiable net assets are consolidated at fair value. This means that their carrying amount in the consolidated financial statements differs from their tax base, normally giving rise to a deferred tax liability.

Calculation of deferred tax arising on acquisition:

	$m
Fair values of Sweety's identifiable net assets excluding deferred tax	20.0
Less tax base	(15.0)
Temporary difference arising on acquisition	5.0
Net deferred tax liability arising on acquisition (30% × $5m)	1.5

Calculation of goodwill:

Purchase consideration	30.0
Fair value of net assets (net of deferred tax)	(20.0)
Deferred taxation	1.5
Goodwill arising on acquisition	11.5

(W4) Associate

Tutorial note

Associates are accounted for using the equity method.

	$m
Balance at 1 December 20X2	nil
Profit for period	12
Dividend received ($10m × 30%)	(3)
Cost of acquisition (bal. fig.)	71
Balance at 30 November 20X3	80

Therefore, cash paid for the investment is $71 million, and the cash dividend received is $3 million.

(W5) Taxation

Tutorial note

When calculating the tax paid during the year, include the opening and closing deferred tax balances in your workings. Also, remember that deferred tax charges may have been recorded in other comprehensive income.

	$m
Balance at 1 December 20X2 ($31m + $138m)	169
Charge for year (P/L)	46
Deferred tax on acquisition (W3)	1.5
Tax on revaluation PPE	2
Tax on financial assets	1
Cash paid (bal. fig.)	(135.5)
Balance at 30 November 20X3 ($35m + $49m)	84

(W6) Retirement benefit

Tutorial note

The service cost component and net interest component are non-cash expenses. These must be added back to profit in the reconciliation between profit before tax and cash generated from operations.

	$m
Opening balance at 1 December 20X2	74
Remeasurement component	4
Current year service cost plus interest	11
Contributions paid	(9)
Closing balance at 30 November 20X3	80

The $11 million service cost and interest figure above includes the carrying amount of the subsidiary's defined benefit obligation at the acquisition date. Therefore, the actual expense is $10m ($11m – $1m). This is added back in the reconciliation between profit before tax and cash generated from operations.

(b) Cash and cash equivalents comprise cash in hand and demand deposits, together with short-term, liquid investments which are readily convertible to a known amount of cash and which are subject to an insignificant risk of changes in value. IAS 7 *Statement of Cash Flow* does not define 'short term' but does state 'an investment normally qualifies as a cash equivalent only when it has a short maturity of, say, three months or less from the date of acquisition'.

Consequently, equity or other investments which do not have a maturity date are normally excluded from cash equivalents.

Tutorial note

Remember to apply the definition of 'cash equivalents' to the scenario.

As regards the deposits, the following is the case:

(i) Although the principal ($3 million) will be recoverable with early withdrawal, the entity will lose all accumulated interest over the term, which seems to be a significant penalty. The cash is not needed to meet short-term cash commitments and so would not qualify as a cash equivalent.

(ii) Although the deposit is stated to have a 12-month maturity period, it can be withdrawn with 21 days' notice. Although this incurs a penalty, the reduction in the rate of interest from 3% to 2% is unlikely to be considered significant and is in line with the bank's short-term deposit rate. The intention of management is to keep these funds available for short-term cash needs and so this deposit is likely to qualify as a cash equivalent.

Marking scheme

		Marks
(a)	Finance costs	1
	Associate's profit	1
	Depreciation	1
	Profit on disposal of PPE/financial assets	1
	Impairment of intangibles	2
	Pension expense	1
	Working capital movements	3
	Cash paid to pension	1
	Interest paid	1
	Tax paid	2
	Sale and purchase of financial asset	1
	Purchase of PPE	2
	Purchase of subsidiary	1
	Proceeds from PPE disposal	1
	Dividend from associate	1
	Purchase of associate	1
	Proceeds from shares	1
	Borrowings	1
	Dividends paid	1
	Dividends paid to NCI	1
	Net movement in cash	1
		26
	Maximum	**25**
(b)	Cash and cash equivalents – 1 mark per point	**5**
Total		**30**

19 TRAVELER  *Walk in the footsteps of a top tutor*

Key answer tips

This is a good question for testing your knowledge of a number of consolidation issues. In particular, this group uses both the share of net assets method and the fair value method to value the non-controlling interest at acquisition. This has important implications for subsequent goodwill impairments – goodwill calculated under the share of net asset method must be grossed up to include the non-controlling interest's share when performing an impairment review.

This question also involves the parent company increasing its shareholding in a subsidiary from 60% to 80%. Goodwill is calculated on the date that control is achieved and is not re-calculated. Instead, this increase in the group's shareholding is accounted for in equity.

(a) Consolidated Statement of Financial Position at 30 November 20X1

	$m
Assets:	
Non-current assets:	
Property, plant and equipment (W8)	1,845
Goodwill (W3)	69.2
Financial assets ($108m + $10m + $20m)	138
Current assets ($1,067m + $781m + $350m)	2,198
Total assets	4,250.2
Equity and liabilities	
Equity attributable to owners of parent	
Share capital	1,120
Retained earnings (W5)	1,058
Other components of equity (W5)	91.7
	2,269.7
Non-controlling interest (W4)	343.5
	2,613.2
Total non-current liabilities ($455m + $323m + $73m)	851.0
Current liabilities ($274m + $199m + $313m)	786.0
Total liabilities	1,637.0
Total equity and liabilities	4,250.2

Workings

(W1) Group structure

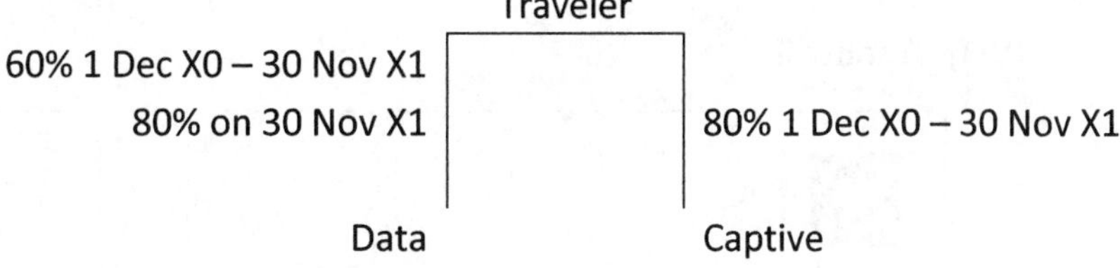

(W2) Net assets

Tutorial note

The identifiable net assets of a subsidiary are consolidated at fair value. Make sure that fair value adjustments are processed through your net asset workings.

Data

	Acq'n date	**Rep date**
	$m	$m
Share capital	600	600
Retained earnings	299	442
Other Equity	26	37
Fair value adjustment – Land (bal. fig)	10	10
	935	1,089

Of the net asset movement of $154 million ($1,089m – $935m), $11 million ($37m – $26m) relates to other components of equity and the remaining $143 million relates to retained earnings.

Captive

	Acq'n date	**Rep date**
	$m	$m
Share capital	390	390
Retained earnings	90	169
Other Equity	24	45
Fair value adjustment – Land (bal. fig)	22	22
	526	626

Of the net asset movement of $100 million ($626m – $526m), $21 million ($45m – $24m) relates to other components of equity and the remaining $79 million relates to retained earnings.

(W3) Goodwill

Tutorial note

Pay attention to whether the NCI at acquisition is being measured at its share of the subsidiary's identifiable net assets or at fair value.

Remember that goodwill is calculated at the date control is achieved over another company. It is not recalculated for any further share purchases.

Data

	$m
Fair value of consideration for 60% interest	600
Fair value of non-controlling interest	395
Fair value of identifiable net assets acquired (W2)	(935)
Goodwill at acquisition	60
Impairment (W6)	(50)
Goodwill at reporting date	10

Captive

	$m
Fair value of consideration	541
NCI at acquisition ($526 × 20%)	105.2
Less fair value of identifiable net assets (W2):	(526)
Goodwill	120.2
Impairment (W6)	(61)
	59.2

Total goodwill at the reporting date is $69.2m ($10 + $59.2).

The assets transferred as part of the consideration need to be removed from non-current assets, and the gain on disposal needs to be calculated. The sale consideration of $64 million has been recorded in profit. The carrying amount of the asset is $56 million, giving a gain on disposal of $8 million.

The adjustment required to arrive at the gain is:

Dr Retained earnings (W5) $56m

Cr PPE (W8) $56m

(W4) Non-controlling interest

	$m
NCI in Data at acquisition (W3)	395
NCI % of Data's post acquisition net assets (40% × $154m (W2))	61.6
Reduction in NCI (W7)	(228.3)
Impairment of Data goodwill (W6)	(10)
NCI in Captive:	
NCI in Captive at acquisition (W3)	105.2
NCI % of Captive's post-acquisition net assets (20% × $100m (W2))	20.0
	343.5

(W5) Reserves

Retained earnings

	$m
Traveler	1,066.0
Sale of non-current asset (W3)	(56.0)
Impairment of Data goodwill (W6)	(40)
Impairment of Captive goodwill (W6)	(61)
Post-acquisition retained earnings:	
Data (60% × $143m (W2))	85.8
Captive (80% × $79m (W2))	63.2
	1,058

Other components of equity

	$m
Traveler	60.0
Data (60% × $11m (W2))	6.6
Captive (80% × $21m (W2))	16.8
Positive movement in equity (W7)	8.3
	91.7

(W6) Impairment of goodwill

Tutorial note

Pay close attention to whether the non-controlling interest has been valued using the share of net assets method or the fair value method.

If the share of net assets method has been used, then only the goodwill attributable to the parent has been calculated. When performing an impairment review, this goodwill must be notionally grossed up to include the NCI's share.

Data

	$m
Goodwill (W3)	60
Identifiable net assets (W2)	1,089
Total	1,149
Recoverable amount	(1,099)
Goodwill impairment	50

The goodwill impairment relating to Data will be split 80%/20% between the group and the NCI. Thus retained earnings will be debited with $40 million (W5) and NCI with $10 million (W4).

Tutorial note

It could be argued that a 60:40 allocation between group and NCI is also appropriate as this was how profits that arose in the year have been apportioned and the impairment is a loss that arose in the year, albeit calculated at the year end.

Captive

	$m	$m
Goodwill (W3)	120.2	
Notional NCI ($120.2 × 20/80)	30.1	
Total notional goodwill		150.3
Identifiable net assets (W2)		626.0
Total		776.3
Recoverable amount		(700.0)
Impairment		76.3

The impairment is allocated to the notional goodwill. However, only 80% of the notional goodwill has been recognised in the consolidated statements and so only 80% of the impairment is accounted for. This means that the goodwill impairment recognised is $61m ($76.3 × 80%). This expense is all attributable to the group and therefore retained earnings (W5) must be debited with $61m.

(W7) Increase in shareholding

Tutorial note

If the group increases its shareholding in a subsidiary, goodwill is not recalculated. Instead, this transaction is accounted for in equity. The difference between the cash paid and the decrease in the NCI is recorded in other components of equity.

	$m	$m
Fair value of consideration		220
NCI in Data at acquisition (W4)	395	
NCI % of Data's net assets movement (W4)	61.6	
NCI per share purchase	456.6	
Reduction in NCI (20/40 × $456.6m)		228.3
Positive movement in equity (W5)		8.3

(W8) Property, plant and equipment

	$m
Traveler	439
Data	810
Captive	620
Increase in value of land – Data (W2)	10
Increase in value of land – Captive (W2)	22
Less disposal of asset (W3)	(56)
	1,845

(b) Disclosure of the impact of fair value uplifts

IAS 2 *Inventories* requires the carrying amount of inventories sold to be recognised as an expense in the period in which the related revenue is recognised. Cost of sales are costs previously included in the measurement of inventory which has now been sold plus unallocated production overheads and abnormal amounts of production costs of inventories.

IFRS 3 *Business Combinations* requires an acquirer to measure the identifiable assets acquired in a business combination at their fair values at the date of acquisition. Therefore, the carrying amount of the inventories originating from the acquisition of the subsidiary is their acquisition-date fair value. Consequently, the entire carrying amount of inventory, including the effects of the fair value step-up, should be presented as cost of sales.

IAS 1 *Presentation of Financial Statements* sets out minimum levels of required items in the financial statements by requiring certain items to be presented on the face of, or in the notes to, the financial statements and in other required disclosures.

IAS 1 provides little further guidance on the presentation of line items in financial statements, such as the level of detail or number of line items that should be presented in the financial statements. The absence of specific requirements arises from the fact that the guidance in IAS 1 relies on management's judgement about which additional line items, headings and subtotals:

(a) are relevant to an understanding of the entity's financial position/ financial performance; and

(b) should be presented in a manner which provides relevant, reliable, comparable and understandable information.

IAS 1 allows entities to include additional line items, amend descriptions and the ordering of items in order to explain the elements of financial performance due to various activities, which may differ in frequency and predictability.

Transactions like business combinations may have a significant impact on profit or loss and these transactions are not necessarily frequent or regular. However, the practice of presenting non-recurring items may be interpreted as a way to present 'extraordinary items' in the financial statements despite the fact that 'extraordinary items' are not allowed under IAS 1. It can also be argued that additional lines and subtotals, as permitted by IAS 1, may add complexity to the analysis of the financial statements, which may become difficult to understand if entities use sub-totals and additional headings to isolate the effects of non-recurring transactions from classes of expense or income.

To conclude, the cost of the inventories sold should be presented as a cost of sale and not split in the manner proposed by Traveler.

Marking scheme		
		Marks
(a)	Property, plant and equipment	2
	Goodwill	3
	Other assets/liabilities	2
	Share capital	1
	Retained earnings	5
	Other components of equity	3
	Non-controlling interest	4
		23
(b)	Fair value adjustment disclosure – 1 mark per point	**7**
Total		**30**

20 ROSE  *Walk in the footsteps of a top tutor*

Key answer tips

This question involves consolidating an overseas subsidiary.

When consolidating a subsidiary with a different functional currency to that of the group, its assets and liabilities are translated at the closing exchange rate. Translation differences arise on goodwill and the opening net assets and profit of the subsidiary. Current year exchange differences are recorded in other comprehensive income. The cumulative exchange gains and losses are held in equity.

This question also involves the parent company increasing its shareholding in a subsidiary from 70% to 80%. This results in a decrease in the NCI holding from 30% to 20%, a decline of one third. Such transactions are accounted for within equity and no adjustments are made to goodwill.

(a) Rose plc

Consolidated Statement of Financial Position at 30 April 20X1

Assets	
Non-current assets	$m
Property, plant and equipment (W11)	633
Goodwill ($16m + $6.2m) (W3)	22.2
Intangible assets ($4m – $1m) (W2)	3
Current assets ($118m + $100m + D330m/5)	284
Total assets	942.2

Equity and liabilities:	
Share capital	158
Retained earnings (W5)	267.37
Translation reserve (W7)	10.27
Other components of equity (W6)	4.73
Non-controlling interest (W4)	89.83
Total equity	530.2
Non-current liabilities ($56m + $42m + D160m/5)	130
Current liabilities ($185m + $77m + D100m/5)	282
Total equity and liabilities	942.2

Workings

(W1) Group structure

Rose

70% 1 May X0 – 30 April X1
80% 30 April X1
Petal

52% for full year
Stem

(W2) Net assets

Tutorial note

The identifiable net assets of a subsidiary at acquisition are recognised at fair value.

Petal

	Acq'n date	**Rep date**
	$m	$m
Share capital	38	38
Other equity	3	4
Retained earnings	49	56
FV adjustment – land (bal. fig)	30	30
FV of recognised net assets	120	128
FV adjustment – patent	4	4
Amortisation ($4m/4 years)	–	(1)
FV of identifiable net assets	124	131

Of the net asset increase of $7 million ($131m – $124m), $1 million ($4m – $3m) relates to other components of equity and the remaining $6 million relates to retained earnings.

Stem

	Acq'n date	**Rep date**
	Dinars m	Dinars m
Share capital	200	200
Other equity	–	–
Retained earnings	220	300
FV adjustment – land (bal. fig)	75	75
	495	575

The net asset increase of D80 million (D575m – D495m) all relates to retained earnings because Stem has no other components of equity.

(W3) Goodwill

Tutorial note

Goodwill is calculated on the date control is achieved. It is not recalculated when further share purchases are made.

Goodwill in an overseas subsidiary should be translated each year at the closing exchange rate.

Petal

	$m
Fair value of consideration	94
Fair value of NCI at acquisition	46
Fair value of identifiable net assets acquired (W2)	(124)
Goodwill	16

Stem

	Dinars m
Fair value of consideration ($46m × 6 (acquisition rate))	276
Fair value of NCI at acquisition	250
Fair value of identifiable net assets acquired (W2)	(495)
Goodwill	31

Goodwill is deemed to be an asset of the subsidiary and is translated at the closing rate at each reporting date. Goodwill in Stem is therefore $6.2m (D31m/5).

(W4) Non-controlling Interest

	$m
Petal at acquisition (W3)	46
NCI % of post-acquisition net assets (30% × ($131m – $124m)) (W2)	2.1
Reduction in NCI due to share purchase (W10)	(16.03)
Stem at acquisition (D250m/6) (W3)	41.67
NCI % of post-acquisition net assets (48% × D80m/5.8) (W2)	6.62
Exchange gain – goodwill (W8)	0.49
Exchange gain on net assets (W9)	8.98
	89.83

(W5) Retained earnings

	$m
Rose	256
Rose's share of post-acquisition retained earnings:	
Petal (70% × $6m) (W2)	4.2
Stem (52% × D80m/5.8) (W2)	7.17
	267.37

(W6) Other components of equity

	$m
Rose	7
Petal – negative movement in equity (W10)	(2.97)
Share of Petal's post-acquisition other components (70% × $1m) (W2)	0.7
	4.73

(W7) Translation reserve

	$m
Exchange gain on goodwill (W8)	0.54
Exchange gain on net assets (W9)	9.73
	10.27

(W8) Exchange gain on Stem's goodwill

Tutorial note

If goodwill is calculated using the fair value method, the exchange gain or loss (and any impairment) must be apportioned between the group and the NCI.

	Dinars m	Exchange rate	$m
Goodwill at 1 May 20X0 (W3)	31	6.0	5.17
Impairment	–	5.8	–
Exchange gain (bal. fig)	–		1.03
Goodwill at 30 April 20X1	31	5.0	6.2

The exchange gain is allocated between the group and the NCI as follows:

Group: $1.03m × 52% = $0.54m (W7)

NCI: $1.03m × 48% = $0.49m (W4)

(W9) Exchange gain on Stem's opening net assets and profit

Tutorial note

Exchange gains or losses arising on the opening net assets and profit of an overseas subsidiary must be apportioned between the group and the NCI.

	Dinars m	Exchange rate	$m
Net assets at 1 May 20X0 (W2)	495	6.0	82.5
Profit for the year (W2)	80	5.8	13.79
Exchange gain (bal. fig)	–		18.71
Net assets at 30 April 20X1 (W2)	575	5.0	115.0

The exchange gain on the opening net assets and profit is allocated between the group and the NCI as follows:

Group: $18.71m × 52% = $9.73m (W7)

NCI: $18.71m × 48% = $8.98m (W4)

(W10) Increase in ownership

Tutorial note

Goodwill is not recalculated when the group increases its shareholding in a subsidiary. Instead, the difference between the consideration for the additional shares and the reduction in the NCI is accounted for in other components of equity.

	$m
Fair value of consideration	19
Reduction in NCI in Petal (10/30 × ($46m + $2.1m) (W4))	(16.03)
Negative movement (debit) in equity	2.97

(W11) Property, plant and equipment

	$m
Rose	385
Petal	117
Stem (D430m/5)	86
Petal fair value adjustment (W2)	30
Stem fair value adjustment (D75m/5) (W2)	15
	633

(b) Foreign exchange

Tutorial note

To score highly, this question requires a detailed knowledge of IAS 21. However, solid marks can still be obtained for demonstrating a basic understanding of the standard.

Monetary items

Monetary items are units of currency held and assets and liabilities to be received or paid in a fixed or determinable number of units of currency. This would include foreign bank accounts, receivables, payables and loans. Non-monetary items are other items which are in the statement of financial position, such as non-current assets, inventories and investments in equity.

Monetary items are retranslated using the closing exchange rate (the year-end rate). The exchange differences on retranslation of monetary assets must be recorded in profit or loss. IAS 21 *The Effects of Changes in Foreign Exchange Rates* is not specific under which heading the exchange gains and losses should be classified.

Non-monetary items

Non-monetary items which are measured in terms of historical cost in a foreign currency are translated using the exchange rate at the date of the transaction. If non-monetary items are measured at fair value in a foreign currency then this amount must be translated using exchange rates at the date when the fair value was measured. Exchange differences on such items are recorded consistently with the recognition of the movement in fair values. For example, exchange differences on an investment property, a fair value through profit and loss financial asset, or arising on impairment will be recorded in profit or loss. Exchange differences on the upwards revaluation of property, plant and equipment would be recorded in other comprehensive income.

Overseas subsidiaries

When translating a foreign subsidiary, the exchange differences on all the net assets, including goodwill, are recorded in other comprehensive income and are held in equity. The proportion belonging to the shareholders of the parent will usually be held in a separate translation reserve. The proportion belonging to the non-controlling interest is not shown separately but subsumed in the non-controlling interest figure in the consolidated financial statements.

If Rose were to sell all of its equity shares in Stem, the cumulative exchange differences belonging to the equity holders of Rose will be reclassified from equity to profit or loss. In addition, the cumulative exchange differences attributable to the non-controlling interest would be derecognised but would not be reclassified to profit or loss.

Marking scheme		
		Marks
(a)	Amortisation of patent	1
	Acquisition of further interest	5
	Stem – translation and calculation of goodwill	6
	Retained earnings and other equity	4
	Non-controlling interest	3
	Property, plant and equipment	2
	Other assets/liabilities	1
		22
(b)	Currency issues – 1 mark per point	**8**
Total		**30**

SECTION A QUESTIONS – REPORTING AND ETHICAL IMPLICATIONS

21 AGENCY GROUP (SEP/DEC 2021)  *Walk in the footsteps of a top tutor*

Key answer tips

This is a typical SBR exam question 2 with some financial reporting knowledge and application (foreign currency principles in group accounts, intangible assets and revenue recognition) coupled with associated ethical issues.

Spend your time on each requirement in proportion to the marks allocated to it. Use most of your allotted time on (a) (ii) the ethics requirement (6 marks plus 2 professional marks) and least time on (a)(i) (3 marks).

(a) (i) Foreign exchange

Tutorial note

Identifying that the foreign currency gains are incorrectly treated (they should be taken to other comprehensive income rather than the P/L) is the key learning point here. Candidates should spot this issue fairly easily, and if not, must revise the foreign currency consolidation principles as this is a fundamental concept.

The content regarding the disposal of the subsidiary and the subsequent recycling out of OCI and into profit, whilst relevant, takes the discussion further than most candidates would.

IAS 21 *The Effects of Changes in Foreign Exchange Rates* requires gains and losses to be reclassified from equity to the statement of profit or loss (SOPL) as a reclassification adjustment. When a group has a foreign subsidiary, a group exchange difference will arise on the re-translation of the subsidiary's goodwill and net assets. In accordance with IAS 21, such exchange differences are recognised in other comprehensive income (OCI) and so accumulate in other components of equity (OCE). On the disposal of the subsidiary, IAS 21 requires that the net cumulative balance of group exchange differences be reclassified from equity to the SOPL as a reclassification adjustment. Mr Raavi should not have included the exchange gains arising on the re-translation of the foreign subsidiary in the SOPL as it is currently only held for sale. When the subsidiary is then sold, the gains accumulated in OCE may be reclassified to profit or loss.

(ii) Ethics

Tutorial note

Do not think about the financial reporting requirements and the ethics issues as mutually exclusive. Good answers will always strive to find the motivations for any incorrect accounting treatments (in this case, within in (a)(i)) and link them to potential ethical issues.

*Be as specific as possible here. The requirement asks for the ethical issues caused by **Ms Malgun's** actions when managing Mr Raavi. Therefore, use the actual names, roles and details provided within the scenario to demonstrate how the actions of Ms Malgun cause ethical threats (e.g. Ms Malgun's expertise, the profit related payment received by Ms Malgun, Ms Malgun's delegation to an inexperienced Mr Raavi). Rote learned ethics answers do not score well, application to the scenario does.*

Although Mr Raavi is a student accountant, he is bound by the same ethical codes as a qualified accountant. Mr Raavi is employed on the basis that either he or Agency Co can choose to terminate his employment for no reason. Even though the jurisdiction has laws which protect such employees from termination due to discrimination, it can be argued that the ability to terminate employment benefits the employer more than the employee. Thus, a primary issue is whether this type of employment contract is fair to the employee and whether it can result in unethical behaviour.

It can be argued that fear of termination acts as a motivation for Mr Raavi to act unethically and that this type of employment has provided Mr Raavi with an opportunity as he had struggled to be employed. It is arguable whether fear of losing his job is an effective motivator for Mr Raavi. Also, allowing employees to be arbitrarily dismissed amounts to treating them with very little respect. The employer's ability to terminate a contract without reason undermines Mr Raavi's potential to set and achieve goals for himself. Mr Raavi's ability to terminate employment without cause, on the other hand, has comparatively little effect on the company's ability to set and achieve its goals.

Competitive markets are more likely to see unethical behaviour especially if unethical behaviour benefits the organisation. Accountability can have a major influence on ethical behaviour. People may behave unethically if they do not have responsibility for their actions. Mr Raavi is only an ACCA student accountant and therefore would not bear the ultimate responsibility for the inaccurate accounting for foreign exchange gains. Ms Malgun obviously knew that the accounting was inaccurate but because it benefited the company and helped the performance targets, she was prepared to overlook it. Also, this can be an unintended consequence of performance related pay as Ms Malgun is partly remunerated through pay related to profit targets. However, in order to preserve her position, she disciplined Mr Raavi after the financial statements had been published, thus displaying a lack of integrity and professional values in her dealings with Mr Raavi and stakeholders.

Ms Malgun should not have left the preparation of the year-end financial statements to Mr Raavi as he is a student accountant and has only been with the company for 3 months. She has significant experience and expertise in their preparation. Work pressure can influence ethical behaviour. Difficult performance goals and time pressure make unethical behaviour more likely. When employees are under pressure, this not only affects their wellbeing and motivation, but also their behaviour. Ms Malgun is an expert in IFRS standards and should have ensured that she allocated some time to assist Mr Raavi in the preparation of the year-end financial statements. It is the responsibility of both Ms Malgun and Mr Raavi to engage in fair and accurate reporting with regard to the truthfulness of the data they provide as well as its completeness. It is ethically important for accountants to present the financial information in a way which is clear and honest.

Competition can influence unethical behaviour. Individuals are more inclined to engage in unethical behaviour when their organisation is in competition with other organisations or they have been given targets which have to be met. When unethical behaviour leads to a gain for a company, managers choose less severe disciplinary measures for their employees. Thus, although Ms Malgun knew of the error in the financial statements, she only reprimanded Mr Raavi after the financial statements had been published and even then, she then offered him a full-time contract instead of his current temporary contract.

(b) Sale of licence

Tutorial note

If this question considered the disposal of property, plant and equipment, most candidates would identify that Agency would record a gain or loss on disposal (not revenue). SBR will test similar situations for other, more complicated types of non-current asset (e.g. intangibles, financial assets). However, the result is no different to that of the disposal of PPE – a gain or loss on disposal recorded in profit calculated as proceeds less carrying amount.

The disposal of an intangible asset, as decribed in this scenario, will have the same outcome. Do not let the complications described in the scenario (e.g.variable consideration, development costs) prevent you from identifying this achievable conclusion.

Agency Co had correctly capitalised development costs for Headon at a carrying amount of $30 million. IAS 38 *Intangible Assets* states that an intangible asset, in this case a proportion of the development costs, may be derecognised on disposal or when no future economic benefits are expected from its use or disposal. The gain or loss arising on derecognition is the difference between the net proceeds and the carrying amount of the asset. Gains are not classified as revenue. The amount of gain or loss arising from the derecognition will be affected by the determination of the transaction price with reference to IFRS 15 *Revenue from Contracts with Customers*.

In assessing whether an entity's promises to transfer goods or services to the customer are separately identifiable, the objective of IFRS 15 is to determine whether the nature of the promise is to transfer each of those goods or services individually or, instead, to transfer a combined item.

Kokila Co can benefit from the licence without Agency Co's manufacturing service because there are other entities which can provide the manufacturing service. Therefore, Agency Co's promises to grant the licence and to provide the manufacturing service are separately identifiable.

Tutorial note

As per IFRS 15, variable consideration will only be recorded if it is highly probable that a signicant reversal will not occur. Here, the reversal of the variable consideration can only be refuted with confidence once the target of $35m sales has been met.

The consideration for the licence comprises the up-front payment of $15 million and a variable consideration of $3 million. Initially, only the up-front payment will be recognised as proceeds, which is used to calculate any gain or loss arising on the disposal of the South American development costs. The variable consideration will be recognised in SOPL when it occurs, i.e. when South American sales exceed $35 million. The performance obligation needs to be satisfied before the payment is recognised.

Judgement is required to determine the portion of the carrying amount of the intangible asset to derecognise, relative to the amount retained. Therefore, a gain is recognised on disposal of the South American development costs of $9 million ($15m – ($30m × 20%)).

(c) Drug development

Tutorial note

*Remember the PIRATE criteria! Development costs can only be capitalised if the project is **profitable**, the company **intends** to use or sell the product, **resources** are available to complete the project, the company has the **ability** to use or sell the product, the project is **technically feasible** and the **expenditure** is identifiable.*

Apply the rules to Agency's development costs and make a conclusion on the accounting treatment.

Development costs are capitalised as an intangible asset if certain criteria in IAS 38 are met.

There is no definitive starting point for the capitalisation of internal development costs and, therefore, Agency Co must use its judgement, based on the facts and circumstances of each product. A strong indication that Agency Co has met all of the IAS 38 criteria arises when regulatory approval is issued for the biosimilar drug as it proves the technical feasibility of the asset. This is often the most difficult criterion to demonstrate.

Another criterion to be met is that the asset should generate probable future economic benefits and demonstrate the existence of a market, or the usefulness of the asset if it is to be used internally. At present, this criterion has not been met as the product is aimed at a small group of people who will only pay a notional amount if it is an effective product.

In addition, regulatory approval has only been applied for, and there is a concern over the limited market and revenue stream. Thus, the costs are unlikely to meet the capitalisation criteria and all costs to date will be written off to profit or loss.

ACCA marking guide

		Marks
(a) (i)	Discussion and appropriateness of the accounting policy	3
(ii)	Application and discussion of ethical principles to scenario which includes:	6
	Employment contract	
	Accounting policy and profit related pay	
	Time pressures	
	Competition	
	Less severe discipline	
		9
(b)	Discussion of key principles of IFRS 15 and relate to scenario	2
	Derecognition of intangible asset and IAS 38	2
	Calculation of gain	1
		5
(c)	Setting out principles for capitalisation	1
	Application of principles to scenario	3
		4
	Professional marks	2
Total		**20**

Examiner's comments

Requirement (a) was conveniently split into two parts, so providing a helpful guide as to how long to spend on each aspect.

a) i) Three marks equates to just over five minutes, so your answer should be brief. On disposal of the foreign subsidiary, the related net exchange differences are reclassified from equity to the statement of profit or loss. So, had the subsidiary been disposed, the accounting treatment would have been appropriate.

However, this was not a disposal – the subsidiary was reclassified as held for sale. Your answer could have explained how the subsidiary should be accounted for under IFRS 5 *Non-current Assets Held for Sale and Discontinued Operations* and credit would be available for this. However, given the brevity of the requirement, and the focus on the exchange differences in the question, better (time-managed) answers explained that since no sale had yet been made, transfer of the accumulated foreign exchange gains from the other components of equity was not appropriate.

a)ii) This second requirement asks for a discussion of the ethical issues. Part (a)(ii) has a total of eight marks (6 marks plus the two professional marks for the quality of your discussion). A well planned answer that covers all the key areas and meets all the requirements is more likely to gain both professional marks. A discussion of ethical issues will include the identification of threats to impartiality, for example. You may want to begin by summarising the key issues from the scenario, and then link these with concerns you may identify.

Note that these issues don't just stem from what the finance director has done, but also the pressures placed on the student, and the systemic pressures placed on the finance director by the board. Remember that the requirement has six marks, so seven separate issues should have a very good chance of gaining a high score.

b) For five marks, this question offers candidates a lot to describe: principles of derecognition under IAS 38 *Intangible Assets*, and principles of IFRS 15 *Revenue from Contracts with Customers*. Good answers would cover each aspect of the question in turn, leading to a short calculation of the gain on disposal of the development costs. Candidates who misread the requirement described the accounting requirements for Kokila Co with some answers describing lease accounting (wrongly assuming Agency Co retained control of the entire rights).

c) The scenario describes a number of situations which should be familiar to candidates from their assumed knowledge of IAS 38 *Intangible Assets*. Candidates should be expected to apply their knowledge of the recognition requirements relating to development costs to the information provided in the scenario, and not merely list out the requirements. In this case what is key to the treatment as research or development is whether regulatory approval of the drug is achieved: without this, technical feasibility is not assured. Better answers considered the effectiveness of the asset in generating future economic benefit where the product is aimed at a small group of people who will only pay a notional amount. This last point was overlooked by quite a few candidates.

22 BISMUTH (MAR/JUN 2021)  *Walk in the footsteps of a top tutor*

Key answer tips

This question includes some tricky, modern day accounting issues. However, do not get too bogged down in the technical bits. State the rules, apply them to the scenario and move on. In the Qn 2 style questions, you must get answers to the ethics part. There are 5 marks each for the accounting issues but 8 marks plus 2 professional marks for the ethics section. You must get answers to the ethics requirement to enable the marker to award the professional marks.

(a) Impairment testing of mines

Tutorial note

The important issue here is that an assessment as to whether the mines are impaired occurs under IAS 36. You must compare the carrying amount to the recoverable amount of the mines.

If you make a mistake (e.g. with the treatment of the decommissioning costs) it is still possible to conclude that the mine is impaired. A description of the accounting treatment of the impairment using your calculated figures will score subsequent OFR (own figure rule) marks.

N.B. If you erroneously left the decommissioning costs out of both the carrying amount and the recoverable amount, you will arrive at exactly the same impairment charge as provided in the answer!

Most liabilities are ignored when calculating recoverable amounts in impairment testing. However, certain liabilities, such as decommissioning liabilities, cannot be separated from the related assets.

IAS 36 *Impairment of Assets* requires the carrying amount of a recognised liability to be deducted from both the carrying amount of a cash generating unit (CGU) and the amount determined using the value-in-use (VIU). The recoverable amount of the asset should be determined using the VIU model in IAS 36.

The amount of the decommissioning provision is used to calculate the recoverable amount by deducting it from the VIU amount. The recoverable amount is then compared to the carrying amount of the CGU which should be adjusted to include the decommissioning provision in accordance with IAS 37 *Provisions, Contingent Liabilities and Contingent Assets.*

Cash flow projections should be based on reasonable and supportable assumptions, the most recent budgets and forecasts, and extrapolation for periods beyond budgeted projections. IAS 36 presumes that budgets and forecasts should not go beyond five years; for periods after five years, extrapolation should be used from the earlier budgets. In this case, the mines have a useful life of five years or less and, therefore, the cash flow projections can be used in the impairment testing.

At 31 December 20X7	**$m**
Present value of future cash inflows from the sale of components for re-use	20
Present value of future cash inflows from sale of mining output	203
Present value of future cash outflows from operating the mines	(48)
Carrying amount of decommissioning provision	(53)
Recoverable amount (NPV of cash flows)	122
Carrying amount of the mines	200
Carrying amount of decommissioning provision	(53)
Net carrying amount of mines	147

The recoverable amount is less than the carrying amount and, hence, there is an impairment charge of $25 million ($147 million – $122 million).

(b) Class A and Class B shares

Tutorial note

Part (b) is particularly tricky and can take a while to decipher what is going on. Remember, it is only worth 5 marks. A maximum of 9 minutes to think about and write your answer. Therefore, keep your answer as simple as possible.

Answer the question – are Share A and Share B debt or equity? Use the definitions as per financial liabilities or equity instruments to help structure your opinion (e.g. to be a liability an obligation must exist so look for indications within the terms that suggest an obligation is or is not present). Present an argument for A, present an argument for B and quickly move on to the next requirement.

Do not think you must have an answer that uses exactly the same arguments as provided here within the published answer. The marker knows this is technically difficult and will reward candidates who show perseverance and the courage to provide an argument either way.

IAS 32 *Financial Instruments: Presentation* states that a financial instrument is a financial liability if it provides that, on settlement, the entity will deliver either:

(i) cash or another financial asset, or

(ii) its own shares whose value is determined to exceed substantially the value of the cash or other financial asset.

Bismuth Co has discretion over whether 'rewards' are payable on class A shares and class B shares. The rewards are essentially a dividend paid on the investment. This would seem to indicate that both instruments should be classified as equity. The Bitcoin can be readily converted into cash in Bismuth Co's jurisdiction and therefore can be treated in the same way as legal tender or cash (also known as fiat money).

The possibility of Bismuth Co listing on a stock exchange is a contingent settlement provision. Bismuth Co is able to avoid listing shares on a stock exchange if it so chooses but is unlikely to do so, as the listing is deemed to be highly probable. Thus, the class A shares will be classified as a liability because the value of the share settlement of 1,000 class A instruments at 2 Bitcoin substantially exceeds that of the 'cash' settlement option of 1 Bitcoin for the same number of instruments and Bismuth Co is implicitly obliged to redeem the instruments for a 'cash' amount of 1 Bitcoin.

If Bismuth Co fails to exercise its call option on the class B shares, it must transfer an additional reward to the holder. An obligation must be established through the terms and conditions of the financial instrument. Anything outside the contractual terms is not relevant to the classification process in accordance with IAS 32. Therefore, the potential failure to exercise the call option does not affect the classification of class B shares as equity as there is no unavoidable contractual obligation to pay the reward or to call the instrument. Also, if the call option is not exercised, the reward payable will only constitute an increase in the dividend rate and not a redemption of the class B shares. Hence the class B shares constitute equity shares.

(c) Blockchain technology

Tutorial note

As always the ethics part has 2 professional marks associated with it, which makes it even more important to get an answer to the scenario. If you do not attempt the question, you cannot be awarded the professional marks.

The scenario here is very contemporary, focussing on issues arising from the implementation of Blockchain technology. Do not let this distract you from the main task of discussing the ethical issues. Candiates do not need a detailed understanding of how the technologies work, but should appreciate how it may affect the accountants involved. There are some very achieveable ethical conundrums to consider here regarding confidentiality, conflicts of interest and due competence and care.

The digital age and the problems it presents for accountants does seem to be a regular occurance within recent examinations (see the next question too).

Ms Pleasant is in a difficult position as regards information gained at a previous employer. In general, she should respect the confidentiality of information acquired as a result of professional and business relationships and, therefore, not disclose any such information to third parties without proper and specific authority, unless there is a legal or professional right or duty to disclose. In addition, she should not use the information for her personal advantage. However, the situation will depend upon the nature of the confidentiality agreement with her previous employer. This agreement may have been made in order to protect commercially sensitive information and to prevent her from sharing such information with Bismuth Co. However, if the agreement is not clear or specific, then it will be left up to the ethical conscience of Ms Pleasant as to whether she should disclose the information. The purpose of the agreement is to prevent the disclosure of this type of sensitive information and the chief accountant's ethical conscience should prevail. In addition, the confidentiality agreement may be legally binding.

Opportunities and challenges presented by technology, and new business models, require an evolving level of digital literacy by accountants. Accountants should provide relevant, decision-useful analysis to ensure that the right technological applications are adopted in the best interests of the business. New business models present opportunities for professional accountants to provide relevant advice on regulatory matters. This development requires a growing set of competencies. These competencies relate to, not only financial matters, but also social impact assessment, environmental accounting or other non-financial capital valuation techniques. Mr Fricklin is obviously not aware of the importance of the entity being environmentally aware as he has told the chief accountant not to worry about ethically sourced material data. Professional accountants need to expand their competency areas to include digital and social awareness. The fundamental principle of professional competence and due care requires that a professional accountant only undertake significant tasks for which the professional accountant has, or can obtain, sufficient specific training or experience. A professional accountant should not intentionally mislead an employer as to the level of expertise or experience possessed such as is the case with Mr Fricklin who has told the board that he has 'in depth knowledge' of the technology.

Ms Pleasant is in a difficult position as regards the competence and sabotage of the project by Mr Fricklin, as an act of 'whistleblowing' can cause a conflict of interest between the personal, organisational and societal spheres. This conflict stems from the way in which a whistle-blower is viewed. The chief accountant could be viewed as someone sharing knowledge of misconduct for the benefit of others or as someone who is acting 'disloyal' to their superior. Ms Pleasant will be torn between loyalty to Mr Fricklin and her own moral commitment.

As long as her motivations are sound and she is confident in the system and her knowledge, she should not hesitate to relay such information as she is helping to create an environmentally aware project which will enhance the company's business.

Tutorial note

The list of points raised here are not necessarily exhaustive. If you raise other ethical issues which are reasonably justified by reference to specifics within the scenario, then the may gain credit as well.

ACCA marking guide

		Marks
(a)	– Discussion and application of IAS 36 principles to scenario	3
	– Calculation of impairment	2
		5
(b)	– Discussion and application of IAS 32 principles to scenario	3
	– Contractual obligation discussion	2
		5
(c)	Discussion of the following key ethical principles and application to the scenario:	
	- Confidentiality	3
	- Competence	3
	- Whistleblowing	2
		8
	Professional marks	2
Total		**20**

Examiners comments

(a) This part of the question was generally answered quite well, although many candidates did not deduct the decommissioning provision from both the carrying amount and the recoverable amount of the mines. Most candidates did identify that there was an impairment loss often based upon inaccurate calculations. The own figure rule was used to assess the acceptability of candidates' conclusions.

However, there was little discussion of the acceptability of the use of the cash flow projections in the impairment assessment.

(b) Many candidates discussed the issues but came to the wrong conclusion. This would simply mean that no marks would be given for the incorrect conclusion but with marks for sensible discussion still being available. This was an area were several candidates struggled. Most candidates produced a definition of the financial liability and identified that cryptocurrency could be treated as a 'cash' settlement. However, fewer candidates recognised that the class A shares should be classified as a liability with the class B shares being classified as equity. Marks were awarded for the application of the definitions of equity and liability to the scenario on the basis of one mark per valid and well discussed point up to a maximum of 5 marks.

(c) Generally, one mark is allocated for each well discussed point raised by candidates. If candidates just listed ethical principles without application to the scenario, then a maximum of two marks would have been given. Marks are allocated as a result of using the scenario to demonstrate an understanding of the ethical issue. The actions required by the chief accountant in the published answer were more subtle in this question and looked at the act of whistleblowing and the issue surrounding such a process. However, if candidates discussed actions such as seeking advice from a colleague or ACCA, then these were appropriate answers and were awarded credit. Many candidates seem to think that accountants should resign immediately if they meet an ethical dilemma. The professional marks were awarded for a realistic discussion of the ethical issues set out in the scenario together with sensible and appropriate actions. Most candidates identified the key ethical issues in this scenario and achieved good marks, but fewer were able to suggest reasonable actions to resolve the situation.

Also, some candidates simply cut and pasted large sections of the exhibit and then stated 'this is an ethical issue'. This action would attract no marks. Candidates have to be sensible when using the cut and paste tool. Any examination would not reward a candidate for simply repeating the question back to the examiner. If candidates wish to use the cut and paste tool, then its use should be restricted to parts of a sentence that are relevant and they should add their own comments, and in this question, appropriate actions. It is very easy for a marker to recognise answers that have been cut and pasted.

23 CALIBRA (SEP/DEC 2020)  *Walk in the footsteps of a top tutor*

Key answer tips

It would be easy to get bogged down in the tricky accounting issues in part (a) and the journals in part (b), but these two requirements are only worth 8 marks. Part (c) is worth 10 marks plus 2 professional marks – it is much easier to score well here, so leave yourself plenty of time to attempt it thoroughly.

(a) Revenue recognition

Control of the apartment block passes to the customer on completion. This is the point at which revenue should be recognised. Calibra is therefore incorrect to recognise revenue on receipt of payment.

There is a two year delay between payment and the transfer of the underlying asset. This means that, in accordance with IFRS 15 *Revenue from Contracts with Customers,* these advanced payments contain a significant financing component. In such cases, the revenue recognised should be the amount that the customer would have paid if they had paid cash at the date the good was transferred – i.e. $9.55 million.

Tutorial note

Discuss the accounting treatment over the two year period – not just the initial entries on receipt of the cash.

On receipt of the payment, Calibra Co should recognise a liability of $8.5 million. It should subsequently accrue interest on this liability at 6% each year, which will increase the carrying amount of the liability. After two years, the liability will have a carrying amount of $9.55 million. When control of the apartment building is transferred, the liability is derecognised, and revenue of $9.55 million recognised in the statement of profit or loss.

Borrowing costs

Tutorial note

This topic would have surprised many students because it is rarely examined. SBR has a big syllabus, but it is vital that you study it all.

IAS 23 *Borrowing Costs* states that borrowing costs that are directly attributable to the acquisition, construction or production of a qualifying asset form part of the cost of that asset. A qualifying asset is one that takes a long time to get ready for use.

Apartment buildings take two years to construct so are qualifying assets. Calibra Co's business model is construction and, therefore, the applicable borrowing costs should be included in the cost of its inventory. Any other borrowing costs are recognised as an expense.

(b) Journal entries

Tutorial note

Many students struggle with journal entries, even though this is assumed knowledge for SBR. Make sure that the debits and credits balance.

Below are the journals produced by the examining team. The scenario says that cash received is posted to revenue, so your first journal might instead be:

Dr Revenue $8.5m

Cr Liability $8.5m

Removes the incorrect entry to revenue and records a liability.

	Dr ($m)	Cr ($m)
Cash	8.5	
Liability		8.5
Records liability on receipt of cash (1/1/X8)		
Inventory	0.51	
Liability		0.51
Interest accruing on liability to 31/12/X8 (6% × 8.5m) included in the costs of inventory		
Inventory	0.54	
Liability		0.54
Interest accruing on liability to 31/12/X9 (6% × ($8.5m + $0.51m)) included in the costs of inventory		
Liability	9.55	
Revenue		9.55
Revenue arising on sale of apartment block.		

The balance on the contract liability at 31/12/X9 would be $9.55 million ($8.5m + $0.51m + $0.54m). When control passes to the customer, Calibra Co derecognises the liability and recognises revenue of $9.55 million.

(c) Ethics

Tutorial note

This is an unusual scenario and you may not have heard about distributed ledgers before. However, this does not mean that you can't answer the question. All that is required is knowledge of the ACCA ethical code and the ability to apply this.

ACCA's model solution makes continuous reference to the scenario. Try and do the same – it stops your answer becoming too generic and makes it more likely that you will be awarded the two professional marks.

Make explicit reference to the principles in the ACCA ethical code that are under threat – such as confidentiality and objectivity.

The chief accountant should not claim to have an understanding of distributed ledgers if he only has a basic knowledge. He should have seen evidence of whether the technology can be scaled up to the requirements of the directors before promising that he can facilitate the move. Also, he must convince himself that the reliability of the due diligence on the sale of property shares and that local regulations are complied with. In order to maintain integrity, professional accountants must be honest about whether they are comfortable with their knowledge of managing projects such as this. The chief accountant should not manage the project if he has doubts as to his knowledge as there may be significant issues as the project progresses. There may be a need to engage specialist consultancy input from distributed ledger experts. Similarly, the chief accountant should behave in a professional manner and determine whether the data on the distributed ledger breaks any confidentiality principles. He will need to consider the fact that local regulations may be violated and the repercussions thereof. The technology allows resale of the shares in the property and given the chief accountants worries over due diligence, illegal transfers of title ownership could be costly and time consuming to resolve. The chief accountant must also exercise independence of mind and not bow to political pressure from the board even though it may be a high-profile project for the company. He should inform the board of his reservations based upon his opinion and technical knowledge.

Tutorial note

The model answer written by ACCA is comprised of two large paragraphs. We would recommend keeping your points separate with plenty of white space between each one. This helps you keep track of how much you have written. It also makes the marker's job easier!

One of the main concerns for accounting professionals is the fear of losing objectivity in their judgment due to pressures from clients, employers, or other stakeholders. This occurrence would create a loss of professional identity for the person concerned. Some individuals are more vulnerable to loss of objectivity than others. Young accountants at the beginning of their career could be considered a vulnerable group, as they may be more easily influenced due to a perceived lack of experience and pressures from senior colleagues. The accountant has only just qualified and so might be inexperienced to be in the position of chief accountant. In this case, he has created a self-interest threat as the chief accountant has a personal interest in allowing Bodoni Co to pay the reduced amount 1 month after the contract for the purchase of the apartment block has been signed, as he wishes a good reference from the client when he applies for the permanent position. The pressure of applying for this position has inappropriately influenced his professional judgement and behaviour. Additionally, there is a threat to the chief accountant's objectivity which stems from a self-interest threat from the fear of losing Bodoni Co as a client which in turn would affect the accountant's chances of securing his position on a permanent basis.

ACCA marking guide		
		Marks
(a)	Application of the following discussion to the scenario:	
	– Revenue	3
	– Borrowing costs	2
		5
(b)	Journal entries	3
(c)	Discussion and application of ethical principles to scenario	10
	Professional marks	2
Total		**20**

Examiner's comments

In part (a), a significant number of candidates outlined the option of recognition 'over time', with some suggesting (incorrectly) that revenue can be recognised over the two-year period using some systematic method. Some candidates repeated the journal entries in both part (a) and part (b) which is wasting time. Make sure you read through all question requirements to avoid this.

Most answers to part (b) were clear and gained full marks, although some answers neglected to show the ultimate derecognition of the liability and recognition of revenue from the contract.

Answers to part (c) were in general good and many candidates provided a clear identification of the ethical issues and suggestions to resolve them. Conversely, a presentation of a "boiler plate" list of ethical responsibilities did not meet the requirements and gained very few marks, if any, unless applied to the two scenarios. Some candidates repeated too much information from the question without adding any new insights or concerns, which limited scope for marks. Overall, it is pleasing to see most answers identifying the threats and recommending appropriate actions to mitigate these and maintain ethical standards.

24 BAGSHOT (MAR 2020)  *Walk in the footsteps of a top tutor*

Key answer tips

The accounting issues tested this question are not technically demanding: provisions and related party transactions. Part (b) on ethics concentrates on a different issue than most recent SBR exams: confidentiality. Make sure that you are confident applying the ACCA *Code of Ethics and Conduct* to any situation that an accountant may face.

(a) (i) Restructuring

Tutorial note

State the criteria that must be satisfied for a provision to be recognised.

A provision for restructuring costs should only be recognised in the financial statements of Bagshot Co where all of the following criteria are met:

- A reliable estimate can be made of the amount of the obligation
- It is probable that an outflow of resources embodying economic benefits will be required to settle the obligation
- There is a present obligation as a result of a past event.

IAS 37 *Provisions, Contingent Liabilities and Contingent Assets* states that it would be extremely rare that no reliable estimate can be made.

Tutorial note

The principles governing the measurement of provisions are also relevant here.

A best estimate of the expenditure required to settle the present obligation should be provided as at 31 December 20X5 should all criteria be met. In the case of a restructuring provision, this should only include direct expenditure arising from the restructuring and not associated with ongoing activities. Hence the relocation costs would not be included as, although they relate directly to the restructuring, the costs would be classified as an ongoing activity.

Tutorial note

Apply the principles from the accounting standard to the scenario. Is there an obligation from a past event? Is payment probable?

It is not clear yet that restructuring payments are probable. Mrs Dawes has indicated that alternative strategies are possible and further clarification is required. Only then may it be determined that such restructuring payments are probable.

Tutorial note

Obligations can be legal or constructive. A constructive obligation arises when an entity's past behaviour creates expectations about its behaviour in the future.

A constructive obligation for restructuring only arises where a detailed formal plan exists and a valid expectation to those affected by the restructuring that it will take place has occurred. A plan is in place but management does not yet appear committed as alternative strategies are possible. It is unlikely therefore that the plan is detailed and specific enough for these criteria to be satisfied. For example, the specific expenditure to be incurred, the date of its implementation and timeframe which should not be unreasonably long must be identified. With alternative strategies available, this does not appear to be the case. Furthermore, Mr Shaw is the only member of staff who has been notified and no public announcement has been made as at the reporting date. Consequently, there is no obligation in existence as at 31 December 20X5 and no provision can be recognised.

Mrs Dawes has identified that a final decision on the restructuring and communication is likely to take place before the financial statements are authorised. This would almost certainly be a material event arising after the reporting date but should be treated as non-adjusting. Accordingly, Bagshot Co should disclose the nature of the restructuring and an estimate of its financial effect but recognition of a restructuring provision is still prohibited.

(ii) Stewardship

Tutorial note

Stewardship is an important principle. According to the Conceptual Framework, one of the main purposes of financial reporting is to enable user groups to assess management's stewardship of an entity's resources.

Stewardship is an ethical principle which embodies the responsible planning and management of resources. The directors of Bagshot Co perform a stewardship role in that they are appointed by the shareholders to manage Bagshot Co on their behalf. The directors therefore assume responsibilities to protect the entity's resources from unfavourable effects of economic factors such as price and technological changes and to ensure that Bagshot Co complies with all laws, regulations and contractual obligations. Group results have been disappointing in recent years although no specific causes have been identified. It could be argued, therefore, that the restructure is acting in good faith and reflecting good principles of stewardship. It is anticipated that long-term shareholder value will be enhanced from the proposals.

Tutorial note

The effectiveness of stewardship can only be assessed if an entity's financial statements faithfully represent its performance, position and cash flows.

A second factor of good stewardship is that it is important that investors, both existing and potential, and lenders have reliable and accurate information about the entity's resources so that they can assess how efficiently and effectively the entity's management and governing board have discharged their responsibilities. It is important therefore that the financial statements are transparent, objective and comply fully with IFRS Standards. Mrs Dawes wants Bagshot Co to include a restructuring provision as at 31 December 20X5 even though no obligation arises. Whilst prudence is a guiding principle when dealing with issues of uncertainty, excessive prudence cannot be justified. As a qualified member of ACCA, it should be apparent to Mrs Dawes that no provision should be recognised and to include one would be misleading to the stakeholders of Bagshot Co.

(iii) Related parties

Mrs Shaw's acquisition of the equity shares in Bagshot Co would be deemed a related party transaction if the acquisition enabled her to control or have significant influence over Bagshot Co.

Tutorial note

Control is assumed when an investor owns more than 50% of the voting rights of the investee. Significant influence is assumed if the holding is between 20% and 50%.

A person is a related party of an entity that they control or have significant influence over. Mrs Shaw has a 5% interest, which is way below the threshold to exercise control. Mrs Shaw has a holding of less than 20% of the voting power so it is very unlikely that she has significant influence over the entity.

Bagshot Co's directors would be related parties of Bagshot Co. However Mrs Shaw is unaware of the proposed restructure which suggests that she does not have a board position.

Mrs Shaw would be deemed to be a close family member of Mr Shaw and so would be a related party of Bagshot Co if it was concluded that Mr Shaw is a member of key management personnel of Bagshot Co.

Tutorial note

Close family includes children, spouses or domestic partners.

Mr Shaw is the head accountant of Bagshot Co but it seems highly unlikely that he would be deemed to be key management personnel. There is no evidence that he has authority or responsibility for planning, directing and controlling the activities of Bagshot Co. Nor does he appear to be a director of the entity.

Tutorial note

Make sure that you reach an explicit conclusion.

Based on the above, it can be concluded that Mrs Shaw's acquisition of the 5% of the equity in Bagshot Co is not a related party transaction.

(b) Ethics

Tutorial note

Explain which principles in the Code of Ethics have been breached – such as objectivity, integrity and confidentiality.

Mr Shaw is facing a number of ethical dilemmas arising from the scenario. Mrs Dawes's insistence that a restructuring provision should be included could constitute an intimidation threat to objectivity, although her motivation for including the provision early is unclear. Mr Shaw is also a qualified member of ACCA and therefore should be aware that the treatment is inconsistent with international accounting standards. Mr Shaw must adhere to the ACCA Code of Ethics and prepare financial statements diligently which are objective and fully comply with IFRS Standards. He must not comply with Mrs Dawes's requests and should politely remind her of her professional responsibilities as a member of ACCA. Non-compliance with accounting standards would be a breach of a range of ethical principles including professional competence, professional behaviour and objectivity. Assuming that Mrs Dawes is aware of the error, her integrity would also be questionable.

Tutorial note

Insider trading is an important issue in real life, although it has not been regularly examined in SBR.

Mr Shaw could be accused of insider trading were he to inform his wife of the proposed restructure. Insider trading involves the use of non-publicised information in order to make decisions on financial investments based on the information which others do not yet know about. It is clear that such behaviour would not be ethical since Mrs Shaw would be in an advantageous position to make investment decisions which could impact unfairly on the other shareholders. Insider traders have information which others do not have such that the other stakeholders may act differently and make different decisions should they have been privy to the same information. Such activities are seen as fraudulent and are likely to be in breach of local money laundering regulations.

Tutorial note

Clearly recommend actions to be taken. They can be very simple – e.g. do not disclose the confidential information.

Mr Shaw has become privy to confidential information regarding Bagshot Co. One of ACCA's key ethical principles is that of confidentiality. Information must not be disclosed to others unless there is a legal or professional right or duty to disclose. Professional accountants must also ensure that they do not use confidential information for their own personal benefit. Mr Shaw has self-interest threats arising both from his wife's ownership of the shares and from his nephew facing potential redundancy. His wife could use the information to consider whether she may wish to sell her 5% ownership interest. Mr Shaw may also feel pressure to inform his nephew of the potential redundancy he may be facing. This may allow his nephew to obtain an unfair advantage over fellow employees by, for example, examining other opportunities in the labour market. Mr Shaw must not disclose the confidential information to his wife or his nephew.

ACCA Marking scheme

			Marks
(a)	(i)	Discussion of IAS 37 criteria and restructuring	3
		Application of above to scenario	2
		Identification of non-adjusting event	1
			6
	(ii)	What is meant by good stewardship	2
		Examples of good stewardship	2
			4
	(iii)	Control/significant influence criteria	2
		Recognition of close family member	1
			3
(b)		Intimidation threat	1
		Insider trading	2
		Confidentiality	2
			5
		Professional marks	2
Total			**30**

Examiner's comments

Despite there being 6 marks available for answering part (a) (i), many answers were the same length as for (a) (iii) despite the latter having only 3 marks. Answers to part (a) (ii) were rather weak; many candidates overlooked the 'knowledge' aspect of explaining what constitutes a related party; most answers did not consider the relevance of the proportion of shares held. Such answers jumped straight to considering the position held by Mr Shaw and assumed that he was in a position of key management (despite not being a director). Many answers gave the wrong conclusion as a result. Answers to part (b) were generally good, with a clear identification of the ethical issues and suggestions to resolve them (which in this case includes simply maintaining confidentiality).

25 STENT (SEP/DEC 2019)  *Walk in the footsteps of a top tutor*

Key answer tips

Your discussion of the three accounting issues can only score you 11 marks. Make sure that you manage your time carefully. Your answers should be much briefer than the model answer below. Don't forget to comment on the gearing impact – this will earn you three quick marks.

Easy marks can be obtained in ethics questions for discussing the actions that the accountants in the scenario should take.

(a) Cash advance

Tutorial note

Directors are members of key management personnel and therefore are related parties of the reporting entity.

IAS 24 *Related Party Disclosures* requires an entity's financial statements to contain disclosures necessary to draw attention to the possibility that its financial statements may have been affected by the existence of related parties and by transactions and outstanding balances with such parties.

The finance director of Stent Co is a related party of Stent Co. The finance director controls Budster Co and therefore Stent Co and Budster Co are related parties of one another. As such, Stent Co must disclose the nature of the related party relationship with Budster Co as well as information about all transactions and outstanding balances between Stent Co and Budster Co.

According to the *Conceptual Framework*, the advance from Budster Co is a liability: Stent Co has a present obligation (legally enforceable as a consequence of a binding contract), the settlement of which involves Stent Co giving up resources embodying economic benefits in order to satisfy the claim.

Tutorial note

Bar some exceptions, IFRS Standards do not permit offsetting.

Except when it reflects the substance of the transaction or other event, offsetting detracts from the ability of users to understand the entity's transactions and to assess the entity's future cash flows. IAS 1 *Presentation of Financial Statements* states that an entity shall not offset assets and liabilities, unless required or permitted by an IFRS Standard. Offsetting a financial asset and a financial liability is permitted according to IAS 32 *Financial Instruments*: *Presentation* when, and only when, an entity has a legally enforceable right to set off the recognised amounts and intends either to settle on a net basis, or to realise the asset and settle the liability simultaneously. No such agreement is evident in this case, so Stent Co should report the receivables and the advance separately.

If the error was not corrected, Stent Co would be showing a lower current asset figure and concealing the liability. If disclosed as a current liability it might be included in the debt element of the gearing calculation, thus increasing gearing.

Convertible redeemable preference shares

Tutorial note

Memorise the definitions of financial assets, financial liabilities and equity. The classification of financial instruments is a popular exam topic.

IAS 32 defines an equity instrument as any contract which evidences a residual interest in the assets of an entity after deducting all of its liabilities. An equity instrument has no contractual obligation to deliver cash or another financial asset, or to exchange financial assets or financial liabilities under potentially unfavourable conditions. If settled by the issuer's own equity instruments, an equity instrument has no contractual obligation to deliver a variable number of shares.

A critical feature in differentiating a financial liability from an equity instrument is the existence of a contractual obligation of the issuer either to deliver cash or another financial asset to the holder, or to exchange financial assets or financial liabilities with the holder, under conditions which are potentially unfavourable to the issuer.

The preference shares offer the holder the choice of conversion into ordinary shares as well as redemption in two years' time. Stent should separately recognise a financial liability (a contractual arrangement to deliver cash or another financial asset) and an equity instrument (a call option granting the holder the right, for a specified period of time, to convert it into a fixed number of ordinary shares of the entity).

Tutorial note

Don't just tell the examiner that the instrument should be split into liability and equity components. Explain how these components are measured.

Stent Co would measure the fair value of the consideration in respect of the liability component based on the fair value of a similar liability without any associated equity conversion option. The equity component is assigned the residual amount.

Tutorial note

Remember to comment on gearing. The gearing ratio will deteriorate if liabilities increase.

Correction of the error would increase non-current debt (the present value of the future obligations) and decrease equity. This will increase gearing.

Deferred tax asset

Tutorial note

Recognition of a deferred tax asset in respect of unused tax losses is a common exam topic. Make sure that you memorise the key principle below.

In accordance with IAS 12 *Income Taxes*, a deferred tax asset shall be recognised for the carry-forward of unused tax losses to the extent that it is probable that future taxable profit will be available against which the unused tax losses can be utilised.

However, the existence of unused tax losses is strong evidence that future taxable profit may not be available. Therefore, when an entity has a history of recent losses, the entity recognises a deferred tax asset arising from unused tax losses only to the extent that it has convincing evidence that sufficient taxable profit will be available against which the unused tax losses can be utilised. In such circumstances, the amount of the deferred tax asset and the nature of the evidence supporting its recognition must be disclosed.

The directors of Stent Co should consider whether it is probable that Stent Co will have taxable profits before the unused tax losses or unused tax credits expire, whether the unused tax losses result from identifiable causes which are unlikely to recur; and whether tax planning opportunities are available to the entity which will create taxable profit in the period in which the unused tax losses or unused tax credits can be utilised. To the extent that it is not probable that taxable profit will be available against which the unused tax losses or unused tax credits can be utilised, the deferred tax asset should not be recognised.

Tutorial note

Don't forget gearing. The carrying amount of equity equals the carrying amount of net assets – so a reduction in assets causes a corresponding reduction in equity, meaning that the gearing ratio will deteriorate.

The removal of a deferred tax asset would reduce net assets and, therefore, equity. Gearing would increase.

(b) Ethical aspects

Tutorial note

Do not attempt the ethics requirement first. If you work through and understand the accounting errors made then you will have more specific comments to make about ethics in part (b). This will improve the quality of your answer and also make it more likely that you will receive the professional marks available.

The ACCA Rulebook contains the bye-laws, regulations and *Code of Ethics and Conduct*, which every ACCA member should follow. The accountant may feel pressured by the finance director's comments on job security given the accountant has only been in her position for a few months. The accountant should comply with the fundamental ethical principles set out in the ACCA Rulebook: to act with integrity, objectivity, professional competence and due care, confidentiality and professional behaviour. The accountant should be mindful of any threats to these fundamental ethical principles. In doing so, the accountant should consider the relevant facts, the ethical issues involved, the fundamental principles which are threatened, whether internal procedures exist which mitigate the threats, and what alternative courses of action could be taken.

Tutorial note

Comment on the ethical principles that are threatened in the scenario and explain why this is the case.

In this case, all fundamental ethical principles with the exception of confidentiality appear under threat. The finance director appears to be allowing bias and undue influence from the pressures imposed by debt covenant gearing and overdraft limits into the choice of accounting treatment, rather than following accounting standards. The company is in a precarious position, reporting losses in the year. The finance director should act professionally, in accordance with applicable technical and professional standards, comply with relevant laws and regulations, and avoid any action which discredits the profession.

The accountant faces an intimidation threat to objectivity given the comments from the finance director, who presumably has an influence over career prospects. Assuming the accountant wishes to keep her job, this intimidation threat also gives rise to a self-interest threat to objectivity.

Tutorial note

What should the accountant do now?

Before acting, the accountant should speak with the finance director, try to confirm the facts, and discuss the treatment with the finance director and explain the risks of non-compliance. A record of conversations and actions should be kept. Stent Co may also have internal procedures which mitigate the threats. It may be that the finance director is not technically up-to-date, in which case a safeguard would be to undergo continuing professional development. If the finance director refuses to comply with accounting standards, then it would be appropriate to discuss the matter with other directors or an audit committee (if applicable), to seek a solution, then seek professional advice from ACCA, and consider legal advice if necessary. A final consideration for the accountant, if matters cannot be satisfactorily resolved, would be resignation.

Tutorial note

Resignation is often a last resort!

ACCA marking guide

		Marks
(a)	– application of the following discussion to the scenario:	
	cash advance from related party	4
	preference shares: convertible	4
	deferred tax asset	3
		11
(b)	– discussion of ethical principles	2
	– application of ethical principles to the scenario, and recommended action	5
		7
	Professional marks	2
Total		**20**

Examiner's comments

A surprising number of candidates failed to comment on the impact of gearing; otherwise however, answers to part (a) were good. Most candidates identified the accounting errors in the described scenario; although in some cases failed to identify the need for a related party disclosure. Candidates' explanation for the accounting treatment of convertible preference shares often lacked application to the scenario.

Marks were divided between identification of ethical issues and actions that the accountant should take to resolve the issues. Answers were generally good, with a clear identification of the ethical issues and suggestions to resolve them. However candidates that combined both parts (a) and (b) tended to repeat themselves; and some answers to part (b) were segmented on the basis of the accounting issues, which again lead to repetition, since the ethical issues in most cases related to all of the three accounting issues. Despite these issues, the question was very well-answered in general.

26 HUDSON (MAR/JUN 2019)  *Walk in the footsteps of a top tutor*

Key answer tips

Question 2 in the SBR exam requires students to discuss the accounting and ethical implications of particular transactions. Pay careful attention to the mark allocation because these are lower in question 2 than in other parts of the paper. For instance, part (b) is only worth 5 marks and so you only need to write five separate points. It would be easy to write too much here and therefore waste time.

Remember that your answer to part (c) must be specific to the scenario. Comment on the particular errors made by Hudson, the specific ethical principles breached, and the actions that should be taken. If you do this then you will be awarded 2 professional marks.

(a) Settlement costs

Tutorial note

On first read through this question seems quite tricky. However, there are easy marks if you adopt a logical approach. Begin your answer by describing the nature of a remeasurement component.

According to IAS 19 *Employee Benefits,* the remeasurement component is presented in other comprehensive income. It comprises:

- Actuarial gains and losses
- Returns on plan assets not included in the net interest component
- Changes in the asset ceiling not included within the net interest calculation.

Actuarial gains and losses result from differences between actuarial assumptions and what actually occurred during the period. These will arise in instances such as unexpected movements on interest rates, unexpectedly high or low rates of employee turnover or unexpected increases or decreases in wage growth.

The effects of the redundancy exercise are not part of the remeasurement component.

A redundancy exercise is an example of a curtailment because it significantly reduces the number of employees covered by the plan. Per IAS 19, the present value of the change in the defined benefit obligation as a result of a curtailment is a past service cost and should be recognised in profit or loss.

Tutorial note

Make sure that you discuss both the basic enhancement and the additional enhancement.

The basic enhancement is an obligation that Hudson must pay as compensation for terminating the employee's services regardless of when the employee leaves the entity. IAS 19 *Employee Benefits* requires such payments to be recognised at the earlier of when the plan of termination is announced and when the entity recognises the associated restructuring costs associated with the closure of Wye. Hudson should therefore have provided in full for the cost of the basic settlement regardless of whether the staff have left or not. This should be recognised as part of the past service cost in the profit or loss of Hudson for the year ended 31 December 20X2.

The additional pension enhancement is only received by employees who complete service up to the closure of division Wye. In effect, the enhancement is in exchange for the period of service until redundancy. Hudson should estimate the number of employees who will remain with Hudson until the closure of Wye and spread the estimated total cost over the period of service. This should be included within the current service cost, thus having an adverse effect on the profit or loss in both 20X2 and 20X3.

Redundancy costs

As set out in IAS 37 *Provisions, Contingent Liabilities and Contingent Assets*, an 'obligating event' must have arisen before a provision can be recognised. With regards to restructuring, a present obligation from a past event arises if:

- a detailed formal plan for the restructuring is in place, and
- a valid expectation has been created in those affected that the restructuring will be carried out, either by starting to implement the plan or publicly announcing its main features.

Tutorial note

Apply the criteria in IAS 37 to Hudson.

In the case of Hudson, a valid expectation has been created because the restructuring has been announced, the redundancies have been confirmed and the directors have approved the restructuring in a formal directors' meeting. A restructuring provision should therefore be recognised.

Tutorial note

Many students will simply discuss ***whether*** *a provision should be recognised, and omit any reference to how the provision should be measured.*

IAS 37 specifies that only the direct expenditure which is necessary as a result of restructuring can be included in the restructuring provision. This includes costs of making employees redundant and the costs of terminating certain contracts. However, the provision cannot include the costs of retraining or relocating staff, marketing or investment in new systems and distribution networks, because these costs relate to future operations.

(b) Deferred tax

Tutorial note

State the principles from IAS 12 with respect to the recognition of a deferred tax asset for unused tax losses. The question is only worth five marks – you would not be expected to reproduce the content below.

IAS 12 *Income Taxes* says that a deferred tax asset shall be recognised for the carry forward of unused tax losses and unused tax credits to the extent that it is probable that future taxable profit will be available against which the unused tax losses and unused tax credits can be utilised. However, the existence of unused tax losses is strong evidence that future taxable profit may not be available. Therefore, when an entity has a history of recent losses, the entity recognises a deferred tax asset arising from unused tax losses or tax credits only to the extent that the entity has sufficient taxable temporary differences or there is convincing other evidence that sufficient taxable profit will be available against which the unused tax losses or unused tax credits can be utilised by the entity.

Tutorial note

Use the information from the scenario to explain whether it is probable that Hudson will make taxable profits before its tax allowable losses expire.

Hudson operates under a tax jurisdiction which only allows losses to be carried forward for two years. The maximum total losses that can be utilised are therefore equal to total unused losses for 20X1 and 20X2. Losses incurred before 20X1 can no longer be carried forward and so no deferred tax asset should be recognised in respect of them.

The directors of Hudson should base their forecast of future profitability on reasonable and supportable assumptions. There appears to be evidence that this is not the case. Hudson has a recent history of trading losses and there is little evidence that there will be an improvement in trading results within the next couple of years. The market is depressed and sales orders for the first quarter of 20X3 are below levels in any of the previous five years. It is also likely that Hudson will incur various costs in relation to the restructuring which would increase losses into 20X3 and possibly 20X4. Only directly attributable expenses such as redundancies should be included within a provision and expensed in 20X2 which would increase the current year loss. On-going expenses may be incurred such as retraining and relocating costs but these should only be expensed from 20X3. The forecast profitability for 20X3 and subsequent growth rate therefore appear to be unrealistically optimistic.

Tutorial note

Reach an explicit conclusion about whether a deferred tax asset can be recognised.

Given that losses can only be carried forward for a maximum of two years, it is unlikely that any deferred tax asset should be recognised.

(c) Ethics

Tutorial note

Your answer must be specific to Hudson. Discuss particular issues in the scenario that increase the likelihood of financial statement manipulation (e.g. performance related bonuses).

Directors have an ethical responsibility to produce financial statements which are a faithful representation of the entity's transactions. The directors of Hudson are paid a bonus based upon earnings before interest, tax depreciation and amortisation (EBITDA) and so a self-interest threat to objectivity arises. The directors have an incentive to manipulate the financial statements in order to try to minimise the losses and maximise profits. Similarly the directors have an incentive to maximise assets and minimise liabilities so that Hudson complies with its debt covenants.

Tutorial note

Discuss the particular errors made by Hudson – such as the treatment of the pension enhancements, the restructuring provision, and the deferred tax asset.

There is evidence that the directors are willing to manipulate the financial statements in a way directly contrary to the ethical principles of integrity and objectivity. The expenses arising from the basic and additional pension enhancements should be recorded in profit or loss but the directors wish to recognise this within other comprehensive income despite knowing that it is contrary to IFRS Standards. This would improve profitability.

The directors also have not recognised a restructuring provision despite the terms being communicated to staff. As a result, profit and net assets are overstated. This may make it more likely that the bonus target is met and that the debt covenants are not breached. It is possible that restructuring would be treated as an exceptional cost in profit or loss and may therefore not impact the bonus. It would therefore be useful to examine the precise terms of the contracts in order to assess the potential impact on the bonus.

The deferred tax asset is based upon forecasts for too long a period and is also based on unrealistic assumptions. Net assets will be overstated, helping Hudson to meet its debt covenant obligations.

The directors' explanation for their proposed treatments are not justified. Directors are appointed to run the business on behalf of the company's shareholders who are the primary stakeholder. It will be in the shareholders' interests for the company to be profitable and to maintain net assets within the debt covenant stipulations. However, this should not be at the expense of the credibility and transparency of the financial statements. Deliberate manipulation of financial statements will reduce stakeholders' confidence in the reliability of the financial statements and the accountancy profession as a whole.

Tutorial note

Discuss the specific ethical principles that the directors are contravening. Do not simply list all of the ethical principles in the ACCA Code of Ethics and Conduct.

The directors' actions with regard to the accountant are contrary to the ethical principles of professional behaviour. It appears that the directors have put the accountant under undue pressure to falsify the financial statements to meet their own needs. An intimidation threat to objectivity arises from the directors' implying that the accountant would lose their job should they not comply with the directors' instructions.

Tutorial note

State the actions needed to resolve the above.

The accountant would also be bound by the ACCA *Code of Ethics and Conduct* and must adhere to the same ethical principles. They must not therefore comply with the directors' instructions and should instead remind the directors of their obligations to comply with this code. Should the accountant feel unable to approach the directors directly, they could consider talking to those charged with governance and, in particular, non-executive directors to explain the situation. The accountant could also seek help from the ACCA ethical helpline and take legal advice. Ultimately, if the situation cannot be resolved, the accountant could consider resigning and seeking employment elsewhere.

ACCA marking guide

		Marks
(a)	– application of the following discussion to the scenario:	
	what should be included in the remeasurement component	2
	correct treatment of the basic enhancement	2
	correct treatment of the additional pension enhancement	2
	– discussion of restructuring costs	2
	Maximum	8
(b)	– an explanation of IAS 12 principles	2
	– application of above discussion to the scenario	3
	Maximum	5
(c)	– application of the following discussion of accounting issues to the scenario:	
	termination payments	2
	tax losses	1
	– consideration of the ethical implications and their resolution	2
	Maximum	5
	Professional marks	2
Total		**20**

Examiner's comments

Better answers apply ethical principles to the scenario. Indeed, it was pleasing to see fewer answers merely 'listing out' rote-learned ethical requirements in this sitting. Most candidates identified that there was a second requirement to outline the implications for the accountant and many answers included suggestions for how the accountant might resolve the ethical issue.

27 FISKERTON (DEC 2018)  *Walk in the footsteps of a top tutor*

Key answer tips

Read the question properly. Part (a) has three requirements: discuss the accounting treatment of the building, explain the impact on the financial statements, and explain the impact on debt covenants. You will miss out on valuable marks if you only discuss the correct accounting treatment.

Part (b) tests revenue recognition. To answer this you need to know the criteria for when revenue is recognised over time.

Nearly half of the available marks in this question are allocated tor ethics (part (c)). Do not neglect this. Make sure that your answer details with the specific accounting issues in the question, and the specific ethical principles that have been breached.

(a) Accounting treatment

According to IFRS 16 *Leases*, the lease is a finance lease. This is because the lease term is equal to the useful life and its residual value is deemed to be minimal. As such, the property should not be held as an investment property but instead derecognised. The fair value gain of $8 million must be reversed. Fiskerton should record a lease receivable equal to the net investment in the lease.

Tutorial note

If the lease was an operating lease then the property should have been presented as an investment property. Rental income would be recognised in profit or loss on a straight line basis.

Note that the fair value gains were incorrectly calculated since adjustments should have been made for the differences between the Halam building and the one sold due to the different location and quality of the materials between the two buildings.

Tutorial note

IFRS 13 Fair Value Measurement states that fair value is the price received when an asset is sold in an orderly transaction between market participants at the measurement date. When deciding on a sale/purchase price, participants would factor in the condition and location of an asset and any restrictions on its use.

A more accurate reflection of fair value would have been $22 million.

Impact on financial statements

Tutorial note

Easy marks are available for recalculating the gearing ratio.

The incorrect treatment has enabled Fiskerton to remain within its debt covenant limits. Gearing per the financial extracts is currently around 49.8% (50/(10 + 20.151 + 70.253)). Fair value gains on investment properties are reported within profit or loss. Retained earnings would consequently be restated to $62.253 million ($70.253m – $8m). Gearing would subsequently become 54.1% (50/10 + 20.151 + 62.253). Furthermore, retained earnings would be further reduced by correcting for rental receipts. These presumably have been included in profit or loss rather than deducted from the net investment in the lease. This would in part be offset by interest income which should be recorded in profit or loss at the effective rate of interest.

After correcting for these errors, Fiskerton would be in breach of its debt covenants. They have a negative cash balance and would appear unlikely to be able to repay the loan. Serious consideration should therefore be given as to whether Fiskerton is a going concern. If it is determined that Fiskerton is not a going concern then non-current assets and non-current liabilities should be reclassified to current and recorded at their realisable values.

Tutorial note

According to IAS 1 Presentation of Financial Statements, going concern uncertainties must be disclosed in the financial statements.

If Fiskerton can renegotiate with the bank then the uncertainties surrounding their ability to continue to trade must be disclosed.

(b) Revenue

Tutorial note

Do not simply recite the five steps of the revenue recognition model. A lot of this is irrelevant to answering the question. The requirement asks you about the timing of revenue recognition – so only the fifth step is relevant.

Make sure that you know the criteria for recognising revenue over time.

According to IFRS 15 *Revenue from Contracts with Customers*, at the inception of the contract, Fiskerton must determine whether its promise to construct the asset is a performance obligation satisfied over time.

During the production of the asset Fiskerton only has rights to the initial deposit and has no enforceable rights to the remaining balance as construction takes place. Therefore Fiskerton would not be able to receive payment for work performed to date. As such, revenue should not be recognised over time but at the point in time when control passes to the customer (most likely on delivery of the asset to the customer).

(c) Ethics

It is concerning that the property has been incorrectly classified as an investment property. Accountants have an ethical duty to be professionally competent and act with due care and attention. It is fundamental that the financial statements comply with the accounting standards and principles which underpin them. This may be a genuine mistake but even so would not be one expected from a professionally qualified accountant. The financial statements must comply with the fair presentation principles embedded within IAS 1 *Presentation of Financial Statements.*

Tutorial note

*Outline the **specific** ethical principles that have been breached.*

The managing director appears to be happy to manipulate the financial statements. A self-interest threat to objectivity arises from the issue over the debt covenants. It is likely that the managing director is concerned about his job security should the bank recall the debt and deem Fiskerton to no longer be a going concern. It appears highly likely that the revaluation was implemented in the interim financial statements to try to maintain a satisfactory gearing ratio. Even more concerning is that the managing director has deliberately overstated the valuation for the year-end financial statements, even though he is aware that it breaches accounting standards. Such deliberate manipulation is contrary to the ethical principles of integrity, professional behaviour and objectivity. It appears that the managing director is trying to defraud the bank by misrepresenting the liquidity of the business to avoid repayment of the loan.

Tutorial note

Make explicit reference to the impact of the revenue error on the financial statements.

The sales contract is further evidence that the managing director may be attempting to manipulate the financial statements. The proposed treatment will overstate both revenue and assets which would improve the gearing ratio.

A governance issue arises from the behaviour of the managing director. It is important that no one individual is too powerful and domineering in running an entity's affairs. An intimidation threat arises from the managing director pressurising the accountant to overstate revenue from the contract. It was also the managing director who implemented the excessive revaluations on the property. It would appear that the managing director is exercising too much power over the financial statements.

Tutorial note

Outline specific actions that the accountant should take.

The accountant must not be influenced by the behaviour of the managing director and should produce financial statements which are transparent and free from bias. Instead, the managing director should be reminded of their ethical responsibilities. The accountant may need to consider professional advice should the managing director refuse to correct the financial statements.

Marking guide

			Marks
(a)	–	application of the following discussion to the scenario:	
		correct accounting treatment of the lease	3
		implications for the financial statements	2
		implications for the debt covenant	2
			7
(b)	–	consideration of whether it is performance satisfied over time or at a point in time and application to the scenario	3
	–	conclusion and implications for revenue	1
			4
(c)	–	application of the following discussion of ethical issues to the scenario:	
		classification of property as investment property	2
		revaluation and manipulation of the debt covenant	3
	–	consideration of the ethical implications and their resolution	2
			7
	Professional		2
Total			**20**

Examiner's comments

Many candidates felt that the investment property classification was justified. Where a candidate concluded, with some justification, that the property was an investment property, some marks were awarded. Where candidates made a reasonable attempt at calculations, then the Own Figure Rule was used to justify the conclusions reached by the candidate.

The second part of the question required a discussion as to whether revenue arising from a sales contract should be recognised on a stage of completion basis under IFRS 15. Any mention of IFRS 15 in a question seems to prompt a regurgitation of the five steps to revenue recognition. This type of answer gains very few marks as this level of exam requires candidate knowledge of the specific requirement in IFRS 15. Thus in this case, candidates should have stated that the entity should determine whether its promise to construct the asset is a performance obligation satisfied over time. Generally, candidates obtained at least half marks on this part.

The final part of the question was generally well answered and full marks were often awarded. The main issue was that some candidates simply quoted ethical guidance without applying it to the scenario. Also, the professional marks were awarded for the quality of ethical discussion and thus where candidates did not apply ethical guidance to the scenario, further marks were lost.

28 FARHAM (SEP 2018)  *Walk in the footsteps of a top tutor*

Key answer tips

This question shows the marks available for each part. Use this to help you with timings. Almost half of the marks are for ethics, so make sure that you write enough. You will score one mark for each valid point that you make.

Ethical issues are never clear-cut. To score the two professional marks, your discussion must demonstrate an understanding of the reality of a problem.

(a) Factory subsidence

Tutorial note

Use subheadings so that it is clear which issue you are addressing.

In accordance with IAS 36 *Impairment of Assets,* the subsidence is an indication of impairment in relation to the production facility.

The impairment review would be performed on a suitable cash generating unit as presumably the factory, as a standalone asset, would not independently generate cash flows for Farham.

Tutorial note

A cash generating unit is the smallest group of assets that generate cash flows that are independent from the rest of the business.

The recoverable amount of the unit would need to be assessed as the higher of fair value less costs to sell and value in use.

Reference to IFRS 13 *Fair Value Measurement* would be required in estimating the fair value of the facility. This may involve considering whether similar facilities have been on the market or recently sold.

Value in use would be calculated by estimating the present value of the cash flows generated from the production facility discounted at a suitable rate of interest to reflect the risks to the business.

Where the carrying amount exceeds the recoverable amount, impairment has occurred. Any impairment loss is allocated to reduce the carrying amount of the assets of the unit. This cannot be netted off the revaluation surplus as the surplus does not specifically relate to the facility impaired. As such the impairment should be recorded in profit or loss.

No provision should be recognised for the costs of repairing the factory. To recognise a provision, IAS 37 *Provisions, Contingent Liabilities and Contingent Assets* would require a legal or constructive obligation to repair the factory. No such obligation exists.

Sale of Newall

The disposal of Newall appears to meet the criteria to be held for sale as per IFRS 5 *Non-current Assets Held for Sale and Discontinued Operations*. Management has shown commitment to the sale by approving the plan and reporting it to the media. A probable acquirer has been found, the sale is highly probable, and it is expected to be completed six months after the year end (well within the 12-month criteria).

Tutorial note

A disposal group is a group of assets that will be disposed of in a single transaction.

Newall would be treated as a disposal group because a single equity transaction is the most likely form of disposal.

If Newall is deemed to be a separate major component of business or geographical area of the group, the losses of the group should be presented separately as a discontinued operation within the consolidated financial statements of Farham.

Assets held for sale are valued at the lower of carrying amount and fair value less costs to sell. The carrying amount consists of the net assets and goodwill relating to Newall less the non-controlling interest's share.

Assets within the disposal group which are not inside the scope of IFRS 5 are adjusted for in accordance with the relevant standard first. This includes leased assets. The right-of-use asset deemed surplus to requirements will most likely be written off with a corresponding expense recognised in profit or loss.

Any further impairment loss recognised to reduce Newall to fair value less costs to sell would be allocated first to goodwill and then on a pro rata basis across the other non-current assets of the group.

Tutorial note

A constructive obligation is where an entity's past behaviour and practice indicates to other parties that it will accept certain responsibilities.

The chief operating officer is wrong to exclude any form of restructuring provision from the consolidated financial statements. The disposal has been communicated to the media and a constructive obligation exists. However, only directly attributable costs of the restructuring should be included and not ongoing costs of the business. The legal fees and redundancy costs should be provided for. Future operating losses should not be provided for because no obligating event has arisen. No provision is required for the impairments of the owned assets as this would have been accounted for on remeasurement to fair value less costs to sell.

Tutorial note

If the lease will be terminated then the lease term has changed.

If the early termination penalty is likely to be paid then the lease term has changed. Per IFRS 16 *Leases*, the lease liability must be remeasured and should now include the present value of the penalty (but should exclude any payments scheduled after this date). When the lease liability is remeasured, a corresponding adjustment is posted against the right-of-use asset. If the right-of-use asset has been written down to zero an expense should instead be charged to profit or loss.

(b) Ethics

Tutorial note

Financial statement errors are an ethical issue, even if they were accidental. Accountants have a responsibility to be professionally competent so that primary user groups are not misled.

Accountants have a duty to ensure that the financial statements are fair, transparent and comply with accounting standards. The accountant has made mistakes that would be unexpected from a professionally qualified accountant. In particular, the accountant appears unaware of which costs should be included within a restructuring provision and has failed to recognise that there is no obligating event in relation to future operating losses. Accountants must carry out their work with due care and attention for the financial statements to have credibility. They must therefore ensure that their knowledge is kept up to date and that they do carry out their work in accordance with the relevant ethical and professional standards. Failure to do so would be a breach of professional competence. The accountant must make sure that they address this issue through, for example, attending regular training and professional development courses.

Tutorial note

Discuss the specific impact of the errors on the financial statements.

There are a number of instances which suggest that the chief operating officer is happy to manipulate the financial statements for their own benefit. She is not willing to account for an impairment loss for the subsidence despite knowing that this is contrary to IFRS Standards. She is also unwilling to reduce the profits of the group by properly applying the assets held for sale criteria in relation to Newall nor to create a restructuring provision. All of the adjustments required to ensure the financial statements comply with IFRS and IAS Standards will reduce profitability. It is true that the directors do have a responsibility to run the group on behalf of their shareholders and to try to maximise their return. This must not be to the detriment, though, of producing financial statements which are objective and faithfully represent the performance of the group. It is likely that the chief operating officer is motivated by bonus targets and is therefore trying to misrepresent the results of the group. The chief operating officer must make sure that she is not unduly influenced by this self-interest threat to her objectivity.

The chief operating officer is also acting unethically by threatening to dismiss the accountant should they try to correct the financial statements. It is not clear whether the chief operating officer is a qualified accountant but the ethical principles should extend to all employees and not just qualified accountants. Threatening and intimidating behaviour is unacceptable and against all ethical principles. The accountant faces an ethical dilemma. They have a duty to produce financial statements which are objective and fair but to do so could mean losing their job.

Tutorial note

Remember to discuss actions that the accountant should take.

The accountant should approach the chief operating officer and remind them of the basic ethical principles and try to persuade them of the need to put the adjustments through the consolidated accounts so that they are fair and objective. Should the chief operating officer remain unmoved, the accountant may wish to contact the ACCA ethical helpline and take legal advice before undertaking any further action.

Marking scheme		
		Marks
(a)	Subsidence as impairment indicator	2
	Fair value	2
	Allocation of impairment loss	1
	Held for sale criteria, valuation and impairment	3
	Required accounting treatment	3
		11
(b)	Discussion of ethical principles	2
	Application of ethical principles to scenario	5
		7
	Professional marks	**2**
Total		**20**

Examiner's comments

Candidates with good exam technique should briefly plan the content of their written answer to avoid repetition: writing the same point twice loses valuable time and certainly will not score marks twice. Good practice is to have separate headings for each 'situation', with lines left in between them for ease of marking.

Part (b) was well-answered in most cases, with better answers applying ethical principles to the scenario. It was pleasing to see fewer answers merely 'listing out' rote-learned ethical requirements in this sitting.

29 CLOUD  *Walk in the footsteps of a top tutor*

Key answer tips

There are two professional marks awarded for the application of ethical principles. Make sure that your discussion of ethics relates to the specific circumstances and transactions in the question. Do not just regurgitate the ACCA Code of Ethics, but do have a think about what ethical principles Cloud's directors and staff might be breaching.

Presentation of loan in statement of cash flows

Tutorial note

Begin by defining the relevant categories of cash flows. Use these definitions to decide whether the cash receipt has been appropriately presented.

IAS 7 *Statement of Cash Flows* says that cash flows from operating activities are those related to the revenue-producing activities of an entity, such as cash received from customers and cash paid to suppliers. Cash flows from financing activities are those that change the equity or borrowing structure of an entity.

The cash received from the bank is a borrowing. As such, it should be reported as a cash flow from financing activities.

The current treatment is over-stating Cloud's operating cash flows, which is likely to make Cloud look more liquid than it really is. It may also improve perceptions of its long-term sustainability.

Share sale

Tutorial note

A profit or loss on the sale of shares in a subsidiary arises in the consolidated financial statements only if control is lost.

If a share sale results in loss of control over a subsidiary then a profit or loss on disposal should be recorded. If there is no loss of control then there should be no profit or loss on disposal and no remeasurement of goodwill. Instead the transaction is accounted for in equity, as an increase to the non-controlling interest (NCI).

Cloud has incorrectly recorded a profit on disposal in the consolidated statement of profit of loss. This is over-stating profits and should be removed.

Tutorial note

Use the figures to calculate the adjustments required to equity.

Cloud should account for an increase to the NCI. This will be calculated as the percentage of the net assets and goodwill sold to the NCI. This amounts to $1.5 million (5% × ($5m + $25m)). The difference between the cash proceeds and the increase to the NCI is accounted for as an increase of $0.5 million ($2m – $1.5m) in other components of equity.

Revaluation of property, plant and equipment

IAS 16 *Property, Plant and Equipment* states that revaluation gains on property, plant and equipment are recorded in other comprehensive income (OCI) and held in a revaluation reserve in equity (other components of equity). Revaluation losses are charged to OCI to the extent that a revaluation reserve exists for that specific asset. Any revaluation loss in excess of the balance on the revaluation reserve is charged to profit or loss.

Tutorial note

You need to work out the revaluation reserve created by the prior year revaluation. Any revaluation loss in excess of the reserve balance is charged to profit or loss.

At 31 December 20X0, there was a revaluation gain of $4 million being the difference between the carrying amount of $8 million ($10m × 4/5) and the fair value of $12 million. This revaluation gain would have been recognised in other comprehensive income and held in a revaluation surplus in equity.

At 31 December 20X1 the carrying amount of the asset before the revaluation was $9 million ($12 million × 3/4).

The revaluation loss is \$5 million (\$9m – \$4m). Of this, \$4 million should be charged to other comprehensive income because that is the balance in the revaluation reserve. The remaining loss of \$1 million should be charged against profit or loss. Cloud's error means that profits are currently over-stated by \$1 million.

Tutorial note

Some entities perform a reserve transfer in respect of the excess depreciation arising from revaluations. This policy is optional. If you need to consider the impact of a reserve transfer then it will be explicitly mentioned in the question.

Ethics

The directors have a responsibility to faithfully represent the transactions that the entity has entered into during the year. This is because various user groups rely on the financial statements to make economic decisions. Accountants are trusted as professionals and it is important that this trust is not broken. Therefore, it is vital that the principles outlined in the ACCA *Code of Ethics* are understood and followed.

The directors receive a bonus based on profits and operating cash flows. This might impair their objectivity when accounting for transactions that have taken place during the year.

Tutorial note

Make specific reference to the accounting errors that Cloud has made. These errors increase cash flows from operating activities and profit – what does that suggest?

The error in the statement of cash flows increased cash flows from operating activities. The errors relating to the share sale and the downwards revaluation of property, plant and equipment have over-stated profit for the year. It seems likely that the misstatements were deliberate in order to meet the bonus target.

It is unclear if it was the finance director who processed these incorrect accounting entries, or if it was other members of the accounts department. However, the other accountants still have an ethical responsibility not to mislead the users of the financial statements. It may be that they are intimidated by the dominant finance director. They should consider reporting any concerns to the other directors, if possible, or they could highlight these issues to the audit committee or the external auditors.

Of course, it may be that the misstatements were legitimate mistakes rather than a deliberate attempt to meet profit and cash flow targets. Nonetheless, accountants have a responsibility to ensure that they are professionally competent. Thus, possessing insufficient knowledge of IFRS and IAS Standards constitutes an ethical issue. If this is the case then the finance director and/or relevant members of the accounts department need to actively seek out opportunities to continue their professional development.

Marking scheme	
	Marks
Cash flow classification – 1 mark per point	3
Share sale – 1 mark per point	4
Downwards revaluation – 1 mark per point	4
Ethical implications – 1 mark per point	7
Professional marks	2
Total	**20**

30 GARDEN  *Walk in the footsteps of a top tutor*

Key answer tips

You score one mark for each valid point that you make – set out your work neatly so that you can keep track of whether you've written enough (or too little or too much) for each issue.

(a) Share-based payment

Tutorial note

Outline the rules regarding the accounting treatment of equity-settled share-based payments and then apply these to the information given.

The directors have been granted share-options so this is an equity-settled share-based payment transaction. According to IFRS 2 *Share-based Payment,* the expense should be based on the fair value of the options at the grant date, which is $4 per option. The expense should be spread over the three year vesting period, based on the number of options expected to vest. One third of the vesting period has passed so the finance director is incorrect in stating that no expense should be recognised in the current financial year.

Tutorial note

Always show full workings for any calculations. That way you may still score some marks, even if you make a mistake.

The expense that should be recognised in the year-ended 30 November 20X6 is:

5 directors × 600,000 options × $4 × 1/3 = $4 million.

An expense of $4 million should be recognised in profit or loss and a corresponding entry made to equity. This will reduce the reported profits of Garden.

Tutorial note

Don't forget that any transaction with a director is a related party transaction. Disclosures are therefore required.

IAS 24 *Related Party Disclosures* requires that key management personnel, which includes all directors, are related parties of the reporting entity. With regards to key management personnel, an entity is required to disclose employee benefits, including share-based payments.

The directors' son

Tutorial note

Do the payments to the son of the two directors need to be disclosed? Identify the relevant provisions of IAS 24 and use them to explain why disclosure is or is not required.

Directors are key management personnel and therefore are related parties of the reporting entity. IAS 24 also says that the close family members of key management personnel would be related parties of the reporting entity. The definition of close family members includes children.

The son of the finance and sales directors is therefore a related party of Garden. The salary paid to him would need to be disclosed in a note to the financial statements. A statement could be made that the transaction is on market value terms as long as this can be substantiated.

Operating segments

Tutorial note

The retail outlets have been aggregated with the rest of Garden's trading operations. Is this correct? State the rules regulating when aggregation of operating segments is appropriate and then apply these to the scenario.

According to IFRS 8 *Operating Segments*, an operating segment is a component of an entity that engages in business activities, and which has discrete financial information available that is monitored by the entity's chief decision maker. It would therefore seem that the retail outlets are an operating segment.

Operating segments can be aggregated if they have similar economic characteristics. Such segments would normally have similar long-term margins and also be similar in terms of the products that they sell, the customers that they sell to, and the distribution methods used.

The retail outlets have a different margin to the rest of Garden's activities. Furthermore, the retail stores sell to customers face-to-face, whereas the rest of Garden's businesses is conducted online with goods despatched to customers via couriers. This suggests that the retail outlets do not have economic characteristics similar to the other operating segments. As such, the retail outlets should be disclosed as a separate segment (assuming they exceed the quantitative thresholds outlined in IFRS 8).

IAS 24 *Related Party Disclosures* says that a close family member of a director is a related party of the reporting entity. However, the definition of a close family member does not include friends. This means that the purchase of the trade and assets of the retail business should not be disclosed as a related party transaction.

(b) Ethical and professional issues

The purpose of financial statements is to give a faithful representation of the company's position and performance to enable investors, lenders and other users to make economic decisions. Accountants have a social and ethical responsibility to issue financial statements which do not mislead the public. Deliberate falsification of financial statements is unethical. Any manipulation of the accounts will harm the credibility of the profession since the public assume that professional accountants will act in an ethical capacity.

A faithful representation is normally deemed to have been provided if the financial statements are prepared in accordance with International Financial Reporting Standards. It would seem that the financial statements currently breach a number of key standards, such as IFRS 2 *Share-based Payments*, IAS 24 *Related Party Disclosures* and IFRS 8 *Operating Segments*.

Tutorial note

Make specific reference to the transactions in the question. What is the impact of the mistakes/omissions on the financial statements?

Omitting the share-based payment transaction from the financial statements has inflated profit for the year, which could impact shareholder perception of the underlying performance of Garden. Moreover, the shareholders have already been critical about director remuneration, so omitting the transaction may have been a tactic for deliberately concealing this additional benefit.

It would also seem that the recruitment and remuneration of the son of the finance and sales directors is being deliberately concealed. Although it is claimed that he is being paid a salary that is in line with market rates, questions may still be asked about the appointment, such as: Is this the best person for the job? Is this role really required? Is this the best use of company money? Some users of the financial statements might conclude that the directors are putting their own interests, and the interests of their family members, above those of the other company shareholders.

Garden's finance director has wrongly aggregated the entity's operating segments. This might be an attempt to hide the poor performance of the newly acquired retail outlets, thus avoiding further criticism and scrutiny of the transaction. Whilst the trade and assets were not purchased from a related party, the fact that the transaction took place with a close friend of one of the directors raises questions about integrity and the extent to which the directors more generally are effectively and efficiently using the entity's resources.

Tutorial note

Note that the question requires you to answer from the perspective of the accountant. Explicitly state the ethical principles that have been breached. Try and come up with practical steps that the accountant should take to resolve the ethical issues.

The accountant should remind the directors that professional ethics are an integral part of the framework from which professional accountants operate. They must adhere to ethical guidelines such as the ACCA's *Code of Ethics and Conduct*. It would appear that the financial statements are being deliberately manipulated, probably to avoid further criticism from shareholders about the running of the company and the stewardship of its assets. This would contravene the principles of integrity, objectivity and professional behaviour. Records of discussions between the accountant and the directors should be kept and, if disagreements remain, advice should be sought by the accountant from ACCA. If no effective channel for internal reporting of concerns exists then the accountant may need to consider resignation.

Marking scheme		
		Marks
(a)	Share-based payment	4
	Related parties	3
	Operating segments	4
		11
(b)	Discussion of ethical principles	2
	Application of ethical principles to scenario	5
		7
	Professional marks	**2**
Total		**20**

31 CHERRY  *Walk in the footsteps of a top tutor*

Key answer tips

There are two marks available for the application of ethical principles. To get these you should tailor your answer to the specific transactions in the question.

Do not write everything that you know about each accounting standard or you will run out of time. Instead, jot down the rules and principles that are relevant to the scenario and then apply these.

Remember that one mark is awarded per valid point that you make. Make sure that you are writing enough to pass.

(a) Change in accounting policy for pension scheme

Tutorial note

If an entity talks about changing its accounting policies then there will be marks available for referring to IAS 8 Accounting Policies, Changes in Accounting Estimates and Errors. Try and remember that entities can only depart from IFRS and IAS Standards if compliance would be misleading.

IAS 8 *Accounting Policies, Changes in Accounting Estimates and Errors* only permits a change in accounting policy if the change is:

- required by an IFRS Standard or
- results in the financial statements providing reliable and more relevant information.

A retrospective adjustment is required unless the change arises from a new accounting policy with transitional arrangements to account for the change.

It is possible to depart from the requirements of IFRS and IAS Standards but only in the extremely rare circumstances where compliance would be so misleading that it would conflict with the overall objectives of the financial statements. This override is rarely, if ever, invoked.

Tutorial note

Use the relevant accounting standard, IAS 19 Employee Benefits, to explain why the directors' policy change is not allowed.

IAS 19 *Employee Benefits* requires all gains and losses on a defined benefit scheme to be recognised in profit or loss except for the remeasurement component which must be recognised in other comprehensive income.

The amendment to the pension scheme is a past service cost and must be expensed to profit or loss. Additionally, it appears that the directors wish to manipulate other aspects of the pension scheme such as the current service cost and, since the scheme is in deficit, the net finance cost. The directors are deliberately manipulating the presentation of these items by recording them in OCI rather than in profit or loss.

Trademark

Tutorial note

Don't rush into calculations. Easy marks are available for using IAS 38 Intangible Assets to explain why Cherry's treatment of the brand is incorrect.

IAS 38 *Intangible Assets* states an intangible asset with a finite useful life should be amortised on a systematic basis over that life. The amortisation method should reflect the pattern of benefits and it should be reviewed at least annually. A change in amortisation method is adjusted prospectively as a change in estimate under IAS 8 *Accounting Policies, Changes in Accounting Estimates and Errors.*

Expected future reductions in sales could be indicative of a higher rate of consumption of the future economic benefits embodied in an asset. Hence, the trademark should have been amortised over a remaining 2.5 year period (from 1 December 20X5 until 31 May 20X8).

At the date of the estimate change the trademark had a carrying amount of \$2.1 million (\$3m × 7/10). The amortisation charge in the current period should have been \$0.84 million (\$2.1m/2.5 years). This means that Cherry's profits and intangible assets are currently overstated by \$0.54 million (\$0.84m – \$0.3m).

The correcting entry required is:

Dr Amortisation expense (P/L) \$0.54m

Cr Intangible assets \$0.54m

Tutorial note

Reducing the expected useful economic life of an asset is an indication that it might be impaired. You should discuss impairment, even though you are not given enough information to calculate it.

IAS 36 *Impairment of Assets* states that an entity should assess annually whether there is any indication that an asset may be impaired. If any such indication exists, the entity should estimate the recoverable amount of the asset. Thus, Cherry should test the trademark for impairment by comparing its carrying amount to its recoverable amount. The recoverable amount is the higher of fair value less costs to sell, and value in use. If the trademark is impaired then the current over-statement of Cherry's profits and assets is even greater.

Sale and leaseback

Tutorial note

Remember that lessees are required to recognise a right-of-use asset and a lease liability. Cherry has not done this. Comment on this to score some easy marks. The calculation of the correct profit on disposal is trickier. Revisit the Study Text if you cannot remember how to do this.

Sale and leaseback transactions are accounted for under IFRS 16 *Leases*. If the transfer of the asset represents a sale then the seller-lessee measures the right-of-use asset at the proportion of the previous carrying amount that relates to the rights retained after the sale. This means that the seller-lessee recognises a profit or loss based only on the rights transferred.

If the transfer does not qualify as a sale then the seller-lessee continues to recognise the underlying asset and will also recognise a financial liability equal to the proceeds received.

It would seem that the transfer does represent a sale because Cherry is only leasing the asset back for a fraction of its remaining useful life and so the buyer-lessor seems to have obtained control of the underlying asset.

Cherry must initially measure the right-of-use asset at $1.26 million (($1.8m/$5m) × $3.5 million).

The lease liability will be initially measured at the present value of the lease payments, which is $1.80 million.

Cherry has recorded a profit on disposal of $1.5 million but this should have been $0.96 million ($1.5m × (($5m – $1.8m)/$5m). Therefore, the profit on disposal must be reduced by $0.54 million.

The correcting entry required is as follows:

Dr Right of use asset $1.26m

Dr Profit or loss $0.54m

Cr Lease liability $1.80m

In the next reporting period, depreciation on the right-of-use asset and interest on the lease liability will be recorded in profit or loss.

(b) Ethics

Tutorial note

Make sure that you discuss why the directors are behaving unethically.

The current accounting treatments cannot be justified. The directors have an ethical responsibility to produce financial statements which are a fair representation of the entity's performance and position and which comply with all accounting standards. The errors made by Cherry under-state its liabilities and over-state its assets and profits.

There is a clear self-interest threat arising from the bonus scheme. The directors' change in policy with regards to pensions appears to be motivated by an intention to overstate operating profit to maximise their bonus potential.

Tutorial note

State the specific principles from the ethical code that the directors are breaching.

Such treatment is against the ACCA ethical principles of objectivity, integrity and professional behaviour.

The objectivity of the financial controller is also being compromised. The implicit threat to reduce her bonus would seem to give rise to both self-interest and intimidation threats.

The financial controller should remind the directors of their ethical responsibilities and should persuade them to change the current accounting treatment of all three of the transactions. If she feels she cannot discuss this with the directors then she should discuss the matters with the audit committee. The financial controller should document her discussions.

Marking scheme		
		Marks
(a)	Change in pension policy	3
	Intangible asset	4
	Sale and leaseback	5
		12
(b)	Discussion of ethical principles	2
	Application of ethical principles to scenario	4
		6
	Professional marks	**2**
Total		**20**

32 ANOUK

Key answer tips

This question requires knowledge of three key accounting standards – IFRS 9 *Financial Instruments*, IAS 32 *Financial Instruments: Presentation*, and IFRS 16 *Leases*. If you are unfamiliar with these, then you should revisit the Study Text. In Strategic Business Reporting, marks are awarded for demonstrating knowledge of the relevant accounting standards and also for applying this knowledge to the scenario.

When discussing the ethical implications remember that generic comments about the *Code of Ethics* will not score highly. You must explain the particular ethical issues facing Anouk and outline how the financial controller should address these.

Receivables

Tutorial note

Many students forget that receivables are a financial instrument and therefore make no reference to IFRS 9 Financial Instruments. However, you could still score well if you applied basic accounting principles to the scenario.

IFRS 9 *Financial Instruments* suggests that the trade receivables should be derecognised from the financial statements when the following conditions are met:

- There are no further rights to receive cash
- The risks and rewards of ownership have substantially transferred.

The factor has full recourse for a six-month period so Anouk still has the irrecoverable debt risk. Furthermore, Anouk has the right to receive further cash payments from the factor, the amounts to be received being dependent on when and if the customers pay the factor. Anouk therefore still has the risks associated with slow payment by their customers. As such, the receivables must not be derecognised from the financial statements on 31 December 20X1. Instead the proceeds of $8 million (20% × $40m) should be treated as a short-term liability.

Accounting for the legal form of the transaction will understate receivables and understate liabilities. This makes it less likely that Anouk will break its loan covenants.

Debt or equity

Tutorial note

This is a very popular exam topic. It is essential to memorise the definitions of equity and financial liabilities.

IAS 32 *Financial Instruments: Presentation* uses principles-based definitions of a financial liability (debt) and of equity. The key feature of debt is that the issuer is obliged to deliver either cash or another financial asset to the holder. The contractual obligation may arise from a requirement to repay principal or interest or dividends. Equity is any contract which evidences a residual interest in the entity's assets after deducting all of its liabilities. A financial instrument is normally an equity instrument if the instrument includes no contractual obligation to deliver cash or another financial asset to another entity (such as ordinary shares).

Anouk's decision to classify B-shares as non-controlling interests is incorrect. Anouk has a clear contractual obligation to buy B-shares from the non-controlling interest under agreed terms and does not have an unconditional right to avoid delivering cash to settle the obligation. The minority shareholders' B-shares should therefore be treated as a financial liability in the consolidated financial statements.

The current treatment of the B shares over-states Anouk's equity and understates its liabilities. This makes it less likely that Anouk will break its loan covenants.

Crane contract

Tutorial note

It is important that entities correctly identify a contract that contains a lease because lessees are required to recognise a liability and a right-of-use asset in respect of all leases (unless short-term or of low value).

IFRS 16 *Leases* says that a contract contains a lease if it **'conveys the right to control the use of an identified asset for a period of time in exchange for consideration'** (IFRS 16, para 9). To have control, the contract must give the customer the right, throughout the period of use, to:

- substantially all of the identified asset's economic benefits, and
- direct the identified asset's use.

Although the crane used by Anouk can be substituted, the supplier is unlikely to benefit from this due to the costs involved. Therefore it can be concluded that Anouk has the right to use an identified asset over the contract term.

Anouk has the right to direct the use of the crane because it decides how the crane will be used. The restriction on operating during high winds, as outlined in the contract, defines the scope of Anouk's use, rather than preventing Anouk from directing use. Therefore Anouk controls the Crane over the period of use.

Tutorial note

Do not stop once you have concluded that the contract contains a lease. You need to discuss the correct accounting treatment.

Based on the above discussion, it would seem that the contract contains a lease. A lease liability should have been recognised at the commencement of the lease for the present value of the payments to be made. A right-of-use asset should be recognised for the same value, plus any associated direct costs.

Anouk has posted no accounting entries and so is currently understating both its assets and liabilities. Once again, this makes it less likely that the loan covenants will be breached.

Ethics

It is important that stakeholders of a company can rely on financial statements to make informed and accurate decisions. The directors of Anouk have an ethical responsibility to produce financial statements which comply with accounting standards, are transparent, and are free from material error.

Tutorial note

Make specific reference to the errors in Anouk's financial statements.

The current accounting treatment of all three transactions understates Anouk's reported liabilities. The current accounting treatments, if uncorrected, may mislead Anouk's stakeholders. Any adverse publicity could lead to a loss of public trust in the accounting profession.

Tutorial note

Make specific reference to the ethical principles that the directors are breaching.

It would seem likely that the directors are deliberately circumventing the terms of the covenants, particularly as they have concealed documents from the financial controller. Such actions are a clear breach of the fundamental principles of objectivity and integrity as outlined in the ACCA *Code of Ethics and Conduct*.

Tutorial note

Outline practical steps that the financial controller should take to resolve the issues.

The financial controller should remind the directors of their ethical responsibilities and remind them that Anouk's financial statements must fully comply with accounting standards. Records of these discussions should be kept. If disagreements remain, the financial controller should seek advice from ACCA. The financial controller may need to consider resignation if no effective channel for internal reporting of concerns exists.

Marking scheme	
	Marks
Receivables and factoring – 1 mark per point	4
Debt or equity – 1 mark per point	4
Lease contract – 1 mark per point	4
Ethical implications – 1 mark per point	6
Professional marks	2
Total	**20**

SECTION B

33 STEM (SEP/DEC 2021)  *Walk in the footsteps of a top tutor*

Key answer tips

This question tested knowledge of two main standards – IFRS 16 *Leases* and IAS 28 *Investments in Associates and Joint Ventures.* Assuming the candidate's knowledge of the basics of these topics is to the required standard, this question could provide some achievable marks. There is quite a lot of data to process so, as always, watch your timing. However, many of the significant figures have been provided directly in the question without the need for time-wasting calculations. Use this to your advantage.

(a) Company cars

Tutorial note

This requirement asks for consideration of the effect on 3 areas of the financial statements (EBITDA, profit before tax and the statement of financial position) caused by 3 separate methods of financing the provision of company cars to its staff. This gives 9 distinct tasks to address. If candidates can address all 9 tasks in their time allocation then, with a mark allocation of 13, a score of at least 9/13 should be well within reach. Focus on providing an answer that addresses each required task within the time. The risk here is that candidates exhibit poor time-management by extensively discussing only 1 or 2 of the financing options.

Option 1: Leased for a four-year period

Tutorial note

Get the basics across for a lease – initial recognition and subsequent treatment of the right of use asset and lease liability.

At 1 January 20X7, a right-of-use asset and lease liability of $50,803 would be recognised according to IFRS 16 *Leases*. The annual lease component of the lease payments is $14,016 (12 × ($1,403 – $235)) and the service component is $2,820 (12 × $235). At 31 December 20X7, operating expenses will comprise the service component of $2,820 and depreciation of $12,701 ($50,803/4). An interest expense of $2,274 will be recognised as a finance cost. The lease liability recognised will be $50,803 less the annual payments of $14,016 plus the interest element of $2,274 i.e. $39,061. The closing lease liability will be split between its non-current and current liability in the statement of financial position. IFRS 16 requires a company to recognise interest on lease liabilities separately from depreciation on leased assets.

Option 2: Purchased on 1 January 20X7

If the cars were purchased on 1 January 20X7, then depreciation of $11,380 ($75,274 – $29,753 = $45,521/4 = $11,380) would be charged and interest of $3,764 ($75,274 × 5%) would also be charged. The cars would have to be serviced at a cost of $2,820.

Tutorial note

For option 2 discussion of the initial recognition of the vehicles (at cost) as per IAS 16 Property, Plant and Equipment, and the loan liability measured at amortised cost per IFRS 9 Financial Instruments is likely to achieve marks as well.

Option 3: Leased on a 12-month agreement

Tutorial note

State the rules for the 12-month lease and apply them to the scenario.

Instead of applying the recognition requirements of IFRS 16 *Leases*, a lessee may elect to account for lease payments as an expense on a straight-line basis over the lease term for the following two types of leases:

(i) leases with a lease term of 12 months or less and containing no purchase options, and

(ii) leases where the underlying asset has a low value.

The effect of applying the IFRS 16 exemption would be that neither an asset nor a liability will be recognised and therefore it will not affect the statement of financial position. Neither a right of use asset nor lease liability will be recognised if this exemption is applied. Instead, an expense will be recognised in the statement of profit or loss.

The cost of the short-term lease would be included in operating expenses at $22,800 (12 × $1,900).

Tutorial note

The approach in the official answer deals firstly with the accounting issues for each option, then considers the resulting impacts on the requested financial indicators (as below). Do not worry if you have used an alternative approach, such as, for each option, addressing the accounting treatment and the impacts on the financial information together, as this would be equally acceptable.

It can be seen that the impact on EBITDA is greatest if 12-month leases are chosen. This is because the cost is shown in operating expenses. Additionally, profit before tax is lower under this option. EBITDA does not include lease interest when IFRS 16 is used and thus is naturally higher.

There will be no effect on EBITDA if Stem Co leases or buys the cars and, further, the impact on profit before tax is minimal with profit being lower if Stem Co purchases the cars.

If 12-month leases are chosen, then there will be no recognition of an asset for the cars which will result in a higher asset base for the four-year lease/purchase of cars, which will affect ratios such as asset turnover. Similarly, a liability will not be recognised in the case of the 12-month lease which will mean higher financial liabilities for the four-year lease/purchase, which will affect financial leverage (gearing).

The carrying amount of the leased cars will typically reduce more quickly than the carrying amount of lease liabilities. This is because, in each period of the lease, the leased car is depreciated on a straight-line basis, and the lease liability is reduced by the amount of lease payments made and increased by the interest which reduces over the life of the lease. Consequently, although the amounts of the lease asset and lease liability are the same at the start and end of the lease, the amount of the asset would typically be lower than that of the liability throughout the lease term. This will result in a further reduction in reported equity as compared to 12-month leases. This will be similar to the effect on reported equity which arises from financing the purchase of the cars through a loan.

	Option 1: Lease over 4 years	**Option 2: Purchase with loan**	**Option 3: 12-month leases**
	($)	($)	($)
Profit before accounting for cars	100,000	100,000	100,000
Service cost	(2,820)	(2,820)	
Operating expense			(22,800)
EBITDA	**97,180**	**97,180**	**77,200**
Depreciation	(12,701)	(11,380)	
Interest	(2,274)	(3,764)	
Profit before tax	**82,205**	**82,036**	**77,200**

Statement of financial position

PPE	38,102	63,894	0
	(50,803-12,701)	(75,274-11,380)	
Lease/Loan Liability	39,061	79,038	0
	(see explanation)	(75,274 + 3,764)	

(b) **(i)** **Equity method**

Tutorial note

Make sure you answer both parts of the requirement here. It is easy to forget to compare the equity method used for an associate to using the cost or fair value. Do not be afraid to provide your own opinion regarding the relevance of the equity accounting treatment, even if your opinion seems to contradict the preferred option of the standard. As long as you justify your stance, a conclusion of some sort is better than no conclusion at all!

The equity method is a measurement method and not a consolidation method, as the equity-accounted entity remains as a single line in the investor's statement of financial position and, in IFRS standards, consolidation is based on the existence of control. Equity accounting is a measurement method for investments where there is 'significant influence' and recognises an associate's profits which have not been received and could not be successfully demanded. The equity method consists of the cost of the investment in the associate, plus the parent's share of the associate's post-acquisition movement in net assets. The equity method provides better information than that provided by cost, but it can be argued that, where investments are listed, there is no reason not to use fair value. The equity method is likely to be better than cost because cost is, in isolation, an uninformative basis for decision-making. However, if an investment is listed, then its fair value would be easier to establish and more intuitively appealing than the numbers derived from the equity method. If the associate is unlisted, then there might be questions about the verifiability of fair value. However, even then, there appears to be no reason why the equity method should be preferred to IFRS 13 *Fair Value Measurement*.

(ii) **Emphasis Co**

Tutorial note

This requirement calls for a discussion of the classification of Emphasis Co as a joint venture and the accounting of the shareholding in Emphasis. The classification part should provide some relatively easy marks for those that had studied the fundamental concepts surrounding joint ventures.

The following are the characteristics of a joint venture:

- Joint ventures are joint arrangements which are structured through a separate vehicle which confers legal separation between the joint venture and the assets and liabilities in the vehicle.
- The entity must be under the joint control of the venturers, which is the contractually agreed sharing of control of an arrangement, which exists only when decisions about the relevant activities require the unanimous consent of the parties sharing control.
- The venturers must be able to exercise joint control of the entity.
- The purpose of the entity must be consistent with the definition of a joint venture.

  Emphasis Co is a joint venture. Its activities are conducted through a separate legal entity and the parties participating in the decision-making exercise control through their equity investments. This control is determined by the ability to appoint board members. This means that the significant decisions require the unanimous consent of all of the parties. The company holding 20% of the equity can only appoint one board member but does have the ability to prevent the remaining companies from making significant decisions without its consent.

Each party to the joint venture (or each 'joint venturer') recognises an investment, which is accounted for using the equity method in accordance with IAS 28 *Investments in Associates and Joint Ventures.*

Tutorial note

The accounting element includes a tricky issue where the joint venturer initially contributes less than the proportionate fair value of the net assets of the joint venturer. If you found yourself struggling with the bargain purchase, have a guess (there's no negative marking), but make sure you prioritise the classification element, where marks for the fundamentals will be awarded.

According to IAS 28, where an investor's investment is less than their share of the fair value of the identifiable net assets acquired, this results in a gain to the investor and is referred to as a bargain purchase. IAS 28 states that on the acquisition of the investment in an entity, any difference (whether positive or negative) between the cost of acquisition and the investor's share of the fair values of the net identifiable assets of the entity is accounted for like goodwill in accordance with IFRS 3 *Business Combinations*. Thus, any excess fair value of the identifiable net assets over the cost of the investment paid by Stem would be recognised as a bargain purchase gain in earnings on the investment date, which is consistent with the accounting for bargain purchases in business combinations.

However, bargain purchases are rare. Therefore, before recognising a gain on a bargain purchase, Stem Co should reassess whether it has correctly identified all of the assets acquired and all of the liabilities assumed as part of the investment, in order to ensure that all identifiable assets or liabilities are properly recognised. In addition, Stem Co should reconsider and challenge all valuations to verify that the identifiable net assets are properly measured. Stem Co should try to understand why the other parties would contribute assets of higher value than those contributed by Stem Co. Usually, investors act in an economically rational manner. There may be strategic reasons for such actions. For example, Stem Co may have specialised knowledge of the industry. Also, the fair value of the net identifiable assets of Emphasis Co may have increased before the finalisation of the agreement.

Stem Co contributed cash of $150,000 to Emphasis Co. The carrying amount of the net assets contributed by the investors was $310,000 but it is the fair value that is more relevant. The fair value of the net assets contributed was $470,000. Therefore, Stem Co's share of the fair value of the identifiable assets of Emphasis Co is 40% of $470,000, i.e. $188,000. This exceeds the contribution of $150,000. Once Stem Co has reassessed whether it has correctly identified all of the assets acquired and all of the liabilities assumed as part of its investment in Emphasis Co, Stem Co will record the investment at $188,000 and will record a gain of $38,000 ($188,000-$150,000).

Dr Investment in Emphasis Co	$188,000
Cr Cash	$150,000
Cr Profit or loss	$38,000

Marking scheme

		Marks
(a)	Discussion and application of principles to scenario:	
	IFRS 16 *Leases*	3
	Purchasing cars	2
	12-month leases	2
	Impact on EBITDA and profit	3
	SOFP	3
		13
(b) (i)	Discussion of key principles of equity accounting:	
	Nature	2
	Cost	1
	Fair value	1
		4
(ii)	Discussion of key principles of joint venture accounting including a well-argued conclusion	5
	Discussion of bargain purchase	2
	Accounting for bargain purchase	1
		8
Total		**25**

Examiner's comments

a) Part (a) appeared surprisingly challenging for candidates, which is concerning given 13 marks were available for this, and the area of leases is examined relatively often. Much of it was assumed knowledge from Financial Reporting and we would have expected strong application of this knowledge.

Some candidates incorrectly treated the transactions as if the company were leasing cars to managers rather than leasing cars for the managers' use. Even with this misinterpretation, a good description of the principles and underlying treatment of each option would still earn marks.

The question provides sufficient detail for candidates to use the spreadsheet function to calculate the accounting treatments for options 1 and 2, and then summarise the impact of all three options on the three aspects (EBITDA, profit before tax and the statement of financial position). Present values were provided, so in the case of option 1, candidates needed only to calculate the unwinding of the lease liability and depreciation of the right of use asset for the first year. No implicit interest rate is provided, nor required. Instead, the question tells us the correct amount of interest for the year. The monthly payments and service charge element within this amount are also provided, so the closing lease liability can be calculated once annual amounts are worked out.

For option 2, the calculations were simpler since the cars' fair value and residual value, and the implicit interest rate of the loan are all provided. Candidates needed only to work out the depreciation charge, using the stated residual value and interest charge, given no repayment was made until the first day of the following year. This is FR level knowledge and should have been straightforward. For option 3, the annual cost is the only calculation.

The weakest part of most answers was the description of the impact of each option on EBITDA, profit before tax and the statement of financial position. A good answer would use a table approach, in which the impact on each aspect could be shown succinctly.

Note how this presentation separates EBITDA, which is not impacted by depreciation or interest, from profit before tax. Candidates should link the figures included in the above table to their previous workings, to save time and avoid errors. Once complete, a description of the impact of each option on each aspect of the financial statements is a much simpler task. Unfortunately, too many answers did not make sufficient use of the spreadsheet functions available. In a surprisingly high number of cases the spreadsheet was not used at all. Presentation in these cases was very weak; with answers limited to note form or without any structure, and with little attempt to present workings in a way that could be understood.

In some cases, candidates did not seem to know what EBITDA was despite it being written out in full in the requirements; and a number of answers excluded any calculations or explanation of the impacts on EBITDA, profit before tax and SOFP. Whilst calculations were not explicitly required in the question (which asked for an explanation), these aided the explanation of the impact, and most answers provided calculations. Candidates who did not achieve high marks in this question need to be much more familiar with the advantages of answering it using the spreadsheet function. The accounting profession expects the use of spreadsheets at a high level, and candidates need to consider not only the use of formulae to save time, but also an appropriate layout of a spreadsheet working. A worrying number of answers did not use the formula function at all or presented their workings poorly, making it hard for the marker to follow, or impossible to mark without suitable workings and explanation. It is vital for candidates to avoid treating the spreadsheet as a word processor.

b)i) This part had only four marks and required no reference to the scenario. As such, it provides an opportunity for candidates to show their knowledge of the equity accounting measurement method, and to compare this with the cost or fair value measurement bases. Good answers would describe the need for significant influence (as opposed to control) and the principles that apply where such an influence exists.

To gain good marks, candidates should ensure they have met all the requirements of the question. Whilst most candidates described the equity method and the underlying accounting principles, fewer then contrasted this sufficiently to the cost and fair value measurements and where these may be more useful to the users. Those that did not provide answers to both limited their opportunity for marks.

b)ii) This requirement continues the theme of part (b)(i) by requiring a discussion as to whether the newly-formed legal entity (Emphasis Co) should be classified as a joint venture, and how it should be accounted for at the date of formation. The majority of candidates scored well in explaining the characteristics of a joint venture, and then discussed why this applied to Emphasis Co.

Good answers would have identified that whilst the 20% holding only appointed one board member, this member was key as it can prevent the other two parties from making significant decisions – without that member's consent decisions are not unanimous. Weaker answers incorrectly identified Emphasis Co as an associate, focusing on the 40% holding rather than the other characteristics of the agreement.

The accounting method was therefore to apply the equity method under IAS 28 *Investments in Associates and Joint Ventures*. Under IAS 28, where there is a difference between the investment in the joint venture and the share of the fair value of its net assets, this is accounted for like goodwill (in accordance with IFRS 3 *Business Combinations*). In this case, a bargain purchaseis recorded as a gain in earnings on the investment date. Few candidates identified this bargain purchase, and also made no comments relating to the need to reassess whether all identifiable assets and liabilities are identified (since bargain purchases are rare). A simple calculation of the gain would have maximised potential for marks. Generally, if given figures in a scenario, candidates are expected to use them in their answer.

34 SYMBAL (SEP/DEC 2021)  *Walk in the footsteps of a top tutor*

Key answer tips

Another SBR examination question featuring contemporary issues– this time crypto assets and ICOs. A number of recent technical articles have been written on these subjects, so please take note of their examinability.

The financial reporting scenarios in requirements (b-d) are difficult and candidates are unlikely to feel confident as they produce their answers. Use the mark allocations to help with the timing. Address the requirements and follow the specific tips outlined in the tutorial notes.

(a) Principles of good disclosure

Tutorial note

If you're not feeling confident when attempting a current issues discussion question like this one, it is important that you do not give up entirely. Not all answers need detailed technical knowledge. For tasks like this, the examiner wants to see indications that you have properly considered the practical implications presented by the issues raised for accountants in practice. Common sense points relating to the purpose of disclosures in general can be applied to this question. Disclosures should provide useful information, be entity-specific, concise, highlight important matters and should consider materiality. Application of these general disclosure points to the issue of crypto assets will ensure candidates score well.

This requirement carries 2 professional marks. Candidates must attempt the question fully to give the marker the chance to award these marks. If you give up, you'll throw those marks away too.

It is also important to note that these answers are not exhaustive. Relevant points made that may not be represented within this published answer will still score marks. Therefore, within your time allocation, make as many sensible points as possible. You may do better than you think. However, one thing is for sure, a blank answer will score zero!

There is significant interest in crypto assets with implications for both new and traditional investors. There is a growing need for clarity regarding the accounting and related disclosures relating to these new investments. The general disclosure principles which should be used to help investors can include that the disclosures should be entity-specific as information tailored to an entity's own circumstances is more useful than generic information which is readily available outside the financial statements. Thus, detailed information concerning the company's holding of crypto assets and Initial Coin Offerings (ICO) should be disclosed. The company's involvement in ICO's or other issues of crypto assets should be described as simply and directly as possible without a loss of material information and without unnecessarily increasing the length of the financial statements. Additionally, the information disclosed should be organised in a way which highlights important matters which includes providing disclosures in an appropriate order and emphasising the important matters within them. It is important that the terms of an ICO are disclosed so that investors can determine the rights associated with it.

The information about crypto assets should be linked when relevant to other information in the financial statements or to other parts of the annual report to highlight relationships between pieces of information and improve navigation through the financial statements. Commodity broker-traders holding crypto-assets as inventory at fair value less costs to sell, in addition to the general IAS 2 *Inventories* requirements, will need to disclose the carrying amount of such inventories carried at fair value less costs to sell. In addition, IFRS 13 *Fair Value Measurement* disclosure requirements for recurring fair value measurements would also apply. The information about crypto assets should be provided in a way which optimises comparability among entities and across reporting periods without compromising the usefulness of the information. Holders of crypto assets classified as intangible assets under IAS 38 *Intangible Assets* will need to disclose, by class, a reconciliation between the opening and closing carrying amounts, whether the useful life is assessed as indefinite, and, if so, the reasons supporting the indefinite useful life assessment, and a description of individually material holdings.

Finally, the proper application of materiality is key to determining what information to disclose. The judgmental nature of materiality assessments could lead to entities omitting useful information concerning crypto assets from the financial statements. Similarly, difficulties in exercising judgement around materiality could contribute to 'disclosure overload'.

(b) Development costs

Tutorial note

Candidates must apply the principles of IAS 38 Intangible Assets to the development and promotional costs associated with the unusual situation of the ICO of Symbal. However, be aware that judgement should be applied and a definite conclusion may not always be possible based upon the information provided. Weighing up the treatment whether or not the costs meet the definition of an intangible asset will help provide further facets to an answer.

Also, it is worth noting that similar conclusions can be made if the candidate applied the definition of an asset, as outlined within the Conceptual Framework. This alternative viewpoint may help a candidate arrive at a valid conclusion even if their specific knowledge of IAS 38 falls short.

If the costs do not satisfy the requirements of IAS 38 they are recognised as expenses. The costs satisfy the requirements for recognition of intangible assets if, and only if, it is probable that the future economic benefits which are attributable to the asset will flow to the entity and the cost of the asset can be measured reliably. The probability of future economic benefits must be based on reasonable and supportable assumptions about conditions which will exist over the life of the asset.

In making the decision on recognition of the costs incurred, Symbal Co should evaluate whether after the issue of the tokens, it is still capable of controlling the trading platform and whether it may reasonably expect future economic benefits from the token holders. It is important to know whether Symbal Co will be able to get future economic benefits from token holders by providing them with future services other than another issue of tokens.

If costs incurred will not ensure further economic benefits, they should be immediately recognised as an expense in profit or loss. In this case, Symbal Co promises to produce gains for investors from trading the tokens on the platform and in return, the company takes a percentage of the profit as a fee. Thus, the company can reasonably expect further economic benefits after the issue of tokens. The costs may be recognised as an intangible asset and amortised over the useful life of these assets. However, IAS 38 states that an entity should expense promotional activity costs when incurred. Thus, these costs should be excluded from the intangible asset.

If, during future reporting periods, new circumstances are revealed, which indicate that there may be no more future economic benefits, then the value of the intangible asset would be impaired and written down.

(c) ICO arrangements

Tutorial note

Another tricky scenario that candidates are unlikely to feel confident attempting to answer. My advice is to keep your answer structured and as simple as possible.

Keep the answer structured by using the requirement to your advantage. The requirement explicitly mentions the $1m pre-sale agreement, and the $10m raised by the ICO. Effectively identifying these transactions as separate issues to consider. Tackle them one at a time and use sub-headings to make it easier for the marker to spot that you have addressed each issue.

If you are struggling to find a standard that fits the bill, fall back on the definitions of the elements of the financial statements as identified within the Conceptual Framework. This may help to develop a conclusion.

Year ended 31 March 20X7

The success of the ICO is not within the control of Symbal Co as the ICO can be abandoned if the minimum fundraising level of $9 million is not reached. Neither does the investor have the right to be repaid $1 million in cash prior to 30 April 20X7. However, on the basis that the occurrence of a successful ICO is beyond the control of the entity, the agreement contains a financial obligation, because it represents a contractual obligation to deliver cash or another financial asset to another entity if the ICO does not occur by 30 April 20X7. At 31 March 20X7, the $1 million is viewed as a financial liability of Symbal Co in accordance with IAS 32 *Financial Instruments: Presentation* at initial recognition.

Year ended 31 March 20X8

At 30 April 20X7, the funds paid by the holders of tokens of $10 million have the one-off right to 10% of profits from the year ended 31 March 20X8 but they do not have the right to their redemption or residual interest in the assets. Due to this reason, the company should not record any inflows as a financial liability or equity but record them as income by the following accounting entry.

Dr Bank $10 million

Cr Other financial income $10 million

Also at 30 April 20X7, the liability of $1 million recorded for the pre-sale agreement will be reversed and recorded as income.

Initially, at 30 April 20X7, the commitment to the holders of tokens to pay 10% of annual profits for the year ended 31 March 20X8 is considered by Symbal Co to be a contingent liability. IAS 37 *Provisions, Contingent Liabilities and Contingent Assets* defines a contingent liability as a possible obligation depending on whether some uncertain future event occurs. The recognition of the liability depends on whether there are annual profits. Therefore, a liability should be recognised if the company earns profits during the reporting period to 31 March 20X8. Symbal Co will recognise a financial liability to the holders of tokens and an expense to profit or loss.

The tokens are not equity instruments as they do not have a residual interest in the assets of the entity after deducting all of its liabilities and they have a contractual obligation to deliver cash.

(d) Tokens granted to directors

Tutorial note

The requirement here helps by confirming that IFRS 2 is not appropriate and clarifies that Symbal should be applying IAS 19 Employee Benefits. This provides a basic structure to the answer – discuss why IFRS 2 is not relevant (the scenario provides plenty of indicators that the tokens are not shares, therefore the tokens cannot be a share-based payment) and discuss why IAS 19 is relevant.

The dates involved are short term, therefore the tokens are equivalent to a bonus for the directors and are accrued for.

When assessing the accounting treatment of such arrangements, an entity should consider the characteristics of the ICO tokens generated. Equity is the residual interest in the assets of an entity after deducting all of its liabilities. Unless the ICO tokens meet the definition of equity, the arrangements would not meet the definition of a share-based payment arrangement in accordance with IFRS 2 *Share-based Payment*. Instead, they would fall within the scope of IAS 19 *Employee Benefits* as a non-cash employee benefit. IAS 19 can then be used to determine the recognition, as well as the measurement, of the employee benefit.

The tokens do not meet the definition of the equity of Symbal Co as they do not grant the directors a residual interest in the net assets of Symbal Co. Therefore, the arrangements do not meet the definition of a share-based payment arrangement in accordance with IFRS 2. Instead, it is a non-cash short term employee benefit. Short-term employee benefits are those expected to be settled wholly before twelve months after the end of the annual reporting period during which employee services are rendered. The substance of the arrangement is an exchange of employee services for the tokens.

The arrangement includes a condition that the directors should be in employment at 31 March 20X7. Symbal Co should recognise a liability and short-term employee benefit expense at 31 March 20X7.

Symbal Co would measure the amount that it expects to pay by using the fair value of the tokens to be delivered to the employees, or by using the estimated cost of the goods or services which it expects to deliver in the future. This amount would be $250,000 ((5 × $50,000).

Thus, at 31 March 20X7

Dr Employee costs	$250,000
Cr Short-term employee benefit liability	$250,000

Marking scheme		
		Marks
(a)	Discussion of key principles of disclosure for crypto assets	6
(b)	Discussion of:	
	Principles of IAS 38	2
	Application to scenario	3
		5
(c)	Application of the following discussion to the scenario of:	
	Pre-sale agreement/IAS 32	3
	ICO and profit element	3
		6
(ii)	Discussion of key principles of the award – IAS 19/IFRS 2	3
	Accounting for the award	3
		6
	Professional marks	2
Total		**25**

Examiner's comments

This question scenario was based around a contemporary issue in financial reporting and referred to in the SBR syllabus under current issues as broadly 'accounting for digital assets'. This area of the syllabus has been specifically created in response to employers wanting to employ candidates who understand new concepts in this digital age. However, much of the question was not specifically about digital assets or indeed the Initial Coin Offering (ICO) but examined wider issues, like the principles of good disclosure, the recognition criteria of IAS 38 *Intangible Assets* and IAS 19 *Employee Benefits*. It was disappointing that so many candidates could not apply their financial reporting knowledge to the given scenario. Instead they often focussed exclusively on crypto currency, choosing to discuss everything they knew about crypto currencies without specific application to the requirement. This gained few, if any marks.

It is also worth stating that the scenario provided a diagram that illustrated in simple terms the relationship between the investors in an Initial Coin Offering (ICO) and Symbal Co who issued the tokens and managed the trading platform. This was designed to assist candidates and sat alongside the narrative description of the relationships shown in the diagram. There are also recent technical articles written by the SBR examining team specifically covering Initial Coin Offerings and crypto currencies so candidates should have been prepared to see them in an SBR exam. We have always stressed to learning providers and candidates that it is vital that candidates read the articles produced by the examining team. However, we would reiterate that although the scenario was deliberately relevant and current, as candidates should expect, it was examining other core syllabus areas and not just digital assets.

a) This part of the question required candidates to simply explain the principles of good disclosure and apply them to crypto assets. The candidates were told they did not need to refer to any exhibit as it was a high level discussion that was expected and required. It was uncomplicated and marks were awarded for basic principles.

Good candidates were able to match basic disclosure principles disclosures with the challenges brought by crypto assets and their relatively recent rise to prominence. There were, encouragingly, many candidates who advised treatment as intangible assets as opposed to cash or investments. Marks were awarded for this despite not being specifically asked for as it was relevant. The published answer does not cover all the points that could be awarded marks, but credit was given for appropriate discussion of the principles of good disclosure, which may have been IFRS standard specific.

Weaker candidates tended to list out everything they knew about crypto assets without actually addressing the requirements. Some candidates simply regurgitated the article on crypto currency without any application at all and certainly no mention of what constituted good disclosure. This type of rote learned knowledge will never be sufficient to score well in an SBR exam and will always severely restrict any marks that can be awarded. As the 2 professional marks were awarded here, those who did not address the required disclosure aspect lost these marks.

b) This part of the question required candidates to discuss the basic principles of IAS 38 *Intangible Assets* and apply them to the costs of setting up an ICO. The candidate did not therefore need to understand an ICO to be able to apply basic knowledge and principles of IAS 38, much of which is assumed knowledge from Financial Reporting level. The principles are the same whatever the context and scenario. There were some very good answers which separated out the development and promotional costs and their differing treatment. Weaker answers often treated all the elements identically or just listed out the definition of intangibles from IAS 38.

c) This part of the question was answered poorly by many candidates. The question required candidates to deal with an advanced payment for tokens to be issued in an ICO and then how to treat the receipt of monies received from an ICO. This recent technical article may have helped some candidates however application of basic principles to the scenario should have been sufficient to score well.

Candidates did not have to have any in-depth understanding of an ICO, just to apply basic principles to discuss how the proceeds should be recognised, i.e income, liability or equity. Many candidates were unable to do this and omitted answers altogether. This is becoming an increasing issue with the SBR exam, in that candidates cannot apply principles to a scenario, familiar or otherwise. There were many signposts provided in the scenario for example 'no other rights such as redemption or any residual interest'. This should have been a clear steer that the tokens and monies raised are neither a financial liability or equity but instead would be recognised as income. Further discussion on the financial obligation to repay the $1million received credit as did discussion of the principles of a contingent liability and financial liabilities with regards the payment of 10% profit to token holders. Many candidates treated the initial $1m receipt as a sale and then ignored the remaining element of the transaction or treated it as equity. Candidates have problems generally with dealing with the difference between revenue and equity. Better candidates applied the principles of IAS 37 *Provisions, Contingent Liabilities and Contingent Assets* and realised that there was a contingent liability. A few candidates did mention how the transaction should be treated in the second year (20X8) too and they earned higher marks.

d) Despite the question specifically stating that the tokens would be treated as part of IAS 19, many candidates described the different types of share-based payments and then just added either no comment or a single line in relation to employee benefits. This part of the question generated very poor answers overall despite the fact that the requirement provided these clear signposts. The SBR exam increasingly details specifically the IFRS standards that are to be applied to the scenario. Choosing to ignore this will mean any marks awarded must be restricted. It would be useful for both candidates and tutors to be mindful of this.

35 SITKA (MAR/JUN 2021)  *Walk in the footsteps of a top tutor*

Key answer tips

This question requires application of a range of core IFRS Standards, most notably IFRS 15 *Revenue from Contracts with Customers,* IAS 38 *Intangible Assets*, IFRS 16 *Leases* and IFRS 13 *Fair Value Measurement* to a modern, technology-driven industry. It also drew upon a less commonly tested standard, IAS 27 *Separate Financial Statements.*

Remember to state the relevant rules from the core standards for some easy marks.

(a) (i) Software contracts and updates

Tutorial note

As is the current exam trend, the scenario focuses on a modern phenomenon of licencing software. Despite this contemporary setting, candidates should follow a well-worn exam approach – state the rule and then apply the rule.

Application to the situation of IFRS 15 fundamentals such as identifying the performance obligation and recognising revenue over time will score well.

IFRS 15 *Revenue from Contracts with Customers* states that goods or services which are promised to a customer are distinct if both of the following criteria are met:

- the customer can benefit from the good or service either on its own or together with other resources, and
- the entity's promise to transfer the good or service to the customer is separately identifiable from other promises in the contract.

The updates are integral to Cent Co's ability to derive benefit from the licence during the four-year contract, because the entity works in an industry in which technologies change rapidly. The determination of whether licence and updates are separate performance obligations requires judgement. In this case, the updates improve the effectiveness of software without being essential. However, for the updates to be combined with the licence, they should fundamentally change the functionality of the software or be essential to its functionality.

Although the software can function on its own without updates, the benefits of using the software would be significantly reduced. The frequency of the monthly updates indicates that they are essential to the effective operation of the software. However, Sitka Co should consider not only the frequency but also whether Cent Co accepts the updates. Updates are made available every month but Cent Co has only updated its software on two occasions which seems to indicate that the software is functional without updates.

To conclude, the benefit which Cent Co could obtain from the licence over the four-year term without the updates would be significantly reduced, the contract to grant the licence and to provide the expected updates is, in effect, a single promise to deliver a combined item to Cent Co. As Cent Co simultaneously receives and consumes the benefits of the entity's performance as it occurs, the performance obligation is satisfied over time. As the contract is a single promise, the revenue of $3 million will be allocated over the four-year time period. Sitka Co should disclose the method used to recognise revenue together with the judgements used to determine the timing of the satisfaction of performance obligations, in the financial statements for the year ended 31 December 20X7. It should not and cannot allocate $2.5 million to the monthly updates and the residual amount of $0.5 million to the licence of software as this does not faithfully reflect the stand-alone selling price of the software.

Tutorial note

This is another example where conclusions that are different to those made in the model answer can still score well. You will be awarded marks for any well-argued points you make.

Note: If the conclusion was that the software could function without updates (since they are not essential to functionality, and Cent Co has only updated twice, which could indicate the software is functional without updates), then two performance obligations would be identified and the contract price allocated to each performance obligation. This approach to an answer, if well argued, would have been given credit.

(ii) Cent Co – why no intangible or lease?

Tutorial note

Read the requirement properly here – the perspective has shifted from Sitka Co to Cent Co.

Cent Co pays fees to Sitka Co to access and use its software. The recognition criteria for an intangible asset, in accordance with IAS 38 *Intangible Assets,* are identifiability, control over a resource and existence of future economic benefits. These need to be considered when determining whether an intangible asset is created. The current arrangement with Sitka Co is likely to satisfy the identifiability and existence of future economic benefits criteria, but it is questionable whether the control criterion is satisfied. IAS 38 states that 'an entity controls an asset if the entity has the power to obtain the future economic benefits flowing from the underlying resource and to restrict the access of others to those benefits'. Cent Co does not own the rights to the software at any time.

Thus, Cent Co should not recognise an intangible asset because Cent Co does not control the resource.

The contract is not a lease contract, in accordance with IFRS 16 *Leases,* as Cent Co does not have the right to direct the use of an asset by having decision-making rights to change how and for what purpose the asset is used throughout the four-year contract. At 1 January 20X7, the contract gave Cent Co only the right to receive access to Sitka Co's software in the future and is therefore a service contract which is expensed over the four-year period.

(b) Part-disposal of Martett Co

Tutorial note

Even without detailed knowledge of the specifics of IAS 27, you would be able to reach reasonable conclusions using common sense (on disposal, a gain or loss will be recorded) or by drawing on knowledge from other standards (e.g. IFRS 9 Financial instruments). Don't worry if you're not mentioning all the technical points from IAS 27 referenced here.

IAS 27 *Separate Financial Statements* requires an entity which prepares separate financial statements to account for investments in subsidiaries, joint ventures and associates either:

– at cost

– in accordance with IFRS 9 *Financial Instruments*

– using the equity method as described in IAS 28 *Investments in Associates and Joint Ventures.*

After the partial disposal, Marlett Co is not a subsidiary, joint venture or associate of Sitka Co but is an investment in an equity instrument. Therefore, IFRS 9 is used to account for the retained interest. Investments in equity instruments should be measured at fair value. However, IFRS 9 also states that an entity can make an irrevocable election at initial recognition to present subsequent changes in fair value in other comprehensive income. This can only occur if the investment is neither held for trading nor contingent consideration. In this case, Sitka Co could make such an election at 1 July 20X7. IAS 28 specifies how an entity should account for a transaction which results in discontinuing the use of the equity method because the investment ceases to be an associate or joint venture but retaining an interest which is a financial asset. Here the entity recognises in profit or loss any difference between:

– the fair value of the retained interest and any proceeds from disposing of a part interest in the associate or joint venture, and

– the carrying amount of the investment at the date the equity method is discontinued.

Thus, Sitka Co would make a profit of \$(10 + 3.5 – 12) million, i.e. \$1.5 million. This applies regardless of whether the entity elects to present in OCI subsequent changes in fair value of the retained interest. Sitka Co should only present any difference in OCI to subsequent changes in fair value which arise after initial recognition. Such a difference is not a result of a change in fair value but instead results from a change in the measurement basis of the retained interest when an entity loses control of an investee. The difference also meets the definition of income or expenses in the *Conceptual Framework for Financial Reporting* (2018).

(c) Acquisition of Billings

Tutorial note

IFRS 13 Fair Value Measurement takes a market perspective. Therefore, the highest and best use must be taken from the perspective of those operating within the specific industry.

IFRS 13 *Fair Value Measurement* states that the fair value is the price which would be received to sell an asset or paid to transfer a liability in an orderly transaction between market participants at the measurement date. However, IFRS 13 also uses the concept of the highest and best use which is the use of a non-financial asset by market participants which would maximise the value of the asset or the group of assets and liabilities within which the asset would be used. The fair values of the two assets would be determined based on the use of the assets within the buyer group which operates in the industry. The fair value of the asset group of $230 million is higher than the asset group for the financial investor of $200 million. The use of the assets in the industry buyer group does not maximise the fair value of the assets individually but it maximises the fair value of the asset group. Thus, even though Qbooks would be worth $50 million to the financial investors, its fair value for financial reporting purposes is $30 million as this is the value placed upon Qbooks by the industry buyer group.

ACCA marking guide

			Marks
(a) (i)	(i)	Discussion and application of the following to the scenario:	
		IFRS 15	2
		Updates of software	3
		Single performance obligation	1
		Revenue allocated over time	1
		Cannot use residual value	1
			8
(a)	(ii)	Discussion and application of the following to the scenario:	
		IAS 38	2
		IFRS 16	1
		Service contract	1
			4
(b)	Discussion and application of the following to the scenario:		
	IAS 27		2
	IFRS 9		3
	IAS 28		2
	Calculation of profit or loss		1
	Principles of OCI		1
			9
(c)	Discussion and application of the following to the scenario:		
	IFRS 13 highest and best use		2
	Grouping of fair values		2
			4
Total			**25**

Examiners comments

(a) (i) 8 marks were available here, so your answer should be sufficiently detailed to earn these marks, whilst applying the guidance in IFRS 15 *Revenue from Contracts with Customers* for identifying distinct performance obligations. Since the determination of whether the licence and updates are separate performance obligations requires judgement, a good answer would discuss both sides of the argument. However, this was not necessary to gain maximum marks so long as the answer fully explained the rationale for either a single performance obligation or for two separate ones. Marks were available for calculations of revenue, provided they were supported with a valid argument.

(a) (ii) The requirement to part (a) (ii) asked for an explanation as to why the right to receive access to the software was unlikely to be an intangible asset or a lease. Both items require explanation: why the right is not likely to be an intangible asset, nor a lease.

Given there are four marks available, this suggests two marks for each. It may help if your answer is split into two sections (intangible asset and lease).

(b) had 9 marks available including marks for the calculation of the disposal gain. The first part of the question (on the disposal of the 45% interest) was not as well-answered as the subsequent measurement of the 15% interest. Many answers approached this first part from a group perspective, despite the question stating the need to discuss accounting treatment in the separate financial statements of Sitka Co. This meant applying IAS 27 *Separate Financial Statements,* and the question referred to this, as well as stating that the company had elected to measure the investment using the equity method. Be sure that you read the question scenario carefully before starting your answer. Calculation of the disposal gain was generally well-answered. Most candidates accounted for the subsequent measurement of the 15% interest in line with IFRS 9 *Financial Instruments* (measurement at fair value). However, few answers discussed the election at initial recognition to present changes in fair value in other comprehensive income (if not held for trading).

(c) Most answers included a definition of fair value according to IFRS 13, and then applied the principle of highest and best use. Fewer answers then expanded further on applying this principle to the group of assets/liabilities within which the asset would be used, rather than individually, and how this lead to the highest and best use.

36 COLAT (MAR/JUN 2021)  *Walk in the footsteps of a top tutor*

Key answer tips

This question combined the interpretation (in the sustainability requirement (a)) and the current issues (through the consideration of the impacts of natural disasters tested in (c)).

The interpretation requirements will always have 2 professional marks associated with them, making it extra important to attempt that part!

(a) Sustainability

Tutorial note

The requirement specifically states that there is no need to use the exhibits to answer this requirement. So don't make things hard for yourself by trying to link the content in the scenario. The exhibits are provided for later requirements.

Make sure you answer the question! Tell the examiner how sustainability is important ***to investors****. Do not simply provide a generic answer here – meaning do not just discuss everything you know about sustainability reporting, with no context. By addressing the specific context of the requirement (the investors perspective), you will guarantee a good mark and ensure you grab those elusive professional marks.*

Sustainability has become an increasingly crucial aspect of investing. There is a growing recognition that sustainability can have a significant effect on company financial performance. Investors are increasingly integrating consideration of sustainability issues and metrics into their decision-making. Investors require a better understanding of the wider social and environmental context in which the business operates. This creates a greater trust and credibility with investors and a reduced risk of investors using inaccurate information to make decisions about the company.

Investors have shown an appetite for products which recognise and reflect the relationship between their investments and social and environmental conduct. Investors need to completely understand the nature of the companies in which they are looking to invest and need to incorporate material sustainability factors into investment decisions. They need to understand whether there are material risks or opportunities connected with sustainability factors which do not appear in traditional financial reports.

Their materiality will differ from sector to sector, industry to industry. Sustainability is often unique to the sector. This analysis can be the deciding factor between otherwise identical companies. If the company is viewed poorly based on its sustainability performance, it could lead to a non-investment decision. The increasing availability of data from companies offers the opportunity for rating and ranking analysis, as well as observing trends. These advances have led to the quantitative application of sustainability data in investment analysis and decision making. Companies need a greater knowledge of investor needs and perspectives to help make reporting more relevant to investors and to clearly communicate the financial value of the company's sustainability efforts.

(b) Impairment

Tutorial note

The old tutor mantra of 'read the requirement properly' is applicable here.

*To score marks, you must address the **factors** indicating impairment. You do not need a detailed description of the accounting for potential impairments or an impairment calculation. Always answer the question set!*

If Colat Co determines that the events resulting from a natural disaster have triggered impairment indicators, an impairment test must be performed in accordance with IAS 36 *Impairment of Assets* for the respective assets and/or cash-generating units. In this instance, a decline in customer demand has taken place because of the damage in reputation resulting from the disaster. Also, the share price of Colat Co has declined which again may indicate that the carrying amount of the entity's net assets is higher than its market capitalisation. Finally, damage to the manufacturing facility is a direct indicator and the increase in operating costs resulting from the replacement of a supplier in the region with an international supplier is an indirect indicator. The increase in costs as an indicator of impairment depends on the significance and duration of the expected change. Short-term, temporary disruptions are not necessarily indicative of an impairment for assets with a long-term remaining useful life. As a result of the above impairment indicators, an impairment test must be performed in accordance with IAS 36.

(c) (i) Destruction of the non-current assets and decommissioning of the power plant

The destruction of a non-current asset (NCA) results in the derecognition of that asset as opposed to an impairment as there will be no future economic benefits expected either from its use or disposal. Therefore, the NCA of $250 million would be derecognised. As regards the decommissioning of the power plant, IAS 37 *Provisions, Contingent Liabilities and Contingent Assets* requires that a liability is recognised as soon as the obligation arises, which will normally be at commencement of operations. Similarly, IAS 16 *Property, Plant and Equipment* requires the initial cost of an item of property, plant and equipment to include an estimate of the amount of the costs to dismantle and remove the item and restore the site on which it is located. As regards the change in the useful life of the power plant, the present value of the decommissioning liability will increase because of the shorter period over which cash flows are discounted. This increase is added to the carrying amount of the asset, which is tested for impairment. The remaining carrying amount is depreciated prospectively over the following eight years.

(ii) Environmental damage and government compensation

Colat Co has, in the past, put right minor environmental damage which it has caused but it has never been involved in a natural disaster on this scale and there is no legal obligation. A constructive obligation for the environmental costs will only result in the recognition of a provision if there is an established pattern of past practice, published policies or a specific current statement that Colat Co will pay for the damage. In this case, the entity has not indicated to other parties that it will accept certain responsibilities and as a result, it has not created a valid expectation. IAS 37 states that a provision should be recognised only when there is a present obligation resulting from past events. The future expected costs would not meet the definition of a provision as there is no legal obligation nor a constructive obligation. In the case of the natural disaster, Colat Co is not at fault and therefore there will be no obligation to correct the environmental damage which may be put right by the government.

IAS 20 *Accounting for Government Grants and Disclosure of Government Assistance* states that a government grant is recognised only when there is reasonable assurance that the entity will comply with any conditions attached to the grant and the grant will be received. A grant receivable as financial support should be recognised as income in the period in which it is receivable. In this case, Colat Co has only received acknowledgement of its application for a grant on 1 March 20X8 and, therefore, there is no reasonable assurance that the grant will be received. Further, it is not probable that the grant will be received and it should not be disclosed in the financial statements.

(iii) Hedge of commodity price risk in aluminium

Tutorial note

IFRS 9 states that, to apply hedge accounting to forecasted hedge items, the transactions must be highly probable to occur. If the transactions are no longer highly probable, hedge accounting cannot be applied.

Prior to the disaster, Colat Co hedges commodity price risk in aluminium and such transactions constituted 'highly probable' hedged transactions in cash flow hedges under IFRS 9 *Financial Instruments*. However, the purchases which were considered highly probable prior to the natural disaster are now not expected to occur. Colat Co should follow hedge accounting principles up until the date of the natural disaster and then should cease hedge accounting. As the forecast transaction is no longer expected to occur, Colat Co should reclassify the accumulated gains or losses on the hedging instrument from other comprehensive income into profit or loss as a reclassification adjustment.

(iv) Potential insurance policy proceeds

Tutorial note

This question relies heavily on knowledge of IAS 37 Provisions, Contingent Liabilities and Contingent Assets. This is a standard that you would have first encountered in the ACCA Financial Reporting (FR) paper. Prior learning is crucial within the SBR examination and comes up regularly. Make sure you know your FR standards.

IAS 37 does not permit the recognition of contingent assets. Accordingly, an insurance recovery asset can only be recognised if it is determined that the entity has a valid insurance policy which includes cover for the incident and a claim will be settled by the insurer. The recognition of the insurance recovery will only be appropriate when its realisation is virtually certain, in which case the insurance recovery is no longer a contingent asset. Decisions about the recognition and measurement of losses are made independently of those relating to the recognition of any compensation which might be receivable. It is not appropriate to take potential proceeds into account when accounting for the losses. The potential receipt of compensation should be assessed continually to ensure that it is appropriately reflected in the financial statements. The asset and the related income are recognised in the period in which it is determined that a compensation will be received which means reviewing the situation after the end of the reporting period and before the date of approval of the financial statements.

In this case, as it appears probable that the insurance claim for the loss of the non-current assets would be paid and as this information was received before the financial statements were approved, the potential proceeds ($280 million) should be disclosed in the financial statements for the year ended 31 December 20X7. There would be no disclosure of the insurance recovery related to the relocation costs or the lost revenue as the recovery is not virtually certain. The insurance policy does not cover environmental damage which is the responsibility of the government.

ACCA marking guide			
			Marks
(a)		Discussion of:	
		Integration of sustainability issues	4
			4
(b)		Discussion of impairment indicators	2
		Conclusion	1
			3
(c)	(i)	Discussion and application to scenario:	
		Derecognition of NCA	1
		Change in accounting for decommissioning	3
			4
	(ii)	Discussion and application to scenario of liability for environmental damage	2
		Government grant	2
			4
	(iii)	Discussion and application to scenario:	
		Hedged transaction	2
		Accounting treatment	2
			4
	(iv)	Discussion and application to scenario:	
		Contingent asset	2
		Disclosure	2
			4
Professional marks			2
Total			**25**

Examiners comments

a) The question starts with a 4 mark requirement (a) to discuss why sustainability is important to an investors' analysis. It was clearly stated that there was no need to refer to the scenario in this section, and most answers followed that guidance. Referring to the scenario risks answering subsequent parts of the question, so it is recommended that candidates use the advice and stick to a general discussion. Better answers focused on the investors' perspective, and how sustainability information can enhance the more quantitative "traditional" financial statements. Fewer answers considered how sustainability information can be used to rank or rate potential investments or be a deciding factor in otherwise identical investments.

b) This part was well-answered, and there were a number of events within the scenario which could have been used to illustrate the need. Most candidates scored full marks by identifying and explaining the importance of three key external indicators: a fall in demand, a fall in share price and the implications of storm damage.

c) asked for a discussion of four events described in the scenario. Each was awarded 4 marks, so time spent on each item should have been allocated evenly. Doing so may have helped in your time management: this question is often the last attempted and therefore time may be constrained.

For (c) (i), two issues were raised (logically each earning 2 marks): the destruction of the non-current assets and decommissioning of the power plant. Whilst answers were generally good, some incorrectly suggested impairing the destroyed assets, which would be irrelevant since there would be no value in use nor net selling price. Decommissioning costs were often correctly identified as a provision, although some answers failed to discuss how the provision would be added to the carrying amount of the asset once the obligation arises (on commencement). Most answers picked up on the need for a change in depreciation (prospective adjustment), although fewer recognised the impact of the shorter life on the present value of the decommissioning liability.

Part (c) (ii) related to the cost of repairing environmental damage and the potential receipt of government compensation. These are two separate issues, so are likely to be awarded 2 marks each. Whilst most answers identified that there was no legal obligation for the environmental repairs, fewer considered whether a constructive obligation existed given past behaviour. The difference in scale and the fact that no announcement or valid expectation was raised means this is not likely to be a constructive obligation. Accounting for the government grant was less well-explained as some answers suggested disclosure despite there being no evidence of probable receipt (confirmation of receipt of application is not a confirmation that the grant will be paid, and the question states 'no approval'). Contingent assets require probable receipt for disclosure, and this aspect is also covered in (c) (iv). Fewer answers explained how, under IAS 20 *Accounting for Government Grants and Disclosure of Government Assistance,* a grant is only recognised when reasonable assurance is gained that any attached terms have been complied with and that the grant will be received.

For part (c) (iii), required discussion over the treatment of the hedging of commodity price risk in aluminium. This part was often the least well-answered and the shortest, despite also having 4 marks available. Whilst most answers correctly suggested derecognition of the hedge, any further knowledge of the correct hedge accounting was often weak. Answers often overlooked the accounting treatment prior to the disaster, and how after the disaster (and after derecognition) accumulated gains would need reclassifying from OCI to profit or loss.

Part (c) (iv) required a discussion on potential insurance policy proceeds. There were two situations for insurance claims with differing outcomes at the date of financial statement approval, and both should have been covered to increase potential for the 4 marks. Candidates in general were aware of the need to distinguish between the claim for the non-current asset losses (whose receipt post-reporting date was probable), and the two other claims for relocation costs and lost revenue (for which significant uncertainty existed). However, the recommended treatment of each was mixed. For the non-current asset loss, some incorrectly suggested recognition (contrary to IAS 37 *Provisions, Contingent Liabilities and Contingent Assets*) rather than disclosure. Very few explained that virtual certainty is required for recognition (in which case IAS 37 no longer applies). Likewise, many answers suggested the claims with significant uncertainty could be disclosed as a note, rather than not being disclosed. These are quite fundamental and suggest a lack of knowledge of aspects of IAS 37 relating to contingent assets. Better answers began with a clear description of the requirements under IAS 37, and then applied these to the different claims.

37 CORBEL (SEP/DEC 2020)  *Walk in the footsteps of a top tutor*

Key answer tips

This question requires application of a range of core IFRS Standards, most notably IAS 36 *Impairment of Assets,* IAS 38 *Intangible Assets* and IFRS 5 *Non-current Assets Held for Sale and Discontinued Operations.* Remember to state the relevant rules from the standards for some easy marks. Do not worry if your conclusion is different from the model answers – you will be awarded marks for any well-argued points you make.

(a) IAS 38 *Intangible Assets*

Tutorial note

There are many different ways of approaching this question – any well discussed point will score one mark.

You might have concentrated on issues to do with identifying intangibles, or recognising internally generated intangibles. Alternatively, you might have spent more time discussing the difficulty involved in determining amortisation rates, or fair values, or value-in-use amounts for impairment review.

Below is a selection of comments that would be credit worthy.

The importance of intangible assets is reflected in the increasing proportion of a company's market value being attributable to them. However, there are many challenges involved in recognising and measuring intangible assets, such as brands, in the statement of financial position.

According to IAS 38 *Intangible Assets* are recognised at cost. For purchased intangibles, this is easy to determine. However some intangible assets, including many brands, are internally generated. IAS 38 prohibits the recognition of internally generated intangible assets (except those arising from development activity) because the cost of the asset cannot be determined.

Once an intangible asset has been recognised, it can be measured using a cost model (cost less amortisation and impairment) or using a revaluation model (fair value less amortisation and impairment).

Whichever model is used, determining the useful life of intangible assets is often subjective.

Many intangible assets are not traded on a stand-alone basis and so there is rarely an active market for them. This makes it difficult to determine a fair value. For these intangible assets, IAS 38 prohibits the revaluation model.

IFRS 3 *Business Combinations*

It was noted above that internally generated brands are not recognised in the statement of financial position. One exception to this rule is a business combination. If a company acquires control over another company, IFRS 3 *Business Combinations* requires that the subsidiary's identifiable net assets at the acquisition date are measured in the consolidated financial statements at fair value – even those that have not been recognised in the subsidiary's separate financial statements. Many intangible assets are unique and therefore it is not easy to identify and assess their value. Valuation methods are often complex and subjective and the measurement is more subjective when the intangible assets are not based on legally enforceable rights. In some cases, the acquirer does not intend to use the intangible assets (for example, Corbel has acquired brands for defensive reasons) and this raises further issues with regards to arriving at a value.

(b) (i) Jengi brand

Tutorial note

State the rule and then apply the rule.

IFRS 3 *Business Combinations* says that the acquirer must recognised identifiable intangible assets acquired in a business combination separately from goodwill. To be identifiable, the asset must be separable or arise from contractual or legal rights.

The Jengi brand is intangible because it has no physical substance. It meets the definition of an asset because it has the potential to generate future economic benefits by increasing sales volumes and the ability to charge premium prices. Brands are separable because they can be disposed of. As such, the brand is a separable intangible asset and must be recognised separately from goodwill.

Cash generating units

Tutorial note

Start with the definition of a cash generating unit.

IAS 36 *Impairment of Assets* defines a cash generating unit (CGU) as the smallest identifiable group of assets that generates cash inflows that are largely independent of the cash inflows from other assets or other groups of assets. As such, brands rarely qualify as a separate CGU.

The brand is most likely to qualify as a corporate asset. This is because it does not generate cash flows independently of other assets, but is also not attributable to just one single cash generating unit. Instead, it provides benefits across the business.

This means that the brand should be allocated to each of Corbel Co's cash generating units that are expected to benefit from the synergies of the combination.

(ii) Intangible assets with an indefinite useful life

Tutorial note

Easy marks are available for stating principles from IAS 38 Intangible Assets regarding the meaning of definite and indefinite, and how to account for assets which have an indefinite useful life.

IAS 38 *Intangible Assets* states that intangible assets have an indefinite useful life when there is no foreseeable limit to the period the asset is expected to generate net cash inflows for the entity. An intangible asset with an indefinite useful life is not be amortised.

IAS 36 *Impairment of Assets*, requires an entity to test an intangible asset with an indefinite useful life for impairment on an annual basis.

The useful life of an intangible asset that is not being amortised should be reviewed each period to determine whether events and circumstances continue to support an indefinite useful life assessment for that asset. If they do not, the change in the useful life assessment from indefinite to finite should be accounted for as a change in an accounting estimate in accordance with IAS 8 *Accounting Policies, Changes in Accounting Estimates and Errors*.

Locust and Clara

Corbel Co should consider various factors to determine whether the brand names can be considered to have a useful life. These will include the extent to which Corbel Co is prepared to support the brand and the extent to which the brand has long-term potential and has had proven success. Perfume is subject to market and fashion trends and therefore, an assessment of how resistant the brands are to change should be made. Also Corbel Co has purchased the brands as a defensive measure to prevent rival companies acquiring them. Therefore, there may be a doubt as to the support that Corbel Co may be prepared to give to the brands.

Tutorial note

Even without detailed knowledge of IAS 38 Intangible Assets, you should be able to reach reasonable conclusions using common sense.

The Locust perfume has been sold successfully in the market for many years and could be deemed to have an indefinite life.

The Clara perfume is linked to the popularity of the actor and therefore, it is difficult to assess whether the brand has an indefinite life as it is likely to be dependent upon the longevity of the popularity of the actor. In the case of the Clara perfume, it is difficult to state that the brand will have an indefinite life. Thus Clara is likely to have a finite life.

(iii) Proposed closure

Tutorial note

Easy marks are available for discussing the principles around non-current assets held for sale and discontinued operations.

IFRS 5 *Non-current Assets Held for Sale and Discontinued Operations* states that an asset or disposal group should be classified as held for sale if its carrying amount will be recovered mainly through a sales transaction. It must be available for immediate sale in its current condition and the sale must be highly probable.

There is a formal plan for closure and an active search for a buyer so the sale is likely to qualify as highly probable. Once the liquidation sale is over the stores will be available to immediate sale – this is the point at which they should be classified as a disposal group held for sale.

IFRS 5 states that immediately before classifying a disposal group as held for sale, the carrying amounts of the assets and liabilities within the group are measured in accordance with the applicable IFRS Standards. After classification as held for sale, disposal groups are measured at the lower of carrying amount and fair value less costs to sell.

The six stores represent a component of Corbel Co because they are a separate geographical area of operations (Italy). As such, once classified as held for sale, they should be presented as a discontinued operation in the statement of profit or loss.

There may be a need to provide for the additional costs of closure such as redundancy costs, under IAS 37 *Provisions, Contingent liabilities and Contingent Assets.*

Suggested closure

Tutorial note

Without formal plans and formal announcements, the suggested closures are unlikely to fall within the scope of IFRS 5 Non-current Assets Held for Sale and Discontinued Operations or IAS 37 *Provisions, Contingent Liabilities and Contingent Assets.*

Although there has been a local newspaper article that Corbel Co is to shut 30 stores with a loss of 500 jobs across the world over the next five years, there has been no formal announcement by Corbel Co. This means that a sale is not highly probable. As such, these stores would not qualify as held for sale and cannot be presented as discontinued operations. These stores should continue to be recognised and depreciated as normal.

Without formal plans, it is feasible that the closure of the additional 24 stores will not take place. This means that no obligation exists to restructure and, as per IAS 37 *Provisions, Contingent Liabilities and Contingent Assets,* no restructuring provision should be recognised.

(iv) Primary store

Tutorial note

State basic impairment principles for easy marks.

An entity needs to assess at the end of each reporting period whether there is any indication that an asset may be impaired. An indication of impairment is whether the performance of the asset is worse than expected.

The primary store is performing in line with expectations, so it would appear that there is no indication of impairment and no impairment test is required.

Tutorial note

The carrying amount of an asset should not exceed the benefits it will bring to the entity, whether directly or indirectly. Although the primary store makes a loss, this was expected and so were additional indirect benefits – this would all have been factored into the price Corbel paid. If a profit was expected, then Corbel might have paid more for the store, and thus the carrying amount would have been higher – in such circumstances an impairment review would have been needed.

If Corbel Co feels that the primary store benefits all the other stores from a brand perspective, there is an argument for treating the store as a corporate asset and allocating its carrying amount to the cash generating units when testing for impairment. However, it is likely that management assesses performance on a store-by-store basis – this adds weight to the argument that each store, including the primary store, is a separate cash generating unit because of their ability to generate cash flows independently from other company assets.

The amount of internet sales included when calculating value in use for the purposes of testing the primary store for impairment will depend on the quantity of sales that are sourced directly from it. Where Internet sales are sourced from a central warehouse or another store, the cash inflows should be excluded from the primary store's impairment assessment and included in the appropriate CGU.

ACCA marking guide

			Marks
(a)	Listing of major challenges		
	1 mark per point up to maximum		5
(b)	Discussion and application of the following to the scenario:		
	(i)	Treatment of brand on acquisition	2
		Allocation of brand to CGU	2
			4
	(ii)	Intangible assets with indefinite life principles	2
		Application to scenario	4
			6
	(iii)	NCA held for sale-principles	3
		Application to scenario	3
			6
	(iv)	Impairment principles	2
		Impairment of primary store	2
			4
Total			**25**

Examiner's comments

With regards to part (a), candidates are reminded that there will be other challenges outside of the suggested answer that would have scored marks. It is always a good idea to refer to the Conceptual Framework in answering such a question. For example, answers mentioning relevance, reliability, materiality, verifiability etc would have gained marks. The use of the Conceptual Framework is recommended in answering many questions even though it may not be specifically referred to in the question or the answer. Generally, in this type of question, candidates will score 1 mark for each well explained point.

With regards to part (b), if there is little reference to the scenario, there is a risk of missing key marks. Also, the scenario and requirements are linked – the requirement is based upon the scenario. It is very difficult to score good marks without using the scenario.

Only the relevant sections of the IFRS standard should be discussed. There is no point in setting out the terms of an IFRS standard if they are not relevant. In theory, a candidate could rote learn the whole of an IFRS standard and reproduce it in the exam, leaving the examiner to mark the relevant parts. This is a poor strategy as very few marks would be given if the examiner has to decide the relevancy of a rote learned answer

38 HANDFOOD (SEP/DEC 2020)  *Walk in the footsteps of a top tutor*

Key answer tips

This questions tests areas many students will be less familiar with – the SMEs Standard and the calculation of a service cost on an 'other long term benefit'. As such, you might find it tricky. However, part (a) in particular is less demanding than usual in terms of the level application skill required – but you do need to have the relevant knowledge. Question spotting in SBR (i.e. predicting what topics will be tested) is dangerous – study the whole syllabus!

(a) (i) Nature of the SME's Standard

The principal aim when developing the SMEs Standard was to provide a framework that generated relevant, reliable and useful information and the provision of a high quality and understandable accounting standard suitable for SMEs. The Standard itself is self-contained, and incorporates accounting principles based on full IFRS standards. It comprises a single standard divided into simplified sections for each relevant IFRS standard but which have also omitted certain IFRS standards such as earnings per share and segmental reporting. In addition, there are certain accounting treatments that are not allowable under the SMEs Standard. For example, there is no separate guidance for non-current assets held for sale.

To this end, the SMEs Standard makes numerous simplifications to the recognition, measurement and disclosure requirements in full IFRS standards. Examples of these simplifications are:

- Intangible assets must be amortised over their useful lives. If the useful life is not determinable then it is presumed to be 10 years.
- The cost model (investment is measured at cost less any accumulated impairment losses) can be used for investments in associates. This model may not be used for investments for which there is a published price quotation, in which case the fair value model must be applied.

The disclosure requirements in the SMEs Standard are also substantially reduced when compared with those in full IFRS standards partly because they are not considered appropriate for users' needs and for cost-benefit considerations.

(ii) Information asymmetry

IFRS for SMEs decreases information asymmetry between the firm and the users, because of its recognition, measurement and disclosure requirements. However, there are certain facts and information in companies which is not disclosed by them to investors under any accounting standards. SMEs have access to all relevant information, while investors lack much of the relevant information. Unfortunately, lack of relevant information will have an adverse effect on the decision-making of the investor. Information related to the SME's credit, project risk and benefits are known more by the SME than by the investor giving the SME an information advantage. Therefore, investors are in a relatively disadvantaged position, and if they, for example, are financial institutions, they will raise lending rates to reduce potential risk of credit losses or may not invest at all. The more incomplete and the less transparent the information from the SME, the higher will be the risk related to the investment and the higher will be the return that the investor requires. The access to investment by SMEs could be determined by the quality of financial statements, information asymmetry and perceived risk. Quality financial statements reduce the level of information asymmetry which reduces perceived risk.

(iii) Integrated reporting

Integrated reporting could help SMEs better understand and better communicate how they create value. It can provide a roadmap for SMEs to consider the multiple capitals that make up its value creation. An integrated report represents a more complete corporate report which will help SMEs understand their business so they can implement a business model that will help them grow. SMEs use a range of resources and relationships to create value. An integrated reporting approach helps SMEs build a better understanding of the factors that determine its ability to create value over time. Integrated thinking helps SMEs gain a deeper understanding of the mechanics of their business. This will help them assess the strengths of their business model and spot any deficiencies. These will create a forward-looking approach and sound strategic decision making.

Some SMEs have few tangible assets and operate in a virtual world. As such, conventional accounting will fail to provide a complete picture as to its ability to create value. Capitals, such as employee expertise, customer loyalty, and intellectual property, will not be accounted for in the financial statements which are only one aspect of an SME's value creation. As a result, SME stakeholders can be left with insufficient information to make an informed decision.

Integrated reporting will include key financial information but that information is alongside significant non-financial measures and narrative information. Integrated reporting can help fulfil the communication needs of financial capital and other stakeholders and can optimize reporting.

(b) (i) Current service cost

Tutorial note

*The benefit in the question is **not** a pension. Pensions are a type of post-employment income.*

The benefit is paid to current employees but will not be settled within 12 months of the current reporting period. It is therefore an 'other long-term benefit'.

The accounting treatment for other long-term benefits is similar to defined benefit pension schemes, although remeasurement components are recognised in profit or loss. As such, Handfood is incorrect to recognise this in amount in other comprehensive income.

Handfood Co should recognise a liability for its obligations as a result of the additional employee benefit. The company will measure the benefit liability at the present value of its obligations at the reporting date. This amount is the estimated amount of benefit that employees have earned in return for their service in the current and prior periods.

Service costs, net interest and remeasurements should be recognised in profit or loss.

Handfood Co should recognise a current service cost expense of $7,700 in profit or loss as set out below:

	$000
Expected final salary $1.1million × $(1.03)^4$	1,238
Benefit for the current year (1% × $1.238 million)	12.4
Adjusted benefit for the current year (75% × $12,400)	9.3
Current service cost (($9,300 × 0.823) discounted at 5% over 4 years)	7.7

This figure will be unwound each year and the movement recorded as the current service cost (in so far as no other changes to the assumptions are made).

Tutorial note

The above calculation is the model answer produced by ACCA. However, alternative methods would have been accepted.

Some candidates may have allocated the service cost over the five year service period, and recognised one fifth in each reporting period. ACCA have confirmed that this approach would have scored full marks.

Some candidates may have concluded that the obligating event occurred on 1 January 20X2 and that the service cost should be recognised at that date. The present value of this of this would be $7,300. Interest on this amount is then recognised over the first year, equating to $400. These two amounts total $7,700, as per the calculation above. ACCA have confirmed that this approach would also have scored full marks.

(ii) An increase in employees' salaries above 3% per annum and a decrease in the probability of employees leaving the company would have the same effect on the additional benefit liability. The changes in the assumptions would both increase the benefit liability (discounted) at 31 December 20X3. This would in turn increase the current service cost for the year in profit or loss as the benefit payable on 1 January 20X7 will have increased as will the number of employees to whom the benefit will be payable.

Interest, which is calculated on the opening balance of the benefit obligation, will not be affected by the changes in assumptions. It will be charged to profit or loss at $385 ($7,700 × 5%). Actuarial gains or losses arise when the assumptions change. In this case because, of the changes in assumptions, an actuarial loss will arise because of the increase in benefits payable and the obligation and this will be charged to profit or loss.

ACCA marking guide			
			Marks
(a)	(i)	Discussion of IFRS for SMEs:	
		Simplifications and omissions	2
		Disclosure	1
		Recognised concepts	1
			4
	(ii)	Discussion of:	
		Information asymmetry issues and investors knowledge	4
	(iii)	Discussion of Integrated Reporting:	
		Better understanding	2
		Better communication	1
		Nature of IR	2
			5
(b)	(i)	Discussion of principles of accounting for additional benefit liability/current service cost	4
		Calculation of current service cost 20X2	2
			6
	(ii)	Discussion of effect of change in assumptions	4
	Professional marks		2
Total			**25**

Examiner's comments

It is understandable that in a time pressured exam, a candidate will resort to simply answering questions with rote knowledge. However, the SBR exam is looking for application of that knowledge and in this case, the context was SMEs. If a candidate simply described the 'capitals' in part (a) (iii) without any reference to SMEs, then the marks were reduced accordingly. Maximum marks will never be achieved if candidates do not apply their knowledge.

Part (a) of the question attracted professional marks. Candidates are not awarded these marks simply for answering the question, although this obviously helps and is another reason to ensure all questions, and parts of questions, are attempted. The marks were awarded for the quality of the discussion in part (a). This part contained requirements relating to investors and the investment decision. Therefore, if candidates did not discuss the 'investor perspective', then professional marks would not be awarded. These two marks can and often are the difference between pass and fail.

Part (b) (i) was not well answered, maybe because of time pressures or maybe because the principles were not understood. Candidates could still score a pass mark in this part of the question if they discussed the principles behind the calculation and candidates scored well when this was attempted.

Part (b) (ii) could have been answered without an attempt at part (b) (i), if the candidate had used basic principles.

39 LERIA (MAR 2020)  *Walk in the footsteps of a top tutor*

Key answer tips

This question requires application of a range of core IFRS Standards. You should be able to score high marks on all parts if you have a good knowledge of the core principles in each. Remember to state the relevant rules from the standards for some easy marks.

(a) (i) Held for Sale

Tutorial note

Assessment of whether an asset qualifies to be categorised as 'held for sale' is a very common exam requirement. Make sure that you are aware of the qualifying criteria and can apply these to any scenario.

IFRS 5 *Non-current Assets Held for Sale and Discontinued Operations* requires a non-current asset to be classified as held for sale if its carrying amount will be recovered principally through a sale transaction rather than through its continuing use. It must be available for immediate sale in its present condition, and its sale must be highly probable within 12 months of classification as held for sale. The standard only foresees an exemption to this rule if the sale is delayed by events or circumstances which are beyond the entity's control, which is unlikely to be the case in this instance. Leria Co has entered into a firm sales commitment but the sale will occur after the 12-month threshold. Therefore, the stadium cannot be classified as held for sale.

(ii) Barrier improvements

The $2 million to be spent on crowd barrier improvements to the stadium should not be treated as a reduction of the asset's carrying amount at 31 October 20X5.

IAS 37 *Provisions, Contingent Liabilities and Contingent Assets* states that a provision can only be recognised where there is a present obligation (legal or constructive) as a result of a past event. There is no present obligation because Leria Co may decide not to carry out the improvements. Therefore the $2 million should be added back to the carrying amount of the stadium and a corresponding credit made to profit or loss.

Tutorial note

You may not have approached this question through IAS 37. Instead, you might have discussed principles around offsetting – that is valid too.

Note: when provisions are recognised they should be presented as a liability on the statement of financial position. Liabilities and assets should not be offset (except under specific circumstances).

(iii) Sale and leaseback

A sale and leaseback transaction occurs where an entity transfers an asset to another entity and leases that asset back from the buyer/lessor.

The accounting treatment depends on whether a sale has occurred. Under IFRS 16 *Leases*, an entity must apply the IFRS 15 *Revenue from Contracts with Customers* requirements to determine when a performance obligation is satisfied.

Tutorial note

If it is concluded that the transfer of an asset is not a sale, then the seller/lessee will continue to recognise the underlying asset. The seller/lessee will recognised a financial liability equal to the proceeds received.

In this case it seems that a sale will occur on 30 November 20X6 because of the binding sale commitment.

Tutorial note

Clearly show all workings. The markers will be able to award you credit, even if you have made mistakes.

Leria Co should account for the sale and leaseback as follows:

- Derecognise the $18.92 million (W1) underlying asset
- Recognise the $30 million proceeds from the sale
- Recognise a right-of-use asset at $16.4 million (W2)
- Recognise a lease liability at $26 million
- Recognise a profit on disposal of the underlying asset of $1.48 million (W3).

(W1) Carrying amount of the underlying asset

Carrying amount of stadium is $20 million ($18m + $2m).

Depreciation for year to 31 October 20X6 is $1 million ($20m × 5%).

Depreciation for November 20X6 is $0.08 million (($20m – $1m) × 5% × 1/12).

The carrying amount at the sale date = $20m – $1m – $0.08m = $18.92m

(W2) Right-of-use asset

The right-of-use asset is recorded at the proportion of the asset's previous carrying amount that relates to the rights retained. This is $16.4 million (($26m/$30m) × $18.92m).

(W3) Profit on disposal

The profit on disposal relates solely to the rights transferred. This amounts to $1.48 million ($30m + $16.4m – $18.92m – $26m).

(b) (i) Intangible amortisation

IAS 38 *Intangible Assets* sets out a rebuttable presumption that amortisation based on revenue generated by an activity which includes the use of an intangible asset is not appropriate. This is because revenue is influenced by many factors that are not linked to the asset's economic consumption, such as inflation.

Tutorial note

You can still score well in the SBR exam without knowing every rule in each examinable standard. For example, many students will be unaware of the rebuttable presumption regarding revenue-based methods of amortisation but this does not matter. As long as you understand the underlying principles behind amortisation – matching the cost of an asset to the benefits it produces – then you are capable of producing a good answer to this question.

However, this presumption can be overcome when it can be demonstrated that revenue and the consumption of the economic benefits of the intangible asset are highly correlated. The intellectual property embodied in the television programmes will generate cash flows through the television channel subscriptions and the estimated revenues for a television programme determine the amount to be spent on producing the television programme. Therefore, in this case, revenue reflects a proxy for the pattern of consumption of the benefits received. Revenue and consumption of the economic benefits of the intangible asset seem highly correlated and therefore a revenue-based amortisation method seems appropriate.

The industry practice method is also acceptable and conceptually sound as it is based on an analysis of the remaining useful life of the programme and the recoverable amount. Such an approach does not contradict IAS 38's prohibition on revenue-based amortisation because it is not based on direct matching of revenue and amortisation.

The useful life of an asset is required to be reassessed in accordance with IFRS Standards at least at each financial year end. Where this results in a change in estimate, this is will be accounted for prospectively from the date of reassessment.

IAS 38 also states that if a pattern of amortisation cannot be measured reliably, the straight-line method must be used.

(ii) Player contracts

When a player's contract is signed, management should make an assessment of the likely outcome of performance conditions. Contingent consideration will be recognised in the players' initial registration costs if management believes the performance conditions will be met in line with the contractual terms. Periodic reassessments of the contingent consideration should be made. Any contingent amounts which the directors of Leria Co believe will be payable should be included in the players' contract costs from the date management believes that the performance conditions will be met. Any additional amounts of contingent consideration not included in the costs of players' registrations will be disclosed separately as a commitment. Amortisation of the costs of the contract will be based upon the length of the player's contract.

Tutorial note

The paragraph above is the model answer published by ACCA.

Please note that contingent consideration is not mentioned in either IAS 16 Property, Plant and Equipment or IAS 38 Intangible Assets. As such, the accounting treatment of contingent consideration payable on the acquisition of these assets is not clear-cut and alternative conclusions to ACCA's answer would be acceptable. For instance, you might have argued that changes in the contingent consideration believed to be payable would be recorded in the statement of profit or loss. Or you might have argued that the contingent costs would only be capitalised once the conditions had been satisfied. These approaches are acceptable. Whatever accounting policy is used, it must be applied consistently to all similar transactions.

The costs associated with the renegotiation of a playing contract should be added to the residual balance of the players' contract costs at the date of signing the contract extension. The revised carrying amount should be amortised over the remaining renegotiated contract length.

Tutorial note

An injury is an indication of impairment because the benefits received from the asset will be lower than expected. In other words, the entity is likely to have overpaid and so the carrying amount of the asset will be too high.

Where a player sustains a career threatening injury and is removed from the playing team, then the carrying amount of the individual would be assessed against the best estimate of the individual's fair value less any costs to sell and an impairment charge made in operating expenses reflecting any loss arising.

Tutorial note

A cash generating unit is the smallest group of assets that generate cash flows distinct from the rest of the business.

It is unlikely that any individual player can be a separate single cash generating unit (CGU) as this is likely to be the playing squad. Also, it is difficult to determine the value-in-use of an individual player in isolation as players cannot generate cash flows on their own unless via a sale.

ACCA Marking scheme			
			Marks
(a)	(i)	Held for sale guidance	3
	(ii)	Accounting for barrier improvements	3
	(iii)	Sale and leaseback principles	4
		Accounting treatment	3
			13
(b)		Potential amortisation of the intangible asset	5
		Performance conditions and contract costs	5
		Value in use of a player/CGU	2
			12
Total			**25**

Examiner's comments

Part (a) (i) tended to be well-answered, provided candidates carefully reviewed the scenario to identify the contract commencing beyond the 12 month limit under IFRS 5 *Non-current Assets Held for Sale and Discontinued Operations*. Part (a) (ii) was consistently well-answered: most candidates identified and justified a lack of obligating event and recommended the accounting correction required. However, some answers needlessly extended beyond the requirements by considered the treatment in the following reporting period, which was not asked for. The quality of answers to part (a) (iii) (the sale and leaseback) varied the most. Some answers omitted a relatively basic calculation of the carrying amount at disposal date, whilst others incorrectly took the present value of the lease obligations as the carrying value of the right of use asset. In both cases, this limited opportunities for marks. In part (b) (i), few answers considered the principles behind amortisation, and more specifically an application of those principles to this situation. Answers were often limited to a basic recommendation of amortising over the useful life of the asset, with little development or argument for alternative amortisation methods, other than suggesting use of a straight line approach if the consumption pattern is not reliably measurable. Answers to part (b) (ii) were relatively well-answered. Candidates generally justified why a footballer cannot be a CGU and the need for impairment testing of an injured player. Most identified the contract as an intangible asset. Fewer were confident regarding when and how to recognise the contingent payments.

40 ECOMA (MARCH 2020)  *Walk in the footsteps of a top tutor*

Key answer tips

Part (a) tests the topic of sustainability. This is part of the 'analysis' section of the syllabus, so two professional marks are available.

(a) Sustainability information

Tutorial note

Prior to the question being set, the examining team produced an article about sustainability reporting. It is important to read widely, and to regularly check the ACCA website for new articles.

There is increasing interest by investors in understanding how businesses are developing environmental, social or governance (ESG) goals. The positioning of the ESGs in relation to the overall corporate strategies is information which investors feel is very relevant to the investment decision which in turn will lead to capital being channelled to responsible businesses.

Sustainability practices will not all be equally relevant to all companies and investors' expectations are likely to focus on companies realising their core business activities with financial sustainability as a prerequisite for attracting investment. Because institutional investors have a fiduciary duty to act in the best interests of their beneficiaries, such institutions have to take into account sustainability practices. Companies utilising more sustainable business practices provide new investment opportunities. Investors realise that environmental events can create costs for their portfolio in the form of insurance premiums, taxes and the physical cost related with disasters. Social issues can lead to unrest and instability, which carries business risks which may reduce future cash flows and financial returns.

Investors screen the sustainable policies of companies and factor the information into their valuation models. Investors may select a company for investment based on specific policy criteria such as education and health. Investors may evaluate how successful a company has been in a particular area, for example, the reduction of educational inequality. This approach can help optimise financial returns and demonstrate their contribution to sustainability. Investors increasingly promote sustainable economies and markets to improve their long-term financial performance. However, the disclosure of information should be in line with widely-accepted recommendations such as the Global Reporting Initiative (GRI) and the UN Global Compact. Integrated reporting incorporates appropriate material sustainability information equally alongside financial information, thus providing reporting organisations with a broad perspective on risk.

Investors often require an understanding of how the directors feel about the relevance of sustainability to the overall corporate strategy, and this will include a discussion of any risks and opportunities identified and changes which have occurred in the business model as a result.

Investors employ screening strategies, which may involve eliminating companies which have a specific feature, for example, low pay rates or eliminating them on a ranking basis. The latter may be on the basis of companies which are contributing or not to sustainability. Investors will use related disclosures to identify risks and opportunities on which they wish to engage with companies. Investors will see potential business opportunities in those companies which address the risks to people and the environment and those companies which develop new beneficial products, services and investments which mitigate the business risks related to sustainability. Investors are increasingly seeking investment opportunities which can make a credible contribution to the realisation of the ESGs.

(b) (i) Roof

Tutorial note

State the criteria that must be satisfied for a provision to be recognised and then apply these to the scenario.

IAS 37 *Provision, Contingent Liabilities and Contingent Assets* requires a provision to be recognised if there is a present obligation from a past event, the settlement of which will result in the probable outflow of measurable economic resources. Ecoma Co cannot make a provision of $16 million because it is under no obligation to replace its roof.

Head office

Tutorial note

In accordance with IFRS 16 Leases, a lessee must recognise a lease liability and a right-of-use asset for all leases except those that are short-term or low value.

The head office is a lease. In accordance with IFRS 16 *Leases,* Ecoma Co will have recognised a lease liability and a right-of-use asset in its statement of financial position.

Tutorial note

If assets are unused, idle or damaged then an impairment review should be performed.

Vacating the lease means that the right-of-use asset will provide no further economic benefits. This is an indicator of impairment and, in accordance with IAS 36 *Impairment of Assets*, an impairment review must be performed.

The carrying amount of the right-of-use asset must be compared with its recoverable amount. Recoverable amount is the higher of two figures: fair value less costs to sell, and value in use. If the lease cannot be sold or sublet, then the recoverable amount is likely to be nil. Any write down of the right-of-use asset to recoverable amount will be recorded as an expense in the statement of profit or loss.

(ii) Pension scheme

Tutorial note

The requirement asks you to 'advise' on the principles of accounting for the pension scheme. As such, most of the marks are for discussion of the correct accounting treatment.

At each financial year end, the plan assets and the defined benefit obligation are remeasured. The obligation is measured at present value, and the assets are measured at fair value.

The amount of pension expense to be recognised in profit or loss is comprised of the net interest component and service costs. Net interest is calculated by multiplying the opening net defined benefit liability by the discount rate at the start of the annual reporting period. Service costs are the current service costs, which is the increase in the present value of the defined benefit obligation resulting from employee services in the current period, and 'past-service costs'.

Ecoma Co's past-service costs are the changes in the present value of the defined benefit obligation for employee services in prior periods which have resulted from the plan amendment and should be recognised as an expense. IAS 19 *Employee Benefits* requires all past service costs to be recognised as an expense at the earlier of the following dates:

(a) when the plan amendment or curtailment occurs, and

(b) when the entity recognises related restructuring costs or termination benefits.

These costs should be recognised regardless of vesting requirements. Thus, the past service cost of $9 million will be recognised at 30 September 20X5.

Remeasurement gains and losses are recognised in other comprehensive income.

The table below reflects the change in the net pension obligation for the period. The statement of profit or loss will be charged with the net interest component of $3.2 million and the total service cost of $27 million ($18 million + $9 million). Benefits paid have no effect on the net obligation as both plan assets and obligations are reduced by $6 million. OCI will be credited with the $1.2 million remeasurement gain. This gain cannot be reclassified to profit or loss.

Tutorial note

You need to set up a working like the one below in order to calculate the remeasurement component.

	$m
Net pension obligation at 30 September 20X4	59.0
Net interest component ($59m × 5.5%)	3.2
Current service cost	18.0
Past service cost	9.0
Contributions	(10.0)
Remeasurement (bal. fig.)	(1.2)
Net pension obligation at 30 September 20X5	24.0

(iii) Profit adjustments

Tutorial note

You are asked to 'calculate' the impact of the adjustments. No explanation or discussion is required.

	$m
Draft profit	25.0
Net interest component	(3.2)
Current and past service costs	(27.0)
Revised loss before tax	(5.2)

Marking scheme			
			Marks
(a)		Relevance	2
		Opportunities	1
		Valuation models	2
		Risks	2
		Screening strategies	1
			8
(b)	(i)	Provision	2
		Impairment	4
			6
	(ii)	Accounting for the pension scheme	4
		Calculations	3
			7
	(iii)	Calculation of impact on earnings	2
		Professional marks	2
Total			**25**

Examiner's comments

Part (a) was generally well-answered; with better answers suggesting that candidates are reading around this subject (including the SBR technical article on Sustainable Development Goals from the ACCA website). Very few candidates related disclosure with the Global Reporting Initiative (GRI) and the UN Global Compact.

Part b (ii) required an explanation with calculations of the principles of accounting for changes in the vesting period of a defined benefit pension scheme, including past service cost adjustments in the year. Answers to this part were often good, with some answers presenting clear net liability workings, and descriptions of the accounting requirements. However candidates often applied the incorrect discount rate to calculate net interest, and sometimes applied the incorrect signage (deducting service costs from the net obligation for example). Weaker attempts wasted valuable time describing the differences between defined contribution and defined benefit schemes which gained no marks as it was not a requirement

Part b(iii) asked for a calculation of the impact of the items in b(ii) on a given profit before tax. This was, surprisingly, often omitted with some errors in adding or subtracting adjustments orcandidates may have run out of time. Time management is vital to ensure that all requirements of the question are met: in this case b (iii) was a relatively simple task following on from the answer to task b (ii).

41 DIGIWIRE (SEP/DEC 2019)  *Walk in the footsteps of a top tutor*

Key answer tips

This is a big question. In SBR you have just under two minutes per mark, so there is simply not enough time to write a detailed answer like the one provided below. Students generally score better when they attempt all requirements, so aim to spread your time across each part of the question (rather than writing a very detailed answer to part (a) and then leaving parts (b) and (c) unanswered).

(a) (i) Revenue recognition: Clamusic Co shares

Tutorial note

Start with the relevant principle from the relevant accounting standard.

IFRS 15 *Revenue from Contracts with Customers* requires that non-cash consideration received should be measured at the fair value of the consideration received.

Tutorial note

An active market is one where there are regular sales of identical assets and liabilities. There is unlikely to be an active market for unlisted shares.

The fair valuation of shares in an unlisted start-up company is problematic. However, IFRS 13 *Fair Value Measurement* gives advice on how to measure unlisted shares. It sets out three approaches: (i) the market approach, such as the transaction price paid for identical or similar instruments of an investee; (ii) the income approach, for example, using discounted cash flows; and (iii) the adjusted net asset approach.

Tutorial note

The valuation provided in the following paragraph is just one possible answer. Alternative valuations score just as many marks as long as justification is provided.

In this case, the market approach has been used and the range of fair values is significant based upon the professional valuation report. The range of fair values for a 7% holding of shares would be $280,000 to $350,000 (7% of $4–$5 million) at the date of the contract and $420,000 to $490,000 (7% of $6–$7 million) at the year end. As the fair valuation is based upon a similar listed company and is based upon a controlling interest, a discount on the valuation of the shares should be applied to reflect the lack of liquidity and inability to participate in Digiwire Co's policy decisions. Thus an estimated value of the shares can be made which takes into account the above facts. This could be the mid-point of $315,000 (($280,000 + $350,000)/2) at the date of the contract and $455,000 (($420,000 + $490,000)/2) at the year end.

Tutorial note

Remember that revenue is recognised either over-time or at a point in time.

At contract inception the shares will be recognised at $315,000. However, a corresponding entry should not be made to revenue. Digiwire Co retains an active role in the updating and maintenance of sold licence to ensure its continuing value to the client. As such, the customer is benefitting from Digiwire's continuing performance as Digiwire performs. In accordance with IFRS 15 *Revenue from Contracts from Customers*, revenue should be recognised over time – most likely over the three year contract term. Any difference between the initial carrying amount of the shares and the revenue recognised is recorded as a contract liability.

Clamusic Co share valuation at 31 December 20X6

Tutorial note

An investment in the equity instruments of another entity is a financial asset (unless the investor has control, joint control, or significant influence over the investee).

Equity investments in scope of IFRS 9 *Financial Instruments* should be measured at fair value in the statement of financial position, with gains and losses on remeasurement recognised in profit or loss. If an equity investment is not held for trading, an entity can make an irrevocable election at initial recognition to measure it at fair value through other comprehensive income (FVTOCI) with only dividend income recognised in profit or loss.

The shares will be remeasured to $455,000 (($420,000 + $490,000)/2) at 31 December 20X6. A gain of $140,000 ($455,000 – $315,000) will be recorded in profit or loss or other comprehensive income dependent upon any election being made. If Digiwire Co elects to present the remeasurements through other comprehensive income, the gain will never be reclassified to the statement of profit or loss.

(ii) Revenue: royalties

IFRS 15 states that revenue from a sales-based royalty should be recognised when the subsequent sale occurs.

At the end of the first year of the contract, revenue from royalties can be calculated based upon the sales for the period. This would be $50,000 (5% × $1 million).

The *Conceptual Framework* support

Tutorial note

The question is quite vague about what areas of the Conceptual Framework should be discussed. Alternative answers, such as discussions of the definitions of the elements, would therefore be awarded marks.

The *Conceptual Framework* states that an item which meets the definition of an element should be recognised if recognition provides useful financial information. In other words:

(a) relevant information; and

(b) a faithful representation of the underlying transaction.

Tutorial note

Do not just recite key principles from the Conceptual Framework. Make sure that you apply these principles to the accounting treatment of the sales-based royalty.

Recognition of royalties earned during the year in the statement of profit or loss will help users of the financial statements to assess Digiwire Co's economic performance and thus make investment decisions. The sales made in the year can be accurately measured and so the royalty can be accurately calculated – thus a faithful representation of the income earned in the period is possible.

Future royalty incomes, relating to years two or three of the contract, should not be recognised because Digiwire has not yet performed in those economic periods. Moreover, future royalties cannot be measured with any certainty and so estimation and recognition of these would not provide a faithful representation of revenue earned in the period. The principles in the *Conceptual Framework* relating to recognition are therefore consistent with the approach taken by Digiwire Co.

(b) (i) FourDee Co

Tutorial note

Make sure that you know the definition of joint control because this principle is regularly tested in SBR.

IFRS 11 *Joint Arrangements* defines joint control as the contractually agreed sharing of control of an arrangement, which exists only when decisions about the relevant activities require the unanimous consent of the parties sharing control. This would seem to be the case with FourDee Co because decisions are made by a unanimous vote of the two parties that share control.

Tutorial note

There are two types of joint arrangements: joint ventures and joint operations. Joint ventures are usually a separate company.

The investment in FourDee Co would seem to qualify as a joint venture. This is because FourDee Co is a separate company so the venturers have rights to the net assets of the arrangement

Tutorial note

The accounting treatment of a joint venture is the same as the accounting treatment of an associate.

A joint venturer accounts for an investment in a joint venture using the equity method in accordance with IAS 28 *Investments in Associates and Joint Ventures*. This means that the investment is initially recognised at cost. The venturer will subsequently recognise its share of the joint venture's profits and other comprehensive income.

(ii) Derecognition of assets

Tutorial note

According to the Conceptual Framework, assets are derecognised when the entity no longer has control. Liabilities are derecognised when there is no longer a present obligation to transfer an economic resource.

Digiwire Co has exchanged non-monetary assets for its investment in FourDee Co, and thus needs to de-recognise the assets it is contributing to FourDee Co. The carrying amount of $6 million of the property is derecognised but the intellectual property of Digiwire Co has been generated internally and does not have a carrying amount. The cryptocurrency is recorded as an asset in the financial statements of Digiwire Co at $3 million and must also be derecognised.

Profit on disposal

When a joint venturer contributes a non-monetary asset to a joint venture in exchange for an equity interest in the joint venture, the joint venturer recognises a portion of the gain or loss on disposal which is attributable to the other parties to the joint venture (except when the contribution lacks commercial substance). As such, Digiwire Co is required by IAS 28 to limit the profit on disposal of its non-monetary assets to 50% because, effectively, Digiwire has only disposed of 50% of the assets contributed to the joint venture.

Thus the carrying amount of the joint venture in Digwire's financial statements at 31 December 20X6 will be $11.5 million (($6m + $3m carrying amounts derecognised for property and cryptocurrency) + (($4m – $3m)/2) + (($10m – $6m)/2)). A gain of $2.5 million will be recorded in profit or loss.

(iii) Cryptocurrency

Tutorial note

Some companies accept cryptocurrency as a form of payment. However, as yet, cryptocurrency is not widely accepted.

Cryptocurrency is not cash or cash equivalents as its value is exposed to significant changes in market value and there is no contractual right to receive either cash or cash equivalents. Therefore, cryptocurrency does not meet the definition of a financial asset per IAS 32 *Financial Instruments: Presentation*.

IAS 38 *Intangible Assets* defines an intangible asset as an identifiable non-monetary asset without physical substance. Cryptocurrency would seem to meet this definition.

If the cryptocurrency is to be recognised as an intangible asset then it could be measured at cost less amortisation and impairment. If the useful life was determined to be indefinite then no amortisation would be charged. Because there is an active market for the cryptocurrency, it would be possible for it to be measured at fair value instead. If measured at fair value then any gains on remeasurement would be presented in other comprehensive income and the gain would not be reclassified through profit or loss when the cryptocurrency is derecognised.

Tutorial note

Remember that the Conceptual Framework provides useful guidance to preparers of financial statements when an IFRS Standard offers a choice of accounting policy or when no IFRS Standard exists for a particular transaction.

When offered a choice of measurement base, the *Conceptual Framework* states that consideration should be given to the characteristics of the asset and the way in which it contributes to future cash flows. Cryptocurrency has a volatile market value and is often traded in the short-term. As such a current value measurement (such as fair value) is likely to provide more relevant information that historical cost.

The *Conceptual Framework* states that profit or loss is the primary source of information about economic performance during the reporting period and that income and expenses would normally be presented in this statement. Income or expenses might be presented in other comprehensive income if they result from a current value remeasurement and if presentation in other comprehensive income increases the relevance of profit or loss. However, if cryptocurrency is held as an investment, then economic returns earned in the period are likely to be of interest to investors when assessing overall economic performance. Therefore, gains and losses on remeasurement of cryptocurrency to fair value should probably be recorded in profit or loss. This treatment would be consistent with financial assets held in the short-term, measured in accordance with IFRS 9 *Financial Instruments*.

(c) IAS 19 *Employee Benefits*

Tutorial note

Basic points will still score you a mark if relevant to the question.

According to IAS 19 *Employee* Benefits, any gain or loss arising on a curtailment is recognised in the statement of profit or loss.

Tutorial note

State the accounting principles regarding a mid-year plan amendment, curtailment or settlement.

When a plan amendment, curtailment or settlement occurs during the annual reporting period, an entity must:

– Determine current service cost for the remainder of the period after the plan amendment, curtailment or settlement using the actuarial assumptions used to remeasure the net defined benefit liability/asset reflecting the benefits offered under the plan and the plan assets after that event.

– Determine net interest for the remainder of the period after the plan amendment, curtailment or settlement using: (i) the net defined benefit liability/asset reflecting the benefits offered under the plan and the plan assets after that event; and (ii) the discount rate used to remeasure that net defined benefit liability/asset.

Tutorial note

Show your workings.

The current service cost would be $96 million ((8 months × $9 million) + (4 months × $6 million)).

The net interest component would be calculated as $1,020,000 (($900,000 × 8/12) + (3.5% × $36m × 4/12)).

Marking guide				
				Marks
(a)	(i)	–	application of the following discussion to the scenario:	
			IFRS 15 non-cash consideration and IFRS 13 alternatives to value the shares (including share value calculation at year end)	3
			IFRS 9 remeasurement gains (including calculation)	3
	(ii)	–	application of the following discussion to the scenario:	
			revenue recognised over time	2
			Conceptual Framework	2
				10
(b)	(i)	–	discussion and application of the IFRS 11 requirements to the scenario	3
	(ii)	–	discussion of the derecognition of non-monetary assets and application to the scenario	2
		–	calculation of carrying amount of the joint venture	1
	(iii)	–	discussion of the potential ways in which the cryptocurrency could be accounted for at fair value	4
				10
(c)	Curtailment in P/L			1
	Principles relating to curtailment and impact on service/interest			2
	Calculations			2
				5
Total				**25**

Examiner's comments

Part (c) was the least well-answered, with many candidates choosing to avoid answering altogether. Candidates who were unaware of the amendments should at least have been in a position to critically describe the previous method by which each cost was calculated. Appropriate discussion would have been awarded marks. Part (a) required a valuation of the equity investment, and was generally well-answered. The royalties aspect also required a demonstration of how the *Conceptual Framework for Financial Reporting* supported the suggested treatment. Answers tended to focus on the more general aspects of the *Conceptual Framework*, whilst the answer called for those aspects relating to the scenario, such as recognition requirements. In part (b) very few recognised that the disposal was effectively 50% of the assets contributed (relating to the part attributable to the other party of the joint venture). The final requirement of part (b) tested whether cryptocurrency can be classified as a financial asset or intangible asset, and whether valuation movements should appear in profit or loss. Answers to this were generally weak; and again, some answers ignored this requirement altogether. This is surprising given that there is a technical article on cryptocurrency.

42 GUIDANCE (SEP/DEC 2019)  *Walk in the footsteps of a top tutor*

Key answer tips

Lots of easy marks are available in part (b) and long as you are answering all of the requirements. If you forget to calculate ratios, or neglect to talk about the impact of the transactions on ROE, then you throw away easy marks. Two professional marks are available in part (b) – try and keep you answer as clear and understandable as possible.

(a) Accounting policy choices

If an IFRS Standard allows an entity an accounting choice, the financial statements will be affected by that choice.

The accounting policy chosen might be driven by self-interest. Companies may use the financial choices to increase earnings, and manipulate accounting figures in order to influence contractual outcomes which depend on the accounting figures reported.

Tutorial note

The question does not explicitly refer to the Conceptual Framework. However, the Conceptual Framework provides guidance for preparers of financial statements when an IFRS Standard offers a choice of accounting policy – and so the principles that it outlines are relevant here.

Accounting choices exist to provide companies which operate under different business models with the option of utilising an accounting method which best represents their operations. When an accounting standard offers a choice of accounting policy, the *Conceptual Framework* states that the information provided must be useful – i.e. relevant and a faithful representation of the entity's underlying transactions. A faithful representation means that, to the maximum extent possible, the financial statements are complete, neutral and free from error. A faithful representation is affected by the level of measurement uncertainty in the financial statements.

Comparability is one of the four qualitative characteristics which enhances the usefulness of financial information.

Tutorial note

The other enhancing qualitative characteristics of useful financial information are timeliness, understandability and verifiability.

Accounting information is more useful if it can be compared with similar information from other companies, or from the same company. Where there is flexibility when applying an IFRS Standard, financial statements can become less comparable with other companies. However, if guidance in the *Conceptual Framework* is followed, companies with the same business models or that hold assets or liabilities for similar purposes are likely to measure them in similar, comparable, ways.

Comparability is crucial to improve financial reporting quality but it can be argued that comparability is made more difficult by the fact that the Board allows entities to choose between alternative measurement bases. Environmental, economic, political, cultural, operational differences could be solved with the existence of accounting choices in the standards, but these choices could be at the cost of comparability.

(b) **(i)** **Usefulness of return on equity**

The return on equity (ROE) ratio measures the rate of return which the owners of issued shares of a company receive on their shareholdings in terms of profitability. This metric is especially important from an investor's perspective, as it can be used to judge how efficiently the firm will be able to use shareholder's investment to generate additional revenues.

The net profit margin (net profit/sales) tells how much profit a company makes on every dollar of sales.

Asset turnover (sales/assets) ratio measures the value of a company's sales or revenues generated relative to the carrying amount of its assets. The asset turnover ratio can often be used as an indicator of the efficiency with which a company is deploying its assets in generating revenue.

The equity ratio (assets/equity) indicates the relative proportion of the company's assets that are financed by equity. The equity ratio is a good indicator of the level of leverage used by a company by measuring the proportion of the total assets which are financed by shareholders, as opposed to creditors.

Tutorial note

Calculating the ratios is an easy source of marks.

	20X5	**20X6**
Net profit margin	15%	17.3%
Asset turnover	0.8	1.05
Equity ratio	1.43	2.1
Return on equity	17%	38%

Tutorial note

The return on equity formula provided in the question can be simplified.

Return on equity = net profit/equity

(ii) Setting up of special purpose entity (SPE)

Tutorial note

Remember to comment on the impact on ROE and its constituent elements.

By transferring their assets to a SPE, the asset turnover ratio will be significantly larger making the entity look more efficient. Furthermore, the revaluation reserve has been charged, thus reducing equity, and improving the ROE ratio.

Tutorial note

Use your knowledge from IFRS 10 Consolidated Financial Statements to explain why the treatment of the SPE is incorrect.

IFRS 10 *Consolidated Financial Statements* states that an investor controls a SPE when it is exposed, or has rights, to variable returns from its involvement with the SPE and has the ability to affect those returns through its power over the SPE. Power is the current ability to direct the activities which significantly influence returns. As such, the SPE should be consolidated by Guidance Co in its group financial statements. The property should be included in the group's assets and the charge eliminated from the revaluation reserves. The adjustment will increase shareholder equity, thus reducing ROE.

Miscellaneous transactions – share buyback

Tutorial note

The accounting entry for a share buyback is:

Dr Equity X

Cr Cash X

A major concern about using ROE is when a company buys back its shares. This decreases the equity on the statement of financial position. As the equity portion of ROE shrinks, the ROE metric gets larger. The ROE calculation can become meaningless if a company regularly buys back its shares. As a result there may be better metrics for investors to use (such as the P/E ratio).

Miscellaneous transactions – associate

Tutorial note

The investment in the associate is likely to affect year-on-year comparability. Stripping out the impact of the investment may provide more relevant trend analysis of performance.

Guidance Co has included $4m profit ($32m × 6/12 × 25%) from an associate in the current year's figures. The associate was purchased in the current year. If the share of the results of the associate were excluded, this would allow Guidance Co's profitability to result exclusively from Guidance Co's asset base. It could be argued that the full value of the company's reported profit including the associate could distort the analysis of Guidance Co's performance as compared to the last financial year.

There is no need to adjust for the original $15 million investment in the associate because one asset is merely being replaced by another but total assets, and total equity, remain the same.

Adjusted amounts

Tutorial note

The examiner commented that better quality answers used a table to show the adjustments needed to the 20X6 figures. Label the table. This provides an audit trail for the marker, making it easier for them to give you credit if you make a mistake.

		SPE property	**Shares cancelled**	**Associate**	**Total**
		$m	$m	$m	$m
Net profit before tax	38			(4)	34
Sales	220				220
Assets	210	50	30		290
Equity	100	50	30	(4)	176

Adjusted calculations

	20X5	**20X6 (adjusted)**	**20X6 (unadjusted)**
Net profit margin	15%	15.5%	17.3%
Asset turnover	0.8	0.76	1.05
Equity ratio	1.43	1.65	2.1
ROE	17%	19.3%	38%

Tutorial note

The investor's share of the associate's profit is recognisd in profit or loss and also increases the carrying amount of the investment in the associate. As such, in the adjustments table above, some candidates may also have removed $4 million from the entity's assets. This adjustment was not made by the examining team but would have been acceptable and scored marks.

It can be seen that if the impact of the transactions in the period were eliminated, then ROE, and its component parts, significantly reduce. The buyback of shares and the purchase of the associate were legitimate transactions but they have been eliminated in order to determine comparative metrics. The accounting treatment of the SPE was contrary to IFRS 10 and would have been reversed in any event. Although financial metrics are intended to enable comparisons between companies, the relative performance of any particular company can be affected by transactions both acceptable and unacceptable under accounting standards.

ACCA marking guide				
				Marks
(a)		–	discussion of the issues relating to accounting choice	3
		–	discussion of whether faithful representation and comparability are affected	3
				6
(b)	(i)	–	discussion of the meaning of the return on equity (ROE) and its component parts	3
		–	calculation of ROE for the years ended 31 December 20X5 and 20X6	2
				5
	(ii)	–	application of the following discussion to the scenario:	
			transfer of property to SPE	3
			buy back of shares	3
			purchase of associate	2
			calculation of the impact on ROE and its component parts	4
				12
	Professional marks			2
Total				**25**

Examiner's comments

Answers to part (a) were generally well-presented, with a good description of the need to reflect the characteristics of assets and liabilities, although at a potential cost to comparability (an enhancing qualitative characteristic). Fewer answers considered the need to best represent the business model of the entity. Part (bi) was also well-answered in general, although surprisingly few candidates provided a clear description of the component elements of ROE, despite the requirement clearly asking for it. In part (b) (ii), most candidates identified the impact that the transactions had on the comparability of the current year's ROE. Better answers provided a table in which the original accounting data is adjusted for each transaction. A methodical approach yielded good marks; whilst weaker answers presented unclear workings without any referencing or commentary. Overall, this question was well-answered.

43 CRYPTO (MAR/JUN 2019)  *Walk in the footsteps of a top tutor*

Key answer tips

Part (a) (i) tests a very popular exam topic – the definitions of 'control' and 'joint control'. This should be a source of easy marks. In contrast, part (a) (ii) tests a much more difficult part of the syllabus – embedded derivatives. That said, easy marks are available here for basic knowledge, such as the fact that derivatives are measured at fair value through profit or loss.

Part (b) is about the impact on investor analysis when an entity applies IFRS 16 *Leases*. Two professional marks are available here if your answer is well organised and addresses the question. Make sure that you distinguish between parts (i) and (ii) – discussion of ratios should be kept to the latter part.

(a) (i) Joint control

Before assessing whether an entity has joint control over an arrangement, an entity must first assess whether the parties control the arrangement in accordance with the definition of control in IFRS 10 *Consolidated Financial Statements*. If not, an entity must determine whether it has joint control of the arrangement.

Tutorial note

Control is normally presumed if the investor owns more than 50% of the investee's ordinary shares. However, it is possible to own less than 50% of the ordinary shares and still have control – for instance, if the other shareholdings are dispersed, or if the investor is able to control the decisions made at a board level.

IFRS 10 states that control requires power over the investee which gives the investor the ability to direct the relevant activities. Crypto does not have the ability to direct the relevant activities as it can only block decisions, and cannot make decisions by itself. Also, there is no shareholder agreement which sets out shareholders' voting rights and obligations and thus the other shareholders can act together to prevent Crypto from making decisions in its own interest. As such Crypto does not have control over Kurran.

Tutorial note

Start off with the definition of joint control and there try and apply this to the scenario.

IFRS 11 *Joint Arrangements* defines joint control as 'the contractually agreed sharing of control of an arrangement, which exists only when decisions about the relevant activities require the unanimous consent of the parties sharing control'. It must be clear which combination of parties is required to agree unanimously to decisions about the relevant activities of the arrangement. In the case of Kurran, there is more than one combination of parties possible to reach the required majority. As a result, Crypto does not have joint control.

Tutorial note

The requirement asks you to 'advise the directors of Crypto as to how the above issues should be accounted for.' Make sure you finish your answer by explaining the correct treatment of the investment in Kurran.

IAS 28 *Investments in Associates and Joint Ventures* states that an associate is an entity over which the investor has significant influence. Significant influence is presumed when the investor owns between 20% and 50% of the ordinary shares. Therefore, it appears that Kurran is an associate of Crypto and should be accounted for in the consolidated financial statements using the equity method.

(ii) Embedded derivative

The contract is a hybrid contract. It contains a host contract, which is an executory contract to purchase electricity at a price of 20 million euros. The contract also contains an embedded derivative to sell dollars in the future to buy 20 million euros.

The host contract is not a financial asset. As such the embedded derivative is only separated out if the economic characteristics and risks of the embedded derivative are not closely related to those of the host contract. This would seem to be the case, because neither party to the contract has a functional currency of Euros. As such, it is acceptable to separate the embedded derivative but it should have been measured at fair value through profit or loss, rather than at fair value through other comprehensive income.

Tutorial note

Remember that derivatives are always measured at fair value through profit or loss unless hedge accounting is applied.

Note that it is not mandatory to separate the embedded derivative. Instead the entire hybrid contract can be measured at fair value through profit or loss.

At the date of the modification of the contract, there is a significant change to the contract. The contract no longer contains an embedded derivative and is instead an executory contract (outside the scope of IFRS 9). The embedded derivative component that has been accounted for separately must therefore be derecognised.

Tutorial note

According to the Conceptual Framework, an executory contract is one where neither party has performed any of its obligations (e.g. a purchase contract where the purchaser has not paid and the seller has not started to satisfy the performance obligations in the contract). The contract will be unrecognised until an entity starts to perform – i.e. Crypto will record electricity at the cost of purchase when received from the supplier.

(b) (i) Key changes to lessee accounting

Tutorial note

In previous versions of the lease standard, certain types of lease would require that the lessee did not recognise an asset or a liability. In contrast IFRS 16 Leases requires that a right-of-use asset and a lease liability is recognised for almost all leases. Try and draw out the impact of this on both the statement of financial position and the statement of profit or loss. Why was this change useful for investors, and what impact might it have on their analysis of financial position and financial performance?

Even without knowledge of the rules from the previous version of the lease standard, the preamble to the question gives enough information regarding the prior treatment of lease liabilities (or, more accurately, the non-treatment) to enable candidates to answer the question. Use the content of these introductory paragraphs to generate ideas, as they can contain useful hints towards the direction of travel of an expected answer.

IFRS 16 *Leases* introduces a single lessee accounting model. Upon lease commencement, a lessee recognises a right-of-use asset and a lease liability unless the lease is short-term or of minimal value. The lease liability is initially measured at the present value of the lease payments still to be paid over the lease term, discounted at the rate implicit in the lease. The right-of-use asset is recognised at the same amount, plus any payments made at or before commencement of the lease, plus any initial direct costs.

Investors should bear in mind that some sectors and some companies will be more affected than others. As a result of applying IFRS 16, companies with previous material off-balance sheet leases will report higher assets and liabilities.

IFRS 16 results in more information about leases both on the statement of financial position and in the notes. Investors will no longer have to estimate the assets and liabilities resulting from off-balance sheet leases when calculating financial statement ratios. The standard should therefore make it easier to compare companies that lease assets with those that borrow to buy assets.

IFRS 16 requires a lessee to disclose lease liabilities separately from other liabilities as a separate line item, or together with other similar liabilities, in a manner which is relevant to understanding the lessee's financial position. A lessee will also split lease liabilities into current and non-current portions, based on the timing of payments.

After lease commencement, a lessee measures the right-of-use asset using a cost model less accumulated depreciation (and accumulated impairment if applicable). The lease liability is increased by interest, and reduced by the repayments made. The impact on the statement of profit or loss is a depreciation expense on the right-of-use assert (normally presented as an operating expense) and an interest expense on the lease liability (normally presented as a finance cost). In contrast, entities that previously had off-balance sheet leases would most likely have presented the full lease expense as an operating expense. Applying IFRS 16 is therefore likely to lead to an increase in profits before interest and tax (profits from operations).

(ii) Accounting ratios

The recognition of an asset which was previously unrecognised will result in a higher asset base, which will affect ratios such as asset turnover. The recognition of a liability which was previously unrecognised will result in higher liabilities, which will affect gearing. The recognition of depreciation and interest instead of operating lease expenses will result in higher operating profit because interest is typically excluded from operating expenses and will affect performance ratios. Similarly, profit measures which exclude interest and depreciation but previously included operating lease expense, such as EBITDA, will be higher under IFRS 16.

Tutorial note

Try and think about the impact of IFRS 16 on the constituent parts of each ratio. For example, IFRS 16 will lead to an increase in earnings before interest and tax, but also an increase in the interest expense.

If you are struggling here then make up some numbers so that you can see the impact more clearly.

Interest cover: accounting for leases in accordance with IFRS 16 will increase earnings before interest and tax (EBIT), because the interest expense on the lease liability will most likely be presented as interest. This change in EBIT will not be proportionate to the overall change in interest so the ratio will be change. The actual change in the ratio, however, will depend on the characteristics of the lease portfolio. This is because the interest charge on the lease liability is higher in the earlier years of a lease.

Return on capital employed: it is likely that ROCE will be lower under IFRS 16 because the increase in earnings before interest and tax is unlikely to be proportionate to the increase in capital employed.

Debt to EBITDA: the amount of debt will rise because lease liabilities will be recognised on the statement of financial position. EBITDA will rise because, under IFRS 16, the whole lease expense comprises either depreciation of the right of use asset or interest on the lease liability. The ratio of debt to EBITDA will increase because the increase in debt will be greater than the increase in EBITDA.

ACCA marking guide

			Marks
(a)	(i)	– discussion of the following accounting issues and application to the scenario:	
		the definition of control per IFRS 10 and joint control per IFRS 11	3
		power over the investee	3
		Maximum	6
	(ii)	– discussion of the following accounting issues and application to the scenario:	
		IFRS 9 requirements for embedded derivatives and hybrid	3
		IFRS 9 requirements for contract modifications	2
		Maximum	5
(b)	(i)	– a discussion of the IFRS 16 requirements	3
		– implications for investors	3
		Maximum	6
	(ii)	– a description of the IFRS 16 impact on accounting numbers	2
		– impact on the following ratios:	
		Interest cover	2
		ROCE	1
		Debt to EBITDA	1
		Maximum	6
	Professional marks		2
Total			**25**

Examiner's comments

Answers to the first part of the question were relatively weak. The scenario explained that the company held half of the board's nominations and that the directors sought advice over the applicability of IFRS 11. Most answers focused on this standard, but better answers began by considering the aspect of control: first, whether control was exhibited in accordance with IFRS 10 (individual control), then if joint control existed (IFRS 11), before finally considering the treatment without control, but with significant influence (IAS 28).

The second part was not well-answered, with a significant minority of candidates failing to answer this part at all or providing a very limited answer.

Many candidates explained the key changes on the application of IFRS 16; although the explanation was in some cases limited to a description of the accounting adjustments (the introduction of a right of use asset and corresponding liability) with limited consideration of the investor's viewpoint. Better answers described how certain industries would be more significantly affected, outlined the benefits to the investor of the change (increased comparability, no need to estimate off-balance sheet liabilities), and how disclosures should aid understanding. Answers to the last part of the question were generally good, provided the impact on each stated ratio was linked to the change in accounting treatment.

44 ZEDTECH (MAR/JUN 2019)

Key answer tips

Parts (a) tests principles relating to revenue recognition. It involves very few numbers, and so tests this topic very differently than questions in lower level exams.

Part (b) examines a current issue relating to sustainability reporting and developments but applies it practically to the Zedtech business.

Part (c) covers a technical area that has been added to the syllabus for 2022/23, being deferred tax and leases. Make sure you study this section as new areas tend be a favourite of the examiner.

(a) (i) Principles from IFRS 15 *Revenue from Contracts with Customers*

IFRS 15 *Revenue from Contracts with Customers* states that an entity must first identify the contract with the customer. As part of this, the entity must determine whether it is probable that the consideration which the entity is entitled to in exchange for the goods or services will be collected.

Once an entity has identified the contract with a customer, it evaluates the contractual terms and its customary business practices to identify all the promised goods or services within the contract. It must then determine which of those promised goods or services will be treated as separate performance obligations. A good or service is distinct if the customer can benefit from the good or service on its own, or together with the resources readily available to it.

(ii) 0inventory

As regards 0inventory, it seems that all of the individual goods and services in the contract are distinct because the entity regularly sells each element of the contract separately and is not providing the significant service of integrating the goods and services. Also, as the customer could purchase each good and service without significantly affecting the other goods and services purchased, there is no dependence upon individual elements of the service. Thus hardware, professional services and hosting services should each be accounted for as separate performance obligations.

InventoryX

Regarding InventoryX, the professional services are distinct because Zedtech frequently sells those services on a stand-alone basis. These should be dealt with as a separate performance obligation.

The hardware is integral to the delivery of the hosted software and cannot be used on its own. This means that the provision of the hardware and hosting services together form a single performance obligation.

Collectability

Zedtech has entered into an arrangement and does not expect to collect the full contractual amount such that the contract contains an implied price concession. Therefore, Zedtech needs to assess the collectability of the amount to which it expects to be entitled, rather than the stated contractual amount. Zedtech assesses whether collectability is probable, whether the customer has the ability and intent to pay the estimated transaction price. Zedtech will determine that the amount to which it expects to be entitled is $2.4 million and performs the collectability assessment based on that amount, rather than the contractual price of $3 million.

(b) Factors affecting sustainability reporting of Zedtech

Sustainability has become an increasingly crucial aspect of running a business and, as a consequence, the reporting of sustainability is a hot accounting topic. The UN has produced 17 Sustainability Development Goals (SDGs) and buy in from industry has a part to play in achieving these goals. There is also a growing recognition that sustainability can have a significant effect on a company's financial performance. Entities are more likely to volunteer to disclose the methods and processes that will help to achieve these SDGs through increased sustainability reporting. Therefore, the directors of Zedtech should consider how their operational practices may impact sustainability.

The nature of Zedtech's business creates a variety of factors that the directors should consider which may affect sustainability. Zedtech, as a software development company, operates in a high-tech industry. It provides data-hosting services and online inventory management services. It can be assumed that Zedtech operates using large server networks, possibly utilising cloud storage. This assumption can be ratified through the lease agreement for servers entered into by Zedtech. Online storage of data utilises vast amounts of energy through the powering and maintenance of the servers required. CO_2 emissions are a significant concern. For Zedtech to be considered a sustainable business, it should be actively investigating ways that could reduce Zedtech's carbon footprint e.g. utilisation of renewable energy, strategies of server temperature reduction.

Zedtech has recently started to provide services in a new geographic location. This could create different or unforeseen sustainability risks for Zedtech. Proper research should have been undertaken before entering the market place to ensure operational practices within the region do not expose Zedtech to negative press. For example, if the region has less rigorous labour laws in place, has a reputation for promoting inequality within the work place, operates under poor working conditions or has a negative reputation regarding environmental concerns. The actions performed by Zedtech to ensure the new region operates in a sustainable fashion should form part of any sustainability reporting.

The same considerations applied to the region as a whole, could also be applied to the customers and, if necessary, the suppliers (say if local servers were required to facilitate the contracts) with which Zedtech undertakes business in the new regions. Zedtech cannot declare to be at the forefront of sustainable business if the entities with which they trade do not share the same approach. If that were the case, Zedtech's reputation will be tarnished through association.

The new regions of operation could create the need for more travel and for exporting hardware overseas. This would lead to an increase in Zedtech's carbon footprint.

The 0inventory and InventoryX packages provide hardware to Zedtech's customers. Consideration of the impact to the environment of the production and disposal of the Zedtech hardware would be an important sustainability factor that should be demonstrable. Zedtech would want to promote any use of recycled raw materials and the production of recyclable and biodegradable finished goods.

The main stakeholders in companies (shareholders, financiers, investors, employees, customers, suppliers, governments, and the public) are increasingly integrating consideration of sustainability issues into their decision-making. Stakeholders require a greater understanding of the wider social and environmental context in which the business operates. Creating a positive picture through the adoption of sustainability practices and their subsequent disclosure invokes greater trust and credibility with stakeholders.

In their eagerness to present an image of promoting sustainability, the directors of Zedtech must be wary of overstating their engagement in sustainable practices. If decisions by stakeholders are influenced by proclamations included within the sustainability report, which subsequently are proven to have no substance, the resulting backlash could tarnish the reputation of Zedtech, perhaps to greater levels than if Zedtech ignored sustainability issues altogether. Zedtech could find itself subject to swathes of negative press, customer and investor boycotts and even protests at company locations.

As Zedtech is a listed entity, investors, whether current or potential, are clearly an important stakeholder. In recent times, investor groups have shown an appetite for products which recognise and reflect the relationship between their investments and social and environmental conduct. Investors need to completely understand the nature of the companies in which they are looking to invest and like to incorporate sustainability factors into investment decisions.

Analysis of the impact Zedtech has on sustainability could be the deciding factor for potential investors. If the company is viewed poorly based on its sustainability performance, it could lead to a potential investor investing their money elsewhere.

(c) Deferred tax and leases

In accordance with IFRS 16 *Leases*, a lease liability is recognised for $15 million, being the present value of future lease payments. The right-of-use asset is recorded at $19m, being the lease liability plus payments already made ($15m + $4m).

However, the initial advanced payment needs to be considered for deferred tax purposes separately from the recognition of the lease liability and right-of-use asset.

Considering the deferred tax created by the initial recognition of the lease liability firstly, the tax relief granted in this jurisdiction relates to the lease liability of $15m rather than the right-of-use asset. This causes the tax base of the right-of-use asset to be nil (no future tax relief is granted). Its carrying amount is initially $15 million (ignoring the advanced payment) and so a taxable temporary difference of $15 million arises which creates a deferred tax liability.

The tax base of the lease liability is nil ($15m carrying amount less $15m future tax relief). The carrying amount of the lease liability is $15 million, so a deductible temporary difference of $15 million arises, which would create a deferred tax asset.

This transaction is not a business combination and it affects neither accounting profit nor taxable profit. However, equal amounts of deductible and taxable temporary differences are created.

A deferred tax asset would be recognised for $3 million ($15m × 20%), assuming that sufficient future profits are expected against which the difference can be utilised. A deferred tax liability would also be recognised for $3 million.

The entry required is:

Dr Deferred tax assets $3m

Cr Deferred tax liabilities $3m.

The initial advanced payment is considered for deferred tax purposes separately from the recognition of the right-of-use asset and lease liability. The advance rental of $4m is included in the right-of-use asset but not the lease liability. The carrying amount of the right-of-use asset increases by $4m. The tax base is nil. This is a taxable temporary difference of $4 million.

The advance payments do not affect accounting profit, but they do affect taxable profit as tax relief is granted as the cash is paid, so a deferred tax liability will need to be recorded. A deferred tax liability is recognised for $0.8 million ($4m × 20%). A corresponding tax expense is recognised in the statement of profit or loss.

Dr Tax expense (P/L) $0.8m

Cr Deferred tax liabilities $0.8m

Marking guide				
				Marks
(a)	(i)	– discussion of the collectability of consideration		2
		– discussion of performance obligations		3
			Maximum	5
	(ii)	– application of the above principles to:		
		0inventory		2
		InventoryX		3
		– collectability assessment		2
			Maximum	7
(b)	Discussion of the following:			
	– Sustainability reporting developments e.g. SDGs, other initiatives (GRI etc)			1
	– Specific Zedtech factors:			5
	- high tech industry			
	- new region			
	- workers' rights			
	- equality			
	- use of sustainable materials			
	- other sensible, scenario based factors			
	– importance to stakeholders and management			2
			Maximum	8
(c)	Identification of taxable and deductible temporary differences			2
	Journal (deferred tax asset and deferred tax liability)			1
	Deferred tax on advance payment separately accounted			1
	Journal or reference to tax recognised in profit or loss			1
			Maximum	5
Total				**25**

Examiner's comments

Where a question requires a discussion of the principles of IFRS 15 to determine the recognition of for instance two software packages (one with distinct contracts for hardware and software, the other where hardware is integral to the software), candidates should ensure that they apply those principles to the scenario. For example, some candidates are still providing a IFRS 15 'list' rather than further explaining the importance of each step with regard to recognition.

Those candidates that applied the principles of IFRS 15 to the scenario – and distinguished between the separate performance obligations in one contract and the integrated performance obligation in the second contract – scored well in their explanation and application.

45 FILL (DEC 2018)

Key answer tips

Parts (a) and (c) both require reference to the Conceptual Framework. This is a key topic in SBR that is being tested heavily. Make sure that you read Chapter 1 in the Study Text thoroughly.

(a) (i) Conceptual Framework

The *Conceptual Framework* acknowledges two measurement bases: historical cost, and current value. Net realisable value (NRV) is a current value measurement. However, the *Conceptual Framework* is not an accounting standard and so, in order to determine NRV, the directors would need to refer to IAS 2 *Inventories*.

(ii) Net realisable value

IAS 2 defines NRV as the estimated selling price in the ordinary course of business less the costs of completion and costs of sale. In this case, the NRV will be determined on the basis of conditions which existed at the date of the statement of financial position.

NRV will be based upon the most reliable estimate of the amounts which will be realised for the coal. The year-end spot price will provide good evidence of the realisable value of the inventories and where the company has an executory contract to sell coal at a future date, then the use of the forward contract price may be appropriate. However, if the contract is not executory but is a financial instrument under IFRS 9 *Financial Instruments* or an onerous contract recognised as a provision under IAS 37 *Provisions, Contingent Liabilities and Contingent Assets*, it is unlikely to be used to calculate NRV.

Fill should calculate the NRV of the low carbon coal using the forecast market price based upon when the inventory is expected to be processed and realised. Future changes in the forecast market price or the processing and sale of the low carbon coal may result in adjustments to the NRV. As these adjustments are changes in estimates, IAS 8 *Accounting Policies, Changes in Accounting Estimates and Errors* will apply with the result that such gains and losses will be recognised in the statement of profit or loss in the period in which they arise.

(b) Replacement costs

IAS 16 *Property, Plant and Equipment* (PPE) requires an entity to recognise in the carrying amount of PPE, the cost of replacing part of such an item. When each major inspection is performed, its cost is recognised in the carrying amount of the item of PPE as a replacement if the recognition criteria are satisfied. Any remaining carrying amount of the cost of a previous inspection is derecognised. The costs of performing a major reconditioning are capitalised if it gives access to future economic benefits. Such costs will include the labour and materials costs ($3 million) of performing the reconditioning. However, costs which do not relate to the replacement of components or the installation of new assets, such as routine maintenance costs, should be expensed as incurred.

Provision

It is not acceptable to provide the costs of reconditioning equipment as there is no legal or apparent constructive obligation to undertake the reconditioning. As set out above, the cost of the reconditioning should be identified as a separate component of the mine asset at initial recognition and depreciated over a period of two years. This will result in the same amount of expense being recognised as the proposal to create a provision.

Impairment

IAS 36 *Impairment of Assets* says that at the end of each reporting period, an entity is required to assess whether there is any indication that an asset may be impaired. IAS 36 has a list of external and internal indicators of impairment. If there is an indication that an asset may be impaired, then the asset's recoverable amount must be calculated.

Past and future reductions in selling prices may indicate that the future economic benefits which relate to the asset have been reduced. Mining assets should be tested for impairment whenever indicators of impairment exist. Impairments are recognised if a mine's carrying amount exceeds its recoverable amount. However, the nature of mining assets is that they often have a long useful life. Commodity prices can be volatile but downward price movements are more significant if they are likely to persist for longer periods. In this case, there is evidence of a decline in forward prices. If the decline in prices is for a significant proportion of the remaining expected life of the mine, this is more likely to be an impairment indicator. It appears that forward contract prices for two years out of the three years of the mine's remaining life indicate a reduction in selling prices. Based on market information, Fill has also calculated that the three-year forecast price of coal will be 20% lower than the current spot price (part (a) of question).

Short-term market fluctuations may not be impairment indicators if prices are expected to return to higher levels. However, despite the difficulty in making such assessments, it would appear that the mining assets should be tested for impairment.

(c) Control

The *Conceptual Framework* states that an entity controls an economic resource if it has the present ability to direct the use of the economic resource and obtain the economic benefits which flow from it. An entity has the ability to direct the use of an economic resource if it has the right to deploy that economic resource in its activities. Although control of an economic resource usually arises from legal rights, it can also arise if an entity has the present ability to prevent all other parties from directing the use of it and obtaining the benefits from the economic resource. For an entity to control a resource, the economic benefits from the resource must flow to the entity instead of another party.

Although the *Conceptual Framework* gives some guidance on the definition of control, existing IFRS Standards should be used when making the assessment.

IFRS 10 *Consolidated Financial Statements* states that an investor controls an investee when it is exposed, or has rights, to variable returns from its involvement with the investee and has the ability to affect those returns through its power over the investee. Fill does not have control over the mine because its voting power is not sufficient for it to pass operating decisions that will affect the mine's relevant activities and thus its returns.

However, in accordance with IFRS 11 *Joint Arrangements*, it would seem that joint control exists. This is because two of the parties (Fill and the participant that owns 35%) share control and operating decisions require them to unanimously agree. The mine does not appear to be a separate entity and would therefore most likely be classified as a joint operation.

Business Combinations

A business combination is defined in IFRS 3 *Business Combinations* as a transaction or other event in which an acquirer obtains **control** of one or more businesses. A business is defined as an integrated set of activities and assets capable of being managed to provide outputs. The mine does represent a business. However, the Fill's purchase of a 40% interest is not a business combination because Fill does not have control.

That said, IFRS 3 states that the accounting treatment of the acquisition of an interest in a joint operation that meets the definition of a business should apply the same principles as are applied to a business combination unless those principles contradict IFRS 11. In other words, the identifiable net assets of the joint operation should be measured at fair value. However, unlike with a business combination, Fill should not recognise any non-controlling interest. Instead, Fill should only recognise its share of the mine's assets and liabilities. Goodwill would be recognised for the difference between the consideration paid for the interest and Fill's share of the net assets acquired.

Marking guide

			Marks
(a)	–	a discussion of potential measurement basis, NRV and relevant Standards	4
	–	application of IAS 2 to the scenario	3
			7
(b)	–	a discussion of IAS 16 and application to the scenario	4
	–	a discussion of IAS 36 and application to the scenario	4
			8
(c)	–	a discussion of control in the ED Conceptual Framework and other relevant Standards	4
	–	a discussion of a business combination per IFRS 3	2
	–	application of the above discussions to the scenario	4
			10
Total			**25**

Examiner's comments

The key to answering the first part of the question (and most questions) was to use the information in the scenario. The scenario mentioned that the entity sells its coal on the spot and futures markets and that low quality coal is to be extracted in three years' time when the forecast price of coal is to be 20% lower than the current spot price. Candidates could gain marks by simply discussing how this information would impact on coal valuation. In addition, candidates could gain marks by discussing the variety of measurement bases set out in the *Conceptual Framework* and how these might be applied to inventory valuation.

This second part of the question was well answered by candidates. However, the same cannot be said for the third part of the question which tested joint control and whether the *Conceptual Framework* affected the decision over the control of the mine. The wording of the question was such that it gave candidates the scope for a wide discussion of the issues involved. For example, candidates could have discussed the *Conceptual Framework* and the guidance on the definition of control. Additionally, existing IFRS standards also provide help in determining control via IFRS 10 *Consolidated Financial Statements*. IFRS 3 *Business Combinations* discusses the situation where an acquirer obtains control of one or more businesses. Unfortunately most candidates took a narrow approach and discussed mainly IFRS 10 or IFRS 3. However, if a candidate concluded differently to the model answer, and substantiated this, then credit was given.

46 HOLLS (DEC 2018)  *Walk in the footsteps of a top tutor*

Key answer tips

Many students who sat the exam in December 2018 found this question difficult. There are definitely some tricky elements within in. However, part of the problem no doubt resulted from issues with exam technique and exam preparation.

Part (a) is relatively straight-forward, but 'management commentary' is a current issue and many students do not study this area of the syllabus adequately. Current issues feature in every SBR exam; do not neglect them.

Part (b) appears tricky but actually offers some very easy sources of marks. For example, all students sitting SBR should be able to 'provide an explanation of accounting for deferred taxation'. Make sure that you concentrate on the parts of the question that you are most comfortable with.

(a) (i) Management commentary

Tutorial note

Management commentary is listed as a 'current issue' within the SBR syllabus. Do not neglect this area of the syllabus when studying. Current issues feature in every SBR exam.

The IFRS Practice Statement *Management Commentary* provides a broad, non-binding framework for the presentation of management commentary. The Practice Statement is not an IFRS Standard. Consequently, entities applying IFRS Standards are not required to comply with the Practice Statement, unless specifically required by their jurisdiction. Furthermore, non-compliance with the Practice Statement will not prevent an entity's financial statements from complying with IFRS Standards.

Arguments against non-binding approach

Tutorial note

You should be able to generate some points here using common-sense.

A mandatory standard is more likely to guarantee a consistent application of its principles and practices. Some entities will not produce management commentary because its application is non-mandatory. It can therefore be argued that the Board's objectives of enhancing the comparability of financial information will not be achieved unless management commentary is mandatory.

Arguments for non-binding approach

Tutorial note

Remember that a non-binding approach will permit greater flexibility. Whilst this can be a drawback, it can also lead to the disclosure of more relevant information.

It is difficult to create a standard on the MC which is sufficiently detailed to cover the business models of every entity or be consistent with all IFRS Standards. The Practice Statement allows companies to adapt the information provided to particular aspects of their business. This flexible approach could help generate more meaningful disclosures about resources, risks and relationships which can affect an entity's value and how these resources are managed. It provides management with an opportunity to add context to the published financial information, and to explain their future strategy and objectives without being restricted by the constraints of a standard.

Some jurisdictions take little notice of non-mandatory guidance but the Practice Statement provides local regulators with a framework to develop more authoritative requirements.

If the MC were a full IFRS Standard, the integration of management commentaries and the information produced in accordance with IFRS Standards could be challenged on technical grounds, as well as its practical merits.

(ii) Understandability

The *Conceptual Framework* states that financial information should be readily understandable. The MC should therefore be written in plain language and a style appropriate to users' needs.

The form and content of the MC will vary between entities, reflecting the nature of their business, the strategies adopted and the regulatory environment in which they operate. Whatever the form and content, users should be able to locate information relevant to their needs.

Relevance

Tutorial note

Begin by defining 'relevance' as per the Conceptual Framework.

Information has the quality of relevance when it has the capacity to influence the economic decisions of users by helping them evaluate past, present or future events or confirming, or correcting, their past evaluations. Relevant financial information has predictive value, confirmatory value or both.

The onus is on management to determine what information is important enough to be included in the MC to enable users to 'understand' the financial statements and meet the objective of the MC. If the entity provides too much information, it could reduce its relevance and understandability. If material events or uncertainties are not disclosed, then users may have insufficient information to meet their needs.

However, unnecessary detail may obscure important information especially if entities adopt a boiler-plate approach. If management presents too much information about, for example, all the risks facing an organisation, this will conflict with the relevance objective. There is no single optimal number of disclosures but it is useful to convey their relative importance in a meaningful way.

Comparability

Tutorial note

Begin by defining comparability as per the Conceptual Framework.

Comparability is the qualitative characteristic which enables users to identify and understand similarities and differences amongst items. It is important for users to be able to compare information over time and between entities. Comparability between entities is problematic as the MC is designed to reflect the perspectives of management and the circumstances of individual entities. Thus, entities in the same industry may have different perceptions of what is important and how they measure and report it. There are some precedents on how to define and calculate non-financial measures and financial measures which are not produced in accordance with IFRS Standards but there are inconsistencies in the definition and calculation of these measures.

It is sometimes suggested that the effectiveness of the overall report may be enhanced by strengthening the links between financial statements and the MC. However, such suggestions raise concerns about maintaining a clear distinction between the financial statement information and other information.

An entity should ensure consistency in terms of wording, definitions, segment disclosures, etc. between the financial statements and the MC to improve the understanding of financial performance.

(b) Current tax

Current tax is based on taxable profit for the year. Taxable profit is different from accounting profit due to temporary differences between accounting and tax treatments, and due to items which are never taxable or tax deductible. Tax benefits such as tax credits are not recognised unless it is probable that the tax positions are sustainable.

The Group is required to estimate the corporate tax in each of the many jurisdictions in which it operates. The Group is subject to tax audits in many jurisdictions; as a result, the Group may be required to make an adjustment in a subsequent period which could have a material impact on the Group's profit for the year.

Tax reconciliation

Tutorial note

Discuss the tax reconciliation, what it shows, and why it is useful.

The tax rate reconciliation is important for understanding the tax charge reported in the financial statements and why the effective tax rate differs from the statutory rate.

Most companies will reconcile the group's annual tax expense to the statutory rate in the country in which the parent is based. Hence the rate of 22% is used in the tax reconciliation. It is important that the reconciliation explains the reasons for the differences between the effective rate and the statutory rate.

Tutorial note

Remember to state the obvious. The 'other' category is vague and does not provide useful information to financial statement users.

There should be minimal use of the 'other' category. In this case, the other category is significant ($14 million) and there is no explanation of what 'other' constitutes. This makes it harder for investors to predict the Group's tax expense in future periods.

One-off and unusual items can have a significant effect on the effective tax rate, but financial statements and disclosure notes rarely include a detailed discussion of them. For example, the brand impairment and disposals of businesses should be explained to investors, as they are probably material items. The explanation should include any potential reversal of the treatment.

Some profits recognised in the financial statements are non-taxable. In some jurisdictions, gains on disposals of businesses are not taxable and impairment losses do not obtain tax relief. These issues should be explained to investors so that they understand the impact on the Group's effective tax rate.

Tax rates

Tutorial note

To make investment decisions, investors need information that will help them to assess an entity's future cash flows. Tax paid is a significant annual cash flow, so information about different tax rates is important.

As the Group is operating in multiple countries, the actual tax rates applicable to profits in those countries are different from the local tax rate. The overseas tax rates are higher than local rates, hence the increase in the taxation charge of $10 million. The local rate is different from the weighted average tax rate (27%) of the Group based on the different jurisdictions in which it operates. Investors may feel that using the weighted tax rate in the reconciliation gives a more meaningful number because it is a better estimate of the tax rate the Group expects to pay over the long term. Investors will wish to understand the company's expected long-term sustainable tax rate so they can prepare their cash flow or profit forecasts.

Information about the sustainability of the tax rate over the long term is more important than whether the rate is high or low compared to other jurisdictions. An adjustment can be made to an investor's financial model for a long-term sustainable rate, but not for a volatile rate where there is no certainty over future performance.

Tutorial note

Volatility in financial statements makes it harder for investors to predict an entity's future net cash flows.

For modelling purposes, an understanding of the actual cash taxes paid is critical and the cash paid of $95 million can be found in the statement of cash flows.

Deferred taxation

Tutorial note

Easy marks can be obtained for outlining the accounting treatment of deferred tax.

Provision for deferred tax is made for temporary differences between the carrying amount of assets and liabilities for financial reporting purposes and their value for tax purposes. The amount of deferred tax reflects the expected recoverable amount and is based on the expected manner of recovery or settlement of the carrying amount of assets and liabilities, using the basis of taxation enacted or substantively enacted by the financial statement date.

Deferred tax assets are not recognised where it is more likely than not that the assets will not be realised in the future. The evaluation of deferred tax assets' recoverability requires judgements to be made regarding the availability of future taxable income.

Management assesses the available evidence to estimate if sufficient future taxable income will be generated to use the existing deferred tax assets. A significant piece of objective negative evidence evaluated was the loss incurred in the period prior to the period ended 30 November 20X7. Such objective evidence may limit the ability to consider other subjective evidence such as projections for future growth.

Deferred taxes are one of the most difficult areas of the financial statements for investors to understand. Thus there is a need for a clear explanation of the deferred tax balances and an analysis of the expected timing of reversals. This would help investors see the time period over which deferred tax assets arising from losses might reverse. It would be helpful if the company provided a breakdown of which reversals would have a cash tax impact and which would not.

Application of deferred tax rules to Holls

As the proposed tax law was approved, it is considered to be enacted. Therefore, the rate of 25% should be used to calculate the deferred tax liability associated with the relevant items which affect deferred taxation.

Tutorial note

Use the information in the question to calculate the deferred tax balances.

At 30 November 20X7, Holls has deductible temporary differences of \$4.5 million which are expected to reverse in the next year. In addition, Holls also has taxable temporary differences of \$5 million which relate to the same taxable company and the tax authority. Holls expects \$3 million of those taxable temporary differences to reverse in 20X8 and the remaining \$2 million to reverse in 20X9. Thus a deferred tax liability of \$1.25 million (\$5 million × 25%) should be recognised and as \$3 million of these taxable temporary differences are expected to reverse in the year in which the deductible temporary differences reverse, Holls can also recognise a deferred tax asset for \$0.75 million (\$3 million × 25%). The recognition of a deferred tax asset for the rest of the deductible temporary differences will depend on whether future taxable profits sufficient to cover the reversal of this deductible temporary difference are expected to arise. An entity is permitted to offset deferred tax assets and deferred tax liabilities if there is a legally enforceable right to offset the current tax assets against current tax liabilities as the amounts relate to income tax levied by the same taxation authority on the same taxable entity.

After the enactment of a new tax law, when material, Holls should consider disclosing the anticipated current and future impact on their results of operations, financial position, liquidity, and capital resources. In addition, Holls should consider disclosures in the critical accounting estimates section of the management commentary to the extent the changes could materially affect existing assumptions used in making estimates of tax-related balances. Changes in tax laws and rates may affect recorded deferred tax assets and liabilities and the effective tax rate in the future.

Marking guide

			Marks
(a)	(i)	– arguments for and against the non-binding framework	4
	(ii)	– a discussion of understandability, relevance and comparability	3
		– application of the above characteristics to MC	2
			5
(b)		– an explanation of why taxable profits are different from accounting profit	2
		– application of the following explanations to the scenario:	
		tax reconciliation	4
		tax rates	3
		deferred taxation	5
			14
	Professional marks		2
Total			**25**

Examiner's comments

There were a range of answers available to the first part of the question and candidates were given due credit if they were able to justify their conclusions. Many candidates did not actually answer the requirement but instead simply described a management commentary or defined the qualitative characteristics. They did this without applying their knowledge to the preparation of the management commentary. Due credit was given to this type of answer but of course, full marks cannot be awarded unless the question set is actually answered.

The second part of the question caused some candidates concern and yet it was well answered. The syllabus area requires candidates to demonstrate synthesis and evaluation and not simply factual knowledge. The model answer sets out significantly more than was required to gain a good mark. Likewise, candidates were also awarded marks for points raised which were not included in the model answer. By their nature, questions on an investor perspective are going to produce variations in answers because investors have many different perspectives and may even require different information from that provided in the financial statements.

47 SKIZER (SEP 2018)  *Walk in the footsteps of a top tutor*

Key answer tips

The *Conceptual Framework* is an important topic in the SBR syllabus. You need to learn its contents but also practise applying it to each of the examinable IFRS and IAS Standards.

The SBR syllabus requires you to be able to discuss the current framework for integrated reporting, including the objectives, concepts, guiding principles and content of an integrated report. Do not neglect this popular exam topic.

(a) (i) IAS 38 recognition criteria

Tutorial note

You should know the recognition criteria in all of the examinable IFRS and IAS Standards. This is core knowledge.

IAS 38 *Intangible Assets* defines an intangible asset as a non-monetary asset without physical substance. It requires an entity to recognise an intangible asset if:

- it is probable that expected future economic benefits will flow to the entity, and
- the cost of the asset can be measured reliably.

This requirement applies whether an intangible asset is acquired externally or generated internally. The probability of future economic benefits must be based on reasonable and supportable assumptions about conditions which will exist over the life of the asset. The probability recognition criterion is always considered to be satisfied for intangible assets which are acquired separately or in a business combination.

If the recognition criteria are not met, IAS 38 requires the expenditure to be expensed when it is incurred.

Conceptual Framework

Tutorial note

The Conceptual Framework was revised in 2018. Make sure that your knowledge here is up-to-date. The current definitions of assets and liabilities make no reference to the probability of economic inflows or outflows.

According to the *Conceptual Framework,* items are only recognised if they meet the definition of an element. The definition of an asset is **'a present economic resource controlled by an entity as a result of a past event'** (para 4.3).

This does not mean that all items meeting the definition of an element are recognised. An element is only recognised if recognition provides users with useful financial information. In other words recognition must provide:

- relevant information
- a faithful representation of the asset or liability, and resulting income, expenses or equity movements.

Recognition might not provide relevant information if there is uncertainty over the existence of the element or if there is a low probability of an inflow or outflow of economic resources. Recognition of an element might not provide a faithful representation if there is a very high degree of measurement uncertainty.

Consistency

As can be seen, the recognition criteria in the *Conceptual Framework* and IAS 38 are different. This is because the recognition criteria in IAS 38 were based on previous versions of the *Conceptual Framework*, and have not been updated to reflect the 2018 *Conceptual Framework.*

Tutorial note

The recognition criteria in many other IFRS and IAS Standards are also based on the previous version of the Conceptual Framework. The Board may revise these standards in the future.

Both IAS 38 and the *Conceptual Framework* attempt to ensure that financial statements provide information that meets the qualitative characteristics of useful information but do this in different ways. IAS 38 uses practical filters of probability and reliability to exclude information that will not be useful. In contrast, the *Conceptual Framework* refers directly to the qualitative characteristics, and provides guidance on how to apply them.

The *Conceptual Framework* does not override IAS 38. The *Conceptual Framework* is only applied by preparers of financial statements when no standard applies to a particular transaction. Transactions involving intangible assets fall within the scope of IAS 38 and so the recognition criteria in this standard will be applied.

Tutorial note

Remember that one of the key purposes of the Conceptual Framework is to assist the Board when developing or revising an IFRS Standard.

(ii) Implications if recognition criteria were met

Tutorial note

Capitalisation is not optional. Expenditure that meets the criteria in IAS 38 must be recognised as an intangible asset, unless the effect is immaterial.

Skizer should have assessed whether the recognition criteria in IAS 38 were met at the time the entity capitalised the intangible assets. If the recognition criteria were met, then it was not appropriate to derecognise the intangible assets. According to IAS 38, an intangible asset should be derecognised only on disposal or when no future economic benefits are expected from its use or disposal.

If there were any doubts regarding the recoverability of the intangible asset, then Skizer should have assessed whether the intangible assets would be impaired. IAS 36 *Impairment of Assets* would be used to determine whether an intangible asset is impaired.

Further, the reclassification of intangible assets to research and development costs does not constitute a change in an accounting estimate. IAS 8 *Accounting Policies, Changes in Accounting Estimates and Errors* states that a change in accounting estimate is an adjustment of the carrying amount of an asset or liability, or related expense, resulting from reassessing the expected future benefits and obligations associated with that asset or liability. The costs of the stakes in the development projects can be determined and will not have been estimated.

Implications if recognition criteria were not met

Tutorial note

If a mistake was made on initial recognition, then this would constitute a prior period error.

If it is believed that the transactions never met the recognition criteria in IAS 38 then Skizer would have to recognise retrospectively a correction of an error, in accordance with IAS 8.

(iii) Sale of intangible

Revenue is defined in IFRS 15 *Revenue from Contracts with Customers* as income arising from a company's ordinary activities.

There is no indication that Skizer's business model is to sell development projects. Skizer's business model is to jointly develop a product, then leave the production to partners. Moreover, if the asset was for sale in the ordinary course of business then it would have been classified on acquisition as inventory. Skizer recognised an intangible asset, and fully impaired the asset, so it cannot argue that it has thereafter been held for sale in the ordinary course of business.

Tutorial note

Intangible assets are non-current assets. If an asset is held for sale in the ordinary course of business then, per IAS 1 Presentation of Financial Statements, it is presented as a current asset (most likely as inventories).

Furthermore, IAS 38 prohibits presenting the proceeds from the disposal of an intangible asset as revenue.

(b) (i) Issues with intangible assets acquired in a business combination

Tutorial note

This is a tricky requirement, but you are not expected to answer in the same level as detail as the model answer below. Seven separate points across the three issues would be sufficient to score full marks.

Under IFRS 3 *Business Combinations*, acquired intangible assets must be recognised and measured at fair value if they are separable or arise from other contractual rights. Once recognised, IAS 38 requires intangible assets with finite lives to be amortised over their useful lives and intangible assets with indefinite lives to be subject to an annual impairment review in accordance with IAS 36.

However, it is unlikely that all intangible assets acquired in a business combination will be homogeneous and investors may feel that there are different types of intangible assets which may be acquired. For example, a patent may only last for a finite period of time and may be thought as having an identifiable future revenue stream. In this case, amortisation of the patent would be logical. However, there are other intangible assets which are gradually replaced by the purchasing entity's own intangible assets, for example, customer lists, and it may make sense to account for these assets within goodwill. In such cases, investors may wish to reverse amortisation charges. In order to decide whether an amortisation charge makes sense, investors require greater detail about the nature of the identified intangible assets. IFRS Standards do not permit a different accounting treatment for this distinction.

Issues with choice in accounting policy

Tutorial note

Remember that measurement choices within IFRS Standards limit comparability because it is harder to compare one entity with another.

IAS 38 requires an entity to choose either the cost model or the revaluation model for each class of intangible asset. Under the cost model, after initial recognition intangible assets should be carried at cost less accumulated amortisation and impairment losses. Under the revaluation model, intangible assets may be carried at a revalued amount, based on fair value, less any subsequent amortisation and impairment losses.

The revaluation model can only be used if there is an active market for the intangible asset. Such active markets are not common for intangible assets.

Tutorial note

An active market is one where identical assets are regularly traded and prices are readily available.

If an intangible asset is reported using the cost model, the reported figures for intangible assets such as trademarks may be understated when compared to their fair values.

Moreover, the ability to choose the revaluation model or the cost model may limit comparability between different entities.

Capitalisation of development expenditure

Tutorial note

In real life, the distinction between 'research' and 'development' may not be clear cut. Moreover, performance related bonuses or stock market pressure may be incentives to classify research expenditure as development.

IAS 38 requires all research costs to be expensed. Development costs must be capitalised if the technical and commercial feasibility of the asset for sale or use has been established.

If an entity cannot distinguish the research phase of an internal project to create an intangible asset from the development phase, the entity treats the expenditure for that project as if it were incurred in the research phase only. This cautious approach ensures that assets are not overstated.

The problem for investors is that companies do not have a consistent approach to capitalisation. It is often unclear from disclosures how research expenditure was distinguished from development expenditure. It may be that entities allow bias to impact their decision-making in this area.

Intangible asset disclosure can help analysts understand the innovation capacity of companies. Investors can use the disclosure to identify companies with valuable development assets – once these launch in the market they should generate economic benefits, potentially increasing investment returns. However, preparers of financial statements are failing to adequately comply with the disclosure requirements of IAS 38, which limits their usefulness.

(ii) Integrated reporting

Tutorial note

An integrated report communicates an entity's value creation in the short, medium, and long-term. It conceptualises value in terms of a range of capitals (stocks of value), rather than just in terms of financial capital.

Measuring the contribution of intangible assets to future cash flows is fundamental to integrated reporting. This helps explain the gap between the carrying amount of an entity's net assets and its market equity value.

As set out above, organisations are required to recognise intangible assets acquired in a business combination. Consequently, the intangible assets are only measured once for this purpose. However, organisations are likely to go further in their integrated report and disclose the impact on intangible assets as a result of sustainable growth strategies or specific initiatives. It is therefore very useful to communicate the value of intangible assets in an integrated report. For example, an entity may decide to disclose its assessment of the increase in brand value as a result of a corporate social responsibility initiative.

Marking scheme

			Marks
(a)	(i)	Discussion of recognition criteria	**5**
	(ii)	Derecognition criteria and impairment	2
		Reclassification and estimates	2
		If criteria not met	1
			5
	(iii)	Consideration of Skizer's business model	2
		Application of IFRS 15	2
			4
(b)	(i)	Different types of intangibles	3
		Cost or revaluation	2
		Development or research	2
			7
	(ii)	Measurement in financial statements	2
		Discussion of whether IR can supplement financial statements	2
			4
Total			**25**

Examiner's comments

Candidates should be able to discuss the consistency of the Conceptual Framework with each IFRS that is examined. Part (a)(i) is a good illustration of how candidates can be tested on this. Answers to this section were weak in general.

Answers to part (a)(ii) were generally weak. Some candidates missed that the question specifically referred to the recognition criteria being met, in which case derecognition would be inappropriate. Very few candidates identified the need for an impairment review under IAS 36 *Impairment of Assets* if there were doubts over recoverability from the intangible assets.

Answers to part (b) were generally good, where discussion included the accounting choices and subjective aspects of IAS 38 and IFRS 3. However, some answers limited opportunities for marks by not considering both standards. Part (b)(ii) asked for a discussion on whether integrated reporting can enhance reporting for intangible assets. Whilst many candidates were familiar with integrated reporting, fewer applied it to the situation (relating to intangible assets).

48 TOOBASCO (SEP 2018)  *Walk in the footsteps of a top tutor*

Key answer tips

Additional performance measures (APMs) are increasingly prominent in the financial statements of public limited entities. The SBR syllabus states that students need to be able to discuss and apply APMs. Part (a) of this question should be a source of easy marks because lots of common-sense points can be made.

Part (b) is trickier. Many students dislike statements of cash flows and so would struggle to correct the errors made by Daveed. There are four marks available in part (b) (i) and part (b) (ii) – so you only need to post two correct adjustments on each to score a pass mark. Deal with the easiest adjustments first. If you don't understand an issue then leave it and move on.

(a) APMs

(i) APMs are not defined by International Financial Reporting Standards and therefore may not be directly comparable with other companies' APMs, including those in the same industry. If the same category of material items recurs each year and in similar amounts (in this example, restructuring costs and impairment losses) then the reporting entity should consider whether excluding these amounts from underlying profit provides a faithful representation of economic performance.

Under IFRS Standards, items cannot be presented as 'extraordinary items' in the financial statements or in the notes. Thus it may be confusing to users of the APMs to see this term used.

Tutorial note

Many entities are quick to classify expenses as non-recurring. Relatively few entities classify incomes as 'non-recurring'. Why do you think this is?

Items such as restructuring costs or impairment losses should not be labelled as non-recurring where it is misleading. The entity can make an adjustment for a charge or gain which they believe is appropriate, but they cannot describe such adjustments inaccurately.

(ii) The deduction of capital expenditure, purchase of own shares and the purchase of intangible assets from cash flows from operating activities is acceptable because free cash flow does not have a uniform definition.

A clear description of free cash flow and a reconciliation showing how this measure is calculated should be disclosed so that users can draw conclusions about the usefulness of the APM.

Entities should avoid misleading comments when describing APMs. Free cash flow does not normally represent the residual cash flow available as many entities have mandatory debt service requirements which are not normally deducted from the measure. It would also be misleading to show free cash flow per share in bold alongside earnings per share as they are not comparable.

(iii) When an entity presents an APM, it should present the most directly comparable measure calculated in accordance with IFRS Standards with equal or greater prominence. Whether an APM is more prominent would depend on the facts and circumstances. In this case, the entity has omitted comparable information calculated in accordance with IFRS Standards from an earnings release which includes APMs such as EBITDAR. Additionally, the entity has emphasised the APM measure by describing it as 'record performance' without an equally prominent description any measure calculated in accordance with IFRS Standards. Further, the entity has provided a discussion of the APM measure without a similar discussion and analysis of the IFRS Standards measure.

The entity has presented EBITDAR as a performance measure; such measures should be reconciled to profit for the year as presented in the statement of comprehensive income. Operating profit would not be considered the best starting point as EBITDAR makes adjustments for items which are not included in operating profit such as interest and tax.

Tutorial note

Comparability is an important characteristic of useful financial information. The users of financial statements should be able to compare the financial performance and position of one entity with another. They should also be able to compare the same entity year-on-year.

The entity has changed the way it calculates the APM because it has treated rent differently. However, if an entity chooses to change an APM, the change and the reason for the change should be explained and any comparatives restated. A change would be appropriate only in exceptional circumstances where the new APM better achieves the same objectives, perhaps if there has been a change in the strategy. The revised APM should be reliable and more relevant.

(iv) The entity should provide income tax effects on its APMs depending on the nature of the measures. The entity should include current and deferred income tax expense commensurate with the APM and the APM should not be presented net of tax as income taxes should be shown as a separate adjustment and explained.

(b) **(i)** **Adjustment of net cash generated from operating activities for errors in the statement**

Tutorial note

Label your workings so that the marker can understand the adjustments you have made.

	$m
Draft net cash generated from operations (per question)	278
Cash inflows relating to car disposals	30
Effects of changes in foreign exchange rates	28
Reclassification of interest paid	18
Tax credit not recorded	6
Associate's profit – incorrectly included	(12)
Share of associate's profit – non-cash item that should have been deducted from profit.	(4)
Net cash generated from operating activities	344

(ii) Free cash flow reconciliation

Tutorial note

The question tells you how to calculate operating 'free cash flow'. Make sure you read note (vi) carefully.

In note (iv) we are told that the pension deficit payments are 'exceptional'. It is easy to miss this. Daveed excludes exceptional items when calculating free cash flow.

	$m
Net cash generated from operating activities (part (i))	344
Net capital expenditure	(46)
Purchase of associate (W1)	(20)
Dividend received from associate (25% × $4m)	1
Interest received	10
Interest paid	(18)
Pension deficit payments – add back to exclude	27
Free cash flow	298

(W1) Purchase of associate

	$m
Purchase cost (bal. fig.)	20
Share of profit of associate	4
Dividend received	(1)
Carrying amount as at 31 August 20X8	23

(iii) Explanation of adjustments

Tutorial note

There is only one mark available for each issue. Keep your explanations brief.

Purchase and sale of cars

Daveed's presentation of cash flows from the sale of cars as being from investing activities is incorrect as cash flows from the sale of cars should have been presented as cash flows from operating activities ($30 million). IAS 16 *Property, Plant and Equipment* (PPE) states that an entity which normally sells items of PPE which are held for rental to others should transfer such assets to inventories at their carrying amount when they cease to be rented and become held for sale. Subsequent proceeds from the sale of such assets should be recognised as revenue in accordance with IFRS 15 *Revenue from Contracts with Customers* and thus shown as cash flows from operating activities.

Purchase of associate

Cash paid for the investment is $20 million, and cash received from the dividend is $1 million. In order to arrive at the correct figure for net cash generated from operating activities, the incorrect treatment of the profit for the year for the associate must be eliminated ($12 million) and the correct adjustment of $4 million shown in net cash generated by operating activities.

Foreign exchange losses

IAS 7 *Statement of Cash Flows* states that unrealised gains and losses arising from changes in foreign exchange rates are not cash flows. The amounts reported in the statement of cash flows included, in error, the effect of changes in foreign exchange rates arising on the retranslation of its overseas operations. As a consequence, cash generated from operating activities should be increased by $28 million. All exchange differences relating to the subsidiary are recorded in other comprehensive income and taken to a separate component of equity. On disposal of the foreign operation the gains (or losses) are reclassified to the statement of profit or loss.

Pension payments

The pension payments are correctly included in operating cash flows. However, Daveed excludes them when calculating free cash flow. As the tax cash benefit has not been included, net cash generated from operating activities will be adjusted for the $6 million and $27 million ($33m – $6m) will be excluded from the free cash flow calculation.

Interest paid

Interest paid which is capitalised as part of the cost of property, plant, and equipment should be treated as a cash flow from investing activities. Interest paid and capitalised as part of inventory should be classified within operating activities the statement of cash flows. Thus there should be a reclassification of interest paid of $18 million from the operating section to the investing activities section.

Marking scheme			
			Marks
(a)		Discussion of comparability of APMs	1
		Extraordinary items	2
		Free cash flow	2
		EBITDAR	4
		Tax effects	1
			10
(b)	(i)	Adjustment schedule	**4**
	(ii)	Free cash reconciliation	**4**
	(iii)	Purchase of cars	1
		Purchase of associate	1
		Foreign exchange losses	1
		Pension payments	1
		Interest paid	1
			5
		Professional marks	**2**
Total			**25**

Examiner's comments

It was pleasing to see that part (a) was often well-described, reasoned and applied to the scenario. However, answers to part (b) were more varied.

49 PLAYER TWO

Key answer tips

Part (a) of this question tests management performance measures. This topic appears in the SBR specimen paper 1 (the original pilot paper). Make sure that you have read about their use and legitimacy. Marks are available for general points, as well as for raising specific issues with Player Two's performance measures.

Part (b) requires assessment of a financial statement disclosure. Users of the financial statements want information that is entity specific rather than generic. What else do you think Wrap's investors would want to know about the impairment review?

(a) Management performance measures

IAS 1 *Presentation of Financial Statements* permits entities to disclose additional information that is relevant to understanding an entity's performance and position. The *Conceptual Framework* notes that the primary users of financial statements are investors, lenders and other creditors.

Management performance measures are often used internally when assessing management performance. As such, they can help financial statement users to understand management's view about what is important to the entity. However, there are concerns about their use.

It is commonly argued that management performance measures are used to disguise weak financial performance, which may mislead financial statement users. This criticism might apply to Player Two. Basic earnings per share (EPS) is 2.0 cents per share ($2.5m/122.2m), whereas adjusted basic EPS is more than five times higher.

Management performance measures can be particularly misleading if displayed prominently. This is because they may become indistinguishable from figures produced in accordance with IFRS Standards and therefore obtain unwarranted credibility. Although Player Two does not disclose this performance measure on the face of its primary statements the ordering of disclosure notes is important and the disclosure of this information may still mislead investors as to its nature.

Performance measures that use figures prepared in accordance with IFRS Standards are more likely to be comparable with other entities. Entities may differ markedly when calculating management performance measures. For example, the types of adjustments made by Player Two when calculating adjusted basic EPS may differ from those used by other entities, hindering comparability. One company's performance measures may also not be comparable year-on-year.

Some entities do not reconcile their management performance measures back to the financial statements. However, this criticism does not apply to Player Two. As such, it is possible to assess the adequacy and reasonableness of the adjusting items.

Some users may question the appropriateness of the profit adjustments that Player Two has made to arrive at adjusted basic EPS:

- Although amortisation is a judgemental, non-cash expense, the business may need to replace its intangible assets. This will require investment. Moreover, amortisation of brands should reflect their pattern of use. If brands have a definite useful life then the business will need to incur costs in order to protect its brand positioning and market share.
- Restructuring costs were incurred in both the current and prior periods and so they are not a one-off cost. Excluding these amounts from underlying basic EPS ignores the fact that restructuring is a regular part of Player Two's business.
- The existence of impairment charges suggests that the retail stores have performed poorly and are under-utilised. It also suggests a poor outlook for the business in terms of its future net cash inflows. Eliminating this impairment charge when calculating adjusted basic EPS could be argued to provide an over-optimistic representation of Player Two's current and future performance.

(b) Impairment disclosures

Impairment reviews involve judgement and therefore the users of the financial statements must be provided with enough information to assess whether the assumptions used were reliable.

The disclosure note is lacking key information about many of the judgements used. It is very generic and does not provide information that is specific to Wrap's impairment review.

Cash-generating unit

No information has been provided about how the cash generating unit was determined.

No information has been provided about how goodwill was allocated to the cash generating unit.

Value-in-use

The disclosure note does not describe key assumptions factored into the cash flow forecast and therefore the users cannot assess its reliability. Important assumptions might include estimates of future margins or, if relevant, foreign currency movements.

The disclosure does not say whether the forecasts represent past experience or future expectations. It also does not state whether there is any consistency with external sources of information.

The disclosure note does not say how many years the cash flow forecasts covered. This is important because forecasts that cover a longer period are less likely to be reliable.

The note does not say how many years' worth of cash flows have been extrapolated beyond the end of the budgeted period. The longer this period, the less likely it is that the growth rate will be maintained, due to obsolescence issues or the entrance of new competitors to the market.

The disclosure note does not justify the rate of growth used to extrapolate cash flows beyond the period covered by the cash flow forecasts. This is important because the growth rate used seems unrealistically high, particularly when compared to the current economic climate and the sluggish performance of the industry within which Wrap operates.

The disclosure does not state whether the growth rate used is specific to Unit D. Growth could therefore be over or under-stated.

Wrap have disclosed an average discount rate. They should instead disclose the specific rate used to discount the cash flows of Unit D so that users can assess whether it appears reasonable. The discount rate used should reflect the time value of money and the risks specific to the CGU for which future cash flow estimates have not been adjusted.

Sensitivity

The market capitalisation of Wrap is below its net asset value, suggesting that the market is expecting impairment in value. This would contradict the disclosure, which says that a 'reasonably possible change' would not cause impairment.

Sensitivity analysis would therefore be of use to the users so that they assess the likelihood and impact of potential future impairments.

Marking scheme		
		Marks
(a)	Player Two's performance measures	15
(b)	Impairment disclosure	10
Total		**25**

50 MEHRAN  *Walk in the footsteps of a top tutor*

Key answer tips

Part (a) requires an in-depth knowledge of IFRS 13 *Fair Value Measurement*. As with all narrative based questions, you need to demonstrate both your knowledge of the standard and your ability to apply it to real-life scenarios.

(a) (i) IFRS 13 and non-financial assets

Tutorial note

IFRS 13 Fair Value Measurement says that the fair value of a non-financial asset is based on its 'highest and best use'. This is an important concept. Fair value is also a market-based measurement, rather than one which is entity specific.

IFRS 13 *Fair Value Measurement* requires the fair value of a non-financial asset to be measured based on its highest and best use. This is determined from the perspective of market participants. It does not matter whether the entity intends to use the asset differently.

The highest and best use takes into account the use of the asset which is physically possible, legally permissible and financially feasible. IFRS 13 allows management to presume that the current use of an asset is the highest and best use unless factors suggest otherwise.

Land

If the land zoned for agricultural use is currently used for farming, the fair value should reflect the cost structure to continue operating the land for farming, including any tax credits which could be realised by market participants. Thus the fair value of the land if used for farming would be $5.1 million ($5m + $0.1m).

The agricultural land appears to have an alternative use as market participants have considered its use for residential purposes instead. A use of an asset need not be legal at the measurement date, but it must not be legally prohibited in the jurisdiction.

If used for residential purposes, the value should include all costs associated with changing the land to the market participant's intended use. In addition, demolition and other costs associated with preparing the land for a different use should be included in the valuation. These costs would include the uncertainty related to whether the approval needed for changing the usage would be obtained, because market participants would take that into account when pricing value of the land if it had a different use. Thus the fair value of the land if used for residential purposes would be $5.44 million (($7.4m – $0.2m – $0.3m – $0.1m) × 80%).

In this situation, the presumption that the current use is the highest and best use of the land has been overridden by the market factors which indicate that residential development is the highest and best use. Therefore the fair value of the land would be $5.44 million.

Brand

In the absence of any evidence to the contrary, Mehran should value the brand on the basis of the highest and best use by market participants, even if Mehran intends a different use.

Market participants would not discontinue the brand, because their existing brands are less strong. Instead market participants would continue to use the brand in order to obtain the direct benefits.

Mehran's decision to discontinue the brand is therefore not relevant in determining fair value. As such, the fair value of the brand is $17 million.

(ii) IFRS 13 and financial assets

Tutorial note

This part of the question can be answered well using common-sense. How do Mehran's ordinary shares differ from the preferred shares? What impact will these differences have on their fair value?

IFRS 13 *Fair Value Measurement* states that fair value is a market-based measurement, although it acknowledges that observable market transactions might not be available. Whether or not observable information is available, the aim of IFRS 13 is to estimate the price at which an asset would be sold at in an orderly transaction between market participants at the measurement date.

The market approach takes a transaction price paid for an identical or a similar instrument and adjusts it. Using a market approach, Mehran could take the transaction price for the preferred shares and adjust it to reflect certain differences between the preferred shares and the ordinary shares. For example:

- There would be an adjustment to reflect the priority of the preferred shares upon liquidation.
- Mehran should acknowledge the benefit associated with control. This adjustment relates to the fact that Mehran's individual ordinary shares represent a non-controlling interest whereas the preferred shares issued reflect a controlling interest.
- There will be an adjustment for the lack of liquidity of the investment which reflects the lesser ability of the ordinary shareholder to initiate a sale of Erham relative to the preferred shareholder.
- There will be an adjustment for the cumulative dividend entitlement of the preferred shares. This would be calculated as the present value of the expected future dividend receipts on the preferred shares, less the present value of any expected dividend receipts on the ordinary shares.

Mehran should review the circumstances of the issue of the preferred shares to ensure that its price was a valid benchmark. In addition, Mehran should consider whether there have been changes in market conditions between the issue of the preferred shares and the measurement date.

(b) Accounting for provisions

Tutorial note

The question requires you to explain the accounting treatment of provisions. This should be a source of easy marks.

Provisions are defined in IAS 37 *Provisions, Contingent Liabilities, and Contingent Assets* as liabilities where the timing or the amount of the future outflow is uncertain. A provision is recognised if all of the following criteria are met:

- there is an obligation from a past event
- an outflow of economic resources to settle the obligation is probable
- the outflow of economic resources can be measured reliably.

Provisions should be measured at the best estimate of the economic resources required to settle the obligation. They should be remeasured at each reporting date using the best available information. If the time value of money is material then the provision should be discounted to present value. The discount rate used should reflect risks specific to the liability.

Benefits and limitations

Tutorial note

Imagine you are an investor. What useful information about future cash flows and risks can you get from the disclosure? What other information would you like to know?

Provisions involve uncertainty. Disclosures should provide important information to help users understand the nature of the obligation, the timing of any outflow of economic benefits, uncertainties about the amounts or timing involved, and major assumptions made.

The disclosure note splits the provision between current and non-current liabilities. This helps users of the financial statements assess the timing of the cash outflows and the potential impact on Mehran's overall net cash inflows. It would be useful to provide further information about the expected timing of the outflows classified as a non-current liability.

Financial reporting focusses on past events, but provisions disclosures also provide important information about the future. This disclosure note informs investors about restructuring activities within stores, but also in Finance and IT. Whilst this restructuring will incur costs, investors may value Mehran's efforts to streamline its operations and improve efficiency.

The disclosure shows that provisions, as a total balance, increased year on year. Liabilities always entail risk because there is an obligation to make payments to settle the obligation even if the company has insufficient liquid resources to do so. Provisions might be viewed as particularly risky, because they are estimated and therefore the actual cash outflows required might be significantly higher than estimated. Some investors may be deterred from investing in companies with substantial provisions.

With regards to the refund provision, the amount utilised in the reporting period is less than the provision at the start of the year. This suggests that, in the prior year, management had over-estimated the refund provision. This information may cast doubt on management's ability to accurately estimate its provisions and increase uncertainty regarding Mehran's future cash flows.

Further information could be provided to help users assess the adequacy of the provisions made. Part of the restructuring provision is classified as non-current but no information is provided about discount rates. Very little information is provided about any uncertainties that would impact the measurement of the provision, or the assumptions made. This hinders the ability of the users to assess the adequacy of management's estimates.

Marking scheme			
			Marks
(a)	(i)	Non-financial assets and fair value – 1 mark per point	9
	(ii)	Financial assets and fair value – 1 mark per point	6
(b)		Provisions accounting – 1 mark per point	3
		Benefits and limitations – 1 mark per point	5
		Professional marks	2
Total			**25**

51 CARSOON

Key answer tips

Part (a) of this question requires a good knowledge of IFRS 9 *Financial Instruments* and IFRS 15 *Revenue from Contracts with Customers.* Part (b) examines the accounting implications of a contemporary scenario, and so it falls within the 'current issues' section of the syllabus.

(a) (i) Financial asset

According to IFRS 9 *Financial Instruments,* debt instruments measured at FVOCI are measured at fair value in the statement of financial position. Interest income is calculated using the effective interest rate. Fair value gains and losses on these financial assets are recognised in other comprehensive income (OCI).

Expected credit losses (ECLs) do not reduce the carrying amount of the financial assets, which remains at fair value. Instead, an amount equal to the ECL allowance is recognised in OCI.

When these financial assets are derecognised, the cumulative gains and losses previously recognised in OCI are reclassified from equity to profit or loss.

The fair value of the debt instrument therefore needs to be ascertained at 28 February 20X7. IFRS 13 *Fair Value Measurement* states that Level 1 inputs are unadjusted quoted prices in active markets for identical assets or liabilities which the entity can access at the measurement date. The standard sets out that adjustment to Level 1 prices should not be made except in certain circumstances. It would seem that a Level 1 input is available so there is no reason to use the 'in house' model.

Therefore the accounting for the instrument should be as follows:

- The bonds will be initially recorded at $6 million
- Interest of $0.24 million will be received and credited to profit or loss.
- At 28 February 20X7, the bonds will be valued at $5.3 million. The loss of $0.7 million will be charged as an impairment loss of $0.4 million to profit or loss and $0.3 million to OCI.
- When the bond is sold for $5.3 million on 1 March 20X7, the financial asset is derecognised and the loss in OCI ($0.3 million) is reclassified to profit or loss.

(ii) Revenue recognition

IFRS 15 *Revenue from Contracts with Customers* specifies how to account for costs incurred in fulfilling a contract which are not in the scope of another standard. These are divided into those which give rise to an asset and those which are expensed as incurred. Entities will recognise an asset when costs incurred to fulfil a contract meet certain criteria, one of which is that the costs are expected to be recovered. For costs to meet the 'expected to be recovered' criterion, they need to be either explicitly reimbursable under the contract or reflected through the pricing of the contract and recoverable through the margin.

General and administrative costs cannot be capitalised unless these costs are specifically chargeable to the customer under the contract. Similarly, wasted material costs are expensed where they are not chargeable to the customer. Therefore a total expense of $15 million will be charged to profit or loss and not shown as assets.

A penalty is a form of variable consideration. The penalty payable should be estimated and deducted from the transaction price if it is highly probable that a significant reversal in the amount of revenue recognised will not occur when the uncertainty is resolved.

The construction of the separate storage facility is a distinct performance obligation; the contract modification for the additional storage facility would be, in effect, a new contract which does not affect the accounting for the existing contract. When the contract is modified for the construction of the storage facility, an additional $7 million is added to the consideration which Carsoon will receive. The performance obligation has been satisfied so this revenue can be recognised in full.

(b) Financial reporting implications

The flood has damaged production machinery and caused a decline in production output. Per IAS 36 *Impairment of Assets*, this is an indication of impairment. As such, an impairment review must be performed in which the carrying amount of the assets is compared to the recoverable amount. The recoverable amount is the higher of fair value less costs to sell and value in use. Individual assets do not generate cash flows, so it is likely that the assets will need to be tested as part of the cash generating unit to which they belong. Any impairment of the cash generating unit will be firstly allocated to goodwill and then to other assets in proportion to their carrying amounts. No asset can be impaired below the higher of zero and its recoverable amount. Impairment losses are charged to profit or loss, unless they relate to an asset for which a specific revaluation surplus exists.

According to IAS 2 *Inventories*, inventory must be valued at the lower of cost and net realisable value (NRV). If the damaged inventory cannot be sold then it should be written off entirely and the loss charged to cost of sales in the statement of profit or loss. If the inventory can be fixed and resold then the necessary costs should be factored in when determining NRV.

IAS 37 *Provisions, Contingent Liabilities and Contingent Assets* states that contingent assets are disclosed in the financial statements if economic benefits are probable. As such, Sinkton should disclose information about the insurance claim and an estimate of the proceeds that will be received.

According to IAS 37, recognition of a provision is dependent on the existence of a present obligation arising from a past event. As such, no provision can be recognised for future operating losses. Moreover, a provision cannot yet be recognised for restructuring. This is because, at the reporting date, there is no detailed, formal plan in place and therefore Sinkton does not have a constructive obligation to restructure.

As a result of the flooding, it would seem that the useful life of the building has reduced. The useful life of an asset, per IAS 8 *Accounting Policies, Changes in Accounting Estimates and Errors*, is an accounting estimate. As such, amending the useful life is accounted for prospectively and will lead to higher depreciation charges in profit or loss for the remainder of the current period and in future periods.

Cash flow problems may give rise to going concern uncertainties. IAS 1 *Presentation of Financial Statements* states that going concern uncertainties should be disclosed in the notes to the financial statements.

Marking scheme

			Marks
(a)	(i)	Financial asset – 1 mark per point	8
	(ii)	Revenue – 1 mark per point	7
(b)	Natural disasters – 1 mark per point		10
Total			**25**

52 SKYE

Key answer tips

Part (a) requires a good knowledge of two key topics: classifying a financial instrument as debt or equity, and deferred tax. Part (b) is about the *Conceptual Framework*, which is a fundamental part of the SBR syllabus.

(a) (i) Debt or equity

Tutorial note

This is a very common exam topic. Make sure that you know the definition of a financial liability and are able to apply it. Revisit the Study Text if your knowledge is lacking.

IAS 32 *Financial Instruments: Presentation* states that a financial liability is a contractual obligation to deliver cash or another financial asset to another entity. Equity is any contract which evidences a residual interest in the assets of an entity after deducting all of its liabilities.

In the case of the B shares, Skye has no obligation to transfer cash or another asset to the holders of the instruments. Therefore the B shares should be classed as equity. The fact that Skye has not refused redemption in the past does not cause the B shares to be classified as a liability since this does not create a contractual obligation on Skye.

The preference shares create an obligation for Skye because of the put option clause in the agreement. The fact that Skye may not be in a position to satisfy the put option feature because of insufficient distributable reserves does not negate the fact that Skye has an obligation.

(ii) Deferred tax

Tutorial note

Deferred tax is calculated by comparing the carrying amount of an asset or liability with its tax base. An important first step is therefore to calculate the carrying amount of the property at the reporting date. Remember that the overseas property is a non-monetary item and so is initially translated into the functional currency of Skye at the historic rate and is not retranslated.

According to IAS 12 *Income Taxes*, deferred tax is accounted for on temporary differences between the financial reporting treatment of a transaction and the tax treatment.

The property of the overseas branch is written down at different rates in the financial statements than it is for tax purposes, giving rise to a temporary difference. A temporary difference may also arise if the carrying amounts of the non-monetary assets of the overseas branch are translated at different rates to the tax base.

The property is a non-monetary asset and so, according to IAS 21 *The Effects of Changes in Foreign Exchange Rates*, is translated into Skye's functional currency using the historic rate and is not retranslated. This means that the asset would initially be recorded at $1.2 million (D6m/5).

IAS 16 *Property, Plant and Equipment* requires that the asset is depreciated over its useful life. The carrying amount of the asset at the reporting date is therefore $1.1 million ($1.2m × 11/12).

The tax base of the property at the reporting date is D5.25 million (D6m × 7/8). If translated at the closing rate, this gives $0.875 million (D5.25m/6).

There is a taxable temporary difference of $0.225 million ($1.1m – $0.875m). The deferred tax balance will be calculated using the tax rate in the overseas country. The deferred tax liability arising is $45,000 ($0.225m × 20%), which will increase the tax charge in profit or loss.

(b) (i) Prudence

Tutorial note

You should be able to give a definition of prudence for some easy marks.

Prudence is the inclusion of a degree of caution in the exercise of the judgements needed in making the estimates. Prudence is generally taken to mean that assets or income are not overstated and liabilities or expenses are not understated.

Exercising prudence can lead to increased subjectivity in the financial statements, which will affect the evaluation of the entity's performance. Deliberate understatement or deliberate overstatement of the financial statements, even in the name of prudence, is not neutral. Overstating liabilities and expenses in the current period will lead to higher reported profits in the next reporting period. As such, this would not offer a faithful representation of an entity's financial performance and position.

However, to offer a faithful representation, financial statements should be free from bias. Preparers of financial statements have a natural bias towards optimism – often as a result of incentives to report higher profits and/or assets – and therefore prudence might counteract this. Investors are often concerned about financial risk relating to potential losses and so some form of conservatism certainly has a role to play in financial reporting.

(ii) Measurement

Tutorial note

The purpose of financial reporting is to provide information to users that will help them to make decisions about advancing economic resources to an entity. To be useful, the information must embody the fundamental qualitative characteristics.

The *Conceptual Framework* identifies two broad measurement bases: historical cost and current value.

When selecting a measurement base, preparers of the financial statements should ensure that the resulting financial information is as useful as possible to primary user groups. To be useful, financial information must be relevant and it must faithfully represent an entity's underlying transactions.

To maximise relevance, preparers of financial statements should consider the characteristics of the asset or liability they are measuring. In particular, they should consider how the asset contributes to future cash flows, and whether those cash flows are sensitive to market factors.

Depreciated cost is unlikely to provide relevant information about an asset with a volatile market value that will be traded in the short-term. Similarly, reporting an asset or liability at fair value will not provide relevant information if the item is held to collect contractual cash flows.

In order to faithfully represent an entity's transactions, consideration must be given to measurement uncertainty. This arises when estimation techniques are used. If measurement uncertainty is too high then information provided by that measurement basis is unlikely to be useful.

When selecting a measurement basis, preparers of financial statements should consider whether the benefits of the information it provides to the users of the financial statements outweigh the costs providing that information.

Tutorial note

Don't forget about the enhancing qualitative characteristics of useful financial information. These should be maximised where possible.

Consideration should also be given to the enhancing qualitative characteristics of useful financial information. Using the same measurement basis as other entities in the same sector would enhance comparability. Using many difference measurement bases in a set of financial statements reduces understandability. Verifiability is maximised by using measurement bases that can be corroborated.

Marking scheme			
			Marks
(a)	(i)	Debt or equity – 1 mark per point	6
	(ii)	Deferred tax – 1 mark per point	7
(b)	(i)	Prudence – 1 mark per point	6
	(ii)	Selecting a measurement base – 1 mark per point	6
Total			**25**

53 WHITEBIRK

Key answer tips

Part (a) (i) should be relatively straight forward because it tests knowledge from the Financial Reporting paper. However, part (a) (ii) requires knowledge of the differences between full International Financial Reporting Standards and the IFRS for SMEs Standard. Many students neglect this area of the syllabus. All of the examinable content can be found in the Study Text.

You can score relatively well on the practical considerations in part (b) using common sense. The financial statement implications, however, are trickier. Try and refer to specific accounting standards, otherwise your answer is likely to be too generic.

(a) (i) Borrowing costs

IAS 23 *Borrowing Costs* requires borrowing costs incurred when acquiring or constructing an asset to be capitalised if the asset takes a substantial period of time to be prepared for its intended use or sale.

The definition of borrowing costs includes interest expense calculated by the effective interest method, finance charges on leases and exchange differences arising from foreign currency borrowings relating to interest costs.

Borrowing costs should be capitalised during construction and include the costs of funds borrowed for the purpose of financing the construction of the asset, and general borrowings which would have been avoided if the expenditure on the asset had not occurred. The general borrowing costs are determined by applying a capitalisation rate to the expenditure on that asset.

The weighted-average carrying amount of the machine during the period is $3.5 million ($2m + $3m + $4m + $5m) / 4). The capitalisation rate of the borrowings of Whitebirk during the period of construction is 9% per annum. The total amount of borrowing costs to be capitalised is the weighted-average carrying amount of the stadium multiplied by the capitalisation rate. This amounts to $0.1 million ($3.5 million × 9% × 4/12).

(ii) Research and development

According to IAS 38 *Intangible Assets*, research expenditure does not give rise to probable economic benefits and therefore no intangible asset should be recognised. The $1 million research expenditure should be written off to profit or loss.

IAS 38 requires development expenditure to be capitalised as long as certain criteria are met. The project must give rise to probable economic benefits, the entity must have sufficient resources to complete development, and the expenditure incurred must be able to be measurable. Assuming the criteria are met, the $0.5 million expenditure should be capitalised as an intangible asset. The asset should be amortised to profit or loss to reflect its pattern of use by the entity.

SMEs Standard

Borrowing costs

In accordance with the SMEs Standard, borrowing costs are always expensed to the statement of profit or loss. Therefore, none of the borrowing costs incurred as a result of the construction of the machine can be capitalised.

Research and development expenditure

The SMEs Standard states that an entity must recognise expenditure incurred internally on an intangible item, including all expenditure on both research and development activities, as an expense when it is incurred. Thus the expenditure of $1.5 million on research and development would all be written off to profit or loss.

(b) (i) Practical considerations

When implementing a new accounting standard, an entity should prepare an impact assessment and project plan. The entity may need to spend money on training staff, or on updating or replacing its systems. New processes and controls may need to be developed and documented.

New accounting standards will most likely contain new recognition, measurement and disclosure requirements. If the impact of these is not communicated then investors' assessments of how management has discharged its stewardship responsibilities may change and this could affect their investment decisions. As such, management should communicate the impact of a new standard to investors and other stakeholders – particularly if it will result in lower profits or increased liabilities.

Banking agreements often specify maximum debt levels or financial ratios based on figures reported in the financial statements. New financial reporting requirements can affect those ratios, causing potential covenant breaches.

Dividends could be affected. Many jurisdictions have regulations, which restrict the amount which can be paid out in dividends. This restriction is normally based on accounting profits.

The impact of adopting a new IFRS Standard should be communicated to analysts. Some governments use information prepared under IFRS standards for statistical and economic planning purposes.

Competitive advantage could be lost if a new financial reporting standard requires extensive disclosures.

Bonus schemes may need to be re-assessed because the new standard could affect the calculation of performance-related pay.

Financial statement implications

Where there is the introduction of a new accounting standard, the financial statements will need to reflect the new recognition, measurement and disclosure requirements which, in turn, will mean that entities will need to consider the requirements of IAS 8 *Accounting Policies, Changes in Accounting Estimates and Errors*. IAS 8 contains a requirement that changes in accounting policies are fully applied retrospectively unless there are specific transitional provisions contained in the new IFRS Standard being implemented.

IAS 1 *Presentation of Financial Statements* requires a third statement of financial position to be presented if the entity retrospectively applies an accounting policy, restates items, or reclassifies items, and those adjustments had a material effect on the information in the statement of financial position at the beginning of the comparative period.

IAS 33 *Earnings per Share* requires basic and diluted EPS to be adjusted for the impacts of adjustments resulting from changes in accounting policies accounted for retrospectively and IAS 8 requires the disclosure of the amount of any such adjustments.

A change in an accounting standard can change the carrying amounts of assets and liabilities, which will have deferred tax consequences.

(ii) First time adoption of IFRS Standards

IFRS 1 *First-time Adoption of IFRS* says that an entity must produce an opening statement of financial position in accordance with IFRS Standards as at the date of transition. The date of transition is the beginning of the earliest period for which an entity presents full comparative information under IFRS Standards in its first financial statements produced using IFRS Standards.

At the date of transition, the entity must:

- recognise all assets and liabilities required by IFRS Standards
- derecognise assets and liabilities not permitted by IFRS Standards
- reclassify assets, liabilities and equity in accordance with IFRS Standards
- measure assets and liabilities in accordance with IFRS Standards.

Gains or losses arising on the adoption of IFRS Standards at the date of transition should be recognised directly in retained earnings.

Marking scheme		
		Marks
(a)	(i) IAS 23 and IAS 38 – 1 mark per point	8
	(ii) IFRS Standards vs. IFRS for SMEs Standard – 1 mark per point	4
(b)	(i) Practicalities of implementing new IFRS Standards – 1 mark per point	10
	(ii) IFRS 1	3
Total		**25**

54 BUSINESS COMBINATIONS  *Walk in the footsteps of a top tutor*

Key answer tips

The two requirements in part (a) are worth a lot of marks. Broadly speaking, you will be awarded one mark for every valid point that you make. Ensure that you are making enough points to achieve at least a pass mark.

Always thoroughly read the model answer and learn from any mistakes that you made. If you lack the required technical knowledge then revisit the Study Text.

(a) (i) Saag and Aloo

Tutorial note

Should Saag have been accounted for Aloo as a business combination or an asset acquisition? This requires knowledge of the definition of a business per IFRS 3 Business Combinations. State this definition, and then apply it to the information provided in the question.

IFRS 3 *Business Combinations* defines a business as an integrated set of activities and assets that can be managed to provide goods or services, generate investment income (such as dividends or interest), or generate other income from ordinary activities. To meet this definition, the acquisition must comprise inputs and processes that significantly contribute to the **ability** to turn those inputs into outputs. To qualify as a business, outputs are not required.

The Board has introduced an optional concentration test that helps entities to conclude whether an acquisition is not a business. The concentration test is met if substantially all of the fair value of the total assets acquired is concentrated in a single identifiable asset or group of similar identifiable assets.

The optional concentration test is not met because the fair value of the total assets acquired is split between land and buildings, and equipment. These are different classes of PPE.

As such, Saag must engage in a more detailed assessment of whether Aloo constitutes a business.

Aloo does not currently produce outputs. The acquired processes are therefore only substantive if there is a knowledgeable and experienced workforce able to convert other acquired inputs into outputs. Although such a workforce has been transferred, in the absence of inventories or intellectual property this workforce is incapable of producing outputs. As such, the purchase of Aloo does not constitute a business combination and so the proposed treatment is incorrect.

(ii) Bimbi and Lental

Tutorial note

Remember that the acquirer in a business combination is the entity that exercises control. Easy marks can be obtained for stating the definition of control in IFRS 10.

IFRS 3 *Business Combinations* requires an acquirer to be identified in all business combinations. The acquirer is the combining entity which obtains control of the other combined entity.

IFRS 10 *Consolidated Financial Statements* says that an investor controls an investee when it is exposed, or has rights, to variable returns from its involvement with the investee and has the ability to affect those returns through its power over the investee.

Sometimes it is straightforward to assess power by looking at the voting rights obtained. When the parent acquires more than half of the voting rights of the entity, it normally has power if the relevant activities of the investee are directed by a vote.

There is a presumption that an entity achieves control over another entity by acquiring more than one half of the voting rights, unless it can be demonstrated that such ownership does not constitute control.

Tutorial note

In more complicated scenarios, like the one in this question, IFRS 3 sets out further rules for determining the acquirer in a business combination.

You may struggle to remember the rules off by heart. If this is the case, then use your common sense. Which company issued equity in the transaction? Which company is the bigger of the two? Which company seems to control the other? As always, try and reach a justified conclusion.

If the guidance in IFRS 10 does not clearly indicate which of the combining entities is the acquirer then the indicators listed in IFRS 3 should be considered.

The acquirer is usually the entity which transfers cash or other assets. In this scenario, as Bimbi is the entity giving up a cash amount corresponding to 45% of the purchase price, this represents a significant share of the total purchase consideration.

When there is an exchange of equity interests in a business combination, the entity which issues the equity interests is normally the acquirer. In this case, as the majority of the purchase consideration is settled in equity instruments, Bimbi would appear to be the acquirer.

The acquirer is usually the combining entities whose shareholders retain or receive the largest portion of the voting rights in the combined entity. The shareholders of Bimbi, the smaller of the two combining entities, appear to have obtained control since their share amounts to 51% of the voting rights after the transaction. A controlling ownership, however, does not necessarily mean that the entity has the power to govern the combined entity's financial and operating policies so as to obtain benefits from its activities.

Additionally, the acquirer could be deemed to be the entity whose owners have the ability to appoint or remove a majority of the members of the governing body of the combined entity. Five out of six members of the board here are former board members of Bimbi, which again suggests that Bimbi is the acquirer.

Additionally, the acquirer could be deemed the entity whose former management dominates the management of the combined entity. However, the management team consists of the COO plus two former employees of Lental as compared to two former employees of Bimbi. Therefore, the former management of Lental has a greater representation. Although the board nominates the management team, the COO will have significant influence through his share ownership and the selection of the team.

IFRS 3 also says that the acquirer is often the larger entity. As the fair value of Lental ($90 million) is significantly greater than Bimbi ($70 million), this would point towards Lental as the acquirer.

The arguments supporting Bimbi or Lental as the acquirer are finely balanced and therefore it is difficult to identify an acquirer in this case. It can be argued that Bimbi can be identified as the acquirer, on the basis that:

- Bimbi issued the equity interest
- Bimbi is the entity transferring the cash or other assets and
- Bimbi has the marginal controlling interest (51%).

(b) Kata

Tutorial note

You have enough information to calculate the impact that consolidating Kata, or using the equity method, would have on the consolidated financial statements.

Subsidiary

If accounted for as a subsidiary:

- The assets, liabilities, incomes and expenses of Kata would be consolidated in full.
- Goodwill of $1.92 million (W1) would be recognised.
- The group would recognise its share of Kata's post-acquisition retained earnings. This amounts to $0.27 million (45% × ($2m – ($2.4m – $1.0m)).
- The group would recognise a non-controlling interest in respect of Kata of $1.65 million (W2).

Associate

If accounted for as an associate, the investment in Kata at the year-end would be carried at $3.27 million (W3).

In the statement of profit or loss, the group would show its share of Kata's profit of $0.27 million (W3).

Comparison of impact

Tutorial note

Don't just calculate figures. Make sure that you explain and compare the likely impact of the classification decision on the users' perceptions of the consolidated financial statements.

Assets

Consolidating Kata would lead to a higher non-current asset position than if equity accounting was used (PPE of $14 million and goodwill of $1.92 million compared with an investment in the associate of $3.27 million).

This will make the group look more asset rich, which may help it to raise finance in the future.

However, consolidating Kata's large PPE balance may have a detrimental impact on the group's non-current asset turnover, thus making the group look less efficient at generating profits.

Liabilities

Consolidating the loans of Kata may have a negative impact on the group's gearing ratio. This may have the effect of making the group look riskier than if equity accounting was used. A higher gearing ratio may make it harder for the group to raise finance in the future.

Profit or loss

Consolidating the incomes and expenses of Kata line by line will impact key profit or loss figures, such as revenue, gross profit and profit from operations. Increased revenues will make the group's market share look more impressive.

Kata is profitable so consolidating its results will improve the group's profit from operations. This may have a positive impact on investor perception.

If Kata was accounted for using the equity method, the group would simply shows its share of Kata's profits as a single line below profit from operations. This would therefore have no impact (positive or negative) on the group's operating profit.

Workings

Tutorial note

Always show your workings.

(W1) Goodwill

	$m
Consideration	3.0
NCI at acquisition (55% × $2.4m)	1.32
Fair value of net assets at acquisition	(2.40)
Goodwill	1.92

(W2) Non-controlling interest

	$m
NCI at acquisition	1.32
NCI % of post-acq'n net assets 55% × ($3m – $2.4m)	0.33
	1.65

(W3) Investment in associate

	$m
Cost	3.0
Group % of post-acq'n P/L 45% × ($2m – ($2.4m – $1.0m))	0.27
	3.27

Note: The same answer could be obtained by taking the group's share of the post-acquisition movement in the associate's net assets (equivalent to the movement in its share capital and retained earnings).

Marking scheme

			Marks
(a)	(i)	Business combinations – 1 mark per point	7
	(ii)	Identifying the acquirer – 1 mark per point	8
(b)		Comparison of consolidation and equity accounting – 1 mark per point	8
		Professional marks	2
Total			**25**

55 MARGIE  *Walk in the footsteps of a top tutor*

Key answer tips

This is a multi-part question which focuses upon application of IFRS 2 *Share-based Payment*. Each part is self-contained, so can be answered in the order you prefer. Remember to clearly identify which part you are answering, particularly if you are answering them out of order. The marks attributable for each part of the question give a good indication of how to allocate your time.

(a) (i) Share-appreciation rights

Tutorial note

There are key differences between the accounting treatment of cash-settled share-based payments and equity-settled share-based payments. Make sure that you learn the rules thoroughly.

The scope of IFRS 13

IFRS 13 *Fair Value Measurement* applies when another IFRS or IAS Standard requires or permits fair value measurements or disclosures about fair value measurements. IFRS 13 specifically excludes transactions covered by certain other standards including share-based payment transactions within the scope of IFRS 2 *Share-based Payment*.

Thus share-based payment transactions are scoped out of IFRS 13.

Accounting for the SARs

Tutorial note

The question asks you to 'advise'. Lots of students jump straight into calculations – don't forget the words!

For cash settled share-based payment transactions, the entity should recognise an expense and liability as service is rendered. The fair value of the liability is measured at each reporting date. Any changes in fair value are recognised in profit or loss in the period.

Tutorial note

Show all workings. This will help you to score marks even if you make a mistake.

The SARs would have been accounted for during the vesting period as follows:

Year	Expense	Liability	Calculation
	$	$	
30 April 20X3	641,250	641,250	(300 × 95%) × 500 × $9 × ½
30 April 20X4	926,250	1,567,500	(300 × 95%) × 500 × $11

Until the liability is settled, the entity must re-measure the fair value of the liability at the end of each reporting period and at the date of settlement, with any changes in fair value recognised in profit or loss for the period.

	$
Liability 1 May 20X4	1,567,500
Cash paid (60 × 500 × $10.50)	(315,000)
Expense (bal. fig.)	97,500
Liability 30 April 20X5 ((285 – 60) × 500 × $12)	1,350,000

The fair value of the liability would be $1,350,000 at 30 April 20X5 and the expense for the year would be $97,500.

(ii) Share transactions

Tutorial note

This part of the question contains two separate transactions – one with shareholders and one with a supplier. Ensure that you address both issues in turn.

A share-based payment is when an entity receives goods or services in exchange for equity instruments or cash based on the value of equity instruments

The shares issued to the employees were issued in their capacity as shareholders and not in exchange for their services. The employees were not required to complete a period of service in exchange for the shares. Thus the transaction is outside the scope of IFRS 2 *Share-based Payment*.

As regards to Grief, Margie approached the company with the proposal to buy the building in exchange for shares. As such the transaction comes under IFRS 2. Grief is not an employee so the transaction will be recorded at the value of the goods received. This means that the building is recognised at its fair value and equity will be credited with the same amount.

(iii) Wheat contract

Tutorial note

Determine whether or not the transaction falls within the scope of IFRS 2. If not, explain why not and then continue by discussing the required accounting treatment.

The arrangement is not within the scope of IFRS 2 *Share-based Payment* because Margie is not expecting to take delivery of the wheat.

This contract is within the scope of IFRS 9 *Financial Instruments* because it can be settled net and was not entered into for the purpose of the receipt or delivery of the item in accordance with the entity's expected purchase, sale, or usage requirements.

The contract is a derivative because it meets the following criteria:

- Its value changes compared to an underlying item
- It required no, or a low, initial investment
- It is settled in the future

Tutorial note

Don't stop your answer once you've concluded that the contract is a derivative. Make sure that you explain how derivatives are initially and subsequently measured.

IFRS 9 *Financial Instruments* requires derivatives to be measured at fair value through profit or loss, unless the entity applies hedge accounting.

The contract will be initially recognised at fair value. This will probably be nil as, under the terms of a commercial contract, the value of 2,500 shares should equate to the value of 350 tonnes of wheat.

Derivatives are remeasured to fair value at each reporting date, with the gain or loss reported in the statement of profit or loss. The fair value will be based on the values of wheat and Margie shares. The fair value gain or loss should be recorded in the statement of profit or loss.

(b) Share-based payment

Tutorial note

Start with the definition of an 'expense'.

The *Conceptual Framework* defines an expense as a decrease in economic benefits that result in decreases in equity (other than those related to distributions to equity participants).

In the case of a cash-settled share-based payment, the entity has an obligation to pay cash in the future. This therefore meets the definition of an expense.

However, in the case of an equity-settled share-based payment, the entity is providing equity as payment for the good or service received. There is no apparent reduction in an asset or increase in a liability in accordance with the definition of an expense. In fact, an equity-settled share-based payment has no net impact on equity (expenses reduce retained earnings, but the other side of the transaction increases other components of equity). Although IFRS 2 *Share-based Payment* requires the recognition of an expense for equity-settled schemes, it can be argued that this is not in accordance with the definitions in the *Conceptual Framework*.

The Board refute the above. They argue that employee service is an asset that is received by the reporting entity but then simultaneously consumed. In other words, in accordance with the definition of an expense, there is a decrease in the assets of the reporting entity.

Non-refundable deposits

Tutorial note

Start with the definition of a 'liability'.

The *Conceptual Framework* defines a liability as a present obligation from a past event to transfer an economic resource.

In this example, there is no obligation to repay the cash because the deposit is non-refundable. Some commentators believe that the deposit amount should therefore be recognised immediately as income.

Nonetheless, the seller has an obligation to transfer the related goods or services to the customer. These goods or services are economic resources because they have the potential to produce economic benefits. As such, a non-refundable deposit received would seem to meet the definition of a liability.

That said, it can be argued that the liability to transfer goods or services should be recognised at the cost to the entity of providing these, rather than the price that was charged to the customer.

Internally generated brands

Tutorial note

This part is about the recognition of an asset. Therefore state the definition of an asset and the principles that govern the recognition of elements in the financial statements.

The *Conceptual Framework* defines an asset as a resource controlled by an entity as a result of a past event. Brands, whether internally generated or purchased, meet the definition of an asset. This is because they are controlled by the entity, normally through trademarks, and they have the potential to bring economic resources.

The *Conceptual Framework* says that items are recognised in the financial statements if recognition provides relevant information and a faithful representation of the underlying transaction. Recognition of a brand in the financial statements would most likely provide relevant information. Non-recognition arguably understates the financial value of the reporting entity to the primary users of the financial statements. However, the cost of an internally generated brand cannot be measured reliably because brand expenditure cannot be differentiated from the day-to-day operating costs of the business. This measurement uncertainty means that it is not possible to represent the brand faithfully in the financial statements.

The prohibition in IAS 38 on recognising internally generated brands would appear to be consistent with the *Conceptual Framework*.

Marking scheme

			Marks
(a)	(i)	Share appreciation rights – 1 mark per point	6
	(ii)	Share transactions – 1 mark per point	5
	(iii)	Wheat contract – 1 mark per point	7
(b)	Conceptual Framework – 1 mark per point		7
Total			**25**

56 KAYTE

Key answer tips

Broadly speaking, you will be awarded one mark for every valid point that you make. Ensure that you are making enough points to achieve at least a pass mark.

As always, make sure that you thoroughly debrief the answer and learn from any mistakes that you made.

(a) Vessels

Residual values

IAS 16 *Property, Plant and Equipment* defines residual value as the estimated amount which an entity would currently obtain from disposal of the asset, after deducting the estimated costs of disposal, if the asset were already at the age and in the condition expected at the end of its useful life. IAS 16 requires the residual value to be reviewed at least at the end of each financial year end. If the estimated residual value is higher than an asset's carrying amount then no depreciation is charged.

Vessels with 10 year useful life

Kayte's calculation of the residual value of the vessels with a 10-year useful life is not acceptable under IAS 16 *Property, Plant and Equipment*. Undesirable volatility is not a convincing argument to support the use of a residual value equivalent to half of the acquisition cost. The residual value should be the value at the reporting date as if the vessel were already of the age and in the condition expected at the end of its useful life. Kayte should prepare a new model to determine residual value which would take account of broker valuations at the end of each reporting period.

Vessels with 30 year useful life

As regards the vessels which are kept for the whole of their economic life, a residual value based upon the scrap value of steel is acceptable. Therefore the vessels should be depreciated based upon the cost less the scrap value of steel over the 30-year period.

When major planned maintenance work is to be undertaken, the cost should be capitalised. The engine overhaul will be capitalised as a new asset which will then be depreciated over the 10-year period to the next overhaul. The depreciation of the original capitalised amount will typically be calculated such that it had a carrying amount of nil when the overhaul is undertaken.

This is not the case with one vessel, because work was required earlier than expected. In this case, any remaining carrying amount of the old engine and overhaul cost should be expensed immediately.

Funnels

The initial carve out of components should include all major maintenance events which are likely to occur over the economic life of the vessel. Sometimes, it may subsequently be found that the initial allocation was insufficiently detailed, in that not all components were identified. This is the case with the funnels. In this situation it is necessary to determine what the carrying amount of the component would currently be had it been initially identified. This will sometimes require the initial cost to be determined by reference to the replacement cost and the associated accumulated depreciation charge determined using the rate used for the vessel. This is likely to leave a significant carrying amount in the component being replaced, which will need to be written off at the time the replacement is capitalised.

(b) (i) Selection of KPIs

The Integrated Reporting Framework does not specify which KPIs should be disclosed, or how they should be disclosed, but instead leaves this to management judgement. However, the Integrated Reporting Framework does identify characteristics of useful quantitative indicators.

KPIs should be focussed on matters that management have identified as material. They should be consistent with the KPIs used internally by management.

KPIs should be presented with comparative figures so that users of the <IR> can appreciate trends. Targets should also be disclosed, as well as projections for future periods.

The KPIs selected should be consistent with those used within the industry in which the entity operates.

The same KPIs should be reported each period, unless they are no longer material. KPIs should be calculated in a consistent manner in each reporting period.

Qualitative information and discussion is required to add context to KPIs, such as the assumptions used and the reasons for significant trends.

(ii) Interpretation of KPIs

Tutorial note

Imagine that you are a user of Kayte's <IR> – what conclusions might you draw? There are no right or wrong answers here. You will score one mark for every sensible point that you make. Make sure that you say at least seven different things.

The average employee salary has risen by 1.2%. This is less than the rate of inflation. Although the statistic could be skewed by high earners, it suggests that employees are earning less in real terms than they were a year ago.

Despite this, revenue per employee has increased by 14%. This suggests that there have been large scale measures to improve efficiency. There may be many reasons for this increase, such as technological changes, or new contracts. However, when combined with the small year-on-year pay increase, this extra workload could cause employee dissatisfaction.

The KPIs on sick days corroborate the above. Sick days per employee have increased by 133.3%. This may be suggestive of high levels of stress, potentially caused by the dramatic rise in efficiency, or simply the fact that many employees are not enjoying their jobs. Employee turnover has increased, and it is now in excess of the industry average. Once again, this may suggest dissatisfaction with pay or working conditions. It may be that Kayte's competitors offer more attractive employment terms.

Kayte is reliant on a skilled workforce, but the KPIs suggest that it needs to take measures to reduce absenteeism and to improve employee retention. Kayte appears to be losing a large number of its staff, which is ultimately not sustainable. A lack of experienced staff in the business will have a detrimental impact on the quality of the service provided by Kayte and a negative impact on its reputation. Users of the <IR> may therefore be pessimistic about Kayte's long-term prospects.

Marking scheme			
			Marks
(a)	Vessels– 1 mark per point		11
(b)	(i)	Selection of KPIs – 1 mark per point	4
	(ii)	Interpretation of KPIs – 1 mark per point	8
	Professional marks		2
Total			**25**

57 VERGE  *Walk in the footsteps of a top tutor*

Key answer tips

This question covers a number of different standards that are commonly examined. It is vital that you learn these thoroughly. Make sure that you state the relevant accounting rules for easy marks, before applying them to the information in the scenario.

(a) (i) Operating segments

Tutorial note

IFRS 8 Operating Segments is a standard applicable to listed entities. Its aim is to increase the usefulness of the information provided to the users by disaggregating the highly summarised information provided in the primary financial statements.

Even if you do not have a detailed knowledge of this standard, you should still be able to reach a sensible conclusion as to whether or not segments 1 and 2 should be aggregated.

IFRS *8 Operating Segments* states that reportable segments are those operating segments or aggregations of operating segments for which segment information must be separately reported. Aggregation of one or more operating segments into a single reportable segment is permitted (but not required) where certain conditions are met, the principal condition being that the operating segments should have similar economic characteristics. The segments must be similar in each of the following respects:

- the nature of the products and services
- the nature of the production processes
- the type or class of customer
- the methods used to distribute their products or provide their services
- the nature of the regulatory environment.

Segments 1 and 2 have different customers. The decision to award or withdraw a local train contract rests with the transport authority and not with the end customer, the passenger. In contrast, the decision to withdraw from a route in the inter-city train market would normally rest with Verge but would be largely influenced by the passengers' actions that would lead to the route becoming economically unviable. In view of the fact that the segments have different customers, the two segments do not satisfy the aggregation criteria above.

In the local train market, contracts are awarded following a competitive tender process, and, consequently, there is no exposure to passenger revenue risk. The ticket prices paid by passengers are set by a transport authority and not Verge. By contrast, in the inter-city train market, ticket prices are set by Verge and its revenues are, therefore, the fares paid by the passengers travelling on the trains. In this set of circumstances, the company is exposed to passenger revenue risk. This risk would affect the two segments in different ways but generally through the action of the operating segment's customer.

Therefore the economic characteristics of the two segments are different and so they should be reported as separate segments.

(ii) Revenue recognition

Tutorial note

If a customer is provided with a significant financing benefit, revenue is calculated by discounting the consideration receivable to present value.

Make sure that you pay careful attention to dates in this question. This is important for the discounting calculations as well as for determining that a prior period error has occurred.

Maintenance services are simultaneously received and consumed. According to IFRS 15 *Revenue from Contracts with Customers,* this means that revenue should be recognised over time based on progress towards the satisfaction of the performance obligation. Thus Verge must recognise revenue as work is performed throughout the contract life.

The length of time between the transfer of the promised services and the payment date suggests that there is a significant financing component. The consideration should be discounted to present value using the rate at which the customer could borrow.

In the year ended 31 March 20X2, Verge should have recorded revenue of \$2.6 million (\$1 million + (\$1.8 million × ($1/1.06^2$))). Since Verge has received \$1 million cash, a receivable of \$1.6 million should have been recognised.

In the year ended 31 March 20X3, revenue should be recorded at \$1.13 million (\$1.2 million × (1/1.06)). In addition, the discount on the receivable recognised in the year ended 31 March 20X2 must be unwound. Consequently, there will be interest income of \$96,000 (\$1.6 million × 6%).

Prior period error

Tutorial note

Students often miss prior period errors. Pay careful attention to dates.

Prior period errors are omissions from, and misstatements in, the entity's financial statements for one or more prior periods arising from a failure to use, or misuse of, reliable information that:

- was available when financial statements for those periods were authorised for issue, and
- could reasonably be expected to have been obtained and taken into account in the preparation and presentation of those financial statements.

Such errors include mathematical mistakes, mistakes in applying accounting policies and fraud. The fact that Verge only included $1 million of the revenue in the financial statements for the year ended 31 March 20X2 is a prior period error.

Verge should correct the prior period error retrospectively. In the financial statements for the year ended 31 March 20X3, the comparative amounts for the prior period should be restated.

(b) Proposed financing

Tutorial note

Start of by explaining the accounting treatment of these transactions. Will they impact profit? Will these instruments be classified as debt, or equity, or both?

Ordinary shares

Ordinary shares do not create a contractual obligation to deliver cash or another financial asset. As such, per IAS 32 *Financial Instruments: Presentation*, they are classified as equity on the statement of financial position. If equity increases then the gearing ratio will improve, which may make Verge's financing structure look less risky to its investors.

Dividends paid on equity shares have no impact on profits because they are charged directly to retained earnings. Dividends are, in substance, the distribution of the entity's profits to its shareholders.

Issuing equity shares will increase the number of ordinary shares in the basic earnings per share calculation. If the entity is not able to grow its profits then basic earnings per share may fall year-on-year. Investors might perceive this negatively because it is an indication that their future dividend returns will fall.

Convertible bonds

A bond that is redeemed in the form of cash or a fixed number of the entity's own equity shares has characteristics of debt and equity. According to IAS 32 *Financial Instruments: Presentation,* the issuer should 'split' the bond into a liability component and an equity component. The liability component is calculated by taking the cash repayments and discounting them to present value using the rate on a similar non-convertible bond. The difference between the cash proceeds and the liability component on the issue date is classified as equity.

The liability component is normally much larger than the equity component. As such, the issue of the bond is likely to make the gearing ratio deteriorate, increasing investors' perception of risk. This is because liabilities necessitate mandatory repayments, whereas equity does not.

If the convertible bond is issued then an annual Interest expense will be charged to profit or loss. This interest is calculated by applying the effective rate of interest to the liability component. Interest expenses are charged to the statement of profit or loss and so will reduce profits and basic earnings per share. However, whilst in issue, the convertible bonds have no impact on the number of shares used in the basic earnings per share calculation.

Most convertible bonds are dilutive instruments. This is because the entity has a commitment to issue ordinary shares in the future. The maximum number of shares that Verge may issue to redeem the convertible bonds should be included in the diluted earnings per share calculation. Moreover, the earnings figure used in the calculation should be increased by the current year interest on the bond because this will not be charged after redemption.

The disclosure of diluted earnings per share warns current and potential investors that earnings per share will fall when the convertible bond is redeemed. If investors are concerned about the potential drop, and the impact this may have on their investment returns, then they may decide to invest in other companies.

Marking scheme			
			Marks
(a)	(i)	Segment reporting – 1 mark per point	7
	(ii)	Revenue explanation and calculation – 1 mark per point	7
(b)		Finance and impact on financial statements	9
		Professional marks	2
Total			**25**

58 ARON

Key answer tips

This question tests financial instruments. This is a topic that students struggle with so make sure you have thoroughly studied Chapter 12 in the Study Text. Remember that marks are awarded for stating the relevant principles from the relevant accounting standards. Even if you struggle with the calculations for the convertible bond, you would still score solid marks for describing the correct accounting treatment.

(a) Convertible bond

Some financial instruments have both a liability and an equity component. In this case, IAS 32 *Financial Instruments: Presentation* requires that the component parts be accounted for and presented separately according to their substance. The split is made on the issue date.

A convertible bond contains two components:

- a financial liability – the issuer's contractual obligation to pay cash in the form of interest or capital
- an equity instrument – the contract to issue a fixed number of equity shares.

The liability component will be determined by discounting the future cash flows. The discount rate used will be 9%, which is the market rate for similar bonds without the conversion right. The difference between cash received and the liability component is the value of the equity.

	$m
Present value of cash flows	
Year 1 (31 May 20X7) ($100m × 6%) ÷ 1.09	5.50
Year 2 (31 May 20X8) ($100m × 6%) ÷ 1.09^2	5.05
Year 3 (31 May 20X9) ($100m + ($100m × 6%)) ÷ 1.09^3	81.85
Total liability component	92.40
Total equity element	7.60
Proceeds of issue	100.0

The entries required to account for this are:

Dr Cash	$100m
Cr Liability	$92.40m
Cr Equity	$7.60m

The issue cost will have to be allocated between the liability and equity. The entries required are:

Dr Liability	$0.92m
Dr Equity	$0.08m
Cr Cash	$1.00m

After posting the above entries, the liability and equity would have carrying amounts as follows:

	$m	$m
	Liability	**Equity**
Proceeds	92.40	7.60
Issue cost	(0.92)	(0.08)
	91.48	7.52

The equity of $7.52 million will not be re-measured.

The liability component of $91.48 million would be measured at amortised cost. This means that interest is charged at the effective rate of 9.38%. The cash payments reduce the liability.

	Interest	**Cash paid**	
1 June X6	**(9.38%)**	**(6% × $100m)**	**31 May X7**
$m	$m	$m	$m
91.48	8.58	(6.0)	94.06

The finance cost in profit or loss will be $8.58 million. The liability will have a carrying amount on 31 May 20X7 of $94.06 million.

(b) Shares in Smart

Aron has to determine if the transfer of shares in Smart qualifies for derecognition. If substantially all the risks and rewards have been transferred, the asset is derecognised. If substantially all the risks and rewards have been retained, the asset is not derecognised. In this case the transfer of shares in Smart qualifies for derecognition as Aron no longer retains any risks and rewards of ownership.

Aron has obtained a new financial asset which is the shares in Given. Financial assets are initially recognised at fair value. The shares in Given should therefore be initially recognised at $5.5 million. If not held for trading, a designation could be made upon initial recognition to account for this new financial asset at fair value through other comprehensive income.

A profit on disposal of $0.5 million will be recorded in the statement of profit or loss. This is the difference between the initial carrying amount of the Shares in Given and the carrying amount of the shares in Smart that have been derecognised.

The entries required are:

Dr Financial asset (shares in Given)	$5.5m
Cr Financial asset (shares in Smart)	$5.0m
Cr Profit on disposal	$0.5m

Tutorial note

For investments in shares that are measured FVOCI, remeasurements to fair value are recorded in other comprehensive income. This includes remeasurements to fair value immediately prior to disposal. However, the fair value of the shares received in this transaction exceeds the fair value of the shares disposed of. This excess fair value is therefore recognised in profit or loss rather than in other comprehensive income.

In addition, Aron may choose to make a transfer within equity of the cumulative gain recognised up to the disposal date of $400,000.

(c) Investment in bonds

Financial assets are initially measured at fair value, so the investment in the bond will be initially recognised at $10 million.

The entity's business model involves both holding debt instruments to collect their contractual cash flows and also selling the assets. As a debt instrument, it would appear that the contractual terms of the asset comprise the repayment of the principal and interest on the principal amount outstanding. Therefore, the asset should be measured at fair value through other comprehensive income.

Interest income should be recognised in profit or loss using the effective rate of interest. At the reporting date, the asset should be remeasured to fair value with the gain or loss recognised in other comprehensive income. These gains or losses will be recycled to profit or loss if the asset is disposed of.

Interest income of $1.5 million (W1) should be recognised in profit or loss.

Fair value is defined by IFRS 13 *Fair Value Measurement* as the price paid when an asset is sold, or a liability transferred, in an orderly transaction between market participants at the measurement date. IFRS 13 requires entities to prioritise the use of level 1 inputs when measuring fair value, which are defined as quoted prices for identical assets or liabilities in an active market. The quoted price of $9 million appears to be a level 1 input so this is the fair value measurement that should be reported in the financial statements.

Remeasuring the asset to its fair value of $9.0 million will lead to a loss of $2.0 million (W1), which is recorded in other comprehensive income.

Loss allowance

IFRS 9 *Financial Instruments* requires a loss allowance to be recognised on investments in debt that are measured at amortised cost or fair value through other comprehensive income.

If credit risk has not increased significantly since initial recognition, the loss allowance should be equal to 12-month expected credit losses. If credit risk has increased significantly, the loss allowance must be equal to lifetime expected credit losses.

The credit risk of Winston's bonds remains low at the reporting date, suggesting that there has not been a significant increase in credit risk. The loss allowance should therefore be equal to the 12-month expected credit losses of $0.2 million.

When the financial asset is measured at fair value though other comprehensive income, the loss allowance is not adjusted against the asset's carrying amount (otherwise the asset will be held below fair value). Therefore, the loss allowance is charged to profit or loss, with the credit entry being recorded in other comprehensive income (essentially, this adjustment reclassifies $0.2 million of the earlier downwards revaluation from other comprehensive income to profit or loss).

Statement of cash flows

The $10 million cash spent on the financial asset will be presented as a cash outflow from investing activities.

The interest received of $0.5 million will be presented as a cash inflow from investing activities.

Working

(W1) Financial asset

1 June X6	Interest (15%)	Cash received	Total	Loss.	31 May X7
$m	$m	$m	$m	$m	$m
10.0	1.5	(0.5)	11.0	(2.0)	9.0

Marking scheme		
		Marks
(a)	Convertible bond – 1 mark per point	9
(b)	Share exchange – 1 mark per point	6
(c)	Winston bonds – 1 mark per point	10
Total		**25**

59 KLANCET  *Walk in the footsteps of a top tutor*

Key answer tips

Part (a) requires no calculations. To score well, it is important to be able to apply your accounting knowledge to the specific transactions. Do not simply knowledge dump. Instead, state the recognition and measurement rules from the relevant accounting standards before applying them to the scenario. If you struggle to identify which standards are relevant then think about the items involved. What accounting standard is used to account for an investment in shares? What accounting standard is used for purchases when consideration is in the form of shares?

(a) (i) IFRS 8 *Operating Segments*

Tutorial note

Students often neglect IFRS 8 when studying but it is a popular exam topic. Make sure that you are familiar with the definition of an operating segment as well as the rules governing which operating segments must be disclosed.

IFRS 8 *Operating Segments* states that an operating segment is a component of an entity which engages in business activities from which it may earn revenues and incur costs. In addition, discrete financial information should be available for the segment and these results should be regularly reviewed by the entity's chief operating decision maker (CODM) when making decisions about resource allocation to the segment and assessing its performance.

If a function is an integral part of the business, it may be disclosed as a segment even though it may not earn revenue.

According to IFRS 8, an operating segment should be reported if it meets one of the following quantitative thresholds:

1 Its reported revenue, including both sales to external customers and intersegment sales or transfers, is 10% or more of the combined revenue, internal and external, of all operating segments.

2 The absolute amount of its reported profit or loss is 10% or more of the greater, in absolute amount, of (i) the combined reported profit of all operating segments which did not report a loss and (ii) the combined reported loss of all operating segments which reported a loss.

3 Its assets are 10% or more of the combined assets of all operating segments.

The research and development laboratories

Tutorial note

Apply the rules to each of the laboratories in turn. Make sure that you reach an explicit conclusion about whether or not they constitute operating segments.

The first laboratory is not an operating segment. This is because:

- The laboratory does not have a separate segment manager and the existence of a segment manager is normally an important factor in determining operating segments.
- The laboratory is responsible to the divisions themselves, which would seem to indicate that it is simply supporting the existing divisions and not a separate segment.
- There does not seem to be any discrete performance information, which is reviewed by the CODM.

The second laboratory is an operating segment. This is because:

- It has a separate segment manager
- It engages in activities which earn revenues and incurs costs
- Its operating results are reviewed by the CODM and discrete information is available for the laboratory's activities.

The second laboratory should be separately disclosed because its revenues make up more than 10% of the revenues of all operating segments.

(ii) Share transactions

Tutorial note

Take your time and think through which accounting standards are relevant to these transactions. Marks will only be given for discussion of the relevant accounting standards.

Sale of patent

The shares received are in the scope of IFRS 9 *Financial Instruments* and are to be initially measured at fair value. Klancet should derecognise the patent which is transferred to Jancy. Any gain or loss on disposal is recorded in the statement of profit or loss.

The shares should be remeasured to fair value at the year end. Fair value changes are recognised in profit or loss, except for those equity investments for which the entity has elected to report value changes in 'other comprehensive income'.

Klancet should not yet recognise any asset relating to the future royalty stream from the potential sales of the drug, because this stream of royalties is contingent upon the successful development of the drug.

Purchase of patent

Klancet has received a patent in exchange for issuing its own shares. This transaction is within the scope of IFRS 2 *Share-based Payment*.

The transaction is with a supplier, rather than an employee, so Klancet should measure the patent purchased at its fair value and make a corresponding entry to equity (share capital). If Klancet cannot estimate reliably the fair value of the patent then it should measure the transaction at the fair value of the equity instruments granted.

(b) (i) Financial instrument

According to IFRS 9 *Financial Instruments* the financial asset should be initially recognised at its fair value of $5 million. Klancet's business model means that the asset will be measured at fair value through other comprehensive income. Interest income should be calculated using the effective rate of interest. Gains and losses on revaluation to fair value are recorded in OCI.

Bfd	Interest 10%	Receipt*	Subtotal	Loss	Fair value
$m	$m	$m	$m	$m	$m
5.0	0.5	(0.2)	5.3	(0.8)	4.5

* = $5m × 4%

Interest income of $0.5 million is recorded in profit or loss. The asset is revalued to its fair value of $4.5 million, with a loss of $0.8 million recorded in OCI. This revaluation loss will be presented as an item that may be reclassified to profit or loss in the future.

(ii) ***Conceptual Framework***

The *Conceptual Framework* defines an asset as a resource of an entity that has the potential to produce economic benefits. The financial instrument meets the definition of an asset because Klancet has a contractual right to receive cash.

According to the *Conceptual Framework*, an element is recognised in the financial statements if recognition provides relevant financial information, and a faithful representation of the underlying transaction. This would seem to be the case because primary users of the financial statements are interested in the future cash flows that an entity will generate, and this financial instrument gives the entity a contractual right to future cash flows. Moreover, the cost of the asset can be measured reliably. As such, recognition of the asset would appear to be in accordance with the *Conceptual Framework*.

The *Conceptual Framework* states that the statement of profit or loss is the primary source of information about an entity's performance. This statement should enable investors to understand the entity's returns for the period, to assess future cash flows, and to assess stewardship of the entity's resources.

When developing or revising standards, the Board notes that it might require an income or expense to be presented in other comprehensive if it results from remeasuring an item to current value and if this means that:

- profit or loss provides more relevant information, or
- a more faithful representation is provided of an entity's performance.

Klancet's business model involves holding the asset to maturity in order to collect the contractual cash flows unless a better investment becomes available. It does not intend to trade the asset in the short-term and so fair value gains and losses on the instrument are largely irrelevant when assessing Klancet's performance. Presenting the fair value loss of $0.8 million in other comprehensive income therefore ensures that the statement of profit or loss best presents the entity's economic returns during the period. This is consistent with the *Conceptual Framework*.

The *Conceptual Framework* states that income and expenditure included in other comprehensive income should be reclassified to profit or loss when doing so results in profit or loss providing more relevant information. In accordance with IFRS 9, the gains and losses on Klancet's debt instrument will be reclassified to profit or loss when the asset is derecognised. In this regard, the treatment of the debt instrument is, once again, consistent with the *Conceptual Framework*.

Marking scheme			
			Marks
(a)	(i)	Operating segments – 1 mark per point	8
	(ii)	Share transactions – 1 mark per point	6
(b)	(i)	Financial instrument – 1 mark per point	4
	(ii)	Conceptual Framework – 1 mark per point	7
Total			**25**

60 EMCEE  *Walk in the footsteps of a top tutor*

Key answer tips

This question tests a wide variety of standards. Moreover, part (a) (i) requires students to be able to apply those standards to scenarios that they may not have previously considered. This can be difficult at first but you will improve with practice.

(a) (i) Sports teams

Tutorial note

To score well in part (a)(i) it is important to pick up on certain 'trigger' words within the scenario – 'purchasing registrations' suggests that Emcee is buying intangible assets, 'deciding to sell' suggests that assets may need to be classified as 'held for sale', whereas 'player injuries' suggests there could be impairment issues. Many accounting standards can be examined within a single part of the question.

Purchase of player registrations

IAS 38 *Intangible Assets* states that an entity should recognise an intangible asset where it is probable that future economic benefits will flow to the entity and the cost of the asset can be measured reliably.

Tutorial note

If you are unaware of the detail of IAS 38 Intangible Assets, then use your knowledge of the Conceptual Framework instead. The examiner has said that using the Framework to answers questions will score marks.

Therefore, the costs associated with the acquisition of players' registrations should be capitalised at cost. Cost would include transfer fees, league levy fees, agents' fees incurred by the club and other directly attributable costs.

The cost of player registrations would be amortised over the period covered by the player's contract.

Where a playing contract is extended, any costs associated with securing the extension are added to the unamortised balance at the date of the extension and the revised carrying amount is amortised over the remaining revised contract life.

Decisions to sell

Player registrations would be classified as assets held for sale under IFRS 5 *Non-current Assets Held for Sale and Discontinued Operations* when their carrying amount is expected to be recovered principally through a sale transaction and a sale is considered to be highly probable. To qualify, the registrations should be actively marketed by Emcee, which it appears that they are. It would also appear that management commits itself to a plan to sell the registrations and that the assets are available for immediate sale. IFRS 5 requires that it is unlikely that the plan to sell the registrations will be significantly changed or withdrawn.

If classified as held for sale, the player registrations would be measured at the lower of their carrying amount and fair value less costs to sell.

Gains and losses on disposal of players' registrations would be determined by comparing the fair value of the consideration receivable, net of any transaction costs, with the carrying amount and would be recognised in profit or loss. Where a part of the consideration receivable is contingent on specified performance conditions, this amount is recognised in profit or loss when the conditions are met.

Impairment issues

Tutorial note

The question refers to players who are injured, or who will not play again. This is an indication that the registration rights for these players might be impaired.

IAS 36 *Impairment of Assets* states an asset is impaired if its carrying amount exceeds its recoverable amount. Recoverable amount is the higher of the asset's fair value less costs of disposal, and its value in use.

It will be difficult to determine the value in use of an individual player in isolation as that player cannot generate cash flows on their own (unless in a sale transaction). As such, impairments may need to be performed on the cash generating unit to which the player belongs. This is likely to be the team as a whole.

There may be some circumstances where a player is taken out of the team, such as if they sustain a career threatening injury. If such circumstances arise, the carrying amount of the player should be assessed against the best estimate of the player's fair value less any costs to sell.

Any impairment losses would be charged to profit or loss.

The playing registrations which were disposed of subsequent to the year-end for $25 million would be disclosed as an event after the reporting period.

(ii) Deferred tax assets

Tutorial note

This is a common exam scenario. Use the information in the question to decide whether Emcee will receive probable benefits from its unused tax losses.

IAS 12 *Income Taxes* states that a deferred tax asset shall be recognised for the carry-forward of unused tax losses to the extent that it is probable that future taxable profit will be available against which unused tax losses can be utilised.

IAS 12 explains that the existence of unused tax losses is strong evidence that future taxable profit may not be available. Therefore, when an entity has a history of recent losses, the entity recognises a deferred tax asset arising from unused tax losses only to the extent that the entity has sufficient taxable temporary differences or when there is convincing other evidence that sufficient taxable profit will be available against which the unused tax losses can be utilised by the entity.

Emcee recognised losses during the previous five years. In order to use the deferred tax asset of $16 million, Emcee would have to recognise a profit of $53.3 million at the existing tax rate of 30%. In comparison, the entity recognised an average loss of $19 million per year during the five previous years.

Tutorial note

Do Emcee's budgets seem accurate and reliable?

Emcee's budgets and assumptions are not convincing other evidence because the entity does not appear to have been capable of making accurate forecasts in the past and there were material differences between the amounts budgeted and realised for the previous two years. Emcee had presented future budgets primarily based on general assumptions about economic improvement indicators, rather than what was expected to influence the future income and therefore enable the use of the deferred tax asset.

Tutorial note

Are Emcee's losses one-off events, or are they likely to recur?

IAS 12 states that in assessing the probability that taxable profit will be available against which the unused tax losses or unused tax credits can be utilised, a consideration is whether the unused tax losses result from identifiable causes which are unlikely to recur (i.e. one off events). However, Emcee has continued to recognise impairment losses in excess of budget. This places doubts on the likelihood of future profits arising.

Finally, in its financial statements, Emcee disclosed a material uncertainty about its ability to continue as a going concern. This, again, places doubts on the likelihood of future profits and suggests that recognition of a deferred tax asset for unused tax losses would be inappropriate.

In conclusion the liability of $3 million relating to temporary differences can be offset against $3 million of unused tax losses. No further deferred tax asset relating to tax losses should be recognised.

(b) Disclosure and materiality

Tutorial note

There are some fairly common-sense points to be made in part (b) of the question. What problems arise if disclosures are insufficient? What problems arise if there are too many lengthy disclosures?

Importance of optimal level of disclosure

It is important that financial statements are relevant and understandable. Excessive disclosure can obscure relevant information. This makes it harder for users to find the key points about the performance of the business and its prospects for long-term success

Materiality

An item is material if its omission or misstatement will influence the economic decisions of the users of financial statements.

The Board feels that the poor application of materiality contributes to too much irrelevant information in financial statements and not enough relevant information. As such, they have issued a Practice Statement called *Making Materiality Judgements*.

In the Practice Statement, the Board re-iterate that an entity only needs to apply the disclosure requirements in an IFRS Standard if the resulting information is material. When making such decisions, an entity must consider the common information needs of the primary user groups of its financial statements.

When organising disclosure notes, entities should:

- Emphasise material matters
- Ensure material information is not obscured by immaterial information
- Ensure information is entity-specific
- Aim for simplicity and conciseness without omitting material detail
- Ensure formats are appropriate and understandable (e.g. tables, lists, narrative)
- Provide comparable information
- Avoid duplication

Entities may sometimes need to provide additional disclosures, not required by an IFRS Standard, if necessary to help financial statement users understand the financial impact of its transactions during the period.

Marking scheme			
			Marks
(a)	(i)	Player registrations – 1 mark per point	9
	(ii)	Deferred tax assets and losses – 1 mark per point	8
(b)	Disclosure – 1 mark per point		8
			——
Total			**25**
			——

61 GASNATURE  *Walk in the footsteps of a top tutor*

Key answer tips

Use the mark allocation to help you plan your timings. Leaving parts of a question un-attempted is one of the main reasons why students fail exams.

Broadly speaking, you will be awarded one mark for every valid point that you make. If you have not written very much then think about whether there are any key principles from the relevant accounting standard that you haven't written down. Or, alternatively, try and use the *Conceptual Framework* to help you to develop your answer.

As always, thoroughly debrief the model answer and learn from your mistakes. Write down the things you did not know as this will help you to remember them for next time.

(a) (i) Joint arrangements

Tutorial note

In exam questions watch out for scenarios where decision making requires 'unanimous' consent of the parties that share control. This is usually an indication of joint control, suggesting that there is a joint arrangement.

Joint arrangements take two forms: joint operations or joint ventures. Make sure that you are clear on the difference between the two.

A joint arrangement occurs where two or more parties have joint control. Joint control exists when decisions about the relevant activities require the unanimous consent of the parties sharing control.

The classification of a joint arrangement as a joint operation or a joint venture depends upon the rights and obligations of the parties to the arrangement. A joint arrangement which is not structured through a separate vehicle is normally a joint operation. A joint operator accounts for the assets, liabilities, revenues and expenses relating to its involvement in a joint operation.

The arrangement with Gogas is a joint arrangement, because decisions regarding the platform require unanimous agreement of both parties. The joint arrangement with Gogas should be classified as a joint operation because there is no separate vehicle involved. Gasnature should recognise 55% of the asset's cost as property, plant and equipment.

Dismantling

Under IAS 16 *Property, Plant and Equipment* (PPE), the cost of an item of property, plant and equipment must include the initial estimate of the costs of dismantling and removing the item and restoring the site on which it is located.

IAS 37 *Provisions, Contingent Liabilities and Contingent Assets* stipulates how to measure decommissioning and restoration costs and similar liabilities. Where the effect of the time value of money is material, the amount of a provision should be the present value of the expected expenditure required to settle the obligation.

Tutorial note

In their financial statements, joint operators recognise their interest in the assets and liabilities of the joint operation.

Thus Gasnature should account for 55% of the present value of the estimated decommissioning costs. Gasnature will include this in PPE and will also recognise a provision for the same amount.

Because Gasnature is a joint operator, there is also a contingent liability for 45% of the decommissioning costs as there is a potential obligation if some uncertain future event occurs (such as if Gogas goes into liquidation and cannot fund the decommissioning costs). Therefore Gasnature should disclose a contingent liability to the extent that it is potentially liable for Gogas's share of the decommissioning costs.

(ii) Financial instruments

Tutorial note

The answer below uses a lot of technical detail from IFRS 9 Financial Instruments. However, you could reach the same conclusion by using simple accounting principles. Gasnature is buying gas to use in its business – it is therefore a purchase contract.

IFRS 9 *Financial Instruments* applies to contracts to buy or sell a non-financial item that are settled net in cash Such contracts are accounted for as derivatives.

However, contracts which are for an entity's 'own use' of a non-financial asset are exempt from the requirements of IFRS 9.

There are various ways in which a contract to buy or sell a non-financial item can be settled net in cash. These include:

- when the terms of the contract permit either party to settle it net in cash
- when the entity has a practice of settling similar contracts net in cash
- when the entity has a practice of taking delivery of the non-financial asset and selling it in the short-term to generate a profit
- when the non-financial item is readily convertible to cash.

It could be argued that the contract is net settled because the penalty mechanism requires Agas to compensate Gasnature at the current prevailing market price. Further, if natural gas is readily convertible into cash in the location where the delivery takes place, the contract could be considered net settled.

However, the contract will probably still qualify as 'own use' as long as it has been entered into and continues to be held for Gasnature's usage requirements. This means that it falls outside IFRS 9 and should be treated as an executory contract. The gas will be recorded at cost on the purchase date.

(b) Accounting policy choices

Tutorial note

Take time to think about the choices allowed by each standard. This is your gateway into the rest of the question.

IAS 16 *Property, Plant and Equipment*

After initial recognition, IAS 16 allows property, plant and equipment (PPE) to be measured using either:

- the cost model – cost less accumulated depreciation and impairment losses
- the revaluation model – fair value less accumulated depreciation and impairment losses.

Tutorial note

First of all think about the impact on the statement of profit or loss. Remember that revaluation gains on property, plant and equipment are ***not*** *recorded in the statement of profit or loss.*

Assuming that property prices are increasing, an entity that revalues its PPE to fair value will record lower profits than one that uses the cost model. Although the gains arising from the revaluation of PPE are recognised outside of profit, in other comprehensive income, the depreciation charge on the revalued asset will be higher than if the cost model was used. As such, using the revaluation model may have a detrimental impact on stakeholders' assessment of an entity's financial performance. Moreover, the higher asset value recorded in the statement of financial position under the revaluation model might also make the entity look less efficient than one which uses the cost model.

Tutorial note

Think about the impact on the statement of financial position.

However, on the positive side revaluation gains will increase equity which will improve the gearing ratio. This may make the entity look like a less risky investment. Moreover, some stakeholders may place importance on an entity's asset base, as this could be used as security for obtaining new finance. Thus, a higher PPE value in the statement of financial position could be viewed positively.

Another thing to note is that the revaluation model will make the asset position of an entity more volatile than an entity that uses the cost model. Volatility can increase the perception of risk. However, the statement of profit or loss will be much less volatile than the statement of financial position because revaluation gains are recorded in other comprehensive income.

It should be noted that entities using the revaluation model for PPE are required to disclose the carrying amounts that would be recognised if the cost model had been used. Such disclosures enable better comparison with entities that account for PPE using different measurement models.

IAS 20 *Accounting for Government Grants and Disclosure of Government Assistance*

Tutorial note

Your answer does not need to be as detailed as the one presented below.

With regards to asset related grants, two methods of presentation are allowed in the statement of financial position:

- recognise the grant as deferred income and release to profit or loss over the useful life of the asset
- deduct the grant from the carrying amount of the asset and then depreciate the asset over its useful life.

The overall net assets and profit of an entity will not be affected by this choice. However, it could still have an impact on an investor's analysis of the financial statements.

An entity that uses the deferred income method to present asset-related grants will report higher non-current asset assets and higher liabilities than an entity that uses the 'netting off' method.

Reporting a higher level of liabilities may have a detrimental impact on certain ratios, such as the current ratio. More generally, higher liabilities may increase the perception of financial risk, potentially deterring investment.

Reporting higher levels of non-current assets could be viewed positively (as a sign of a strong asset base), or negatively (it may make the entity look less efficient at generating its profit).

With regards to income related grants, two methods of presentation are allowed in the statement of profit or loss:

- present the grant as 'other income'
- present the grant as a reduction in the related expense.

The overall profit of an entity will not be affected by this choice. However, it could still have an impact when analysing financial statements. For instance, an entity that presents grant income by reducing its expenses may be perceived as having better cost control and as operating with greater efficiency than an entity that records its grants within 'other income'.

Cash flows

Accounting policy choices have no impact on the operating, investing or financing cash flows reported in the statement of cash flows.

Marking scheme			
			Marks
(a)	(i)	Joint operation – 1 mark per point	7
	(ii)	Gas contract – 1 mark per point	6
(b)		Accounting choices – 1 mark per point	10
		Professional	2
Total			**25**

62 EVOLVE  *Walk in the footsteps of a top tutor*

Key answer tips

This question tests core accounting standards in quite unusual scenarios. As such, good application skills are required to score well. Make sure that you get the easiest marks by stating your knowledge of the principles from each relevant accounting standard. Many students leave parts of these questions blank – there is no negative marking so you might as well give it your best attempt!

(a) (i) Non-current assets held for sale

IFRS 5 *Non-current Assets Held for Sale and Discontinued Operations* says that an asset should be held for sale if its carrying amount will be recovered primarily through a sale and the sale is highly probable to occur.

IFRS 5 does not require the existence of a binding sales agreement in order to classify a non-current asset as held for sale but only a high probability of its occurrence. IFRS 5 states that the appropriate level of management must be committed to a plan to sell the asset for the sale to be probable. Evolve's acceptance of a binding offer in August 20X6 and the publication of this information thus indicated a high probability of sale. Despite the uncertainties surrounding the sale, the transaction remained highly probable at 31 August 20X6.

Other criteria which indicate that the non-current assets should be shown as held for sale include the fact that a buyer for the non-current assets has been found, the sale occurred within 12 months of classification as held for sale, the asset was actively marketed for sale at a price which has been accepted. Despite the uncertainties at 31 August 20X6, events after the reporting period indicate that the contract was not significantly changed or withdrawn. The fact that the information regarding the uncertainties was not publicly disclosed is irrelevant.

Evolve cannot apply IFRS 5 measurement criteria without classifying the item as held for sale in its statement of financial position particularly as impairment may arise when using such criteria.

Thus as the non-current assets met the criteria to be classified as held for sale, they should have been measured and presented as such in the financial statements. Assets classified as held for sale are presented separately within current assets on the face of the statement of financial position.

(ii) Business combinations

IFRS 3 *Business Combinations* must be applied when accounting for business combinations, but does not apply where the acquisition is not of a business. In this case, the acquisition was essentially that of an asset and therefore the measurement requirements of IFRS 3 would not apply.

Investment property

IAS 40 *Investment Property* states that the cost of an investment property comprises its purchase price and any directly attributable expenditure, such as professional fees for legal services. Hence if Evolve wishes to use the cost basis for accounting for the investment property, the potential gain should not have been recorded in profit or loss or added to the cost of the asset.

The specific fiscal treatment and the tax to be paid were not linked to bringing the asset to the condition necessary for its operations, as the asset would have been operational without the tax. As such, the tax is a cost linked to the activity of Evolve and should be accounted for as an expense in accordance with IAS 12 *Income Taxes* and included in profit or loss for the period.

(b) Materiality

Definition

An item is material if its omission or misstatement might influence the economic decisions of the users of the financial statements.

When an entity is assessing materiality, it is considering whether information is relevant to the readers of its own financial statements – in other words, materiality is entity specific. An entity should assume that the users of its financial statements have a reasonable knowledge of business and accounting

The materiality Practice Statement emphasises that materiality judgements are not just quantitative – transactions that trigger non-compliance with laws, or which impact future operations, may affect user decisions even if the monetary amounts involved are small.

Importance of materiality to financial reporting

The purpose of financial reporting is to provide information that will help investors, lenders and other creditors to make economic decisions about providing an entity with resources.

It is important that management consider materiality throughout the process of preparing financial statements. This should ensure that relevant information is not omitted or misstated. The Practice Statement details a four step process:

- Identify information that might be material
- Assess whether that information is material
- Organise the information in draft financial statements
- Review the draft financial statements.

Management should produce financial statements that are free from error. However the impact of certain transactions might be omitted or simplified as long as the resulting errors are immaterial. The materiality Practice Statement recognises that simplified accounting procedures, such as writing off all capital expenditure below $1,000 to profit or loss, can greatly reduce the burden of financial reporting without causing material misstatements.

The concept of materiality does not just help to determine whether transactions are recognised in the financial statements, but also how they are presented. Management may decide to present some material transactions as separate line items in its financial statements, whereas the effects of other immaterial transactions might be aggregated. The Practice Statement emphasises the importance of these decisions: too much detail can obscure important information, whereas over-aggregation leads to a loss of relevant detail.

Materiality assessments also impact disclosure notes. Guidance in this area is important because financial statements have become increasingly cluttered in recent years as the disclosure requirements in IFRS Standards have expanded. However, as IAS 1 *Presentation of Financial Statements* states, an entity need not provide a specific disclosure required by an IFRS Standard if the information is immaterial. The Practice Statement emphasises that the common information needs of primary user groups should always be considered and that the disclosure requirements in IFRS Standards should not be treated as a simple checklist.

Marking scheme			
			Marks
(a)	(i)	Assets held for sale – 1 mark per point	7
	(ii)	Investment property – 1 mark per point	6
(b)		Materiality – 1 mark per point	10
		Professional marks	2
Total			**25**

63 ARTWRIGHT

Key answer tips

This question tests hedge accounting, which is a topic that students struggle with. The transactions in part (b) are relatively simple. If you struggle, it is important that you revisit the Study Text.

(a) Intangible assets

IAS *38 Intangible Assets* requires an entity to recognise an intangible asset if:

- It is probable that the future economic benefits which are attributable to the asset will flow to the entity, and
- the cost of the asset can be measured reliably.

This requirement applies whether an intangible asset is acquired externally or generated internally.

The probability of future economic benefits must be based on reasonable and supportable assumptions about conditions which will exist over the life of the asset. The price an entity pays to acquire an intangible asset reflects expectations about the probability that the expected future economic benefits from the asset will flow to the entity. This means that the effect of probability is reflected in the cost of the asset and so the probability recognition criterion is always considered to be satisfied for intangible assets that are acquired separately or in a business combination.

In this case, Artwright should recognise an intangible asset for the use of Jomaster's technology. The right should be measured at its cost of $4 million. The intangible asset should be amortised from the date it is available for use. The technology is available for use when the manufacturing of the compound begins. At the end of each reporting period, Artwright is required to assess whether there is any indication that the asset may be impaired.

Due to the nature of intangible assets, subsequent expenditure will rarely meet the criteria for being recognised in the carrying amount of an asset. Thus Artwright continues to expense its own internal development expenditure until the criteria for capitalisation are met and economic benefits are expected to flow to the entity from the capitalised asset. When the drug is sold, the royalty payments are presented in profit or loss.

Business combinations

IFRS 10 *Consolidated Financial Statements* says that: 'An investor controls an investee when the investor is exposed, or has rights, to variable returns from its involvement with the investee and has the ability to affect those returns through its power over the investee'. Therefore it appears that Artwright will control Conew.

Any transaction in which an entity obtains control of one or more businesses qualifies as a business combination and is subject to the measurement and recognition requirements of IFRS 3 *Business Combinations*.

IFRS 3 defines a 'business' as an integrated set of activities and assets that is capable of being conducted and managed to produce returns. A business consists of inputs and processes applied to those inputs which have the ability to create outputs. Processes are included in the acquired group when intellectual property (IP) is accompanied by other resources such as assets or employees or other elements such as protocols and plans which will further help develop the IP to the next phase.

Conew does not meet the definition of a business. It has only one input, and no processes. As such, its inputs and processes are not capable of producing a return. This means that the acquisition of an interest in Conew should be accounted for as an asset acquisition in accordance with IAS 38 *Intangible Assets*.

(b) Hedge effectiveness

If an entity chooses to hedge account then it must assess at inception and at each reporting date whether the hedge effectiveness criteria have been met.

These criteria are as follows:

- **'There is an economic relationship between the hedged item and the hedging instrument**
- **The effect of credit risk does not dominate the value changes that arise from that relationship**
- **The hedged ratio should be the same as that resulting from the quantity of the hedged item that the entity actually hedges and the quantity of the hedging instrument that the entity actually uses.'**

(IFRS 9, para 6.4.1)

IFRS 9 *Financial Instruments* says that the assessment of effectiveness must be forwards-looking.

Derivatives

All derivatives have to be initially recognised at fair value, i.e. at the consideration given or received at inception of the contract. Derivatives A and C appear to have no purchase price, so are initially recognised at nil. Derivative B will be initially recognised at its fair value of $1m.

Derivative A: Artwright has entered into this derivative for speculative purposes. IFRS 9 requires that all derivatives not designated as part of a hedge accounting arrangement are accounted for at fair value through profit or loss. The loss of $20 million that has been incurred has to be immediately recognised profit or loss.

Dr Profit or loss	$20m
Cr Derivative	$20m

Derivative B: If a fair value hedge is effective, then the movement in the fair value of the item and the instrument since the inception of the hedge are normally recognised in profit or loss. However, if the hedged item is an investment in shares that has been designated to be measured at fair value through other comprehensive income (FVOCI), then the fair value movement on the hedged item and the hedging instrument are recognised in other comprehensive income.

The hedged item is an investment of shares designated to be measured at FVOCI. Therefore, the following entries are required at the reporting date:

Dr Financial asset	\$8.5m
Cr Other comprehensive income	\$8.5m
Dr Other comprehensive income	\$10m
Cr Derivative	\$10m

Derivative C: If a cash flow hedge is effective, then the movement in the fair value of the instrument is accounted for through other comprehensive income. However, if the movement on the instrument exceeds the movement on the item, then the excess is recognised in profit or loss.

The following entry is required:

Dr Derivative	\$25m
Cr Other comprehensive income	\$24m
Cr Profit or loss	\$1m

When the raw materials are purchased, the gains recognised in other comprehensive income can be reclassified against the carrying amount of the inventory.

(c) Overseas loan

Tutorial note

There are two issues implicit in part (c): how to account for the loan, and how to translate the figures from dinars into dollars. Make sure that you address both of these issues.

The loan is a financial liability because it contains a contractual obligation to transfer cash. In accordance with IFRS 9 *Financial Instruments*, most financial liabilities are measured at amortised cost. Liabilities at amortised cost should be initially recognised at fair value less transaction costs. The finance cost is calculated using the effective rate of interest and charged to profit or loss.

This loan is denominated in an overseas currency and so must be translated using the rules in IAS 21 *The Effects of Changes in Foreign Exchange Rates*. The overseas loan should initially be translated into the functional currency using the historic (spot) rate. The finance cost is translated at the average rate because it approximates to the actual rate. The cash payment should be translated at the historic (spot) rate (which, because the payment occurs at the reporting date, is the year-end rate). A loan is a monetary liability so is retranslated at the reporting date using the closing rate. Any exchange gain or loss is recognised in profit or loss.

Tutorial note

Complete the amortised cost working in dinars, and then translate each figure into dollars using the appropriate exchange rate.

	Dm	Rate	$m
1 May 20X3	5.0	5	1.000
Finance cost (8%)	0.4	5.6	0.071
Payment	(0.4)	6	(0.067)
Foreign exchange gain (bal. fig.)			(0.171)
30 April 20X4	5.0	6	0.833

The loan is initially recorded at $1 million. The finance cost recorded in the statement of profit or loss is $0.071 million, whilst the cash payment is recorded at $0.067 million. A foreign exchange gain of $0.171 million is recorded in the statement of profit or loss. The liability at the reporting date has a carrying amount of $0.833 million.

Marking scheme		
		Marks
(a)	Intangibles and business combinations – 1 mark per point	8
(b)	Derivatives and hedge accounting – 1 mark per point	9
(b)	Overseas financial liability – 1 mark per point	8
Total		**25**

64 LUCKY DAIRY

Key answer tips

Part (a) (i) of this question tests IAS 41 *Agriculture*. This is a relatively simple accounting standard, albeit one that is not examined frequently. As such, you may lack familiarity with the core principles of the standard.

Part (b) examines integrated reporting. This is an important area of the syllabus so do not neglect it.

(a) (i) Biological assets

According to IAS 41 *Agriculture* a biological asset, such as a dairy cow, is initially measured at fair value less costs to sell. It should be remeasured at each reporting date to its fair value less estimated costs to sell. Gains or losses on remeasurement are recorded in the statement of profit or loss.

As at 31 May 20X1, the herd would have been carried in the statement of financial position at $3.5 million. The heifers purchased in the current year should have been recognised at $1.15 million. At year end, the herd is revalued to its fair value less costs to sell of $5.58 million. A revaluation gain of $0.93 million is recognised in profit or loss (W1).

(W1) Biological assets

	Fair value less costs to sell
	$m
Carrying amount at 31 May 20X1 (70,000 × $50)	3.50
Purchase (25,000 × $46)	1.15
Fair value gain (bal. fig.)	0.93
Carrying amount at 31 May 20X2 (70,000 × 60) + (25,000 × $55)	5.58

(ii) Financial assets

According to IFRS 9 *Financial Instruments*, a loss allowance should be recognised on financial assets that are debt instruments and which are measured at amortised cost or fair value through other comprehensive income.

If the credit risk of a financial asset has not increased significantly since inception, the loss allowance should equal 12-month expected credit losses. If the credit risk of a financial asset has increased significantly since inception, the loss allowance should equal lifetime expected credit losses. An entity must use reasonable forward-looking information when assessing the level of credit risk.

The bonds had a low credit risk at inception. It would seem that credit risk has increased significantly since inception. This is because of the following:

- The financial performance and cash generation of Jags have been poor and this will have impaired its ability to service its financing obligations.
- The entity was close to breaching loan covenants at year end. A breach of covenants would potentially make loans repayable, thus having a detrimental impact on cash flow.
- The decreased bond price appears to be entity specific and therefore reflective of market concerns about Jags and its credit risk
- External agencies are reviewing the credit rating of Jags, suggesting that credit risk has increased since the publication of its latest financial results.

Due to the increase in credit risk, the loss allowance should be equal to lifetime expected credit losses. Increases or decreases in the allowance will be charged to profit or loss.

(b) Statements of cash flows

Statements of cash flows provide valuable information to stakeholders:

- Cash flows are objective and verifiable and so are more easily understood than profits. In contrast, profits can be manipulated through the use of judgement or choice of a particular accounting policy.
- Cash generated from operations is a useful indication of the quality of the profits generated by a business. Good quality profits will generate cash and increase the financial adaptability of an entity.
- Cash flow information has some predictive value. It may assist stakeholders in making judgements on the amount, timing and degree of certainty on future cash flows.

However, the adjustment of non-cash flow items within operating activities is complex and may not be easily understood. Moreover, the classification of cash flows can be manipulated between operating, investing and financing activities. As such, it is only through an analysis of the statement of financial position, statement of comprehensive income and notes, together with cash flow, that a comprehensive understanding of the entity's position and performance can develop.

Integrated reporting

It is true that International Financial Reporting Standards are extensive and their required disclosures very comprehensive. This has led to criticism that the most relevant information can become obscured by immaterial disclosures. An integrated report would increase disclosure as well as imposing additional time and cost constraints on the reporting entity.

However, integrated reporting will provide stakeholders with valuable information which would not be immediately accessible from an entity's financial statements.

Financial statements are based on historical information and may lack predictive value. They are essential in corporate reporting, particularly for compliance purposes but do not provide meaningful information regarding business value. The primary purpose of an integrated report is to explain to providers of capital how the organisation generates value over time.

This is summarised through an examination of the key activities and outputs of the organisation whether they be financial, manufactured, intellectual, human, social or natural.

An integrated report seeks to examine the external environment which the entity operates within and to provide an insight into the entity's resources and relationships to generate value. It is principles based and should be driven by materiality, including how and to what extent the entity understands and responds to the needs of its stakeholders. This would include an analysis of how the entity has performed within its business environment, together with a description of prospects and challenges for the future. It is this strategic direction which is lacking from a traditional set of financial statements and will be invaluable to stakeholders to make a more informed assessment of the organisation and its prospects.

Marking scheme			
			Marks
(a)	(i)	Biological assets – 1 mark per point	6
	(ii)	Financial assets – 1 mark per point	8
(b)	Cash flows and integrated reports – 1 mark per point		9
	Professional marks		2
Total			**25**

UK GAAP FOCUS

65 STEM (SEP/DEC 2021)

Key answer tips

Well prepared candidates who have studied the differences between FRS 102, should have fared well with the UK aspects of this question. Part (a) tests the differences between FRS 102 and IFRS 3, an area with many clear differences e.g. the treatment of transaction costs, amortisation vs impairment.

Part (b) covers joint ventures, which may have proved a little more taxing. The UK treatment of joint ventures is much the same as the international version so plenty of marks for the basic concepts would be available. The only differences caused by the application of FRS 102 are some of the terms used (FRS 102 uses 'joint venture' to cover jointly controlled operations, jointly controlled assets and jointly controlled entities, whereas IAS 28 uses the terms 'joint arrangement' to cover all of these options, and a 'joint venture' becomes solely a jointly controlled entity) and the treatment of the discounted purchase as negative goodwill within the statement of financial position (IFRS takes this to profit as a gain on a bargain purchase).

(a) FRS 102 vs IFRS 3

The key differences between IFRS 3 *Business Combinations* and FRS 102 *The Financial Reporting Standard applicable in the UK and Republic of Ireland* are as follows:

- According to FRS 102, transaction costs are included in the cost of acquisition whereas with IFRS 3, all costs of acquisition are written off as incurred.
- Contingent consideration is also included as part of the acquisition cost if it is probable that the amount will be paid and it can be measured reliably. In accordance with IFRS 3, contingent consideration must be measured at fair value at the time of the business combination and is taken into account in the determination of goodwill.
- FRS 102 states that where control is achieved through a series of transactions, the acquisition cost is the total of the fair values of the assets given, liabilities assumed and equity instruments issued at the date of each transaction. With IFRS 3, the acquirer remeasures any previously held interest at fair value and takes this amount into account in the determination of goodwill. Any resultant gain or loss is recognised in profit or loss or other comprehensive income as appropriate.
- FRS 102 requires negative goodwill to be recognised in profit or loss in the periods expected to benefit from its existence whereas IFRS 3 states that the resulting gain is a bargain purchase which is recognised immediately in profit or loss.
- FRS 102 utilises only the proportionate share method for non-controlling interest and does not allow the fair value method as an option.
- IFRS 3 includes more detailed rules than FRS 102 on fair valuation.

- FRS 102 requires entities to recognise fewer intangible assets acquired in a business combination separately from goodwill. Entities may choose to separately recognise additional intangible assets acquired in a business combination if this provides useful information to the entity and the users of its financial statements.

- FRS 102 requires the acquirer to measure goodwill acquired in a business combination at cost less accumulated amortisation and accumulated impairment losses. Goodwill is considered to have a finite useful life and is amortised on a systematic basis over its life. If, in exceptional cases, an entity is unable to make a reliable estimate of the useful life of goodwill, the life shall not exceed 10 years. With IFRS 3 the goodwill impairment assessment is made each year.

(b) Emphasis Co

FRS 102 defines joint control as the contractually agreed sharing of control over an economic activity, and it exists only when the strategic financial and operating decisions relating to the activity require the unanimous consent of the parties sharing control. Further, a joint venture is a contractual arrangement whereby two or more parties undertake an economic activity which is subject to joint control. Joint ventures can take the form of jointly controlled operations, jointly controlled assets, or jointly controlled entities. A jointly controlled entity is a joint venture which involves the establishment of a corporation, partnership or other entity in which each venturer has an interest. The entity operates in the same way as other entities, except that a contractual arrangement between the venturers establishes joint control over the economic activity of the entity.

Emphasis Co is a jointly controlled entity. Its activities are conducted through a separate legal entity and the parties participating in the decision-making exercise control through their equity investments. This means that the significant decisions require the unanimous consent of all of the parties. The company holding 20% of the equity can appoint a board member and has the ability to prevent the remaining companies from making significant decisions without its consent.

FRS 102 states that a venturer which is a parent shall, in its consolidated financial statements, account for all of its investments in jointly controlled entities using the equity method. Therefore, Stem Co should account for any difference, positive or negative, between the cost of acquisition and the investor's share of the fair values of the net identifiable assets of the entity in accordance with the business combinations regulations of FRS 102, that is, it is accounted for like goodwill. Where an investment is less than their share of the fair value of the identifiable net assets acquired, such a transaction results in a gain to the investor and is referred to as negative goodwill.

However, negative goodwill is rare. Therefore, before recognising such a gain, Stem Co should:

(a) Reassess the identification and measurement of the acquiree's assets, liabilities and provisions for contingent liabilities and the measurement of the cost of the combination.

(b) Recognise and separately disclose the resulting excess on the face of the statement of financial position on the acquisition date, immediately below goodwill, and followed by a subtotal of the net amount of goodwill and the excess.

(c) Recognise subsequently the excess up to the fair value of non-monetary assets acquired in profit or loss in the periods in which the non-monetary assets are recovered. Any excess exceeding the fair value of non-monetary assets acquired should be recognised in profit or loss in the periods expected to be benefited.

Stem Co should try to understand why the other parties would contribute assets of higher value than those contributed by Stem Co. Usually, investors act in an economically rational manner. There may be strategic reasons for such actions. For example, Stem Co may have specialised knowledge of the industry. Also, the fair value of the net identifiable assets of Emphasis Co may have increased before the finalisation of the agreement.

Stem Co contributed cash of $150,000 to Emphasis Co. The carrying value of the net assets contributed by the investors was $310,000 but the fair value of the net assets contributed was $470,000. Therefore, Stem Co's share of the fair value of the identifiable assets of Emphasis Co is 40% of $470,000, i.e. $188,000. This exceeds the contribution of $150,000. Once Stem Co has reassessed whether it has correctly identified all of the assets acquired and all of the liabilities assumed as part of its investment in Emphasis Co, Stem Co will record the investment at $188,000 and will record negative goodwill of $38,000 ($188,000-$150,000) which is recognised in profit or loss in the periods expected to be benefited.

Dr Investment in Emphasis Co	$188,000
Cr Cash	$150,000
Cr SOFP – negative goodwill (shown just below goodwill)	$38,000

Marking scheme		
		Marks
(a)	Discussion of key differences between FRS 102 and IFRS 3:	
	Transaction costs	1
	Contingent consideration	1
	Step acquisition	1
	Bargain purchase	1
	Proportionate method v fair value	1
	Fair value	1
	Intangibles/goodwill	1
		7
(b)	Discussion and application of key principles of joint venture accounting with well-argued conclusion	5
	Discussion of negative goodwill	2
	Accounting of negative goodwill	1
		8
Total		**15**

66 SITKA (MAR/JUN 2021)

Key answer tips

This UK variant question is pretty tough, testing areas that would need detailed knowledge of the UK GAAP content (chapter 24 in your study text). The differences you need to be aware of relate to the **recognition criteria** applied to an intangible asset, the treatment of group investments in separate financial statements and fair values.

For part (c) a comparison of the FRS 102 treatment of fair values versus the international equivalent (IFRS 13) is required. Here, at least, some marks will be given for your core IFRS knowledge. Therefore, even if your UK preparation is found wanting, make sure you discuss the IFRS treatment (and take an educated guess as to what the UK difference may be).

This question shows how important thorough preparation for the UK variant question is. Any of the differences between FRS 102 and IFRS standards could be tested within the examination.

(a) Cent Co pays fees to Sitka Co to access and use its software. The recognition criteria for an intangible asset in accordance with FRS 102 *The Financial Reporting Standard applicable in the UK and Republic of Ireland* are identifiability, the probability that the expected future economic benefits will flow to the entity and reliable measurement. These need to be considered when determining whether an intangible asset is created. The current arrangement with Sitka Co is likely to satisfy the identifiability and measurement criteria but there needs to be an assessment as to whether it is probable that the expected benefits will flow to the entity. FRS 102 states that an entity should assess the probability of expected future economic benefits using reasonable and supportable assumptions which represent management's best estimate of the economic conditions which will exist over the useful life of the asset. Cent Co does not own the rights to the software at any time and cannot run the software on its own hardware. For it to be probable that the expected future economic benefits would flow to the entity, then Cent Co would have to exercise some control over the software. This is not the case.

Thus, Cent Co should not recognise an intangible asset because Cent Co does not control the resource. The contract is not a lease contract as Cent Co does not have the right to direct the use of an asset by having decision-making rights to change how and for what purpose the asset is used throughout the four-year contract. At 1 January 20X7, the contract gave Cent Co only the right to receive access to Sitka Co's software in the future and is therefore a service contract which is expensed over the four-year period.

(b) FRS 102 requires an entity which prepares separate financial statements to account for investments in subsidiaries, joint ventures and associates either

- at cost less impairment,
- at fair value with changes in fair value recognised in other comprehensive income, or
- at fair value with changes in fair value recognised in profit or loss.

Sitka Co has elected to measure its subsidiary at cost less impairment. After the partial disposal, Marlett Co is not a subsidiary, joint venture or associate of Sitka Co but is an investment in an equity instrument. In accordance with FRS 102, investments in non-puttable ordinary shares are measured at fair value if the shares are publicly traded or their fair value can otherwise be measured reliably. Any changes in fair value are recognised in profit or loss.

The carrying amount attributable to the investment at the date when Marlett Co ceased to be a subsidiary will be regarded as the cost on initial measurement of the financial asset of (15%/60% of $12m) $3 million and not its fair value of $3·5 million. Where a parent ceases to control a subsidiary, a gain or loss should be recognised in its individual statement of profit or loss, calculated as the difference between:

(i) the proceeds from the disposal and

(ii) the proportion of the carrying amount of the subsidiary's net assets disposed of as at the date of disposal.

Thus, Sitka Co would make a profit of $(10 – (45%/60% x12)) million, i.e. $1 million. Sitka Co should not present any difference in other comprehensive income as it is not permitted in accordance with FRS 102. Conceptually, the difference meets the definition of income or expenses in FRS 102.

(c) FRS 102 states that the fair value is the amount for which an asset could be exchanged, a liability settled, or an equity instrument granted could be exchanged, between knowledgeable, willing parties in an arm's length transaction.

IFRS 13 *Fair Value Measurement* defines fair value as the price which would be received to sell an asset or paid to transfer a liability in an orderly transaction between market participants at the measurement date. IFRS 13 also uses the concept of the highest and best use which is the use of a non-financial asset by market participants which would maximise the value of the asset or the group of assets and liabilities within which the asset would be used. FRS 102 does not directly specify the use of this concept but often refers to fair value being measured with sufficient reliability.

It can be argued that both standards state that the fair values of the two assets would be determined based on the use of the assets within the buyer group which operates in the industry. The fair value of the asset group of $230 million is higher than the asset group for the financial investor ($200 million). The use of the assets in a group does not maximise the fair value of the assets individually but it maximises the fair value of the asset group. Even though Qbooks would be worth $50 million to the financial investors, its fair value for financial reporting purposes is $30 million as this is the value placed upon Qbooks by the industry buyer group.

Marking scheme			
			Marks
(a)	Discussion and application of the following to the situation:		
	FRS 102		3
	Service contract		1
			4
(b)	Discussion and application of the following to the situation:		
	Separate financial statements		2
	Financial asset		2
	Carrying amount		2
	Calculation of profit or loss		1
	Principles of OCI		1
			8
(c)	Discussion and application of the following to the situation:		
	FRS 102 definition		1
	IFRS 13 highest and best use		2
	Grouping of fair values		2
			5
Total			**17**

67 CORBEL (SEP/DEC 2020)

Key answer tips

High marks can be obtained on this question by using your knowledge of IFRS Standards and then substituting in any UK GAAP differences – such as the fact that FRS 102 does not have a concept of 'held for sale' and does not permit intangibles to have an indefinite life.

(a) Jengi brand name

FRS 102 states that an entity shall assess at each reporting date whether there is any indication that an asset may be impaired. If any such indication exists, the entity shall estimate the recoverable amount of the asset. If there is no indication of impairment, it is not necessary to estimate the recoverable amount. Thus, the brand need not be tested for impairment.

FRS 102 defines a cash generating unit (CGU) as the smallest identifiable group of assets that includes the asset and generated cash flows that are largely independent of the cash inflows from other assets or other groups of assets. However, brands are typically not a separate CGU under FRS 102 and are not tested for impairment individually.

For the purpose of impairment testing, the brand should be allocated to each of Corbel Co's cash generating units that are expected to benefit from the synergies of the combination.

(b) Perfume brand names

FRS 102 states that all intangible assets shall be considered to have a finite useful life. Additionally, if, in exceptional cases, an entity is unable to make a reliable estimate of the useful life of an intangible asset, the life shall not exceed 10 years. Thus, under FRS 102, the perfume brands cannot be considered to have an indefinite life.

Corbel Co should consider various factors to determine the brand names' useful life. These will include the extent to which Corbel is prepared to support the brand and the extent to which the brand has long-term potential and has had proven success, such as the Locust perfume.

Perfume is subject to market and fashion trends and so an assessment of how resistant the brands are to change should be made. Corbel Co has purchased the brands as a defensive measure to prevent rival companies acquiring them. Therefore, there may be a doubt as to the support that Corbel Co may be prepared to give to the brands.

The Clara perfume is linked to the popularity of the actor and therefore its useful life is likely to be dependent upon the longevity of the popularity of the actor.

(c) Proposed store closure

There is no separate guidance in FRS 102 for non-current assets held for sale as it does not have a concept that is comparable to IFRS 5 *Non-current assets Held for Sale*, of assets being classified as 'held for sale'.

Under FRS 102, where an entity intends to sell a non-current asset (NCA)in the near future, the asset should continue to be held in property, plant and equipment unless that asset is being transferred to inventory for sale in the ordinary course of the company's business. The asset will be derecognised at the point of sale or disposal and any profit or loss on disposal recognised accordingly.

This is different to IFRS 5 which requires that a non-current asset be reclassified as 'held for sale' if its carrying amount will be recovered principally through a sale transaction rather than through continuing use. Using IFRS 5, the six stores would be accounted for as a discontinued operation as they represent a component of Corbel Co and are a separate geographical area of operations.

Under FRS 102, the approval and announcement of a plan to close the six Italian stores is an indication that the assets attributable to the sale may be impaired. In addition, the six stores would be classified as a 'disposal group' which is a group of assets that an entity intends to dispose of in a single transaction. FRS 102 sets out the disclosure requirements for situations where an entity has a binding sale agreement at the reporting date for a major disposal of assets or a disposal group. As stated above, FRS 102 states that an entity shall assess at each reporting date whether there is any indication that an asset may be impaired. If any such indication exists, the entity shall estimate the recoverable amount of the asset. If there is no indication of impairment, it is not necessary to estimate the recoverable amount.

Although there has been a local newspaper article that Corbel Co is to shut 30 stores with a loss of 500 jobs across the world over the next five years, there has been no formal announcement by Corbel Co. Without formal plans, it is feasible that the closure of the additional 24 stores will not take place. This means that no obligation exists to restructure and, as per FRS 102, no restructuring provision should be recognised.

(d) Primary store

If Corbel Co feels that the primary store benefits all the other stores from a brand perspective, there is an argument for treating the store as a corporate asset and allocating its carrying amount to the cash generating units when testing for impairment. However, it is likely that management assesses performance on a store-by-store basis -this adds weight to the argument that each store, including the primary store, is a separate cash generating unit because of their ability to generate cash flows independently from other company assets.

The amount of internet sales included when calculating value in use for the purposes of testing the primary store for impairment will depend on the quantity of sales that are sourced directly from it. Where Internet sales are sourced from a central warehouse or another store, the cash inflows should be excluded from the primary store's impairment assessment and included in the appropriate CGU.

ACCA marking scheme		
		Marks
(a)	Treatment of brand on acquisition	2
	Allocation to CGU	2
		4
(b)	Principles	2
	Application	4
		6
(c)	Contrast with IFRS 5	3
	Application of FRS 102 to scenario	3
		6
(d)	Impairment principles	2
	Impairment of primary store	2
		4
Total		**20**

68 LERIA (MAR 2020)

Key answer tips

Part (a) of this question is relatively straight forward – especially if you have learned the UK GAAP content from Chapter 24 of the Study Text. In part (b) it is important to remember that the accounting treatment under FRS 102 and IFRS Standards for many transactions is the same. Alternative answers with regards to the treatment of the contingent consideration would also be allowable.

(a) Intangible assets

FRS 102 only requires recognition of intangible assets other than goodwill arising on a business combination if they are separable **and** arise from legal or contractual rights. IFRS 3 *Business Combinations* says that intangible assets other than goodwill arising from a business combination are recognised at fair value if they are separable **or** if they arise from legal or contractual rights.

Under FRS 102, all intangible assets are considered to have a finite life. The life should not exceed 10 years where a reliable estimate of the life cannot be made. IAS 38 states that an intangible asset can have an indefinite life where there is no foreseeable limit to the period that the asset will generate cash inflows. Such assets are not amortised.

FRS 102 allows an entity to capitalise development expenditure subject to certain criteria. However, an entity may choose to expense this expenditure as incurred. This policy must be applied consistently. However, IAS 38 does not allow this policy choice as intangible assets arising from the development phase of a project must be capitalised if certain criteria are met.

FRS 102 states that if an intangible asset is acquired free of charge or for nominal consideration by way of a grant, the cost of that intangible asset is its fair value at the date the grant is received or receivable. IAS 38 permits a policy choice between recognising the intangible asset at fair value or at a nominal amount.

(b) Contracts

When a player's contract is signed, management should make an assessment of the likely outcome of performance conditions. Thus, the contingent consideration will be recognised in the players' registration costs if management believes the performance conditions will be met in line with the contractual terms. Periodic reassessments of the potential should be completed. Any amounts which the directors of Leria Co believe will be payable should be included in the players' contract costs from the date management believes that the performance conditions will be met. Any additional amounts of contingent consideration not included in the costs of players' registrations will be disclosed separately as a commitment.

Amortisation of the costs of the contract will be based upon the length of the player's contract. The costs associated with an extension of a playing contract should be added to the residual balance of the players' contract costs at the date of signing the contract extension. The revised carrying amount should be amortised over the remaining renegotiated contract length.

If there is no indication of impairment, under FRS 102 then, it is not necessary to estimate the recoverable amount. However, where a player sustains a career threatening injury and is removed from the playing squad, the carrying amount of the individual would be assessed against the best estimate of the individual's fair value less any costs to sell and an impairment charge made in operating expenses reflecting any loss arising.

It is unlikely that any individual player can be separated from the single cash generating unit (CGU) which will be the playing squad. It is difficult to determine the value-in-use of an individual player in isolation as players cannot generate cash flows on their own unless via a sale.

ACCA marking scheme		
		Marks
(a)	Key differences	5
(b)	Performance conditions	5
	Value in use	2
		7
Total		**12**

69 DIGIWIRE (SEP/DEC 2019)

Key answer tips

This is a tricky UK GAAP question. Part (a) tests some relatively small differences between IFRS Standards and FRS 102 that you would only know after thoroughly studying Chapter 24 of the Study Text. Part (c) relies on a knowledge of current issues – a topic that many students neglect. The easiest marks are probably available in part (b) for demonstrating knowledge of the true and fair override and for explaining how this might impact on the usefulness of financial information.

(a) Termination benefits

Where an entity is committed to make payments to employees when it terminates their employment, these payments are categorised as termination benefits. These payments do not carry with them any future economic benefits and are recognised as an expense in profit or loss immediately.

Under FRS 102 *The Financial Reporting Standard applicable in the UK and Republic of Ireland*, if a termination is linked to restructuring, an entity must be demonstrably committed to a termination, which is only the case when the entity has a detailed formal plan for the termination and is without realistic possibility of withdrawal from the plan.

IAS 19 *Employee Benefits* has similar rules regarding terminations linked to restructuring, but gives more detailed guidance on the criteria which demonstrate that the entity is committed to the plan. For example, under IAS 19, it should be unlikely that significant changes to the plan will be made. Also, there should be specific detail regarding numbers of employees, type and amount of benefit, location of the termination and the expected completion date.

(b) Amendments to IAS 19

FRS 102 does not require entities to revise the assumptions for the calculation of current service cost and net interest during the accounting period, even if an entity remeasured the net defined benefit liability or asset in the event of a plan amendment, curtailment or settlement. The calculations are based on the actuarial assumptions as at the start of the financial year. However, it seems inappropriate to ignore any updated assumptions when determining current service cost and net interest for the period.

Therefore, an amendment to IAS 19 if adopted by FRS 102 would change the calculation of net interest and current service cost as follows. When a plan amendment, curtailment or settlement occurs during the annual reporting period, an entity must:

- Determine current service cost for the remainder of the period after the plan amendment, curtailment or settlement using the actuarial assumptions used to remeasure the net defined benefit liability/asset reflecting the benefits offered under the plan and the plan assets after that event.
- Determine net interest for the remainder of the period after the plan amendment, curtailment or settlement using: (i) the net defined benefit liability/asset reflecting the benefits offered under the plan and the plan assets after that event; and (ii) the discount rate used to remeasure that net defined benefit liability/asset.

If Digiwire Co had applied FRS 102 then the current service cost would have been \$108 million (12 months × \$9 million). If Digiwire Co applied the revised IAS 19 requirements, the current service cost would be \$96 million ((8 months × \$9 million) + (4 months × \$6 million)). Thus there will be a reduction in the current service cost of \$12 million.

Similarly, the net interest component calculated under FRS 102 would be \$900,000 (3% × \$30 million). In accordance with the revised IAS 19 requirements, the net interest component would be calculated as \$1,020,000 ((\$900,000 × 8/12) + (3.5% × \$36m × 4/12)). Therefore, applying revised IAS 19 would increase the net interest component by \$120,000 (\$1,020,000 – \$900,000).

The net effect will be to change the re-measurement component by \$11,880,000.

(c) True and fair override

The Companies Act requires that the directors of a company must not approve financial statements unless they are satisfied they give a true and fair view. Where directors and auditors do not believe that a particular accounting policy will give a true and fair view, they are legally required to adopt a more appropriate policy, even if this requires a departure from a particular accounting standard.

The true and fair override is enshrined in FRS 102 and it requires departure from the requirements of a specific accounting standard when compliance would conflict with the objective of financial statements. 'Fair presentation' is where the effects of transactions are represented faithfully so, in effect, there is unlikely to be any substantial difference in practical terms between it and the true and fair concept.

For companies reporting under UK GAAP, FRS 102 and *Companies Act* require that directors make prudent judgements in their consideration of financial statements, particularly where there is uncertainty. Disagreement with a particular standard does not, on its own, provide grounds for departing from it. Where the accounting standards clearly address an issue, but the requirements are insufficient to fully explain the issue, the solution is normally additional disclosure. However, if the financial statements do not represent faithfully the transactions, other events and conditions which they purport to present or could reasonably be expected to represent, then that is where the true and fair override is applied.

Comparability enhances the usefulness of financial information. Thus accounting information would be more useful if it can be compared with similar information from other entities, or from the same entity. Comparability is crucial to improve financial reporting quality but is made more difficult when entities can override accounting standards.

ACCA marking scheme		
		Marks
(a)	FRS 102 vs. IAS 19	3
(b)	Discussion of FRS 102 vs IAS 19 differences	4
	Calculation of impact of differences	4
		8
(c)	True and fair override	3
	Impact on faithful representation and comparability	3
		6
Total		**17**

70 CRYPTO (MAR/JUN 2019)

Key answer tips

If you are studying SBR UK then it is important to thoroughly learn the examinable UK content. This is covered in Chapter 24 of the Study Text. You will find this content easier to learn if you have a solid grasp of the examinable IFRS Standards.

(a) Control

The definition of control in FRS 102 *The Financial Reporting Standard applicable in the UK and Republic of Ireland* is different from the definition in IFRS 10 *Consolidated Financial Statements*.

FRS 102 states that control is the power to govern the financial and operating policies of an entity so as to obtain benefits from its activities. FRS 102 states that control is presumed to exist if an entity owns more than half of the voting rights of another entity. This presumption may be overcome in exceptional circumstances if it can be clearly demonstrated that such ownership does not constitute control.

FRS 102 further states that control also exists when the parent owns half or less of the voting power of an entity but it has:

- power over more than half of the voting rights by virtue of an agreement with other investors
- power to govern the financial and operating policies of the entity under a statute or an agreement
- power to appoint or remove the majority of the members of the board of directors or equivalent governing body and control of the entity is by that board or body; or
- power to cast the majority of votes at meetings of the board of directors or equivalent governing body and control of the entity is by that board or body.

Control can also be achieved by having options or convertible instruments which are currently exercisable or by having an agent with the ability to direct the activities for the benefit of the controlling entity. Control can also exist when the parent has the power to exercise, or actually exercises, dominant influence or control over the undertaking or it and the undertaking are managed on a unified basis.

IFRS 10, however, states that an investor controls an investee when it is exposed, or has rights, to variable returns from its involvement with the investee and has the ability to affect those returns through its power over the investee.

Joint arrangements

FRS 102 now makes a distinction between jointly controlled entities, jointly controlled assets and jointly controlled operations. Under FRS 102, classification as a jointly controlled entity is driven by whether there is the creation of a separate legal entity. Joint control is the contractually agreed sharing of control over an economic activity, and exists only when the strategic financial and operating decisions relating to the activity require the unanimous consent of the parties sharing control.

In contrast, IFRS 11 *Joint Arrangements* outlines the accounting by entities which jointly control an arrangement and classifies the arrangements differently to FRS 102. Under IFRS 11, the arrangements are classified as either a joint venture (representing a share of net assets and equity accounted) or a joint operation (representing rights to assets and obligations for liabilities, accounted for accordingly).

(b) Joint control

FRS 102 defines joint control as the contractually agreed sharing of control over an economic activity. Joint control exists only when the strategic financial and operating decisions relating to the activity require the unanimous consent of the parties sharing control. Before assessing whether an entity has joint control over an arrangement, an entity must first assess whether the parties control the arrangement in accordance with the definition of control in FRS 102. After this assessment, an entity must determine whether it has joint control of the arrangement which, in turn, means an assessment as to whether any party can prevent any of the other parties from making unilateral decisions without its consent. It must be clear which combination of parties is required to agree unanimously to decisions about the relevant activities of the arrangement.

In the case of Kurran, there is more than one combination of parties possible to reach the required majority. As a result, Crypto does not have joint control. Additionally, Crypto does not control Kurran as FRS 102 states that control requires the power to govern the financial and operating policies of an entity so as to obtain benefits from its activities. Crypto does not have the ability to direct the relevant activities as it can only block decisions, and cannot make decisions by itself. Also, there is no shareholder agreement which sets out the shareholders' voting rights and obligations and thus the other shareholders can act together to prevent Crypto from making decisions in its own interest. Crypto does not have joint control as agreement between itself and other board members has to occur for a decision to be made. Therefore, it appears that Kurran is an associate of Crypto.

(c) Translating a foreign operation

FRS 102 sets out one procedure to be followed when translating the results of a foreign subsidiary into the presentation currency of the group:

- all assets and liabilities (whether monetary or non-monetary) for each statement of financial position presented (i.e. including comparatives) are translated at the closing rate at the year-end date
- income and expenses for each statement of comprehensive income (i.e. including comparatives) are translated at exchange rates at the dates of the transactions; and

- all resulting exchange differences are recognised in other comprehensive income and accumulate in equity.

Unlike IAS 21 *The Effects of Changes in Foreign Exchange Rates*, the cumulative exchange differences are not required to be recorded in a separate reserve within equity, although a separate reserve may be used if preferred.

Any accumulated exchange differences on non-wholly owned subsidiaries arising from translation and attributable to non-controlling interests should be allocated to, and recognised as part of, non-controlling interests in the consolidated statement of financial position.

On disposal of the foreign subsidiary, any cumulative exchange differences are not reclassified to profit or loss and simply remain in equity.

ACCA marking scheme		
		Marks
(a)	Control definitions	3
	FRS 102 requirements and IFRS 11 classifications	3
		6
(b)	Control	3
	Power	3
		6
(c)	FRS 102 requirements	2
	Discussion of FRS 102 and IAS 21 and NCI	3
		5
Total		**17**

71 FILL (DEC 2018)

Key answer tips

Students sitting SBR UK might be asked to discuss the accounting treatment of a transaction in accordance with FRS 102. If you know the treatment under IFRS Standards, and you know the differences between IFRS Standards and FRS 102, then you should be able to make a good attempt.

(a) Borrowing costs

Under FRS 102 *The Financial Reporting Standard Applicable in the UK and Republic of Ireland*, an entity **may** adopt a policy of capitalising borrowing costs which are directly attributable to the acquisition, construction or production of a qualifying asset as part of the cost of that asset. A qualifying asset is an asset which necessarily takes a substantial period of time to get ready for its intended use. Fill can capitalise the borrowing costs which relate to the licence. However, as the equipment will be used for other construction projects throughout the UK, the borrowing costs relating to it cannot be capitalised.

Impairment

FRS 102 specifies that a recoverable amount need not be determined unless there are indicators of impairment. There is evidence of a decline in forward prices. Short-term market fluctuations may not be impairment indicators if prices are expected to return to higher levels. However, if the decline in prices is for a significant proportion of the remaining expected life of the mine then it is more likely to be an impairment indicator. It appears that forward contract prices for two years out of the four years of the mine's remaining life indicate a reduction in selling prices and so it would appear that the mining assets should be tested for impairment, especially as the entity wishes to sell the mine. Impairment would be recognised if a mine's carrying amount exceeds its recoverable amount.

Decision to sell

As far as the decision to sell the mine is concerned, FRS 102 does not address assets held for sale; the decision to sell an asset is considered an impairment indicator although continuing and discontinued activities must be analysed. FRS 102 states that an internal indicator of impairment occurs when significant changes with an adverse effect on the entity have taken place during the period, or are expected to take place in the near future, in the extent to which, or manner in which, an asset is used or is expected to be used. These changes include plans to dispose of an asset before the previously expected date. If there is an indication that an asset may be impaired, this may indicate that the entity should review the remaining useful life, the depreciation method or the residual value for the asset.

(b) Business combinations

Under FRS 102, the cost of a business combination includes any costs directly attributable to the business combination, for example, any advisory and legal fees. However, IFRS 3 *Business Combinations* explicitly excludes such costs from the cost of a business combination. Thus, such costs generally form part of goodwill under FRS 102, whereas under IFRS 3, they are recognised as expenses in the period.

If a business combination is acquired in stages, IFRS 3 states that the consideration paid is all measured at the acquisition date fair value in accordance with full IFRS Standards whereas FRS 102 states that the consideration given for each stage is measured at its fair value at the date when the stage was recognised in the financial statements.

Under FRS 102, contingent consideration is included in the cost of a business combination, if its payment is probable and the amount can be measured reliably. IFRS 3 requires the fair value of contingent consideration to be included in the cost of a business combination regardless of whether payment is probable; its fair value is determined by considering the different possible outcomes and estimating the probability of each outcome. Under FRS 102, if the contingent consideration subsequently becomes probable and can be measured reliably, the amount is treated as an adjustment to the cost of the business combination.

Under FRS 102, non-controlling interest (NCI) is measured at its proportionate share of the group carrying amounts of the subsidiary's identifiable net assets. Using this method, goodwill is not included in the carrying amount of non-controlling interest. Under IFRS 3, non-controlling interest is measured using either the fair value method or the proportionate share method. With the fair value method, the NCI's stake in the entity is valued at fair value with the result that all of the entity's goodwill is recognised. The part of the goodwill which is attributable to the equity owned by the NCI is included in the measurement of the non-controlling interest. If the fair value method is used, both goodwill and non-controlling interest are different from those calculated under FRS 102.

Marking scheme		
		Marks
(a)	Borrowing costs	2
	Impairment and decision to sell	5
		7
(b)	Costs	2
	Consideration and stage payments	3
	NCI	3
		8
Total		**15**

72 SKIZER (SEP 2018)

Key answer tips

Students sitting SBR UK might be asked to discuss the accounting treatment of a transaction in accordance with FRS 102. If you know the treatment under IFRS Standards, and you know the differences between IFRS Standards and FRS 102, then you should be able to make a good attempt.

(a) FRS 102 recognition criteria

FRS 102 requires an entity to recognise an intangible asset if:

- it is probable that expected future economic benefits will flow to the entity, and
- the cost of the asset can be measured reliably.

This requirement applies whether an intangible asset is acquired externally or generated internally. The probability of future economic benefits must be based on reasonable and supportable assumptions about conditions which will exist over the life of the asset. The probability recognition criterion is always considered to be satisfied for intangible assets which are acquired separately or in a business combination.

If the recognition criteria are not met, FRS 102 requires the expenditure to be expensed when it is incurred.

Conceptual Framework

According to the *Conceptual Framework,* items are only recognised if they meet the definition of an element. The definition of an asset is **'a present economic resource controlled by an entity as a result of a past event'** (para 4.3).

This does not mean that all items meeting the definition of an element are recognised. An element is only recognised if recognition provides users with useful financial information. In other words recognition must provide:

- relevant information
- a faithful representation of the asset or liability, and resulting income, expenses or equity movements.

Recognition might not provide relevant information if there is uncertainty over the existence of the element or if there is a low probability of an inflow or outflow of economic resources. Recognition of an element might not provide a faithful representation if there is a very high degree of measurement uncertainty.

Consistency

As can be seen, the recognition criteria in the *Conceptual Framework* and FRS 102 are different.

Both FRS 102 and the *Conceptual Framework* attempt to ensure that financial statements provide information that meets the qualitative characteristics of useful information but do this in different ways. FRS 102 uses practical filters of probability and reliability to exclude information that will not be useful. In contrast, the *Conceptual Framework* refers directly to the qualitative characteristics, and provides guidance on how to apply them.

(b) Development projects

Skizer should have assessed whether the recognition criteria in FRS 102 were met at the time the entity capitalised the intangible assets. If the recognition criteria were met, then it was not appropriate to derecognise the intangible assets. According to FRS 102, an intangible asset should be derecognised only on disposal or when no future economic benefits are expected from its use or disposal.

If there were any doubts regarding the recoverability of the intangible asset, then Skizer should have assessed whether the intangible assets would be impaired. Prior to the current year, Skizer was unable to make a reliable estimate of the useful life of the intangible assets. However, FRS 102 states that the life should not exceed 10 years.

Further, the reclassification of intangible assets to research and development costs does not constitute a change in an accounting estimate. Under FRS 102, a change in accounting estimate is an adjustment of the carrying amount of an asset or liability, or related expense, resulting from the assessment of the present status of, and expected future benefits associated with, that asset or liability.

If the directors of Skizer decide that the recognition criteria were not initially met, then Skizer would have to recognise retrospectively a correction of an error.

(c) Differences between UK GAAP and IFRS Standards

Under UK GAAP, an entity may capitalise development expenditure where certain criteria are met. Under IAS 38 *Intangible Assets*, an intangible asset arising from the development phase of an internal project must be capitalised if certain criteria are met.

If an intangible asset is acquired through a business combination and arises from legal or contractual rights, then FRS 102 allows recognition if there is evidence of exchange transactions for similar assets. Under IFRS 3 *Business Combinations*, intangible assets acquired through a business combination are recognised if they are separable, or if they arise from legal or contractual rights.

Under FRS 102, goodwill is amortised over its useful life. If the useful economic life cannot be reliably determined, then the estimate used should not exceed ten years. Under International Financial Reporting Standards, amortisation of goodwill is not permitted. Instead annual impairment testing is required.

Marking scheme		
		Marks
(a)	Recognition criteria – 1 mark per point	6
(b)	Development – 1 mark per point	5
(c)	UK GAAP differences	4
Total		**15**

73 BOBARRA

Key answer tips

Students sitting the UK paper are expected to know Companies Act requirements concerning the preparation of consolidated financial statements. This needs to be learned. However, you would not be expected to reproduce the detail below.

There are not many differences between International Financial Reporting Standards and UK GAAP with regards to related party transactions. There are a couple of marks available for talking about FRS 102 exemptions and whether they apply in this scenario.

(a) Companies Act

The requirements in the Companies Act to prepare group accounts are largely mirrored in FRS 102, which states that consolidated financial statements (group accounts in the Companies Act) are prepared by all parent entities unless one of the following exemptions, which are derived from the Companies Act, applies:

- The parent company is subject to the small companies' regime (see ss.383 to 384 of the Companies Act).

- The parent company is a subsidiary included in a larger group which prepares consolidated financial statements and meets the requirements of ss.400 or 401 of the Companies Act, including:
  - The parent is itself a subsidiary whose immediate parent is established in an EEA state, and whose results are consolidated into the group financial statements of an undertaking established in an EEA state (not necessarily the immediate parent). Companies Act sets out further conditions for this exemption, including that a company, which has any of its securities admitted to trading on a regulated market in an EEA state, is not eligible for this exemption.
  - The parent is itself a subsidiary, its immediate parent is not established in an EEA state, and its results are consolidated into the group accounts of an undertaking (either the same parent or another) drawn up in accordance with the EU Seventh Directive or in an equivalent manner (for example, EU-IFRS accounts). Companies Act sets out further conditions for this exemption, including that a company, which has any of its securities admitted to trading on a regulated market in an EEA state, is not eligible for this exemption.
- All of the parent's subsidiaries are excluded from consolidation under FRS 102.

If an entity is not a parent at the year end, then it is not required to prepare consolidated accounts.

Exclusion of subsidiaries from consolidation

Consolidated financial statements provide information about the group as a single economic entity. They include all subsidiaries of the parent except those excluded on one of the following grounds:

- severe long-term restrictions substantially hinder the exercise of the rights of the parent over the assets or management of the subsidiary. These rights are the rights held by or attributed to the company in the absence of which it would not be the parent company; or
- the subsidiary is held exclusively for resale and has not previously been included in the consolidation.

Companies Act states that a subsidiary may be excluded from consolidation if the necessary information to prepare the group accounts cannot be obtained without disproportionate expense or undue delay. FRS 102, however, states that this does not justify non-consolidation, effectively closing off the statutory option. Subsidiaries are not excluded from consolidation simply because the subsidiary has dissimilar business activities to the rest of the group.

(b) Related parties

The objective of both IAS 24 *Related Party Disclosures* and FRS 102 *The Financial Reporting Standard applicable in the UK and Republic of Ireland* as regards related party disclosures is to ensure that an entity's financial statements contain the disclosures necessary to draw attention to the possibility that its financial position and profit or loss may have been affected by the existence of related parties and by transactions and outstanding balances with such parties.

Individuals

A person or a close member of that person's family is related to a reporting entity if that person:

- has control or joint control over the reporting entity
- has significant influence over the reporting entity; or
- is a member of the key management personnel of the reporting entity or of a parent of the reporting entity.

As regards Bobarra, the finance director is a related party because he controls Bobarra and is a member of the key management personnel. The sales director is also a related party of Bobarra as she is a member of the key management personnel and is a close member (spouse) of the family of the finance director. Their son is a related party of Bobarra as he is a close member (son) of their family. The operations director is also a related party as he is a member of key management personnel and has significant influence (more than 20% of the voting power) over Bobarra.

IAS 24 requires that the disclosure of key management personnel remuneration is broken down into the following categories:

- short-term benefits
- post-employment benefits
- other long-term benefits
- termination benefits
- share-based payments.

FRS 102 simply requires the disclosure of management personnel remuneration in total.

Entities

An entity is related to a reporting entity if the entity is controlled or jointly controlled by a person identified as a related party. Hence, the family trust is a related party of Bobarra. The family trust is controlled by related parties, the finance and sales directors, for the benefit of a close member of their family, i.e. their son. In the absence of evidence to the contrary, the third owner of the shares is not a related party. The person is a passive investor who does not appear to exert significant influence over Bobarra.

A related party relationship exists where the entity and the reporting entity are members of the same group, which means that each parent, subsidiary and fellow subsidiary is related to the others. However, FRS 102 states that disclosures need not be given of transactions entered into between two or more members of a group if any subsidiary which is a party to the transaction is wholly owned by such a member.

The transactions between Bobarra and Drumby would be disclosed as related party disclosures under both IAS 24 and FRS 102. Drumby is not wholly owned by any member of the group and hence the FRS 102 exemption does not apply. However, any transactions between Bobarra, Alucant and Cantor would be covered by the exemption from disclosure in FRS 102 even though the three entities are related parties.

Marking scheme		
		Marks
(a)	Companies Act – 1 mark per point	9
(b)	Related parties – 1 mark per point	7
Total		**16**

74 HARRIS

Key answer tips

One area where there are still large differences between International Financial Reporting Standards and UK GAAP is business combinations. Make sure that you memorise the examinable differences.

Deferred tax is a popular topic for UK specific questions because this section of FRS 102 is worded very differently from IAS 12.

(a) Goodwill

Consideration

IFRS 3 *Business Combinations* requires that contingent consideration is included in the calculation of goodwill at its fair value at the acquisition date. This fair value will incorporate the probability of payment. In contrast FRS 102 says that contingent consideration is only included in the calculation of goodwill if payment is probable.

IFRS 3 requires that any acquisition fees are expensed, whereas FRS 102 states that these should be included in the calculation of goodwill.

Non-controlling interest

Under IFRS 3, the non-controlling interest at the acquisition date can be measured at fair value or at its proportionate share of the fair value of the subsidiary's identifiable net assets. This decision is made on an acquisition by acquisition basis. FRS 102 only allows the proportionate method to be used.

Bargain purchase/negative goodwill

Under IFRS 3 *Business Combinations*, a gain on a bargain purchase is recognised immediately in the statement of profit or loss.

If a bargain purchase arises, FRS 102 requires the entity to:

- Reassess the identification and measurement of the acquiree's assets, liabilities and provisions for contingent liabilities and the measurement of the cost of the combination (this condition is the same as IFRS 3).
- Recognise and separately disclose the resulting excess on the face of the statement of financial position on the acquisition date (i.e. as a negative asset), immediately below goodwill, and followed by a subtotal of the net amount of goodwill and the excess.

- Recognise subsequently the excess up to the fair value of non-monetary assets acquired in profit or loss in the periods in which the non-monetary assets are recovered. Any excess exceeding the fair value of non-monetary assets acquired should be recognised in profit or loss in the periods expected to benefit.

(b) Deferred tax

Under IAS 12 *Income Taxes*, an entity recognises a deferred tax asset or liability for tax recoverable or payable in future periods as a result of past transactions or events. Such tax arises from the difference between the amounts recognised for the entity's assets and liabilities in the statement of financial position and the recognition of those assets and liabilities by the tax authorities plus the carry forward of currently unused tax losses and tax credits.

Under FRS 102, deferred tax is recognised in respect timing differences at the reporting date. Timing differences are differences between taxable profits and total comprehensive income as stated in the financial statements which arise from the inclusion of income and expenses in tax assessments in periods different from those in which they are recognised in financial statements. In addition, FRS 102 states that deferred tax should be recognised on the differences between the tax value and fair value of assets and liabilities acquired in a business combination, even though this impacts neither taxable profits nor total comprehensive income. As such, FRS 102 is said to adopt a 'timing difference plus' approach.

FRS 102 uses the term 'permanent difference', whereas IAS 12 does not use this term.

In practice it is unlikely that the differences between FRS 102 and IAS 12 will cause a significant difference in terms of the recognition and measurement of deferred tax assets and liabilities.

Marking scheme		
		Marks
(a)	Goodwill – 1 mark per point	9
(b)	Deferred tax – 1 mark per point	6
Total		**15**

75 ROWLING

Key answer tips

The UK specific syllabus content is very factual and needs to be learned by students sitting the UK exam. This question concerns the scope of the UK standards FRS 100, FRS 101, FRS 102 and FRS 105. This is core knowledge. If you struggled with this question, revisit the UK content in the Study Text.

The UK Standards

The Financial Reporting Council in the UK has published:

1 FRS 100 *Application of Financial Reporting Requirements*

2 FRS 101 *Reduced Disclosure Framework*

3 FRS 102 *The Financial Reporting Standard applicable in the UK and Republic of Ireland*

4 FRS 105 *The Financial Reporting Standard applicable to the Micro-entities Regime.*

FRS 100

FRS 100 sets out the overall financial reporting requirements, giving many entities a choice depending on factors such as size, and whether or not they are part of a listed group.

FRS 100 identifies whether entities need to produce their consolidated or individual financial statements in accordance with EU approved IFRS Standards or FRS 102.

FRS 101

FRS 101 provides companies with an opportunity to take advantage of reduced disclosures.

FRS 101 permits UK subsidiaries to adopt EU approved IFRS Standards for their individual financial statements but within the reduced disclosure framework. This option is also available for the parent company's individual financial statements.

FRS 102

FRS 102 adopts an IFRS Standard-based framework with proportionate disclosure requirements. It is based on the IFRS for SMEs Standard but with significant changes in order to address company law and to include extra accounting options.

FRS 105

Micro-entities can choose to prepare their financial statements in accordance with FRS 105.

FRS 105 is based on FRS 102 but with some amendments to satisfy legal requirements and to reflect the simpler nature of micro-entities.

For example, FRS 105:

- Prohibits accounting for deferred tax
- Prohibits accounting for equity-settled share-based payments before the issue of the shares
- Simplifies the rules around classifying a financial instrument as debt or equity
- Removes the distinction between functional and presentation currencies.

Intangible assets

Under UK GAAP, where certain criteria are met, an entity **may** capitalise development expenditure. Under IAS 38 *Intangible Assets*, an intangible asset arising from the development phase of an internal project **must** be capitalised if certain criteria are met.

If an intangible is acquired through a business combination and arises from legal or contractual rights then FRS 102 only permits its recognition if there is evidence of exchange transactions for similar assets. Under IFRS 3 *Business Combinations*, intangible assets acquired through a business combination are recognised if they are separable, or if they arise from legal or contractual rights.

Under FRS 102, goodwill is amortised over its useful economic life. If the useful economic life cannot be reliably determined then the estimate used should not exceed ten years. Under International Financial Reporting Standards, amortisation of goodwill is not permitted. Instead annual impairment testing is required.

Marking scheme	
	Marks
1 mark per valid point	15
	—
Total	**15**
	—

76 TOTO

Key answer tips

The recent issue of IFRS 16 *Leases* means that there are now significant differences between International Financial Reporting Standards and UK GAAP with regards to lessee accounting.

IFRS 16 *Leases*

With regards to lessee accounting, IFRS 16 *Leases* says that a lease liability and a right-of-use asset should be recognised at the inception of all leases (unless they are short-term or of low value). The lease liability will be measured at the present value of the lease payments yet to be made – the discount rate used should be the interest rate implicit in the lease. As there are no other costs or payments, the right-of-use asset will be measured at the same value.

Interest on the lease liability will be charged to profit or loss based on the rate implicit in the lease. The right-of-use asset will be depreciated over the three year lease term and this will be recorded in the statement of profit or loss.

FRS 102 *The Financial Reporting Standard applicable in the UK and Republic of Ireland*

FRS 102 classifies leases as finance leases or operating leases. A finance lease is a lease where the risks and rewards of ownership transfer to the lessee. It would seem that the lease is an operating lease, because ownership of the asset does not transfer to Toto at the end of the lease term, and the lease term is much shorter than the asset's useful life.

As such, no asset or liability is would be recognised at the inception of the lease. Instead, lease rentals would be charged to profit or loss on a straight line basis.

Comparison of impact

Liabilities will be higher if the financial statements are prepared using IFRS Standards rather than FRS 102. This will make the entity look more highly geared and, potentially, riskier to investors. Under IFRS 16, some of the lease liability would be classified as current on the statement of financial position, having an adverse impact on the current ratio.

Non-current assets will be higher under IFRS Standards. This could be viewed positively because Toto will appear more asset rich. However, users may conclude that Toto is inefficient at generating returns from its assets, and so invest their money elsewhere.

The total lease expense over the three year period will be the same under both IFRS 16 and FRS 102. However, under IFRS 16, the lease expense is likely to be split between operating expenses (the depreciation on the right-of-use asset) and finance costs (the interest on the lease liability). Under FRS 102 it is likely that the full lease expense will be recorded against operating expenses. As such, IFRS 16 might result in Toto recording higher operating profits.

In the first year of the lease it is likely that IFRS 16 will result in lower profits than FRS 102. This is because IFRS 16 requires recognition of a lease liability and a larger interest expense will be recognised in the first year of the lease when the liability is highest. Lower profits will lead to lower earnings per share, which is a key ratio for assessing company performance and for deriving company valuations.

Marking scheme	
	Marks
1 mark per valid point	15
	—
Total	**15**
	—

77 HOWEY

Key answer tips

Remember you will score one mark per valid point that you make. This means that you would not be expected to reproduce the detail below. However, do try and memorise the key differences between International Financial Reporting Standards and UK GAAP. In particular, it is important to remember that there is no concept of 'held for sale' in FRS 102.

(a) Held for sale and discontinued operations

Held for sale

IFRS 5 *Non-current Assets Held for Sale and Discontinued Operations* sets out requirements for the classification, measurement and presentation of non-current assets held for sale. Under IFRS 5, a non-current asset should be classified held for sale if its carrying amount will be recovered primarily through a sales transaction. At the date of meeting the criteria, such an asset will be measured at the lower of its carrying amount and fair value less costs to sell. Depreciation on the asset ceases.

FRS 102 does not refer to the concept of 'held for sale'. As such the asset will be depreciated or amortised until the disposal date. However, the decision to sell an asset does trigger an impairment review.

Discontinued operations

Under IFRS 5, an operation is classified as discontinued at the date the operation meets the criteria to be classified as held for sale or when the entity has disposed of the operation.

Because the concept of 'held for sale' is absent from FRS 102, an operation is classified as discontinued only if it has been disposed of.

With regards to discontinued operations, IFRS 5 requires a single number to be disclosed on the face of the statement of profit or loss, being the total of (i) the discontinued operations' post-tax profit/loss and (ii) the post-tax gain/loss recognised in the measurement of the fair value less costs to sell or on the disposal of the discontinued operations' assets. A breakdown of this number is required to be given either on the face of the statement of profit or loss or in the notes.

FRS 102 requires disclosure of the results of continuing operations and discontinued operations in separate columns on the face of the income statement.

Subsidiaries acquired exclusively for resale

Under IFRS 5, subsidiaries acquired exclusively with a view to resale that meet the conditions to be classified as held for sale are consolidated. However, their results are presented within the single line item for discontinued operations. In the statement of financial position they are presented as two separate items – assets, including goodwill, and liabilities.

Under FRS 102, subsidiaries acquired exclusively with a view to sell must be measured at either:

- Cost less impairment, or
- Fair value, with gains and losses recognised in profit or loss, or
- Fair value, with gains and losses recognised in other comprehensive income.

(b) Reasons for adopting FRS 102

There are various reasons why an entity might choose to prepare its financial statements in accordance with FRS 102 rather than IFRS Standards:

- FRS 102 is more accessibly worded than IFRS Standards.
- FRS 102 is a single accounting standard that is split into sections (such as 'revenue', 'leases' etc). This means that it is quicker and easier to navigate than IFRS Standards.
- Some accounting concepts are absent from FRS 102, such as 'assets held for sale'. Reducing the number of rules that entities must apply reduces the burden of financial reporting.
- FRS 102 permits some accounting policy choices that will help entities to simplify their financial reporting. For example, entities can choose to write off development expenditure and borrowing costs to profit or loss.
- Some FRS 102 rules are less time-consuming than their IFRS Standard equivalents. For instance, FRS 102 does not require the useful lives of property, plant and equipment to be reassessed annually.
- If other entities in the same sector also prepare financial statements in accordance with FRS 102 then it will make it easier to benchmark performance against them.
- There are far fewer disclosure requirements in FRS 102 than in full IFRS Standards.

Marking scheme		
		Marks
(a)	Held for sale and disc. operations – 1 mark per point	9
(b)	Reasons for adopting FRS 102 – 1 mark per point	6
		—
Total		**15**
		—

78 LOKI

Key answer tips

Although this question requires knowledge of the differences between IFRS Standards and UK GAAP, it also requires a thorough understanding of the impact of different ways of measuring the non-controlling interest. Students often struggle with this area. If you found this question difficult then revisit the chapter on 'basic groups' in the Study Text.

(a) International Financial Reporting Standards

IFRS 3 *Business Combinations* permits the NCI at acquisition to be measured at its fair value or at its proportionate share of the fair value of the subsidiary's identifiable net assets. This choice is made on an acquisition-by-acquisition basis.

Loki opts to measure the NCI at fair value so the calculation of goodwill arising at acquisition is as follows:

	$m
Fair value of consideration	300
Fair value of non-controlling interest	120
Fair value of identifiable net assets acquired	(280)
	——
Goodwill at acquisition	140
	——

Under IFRS Standards, goodwill is not amortised. Instead, IAS 36 *Impairment of Assets* stipulates that it is subject to annual impairment review. An asset, or cash generating unit, is impaired if its carrying amount exceeds its recoverable amount. The calculation of the impairment loss is as follows:

	$m
Goodwill	140
Net assets	260
	——
Total	400
Recoverable amount	(350)
	——
Impairment	50
	——

IAS 36 requires that the impairment is firstly allocated against goodwill. The impairment will be charged to the statement of profit or loss:

Dr Profit or loss	$50m
Cr Goodwill	$50m

The carrying mount of goodwill will therefore be reduced to $90 million ($140m – $50m). The expense will be allocated to the owners of the parent ($35m) and the NCI ($15m) in proportion to their shareholdings.

(b) FRS 102

FRS 102 does not permit the NCI at acquisition to be measured at fair value. As such, the proportionate method must be used. The calculation of goodwill would be as follows:

	$m
Fair value of consideration	300
Non-controlling interest (30% × $280m)	84
Fair value of identifiable net assets acquired	(280)
Goodwill at acquisition	104

In accordance with FRS 102, goodwill is amortised over its estimated useful economic life. By the year ended 31 December 20X2, the goodwill would have a carrying amount of $83.2 million ($104m × 8/10).

When performing an impairment review under FRS 102 (and under IAS 36 if the proportionate method for valuing the NCI has been used), goodwill will need to be notionally grossed up to include the NCI share.

The impairment will be calculated as follows:

	$m	$m
Goodwill	83.2	
Notional NCI ($83.2m × 30/70)	35.7	
Total notional goodwill		118.9
Net assets at reporting date		260.0
Total carrying amount of assets		378.9
Recoverable amount		(350.0)
Impairment		28.9

The impairment is allocated to the total notional goodwill. However, only 70% of the total notional goodwill was recognised and so only 70% of the impairment should be recognised. Therefore, the charge in profit or loss will be $20.2 million ($28.9m × 70%) and goodwill will be reduced to $63 million ($83.2 – $20.2m). All of the charge is attributable to the owners of the parent company.

Marking scheme		
		Marks
(a)	IFRS Standards and impairment – 1 mark per point	6
(b)	FRS 102 and impairment – 1 mark per point	9
Total		**15**

Section 3

SPECIMEN 1 EXAM QUESTIONS

1 KUTCHEN

Background and financial statements

The following group financial statements relate to the Kutchen Group which comprised Kutchen, House and Mach, all public limited companies.

Group statement of financial position as at 31 December 20X6

	$m
Assets:	
Non-current assets	
Property, plant and equipment	365
Goodwill	–
Intangible assets	23
	388
Current assets	133
Total assets	521
Equity and liabilities	
Share capital of $1 each	63
Retained earnings	56
Other components of equity	26
Non-controlling interest	3
	148
Non-current liabilities	101
Current liabilities	
Trade payables	272
Total liabilities	373
Total equity and liabilities	521

Acquisition of 70% of House

On 1 June 20X6, Kutchen acquired 70% of the equity interests of House. The purchase consideration comprised 20 million shares of $1 of Kutchen at the acquisition date and a further 5 million shares on 31 December 20X7 if House's net profit after taxation was at least $4 million for the year ending on that date.

The market price of Kutchen's shares on 1 June 20X6 was $2 per share and that of House was $4.20 per share. It is felt that there is a 20% chance of the profit target being met.

In accounting for the acquisition of House, the finance director did not take into account the non-controlling interest in the goodwill calculation. He determined that a bargain purchase of $8 million arose on the acquisition of House, being the purchase consideration of $40 million less the fair value of the identifiable net assets of House acquired on 1 June 20X6 of $48 million. This valuation was included in the group financial statements above.

After the directors of Kutchen discovered the error, they decided to measure the non-controlling interest at fair value at the date of acquisition. The fair value of the non-controlling interest (NCI) in House was to be based upon quoted market prices at acquisition. House had issued share capital of $1 each, totalling $13 million at 1 June 20X6 and there has been no change in this amount since acquisition.

Initial acquisition of 80% of Mach

On 1 January 20X6, Kutchen acquired 80% of the equity interests of Mach, a privately owned entity, for a consideration of $57 million. The consideration comprised cash of $52 million and the transfer of non-depreciable land with a fair value of $5 million. The carrying amount of the land at the acquisition date was $3 million and the land has only recently been transferred to the seller of the shares in Mach and is still carried at $3 million in the group financial statements at 31 December 20X6.

At the date of acquisition, the identifiable net assets of Mach had a fair value of $55 million. Mach had made a net profit attributable to ordinary shareholders of $3.6 million for the year to 31 December 20X5.

The directors of Kutchen wish to measure the non-controlling interest at fair value at the date of acquisition but had again omitted NCI from the goodwill calculation. The NCI is to be fair valued using a public entity market multiple method. The directors of Kutchen have identified two companies who are comparable to Mach and who are trading at an average price to earnings ratio (P/E ratio) of 21. The directors have adjusted the P/E ratio to 19 for differences between the entities and Mach, for the purpose of fair valuing the NCI. The finance director has determined that a bargain purchase of $3 million arose on the acquisition of Mach being the cash consideration of $52 million less the fair value of the net assets of Mach of $55 million. This gain on the bargain purchase had been included in the group financial statements above.

Acquisition and disposal of 80% of Niche

Kutchen purchased an 80% interest in Niche for $40 million on 1 January 20X6 when the fair value of the identifiable net assets was $44 million. The partial goodwill method had been used and an impairment of $2 million had arisen in the year ended 31 December 20X6. The holding in Niche was sold for $50 million on 31 December 20X6. The carrying amount of Niche's identifiable net assets other than goodwill was $60 million at the date of sale. Kutchen had carried the investment in Niche at cost in its separate financial statements. The finance director calculated that a gain arose of $2 million on the sale of Niche in the group financial statements being the sale proceeds of $50 million less $48 million being their share of the identifiable net assets at the date of sale (80% of $60 million). This was credited to retained earnings.

Business segment restructure

Kutchen has decided to restructure one of its business segments. The plan was agreed by the board of directors on 1 October 20X6 and affects employees in two locations. In the first location, half of the factory units have been closed by 31 December 20X6 and the affected employees' pension benefits have been frozen. Any new employees will not be eligible to join the defined benefit plan. After the restructuring, the present value of the defined benefit obligation in this location is $8 million. The following table relates to location 1.

	$m
Value before restructuring:	
Present value of defined benefit obligation	(10)
Fair value of plan assets	7
Net pension liability	(3)

In the second location, all activities have been discontinued. It has been agreed that employees will receive a payment of $4 million in exchange for the pension liability of $2.4 million in the unfunded pension scheme.

Kutchen estimates that the costs of the above restructuring excluding pension costs will be $6 million. Kutchen has not accounted for the effects of the restructuring in its financial statements because it is planning a rights issue and does not wish to depress the share price. Therefore there has been no formal announcement of the restructuring.

Subsequent acquisition of 20% of Mach

When Kutchen acquired the majority shareholding in Mach, there was an option on the remaining 20% non-controlling interest (NCI), which could be exercised at any time up to 31 March 20X7. On 31 January 20X7, Kutchen acquired the remaining NCI in Mach. The payment for the NCI was structured so that it contained a fixed initial payment and a series of contingent amounts payable over the following two years.

The contingent payments were to be based on the future profits of Mach up to a maximum amount. Kutchen felt that the fixed initial payment was an equity transaction. Additionally, Kutchen was unsure as to whether the contingent payments were equity, financial liabilities or contingent liabilities.

After a board discussion which contained disagreement as to the accounting treatment, Kutchen is preparing to disclose the contingent payments in accordance with IAS 37 *Provisions, Contingent Liabilities and Contingent Assets*. The disclosure will include the estimated timing of the payments and the directors' estimate of the amounts to be settled.

Required:

(a) **(i)** **Explain to the directors of Kutchen, with suitable workings, how goodwill should have been calculated on the acquisition of House and Mach showing the adjustments which need to be made to the consolidated financial statements to correct any errors by the finance director.** **(10 marks)**

(ii) **Explain, with suitable calculations, how the gain or loss on the sale of Niche should have been recorded in the group financial statements.** **(5 marks)**

(iii) **Discuss, with suitable workings, how the pension scheme should be dealt with after the restructuring of the business segment and whether a provision for restructuring should have been made in the financial statements for the year ended 31 December 20X6.** **(7 marks)**

Note: Marks will be allocated in (a) for a suitable discussion of the principles involved as well as the accounting treatment.

(b) **Advise Kutchen on the difference between equity and liabilities, and on the proposed accounting treatment of the contingent payments on the subsequent acquisition of 20% of Mach.** **(8 marks)**

(Total: 30 marks)

2 ABBY

Abby is a company which conducts business in several parts of the world.

Related party transactions

The accountant has discovered that the finance director of Abby has purchased goods from a company, Arwight, which the director jointly owns with his wife and the accountant believes that this purchase should be disclosed. However, the director refuses to disclose the transaction as in his opinion it is an 'arm's length' transaction. He feels that if the transaction is disclosed, it will be harmful to business and feels that the information asymmetry caused by such non-disclosure is irrelevant as most entities undertake related party transactions without disclosing them. Similarly, the director felt that competitive harm would occur if disclosure of operating segment profit or loss was made. As a result, the entity only disclosed a measure of total assets and total liabilities for each reportable segment.

When preparing the financial statements for the recent year end, the accountant noticed that Arwight has not paid an invoice for several million dollars and it is significantly overdue for payment. It appears that the entity has liquidity problems and it is unlikely that Arwight will pay. The accountant believes that a loss allowance for trade receivables is required. The finance director has refused to make such an allowance and has told the accountant that the issue must not be discussed with anyone within the trade because of possible repercussions for the credit worthiness of Arwight.

Subsidiary fair value adjustments

Additionally, when completing the consolidated financial statements, the director has suggested that there should be no positive fair value adjustments for a recently acquired subsidiary and has stated that the accountant's current position is dependent upon following these instructions. The fair value of the subsidiary is $50 million above the carrying amount in the financial records. The reason given for not fair valuing the subsidiary's net assets is that goodwill is an arbitrary calculation which is meaningless in the context of the performance evaluation of an entity.

Goodwill impairment calculation

Finally, when preparing the annual impairment tests of goodwill arising on other subsidiaries, the director has suggested that the accountant is flexible in the assumptions used in calculating future expected cash flows, so that no impairment of goodwill arises and that the accountant should use a discount rate which reflects risks for which future cash flows have been adjusted. He has indicated that he will support a salary increase for the accountant if she follows his suggestions.

Required:

Discuss the ethical and accounting implications of the above situations from the perspective of the reporting accountant. (18 marks)

Professional marks will be awarded in question 2 for the application of ethical principles. (2 marks)

(Total: 20 marks)

3 AFRICANT

(a) Africant owns several farms and also owns a division which sells agricultural vehicles. It is considering selling this agricultural retail division and wishes to measure the fair value of the inventory of vehicles for the purpose of the sale. Three markets currently exist for the vehicles. Africant has transacted regularly in all three markets.

At 31 December 20X5, Africant wishes to find the fair value of 150 new vehicles, which are identical. The current volume and prices in the three markets are as follows:

Market	Sales price per vehicle $	Historical volume – vehicles sold by Africant	Total volume of vehicles sold in the market	Transaction costs per vehicle $	Transport cost to market per vehicle $
Europe	40,000	6,000	150,000	500	400
Asia	38,000	2,500	750,000	400	700
Africa	34,000	1,500	100,000	300	600

Africant wishes to value the vehicles at $39,100 per vehicle as these are the highest net proceeds per vehicle, and Europe is the largest market for Africant's product.

(i) Africant wishes to understand the principles behind the valuation of the new vehicles and also whether their valuation would be acceptable under IFRS 13 *Fair Value Measurement*. **(8 marks)**

(ii) Africant uses the revaluation model for its non-current assets. Africant has several plots of farmland which are unproductive. The company feels that the land would have more value if it were used for residential purposes. There are several potential purchasers for the land but planning permission has not yet been granted for use of the land for residential purposes. However, preliminary enquiries with the regulatory authorities seem to indicate that planning permission may be granted. Additionally, the government has recently indicated that more agricultural land should be used for residential purposes.

Africant has also been approached to sell the land for commercial development at a higher price than that for residential purposes and understands that fair value measurement of a non-financial asset takes into account a market perspective.

Africant would like an explanation of what is meant by a 'market perspective' and advice on how to measure the fair value of the land in its financial statements. **(7 marks)**

Required:

Advise Africant on the matters set out above (in (i) and (ii)) with reference to relevant IFRS Standards.

Note: The mark allocation is shown against each of the two issues above.

(b) Africant is about to hold its annual general meeting with shareholders and the directors wish to prepare for any potential questions which may be raised at the meeting. There have been discussions in the media over the fact that the most relevant measurement method should be selected for each category of assets and liabilities. This 'mixed measurement approach' is used by many entities when preparing financial statements. There have also been comments in the media about the impact that measurement uncertainty and price volatility can have on the quality of financial information.

Required:

Discuss the impact which the above matters may have on the analysis of financial statements by investors in Africant. (8 marks)

Professional marks will be awarded in part (b) for clarity and quality of presentation. (2 marks)

(Total: 25 marks)

4 RATIONALE

The directors of Rationale are reviewing the published financial statements of the group. The following is an extract of information to be found in the financial statements.

Year ended		**31 December 20X6**	**31 December 20X5**
		$m	$m
Net profit/(loss) before taxation and after the items set out below		(5)	38
Net interest expense		10	4
Depreciation		9	8
Amortisation of intangible assets		3	2
Impairment of property	10		
Insurance proceeds	(7)	3	
Debt issue costs		2	
Share-based payment		3	1
Restructuring charges		4	
Impairment of acquired intangible assets		6	8

The directors use 'underlying profit' to comment on its financial performance. Underlying profit is a measure normally based on earnings before interest, tax, depreciation and amortisation (EBITDA). However, the effects of events which are not part of the usual business activity are also excluded when evaluating performance.

The following items were excluded from net profit to arrive at 'underlying profit'. In 20X6, the entity had to write off a property due to subsidence and the insurance proceeds recovered for this property was recorded but not approved until 20X7, when the company's insurer concluded that the claim was valid. In 20X6, the entity considered issuing loan notes to finance an asset purchase, however, the purchase did not go ahead. The entity incurred costs associated with the potential issue and so these costs were expensed as part of net profit before taxation. The entity felt that the share-based payment was not a cash expense and that the value of the options was subjective. Therefore, the directors wished to exclude the item from 'underlying profit'. Similarly, the directors wish to exclude restructuring charges incurred in the year, and impairments of acquired intangible assets.

Required:

(a) **(i)** **Discuss the reasons why an entity may wish to disclose additional performance information in its financial statements and the concerns this may raise.**

(5 marks)

(ii) **Discuss the use and the limitations of the proposed calculation of 'underlying profit' by Rationale. Your answer should include a comparative calculation of underlying profit for the years ended 31 December 20X5 and 20X6.**

(12 marks)

(b) The directors of Rationale are confused over the nature of a reclassification adjustment and understand that the Board has recently revised the *Conceptual Framework* to cover this issue.

Required:

(i) **Discuss, with examples and reference to the *Conceptual Framework*, the nature of a reclassification adjustment** **(5 marks)**

(ii) **Discuss arguments against allowing reclassification of items from other comprehensive income to profit or loss.** **(3 marks)**

(Total: 25 marks)

[illegible]

Section 4

SPECIMEN 1 EXAM ANSWERS

1 KUTCHEN

(a) (i) Goodwill

Goodwill on the acquisition of House and Mach should have been calculated as follows:

House

	$m
Fair value of consideration for 70% interest	42.00
Fair value of non-controlling interest (see below)	16.38
Fair value of identifiable net assets acquired	(48.00)
Goodwill	10.38

Contingent consideration should be valued at fair value and will have to take into account the various milestones set under the agreement. The expected value is (20% × 5 million shares) 1 million shares × $2, i.e. $2 million. This is equity so there will be no remeasurement of the fair value in subsequent periods. The contingent consideration will be recorded in other components of equity. The fair value of the consideration is therefore 20 million shares at $2 plus $2 million (above), i.e. $42 million.

The fair value of the NCI is 30% × 13 million × $4.20 = $16.38 million.

The finance director has not taken into account the fair value of the NCI in the valuation of goodwill or the contingent consideration. If the difference between the fair value of the consideration, NCI and the identifiable net assets is negative, the resulting gain is a bargain purchase in profit or loss, which may arise in circumstances such as a forced seller acting under compulsion. However, before any bargain purchase gain is recognised in profit or loss, and hence in retained earnings in the group statement of financial position, the finance director should have undertaken a review to ensure the identification of assets and liabilities is complete, and that measurements appropriately reflect consideration of all available information.

The adjustment to the group financial statements would be as follows:

Dr Goodwill	$10.38 million
Dr Profit or loss	$8 million
Cr NCI	$16.38 million
Cr OCE	$2 million

Mach

Net profit of Mach for the year to 31 December 20X5 is $3.6 million. The P/E ratio (adjusted) is 19. Therefore the fair value of Mach is 19 × $3.6 million, i.e. $68.4 million. The NCI has a 20% holding, so the fair value of the NCI is $13.68 million.

	$m
Fair value of consideration for 80% interest ($52m + $5m)	57
Fair value of non-controlling interest	13.68
Fair value of identifiable net assets acquired	(55)
Goodwill	15.68

The land transferred as part of the purchase consideration should be valued at its acquisition date fair value of $5 million and included in the goodwill calculation. Therefore the increase of $2 million over the carrying amount should be shown in retained earnings.

Dr PPE	$2 million
Cr Retained earnings	$2 million

The adjustment to the group financial statements would be as follows:

Dr Goodwill	$15.68 million
Dr Retained earnings	$3 million
Cr NCI	$13.68 million
Cr PPE	$5 million

Total goodwill is therefore $26.06 million ($15.68m + $10.38m).

(ii) Niche

The gain or loss on sale should have been calculated as the difference between the proceeds received of $50 million and the carrying amount of the subsidiary in the consolidated financial statements at the date of disposal.

The correct calculation is as follows:

	$m
Sale proceeds	50.0
Goodwill at disposal (W1)	(2.8)
Net assets at disposal	(60.0)
NCI at disposal (W2)	12.0
Loss on sale of Niche in group profit or loss	(0.8)

(W1) Goodwill

	$m
Fair value of consideration for 70% interest	40.0
Non-controlling interest ($44m × 20%)	8.8
Fair value of identifiable net assets acquired	(44.0)
Goodwill at acquisition	4.8
Impairment	(2.0)
Goodwill at disposal	2.8

(W2) NCI at disposal

	$m
NCI at acquisition	8.8
NCI share of post-acquisition net assets 20% × ($60m – $44m)	3.2
NCI at disposal	12.0

(iii) After restructuring, the present value of the pension liability in location 1 is reduced to $8 million. Thus there will be a negative past service cost in this location of $2 million ($10m – $8m). As regards location 2, there is a settlement and a curtailment as all liability will be extinguished by the payment of $4 million. Therefore there is a loss of $1.6 million ($2.4m – $4m). The changes to the pension scheme in locations 1 and 2 will both affect profit or loss as follows:

Location 1

Dr Pension obligation	$2m
Cr Retained earnings	$2m

Location 2

Dr Pension obligation	$2.4m
Dr Retained earnings	$1.6m
Cr Current liabilities	$4m

IAS 37 *Provisions, Contingent Liabilities and Contingent Assets* states that a provision for restructuring should be made only when a detailed formal plan is in place and the entity has started to implement the plan, or announced its main features to those affected. A board decision is insufficient. Even though there has been no formal announcement of the restructuring, Kutchen has started implementing it and therefore it must be accounted for under IAS 37.

A provision of $6 million should also be made at the year end.

(b) The *Conceptual Framework* defines a liability as a present obligation, arising from past events, to transfer an economic resource. IAS 32 *Financial Instruments: Presentation* establishes principles for presenting financial instruments as liabilities or equity. The key feature of a financial liability is that the issuer has a contractual obligation to deliver either cash or another financial asset to the holder. An obligation may arise from a requirement to repay principal or interest or dividends.

In contrast, equity has a residual interest in the entity's assets after deducting all of its liabilities. An equity instrument includes no obligation to deliver cash or another financial asset to another entity. A contract which will be settled by the entity delivering a fixed number of its own equity instruments in exchange for cash or another financial asset is an equity instrument. However, if there is any variability in the amount of equity instruments which will be delivered then such a contract is a financial liability.

Contingent consideration for a business must be recognised at the time of acquisition, in accordance with IFRS 3 *Business Combinations*. IFRS Standards do not contain any guidance when accounting for contingent consideration for the acquisition of a NCI in a subsidiary but the contract for contingent payments does meet the definition of a financial liability under IAS 32. Kutchen has an obligation to pay cash to the vendor of the NCI under the terms of a contract. It is not within Kutchen's control to be able to avoid that obligation. The amount of the contingent payments depends on the profitability of Mach, which itself depends on a number of factors which are uncontrollable. IAS 32 states that a contingent obligation to pay cash which is outside the control of both parties to a contract meets the definition of a financial liability which shall be initially measured at fair value. Since the contingent payments relate to the acquisition of the NCI, the offsetting entry would be recognised directly in equity.

Marking scheme

			Marks
(a)	(i)	– application of the following discussion to the scenario:	
		contingent consideration	2
		NCI	2
		fair value of assets acquired	2
		– goodwill calculations and corrections required	4
	(ii)	– application of the following discussion to the scenario:	
		proceeds	1
		carrying amount of the assets disposed of	1
		– calculation of the gain/loss on disposal of Niche	3
	(iii)	– application of the following discussion to the scenario:	
		present value and past service cost	2
		– calculation of SOPL effect	3
		– consideration of a restructuring provision	2
(b)		– application of the following discussion to the scenario:	
		definition of a liability and IAS 32 (liability v equity)	2
		definition of equity	2
		consideration of contingent payments of Mach	4
Total			**30**

2 ABBY

Related party transaction

The objective of IAS 24 *Related Party Disclosures* is to ensure that an entity's financial statements contain the disclosures necessary to draw attention to the possibility that its financial position and profit or loss may have been affected by the existence of related parties and by transactions and outstanding balances with such parties. If there have been transactions between related parties, there should be disclosure of the nature of the related party relationship as well as information about the transactions and outstanding balances necessary for an understanding of the potential effect of the relationship on the financial statements. The director is a member of the key management personnel of the reporting entity and the entity from whom the goods were purchased is jointly controlled by that director. Therefore a related party relationship exists and should be disclosed.

IFRS 8 *Operating Segments* requires an entity to report financial and descriptive information about its reportable segments. Reportable segments are operating segments or aggregations of operating segments which meet specified criteria. IFRS 8 does not contain a 'competitive harm' exemption and requires entities to disclose the financial information which is provided by the chief operating decision maker (CODM). The management accounts reviewed by the CODM may contain commercially sensitive information, and IFRS 8 might require that information to be disclosed externally. Under IFRS 8, firms should provide financial segment disclosures which enable investors to assess the different sources of risk and income as management does. This sensitive information would also be available for competitors. The potential competitive harm may encourage firms to withhold segment information. However, this is contrary to IFRS 8 which requires information about the profit or loss for each reportable segment, including certain specified revenues and expenses such as revenue from external customers and from transactions with other segments, interest revenue and expense, depreciation and amortisation, income tax expense or income and material non-cash items.

Areas such as impairments of financial assets often involve the application of professional judgement. The director may have received additional information, which has allowed him to form a different opinion to that of the accountant. The matter should be discussed with the director to ascertain why no allowance is required and to ask whether there is additional information available. However, suspicion is raised by the fact that the accountant has been told not to discuss the matter. Whilst there may be valid reasons for this, it appears again that the related party relationship is affecting the judgement of the director.

Subsidiary fair value adjustments

Positive fair value adjustments increase the assets of the acquired company and as such reduce the goodwill recognised on consolidation. However, the majority of positive fair value adjustments usually relate to items of property, plant and equipment. As a result, extra depreciation based on the net fair value adjustment reduces the post-acquisition profits of the subsidiary. This has a negative impact on important financial performance measures such as EPS. Therefore, by reducing fair value adjustments it will improve the apparent performance of new acquisitions and the consolidated financial statements. Accountants should act ethically and ignore undue pressure to undertake creative accounting in preparing such adjustments. Guidance such as IFRS 3 *Business Combinations* and IFRS 13 *Fair Value Measurement* should be used in preparing adjustments and professional valuers should be engaged where necessary.

Goodwill impairment calculation

In measuring value in use, the discount rate used should be the pre-tax rate which reflects current market assessments of the time value of money and the risks specific to the asset. The discount rate should not reflect risks for which future cash flows have been adjusted and should equal the rate of return which investors would require if they were to choose an investment which would generate cash flows equivalent to those expected from the asset. By reducing the impairment, it would have a positive impact on the financial statements. The offer of a salary increase is inappropriate and no action should be taken until the situation is clarified. Inappropriate financial reporting raises issues and risks for those involved and others associated with the company. Whilst financial reporting involves judgement, it would appear that this situation is related to judgement.

Ethics

There are several potential breaches of accounting standards and unethical practices being used by the director. The director is trying to coerce the accountant into acting unethically. IAS 1 *Presentation of Financial Statements* requires all standards to be applied if fair presentation is to be obtained. Directors cannot choose which standards they do or do not apply. It is important that accountants identify issues of unethical practice and act appropriately in accordance with ACCA's *Codes of Ethics*. The accountant should discuss the matters with the director. The technical issues should be explained and the risks of non-compliance explained to the director. If the director refuses to comply with accounting standards, then it would be appropriate to discuss the matter with others affected such as other directors and seek professional advice from ACCA. Legal advice should be considered if necessary.

An accountant who comes under pressure from senior colleagues to make inappropriate valuations and disclosures should discuss the matter with the person suggesting this. The discussion should try to confirm the facts and the reporting guidance which needs to be followed. Financial reporting does involve judgement but the cases above seem to be more than just differences in opinion. The accountant should keep a record of conversations and actions and discuss the matters with others affected by the decision, such as directors. Additionally, resignation should be considered if the matters cannot be satisfactorily resolved.

Marking scheme

	Marks
– application of the following discussion of accounting issues to the scenario:	
related party transactions	2
competitive harm exemptions	2
impairment of financial assets	2
fair value adjustments	2
goodwill impairment review	2
– application of the following discussion of ethical issues to the scenario:	
potential breaches	4
advice to accountant	4
Professional	2
Total	**20**

3 AFRICANT

(a) (i) Vehicle valuation

IFRS 13 *Fair Value Measurement* says that fair value is an exit price in the principal market, which is the market with the highest volume and level of activity. It is not determined based on the volume or level of activity of the reporting entity's transactions in a particular market. Once the accessible markets are identified, market-based volume and activity determines the principal market. There is a presumption that the principal market is the one in which the entity would normally enter into a transaction to sell the asset or transfer the liability, unless there is evidence to the contrary. In practice, an entity would first consider the markets it can access. In the absence of a principal market, it is assumed that the transaction would occur in the most advantageous market. This is the market which would maximise the amount which would be received to sell an asset or minimise the amount which would be paid to transfer a liability, taking into consideration transport and transaction costs. In either case, the entity must have access to the market on the measurement date. Although an entity must be able to access the market at the measurement date, IFRS 13 does not require an entity to be able to sell the particular asset or transfer the particular liability on that date. If there is a principal market for the asset or liability, the fair value measurement represents the price in that market at the measurement date regardless of whether that price is directly observable or estimated using another valuation technique and even if the price in a different market is potentially more advantageous.

In Africant's case, Asia is the principal market as this is the market in which the majority of transactions for the vehicles occur. The most advantageous market would be Europe where a net price of $39,100 (after all costs) would be gained by selling there and the number of vehicles sold in this market is at its highest. Africant would therefore utilise the fair value calculated by reference to the Asian market as this is the principal market.

IFRS 13 makes it clear that the price used to measure fair value must not be adjusted for transaction costs, but should consider transportation costs. Transaction costs are not deemed to be a characteristic of an asset or a liability but they are specific to a transaction and will differ depending on how an entity enters into a transaction.

As such, the fair value of the 150 vehicles would be $5,595,000 ($38,000 – $700 = $37,300 × 150).

(ii) Fair value of land

A fair value measurement of a non-financial asset takes into account a market participant's ability to generate economic benefits by using the asset in its highest and best use or by selling it to another market participant who would use the asset in its highest and best use. The maximum value of a non-financial asset may arise from its use in combination with other assets or by itself. IFRS 13 requires the entity to consider uses which are physically possible, legally permissible and financially feasible. The use must not be legally prohibited. For example, if the land is protected in some way by law and a change of law is required, then it cannot be the highest and best use of the land.

In this case, Africant's land for residential development would only require approval from the regulatory authority and as that approval seems to be possible, then this alternative use could be deemed to be legally permissible. Market participants would consider the probability, extent and timing of the approval which may be required in assessing whether a change in the legal use of the non-financial asset could be obtained.

Africant would need to have sufficient evidence to support its assumption about the potential for an alternative use, particularly in light of IFRS 13's presumption that the highest and best use is an asset's current use. Africant's belief that planning permission was possible is unlikely to be sufficient evidence that the change of use is legally permissible. However, the fact the government has indicated that more agricultural land should be released for residential purposes may provide additional evidence as to the likelihood that the land being measured should be based upon residential value. Africant would need to prove that market participants would consider residential use of the land to be legally permissible. Provided there is sufficient evidence to support these assertions, alternative uses, for example, commercial development which would enable market participants to maximise value, should be considered, but a search for potential alternative uses need not be exhaustive. In addition, any costs to transform the land, for example, obtaining planning permission or converting the land to its alternative use, and profit expectations from a market participant's perspective should also be considered in the fair value measurement.

If there are multiple types of market participants who would use the asset differently, these alternative scenarios must be considered before concluding on the asset's highest and best use. It appears that Africant is not certain about what constitutes the highest and best use and therefore IFRS 13's presumption that the highest and best use is an asset's current use appears to be valid at this stage.

(b) Mixed measurement

Some investors might argue in favour of a single measurement basis for all recognised assets and liabilities as the resulting totals and subtotals can have little meaning if different measurement methods are used. Similarly, profit or loss may lack relevance if it reflects a combination of flows based on historical cost and of value changes for items measured on a current value basis.

However, the majority of investors would tend to favour a mixed measurement approach, whereby the most relevant measurement method is selected for each category of assets and liabilities. This approach is consistent with how investors analyse financial statements. The problems of mixed measurement are outweighed by the greater relevance achieved if the most relevant measurement basis is used for each class of assets and liabilities. The mixed measurement approach is reflected in recent standards; for example, IFRS 9 *Financial Instruments* and IFRS 15 *Revenue from Contracts* with Customers. Historical cost would not have been relevant for all financial assets and has severe limitations for many liabilities; hence, the only viable single measurement method would have been fair value. The *Conceptual Framework* does not propose a single measurement method for assets and liabilities, and instead supports the continued use of a mixed measurement approach.

Most accounting measures of assets and liabilities are uncertain and require estimation. While some measures of historical cost are straightforward as it is the amount paid or received, there are many occasions when the measurement of cost can be uncertain – particularly recoverable cost, for which impairment and depreciation estimates are required. In a similar vein, while some measures of fair value can be easily observed because of the availability of prices in an actively traded market (a so-called 'Level 1' fair value), others inevitably rely on management estimates and judgements ('Level 2' and 'Level 3').

High measurement uncertainty might reduce the quality of information available to investors. High price volatility may make analysing an investment in that entity more challenging. If a relevant measure of an asset or liability value is volatile, this should not be hidden from investors. To conceal its volatility would decrease the usefulness of the financial statements. Of course, such volatile gains and losses do need to be clearly presented and disclosed, because their predictive value may differ from that provided by other components of performance.

Marking scheme			
			Marks
(a)	(i)	– discussion of the principles of IFRS 13	4
		– application of the IFRS 13 principles to Africant	4
	(ii)	– market perspective and highest and best use	4
		– application of highest and best use to Africant	3
(b)	– single v mixed measurement and investor issues		2
	– examples		2
	– investor issues re uncertainty		2
	– investor issues re price volatility		2
	Professional		2
Total			**25**

4 RATIONALE

(a) (i) Reasons for disclosure of additional performance information

IFRS requires an entity to disclose additional information which is relevant to an understanding of the entity's financial position and financial performance. A company may disclose additional information where it is felt that an entity's performance may not be apparent from accounts prepared under IFRS. A single standardised set of accounting practices can never be sufficient information to understand an entity's position or performance. Additional information can help users understand management's view of what is important to the entity and the nature of management's decisions.

Problems caused by disclosure of additional performance information

There are concerns relating to the disclosure of additional information. There is no specific guidance on information which is not required by an IFRS being disclosed in financial statements. Such information may not readily be derived or reconciled back to financial statements. There is also difficulty comparing information across periods and between entities because of the lack of standardised approaches. Also the presentation of additional information may be inconsistent with that defined or specified in IFRS and the entity may present an excessively optimistic picture of an entity's financial performance. Non-IFRS information may make it difficult to identify the complete set of financial statements, including whether the information is audited or not. Additionally, the information may be given undue prominence or credibility merely because of its location within the financial statements. Non-IFRS financial information should be clearly labelled in a way that distinguishes it from the corresponding IFRS financial information. Any term used to describe the information should be appropriate having regard to the nature of the information. The term or label should not cause confusion with IFRS information and should accurately describe the measure.

(ii) Management performance measure

The directors of Rationale are utilising a controversial figure for evaluating a company's earnings. Depreciation and amortisation are non-cash expenses related to assets which have already been purchased and they are expenses which are subject to judgement or estimates based on experience and projections. The company, by using EBITDA, is attempting to show operating cash flow since the non-cash expenses are added back.

However, EBITDA can also be misused and manipulated. It can be argued that because the estimation of depreciation, amortisation and other non-cash items is vulnerable to judgement error, the profit figure can be distorted, but by focusing on profits before these elements are deducted, a truer estimation of cash flow can be given. However, the substitution of EBITDA for conventional profit fails to take into account the need for investment in fixed capital items.

There can be an argument for excluding non-recurring items from the net profit figure. Therefore, it is understandable that the deductions for the impairment of property, the insurance recovery and the debt issue costs are made to arrive at 'underlying profit'. However, IAS 1 *Presentation of Financial Statements* states 'An entity shall present additional line items, headings and subtotals in the statements presenting profit and loss and other comprehensive income when such presentation is relevant to an understanding of the entity's financial performance.' This paragraph should not be used to justify presentation of underlying, adjusted and pre-exceptional measures of performance on the face of the profit or loss statement. The measures proposed are entity specific and could obscure performance and poor management.

Share-based compensation may not represent cash but if an entity chooses to pay equity to an employee, that affects the value of equity, no matter what form that payment is in and therefore it should be charged as employee compensation. It is an outlay in the form of equity. There is therefore little justification in excluding this expense from net profit. Restructuring charges are a feature of an entity's business and they can be volatile. They should not be excluded from net profit because they are part of corporate life. Severance costs and legal fees are not non-cash items.

Impairments of acquired intangible assets usually reflect a weaker outlook for an acquired business than was expected at the time of the acquisition, and could be considered to be non-recurring. However, the impairment charges are a useful way of holding management accountable for its acquisitions. In this case, it seems as though Rationale has not purchased wisely in 20X6.

It appears as though Rationale wishes to disguise a weak performance in 20X6 by adding back a series of expense items. EBITDA, although reduced significantly from 20X5, is now a positive figure and there is an underlying profit created as opposed to a loss. However, users will still be faced with a significant decline in profit whichever measure is disclosed by Rationale. The logic for the increase in profit is flawed in many cases but there is a lack of authoritative guidance in the area. Many companies adopt non-financial measures without articulating the relationship between the measures and the financial statements.

Year ended	**31 December 20X6**	**31 December 20X5**
	$m	$m
Net profit/(loss) before taxation and after the items set out below	(5)	38
Net interest expense	10	4
Depreciation	9	8
Amortisation of intangible assets	3	2
EBITDA	17	52
Impairment of property	10	
Insurance recovery	(7)	–
Debt issue costs	2	
EBITDA after non-recurring items	22	52
Share-based payment	3	1
Restructuring charges	4	
Impairment of acquired intangible assets	6	8
Underlying profit	35	61

(b) (i) The nature of reclassification adjustments

Reclassification adjustments are amounts recorded in profit or loss in the current period which were recognised in OCI in the current or previous periods.

According to the *Conceptual Framework*, income and expenditure included in other comprehensive income should be reclassified to profit or loss when doing so results in profit or loss providing more relevant information. However, when developing or revising an IFRS Standard, the Board may decide that reclassification is not appropriate if there is no clear basis for identifying the amount or timing of the reclassification.

Examples of items recognised in OCI which may be reclassified to profit or loss are foreign currency gains on the disposal of a foreign operation and realised gains or losses on cash flow hedges.

Items which are not reclassified include changes in a revaluation surplus under IAS 16 *Property, Plant and Equipment*, and remeasurement gains and losses on a defined benefit plan under IAS 19 *Employee Benefits*.

(ii) Arguments against reclassification

Those against reclassification believe that it adds complexity to financial reporting because it is not fully understood by user groups. It is also argued that reclassification adjustments do not meet the definitions of income or expense in the *Conceptual Framework* because the change in the asset or liability may have occurred in a previous period.

The lack of a consistent basis in the 2010 *Conceptual Framework* for determining how items should be presented has led to an inconsistent use of OCI across IFRS Standards. Opinions vary but there is a feeling that OCI has become a place where the Board decide to put controversial gains or losses. Many users are thought to ignore OCI, as the changes reported are not caused by recurring trade activities and are therefore irrelevant to predicting future performance.

Marking scheme

			Marks
(a)	(i)	– reasons for disclosures	1
		– problems caused by disclosures	4
	(ii)	– the potential use, misuse and manipulation of EBITDA	5
(b)		– application of use/misuse of EBITDA by Rationale	4
		– calculation of underlying profit of Rationale	3
	(i)	– nature of reclassification adjustment	5
Total	(ii)	– arguments against reclassification	3
			25

Section 5

SPECIMEN 2 EXAM QUESTIONS

1 HILL

Background

Hill is a public limited company which has investments in a number of other entities. All of these entities prepare their financial statements in accordance with International Financial Reporting Standards. Extracts from the draft individual statements of profit or loss for Hill, Chandler and Doyle for the year ended 30 September 20X6 are presented below.

	Hill	**Chandler**	**Doyle**
	$m	$m	$m
Profit/(loss) before taxation	(45)	67	154
Taxation	9	(15)	(31)
Profit/(loss) for the period	(36)	52	123

Acquisition of 80% of Chandler

Hill purchased 80% of the ordinary shares of Chandler on 1 October 20X5. Cash consideration of $150 million has been included when calculating goodwill in the consolidated financial statements. The purchase agreement specified that a further cash payment of $32 million becomes payable on 1 October 20X7 but no entries have been posted in the consolidated financial statements in respect of this. A discount rate of 5% should be used.

In the goodwill calculation, the fair value of Chandler's identifiable net assets was assessed as $170 million. Of this, $30 million related to Chandler's non-depreciable land. However, on 31 December 20X5, a survey was received which revealed that the fair value of this land was actually only $20 million as at the acquisition date. No adjustments have been made to the goodwill calculation in respect of the results of the survey. The non-controlling interest at acquisition was measured using the proportionate method as $34 million ($170m × 20%).

As at 30 September 20X6, the recoverable amount of Chandler was calculated as $250 million. No impairment has been calculated or accounted for in the consolidated financial statements.

Disposal of 20% holding in Doyle

On 1 October 20X4, Hill purchased 60% of the ordinary shares of Doyle. At this date, the fair value of Doyle's identifiable net assets was $510 million. The non-controlling interest at acquisition was measured at its fair value of $215 million. Goodwill arising on the acquisition of Doyle was $50 million and had not been impaired prior to the disposal date. On 1 April 20X6, Hill disposed of a 20% holding in the shares of Doyle for cash consideration of $140 million. At this date, the net assets of Doyle, excluding goodwill, were carried in the consolidated financial statements at $590 million.

From 1 April 20X6, Hill has the ability to appoint two of the six members of Doyle's board of directors. The fair value of Hill's 40% shareholding was $300 million at that date.

Issue of convertible bond

On 1 October 20X5, Hill issued a convertible bond at par value of $20 million and has recorded it as a non-current liability. The bond is redeemable for cash on 30 September 20X7 at par. Bondholders can instead opt for conversion in the form of a fixed number of shares. Interest on the bond is payable at a rate of 4% a year in arrears. The interest paid in the year has been presented in finance costs. The interest rate on similar debt without a conversion option is 10%.

Discount factors

Year	**Discount rate 5%**	**Discount rate 10%**
1	0.952	0.909
2	0.907	0.826

Required

(a) (i) **In respect of the investment in Chandler, explain, with suitable calculations, how goodwill should have been calculated, and show the adjustments which need to be made to the consolidated financial statements for this as well as any implications of the recoverable amount calculated at 30 September 20X6.** **(13 marks)**

(ii) **Discuss, with suitable calculations, how the investment in Doyle should be dealt with in the consolidated financial statements for the year ended 30 September 20X6.** **(7 marks)**

(iii) **Discuss, with suitable calculations, how the convertible bond should be dealt with in the consolidated financial statements for the year ended 30 September 20X6, showing any adjustments required.** **(6 marks)**

(b) Hill has made a loss in the year ended 30 September 20X6, as well as in the previous two financial years. In the consolidated statement of financial position it has recognised a material deferred tax asset in respect of the carry-forward of unused tax losses. These losses cannot be surrendered to other group companies. On 30 September 20X6, Hill breached a covenant attached to a bank loan which is due for repayment in 20X9. The loan is presented in non-current liabilities on the statement of financial position. The loan agreement terms state that a breach in loan covenants entitles the bank to demand immediate repayment of the loan. Hill and its subsidiaries do not have sufficient liquid assets to repay the loan in full. However, on 1 November 20X6 the bank confirmed that repayment of the loan would not be required until the original due date.

Hill has produced a business plan which forecasts significant improvement in its financial situation over the next three years as a result of the launch of new products which are currently being developed.

Required:

Discuss the proposed treatment of Hill's deferred tax asset and the financial reporting issues raised by its loan covenant breach. **(9 marks)**

(Total: 35 marks)

2 GUSTOSO

Gustoso is a public limited company which produces a range of luxury Italian food products which are sold to restaurants, shops and supermarkets. It prepares its financial statements in accordance with International Financial Reporting Standards. The directors of Gustoso receive a cash bonus each year if reported profits for the period exceed a pre-determined target. Gustoso has performed in excess of targets in the year ended 31 December 20X7. Forecasts for 20X8 are, however, pessimistic due to economic uncertainty and stagnant nationwide wage growth.

Provisions

A new accountant has recently started work at Gustoso. She noticed that the provisions balance as at 31 December 20X7 is significantly higher than in the prior year. She made enquiries of the finance director, who explained that the increase was due to substantial changes in food safety and hygiene laws which become effective during 20X8. As a result, Gustoso must retrain a large proportion of its workforce. This retraining has yet to occur, so a provision has been recognised for the estimated cost of $2 million. The finance director then told the accountant that such enquiries were a waste of time and would not be looked at favourably when deciding on her future pay rise and bonuses.

Wheat contract

Gustoso purchases significant quantities of wheat for use in its bread and pasta products. These are high-value products on which Gustoso records significant profit margins. Nonetheless, the price of wheat is volatile and so, on 1 November 20X7, Gustoso entered into a contract with a supplier to purchase 500,000 bushels of wheat in June 20X8 for $5 a bushel. The contract can be settled net in cash. Gustoso has entered into similar contracts in the past and has always taken delivery of the wheat. By 31 December 20X7 the price of wheat had fallen. The finance director recorded a derivative liability of $0.5 million on the statement of financial position and a loss of $0.5 million in the statement of profit or loss. Wheat prices may rise again before June 20X8. The accountant is unsure if the current accounting treatment is correct but feels uncomfortable approaching the finance director again.

Required:

Discuss the ethical and accounting implications of the above situations from the perspective of the accountant. (13 marks)

Professional marks will be awarded in question 2 for the application of ethical principles. (2 marks)

(Total: 15 marks)

3 CALENDAR

Calendar has a reporting date of 31 December 20X7. It prepares its financial statements in accordance with International Financial Reporting Standards. Calendar develops biotech products for pharmaceutical companies. These pharmaceutical companies then manufacture and sell the products. Calendar receives stage payments during product development and a share of royalties when the final product is sold to consumers. A new accountant has recently joined Calendar's finance department and has raised a number of queries.

(a) **(i)** During 20X6 Calendar acquired a development project through a business combination and recognised it as an intangible asset. The commercial director decided that the return made from the completion of this specific development project would be sub-optimal. As such, in October 20X7, the project was sold to a competitor. The gain arising on derecognition of the intangible asset was presented as revenue in the financial statements for the year ended 31 December 20X7 on the grounds that development of new products is one of Calendar's ordinary activities. Calendar has made two similar sales of development projects in the past, but none since 20X0.

The accountant requires advice about whether the accounting treatment of this sale is correct. **(6 marks)**

(ii) While searching for some invoices, the accountant found a contract which Calendar had entered into on 1 January 20X7 with Diary, another entity. The contract allows Calendar to use a specific aircraft owned by Diary for a period of three years. Calendar is required to make annual payments.

On 1 January 20X7, costs were incurred negotiating the contract. The first annual payment was made on 31 December 20X7. Both of these amounts have been expensed to the statement of profit or loss.

There are contractual restrictions concerning where the aircraft can fly. Subject to those restrictions, Calendar determines where and when the aircraft will fly, and the cargo and passengers which will be transported.

Diary is permitted to substitute the aircraft at any time during the three-year period for an alternative model and must replace the aircraft if it is not working. Any substitute aircraft must meet strict interior and exterior specifications outlined in the contract. There are significant costs involved in outfitting an aircraft to meet Calendar's specifications.

The accountant requires advice as to the correct accounting treatment of this contract. **(9 marks)**

Required:

Advise the accountant on the matters set out above with reference to International Financial Reporting Standards.

Note: The split of the mark allocation is shown against each of the two issues above.

(b) The new accountant has been reviewing Calendar's financial reporting processes. She has recommended the following:

- All purchases of property, plant and equipment below $500 should be written off to profit or loss. The accountant believes that this will significantly reduce the time and cost involved in maintaining detailed financial records and producing the annual financial statements.
- A checklist should be used when finalising the annual financial statements to ensure that all disclosure notes required by specific IFRS and IAS Standards are included.

Required:

With reference to the concept of materiality, discuss the acceptability of the above two proposals.

Note: Your answer should refer to IFRS Practice Statement: *Making Materiality Judgements*. **(10 marks)**

(Total: 25 marks)

4 KIKI

(a) Kiki is a public limited entity. It designs and manufactures children's toys. It has a reporting date of 31 December 20X7 and prepares its financial statements in accordance with International Financial Reporting Standards. The directors require advice about the following situations.

(i) Kiki sells $50 gift cards. These can be used when purchasing any of Kiki's products through its website. The gift cards expire after 12 months. Based on significant past experience, Kiki estimates that its customers will redeem 70% of the value of the gift card and that 30% of the value will expire unused. Kiki has no requirement to remit any unused funds to the customer when the gift card expires unused.

The directors are unsure about how the gift cards should be accounted for.

(6 marks)

(ii) Kiki's best-selling range of toys is called Scarimon. In 20X6 Colour, another listed company, entered into a contract with Kiki for the rights to use Scarimon characters and imagery in a monthly comic book. The contract terms state that Colour must pay Kiki a royalty fee for every issue of the comic book which is sold. Before signing the contract, Kiki determined that Colour had a strong credit rating. Throughout 20X6, Colour provided Kiki with monthly sales figures and paid all amounts due in the agreed-upon period. At the beginning of 20X7, Colour experienced cash flow problems. These were expected to be short term. Colour made nominal payments to Kiki in relation to comic sales for the first half of the year. At the beginning of July 20X7, Colour lost access to credit facilities and several major customers. Colour continued to sell Scarimon comics online and through specialist retailers but made no further payments to Kiki.

The directors are unsure how to deal with the above issues in the financial statements for the year ended 31 December 20X7. **(6 marks)**

Required:

Advise the accountant on the matters set out above with reference to International Financial Reporting Standards.

Note: The split of the mark allocation is shown against each of the two issues above.

(b) As a result of rising property prices, Kiki purchased five buildings during the current period in order to benefit from further capital appreciation. Kiki has never owned an investment property before. In accordance with IAS 40 *Investment Property*, the directors are aware that they can measure the buildings using either the fair value model or the cost model. However, they are concerned about the impact that this choice will have on the analysis of Kiki's financial performance, position and cash flows by current and potential investors.

Required:

Discuss the potential impact which this choice in accounting policy will have on investors' analysis of Kiki's financial statements. Your answer should refer to key financial ratios. **(11 marks)**

Professional marks will be awarded in part (b) for clarity and quality of presentation. **(2 marks)**

(Total: 25 marks)

Section 6

SPECIMEN 2 EXAM ANSWERS

1 HILL

(a) (i) Deferred consideration

When calculating goodwill, IFRS 3 *Business Combinations* states that purchase consideration should be measured at fair value. For deferred cash consideration, this will be the present value of the cash flows. This amounts to $29 million ($32m × 0.907). Goodwill arising on acquisition should be increased by $29 million and a corresponding liability should be recognised:

Dr Goodwill	$29 million
Cr Liability	$29 million

Interest of $1.5 million ($29m × 5%) should be recorded. This is charged to the statement of profit or loss and increases the carrying amount of the liability:

Dr Finance costs	$1.5 million
Cr Liability	$1.5 million

Property, plant and equipment (PPE)

During the measurement period IFRS 3 states that adjustments should be made retrospectively if new information is determined about the value of consideration transferred, the subsidiary's identifiable net assets, or the non-controlling interest. The measurement period ends no later than 12 months after the acquisition date.

The survey detailed that Chandler's PPE was overvalued by $10 million as at the acquisition date. It was received three months after the acquisition date and so this revised valuation was received during the measurement period. As such, goodwill at acquisition should be recalculated. As at the acquisition date, the carrying amount of PPE should be reduced by $10 million and the carrying amount of goodwill increased by $10 million:

Dr Goodwill	$10 million
Cr PPE	$10 million

NCI

The NCI at acquisition was valued at $34 million but it should have been valued at $32 million (($170m – $10m PPE adjustment) × 20%). Both NCI at acquisition and goodwill at acquisition should be reduced by $2 million:

Dr NCI	$2 million
Cr Goodwill	$2 million

Goodwill

Goodwill arising on the acquisition of Chandler should have been calculated as follows:

	$m
Fair value of consideration ($150m + $29m)	179
NCI at acquisition	32
Fair value of identifiable net assets acquired	(160)
Goodwill at acquisition	51

Goodwill impairment

According to IAS 36 *Impairment of Assets*, a cash generating unit to which goodwill is allocated should be tested for impairment annually by comparing its carrying amount to its recoverable amount. As goodwill has been calculated using the proportionate method, then this must be grossed up to include the goodwill attributable to the NCI.

	$m	$m
Goodwill	51	
Notional NCI ($51m × 20/80)	12.8	
Total notional goodwill		63.8
Net assets at reporting date:		
Fair value at start of period	160	
Profit for period	52	
		212
Total carrying amount of assets		275.8
Recoverable amount		(250.0)
Impairment		25.8

The impairment is allocated against the total notional goodwill. The NCI share of the goodwill has not been recognised in the consolidated financial statements and so the NCI share of the impairment is also not recognised. The impairment charged to profit or loss is therefore $20.6 million ($25.8m × 80%) and this expense is all attributable to the equity holders of the parent company.

Dr Operating expenses	$20.6 million
Cr Goodwill	$20.6 million

The carrying amount of the goodwill relating to Chandler at the reporting date will be $30.4 million ($51m acquisition –$20.6m impairment).

(ii) Doyle

The share sale results in Hill losing control over Doyle. The goodwill, net assets and NCI of Doyle must be derecognised from the consolidated statement of financial position. The difference between the proceeds from the disposal (including the fair value of the shares retained) and these amounts will give rise to a $47 million profit on disposal. This is calculated as follows:

	$m	$m
Proceeds		140
Fair value of remaining interest		300
		440
Goodwill at disposal		(50)
Net assets at disposal		(590)
NCI:		
At acquisition	215	
NCI % of post-acquisition profit (40% × ($590m – $510m))	32	
NCI at disposal		247
Profit on disposal		47

After the share sale, Hill owns 40% of Doyle's shares and has the ability to appoint two of the six members of Doyle's board of directors. IAS 28 *Investments in Associates and Joint Ventures* states that an associate is an entity over which an investor has significant influence. Significant influence is presumed when the investor has a shareholding of between 20 and 50%. Representation on the board of directors provides further evidence that significant influence exists.

Therefore, the remaining 40% shareholding in Doyle should be accounted for as an associate. It will be initially recognised at its fair value of $300 million and accounted for using the equity method. This means that the group recognises its share of the associate's profit after tax, which equates to $24.6 million ($123m × 6/12 × 40%). As at the reporting date, the associate will be carried at $324.6 million ($300m + $24.6m) in the consolidated statement of financial position.

(iii) Convertible bond

Hill has issued a compound instrument because the bond has characteristics of both a financial liability (an obligation to repay cash) and equity (an obligation to issue a fixed number of Hill's own shares). IAS 32 *Financial Instruments: Presentation* specifies that compound instruments must be split into:

- a liability component (the obligation to repay cash)
- an equity component (the obligation to issue a fixed number of shares).

The split of the liability component and the equity component at the issue date is calculated as follows:

– the liability component is the present value of the cash repayments, discounted using the market rate on non-convertible bonds

– the equity component is the difference between the cash received and the liability component at the issue date.

The initial carrying amount of the liability should have been measured at $17.9 million, calculated as follows:

Date	Cash flow	Discount rate	Present value
	$m		$m
30 September 20X6	0.8	0.909	0.73
30 September 20X7	20.8	0.826	17.18
			17.91

The equity component should have been initially measured at $2.1 million ($20m – $17.9m).

The adjustment required is:

Dr Non-current liabilities $2.1m

Cr Equity $2.1m

The equity component remains unchanged. After initial recognition, the liability is measured at amortised cost, as follows:

1 October 20X5	Finance charge (10%)	Cash paid	30 September 20X6
$m	$m	$m	$m
17.9	1.8	(0.8)	18.9

The finance cost recorded for the year was $0.8 million and so must be increased by $1.0 million ($1.8m – $0.8m).

Dr Finance costs $1.0m

Cr Non-current liabilities $1.0m

The liability has a carrying amount of $18.9 million as at the reporting date.

(b) Deferred tax

According to IAS 12 *Income Taxes*, an entity should recognise a deferred tax asset in respect of the carry-forward of unused tax losses to the extent that it is probable that future taxable profit will be available against which the losses can be utilised. IAS 12 stresses that the existence of unused losses is strong evidence that future taxable profit may not be available. For this reason, convincing evidence is required about the existence of future taxable profits.

IAS 12 says that entities should consider whether the tax losses result from identifiable causes which are unlikely to recur. Hill has now made losses in three consecutive financial years, and therefore significant doubt exists about the likelihood of future profits being generated.

Although Hill is forecasting an improvement in its trading performance, this is a result of new products which are currently under development. It will be difficult to reliably forecast the performance of these products. More emphasis should be placed on the performance of existing products and existing customers when assessing the likelihood of future trading profits.

Finally, Hill breached a bank loan covenant and some uncertainty exists about its ability to continue as a going concern. This, again, places doubts on the likelihood of future profits and suggests that recognition of a deferred tax asset for unused tax losses would be inappropriate.

Based on the above, it would seem that Hill is incorrect to recognise a deferred tax asset in respect of its unused tax losses.

Covenant breach

Hill is currently presenting the loan as a non-current liability. IAS 1 *Presentation of Financial Statements* states that a liability should be presented as current if the entity:

- settles it as part of its operating cycle, or
- is due to settle the liability within 12 months of the reporting date, or
- does not have an unconditional right to defer settlement for at least 12 months after the reporting date.

Hill breached the loan covenants before the reporting date but only received confirmation after the reporting date that the loan was not immediately repayable. As per IAS 10 *Events after the Reporting Period*, the bank confirmation is a non-adjusting event because, as at the reporting date, Hill did not have an unconditional right to defer settlement of the loan for at least 12 months. In the statement of financial position as at 30 September 20X6 the loan should be reclassified as a current liability.

Going concern

Although positive forecasts of future performance exist, management must consider whether the breach of the loan covenant and the recent trading losses place doubt on Hill's ability to continue as a going concern. If material uncertainties exist, then disclosures should be made in accordance with IAS 1.

Marking scheme			
			Marks
(a)	(i)	Discussion 1 mark per point to a maximum	8
		Calculation	5
	(ii)	Discussion 1 mark per point to a maximum	3
		Calculation	4
	(iii)	1 mark for each point to a maximum	6
(b)	1 mark for each point to a maximum		9
Total			**35**

2 GUSTOSO

Provision

IAS 37 *Provisions, Contingent Liabilities and Contingent Assets* states that a provision should only be recognised if:

- there is a present obligation from a past event
- an outflow of economic resources is probable, and
- the obligation can be measured reliably.

No provision should be recognised because Gustoso does not have an obligation to incur the training costs. The expenditure could be avoided by changing the nature of Gustoso's operations and so it has no present obligation for the future expenditure.

The provision should be derecognised. This will reduce liabilities by $2 million and increase profits by the same amount.

Contract

IFRS 9 *Financial Instruments* applies to contracts to buy or sell a non-financial item which are settled net in cash. Such contracts are usually accounted for as derivatives. However, contracts which are for an entity's 'own use' of a non-financial asset are exempt from the requirements of IFRS 9. The contract will qualify as 'own use' because Gustoso always takes delivery of the wheat. This means that it falls outside IFRS 9 and so the recognition of a derivative is incorrect.

The contract is an executory contract. Executory contracts are not initially recognised in the financial statements unless they are onerous, in which case a provision is required. This particular contract is unlikely to be onerous because wheat prices may rise again. Moreover, the finished goods which the wheat forms a part of will be sold at a profit. As such, no provision is required. The contract will therefore remain unrecognised until Gustoso takes delivery of the wheat.

The derivative liability should be derecognised, meaning that profits will increase by $0.5 million.

Ethical implications

The users of Gustoso's financial statements, such as banks and shareholders, trust accountants and rely on them to faithfully represent the effects of a company's transactions. IAS 1 *Presentation of Financial Statements* makes it clear that this will be obtained when accounting standards are correctly applied.

Both of the errors made by Gustoso overstate liabilities and understate profits. It is possible that these are unintentional errors. However, incentives exist to depart from particular IFRS and IAS standards: most notably the bonus scheme. The bonus target in 20X7 has been exceeded, and so the finance director may be attempting to shift 'excess' profits into the next year in order to increase the chance of meeting 20X8's bonus target. In this respect, the finance director has a clear self-interest threat to objectivity and may be in breach of ACCA's *Code of Ethics and Conduct*.

The accountant is correct to challenge the finance director and has an ethical responsibility to do so. Despite the fact that the finance director is acting in an intimidating manner, the accountant should explain the technical issues to the director. If the director refuses to comply with accounting standards, then it would be appropriate to discuss the matter with other directors and to seek professional advice from ACCA. Legal advice should be considered if necessary. The accountant should keep a record of conversations and actions. Resignation should be considered if the matters cannot be satisfactorily resolved.

Marking scheme	
	Marks
Accounting issues – 1 mark per point up to maximum	6
Ethical issues – 1 mark per point up to maximum	7
Professional	2
Total	**15**

3 CALENDAR

(a) (i) Sale of intangible

IFRS 15 *Revenue from Contracts with Customers* defines revenue as income arising from an entity's ordinary activities. Calendar's ordinary activities do not involve selling development projects. In fact, Calendar has made no such sales since 20X0. It would seem that Calendar's business model instead involves developing products for its customers, who then take over its production, marketing and sale. Stage payments and royalties are the incomes which arise from Calendar's ordinary activities and should be treated as revenue.

Based on the above, Calendar is incorrect to recognise the gain as revenue. In fact, IAS 38 *Intangible Assets* explicitly prohibits the classification of a gain on derecognition of an intangible asset as revenue.

IAS 38 defines an intangible asset as an identifiable non-monetary asset without physical substance. Intangible assets held for sale in the ordinary course of business are outside the scope of IAS 38 and are instead accounted for in accordance with IAS 2 *Inventories*. The fact that the development project was classified as an intangible asset upon initial recognition further suggests that it was not held for sale in the ordinary course of business.

If the development was incorrectly categorised in the prior year financial statements as an intangible asset, then, as per IAS 8 *Accounting Policies, Changes in Accounting Estimates and Errors,* this should be corrected retrospectively. However, based on the infrequency of such sales, it seems unlikely that the development was misclassified.

(ii) Contract

IFRS 16 *Leases* says that a contract contains a lease if it conveys the right to control the use of an identified asset for a period of time in exchange for consideration. When deciding if a contract involves the right to control an asset, the customer must assess whether they have:

- The right to substantially all of the identified asset's economic benefits
- The right to direct the asset's use.

Calendar has the right to use a specified aircraft for three years in exchange for annual payments. Although Diary can substitute the aircraft for an alternative, the costs of doing so would be prohibitive because of the strict specifications outlined in the contract.

Calendar appears to have control over the aircraft during the three-year period because no other parties can use the aircraft during this time, and Calendar makes key decisions about the aircraft's destinations and the cargo and passengers which it transports. There are some legal and contractual restrictions which limit the aircraft's use. These protective rights define the scope of Calendar's right of use but do not prevent it from having the right to direct the use of the aircraft.

Based on the above, the contract contains a lease. IFRS 16 permits exemptions for leases of less than 12 months or leases of low value. However, this lease contract is for three years, so is not short term, and is for a high value asset so a lease liability should have been recognised at contract inception. The lease liability should equal the present value of the payments yet to be made, using the discount rate implicit in the lease. A finance cost accrues over the year, which is charged to profit or loss and added to the carrying amount of the lease liability. The year-end cash payment should be removed from profit or loss and deducted from the carrying amount of the liability.

A right-of-use asset should have been recognised at the contract inception at an amount equal to the initial value of the lease liability plus the initial costs to Calendar of negotiating the lease. The right-of-use asset should be depreciated over the lease term of three years and so one year's depreciation should be charged to profit or loss.

(b) Materiality

Calendar's financial statements should help investors, lenders and other creditors to make economic decisions about providing it with resources. An item is material if its omission or misstatement might influence the economic decisions of the users of the financial statements. Materiality is not a purely quantitative consideration; an item can be material if it triggers non-compliance with laws and regulations, or bank covenants. Calendar should consider materiality throughout the process of preparing its financial statements to ensure that relevant information is not omitted, misstated or obscured.

Property, plant and equipment (PPE)

IAS 16 *Property, Plant and Equipment* states that expenditure on PPE should be recognised as an asset and initially measured at the cost of purchase. Writing off such expenditure to profit or loss is therefore not in accordance with IAS 16.

According to IAS 8 *Accounting Policies, Changes in Accounting Estimates and Errors,* financial statements do not comply with International Financial Reporting Standards if they contain material errors, or errors made intentionally in order to present the entity's financial performance and position in a particular way. However, assuming that the aggregate impact of writing off small PPE purchases to profit or loss is not material, then the financial statements would still comply with International Financial Reporting Standards. Moreover, this decision seems to be a practical expedient which will reduce the time and cost involved in producing financial statements, rather than a decision made to achieve a particular financial statement presentation.

If implemented, this policy must be regularly reassessed to ensure that PPE and the statement of profit or loss are not materially misstated.

Disclosure notes

IAS 1 *Presentation of Financial Statements* states that application of IFRS Standards in an entity's financial statements will result in a fair presentation. As such, the use of a checklist may help to ensure that all disclosure requirements within IFRS Standards are fulfilled. However, IAS 1 and the Practice Statement *Making Materiality Judgements* both specify that the disclosures required by IFRS Standards are only required if the information presented is material.

The aim of disclosure notes is to further explain items included in the primary financial statements as well as unrecognised items (such as contingent liabilities) and other events which might influence the decisions of financial statement users (such as events after the reporting period). As such, Calendar should exercise judgement about the disclosures which it prepares, taking into account the information needs of its specific stakeholders. This is because the disclosure of immaterial information clutters the financial statements and makes relevant information harder to find.

Calendar may also need to disclose information in addition to that specified in IFRS Standards if relevant to helping users understand its financial statements.

Marking scheme			
			Marks
(a)	(i)	1 mark per point up to maximum	6
	(ii)	1 mark per point up to maximum	9
(b)	1 mark per point up to maximum		10
Total			**25**

4 KIKI

(a) (i) Gift cards

IFRS 15 *Revenue from Contracts with Customers* says that revenue should be recognised when or as a performance obligation is satisfied by transferring the promised good or service to the customer. When a customer buys a gift card they are pre-paying for a product. Revenue cannot be recognised because the entity has not yet transferred control over an asset and so has not satisfied a performance obligation. As such, cash received in respect of gift cards should be initially recognised as a contract liability.

IFRS 15 refers to a customer's unexercised rights as breakage. The guidance for variable consideration is followed when estimating breakage. In other words, the expected breakage is included in the transaction price if it is highly probable that a significant reversal in the amount of cumulative revenue recognised will not occur once the uncertainty is subsequently resolved. This means that if the company is unable to reliably estimate the breakage amount, then revenue for the unused portion of the gift card is recognised when the likelihood of the customer exercising their remaining rights becomes remote. However, if an entity is able to reliably estimate the breakage amount, then it recognises the expected breakage amount as revenue in proportion to the pattern of rights exercised by the customer.

In relation to Kiki, it appears that the amount of breakage can be reliably determined and so this should be recognised in revenue as the gift card is redeemed. For every $1 redeemed, Kiki should recognise $1.43 ($1 × 100/70) in revenue.

(ii) Royalty

According to IFRS 15, an entity should only account for revenue from a contract with a customer when it meets the following criteria:

- The contract has been approved
- Rights regarding goods and services can be identified
- Payment terms can be identified
- It is probable the seller will collect the consideration it is entitled to.

At inception of the agreement, Kiki and Colour entered an explicit contract which specified payment terms and conditions. Moreover, Colour had a strong credit rating and so payment was probable. As such, it would seem that the above criteria were met. IFRS 15 says that revenue from a usage-based royalty should be recognised as the usage occurs.

Whether a contract with a customer meets the above criteria is only reassessed if there is a significant change in facts and circumstances. In July 20X7, Colour lost major customers and sources of finance. As such, it was no longer probable that Kiki would collect the consideration it was entitled to. From July 20X7, no further revenue from the contract should be recognised.

According to IFRS 9 *Financial Instruments*, non-payment is an indicator that the outstanding receivables are credit impaired. A loss allowance should be recognised equivalent to the difference between the gross carrying amount of the receivables and the present value of the expected future cash flows receivable from Colour. Any increase or decrease in the loss allowance is charged to profit or loss.

(b) Investment properties

In accordance with IAS 40 *Investment Properties,* the buildings should be initially measured at cost.

If the cost model is applied, then the buildings will be measured at cost less accumulated depreciation and impairment losses.

If the fair value model is applied, then the buildings will be remeasured to fair value at each reporting date. Gains and losses on remeasurement are recognised in the statement of profit or loss. No depreciation is charged.

Statement of financial position

Assuming that property prices rise, the fair value model will lead to an increase in reported assets on the statement of financial position. In contrast, investment property measured using the cost model is depreciated, which reduces its carrying amount. This means that the fair value model may make Kiki appear more asset-rich. Some stakeholders may place importance on an entity's asset base, as it can be used as security for obtaining new finance. Moreover investors would expect that the carrying amount of the asset will be recovered in the form of future cash flows, whether directly or indirectly.

As such, a higher carrying amount may increase investor optimism about future returns. However, reporting higher assets can sometimes be perceived negatively. For example, asset turnover ratios will deteriorate, and so Kiki may appear less efficient.

If assets increase, then equity also increases. As such, the fair value model may lead to Kiki reporting a more optimistic gearing ratio. This may reduce the perception of risk, encouraging further investment.

Statement of profit or loss

In times of rising prices, the use of the fair value model will lead to gains being reported in the statement of profit or loss. This will increase profits for the period. In contrast, the depreciation charged under the cost model will reduce profits for the period. Therefore, earnings per share, a key stock market and investor ratio, is likely to be higher if the fair value model is adopted.

However, it should be noted that fair values are volatile. In some years, fair value gains may be much larger than in other years. If property prices decline, then the fair value model will result in losses. As such, reported profits are subject to more volatility if the fair value model is adopted. This may increase stakeholders' perception of risk because it becomes harder to predict future profits. In contrast, the depreciation expense recorded in accordance with the cost model will be much more predictable, meaning that investors will be better able to predict Kiki's future results.

Many entities now present alternative performance measures (APMs), such as EBITDA (earnings before interest, tax, depreciation and amortisation). Other entities present 'underlying profit' indicators, which strip out the impact of non-operating or non-recurring gains or losses (such as the remeasurement of investment properties). Although the use of APMs has been criticised, Kiki may consider them to be useful in helping investors to assess underlying business performance through the eyes of management and to eliminate the impact of certain accounting policy choices.

Statement of cash flows

Accounting policy choices have no impact on the operating, investing or financing cash flows reported in the statement of cash flows.

Disclosure

It should be noted that entities using the cost model for investment properties are required to disclose the fair value. Such disclosures enable better comparisons to be drawn between entities which account for investment property under different models.

Marking scheme			
			Marks
(a)	(i)	1 mark per point up to maximum	6
	(ii)	1 mark per point up to maximum	6
(b)	1 mark per point up to maximum		11
	Professional		2
Total			**25**

Section 7

REFERENCES

This document references IFRS Standards and IAS Standards, which are authored by the International Accounting Standards Board (the Board), and published in the 2022 IFRS Standards Red Book.

The Board (2022) *Conceptual Framework for Financial Reporting*. London: IFRS Foundation.

The Board (2022) IAS 1 *Presentation of Financial Statements.* London: IFRS Foundation.

The Board (2022) IAS 2 *Inventories.* London: IFRS Foundation.

The Board (2022) IAS 7 *Statement of Cash Flows*. London: IFRS Foundation.

The Board (2022) IAS 8 *Accounting Policies, Changes in Accounting Estimates and Errors.* London: IFRS Foundation.

The Board (2022) IAS 10 *Events after the Reporting Period.* London: IFRS Foundation.

The Board (2022) IAS 12 *Income Taxes.* London: IFRS Foundation.

The Board (2022) IAS 16 *Property, Plant and Equipment.* London: IFRS Foundation.

The Board (2022) IAS 19 *Employee Benefits.* London: IFRS Foundation.

The Board (2022) IAS 20 *Accounting for Government Grants and Disclosure of Government Assistance.* London: IFRS Foundation.

The Board (2022) IAS 21 *The Effects of Changes in Foreign Exchange Rates.* London: IFRS Foundation.

The Board (2022) IAS 23 *Borrowing Costs.* London: IFRS Foundation.

The Board (2022) IAS 24 *Related Party Disclosures.* London: IFRS Foundation.

The Board (2022) IAS 27 *Separate Financial Statements.* London: IFRS Foundation.

The Board (2022) IAS 28 *Investments in Associates and Joint Ventures.* London: IFRS Foundation.

The Board (2022) IAS 32 *Financial Instruments: Presentation.* London: IFRS Foundation.

The Board (2022) IAS 33 *Earnings per Share.* London: IFRS Foundation.

The Board (2022) IAS 34 *Interim Financial Reporting.* London: IFRS Foundation.

The Board (2022) IAS 36 *Impairment of Assets.* London: IFRS Foundation.

The Board (2022) IAS 37 *Provisions, Contingent Liabilities and Contingent Assets.* London: IFRS Foundation.

The Board (2022) IAS 38 *Intangible Assets.* London: IFRS Foundation.

The Board (2022) IAS 40 *Investment Property.* London: IFRS Foundation.

The Board (2022) IAS 41 *Agriculture*. London: IFRS Foundation.

The Board (2022) IFRS 1 *First-time Adoption of International Financial Reporting Standards.* London: IFRS Foundation.

The Board (2022) IFRS 2 *Share-based Payment.* London: IFRS Foundation.

The Board (2022) IFRS 3 *Business Combinations.* London: IFRS Foundation.

The Board (2022) IFRS 5 *Non-current Assets Held for Sale and Discontinued Operations.* London: IFRS Foundation.

The Board (2022) IFRS 7 *Financial Instruments: Disclosure.* London: IFRS Foundation.

The Board (2022) IFRS 8 *Operating Segments.* London: IFRS Foundation.

The Board (2022) IFRS 9 *Financial Instruments.* London: IFRS Foundation.

The Board (2022) IFRS 10 *Consolidated Financial Statements.* London: IFRS Foundation.

The Board (2022) IFRS 11 *Joint Arrangements.* London: IFRS Foundation.

The Board (2022) IFRS 12 *Disclosure of Interests in Other Entities.* London: IFRS Foundation.

The Board (2022) IFRS 13 *Fair Value Measurement.* London: IFRS Foundation.

The Board (2022) IFRS 15 *Revenue from Contracts with Customers.* London: IFRS Foundation.

The Board (2022) IFRS 16 *Leases.* London: IFRS Foundation.

The Board (2015) IFRS for *SMEs Standard.* London: IFRS Foundation.

The Board (2022) *IFRS Practice Statement: Management Commentary.* London: IFRS Foundation.

The Board (2022) *IFRS Practice Statement: Making Materiality Judgements.* London: IFRS Foundation.